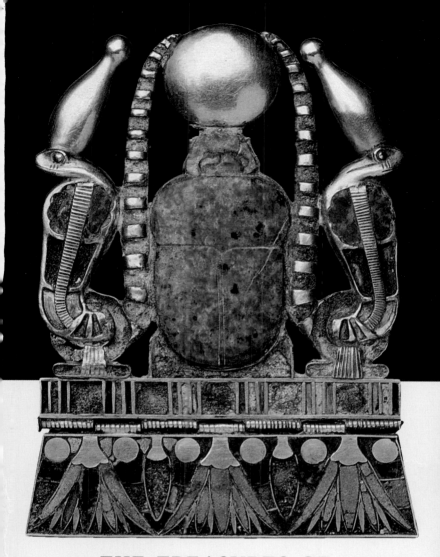

THE TREASURES OF
ANCIENT EGYPT

FROM THE EGYPTIAN MUSEUM IN CAIRO

RIZZOLI
NEW YORK

CONTRIBUTORS

Preface by
Zahi Hawass

Edited by
Alessandro Bongioanni
Maria Sole Croce

Photographs by
Araldo De Luca

Editorial coordination
Laura Accomazzo

Texts
Alessia Amenta
Alessandro Bongioanni
Daniela Comand
Maria Sole Croce
Silvia Einaudi
Marcella Trapani

Graphic design
Patrizia Balocco Lovisetti
Clara Zanotti

*The initials at the end of each
text refer to its author.*

Translation
C.T.M., Milan

First published in the United States of America in
2003 by Universe Publishing, a division of Rizzoli
International Publications, Inc.
300 Park Avenue South, New York, NY 10010
www.rizzoliusa.com

© 2001 White Star S.r.l.
Via Candido Sassone 24 , 13100 Vercelli, Italy

This edition published by arrangement with
White Star S.r.l., Vercelli, Italy

ISBN 0-7893-0986-6
Library of Congress Control Number: 2003104964

Printed in China
Color separation by Fotomec, Turin, Italy.

*1 Pectoral belonging
to Sheshonq II.*

*2 Statue of Menkaura
(detail).*

*3 Funerary bed of
Tutankhamun (detail).*

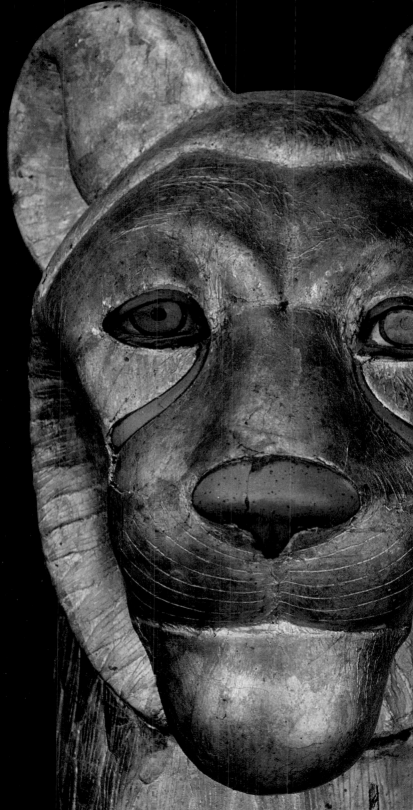

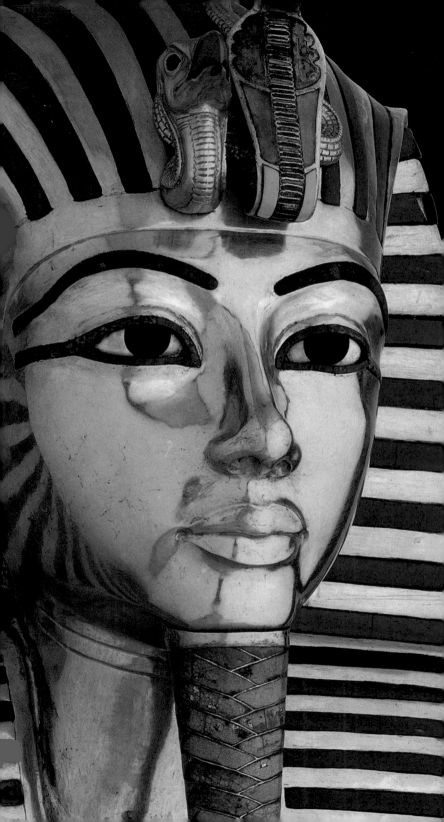

CONTENTS

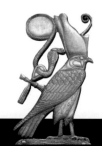

*4 Gold mask of
Tutankhamun.*

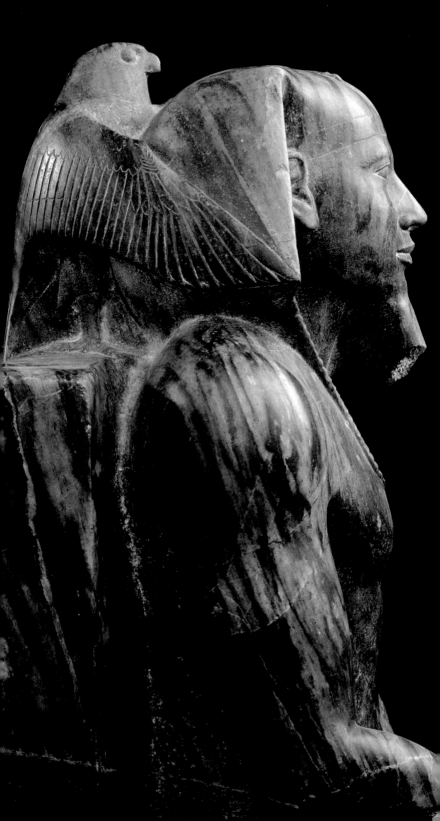

PREFACE

by ZAHI HAWASS

*A*ncient Egypt's cultural wealth has always bedazzled the world. Truly a land of plenty, her vast resources during her glorious years as the kingdom of the pharaohs live today as the artifacts that give humankind a permanent record of the greatness of the ingenious people that lived on the banks of the Nile: this immensely important story is the one told by the treasures in the Egyptian Museum in Cairo, one of the greatest collections in the world. In fact, whenever I enter the garden of the museum, even before I enter the building itself, I can feel the power of the beautiful artifacts and the magic of ancient Egypt. The museum contains the smell and feel of a glorious past, and I can see the glimmer of ancient light shining in the eyes of the museum's statues.

Visiting the Egyptian museum, it is easy to find yourself overwhelmed by the impressive artworks that fill every niche and corner. This is not a new phenomenon. Long ago, a visitor complained to Gaston Maspero, the first director of the Egyptian Museum, that it was too crowded with artifacts. Maspero replied that ancient Egyptians would have liked this. Egyptian temples were crowded with statues, and every available space of a tomb was full

of scenes and hieroglyphic inscriptions. Even the typical Egyptian house was full of furniture and equipment. Thus, the crowding of artifacts in the museum is in keeping with the aesthetic of ancient Egypt itself. Modern Egyptians carry on this ancient custom by hanging pictures on every available wall in their houses.

So, the museum is literally a treasure house. But even more importantly, it plays a key role as guardian of the secrets and legacies of ancient Egypt. The Egyptian scribes are gone, their funerary chapels buried in sand, and their names lost over time, but the Egyptian Museum keeps the legacy of ancient Egypt alive. The treasures of the museum represent one of the world's oldest known civilizations, dating back as early as four thousand years BC. Egypt had writing, centralized government, great towns, and monuments at a time when humans elsewhere were hunting in small bands and tribes. The history of this ancient and glorious past is as intriguing to today's historians as it was to Herodotus, the Greek 'father of history,' who was writing in the fifth century BC.

The collections at the

6 Statue of Khafra.

museum are unique and have been regularly replenished with new finds, from the discoveries of Auguste Mariette in 1853, through the museum's current facilities, opened in 1902, until today. The latest, which I supervised myself, was from the excavations of the Metropolitan Museum at Dahshur, where they found gold and jewelry of Queen Weret, mother of Senusret III. Also on display at the museum now are ten statues that I discovered at Giza and Saqqara over the last ten years. But perhaps most fantastic of all, the five thousand golden artifacts of Tutankhamun and the museum's collection of mummies are unparalleled, and their mystery and magic forever capture our hearts and imaginations.

In total, the museum exhibits some 150,000 artifacts, with another 30,000 held in storage. These artifacts tell us the story of five thousand years of ancient civilization, from predynastic times through the age of the pyramid builders, the Middle Kingdom, the golden age of the Egyptian empire, Akhenaten, Tutankhamun, Rameses II, the Late Period gold of Tanis, to the exquisite Greco-Roman mummy portraits. This guidebook, written by a number of expert Egyptologists, carefully takes you on a tour of this great museum and explains the history of the most important pieces and the story of each discovery. Lavishly illustrated throughout, the beauty of Egyptian art shines with its combination of pleasing proportions and superb craftsmanship.

A friend of mine once asked me why I visit the museum so often. I told him that there were two reasons. The first is that every time I visit I spot something new that I had not noticed before. But besides that, I am in love with the diorite statue of Khafra, builder of the second pyramid at Giza. I like to gaze at the statue's profile with the falcon embracing the head of the king. I feel that the falcon is about to take flight with the king and soar with him into the sky.

The temples, tombs, and artifacts of ancient Egypt are fitting monuments to its power and wealth. From the grandeur and sheer audacity of the Great Pyramid at Giza to the elegance of the finely-crafted statues found in temple caches, the legacy of the pharaohs has provided us with a rich source of knowledge about the distant past and one of the world's first great civilizations. Visiting the museum with this illustrated guide is like experiencing a personalized adventure in the splendid world of the pharaohs.

9 Sarcophagus of Maatkara (detail).

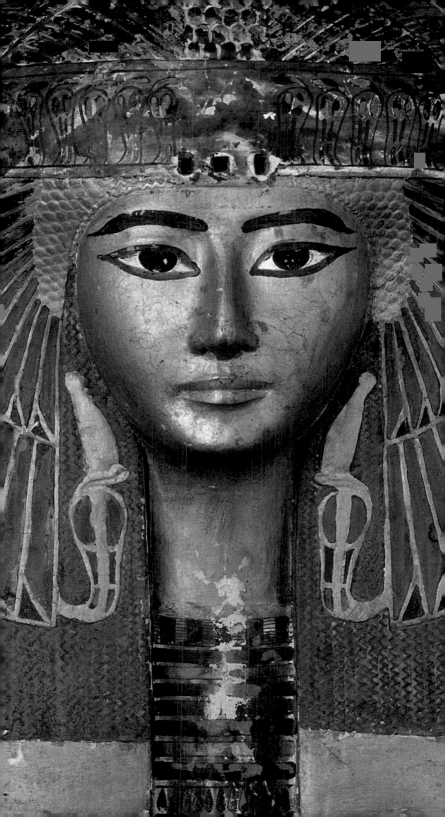

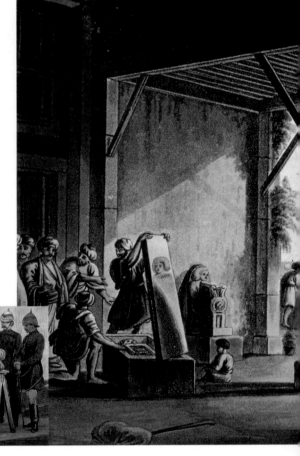

The initial step in the creation of the Egyptian Museum in Cairo was taken in 1835 when Mohammed Ali decided to put an end to the indiscriminate looting of archaeological sites in Egypt. In time, this led to the setting up of the Antiquities Service and to a permanent collection of art objects in the capital. However for 23 years the first

collections of ancient Egyptian objects were little more than stores of items in scattered sites until the initiative of Auguste Mariette officially established the Antiquities Service in 1858 with the aim of discovering and preserving ancient monuments.

Meanwhile, in

Europe the first great collections of Egyptian art were taking shape, for example, in the British Museum and the Louvre; in 1824 in Turin, the world's first great Egyptian museum was created when the Savoy family acquired the collection of the French General

Consul to Egypt, Bernadino Drovetti, which was visited and studied by the great French Egyptologist, Jean-François Champollion.

In 1858 appointed Director of the Antiquities Service, Mariette established the nucleus of the future Cairo museum in rooms belonging to

10

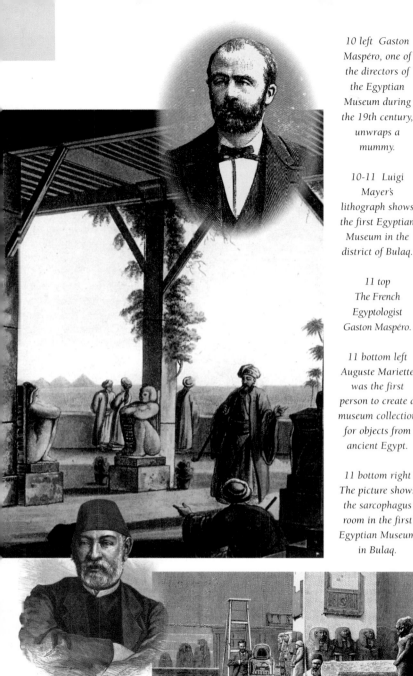

10 left Gaston Maspéro, one of the directors of the Egyptian Museum during the 19th century, unwraps a mummy.

10-11 Luigi Mayer's lithograph shows the first Egyptian Museum in the district of Bulaq.

11 top
The French Egyptologist Gaston Maspéro.

11 bottom left
Auguste Mariette was the first person to create a museum collection for objects from ancient Egypt.

11 bottom right
The picture shows the sarcophagus room in the first Egyptian Museum in Bulaq.

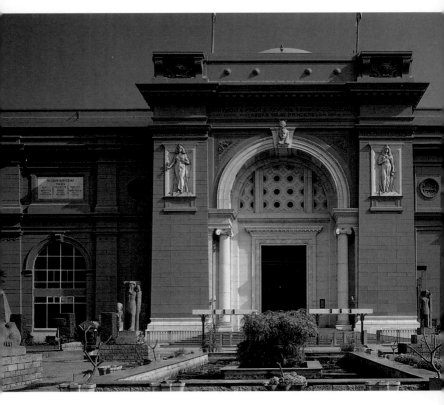

the old River
Company in the
district of Bulaq.
Hoping that the
increasingly large and
splendid art
collections of Egypt
would find a
permanent home in a
suitably impressive
building in the center
of the city, Mariette
dedicated his life to
the museum until his
death in January
1881. His remains
were first laid in the
museum's garden but
transferred in 1891 to
the residence of
Khedive Ismail in
Giza which became
the collections' new

home, and moved
again in 1902 to the
area in front of the
current museum
building in Midan
al-Tahrir.

Designed and
built by the French,
the elegant two-story
building has a
hundred or so rooms
arranged around a
central atrium, and a
vast basement for
storage of the many
finds that continue to
flow in from around
the country. Of the
many works of art
held by the museum,
exhibition of the
grave goods found in
the tomb of

Tutankhamun –
discovered intact in
1923 by Howard
Carter in the Valley of
the Kings – and of the
magnificent silver
sarcophaguses found
in the royal
necropolises at Tanis
quickly brought the
museum worldwide
fame.

Transfer of the
collections to the
museum's current
location began in
March 1902 under
the coordination of
Gaston Maspero where
they were ordered
chronologically on
the ground floor and
by object type on the

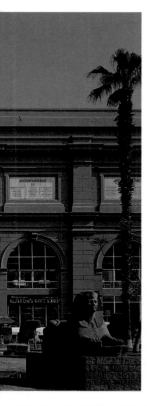

first floor, a system that is still adhered to. The constant increase in size of the collections over the previous century encouraged an exodus of some pieces to other museums such as Luxor, Mellawi and Aswan with the aim of promoting knowledge of ancient Egyptian culture in places other than the capital. The collection in Cairo, however, remains fundamental to scholars around the world as well as to anyone interested in deepening their knowledge by visiting the vast, even overwhelming museum. (A.B.)

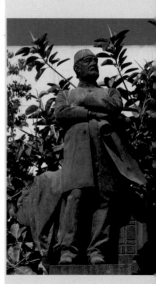

13 top The mausoleum of Auguste Mariette stands in the gardens of the museum.

13 center The ground floor hall has a large and splendid collection of statues: the colossal statue of Amenhotep III and Queen Tiy can be seen in the background.

13 bottom This is one of the side rooms on the ground floor.

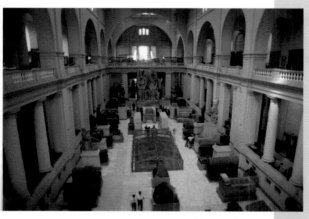

12-13 The photograph shows the current museum building which looks onto the square Midan al-Tahrir.

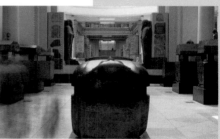

13

This guide presents the collections of the Egyptian Museum in Cairo in accordance with the layout of the museum. The first part is dedicated to the Ground Floor which exhibits the masterpieces of stone sculpture in chronological order from the Pre-Dynastic Period until the Roman Era; the second part introduces the items on the First Floor which illustrates various aspects of the ancient Egyptian civilisation, displaying the objects by theme or by archaeological context. Two general maps (page 20 refers to the Ground Floor and page 254 to the First Floor) give the room numbers and are colour-coded for easy understanding of the chronological periods (Ground Floor) and themes (First Floor). Each colour refers to a chapter that contains a smaller version of the floor map, a historical or theme-based introduction, and a detailed description of the most important objects.

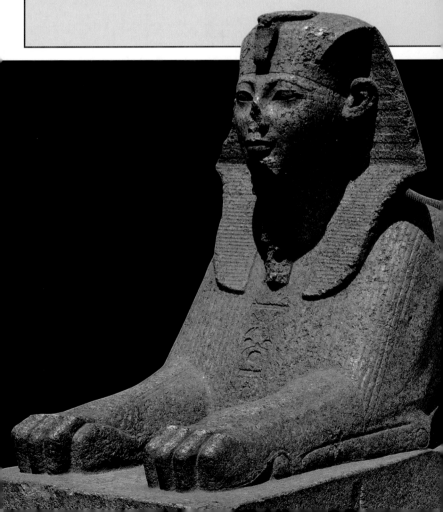

Check:
which room contains the object, next refer to the floor map and then to the relevant chapter.
Or:
consult the illustrated index that starts on page 580 where all the objects in the guide are listed in the order they are displayed in the museum rooms.

PRACTICAL INFORMATION

The Egyptian Museum is open every day from 9 a. m . - 5 p. m. (until 3 p. m. during the holy month of Ramadan). The cost of a full price ticket is LE 20 but LE 10 for students (ID is required).
A separate ticket costing LE 40 is required to visit the mummies on the First floor.
An additional cost of LE 10 is required if you wish to take photographs or LE 100 for the use of a videocamera.

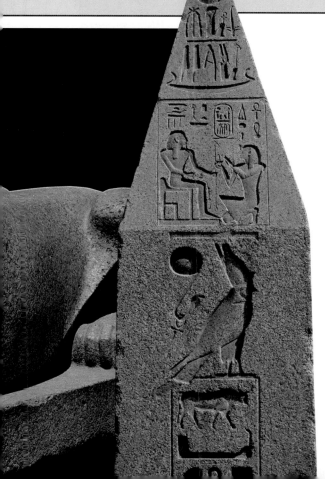

14-15 The museum garden also boasts important finds, such as this granite sphinx of Thutmosis III (262 CM long) found by Auguste Mariette in the Temple of Amun-Ra at Karnak.

15 This fragment of an obelisk of Rameses II in the museum garden was found at Tanis by Auguste Mariette in 1860. It is made of pink granite and stands 325 CM high.

16 Back of the pectoral in the name of Senusret II (detail).

15

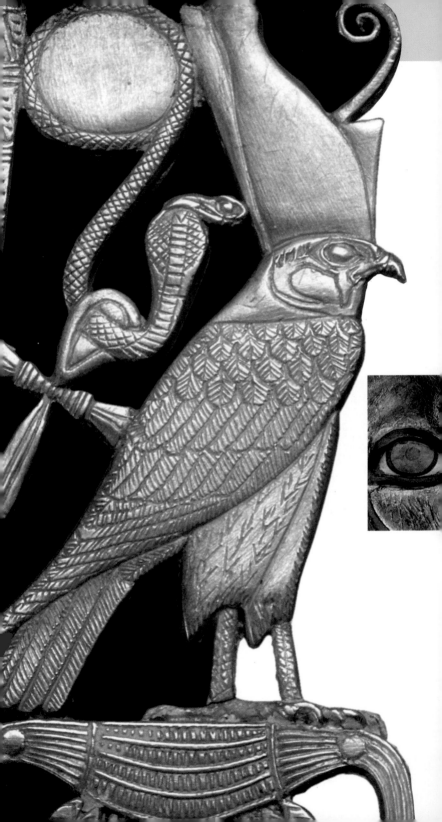

CHRONOLOGY

* PREDYNASTIC PERIOD *
(4000-3000 BC)

Naqada I	(4000-3500)
Naqada II	(3500-3100)

Dynasty 0 (3000 CA)
Narmer

* PROTODYNASTIC PERIOD *
(2920-2575 BC)

First Dynasty (2920-2770)
Aha (Menes ?)
Djer
Djet
Den
Anedjib
Semerkhet
Qa'a

Second Dynasty (2770-2649)
Hetepsekhemwy
Raneb
Nynetjer
Peribsen
Khasekhem (Khasekhemwy)

* OLD KINGDOM *
(2649 - 2152 BC)

Third Dynasty (2649-2575)
Sanakht	2649-2630
Djoser (Netjerikhet)	2630-2611
Sekhemkhet	2611-2603
Khaba	2603-2600
Huni	2600-2575

Fourth Dynasty (2575-2465)
Snefru	2575-2551
Khufu	2551-2528
Djedefra	2528-2520
Khafra	2520-2494
Menkaura	2494-2472
Shepseskaf	2472-2465

Fifth Dynasty (2465-2323)
Userkaf	2465-2458
Sahura	2458-2446
Neferirkare Kakai	2446-2426
Shepseskara	2426-2419
Neferefra	2419-2416
Nyuserra	2416-2392
Menkauhor	2392-2388
Djedkara Isesi	2388-2356
Unas	2356-2323

Sixth Dynasty (2323-2152)
Teti	2323-2291
Pepy I	2289-2255
Merenra	2255-2246
Pepy II	2246-2152

* FIRST INTERMEDIATE PERIOD *
(2152-2065 BC)

Seventh Dynasty
*A shadowy dynasty. Manetho
mentions 'seventy kings of
Memphis who ruled for seventy
days' to indicate the period of
confusion through which
Egypt passed.*

Eighth Dynasty (2150-2135)
*Of the twenty Memphite kings
whose names are known, Qakara
Aba is the only one whose presence
is verified – through the existence
of his pyramid in Saqqara.*

Ninth and Tenth Dynasties
(2135-2040)
*Dynasties in which the
government of much of Egypt
passed into the hands of
the city of Herakleopolis, before
Theban dynasty's reaffirmation.*

Eleventh Dynasty - first part
(2135-2065)
Mentuhotep I	
Antef I	
Antef II	2123-2073
Antef III	2073-2065

* MIDDLE KINGDOM *
(2040-1781 BC)

Eleventh Dynasty - second part
(2065-1994)
Mentuhotep II	
Nebhepetra	2065-2014
Mentuhotep III	2014-2001
Mentuhotep IV	2001-1994

Twelfth Dynasty (1994-1781)
Amenemhat I	1994-1964
Senusret I	1964-1929
Amenemhat II	1929-1898
Senusret II	1898-1881
Senusret III	1881-1842
Amenemhat III	1842-1794
Amenemhat IV	1793-1785
Queen Nefrusobek	1785-1781

Thirteenth Dynasty
(1781 - 1650)
Around seventy ephemeral
rulers are known.
Fourteenth Dynasty (1710-1650)
An unknown number of
ephemeral rulers contemporary to
the Thirteenth and the Fourteenth
Dynasties.
Fifteenth Dynasty (1650-1550)
Main Hyksos kings:
Salitis
Sheshi
Jaqobher
Khian
Apopi
Khamudi
Sixteenth Dynasty (1650-1550)
Minor Hyksos governors ruling
at the same time as the Fifteenth
Dynasty.
Seventeenth Dynasty (1640-1550)
Fifteen Theban kings, among
the most important of whom are:
Antef V
Sobekemsaef I
Sobekemsaef II
Antef VI
Antef VII
Seqenenra Tao I
Seqenenra Tao II
Kamosis

* NEW KINGDOM *
(1550-1075 BC)

Eighteenth Dynasty (1550-1291)

Ahmose	1550-1525
Amenhotep I	1525-1504
Thutmosis I	1504-1492
Thutmosis II	1492-1479
Hatshepsut	1479-1458
Thutmosis III	1479-1425
Amenhotep II	1424-1397
Thutmosis IV	1397-1387
Amenhotep III	1387-1350
Amenhotep IV/	
Akhenaten	1350-1333
Smenkhkare	1335-1333
Tutankhamun	1333-1323
Ay	1323-1319
Horemheb	1319-1291

Nineteenth Dynasty (1291-1185)

Rameses I	1291-1289
Sety I	1289-1279
Rameses II	1279-1212
Merneptah	1212-1202
Amenmeses	1202-1199
Sety II	1199-1193
Siptah	1193-1187
Tausret	1193-1185

Twentieth Dynasty (1187-1075)

Sethnakht	1187-1184
Rameses III	1184-1153
Rameses IV	1153-1147
Rameses V	1147-1143
Rameses VI	1143-1135
Rameses VII	1135-1127
Rameses VIII	1127-1126
Rameses IX	1126-1108
Rameses X	1108-1104
Rameses XI	1104-1075

* THIRD INTERMEDIATE PERIOD *
(1075-664 BC)

Twenty-first Dynasty (1075-945)

Smendes I	1075-1049
Neferkara	1049-1043
Psusennes I	1043-994
Amenemope	994-985
Osorkon the Elder	985-979
Siamun	979-960
Psunennes II	960-945

Twenty-second Dynasty (945-718)

Sheshonq I	945-924
Osorkon I	924-899
Sheshonq II	890 CA
Takelot I	889-883
Osorkon II	883-850
Takelot II	853-827
Sheshonq III	827-775
Pami	775-767
Sheshonq V	767-729
Osorkon V	729-718

Twenty-third Dynasty (820-718)

Petubasty I	820-795
Sheshonq IV	795-788
Osorkon IV	788-760
Takelot III	765-756
Rudamun	752-718

Twenty-fourth Dynasty (730-712)

Tefnakht	730-718
Bakenrenef	718-712

Twenty-fifth (775-653)

Alara	775-765
Kashta	765-745
Peye (Piankhy)	745-713
Shabaka	712-698
Shabatqo	698-690
Taharqa	690-664
Tanutamani	664-653

GROUND FLOOR

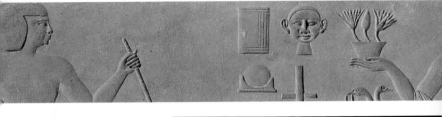

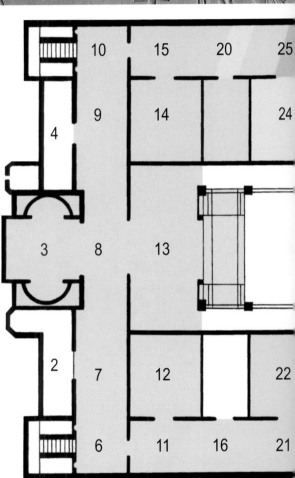

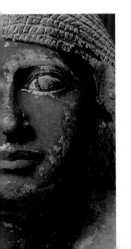

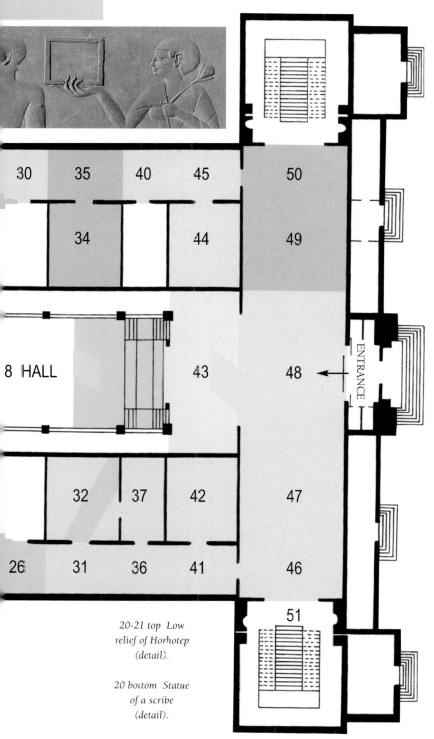

30   35   40   45   50

34   44   49

8 HALL   43   48   ← ENTRANCE

32   37   42   47

26   31   36   41   46

51

*20-21 top Low
relief of Horhotep
(detail).*

*20 bottom Statue
of a scribe
(detail).*

PROTODYNASTIC
AND PREDYNASTIC
PERIODS

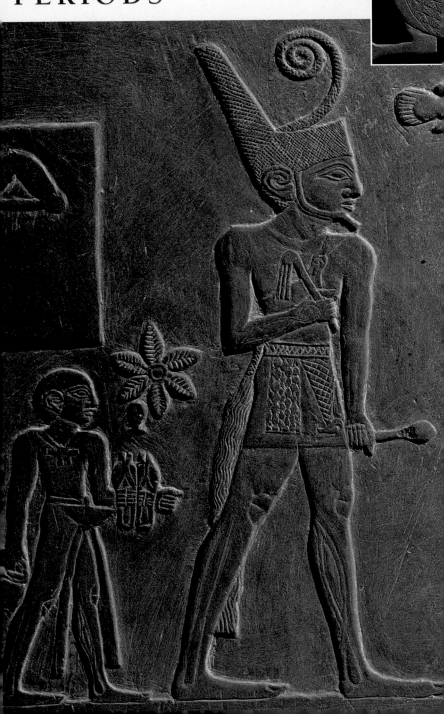

The long gestation period of the Egyptian civilization is still difficult to reconstruct due to lack of documentation and the fragmentary nature of archaeological evidence. Over the millennia, the annual flood of the Nile and its changes of course buried the most ancient sites nearest to the alluvial plain below accumulations of mud; if the regions of northern Egypt, where the river splits into hundreds of emissaries in the delta, have fewer archaeological remains to offer than the south of the country, it is not because they were less populated or more backward. but because the stratification of the alluvial deposits was more widespread.

Transition from the Paleolithic to the Neolithic period occurred in Egypt around 5500 BC. An unexpected increase in rainfall in north-eastern Africa resulted in the spontaneous growth of vegetation in arid zones over desert areas that facilitated human settlements on the edges of the valley and in the oases. Groups of herders and hunters adopted the habits of a settled existence, congregating in more structured communities that provided a subsistence economy increasingly based on agriculture and stock-raising.

In a habitat still populated by giraffes, elephants, rhinoceroses, and ostriches – which disappeared during the Late Predynastic Period – man learned to domesticate goats, pigs, cattle, and donkeys and perhaps even gazelles. The site of Badari in Upper Egypt – to which the culture known as Fayum A corresponds in the north of the country – is the most representative of this period of transition: fireplaces, the remains of domestic and wild animals, sickles, baskets, millstones, and coarse materials document the progress of a society still rooted in the hunting tradition but already able to cultivate the land and to produce functional items adapted to a new lifestyle.

Wheat and barley were already the basis of the Egyptian diet even in this remote epoch. The cultivation of flax soon

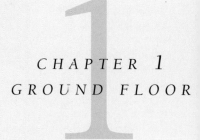

CHAPTER 1
GROUND FLOOR

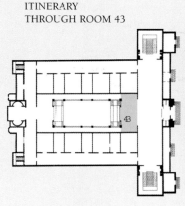

43

22 NARMER'S TABLET
Schist; Height 64 cm, width 42 cm, thickness 2.5 cm; Hierakonpolis

Excavation by J. Quibell (1894); Protodynastic Period (end of IV millenium BC)

developed a flourishing and refined textile industry which was to be a cornerstone, with the production of cereals, of Egypt's wealth during the historical period and the first of the country's produce to be exported.

Pottery production was one of the most important steps forward and was to experience enormous development during the Predynastic Period. Though limited in scope, Badarian pottery was very elegant with bowls in a brilliant red or black, or red with black edges, that was obtained by a process of repeated firing.

Craftsmen carved a wide variety of tools and ornaments from flint, bone, and ivory, for example, combs, arrow heads, fishing hooks, and razors. Many such objects accompanied the deceased on his trip to the Afterlife along with amulets, brooches and beads. Whereas the dead were buried below the houses in very ancient times, later the necropolises were moved to the edge of the desert where sand and the dry climate naturally initiated the process of mummification later obtained with elaborate procedures. The body was laid hunched in an elliptical pit, sometimes wrapped in matting or a

cloth, together with personal objects and a small viaticum of cereals. Beliefs in the Afterlife were not as clearly defined as they were in later centuries, but the presence of grave goods, however simple, is evidence of the ancient Egyptian certainty in a life beyond the grave that was not dissimilar to their earthly existence.

The cultural characteristics of the population of Badari developed during the following Naqada I or

Amratian phase (4000-3500 BC) named after the sites that have left most archaeological evidence. Pottery improved and increased its range of styles and figurative motifs; crockery was more slender and generally colored red with full background painting or covered with cream-colored naturalistic or abstract representations. Crafts used new materials such as copper, turquoise, malachite, and obsidian to create new types of

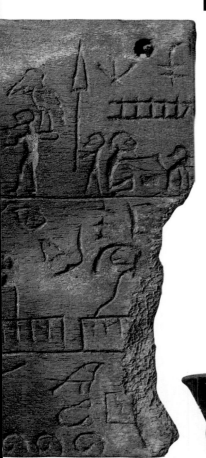

long, entwined necks; these were used to ornament palettes used for cosmetics and the handles of luxury knives. Maceheads, previously prevalently disc-shaped, developed into the shape of a pear, and cylindrical seals began to proliferate. In addition to typical Gerzean production-oval vases made of pink paste colored dark red-pottery took the forms of containers with undulating handles, typical of Palestine, and with an inclined lip, imported from Mesopotamia. These

objects including cosmetic palettes and perfume spoons. This was the era of the first cultural and trading relations with nearby centers, for the most part aimed at the acquisition of raw materials. Despite its poor agricultural potential compared to Egypt, Nubia was a useful market for the supply of high quality materials such as gold, ebony, and ivory.

The Naqada II or Gerzean phase (3500-3100 BC) brought with it rapid progress; the northernmost centers, such as Ma'adi, provided a cultural and commercial communication route between Egypt and south-west Asia. Eastern influences are seen in the adoption of new iconographic and stylistic models such as a bearded hero or heraldic motifs of rampant animals with influences, however, were of short duration. Egyptian artists filtered them through their own styles thereby creating increasingly original expressions of their own culture.

At the end of the Predynastic Period (Naqada III), a process of specialization of trades and an accentuation of social stratification took place. Naqada and Hierakonpolis became important urban centers in the economic and political organization that was to become the cradle of pharaonic civilization. Tombs of the rulers of the Late Predynastic era were found here with signs of the cult of the two deities most closely associated

new cities – each identified by its own animal-standard – were figurative themes widely used and an expression of the new policies of conquest. An effective strategy of alliances by the lords of Hierakonpolis (Dynasty

the exact dynamics that led to the formation of the pharaonic state remain unknown. What is certain is that by this time the monarchy bore the characteristics it was to maintain for 3000 years. The political, economic and religious power in the country was concentrated in the pharaoh, the terrestrial incarnation

with the monarchic institution: Seth at Naqada and Horus at Hierakonpolis.

As in Upper Egypt, a proliferation of small autonomous political entities also occurred in Lower Egypt. These centers were increasingly in competition with one another over trade and the monopoly of profits. Land and sea battles between enemy tribes and the conquest or the foundation of

0) brought the progressive unification of the Two Lands – Upper and Lower Egypt – under a unique, double crown.

Who was the first king of the First Dynasty? Narmer, Menes, Aha: all three are referred to in sources as being founders of the Egyptian civilization but

of the god-falcon Horus; his human and divine essence made him the guarantor of the unity of the state and, in the last analysis, of the equilibrium of the world. Such powers were reflected in the monumental architecture of the royal tombs. The monarchs of the first two dynasties (known as the Thinite Dynasties after their capital, This) were buried at Abydos and Saqqara, sometimes in both cities at once as though to underline the geographical duplicity of the political unity. The tombs had a mastaba superstructure (a parallelepiped tumulus) which was simpler at Abydos than those at Saqqara, with external walls featuring niches and pillars in imitation of the royal palace. The style was Mesopotamian in inspiration and its stylized representation – the *serekh* – with an administration structured in a rigid hierarchy could run the new economic system effectively. Coordination of the various activities made necessary the growth of more suitable tools for management of the complex duties of the bureaucracy, one of which was writing. The first hieroglyphics appeared on seals, labels, vases, and other objects used for concepts that had still to be expressed by figured

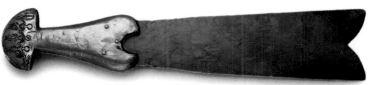

image of Horus above, contained the name of the king in its inscriptions. Later the king's name was to be written in a cartouche. The rich grave goods are evidence of the tendency towards specialization of occupations with the growing demand for luxury goods from the court and other high functionaries, encouraging the formation of a class of skilled artists and craftsmen as well as the creation of larger markets for the acquisition of valuable raw materials. Only a strongly centralized scenes. Votive tablets and funerary stelae give the names of the first pharaohs and of the deities that made up the Egyptian religious world: Horus, Set, Isis, Neith, Hathor, Anubis, Min, and the bull Apis. Despite the very few remains of archaic temples, these objects testfy to the existence of beliefs and religious and funerary rituals that may already be termed "classical". (M.S.C.)

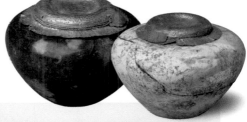

NARMER'S TABLET

SCHIST; HEIGHT 64 CM, WIDTH 42 CM
HIERAKONPOLIS; EXCAVATION BY J. QUIBELL (1894)
DYNASTY 0, REIGN OF NARMER (3000 BC)

ROOM 43

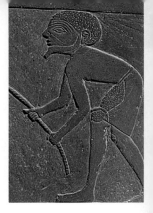

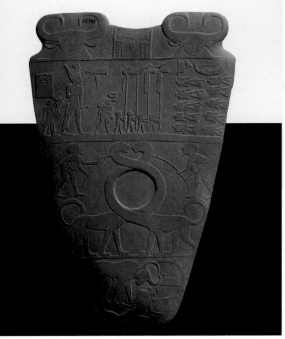

This votive tablet is an item of major artistic and historical importance. Egyptologists have long interpreted the scenes on the sides as a celebration of the annexation of Lower Egypt by King Narmer of Hierakonpolis, however, the dynamics of the events that led to Egypt being ruled by a single monarch are uncertain and it is only possible to have a sketchy idea of the political context in which the rulers of the so-called Dynasty 0 lived.

If it ever really happened that a northern and southern kingdom existed as rivals, then it is probable that the Two Lands had already been united before Narmer's rule and that Hierakonpolis, where many finds refer to the rulers of this city, would have played a prime role in this process. The enterprise immortalized by Narmer more probably refers to a military victory over an area in the Delta identified as *Uash*. The front of the tablet shows the triumphant king reviewing a double line of decapitated prisoners; the pharaoh is followed by a dignitary who holds the royal sandals and is preceeded by another dignitary and the four standards. The standards have been identified as the "followers of Horus", i.e. of the pharaoh; they are very ancient emblems of the first territorial units. Wearing the red crown of Lower Egypt, Narmer is the incarnation of the ruler of the north who strikes against those who rebel; this authority is displayed by the attributes he holds in his hand – the soldier's club and the royal sceptre. He is the powerful bull that attacks the fort and overthrows his enemy, and, as shown in the central register, overcomes the forces against him represented by the wild cats with long entwined necks. The point in which malachite was crushed is the focus of the scene. The name of the king in the *serekh*, flanked by two Hathoric heads, is the main element on both sides of the tablet. On the reverse is the victorious king with the crown of Upper Egypt defeating the enemy of *Uash*; it emphasises the hieroglyphic message that shows Narmer as the falcon Horus holding the man of the papyrus land (the Delta) on a leash. (M.S.G.)

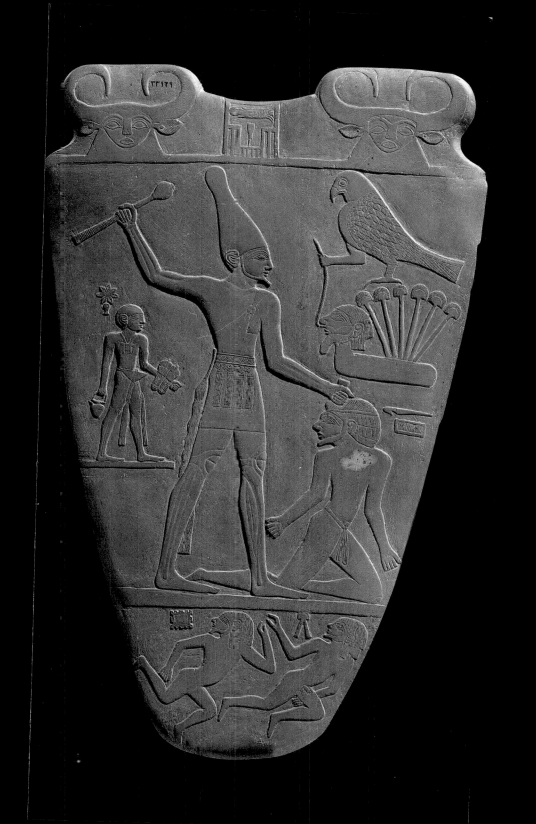

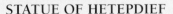

STATUE OF HETEPDIEF

RED GRANITE; HEIGHT 39 CM; MEMPHIS (1888)
END OF THE SECOND – START OF THE THIRD DYNASTY
(SECOND HALF OF THE 27TH CENTURY BC)

ROOM 43

A type of private statuary characterized by compact, unelaborate forms began to appear in the Third Dynasty. The figures were given a solid body and a disproportionately large, though lightly featured, head. Of the statues of this type, that of Hetepdief is notable for the figure's unusual pose; he is not portrayed in the customary fashion seated on a cubic seat but kneeling with his hands open on his thighs.

In Egyptian

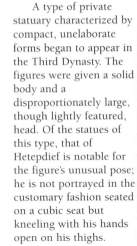

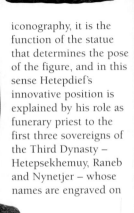

iconography, it is the function of the statue that determines the pose of the figure, and in this sense Hetepdief's innovative position is explained by his role as funerary priest to the first three sovereigns of the Third Dynasty – Hetepsekhemuy, Raneb and Nynetjer – whose names are engraved on the back of his right shoulder. Hetepdief is shown kneeling as a sign of reverence and homage toward the dead kings for whose posthumous cult he was responsible. The perfunctory treatment of the volumes makes the statue rather coarse and heavy and resembles certain examples of archaic sculpture that evidently provided the inspiration for this type of statuary. Only the precise rendition of the hair shows the artist's ability to provide detail, though this is clearly considered to be of secondary importance. (M.S.C.)

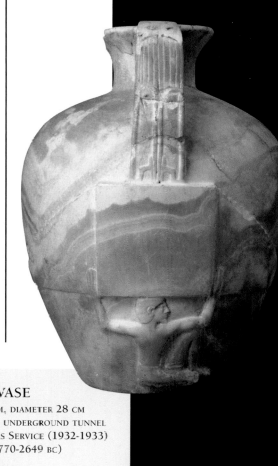

JUBILEE VASE
Alabaster; Height 37 cm, diameter 28 cm
Saqqara, Pyramid of Djoser, underground tunnel
Excavation by the Antiquities Service (1932-1933)
Second Dynasty (2770-2649 bc)

ROOM 43

A large number of very fine alabaster vases, many from the previous dynasties, were found in the grave goods in the underground stores of Djoser's step pyramid at Saqqara. The vase shown here is from the Second Dynasty.

The artist produced an effective and expressive symbol of one of the most important ceremonies of the epoch – the Sed festival or royal Jubilee – during which the king publicly reconfirmed his authority over his lands and regenerated his energies by undertaking a ritual running.

The handles depict the images of the two thrones of Upper and Lower Egypt protected by their respective canopies. The king took his place on the thrones as the absolute lord of the Two Lands after receiving homage from the various deities of Egypt. As images on a flat surface were never portrayed frontally, the thrones are seen in profile although they were in fact placed side by side. They rested on the square base flanked by the two stairways shown on the bulge of the vase. Below, the kneeling god of eternity, Heh, raises his open arms as seen in the hieroglyph *heh* meaning 'millions".

To the north-east of the pyramid, Djoser rebuilt the buildings where the jubilee festivals were celebrated to ensure that the most spectacular and fundamental of the royal attributes would endure for "millions of years". (M.S.C.)

NECKLACE FROM THE THINITE AGE

FAÏENCE AND SCHIST
LENGTH 29 CM
HELUAN; EXCAVATION BY Z. SAAD (1942)
FIRST DYNASTY (2920-2770 BC)

ROOM 43

Right from the earliest of times, jewelery and ornaments were produced in a wide variety of shapes and materials in Egypt.

These necklaces were made from semi-precious stones and destined to accompany the deceased in the Afterlife. They had the double function of being both ornaments and amulets as the quality and cut of the stones used were considered to have magical and apotropaic powers that complemented the article's aesthetic value.

A row of faïence granules (the blue glazing has almost disappeared) with a dung beetle scarab

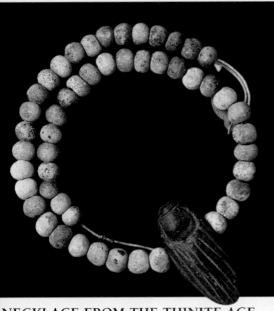

NECKLACE FROM THE THINITE AGE

CARNELIAN
LENGTH 61.5 CM
HELUAN; EXCAVATION BY Z. SAAD (1942)
FIRST DYNASTY (2920-2770 BC)

ROOM 43

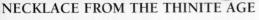

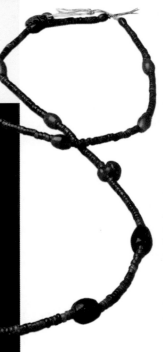

NECKLACE FROM
THE THINITE AGE
FAÏENCE; LENGTH 77 CM
HELUAN; EXCAVATION BY Z. SAAD (1942)
FIRST DYNASTY (2920-2770 BC)

ROOM 43

made from schist in the center (1) is a simple representation of the two meanings of the necklace; the purpose of the scarab was to ensure the wearer of the necklace was eternally reborn in the Afterlife.

The choker with a pendant in the form of a falcon on a boat (3) is made entirely from turquoise faïence. When it was found, the amulet was hung around the neck of the mummy as a last and touching simulacrum of the saving power of the god Horus.

In addition to unrefined materials, jewellers made wide use of expensive stones like carnelian (2), turquoise, amethyst, garnet, and lapis lazuli (4), which were all mined locally except for lapis lazuli which came from Afghanistan. These two necklaces were made during different periods, but both have a central lion's head made from carnelian on a single string of pearls of various sizes, which proves that the model was very fashionable for at least three hundred years. (M.S.C.)

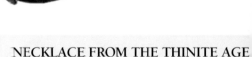

NECKLACE FROM THE THINITE AGE
CARNELIAN, AMETHYST, SEMI-PRECIOUS STONES
LENGTH CM 82
HELUAN; EXCAVATION BY Z. SAAD (1945)
SECOND DYNASTY (2770-2649 BC)

ROOM 43

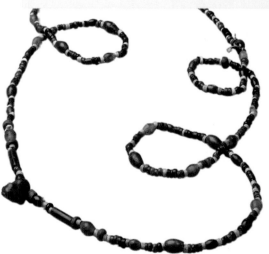

LOTUS FLOWER VASE

PAINTED LIMESTONE; HEIGHT 7 CM
SAQQARA, TOMB OF HEMAKA
EXCAVATION BY W. B. EMERY (1936)
FIRST DYNASTY (2920-2770 BC), REIGN OF DEN

ROOM 43

This charming miniature vase was found with many other exquisitely manufactured objects in the tomb of Hemaka, the treasurer and administrator of King Den. A delicate lotus bloom decorated in bright colors elegantly disguises a small cosmetics container and provides evidence of the extraordinary stone carving skill achieved by ancient Egyptians in this epoch, an art at which they were unsurpassed.

Artistic inspiration was provided to the Nilotic masons by the many forms of nature that surrounded them and which they reproduced with extreme realism. The calyx of the flower is rendered extremely accurately with its petals just open enough to accept a cosmetic or ointment. (M.S.C.)

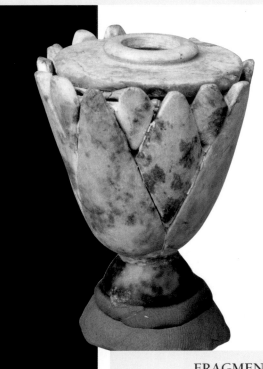

FRAGMENT OF THE "LIBYAN TRIBUTE" TABLET

SCHIST; HEIGHT 19 CM, WIDTH 22 CM
ABYDOS; END OF THE PREDYNASTIC PERIOD (3000 BC CA)

ROOM 43

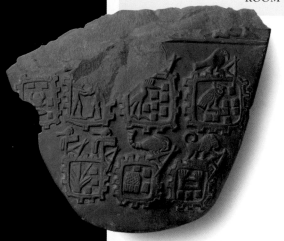

The missing upper section of the tablet prevents complete understanding of the reliefs. A series of animals (the same animals that appear on the standards of the *nomoi*) is shown on one side, each of which sinks a pick into the fortified

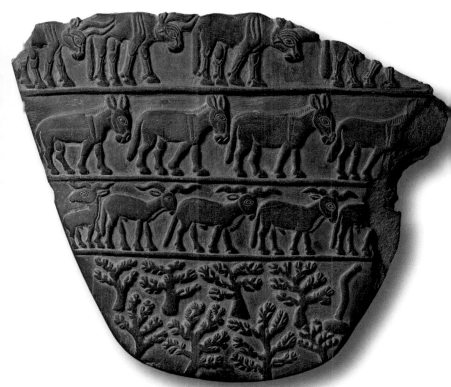

walls of a city. The name of each city is written in hieroglyphs inside the city walls.

At the time this tablet was produced, the expansion of the kingdom of Hierakonpolis northwards was in full swing and perhaps the scene celebrates the victory of the king and his confederates over enemy forts.

It cannot, however, be excluded that the event commemorated refers to the foundation of new cities by the king, perhaps in the subjected territories.

The decoration on the other side shows long trains of animals on three registers and a copse of olive trees accompanied by the hieroglyph that represented the ancient Libyan tribes, the Tjemehu.

In the absence of other elements, the scene is generally interpreted as the payment of a large tribute by the peoples of Libya who were, at least in ancient times, famous for high quality olive oil. We are unable to know if the tribute was a gift of homage to the Egyptian king, whether it was voluntary or not, or if it was booty taken following an Egyptian victory over the Tjemehu, but the second hypothesis is the more probable.

The iconographic rendition of the animals that march in file shows a certain sensibility for the nature of each species. The bulls with their horns lowered seem fretful of the orderly procession they are obliged to follow, whereas the donkeys proceed indifferently, accustomed to long journeys. The procession is concluded by a herd of rams, also docile, the last of which is smaller and has its head facing backwards; this is an expedient used by the artist that cleverly resolves the lack of space available and breaks the monotony of the whole. (M.S.C.)

SENET

INLAID BOXES: IVORY; LENGTH 4 CM, WIDTH 4 CM; ABU ROACH
EXCAVATIONS BY THE FRENCH INSTITUTE OF ORIENTAL ARCHAEOLOGY
FIRST-SECOND DYNASTY (2920-2649 BC)
PIECES: IVORY; HEIGTH 5 CM MAX., DIAMETER 3.5 CM MAX.
SAQQUARA, TOMB OF DJET; EXCAVATIONS BY W. B. EMERY
FIRST DYNASTY (2920-2770 BC), KINGDOM OF DJET

ROOM 43

From the earliest times, the game of *senet* was one of the favorite pastimes of the ancient Egyptians; the abundance of archaeological data has enabled us to learn, more or less, the workings of the game. The two players each have an equal number of pieces, different in both color and shape, which are moved around a rectangular board divided into thirty squares (known in Egyptian as *peru*, "houses") in three lines of ten each. The pieces are moved in accordance with the fall of sticks thrown by the players. The aim of the game is to move all the way around the 30 squares, some of which might enable the player to move forwards or force him backwards if landed on.

The inclusion of *senet* among grave goods and the frequent representation of the game on tomb walls suggest the game had funerary implications beyond simple entertainment.

The tortuous route taken by the pieces on the board may have symbolically reflected the journey of the soul beyond the tomb with each square representing a stop on the way. The reward for successfully concluding the journey would have been eternal life. (M.S.C.)

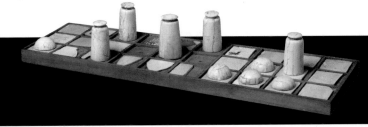

LABEL OF AHA

IVORY; HEIGHT 4.8 CM, WIDTH 5.6 CM
NAQADA; EXCAVATED IN 1897
A FRAGMENT WAS FOUND BY GARSTANG (1904)
FIRST DYNASTY (2920-2770 BC), REIGN OF AHA

ROOM 43

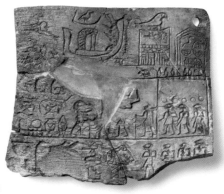

Painstaking by nature, the ancient Egyptians recorded in detail the contents of oil and wine amphoras. The information was engraved directly onto jars or a sealed top or, as in this case, on labels tied to the neck of the container. The small ivory plaque was engraved with a burin and found in the tomb of Queen Neithhotep, Aha's wife.

Horus the falcon is at the top right clutching the hieroglyphs that form the name of the king, Aha, "the Fighter." Below a pavilion, the goddess-cobra Uadjet and the goddess-vulture Nekhbet stand over the hieroglyph *men*, meaning "endure"; this scene might indicate the name of pharaoh Menes (*men*) and be dedicated to the Two Ladies. If that is the case, identification of Aha with Menes (the king cited by the Egyptian historian Manetho as the first pharaoh of the First Dynasty) would be compatible with the version on the Palermo Stone, an important list of the kings of the first five dynasties which begins with Aha. However, it was only with the penultimate king of the First Dynasty that the "Two Ladies" became one of the titles of the royal name, so it is more probable that the double symbol represents the name of the pavilion: *nebty-men*, i.e. "the Two Ladies will endure" (von Beckerath,1984).

The decoration contiues with a boating scene and Horus over the cabin on a boat. A building decorated with a *khakeru* freeze appears in the middle register; the frieze is a stylization of the knotted ends of the plant strips that were used to form the walls. Three long-haired figures appear inside: a dignitary with a long skirt and a staff watches the central scene where two men, perhaps priests, pour water inside what is probably a vase. Various offerings of loaves, jars, and oxen appear on either side.

In the last register, four short-haired figures, perhaps servants, advance towards a group of hieroglyphs that specify the type of oil contained in the vase.
(M.S.C.)

VASE WITH PAINTED DECORATION
CLAY; HEIGHT 22 CM, DIAMETER 15 CM
PROVENANCE UNKNOWN
PREDYNASTIC PERIOD, NAQADA II (3500-3100 BC)

ROOM 43

The vast production of vases by the cultures preceding the historical epoch was enhanced in the final Predynastic period by new forms and decorations and by more advanced production techniques such as the hand-spun wheel.

This vase is an important example of the most common typology during the Gerzean epoch (Naqada II). Its typical features were a very fine paste, closed designs, flat edges, and perforated handles through which a hanging cord could be passed. The pinkish hues of the bottom are decorated with a series of dark red motifs distributed following the surface lines.

The range of figures is mostly based on naturalistic motifs taken from the Nilotic environment and represents the earliest examples of pictorial art from ancient Egypt.

A rowing boat is shown at the height of the handles on both sides with two cabins side by side that fly the standard of a *nome*. The anchor hangs below a long plume at the prow, ready to be dropped into the river whose waters are represented by wavy lines on the handles. The scene is completed by rows of stylized ostriches between thick aloe plants whose leafy branches unite to form a single backdrop to the scenes painted on either side of the vase.
(M.S.C.)

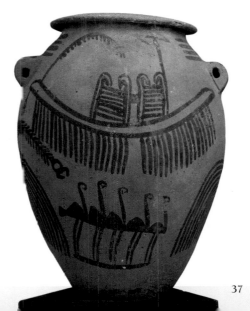

BASKET-SHAPED TRAY

SCHIST

HEIGHT 4.8 CM, LENGTH 22.7 CM, WIDTH 13.8 CM

SAQQARA; EXCAVATION BY W. B. EMERY (1937-1938)

SECOND DYNASTY (2770-2649 BC)

ROOM 43

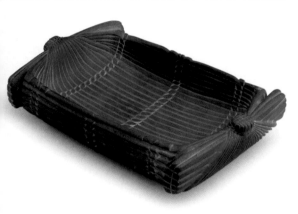

VASE WITH NAMES OF PHARAOHS

SCHIST; HEIGHT 12 CM, DIAMETER 23 CM

SAQQARA, PYRAMID OF DJOSER

EXCAVATION BY THE EGYPTIAN ANTIQUITIES SERVICE (1933)

FIRST DYNASTY (2920-2770 BC)

ROOM 43

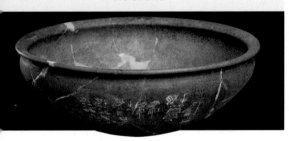

There was no stone that the ancient Egyptian masons and artists were unable to shape with consummate skill. The solidity of stone made any object or figure it was used to depict immortal so it was therefore used in the manufacture of many objects in sets of grave goods.

This small recipient made from green schist is a faithful reproduction of an elegant, though modest, wicker basket. The engraving *nbu* (gold) on one side perhaps means that the stems either were, or "magically" became, gold threads thanks to the force of the word itself; this would make the material more valuable and as imperishable as the golden flesh of the gods. (M.S.C.)

The two falcons on the standards are the "Two Lords" who stand at the start of the *nysut-bity* name of Adj-ib, Mer-pa-bia, "The beloved of the marvellous throne (of the Two Lords)."

The third king, Semerkhet, adds the title *nebty* (the "Two Ladies") to his *nysut-bity* name, (the goddess Nekhbet of al-Kab and the goddess Uadjet of Buto) whose indissoluble link ensured stability.

The *nysut-bity* and *nebty* names of Qaa are the same as the Horus name. The group of signs seen before the list refers to the function of "head cellarman in the house of Horus the harpooner." (M.S.C.)

The inscriptions on this vase are evidence of the identity of the last four kings of the First Dynasty, better known by their "Horus" names: Den, Adj-ib, Semerkhet, and Qaa. Since Den's reign, the first royal name written in the *serekh* and dedicated to Horus was followed by a second name associated with the title *nysut-bity*, "king of Upper and Lower Egypt," "He to whom the *sut* plant and bee belong" (the emblems of Upper and Lower Egypt). Den's *nysut-bity* name was *khasty*, "He to whom the two deserts belong," which were represented by two small sandy hills.

STATUE OF KHASEKHEM

SCHIST; HEIGHT 56 CM
HIERAKONPOLIS; EXCAVATION BY J. QUIBELL (1898)
SECOND DYNASTY (2770-2649 BC),
REIGN OF KHASEKHEM

ROOM 43

Examples of royal statuary from the Thinite epoch are very rare but the high quality of this sculpture of Khasekhem found in a storeroom beneath the temple at Hierakonpolis is typical of the artistic level achieved by the court artists. During the first two dynasties, the formal simplifications and solid volumes of the archaic tradition were maintained in private sculpture but the royal workshops produced more elaborate and innovative works.

The iconography and balance of the proportions in this statue of Khasekhem are precise and careful; the solidity of the work progressively lightens as it rises from the block of the throne until it reaches the tip of the white crown without losing the atmosphere of severity and strictness that was its function. The king is portrayed wearing the costume of the Jubilee, the long clinging cloak that folds across his chest.

A series of straight lines and right angles defines the volumes on the lower part of the statue; the modelling is not very deep and hardly modulated by the light that reflects on the polished surface. Softer, more three dimensional forms are used to create the king's head whose dignified and naturalistic expression is emphasized by strong cheekbones and the muscles at the corners of his mouth.

The outcome of a cruel battle is shown around the base of the throne: the injured bodies of the enemy (47,209 in total according to the hieroglyphs that describe the scene) lie disordered on the battlefield portrayed in their death-throws.

The scenes probably celebrate the victory of Khasekhem over the peoples of Lower Egypt who refused to recognise his authority. We know that at the end of the Second Dynasty Egypt was wracked by serious internal disorder that led to the split between the north and south of the country. Khasekhem, which means "The powerful appears in glory," succeeded in re-establishing the unity of the two kingdoms upon which he changed his name to Khasekhemuy, "The two powers appear in glory." The historical identity of the two characters is not, however, unanimously accepted and some scholars believe they were two separate pharaohs.
(M.S.C.)

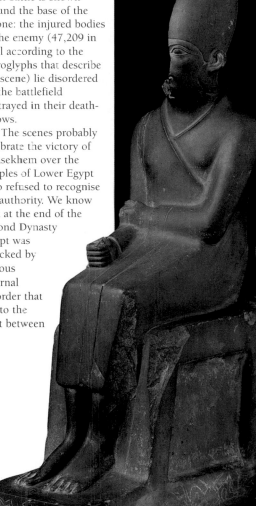

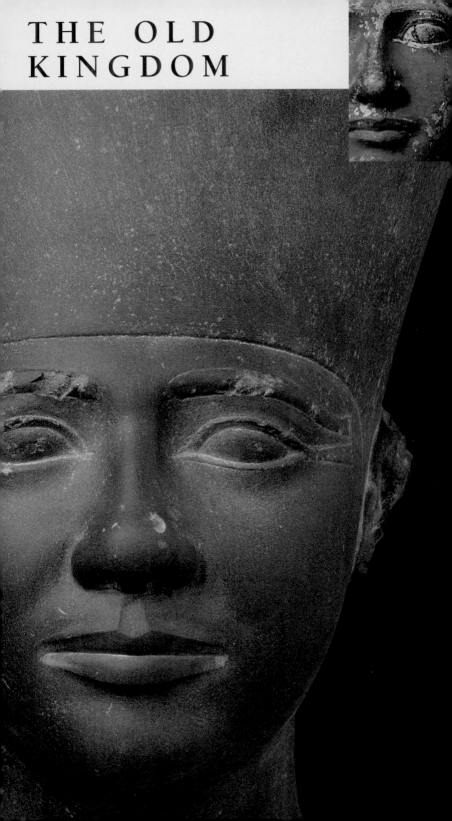

THE OLD
KINGDOM

The Old Kingdom started with the Third Dynasty. It was a period of political and cultural conquests which made the Egyptian state the richest and most powerful of the period.

An energetic policy of expansion in the Sinai and Palestine to the north, and in Lower Nubia to the south, was accompanied by an increase in trade with west Asia, Nubia, and the legendary country of Punt, vaguely localized between Sudan and Eritrea, which supplied exotic goods like incense, ebony, ivory and, leopard skins

Knowledge of Egypts superiority was revealed in the idea that the Egyptian world was governed by universal laws of order and justice (*ma'at*) that had

The legacy of the first two dynasties were confirmed and legitimised in every field by a rich *corpus* of myths that were to form the guidelines of pharaonic ideology from this time on. At the center there was always the figure of the pharaoh whose twin nature (human and divine) guaranteed order on earth and the harmony of the cosmos. The founding myth of pharaonic royalty personified the king as the god-falcon Horus who battled against Seth, the incarnation of evil and chaos, so as to maintain order and justice in the world. The struggle had clear political and religious parallels and reflected the attempt to justify the divine nature of political power though the creation of myths. Seth was the murderer of the

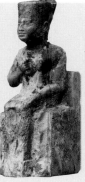

CHAPTER 2
GROUND FLOOR

been laid down by the gods at the moment of creation and that everything outside of *ma'at* was chaos, disorder and anarchy. Only the pharaoh, applying the principles of *ma'at*, could weaken and destroy the external forces that constantly threatened Egypt and ensure the stability of the kingdom and the world. Later traditions were also to regard this epoch as an ideal model, a mythic Golden Age from which to draw inspiration during moments when society's original values or national identity were in crisis.

ITINERARY THROUGH ROOMS
43, 48, 47, 46, 41, 42, 36, 31, 32, 37

43 48
32 37 42 47
31 36 41 46

father of Horus – Osiris, who was the archetype of the dead king – and the defeat of Seth by the heir ensured the continuity of the crown and the stability of the country.

The disparity between the nature of the king and the rest of humanity was at the base of the endurance of the Egyptian civilization over thousands of years;

the sovereign was the prime and final cause of everything that existed and prosperity depended entirely on his benevolence.

Djoser, the first king of the Third Dynasty, was emblematic of this almost mystic conception of royalty. He transferred the capital of the country to Memphis, where it

was strategically located on the boundary between the two Egypts, and created a new type of royal tomb at Saqqara. Advised by the architectural genius, Imhotep – later adored as a semi-god – he conceived a grandiose monument built entirely from stone in the form of a stepped pyramid. The funerary complex was enclosed by a wall with niches and pillars like the facades of the archaic palaces, the *serekh*, and it encompassed, in addition to the pyramid and temple used for worship of the deceased, many buildings

42 FRAGMENT OF PLASTER WITH HIEROGLYPHS
Painted plaster; Height 36 cm; Maydum, Mastaba of Rahotep Excavation by A. Mariette 1871 Fourth Dynasty,

Reign of Snefru (2575-2551 BC)

STATUES OF RAHOTEP AND NOFRET
Painted limestone; Rahotep: height 121 cm;

Nofret: height 122 cm; Maydum, Mastaba of Rahotep; Excavation by A. Mariette 1871 Fourth Dynasty, Reign of Snefru (2575-2551 BC)

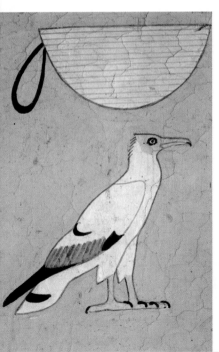

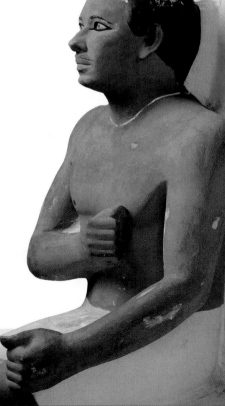

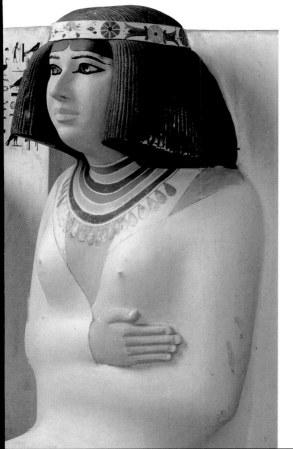

destined to perpetuate the pharaoh's power. The structure faithfully reproduced that of the royal palace but it also contained a small scale reproduction of the rooms in which the king used to celebrate the rite of the Sed, the royal Jubilee, in which his vital forces and authority were renewed. The implications of the new abode beyond the grave were multiple: the use of stone made the structure enduring and its form emphasized the distance between the king and his subjects. It raised the pharaoh toward a new

celestial existence, similar in concept to his earthly life, and re-established the mythical conditions of the creation of the world when the first hill (the pyramid), from which life originated, emerged from the waters of primordial chaos.

The pyramid at Maydum (Huni, end Third Dynasty) and those at Dahshur (Snefru, early Fourth Dynasty) signal the attempt to synthesize a new ideological concept of royalty using pyramidal forms as close as possible to the

perfection achieved by Khufu, Snefru's son, and his successors. The Giza pyramids represent petrified solar rays that lift up the pharaoh and merge him with Ra, the sun god. The architectural symbols of the king's temporal power were secondary. Attention was paid not just to his divine essence, but also to his cult, with the two temples annexed to the pyramid and joined by an ascending ramp.

The following dynasty went further. Originating in Heliopolis, the holy city dedicated to Ra, it legitimized itself claiming direct descent from the sun god by adding the title *Sa-Ra* (Son of Ra) to its royal appellation. The royal tombs and funerary temples of the Fifth Dynasty at Abusir enforced the supremacy of Ra over the other gods. The priesthood of Heliopolis concocted an elaborate theology based on the cult of the sun in open sanctuaries that were essentially based on a pyramidal model but organized around a monumental obelisk – the *benben* – which was a lithic translation of the creative power of the star.

Beginning with Unas, the last pharaoh in this dynasty, the funerary apartments were covered with formulas, spells and exorcisms – the *Texts of*

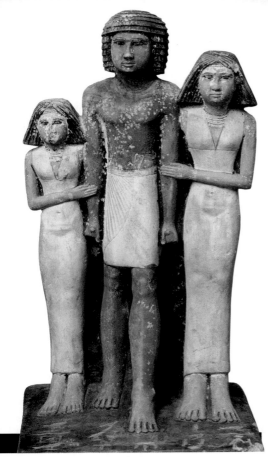

ordinary houses and were decorated with lively scenes of the deceased and his family in the Afterlife. Sowing, harvesting, fishing, and slaughtering of livestock were all themes from daily life that were represented with spontaneity and immediacy.

In addition to these scenes, the custom of carving an autobiography of the deceased on a stela or a statue to carry his memory to future generations was becoming more common. This embryonic form of literature provides wide documentation of military campaigns or missions abroad for which dignitaries were rewarded with honours by the pharaoh.

the Pyramids – that were included to accompany the ruler on his journey to the Afterlife at the end of which he was joined with Ra and assimilated with Osiris, the supreme god of life beyond the tomb.

Egyptian subjects did not aspire to much, but the dignitaries and functionaries closest to the pharaoh were at least given the privilege of a mastaba near the pyramid. For everyone, the Afterlife was based on terrestrial existence. The walls of the tombs were built to resemble

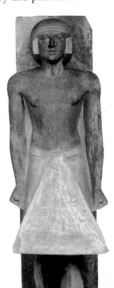

44 TOP STATUE OF MERSUANKH AND TWO DAUGHTERS
Painted limestone; Height 43.5 cm, width 21 cm, depth 20.5 cm; Giza, Mastaba of Mersuankh; Excavation by S. Hassan (1920-1930); End of Fifth Dynasty (second half of 24th century BC)

44 BOTTOM
STATUE OF TY
Painted limestone; Height 198 cm; Saqqara, Mastaba of Ty; Fifth Dynasty, Reign of Niuserra (2416-2392 BC)

However, in order for the deceased to survive on his journey, he needed food and drink, clothes and unguents: a stelae in the tomb positioned above what is known as the "false door" – which allowed communication with the world of the living – showed the deceased in the act of consuming the offerings left during the deceased's burial. A simple representation was all that was needed for the image, imbued with magical power, to become reality and for the deceased, therefore, to consume the offerings left in the tomb. The reading of the texts and the celebration of the funerary rituals depicted on the walls reawoke the vital energy inherent in the iconographic representation, so returning it to the present dimension. In the same way, the statuary absolved the same function: the statue of the deceased was the deceased, the clay figurines in the tomb involved in various activities such as baking bread and making beer were an authentic expression of the functions that would guarantee the dead perpetual provisions during eternal life.

It is clear that the key to understanding pharaonic art in all its forms still resided in the Egyptian conception of the world, both political-religious as well as funerary. Like everything that emanated from the pharaoh, art too, of which he was the principal client and promoter, was an earthly expression of the harmony and perfection of the universe. It was the sovereign who defined the aesthetic canons to which the artists were required to conform so that their work would legitimize the function it

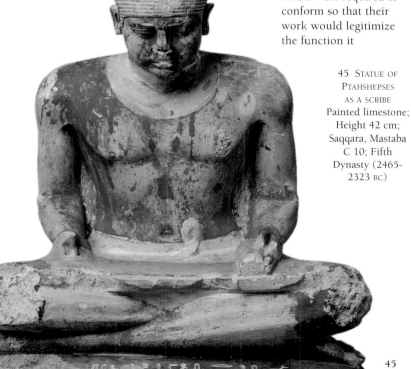

45 STATUE OF
PTAHSHEPSES
AS A SCRIBE
Painted limestone;
Height 42 cm;
Saqqara, Mastaba
C 10; Fifth
Dynasty (2465-
2323 BC)

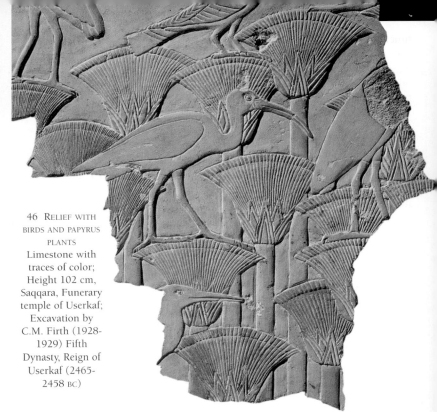

46 RELIEF WITH BIRDS AND PAPYRUS PLANTS
Limestone with traces of color; Height 102 cm, Saqqara, Funerary temple of Userkaf; Excavation by C.M. Firth (1928-1929) Fifth Dynasty, Reign of Userkaf (2465-2458 BC)

represented in accordance with the laws of the universe. There was no opportunity for individual creativeness in the large workshops that toiled for the crown, indeed, it was quite the opposite, for the more that the works conformed to the rigid official conventions, the more they were appreciated.

Representation of the human figure was emblematic of this custom: the iconography used in their depiction transcended every physical characteristic of the individual with the purpose of placing them in an atemporal dimension, aesthetically perfect and technically defined within the limits of an absolute and formal inflexibility. The only concession to the identity of the person was the inscription of his or her name and the representation of the attributes of the function the person had performed.

The use of perspective was not even contemplated because a thing was not what it seemed but what it was. The figure of the individual was conceived as a collection of separate items assembled in such a way that each was shown in its own totality; the end result was the most explicit representation possible of a function that went beyond its contingent appearance.

The cult attributed to the royal and private statues inside the royal funerary temples was also illustrative in this sense. The stone simulacrum was animated by the spirit of the dead – by his *ka* – and the post-death celebration of the cult by the priests allowed the deceased's vital forces to remain active. This form of devotion to ancestors was fairly widespread and is documented by the lists of beneficiaries (kings, queens, and functionaries) conserved in the archives of the temples of the pyramids built by the rulers of the Fifth Dynasty.

These archives are a valuable source of information about the administration and management of the assets of the crown and the temples. As supreme political office coincided administrative activities, particularly in the provinces, where the post of local governor was often associated with that of the high priest.

The tradition of the hereditary transmission of these functions and their related political and financial rewards led to the creation of real "feudal" dynasties whose and south, was to experience a couple of centuries of political and institutional crisis which only ended when Mentuhotep II, a descendant of the Eleventh Theban Dynasty, re-established state unity and inaugurated the Middle Kingdom.
(M.S.C.)

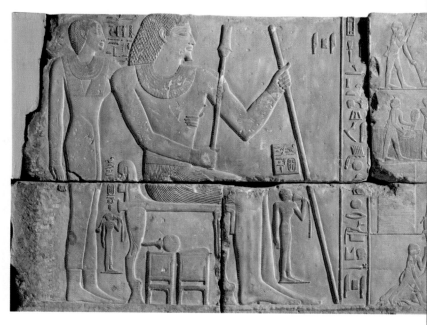

with supreme religious office, much of the revenues from royal properties, recorded in detail, was used to maintain the religious foundations related to the temples and which guaranteed the priesthood a perpetual and substantial source of upkeep and support. The temples, therefore, were a focus of the country's economic and wealth and autonomy were to be at the base of the progressive weakening of central authority at the end of the Old Kingdom, when the power of the local lordlings was great enough to undermine the stability of the central government. Egypt, at the mercy of the struggles between the princes in the provinces in the north

47 RELIEF FROM THE MASTABA OF IPI
Limestone; Height 112 cm, length 502 cm; Saqqara, discovered in 1886; Sixth Dynasty, Reign of Pepy (2289-2255 BC)

PANELS OF HESIRE
WOOD; HEIGHT 114 CM, WIDTH 40 CM
SAQQARA, MASTABA OF HESIRE; REMOVED BY A. MARIETTE
THIRD DYNASTY (2649-2475 BC)

ROOM 43

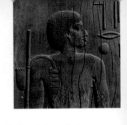

These extraordinary wooden bas-reliefs come from the offerings room in the mastaba of the high functionary, Hesire, north of Djoser's complex at Saqqara. On the east wall, which was protected by another

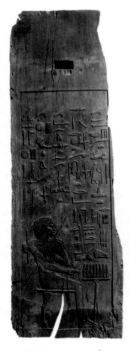

wall, there were eleven false door-niches each containing one of the poses of funerary iconography.

In the reliefs conserved, though probably also in the others, the deceased is shown in the traditional poses of

funerary iconography: seated on a lion's-paws stool before the offerings table or standing in the attitude of a lord surveying his belongings.

The different styles of the wigs and clothes, and particularly the emphasis on the details of each throughout the eleven panels, emphasize the wish of the artist to give a sense of completeness and organization in this impressive narrative set.

The texts along the bottom or framed above the figure provide a list of the funerary offerings and

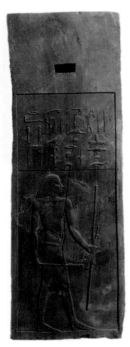

record the titles of the dignitary: Great One of Buto, Chief Dentist, Priest of Horus and Royal Scribe. With proud ostentation, Hesire displays the most prestigious symbols of his functions, the equipment of the scribe, the baton, and the sceptre of power, all elements necessary to perpetuate the prerogatives of his earthly life in the afterlife.

The slender but vigorous anatomical depiction of his body is based on the conventional aesthetic canons of the male figure, while the severe and sunken facial features with pronounced cheekbones and moustache are an important innovation intended to personalize the deceased, though not to portray him as Hesire. No, the physiognomic characterization had another purpose, that of imitating the features of the pharaoh, who was considered to be a model of supreme perfection and the earthly symbol of the harmony of the universe. The face of the limestone statue of Djoser, the contemporary of Hesire, is eloquent testimony of this fact.
(M.S.C.)

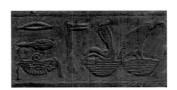

STATUE OF DJOSER

PAINTED LIMESTONE; HEIGHT 142 CM
SAQQARA, *SERDAB* IN THE FUNERARY COMPLEX OF DJOSER
EXCAVATION BY THE ANTIQUITIES SERVICE (1924-1925)
THIRD DYNASTY, REIGN OF DJOSER (2630-2611 BC)

ROOM 48

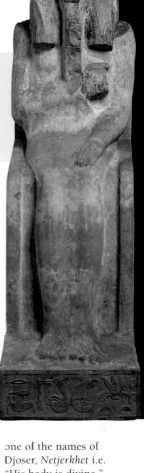

By a happy coincidence, the earliest example of life-size royal sculpture to survive to the modern day is that of the first great pharaoh of the Old Kingdom; his stone image is the most majestic and stately image in the history of Egyptian art. Many others were commissioned by the rulers that succeeded him, but none, across three millennia, ever succeeded in conveying so effectively that sense of dominion, strength, and superhuman power that today still raises awe and reverence in the observer.

The massive throne merged with the ruler's body in a single square block complied with the stylistic norms of pharaonic sculpture; the figure is hardly suggested, being veiled by the ceremonial Jubilee cloak and rigidly locked in a pose that suggests eternity. Djoser's face, on the other hand, is extremely austere and portrayed in every detail:

the high cheekbones, fleshy and pronounced lips, moustache, and ritual beard give the expression an intensity that the sunken (originally inlaid) eyes were supposed to emphasize. And these features can be seen in the faces of the king's subjects, a tradition that was to last centuries, which were based on their master as being the model of aesthetic perfection.

The head is heavily framed by the symbols of his power: the thick three-part wig covered by a short lined headdress (the *nemes*) and the artificial beard. The inscription on the front part of the base bears the titles *Nysut-bity* "King of Upper and Lower Egypt"; *Nebty* 'the two Ladies" i.e. the goddess-cobra Uadjet from Buto in the Delta and the goddess-vulture Nekhbit from the southern city of Elkab, the incarnations of the Two Lands; and finally

one of the names of Djoser, *Netjerkhet* i.e. "His body is divine."

The statue stood in the *serdab*, a room on the north side of the pyramid next to the funerary temple, which allowed the deceased to see the external world through a narrow opening at the height of the statue's eyes and consequently to be present at the ceremonies celebrated in his honor.
(M.S.C.)

THE FAMILY OF NEFERHERENPTAH

Painted limestone; Meretites: height 39 cm
Satmerit: height 53 cm
Neferherenptah: height 65 cm
Itisen: height 37 cm
Giza necropolis, Mastaba of Neferherenptah
Excavation by S. Hassan (1936)
End Fifth-beginning Sixth Dynasty (24th-23rd century bc)

ROOM 47

The increase in the number of mastabas built by Fifth Dynasty dignitaries around the pyramids of their sovereigns required the craft workshops of Memphis to work for a wider and more diversified clientele. As had always happened, the royal models were the primary source of inspiration but the need to explore new means of expression began to appear in private sculpture in ways that were independent of the stylistic conventions of official art.

The political and social balances were altering; increasingly broader sections of the population were receiving benefits and privileges conceded by the pharaoh, and both court and civil art reflected the new political and social conditions. As the number of functionaries and courtiers swelled, they were delegated increasing powers by the central authority. Consequently, the magnificence and grandiosity of Fourth Dynasty art that had expressed a strong and centralized

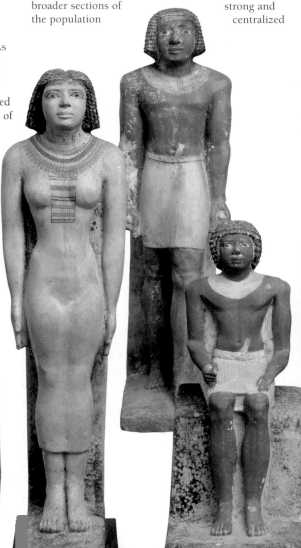

monarchy was gradually diluted by works of more modest craftsmanship, though more vital and less academic, that mirrored the emerging social classes.

Adhesion to the formal traditional rules of sculpture in the Neferherenptah group is evident (static figures, the solid blocks of the limbs, conventional poses) but not absolute.

An attempt has been made to give greater freedom of expression to the whole by treating each family member as a three dimensional structure, valid both as a separate work of art and as an element of a larger composition. The poses of the individuals differ despite respecting the principles of frontality and symmetry: the parents, standing in the

center, display the attributes of their rank (their wigs and neck jewelry) while the children seated on either side formally make up the nuclear family. The female figures are painted yellow as is customary – although the color has been lost from the figure of Meretites – and the tanned bodies of the males are painted with red ocher.

(M.S.C.)

STATUETTE OF A WOMAN PREPARING BEER

PAINTED LIMESTONE; HEIGHT 28 CM
GIZA, MASTABA OF MERESANKH
EXCAVATION BY S. HASSAN (1929-1930)
END OF FIFTH DYNASTY (MID-24TH CENTURY BC)

ROOM 47

The custom of placing a series of statuettes of servants in the mastabas of important courtiers began to establish itself during the Fourth Dynasty. The presence of the figures in the tombs ensured the perpetuation in the Afterlife of the services they offered in their master's earthly household.

This woman is preparing a drink very similar to beer in the manner that was usual in ancient Egypt: barley was mixed with water and dates and was left to ferment; the alcoholic liquid was then filtered and stored in a jar. The realism of the details and the vivid portrayal of the figure have produced a sense of humanity that is absent in official statuary but which

is sometimes present in scenes of everyday life painted on tomb walls.

The statue is a realistic portrait of an actual woman intent on her work. She rests her ample chest on the basket with her large breasts between her rounded arms. Her full face features a prominent nose and bears no sign of the noble idealism seen in the statues of the topmost ranks of Egyptian society. Yet this humble commoner excites sympathy and human warmth and seems content in her work.

The artist has allowed her one feminine touch: the item of jewelry,

probably very simple, that she wears around her neck and which brings a touch of color to a figure that might be defined as "impressionist."

(M.S.C.)

51

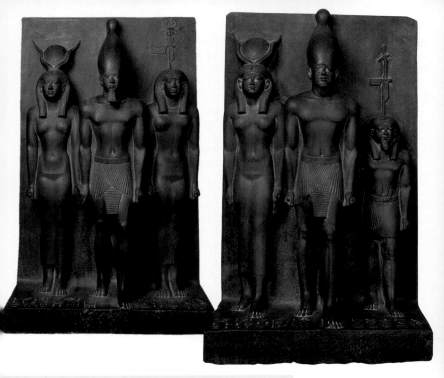

MENKAURA TRIADS

Grey-green schist
Height 93 cm - 95.5 cm - 92.5 cm
Giza, Temple in the Valley of Menkaura
Excavation by George Reisner (1908)
Fourth Dynasty, Reign of Menkaura (2494-2472 bc)

ROOM 47

The three statuary groups of Menkaura fully reflect the classical ideal of court sculpture in which the pharaoh's human nature is transfigured into a divine dimension.

Within a rigid stylistic and compositional schema, the figure of the pharaoh crowned with the white tiara of Upper Egypt is clearly dominant over the other two figures, both in size and because of his central and more forward position looking at the observer. He is

wearing a *shendit*, a short pleated skirt, and grasps two cylindrical objects the function of which is unknown.

To the right is the goddess Hathor wearing a three-part wig crowned by her attribute – cow's horns and a sun disk – and holding the symbol of eternity, the *shen*. The figures to the left of the king are the personifications of the *nomes* of Upper Egypt where the goddess was particularly revered, each of which is crowned by its respective emblem.

The standard with the image of Bat above the Isiac knot represents the province of Diospolis Parva immediately to the south of Abydos (1). The crouching jackal is the emblem of the *nome* of Cinopolis (3) while the small male figure with the *was* sceptre beside the king personifies the *nome* of Thebes (2). A short inscription at the feet of the figures describes the statues: Hathor is "the Lady of the house of the sycamore in all its seats," the sovereign is "the king of Upper and Lower Egypt, Menkaura loved eternally," and both receive offerings "of all good things" from the *nome* represented.

The faces of the figures are identical so that only the attributes of each identify them. Beauty was an immutable value that reflected the perfection of the cosmos, and the gods, of whom the pharaoh was one, were the most complete expression of that beauty.

The superb rendering of the triads, each from a single block of stone, reveals the hand of an expert artist capable of harmoniously modeling the various parts of the body of each figure, of suggesting their forms below their clothing, and of smoothing the delicate volumes. (M.S.C.)

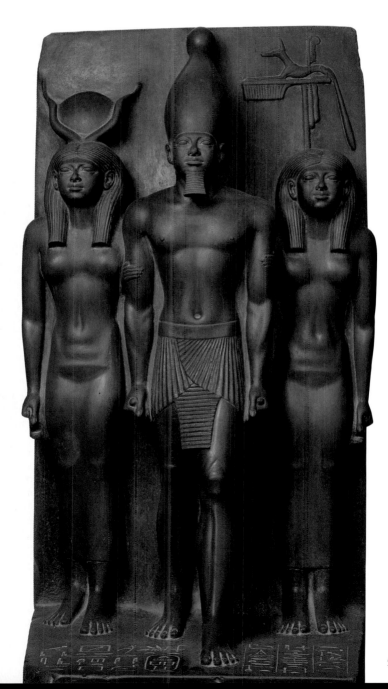

The discovery of the archive of the funerary temple of Neferefra by the University of Prague has shed valuable light on this sovereign who was at first thought not to be of major importance. The collection of papyruses and inscribed tablets is today used to support and integrate existing knowledge, provided by detailed records in the archives of Neferirkara-Kakai, relating to the management of royal properties and the funerary institutions during the Fifth Dynasty. The store where these documents were found also contained other objects including solar barks, small statues of prisoners, and this image of the pharaoh sculpted in pink limestone.

The loss of some parts of the statue does not compromise our understanding of it as a whole, and its small size allows us to have an idea of its carefully balanced structure.

As was traditional, royal portraiture tended to idealize its subject while allowing almost imperceptible touches to provide the face of the sovereign with an individual personality. In this case the nose is small and thin, the cheeks full and marked by slight lines, and the line of the moustache follows the profile of the fleshy, well-formed lips.

The attributes of

STATUETTE OF NEFEREFRA
Painted pink limestone; Height 34 cm
Abusir, Funerary temple of Neferefra
Excavation by the Czechoslovak Mission (1984-1985)
Fifth Dynasty, Reign of Neferefra (2419-2416 bc)

ROOM 47

royalty are the scepter, the uraeus serpent on the king's forehead (on which traces of the wig can be made out), the artificial beard, and the image of the falcon Horus which, as in the statue of Khafra, protects the head of his terrestrial representative with his wings.
(M.S.C.)

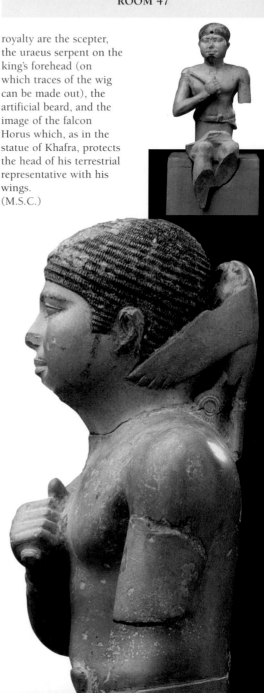

Userkaf, the first pharaoh of the Heliopolitan Fifth Dynasty in Abusir, inaugurated the tradition of associating a solar temple with a funerary temple for the joint cult of the sovereign and Ra. The architectural model of these buildings was based on the Fourth Dynasty funerary complexes in Giza and the substitution of the pyramid with a gigantic obelisk that stood on a podium.

HEAD OF USERKAF

SCHIST; HEIGHT 45 CM
ABUSIR, SOLAR TEMPLE OF USERKAF
JOINT EXCAVATION BY THE
GERMAN AND SWISS INSTITUTES IN CAIRO (1957)
FIFTH DYNASTY, REIGN OF USERKAF (2465-2458 BC)
ROOM 47

This head is an important example of the academic spirit that animated the court artists in Heliopolis who had inherited the sculptural traditions of Menkaura. By using schist as his material, the intention of the sculptor was to emphasize the balance of light and shadow on the polished surfaces without creating excessive chiaroscuro. The simple lines of the crown of Lower Egypt merge with the blurred edges of the face of the young king. Although the king's somatic features resemble those of Menkaura (see the Triad), they, and the rather stereotypical expression of the face, were extremely idealized.

The purpose of the work is to create a sense of harmony and completeness; each element is carefully balanced and positioned, without flaws or contrasts, to portray the sublimity of the ethical and aesthetic ideal embodied by the pharaoh. If the aim of official art was to translate the perfection of divine royalty into perfect artistic creations, the head of Userkaf is a masterpiece.
(M.S.C.)

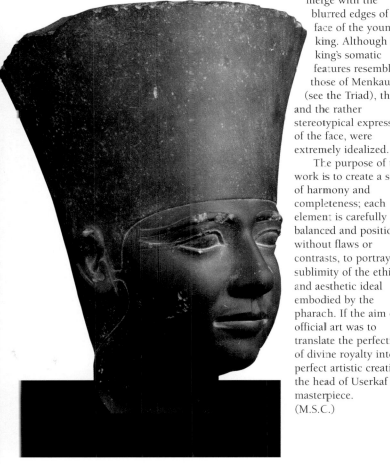

FRAGMENT OF A STATUE OF URKHUI

LIMESTONE WITH TRACES OF COLOR; HEIGHT 35 CM
PROVENANCE UNKNOWN
SIXTH DYNASTY (2323-2152 BC)

ROOM 47

The evident originality of the structural conception of this statue indicates that the work has been severely compromised by the damage it has suffered.

The head of the man seems to lean sideways with a slightly top heavy movement compared to the pose of the torso and shoulders creating a unique model in Egyptian art.

The modeling of the face exceeds the limits of a rather perfunctory execution to give an expressive and realistic portrayal of the man. The features are true, devoid of the idealistic patina that transformed individual characteristics into a mask that could be employed in any type of representation. This effigy of Urkhui is a small masterpiece of humanity. (M.S.C.)

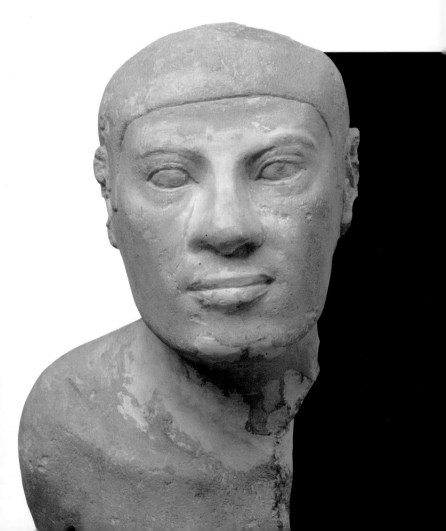

STATUE OF A BEARER

PAINTED WOOD; HEIGHT 36.5 CM
MEIR, TOMB OF NIANKHPEPI
EXCAVATION BY THE ANTIQUITIES SERVICE (1894)
SIXTH DYNASTY, REIGN OF PEPY I (2289-2255 BC)

ROOM 46

The figure of the bearer falls within the category of domestic servants, fated to serve their master for eternity. This one was found with many others in the tomb of a high dignitary of the Sixth Dynasty called Niankhpepi; the inscription of all his titles on the base of the statue informs us that he was referred to as "the Black."

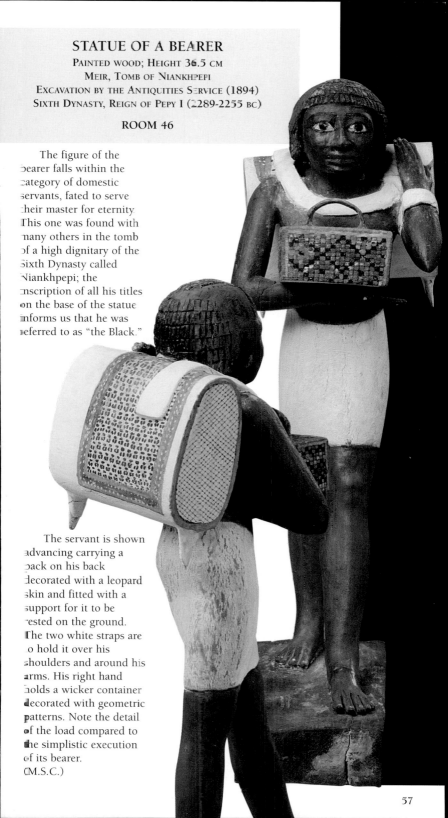

The servant is shown advancing carrying a pack on his back decorated with a leopard skin and fitted with a support for it to be rested on the ground. The two white straps are to hold it over his shoulders and around his arms. His right hand holds a wicker container decorated with geometric patterns. Note the detail of the load compared to the simplistic execution of its bearer.
(M.S.C.)

RELIEF FROM THE MASTABA OF IPI

LIMESTONE; HEIGHT 112 CM, LENGTH 502 CM
SAQQARA, FOUND IN 1886
SIXTH DYNASTY, REIGN OF PEPY I
(2289-2255 BC)

ROOM 46

Inspection scenes are a recurring theme in the decoration of Old Kingdom mastabas. Here we see the nobleman, Ipi, the provincial governor and king's chamberlain, with gathering of cereals (usually spelt, corn, and barley) which are cut and tied in sheaves ready to be carried by donkey to the stores; finally, the grain is packed into silos. by a group of domestic servants and household supervisors as well as his dog. The governor is portrayed in official dress with a finely curled wig, a leopard skin over his left

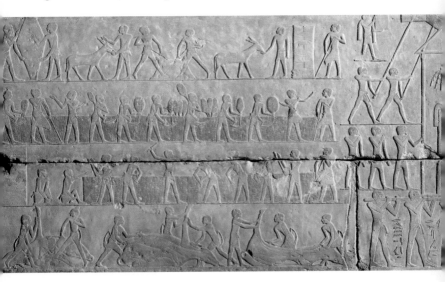

his wife and two daughters presiding over several activities related to his estate.

The four registers are read from the bottom to the top: first there is the slaughter of livestock and the cutting of the meat; then the picking of linen in the fields (the first harvest of the year) followed by the

Caring overseers reward the efforts of the donkeys with strokes and ears of corn, and four foremen with long sticks superintend the labors of the workers.

Later scenes show Ipi being carried in a sedan chair to the port to see in ships laden with goods. On this occasion he is escorted

shoulder, and a staff and a fly whisk in his hands. Note the manner in which the triangular flap of Ipi's skirt is depicted - as seen from above - so as to better show off its style. Zealous servants hold parasols over their master's head while the chief bearer encourages his men.
(M.S.C.)

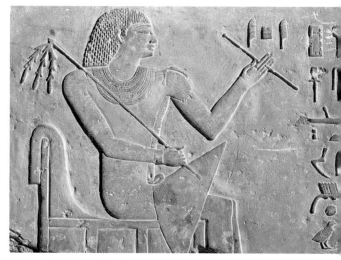

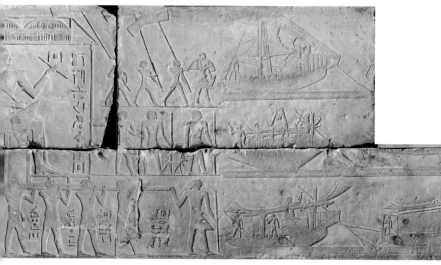

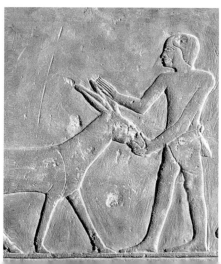

DOUBLE STATUE OF NIMAATSED

PAINTED LIMESTONE; HEIGHT 57 CM
SAQQARA, MASTABA OF NIMAATSED
EXCAVATION BY A. MARIETTE (1860)
SECOND HALF OF THE FIFTH DYNASTY
(START OF THE 24TH CENTURY BC)

ROOM 46

The two statues of Nimaatsed are an extraordinarily effective three-dimensional synthesis of that abstract concept, the *ka*.

In a funerary context, "going to one's *ka*" was the equivalent of dying because the vital force of an individual was not extinguished with death but continued in the *ka*, one's exact physical and spiritual duplicate. The statues of the dead inside tombs are all representations of the deceased's *ka*, which receive the nourishment necessary for their survival through funerary offerings.

In this double sculpture, nothing allows us to distinguish the deceased from his alter ego as they are in concept one and the same, a total symbiosis of roles.

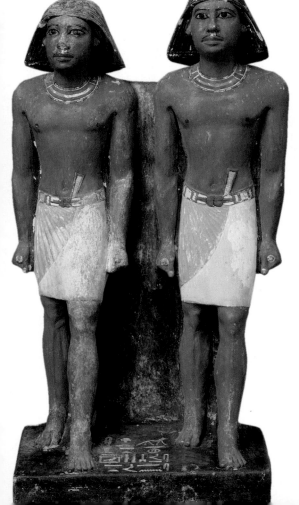

We know from the inscriptions at his feet that Nimaatsed was involved with the execution of justice and that he was linked to the cult of Hathor and Ra in the Solar Temple of the pharaoh Nefeirkara-Kakai. Civil duties were perfectly compatible with religious ones as both functionaries and priests were employed by the state.

The figures are shown in the customary pose of advance with the left leg forward and the arms held down the sides. The powerful body is highlighted by the bright ocher of the skin and the neat lines of the elegant skirt. The artist shunned vivid hues in the depiction of the accessories like the necklace and the material knotted below the navel, preferring combinations of softer tints.

(M.S.C.)

STATUE OF AK AND HETEP-HER-NOFRET

PAINTED LIMESTONE
HEIGHT 49 CM
SAQQARA
FIFTH DYNASTY (2465-2323 BC)

ROOM 46

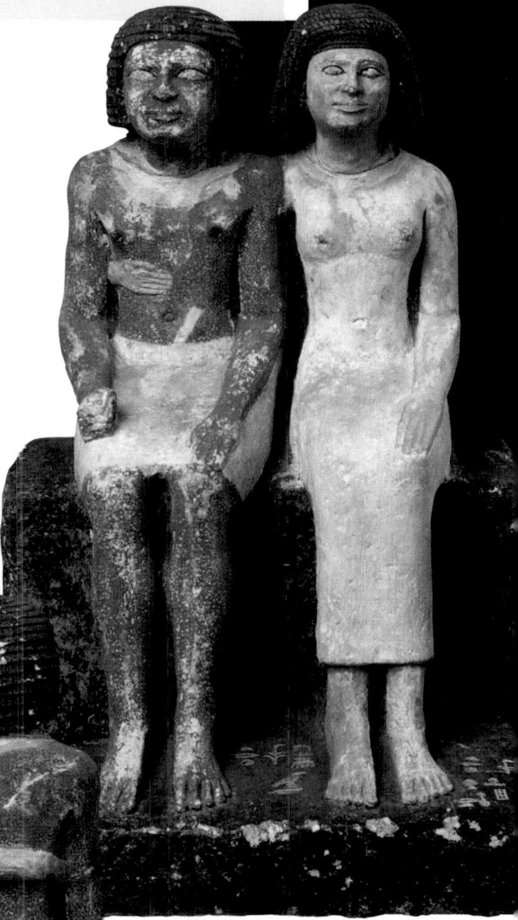

A number of styles of funerary sculpture representing the deceased in their eternal abodes developed over the millennia based on strict and formal artistic canons.

This statuary group of Ak and his consort in the conventional pose of a couple seated on a square seat with a footstool follows one of those styles. The rendition of the figures reflects established stylistic traditions, with the color of the man's flesh being dark ocher and that of the woman yellow, and the clothing are "classical" models of the period.

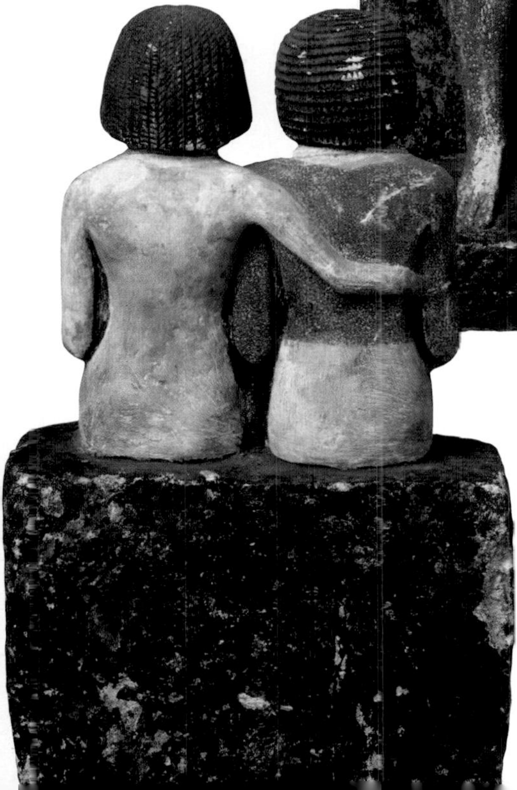

The symmetry of the statue is more apparent than material, in particular if it is seen from behind: the placement of Hetep-her-nofret's hand around her husband is an attempt to instill warm humanity into what would otherwise be a cold an impersonal work. (M.S.C.)

STATUE OF KAEMKED KNEELING

LIMESTONE LINED WITH STUCCO AND PAINTED; HEIGHT 43 CM
SAQQARA, TOMB OF URIRNI
EXCAVATION BY AUGUSTE MARIETTE (1860)
SECOND HALF OF THE FIFTH DYNSTY
(START 24TH CENTURY BC)

ROOM 46

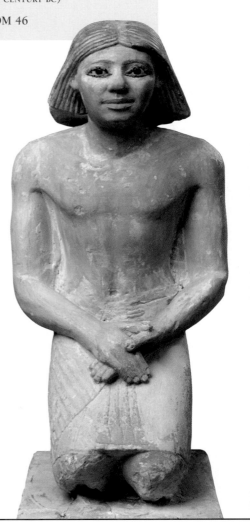

The small statue was found in the tomb of the prince and treasurer, Urirni, with many other statuettes of domestic servants. Kaemked was the prince's funerary priest and is shown here offering devotion and homage to his master. The statue has been well manufactured; for example, note the details of the tassels of the skirt, the setting of the eyes, and the well-designed face; in addition, the hands crossed as a sign of reverence are a new iconographic element.

The pose of a kneeling man was rare for this period and is an example of the artist's desire to introduce innovation, resulting in a work of originality and excellent quality. (M.S.C.)

STATUE OF A SCRIBE

PAINTED LIMESTONE
HEIGHT 51 CM, WIDTH 41 CM, DEPTH 31 CM
SAQQARA; EXCAVATION BY THE ANTIQUITIES SERVICE (1893)
START OF THE FIFTH DYNASTY (MID-25TH CENTURY BC)

ROOM 46

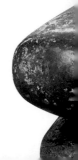

In a civilization in which bureaucracy controlled every aspect of public, private, and religious life, the figure of the scribe was a dominant one. He was above all a bureaucrat but also a literate and cultured man trained in the "House of Life" to exercise the "most important of all professions." Knowledge of his privileged status contrasted with the mass of illiterate citizens that surrounded him is documented by the hundreds of small statues that show the scribe at work. This example represents the scribe in his customary position, cross-legged with a roll of papyrus open on his skirt. The standard pose means that only the features of his face emerge to give the figure any individuality. (M.S.C.)

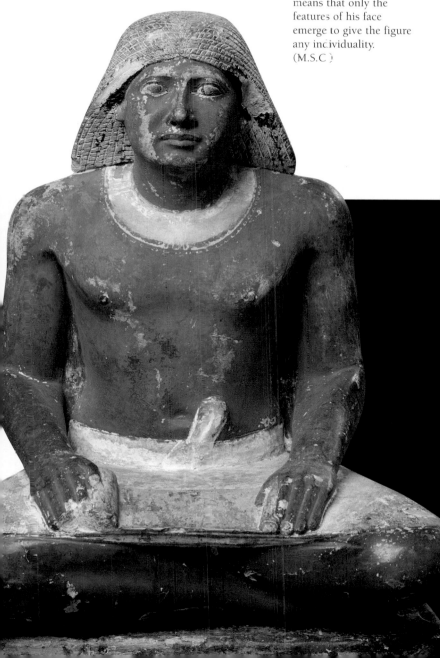

WALL FRAGMENTS
WITH INLAID DECORATIONS

LIMESTONE AND COLORED PASTE
HEIGHT 61.5 AND 62 CM, WIDTH 138 AND 124 CM
MAYDUM, MASTABA OF NOFERMAAT
EXCAVATION BY W.M. FLINDERS PETRIE (1892)
FOURTH DYNASTY, REIGN OF SNEFRU (2575-2551 BC)

ROOM 41

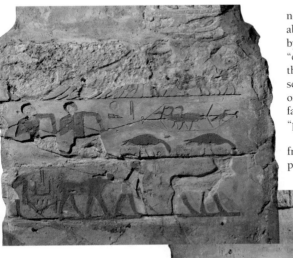

net. The hieroglyphs above the cord pulled by the hunters read *sekh* "close (the net)," while those that describe the scene beneath, in which oxen plough in front of farmers, read *seka*, "plough."

The second fragment shows the prince in two hunting

These two fragments belong to the wall decoration of the mastaba of Nofermaat, one of the sons of the pharaoh Snefru. The technique of inlaying colored paste in limestone has only been found in this tomb, probably because the complex and intricate work required was unable to guarantee satisfactory and long-lasting results. The paste tended to contract once it had dried and fall to the ground.

The subject matter of the scenes is typical of private tombs of the epoch.

There are three registers in the other fragment but the topmost is almost completely ruined leaving only a few traces of plant motifs and animal paws visible. The middle register shows the capture of four geese with the customary hexagonal scenes: a hunter ambushing a panther in the upper register waits for the right moment to throw his hunting sticks; beneath, a hunting dog grips the tail of a fleeing fox less fortunate than the two in front of it. (M.S.C.)

RELIEF FROM THE MASTABA
OF KAEMREHU

PAINTED LIMESTONE
HEIGHT 97 CM, LENGTH 236 CM
SAQQARA, EXCAVATION BY A. MARIETTE
LATE FIFTH DYNASTY (EARLY 24TH CENTURY BC)

ROOM 41

The simple fact that the production and preparation of offerings were painted on tomb walls was enough to ensure the deceased would be supplied with these goods for all eternity. Such scenes are painted with a customary richness of detail in the mastaba of Kaemrehu,

which is then separated from the chaff by farmworkers using forks. The scene below takes place in the granaries of Kaemrehu where the cereals harvested are being measured and recorded by a scribe before being stored.

The middle register shows the grain being

depicts various workshop activities: sculptors preparing funerary statues of Kaemrehu, potters modeling amphoras and jars for offerings, and goldsmiths preparing jewels for the set of grave goods as a scribe notes down the exact quantities of gold used.
(M.S.C.)

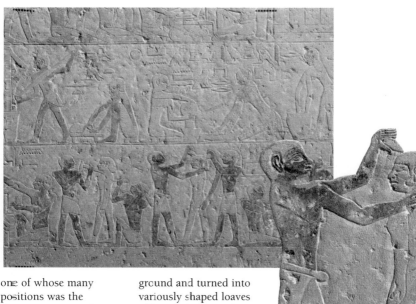

one of whose many positions was the funerary priest in the nearby pyramid of Niuserra at Abusir.

The upper section of the relief is broken, but it is possible to make out a threshing scene in which donkeys tread the ears of corn to separate the grain,

ground and turned into variously shaped loaves of bread. Surviving lists of offerings from the Old Kingdom reveal that there were at least fifteen different types of bread, whereas, during the New Kingdom, there were forty.

The third register

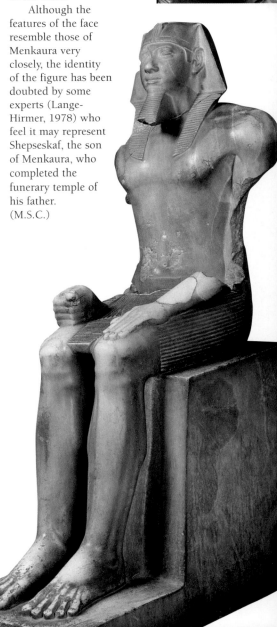

STATUE OF MENKAURA
Alabaster; Height 161 cm
Giza, Lower temple of Menkaura
Excavation by G. Reisner (1908)
Fouth Dynasty, Reign of Menkaura (2494-2472 bc)

SALA 41

A large number of stone statues were found in Menkaura's lower temple that celebrated the various aspects of the pharaoh's divine royalty. The statues provide evidence of a posthumous cult dedicated to this king the existence of which was documented right up until the end of the Old Kingdom.

This impressive but partially damaged alabaster sculpture portrays the pharaoh in all his majesty. Overall, the style is somewhat conventional with the royal attributes clustered around the king's head - the *nemes* headdress with central uraeus serpent and the sacred beard - but the modeling of the body accentuates the king's fine physique which is exaggerated in size when compared to his rather small head.

To compensate the solidity of his muscle-bound body, the soft hues of the alabaster diminish the heaviness of the statue and are a fine example of how the choice of material is essential to the successful outcome of the work.

Although the features of the face resemble those of Menkaura very closely, the identity of the figure has been doubted by some experts (Lange-Hirmer, 1978) who feel it may represent Shepseskaf, the son of Menkaura, who completed the funerary temple of his father.
(M.S.C.)

RELIEF FROM A MASTABA

LIMESTONE
HEIGHT 122 CM, WIDTH 110 CM
MAYDUM
THIRD DYNASTY (2649-2573 BC)

ROOM 41

This relief was found in the mastaba of an unknown noble in the necropolis at Maydum. It demonstrates that the repertoire of figurative styles used to decorate the tomb walls of the Old Kingdom dignitaries had already begun to follow certain dictates by the Third Dynasty. One of the most common themes was scenes in the fields and marshes that illustrated the daily activities carried out on the property of the deceased and which were intended to perpetuate that reality in the afterlife. The three registers on this relief depict various moments of such activities with customary spontaneity and immediacy.

Starting from the bottom, we see the transportation of various animals from one side of a canal to the other. A cage filled with birds is carried on a light papyrus boat and a calf is pulled across by servants. The common method of inducing animals to cross a river was to lead the calves across immediately in front of their mothers and then any male animals. If the calves were too young to swim, their front legs were pulled up on the rear of the boat. A number of cranes and geese are illustrated on the middle register and scenes from the harvest on the upper one. (M.S.C.)

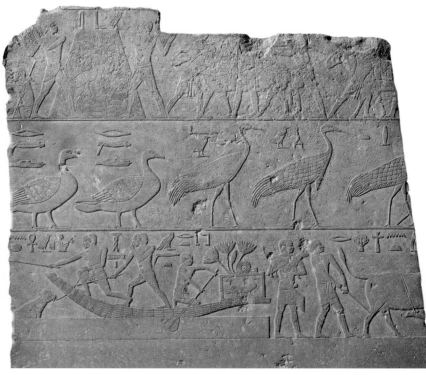

STATUE OF KHAFRA

DIORITE; HEIGHT 168 CM
GIZA, LOWER TEMPLE OF KHAFRA
EXCAVATION BY A. MARIETTE (1860)
FOURTH DYNASTY, REIGN OF KHAFRA (2520-2494 BC)

ROOM 42

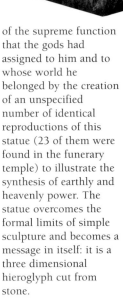

Immensely famous ever since its discovery, this statue of Khafra represents the apotheosis of the sculptural skill of the court artists applied to the sublimation of royal divinity.

The pharaoh is portrayed on a cubic throne carved entirely with symbols of royalty: on the front, lion paws and protomas, and on the sides, the symbol of the *sema-tauy*, the emblem of "Uniting of the Two Lands" (Upper and Lower Egypt) represented respectively by the papyrus plants and the lotus knotted around the hieroglyph of the trachea.

The purpose of the statue was to legitimize and celebrate the universal authority of the sovereign, of whom the throne was one of the most powerful expressions, as the guarantor of the stability and unity of the country. The concept is further emphasized by the presence of the god-falcon Horus who protects the head of the king between his wings as though to underline the perfect symbiosis of the man and the god.

Khafra wished to give an unequivocal sign of the supreme function that the gods had assigned to him and to whose world he belonged by the creation of an unspecified number of identical reproductions of this statue (23 of them were found in the funerary temple) to illustrate the synthesis of earthly and heavenly power. The statue overcomes the formal limits of simple sculpture and becomes a message in itself: it is a three dimensional hieroglyph cut from stone.

The skills of the sculptor succeeded in turning a work of complex ideological content into a masterpiece. As often happens, the choice of stone was a determining factor in the success of the execution; in this case, a high quality stone like the hard and compact diorite was an ideal material to create full but not heavy volumes, with the three dimensional relief rendered softer by the careful polishing of the surfaces. The figure of the pharaoh seems therefore to reflect the light of his own divine essence, an effect that is cleverly emphasized by the dark green veined with white of the diorite. (M.S.C.)

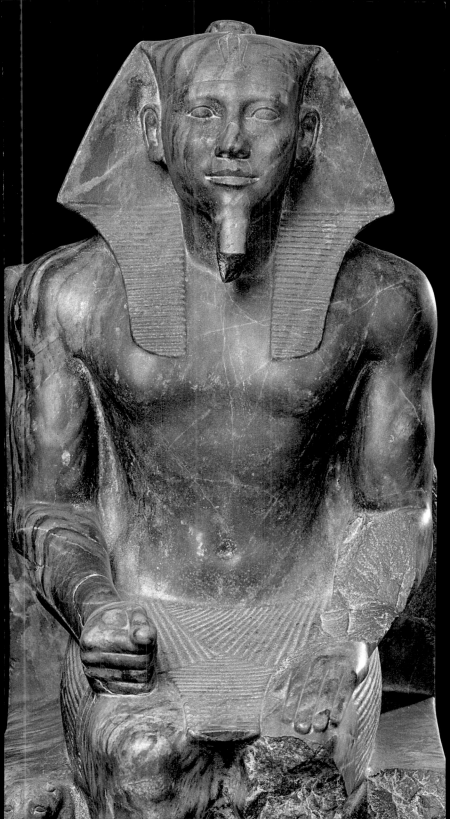

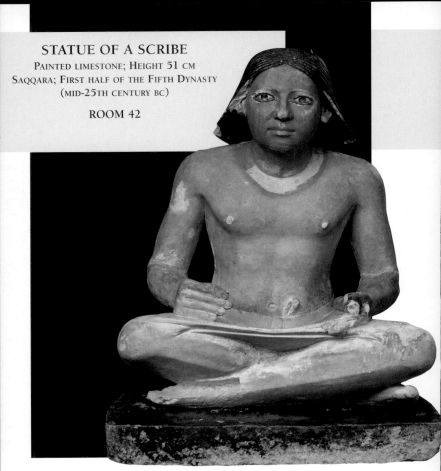

Writing was a skill known by few in ancient Egypt. Besides professional scribes, only the children of the pharaoh, the most learned priests, and a few of the high functionaries were able to read and write. The most ancient statue of a scribe yet to be found – of prince Kauab who lived during the reign of Khufu – was already created in accordance with the iconographic canons that were to remain unaltered over the centuries.

Sadly, the individual in this statue made from painted limestone remains nameless. We see that the artist decided to free the arms and torso of the figure from the stone block that supported it. The scribe is looking ahead as though reflecting on something; he holds the cane pen in his right hand and the papyrus in his left. The pupils of an intelligent man scrupulous in his work shine in the large eyes circled with copper in imitation of make-up. His shoulders are broad and well modeled, his arms polished and hands well cared for. A light, smooth and combed wig with a central parting sweeps back symmetrically to let us see the lobes of his ears.

As often occurred, the position of the body is conventional and gives little indication of the personality of the individual for that function was the role of the aesthetic plane. Only the face portrays the physical reality of the scribe and even that is within the limitations of the stylistic models of the period. (M.S.C.)

STATUE OF A SEATED MAN

PAINTED LIMESTONE; HEIGHT 61 CM
SAQQARA; EXCAVATION BY THE ANTIQUITIES SERVICE (1893)
FIRST HALF OF THE FIFTH DYNASTY (MID-25TH CENTURY BC)

ROOM 42

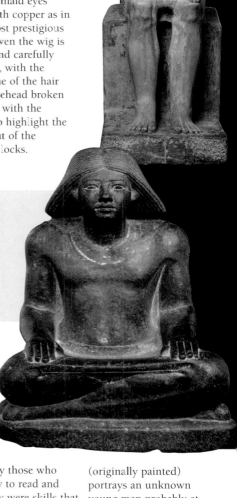

The aesthetic standards that regulated Egyptian sculpture were applied with a certain expressive freedom in this perfectly preserved statue. The human figure is extremely idealized anatomically but his arms are separated from the block of stone to give a more realistic three dimensional effect; the physiognomic characteristics of the head have been carefully created, such as the small but full mouth, the narrow nose, and the large inlaid eyes circled with copper as in all the most prestigious statues. Even the wig is original and carefully portrayed, with the curved line of the hair on the forehead broken on a level with the temples to highlight the layered cut of the overlying locks. (M.S.C.)

STATUE OF A SCRIBE

GREY GRANITE; HEIGHT 48 CM
PROBABLY FROM SAQQARA
FIFTH DYNASTY (2465-2323 BC)

ROOM 42

"..With regard to the position of the scribe, wherever he may work, he will never be wanting..."; this was advice from Kheti, the wise man, to his son in *The Teachings of Kheti*, a book written at the start of the Twelfth Dynasty citing a more ancient text, the *Kemyt*. It confirms that the profession of scribe was traditionally one of the most respectable and profitable.

The great number of figures depicted as scribes is evidence of the status enjoyed by those who knew how to read and write; they were skills that often allowed the most capable to reach important posts in the state bureaucracy.

This granite statue (originally painted) portrays an unknown young man probably at the start of his career; the style of the portrait suggests that it was made during the Fifth Dynasty. (M.S.C.)

STATUE OF KA-APER

SYCAMORE; HEIGHT 112 CM
SAQQARA, MASTABA OF KA-APER
EXCAVATION BY A. MARIETTE (1870);
FIFTH DYNASTY, REIGN OF USERKAF (2465-2458 BC)

ROOM 42

The use of wood as a material in sculpture became more established during the Fourth Dynasty; it was certainly more ductile and versatile but also more perishable. Works like the statues of the priest-reader Ka-aper, which have escaped the wear of time, are rare examples of what was a diffuse type.

The statue was originally covered with a light coat of painted plaster, slight traces of which remain, and portrays with extreme realism the satisfied opulence of a well-to-do man pleased with his social position. The eyes – made from alabaster, crystal, and black stone and ringed with copper in imitation of make-up – vividly bring the face of the priest to life and reflect his self-important personality.

The attitude of the figure more resembles the traditional typologies of bas-reliefs than of stone statues: he is shown in the act of advancing with his staff of power (here substituted with a copy) in one hand, and probably a cylinder in the other, clothed in a long skirt tied below his navel. His short hair accentuates the rounded lines of his head and face merging in a composition of full and smoothed volumes.

Unlike stone statues in which the figure is never completely liberated from the material in which it is carved, wood sculptures are more independent, freed from the dorsal supports and filled spaces between the limbs which were worked separately and applied afterwards.

The firm personalization of the facial features of the figure means that this work falls into the "veristic" artistic school rather than the "idealistic," which tended to cancel the physical characteristics of the individual and conform the figure to an ideal type.

The physiognomy of the statue of Ka-aper is so markedly naturalistic that, when they discovered it, Mariette's workers saw in it the features of the mayor of their village, translated in Arabic as *Sheikh al-Balad*, the name by which the sculpture is still known today. (M.S.C.)

FALSE-DOOR STELA OF IKA

WOOD; HEIGHT 200 CM, WIDTH 150 CM
SAQQARA; EXCAVATION BY THE ANTIQUITIES SERVICE (1939)
FIFTH DYNASTY (2465-2323 BC)

ROOM 42

The perfect state of preservation of this marvellously carved wooden stelae gives us the opportunity to appreciate one of the most important elements of funerary architecture in every detail. The false door represented the point of contact between the worlds of the dead and the living and it was in front of this that the offerings intended to sustain the dead in the Afterlife were placed.

The structure is a faithful representation of a door with a central aperture topped by a cylinder in imitation of a rolled up piece of matting. Two side panels are framed by uprights and architraves and, in the upper part, the funerary niche that portrays Ika, the deceased, with his wife as they "took possession" of the offerings that lay on the table and are listed in the text.

With his titles of "Wab priest", i.e. "pure priest," and "Governor of the Great House," Ika is shown in the aperture of the door with one of his sons, Tjenty, and on the left panel with his other son, Abedu. The two brothers hold their father's emblems as though they were being handed down from father to sons. The

poses, clothing, and attributes of the figures are conventionally represented. Ika's wife, Iymerit, a priestess of Hathor, is shown with her daughter Tjentet smelling a lotus flower whose perfume gave eternal life. The woman wears a clinging dress with shoulders so wide that they leave her breasts visible as was the fashion of the time.

The outer inscriptions and those on the central architrave are the traditional formula of the "reversion of the offerings" to the deceased by the pharaoh and another funerary deity, Anubis or Osiris.

The decision to carve the stela in wood rather than the traditional stone is indicative of the tendency to follow ancient traditions that characterized the Egyptian culture; in this case the wooden panels in the nearby tomb of Hesira (Third Dynasty) probably provided Ika with a ' classical" and influential model as is also suggested by the surprising similarity of the faces and postures. (M.S.C.)

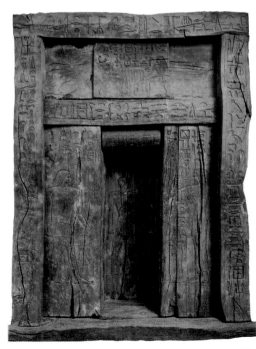

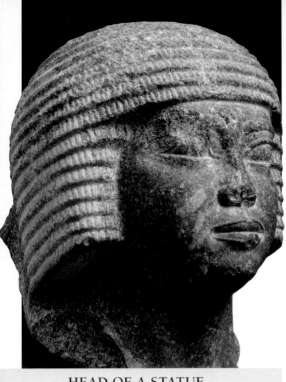

HEAD OF A STATUE
GRANITE
HEIGHT 30.5 CM
GIZA (1938)
FOURTH – SIXTH DYNASTY (2575-2323 BC)

ROOM 36

The loss of the statue to which this head belonged prevents us from knowing either the identity of the individual or the type of sculpture it was, but it does not detract from our appreciation of the work's rigorous formality. The stylistic conventions of official sculpture from the Old Kingdom are presented here with skill and exemplary accuracy.

Stone statues were conventionally sculpted to be viewed from the front, in particular the body, but the head was generally rendered with greater three dimensional effect, often with individual characteristics. In this example, the features are typical of official idealized portraiture but the interpretation has been attenuated by the full volumes of the face and the thick curls of layered wig.

In the absence of further data or comparison of the iconography, the work can be roughly dated to the Fourth or Fifth Dynasty. (M.S.C.)

RESERVE HEAD
LIMESTONE; HEIGHT 25.5 CM
GIZA, WEST NECROPOLIS
FOURTH DYNASTY, REIGN OF KHAFRA (2520-2494 BC)

ROOM 31

About 30 carved limestone heads have been found near the funerary chambers or next to the sarcophaguses in the mastabas of the high dignitaries of the Fourth Dynasty, though their function is still not understood.

It is probable that heads represented the occupants of their respective tombs with emphasis on the features of the deceased's face. Although the heads maintain a formal similarity, they display individual traits. Do not forget that the effigy of the deceased was the deceased and, as such, had to dwell in his funerary abode in an incorruptible and eternal form.

It cannot be excluded that the head, being the most vulnerable part of the body, was particularly at risk during the treacherous journey to the Afterlife that the funerary texts of the epoch describe in such fearful terms, and that therefore it had to be

74

protected by means of rites that included the provision of a "reserve head."

Whatever the purpose of these sculptures, their workmanship reveals a fairly uniform and decidedly singular technique: the head was roughly shaped in the limestone without the creation of any physical details; these were defined at a later stage in a layer of plaster that was spread over the untreated stone model.

This technique of creating a base model to be personalized with the features of the deceased when required, probably allowed the mass production of an object which was, at least in the Fourth Dynasty, greatly

requested.

The treatment of the head and face (apart from the distinctive elements of the individual in question) did not follow the artistic conventions of the time. There was, for example, no element that permitted social identification of the individual represented – an essential element in funerary iconography – such as a name, titles, or a wig symbolizing

professional standing; in addition, the surfaces were left white and the neck was cut cleanly at its base. In the case of missing or broken ears – suggested by some as evidence of a sudden turning against established cult practices – this may simply be explained as the inevitable consequence of the brittle nature of plaster in which these features were modeled before being applied to the head. (M.S.C)

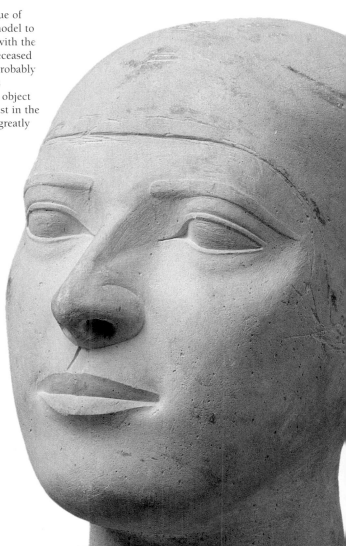

STATUES OF RANOFER

PAINTED LIMESTONE; STATUE ON THE LEFT: HEIGHT 178 CM
STATUE ON THE RIGHT: HEIGHT 186 CM
SAQQARA, MASTABA OF RANOFER; EXCAVATION BY A. MARIETTE (1860)
FIRST HALF OF THE FIFTH DYNASTY
(MID-25TH CENTURY BC)

ROOM 31

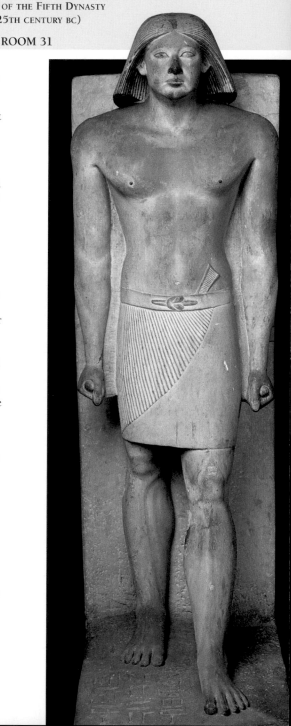

These splendid twin statues of Ranofer were found in two niches in the chapel at his tomb at Saqqara together with that of his wife Hekenu.

The life-size sculptures show the priest of Ptah and Sokari in two phases of his life: in the flush of youth (left) and in old age (right).

The young Ranofer is a handsome, athletic, and muscular man wearing a staid loincloth tied at the waist and a simple but well-cared for wig. The other figure, with hair so short it seems a cap and wearing a long wrapover skirt, has features showing his advanced age such as the folds at the base of the neck, a slight double chin and a prominent stomach, however, these signs are only just perceptible as time did not exist in the funerary world and the appearance of the deceased was always idealized.

The dignitary is portrayed in a typical pose, advancing with his left leg before him, his hands by his sides holding two cylinders, and gazing into the distance beyond earthly life.

Execution of the statue followed the sculptural canons of the day in which a single block of stone was progressively chipped away to form the general volumes of the body until the outline of the figure emerged, then the physical details were defined, and finally the surfaces smoothed to give a gentle, compact relief. The space that separates the individual parts of the body, though, remained filled in accordance with a stylistic convention to which no exception was made. Consequently, the material and the form remain united in a whole that endows the figure with the intrinsic qualities of the stone: eternity and stability. This technique was not used for sculptures made from wood, which was more easily worked. Color was usually applied to stone that was not of high quality, such as limestone, which was unable to achieve the same luminous effects of hard polished stone.

The hand that carved these statues was that of a talented artist able to translate the rigid iconographic conventions of sculpture into a work of excellence. (M.S.C)

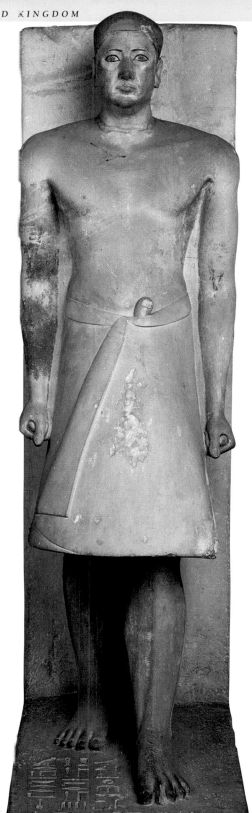

STATUES OF RAHOTEP AND NOFRET

PAINTED LIMESTONE
RAHOTEP: HEIGHT 121 CM; NOFRET: HEIGHT 122 CM
MAYDUM, MASTABA OF RAHOTEP
EXCAVATION BY A. MARIETTE (1871)
FOURTH DYNASTY, REIGN OF SNEFRU (2575-2551 BC)

ROOM 32

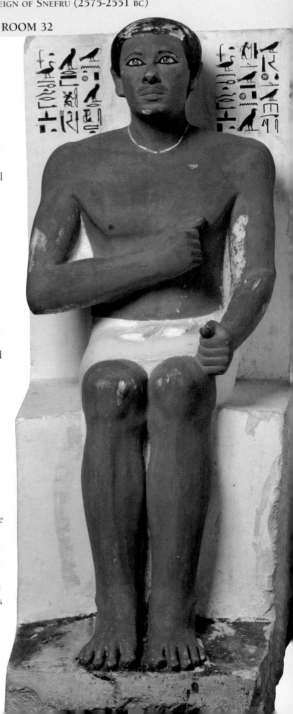

The mastaba of prince Rahotep and his wife is one of the largest from the necropolis of Maydum. Below the east facade, decorated with the customary false-door niche, archaeologists discovered an earlier wall face with a cross-shaped shrine decorated with low reliefs and superbly executed paintings on plaster. It is not known why the earlier wall face was overlaid.

The two statues and the items with which they were discovered are examples of Egyptian art produced during the transition from the Third to the Fourth Dynasty.

With regard to the execution, the pair are a fine illustration of the strict canons that governed the iconography of this period; the couple are portrayed in the unavoidable conventional pose on a square seat painted white to give contrast to the black hieroglyphics. The lower part of the body is treated perfunctorily, almost negligently, while all the artist's attention is concentrated on the upper half, culminating in the brilliant quartz and alabaster eyes. Athletic and moderately

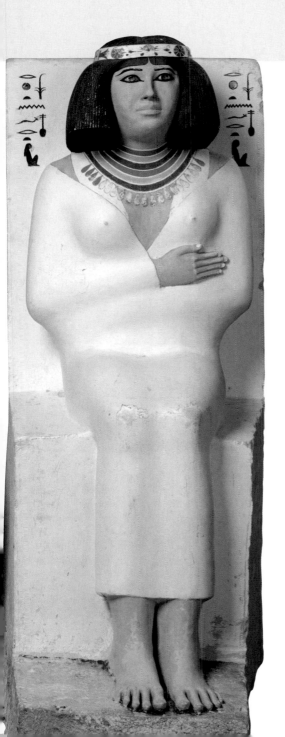

muscular, Rahotep's flesh is colored brick-red; he wears the traditional white loincloth and has very short hair. Nofret is wrapped in a shawl that resembles archaic models and leaves visible the shoulders of her dress. Her pale yellow face is framed by a heavy two-part wig softened by a charming floral diadem.

The prominent forms of the woman emerge voluptuously but discreetly from behind the light material that covers her and create a pleasant contrast with the lean, flaunted physique of her husband; the contrast is further emphasized by the elaborate necklace that adorns her décolleté compared to Rahotep's sober choker.

It is these small technical points that give life to the whole work. The unknown artist was able to distribute the volumes and opulence of the forms and attributes so as to break the static symmetry of the two figures, though without detriment to the intimate communion of the couple.
(M.S.C.)

FALSE-DOOR STELA OF ITETI
Painted limestone; Height 360 cm, width 210 cm
Saqqara, Tomb of Iteti
Excavation by A. Mariette (1861)
Early Sixth Dynasty (2323-2152 bc)

ROOM 32

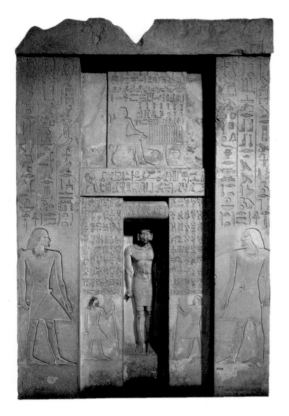

to take the offerings that were placed at his feet in the tomb. Should these be missing, the magical power of the ritual would render the items sculpted on the stela and its uprights real to ensure the deceased would receive the sustenance that was essential to survival in the Afterlife.

Iteti, known as Ankhires, was a high dignitary who lived at the end of the Fifth and start of the Sixth Dynasties. He is shown with titles and names several times on the doorposts in his capacity as palace functionary. The survival of the individual was also linked to the memory of his name which was revitalized each time it was said or even read. The *ka* of Iteti faces the door in the form of a statue in the center of the niche; it is ready to receive the funerary cult whose aim is to fill it with vital energy.

In a shaft dug in the tomb, Mariette found a series of model barks, wooden statues, and stone offerings that, unfortunately, were so fragile they were damaged when picked up, but they were items of enormous historical value regarding the that accompanied the deceased during his eternal existence. (M.S.C.)

The false-door stela was an indispensable item of funerary architecture during the Old Kingdom and was an evolution of the cult niche that used to adorn the external facade of the mastabas in the Thinite kingdom. From the Third Dynasty on, the false-door stela was depicted as a real door with uprights, an architrave, and a roll of matting on the floor at the entrance. The upper panel has a rectangular stela showing the funerary meal and the list of offerings.

The false-door was placed in the chapel of the tomb facing west and represented the point of contact between the worlds of the living and the dead. Having crossed the threshold, the deceased could return from the kingdom of the dead

THE DWARF SENEB AND HIS FAMILY

Painted limestone; Height 43 cm width 22.5 cm
Giza, Tomb of Seneb; Excavation by H. Junker (1926-1927)
Late Fifth – early Sixth Dynasty (24th-23rd century bc)

ROOM 32

The statuary group of the dwarf Seneb and his family was found in a small *naos* in his mastaba in Giza. The crudely realistic sculpture has become famous for the ingenuity of its composition: Seneb's physical deformity is hidden as much as possible by a skilful optical trick: his short legs, crossed below his skirt, are disguised and continue into the figures of his two children. The illusion is completed by the symmetrical representation of his wife's legs, covered down to her ankles, with the result that the artist was seemingly able to provide Seneb with what nature denied him. The Egyptian conception of the world did not allow deviations from the principle of order and balance that had regulated the universe since its creation, and therefore the purpose of every form of art was to represent the mythical archetype. From this point of view, the existence of Seneb's physical defect is not denied but it is hidden so that the aesthetic harmony of the group could be saved.

The figure of the wife with her arm around Seneb's shoulders is very expressive; the lack of color in her eyes does not soften the gentleness of her glance, and the slight movement of her upper body is a gesture of devotion towards her unfortunate husband that seems to want to stop time.

The two children are shown in a typical pose: naked, sucking on a forefinger and, in the case of the boy, with the typical plait of childhood that falls to his shoulder.

The inscriptions on the base and the front of the chair reveal that Seneb was the funerary priest of the pharaohs Khufu and Djedefra and in charge of the royal wardrobe.

The dwarf's tomb was one of the first attempts at building a ceiling dome over a square chamber. Rows of jutting bricks at the corners of the room slowly created the circular plan on which the dome rested. (M.S.C.)

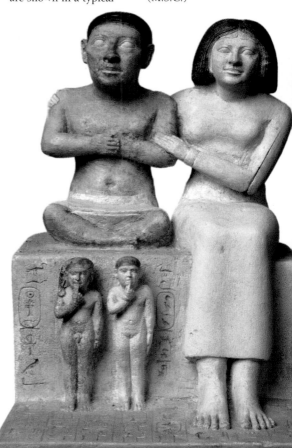

THE "GEESE OF MAYDUM"

PAINTED PLASTER; HEIGHT 27 CM, LENGTH 172 CM
MAYDUM, MASTABA OF NOFERMAAT
EXCAVATION BY A. MARIETTE (1871)
FOURTH DYNASTY, REIGN OF SNEFRU (2575-2551 BC)

ROOM 32

Paint on stucco was a fairly common technique in ancient Egypt as it provided decoration with an economy of both means and diluted with water and a binder such as albumen or vegetable gum, then applied in tempera fashion with broad brushstrokes of palm fibre or, as seen during the late Old Kingdom, with delicate, blended strokes.

Unfortunately, the fragility of the support made the works vulnerable to ageing and to man, and the Geese of Maydum is one of the few examples to have survived.

The fragment comes from the mastaba of

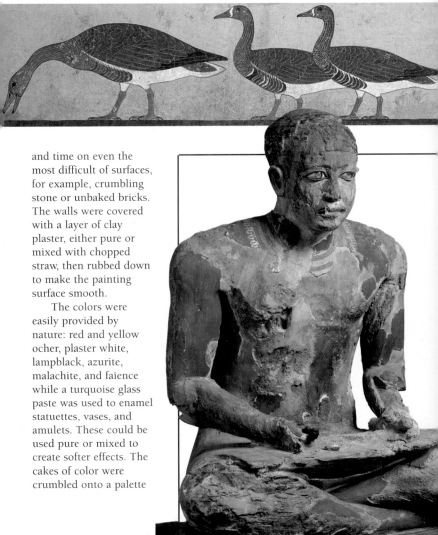

and time on even the most difficult of surfaces, for example, crumbling stone or unbaked bricks. The walls were covered with a layer of clay plaster, either pure or mixed with chopped straw, then rubbed down to make the painting surface smooth.

The colors were easily provided by nature: red and yellow ocher, plaster white, lampblack, azurite, malachite, and faïence while a turquoise glass paste was used to enamel statuettes, vases, and amulets. These could be used pure or mixed to create softer effects. The cakes of color were crumbled onto a palette

Nofermaat and Itet in the necropolis of Maydum where the "cloaked" pyramids begun by Huni, the last pharaoh of the Third Dynasty, were completed by his successor, Snefru, the father of Khufu.

Although animal life was depicted frequently in funerary iconography, rarely did the execution reach the artistic level of these panels. The scene is dominated by six geese in two groups of three against a background of a garden suggested by clumps of grass and flowers. The danger of restricting the painting in order to follow the rules of pictorial symmetry that sometimes stiffened the hand of Egyptian artists is here overcome by the inclusion of different details like the plumage and the tips of the tails.

It is also evident that the intention was to create a rarefied atmosphere in which the harmony of the matching colors was in perfect agreement with the positioning of the geese in the landscape. (M.S.C.)

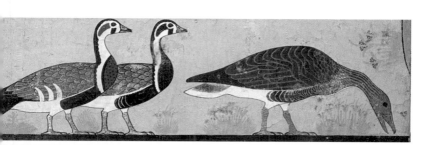

STATUE OF MITRI AS A SCRIBE

WOOD WITH PAINTED STUCCO
HEIGHT 76 CM, WIDTH 50 CM
SAQQARA, MASTABA OF MITRI
EXCAVATION BY THE ANTIQUITIES SERVICE (1925-1926)
LATE FIFTH – EARLY SIXTH DYNASTY
(24TH-23RD CENTURY BC)

ROOM 32

The custom of placing the statue of the deceased in the *serdab* stimulated the creativity of sculptors to produce a wide variety of poses and compositions; even if this did not impede the creation of stereotypes, it was a symptom of the intrinsic dynamism of the Egyptian aesthetic spirit.

The statue of Mitri is emblematic of this. Eleven wooden statues were found in the serdab of his mastaba at Saqqara, which represented the occupant of the tomb and his wife, both separately and together, and in various poses. Five of the statues are now in the Egyptian Museum in Cairo.

The inscription on the base of the statue tells us that Mitri performed important political and religious duties: "Administrator of the nome, Great One of the ten of Upper Egypt and Priest of Maat." The choice of having himself portrayed as a scribe was based on his desire to emphasize the intellectual qualities of a high functionary trained and expert in the use of a pen.

Although much of the color has faded, the necklace of colored semi-precious stone beads creates an effective chromatic contrast with the strong red ocher skin. The modeling of his figure and face keeps his expressiveness intact while the eyes set in limestone and transparent stone and ringed with copper attract the attention of the observer to Mitri's calm gaze and become the focal point of the whole sculpture. (M.S.C.)

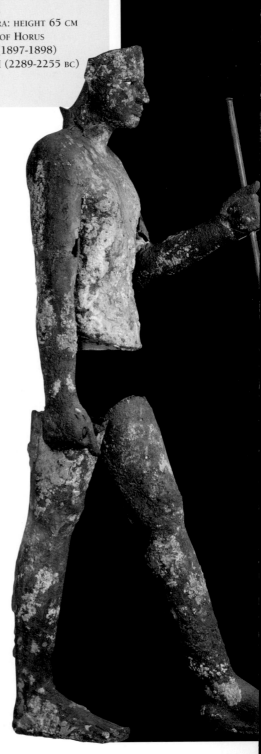

STATUES OF PEPY I AND MERENRA
BEATEN COPPER
PEPY I: HEIGHT 177 CM; MERENRA: HEIGHT 65 CM
HIERAKONPOLIS, TEMPLE OF HORUS
EXCAVATION BY J. QUIBELL (1897-1898)
SIXTH DYNASTY, REIGN OF PEPY I (2289-2255 BC)

ROOM 32

These rare examples of copper statuary produced during the Old Kingdom were found in one of the underground stores of the temple of Horus in Nekhen – the ancient name of Hierakonpolis – together with a statue of King Khasekhemui (Second Dynasty) and a terracotta lion cub made during the Thinite era.

Before storing the two statues, the priests had disassembled them, placed one inside the other, then sealed the resulting combination with a thin layer of engraved copper bearing the titles and names of Pepy I "on the first day of the Jubilee." A "visceral," indissoluble tie bound the two figures, but whereas the identity of the larger statue as Pepy I is given by the inscription, the identity of the smaller statue is still unresolved.

The most common hypothesis is that the athletic young man with the short wig originally decorated with the royal uraeus serpent was Pepy I's son, Merenra, who was publicly associated as his father's successor on the occasion of the Jubilee. The placement of his

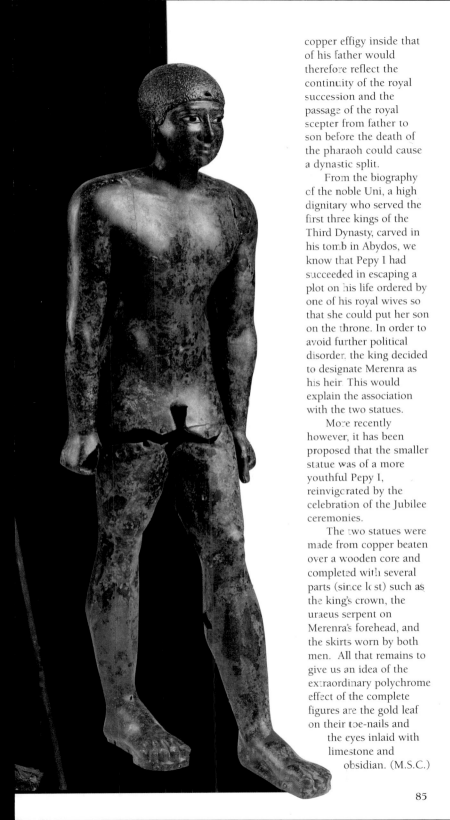

copper effigy inside that of his father would therefore reflect the continuity of the royal succession and the passage of the royal scepter from father to son before the death of the pharaoh could cause a dynastic split.

From the biography of the noble Uni, a high dignitary who served the first three kings of the Third Dynasty, carved in his tomb in Abydos, we know that Pepy I had succeeded in escaping a plot on his life ordered by one of his royal wives so that she could put her son on the throne. In order to avoid further political disorder. the king decided to designate Merenra as his heir This would explain the association with the two statues.

More recently however, it has been proposed that the smaller statue was of a more youthful Pepy I, reinvigorated by the celebration of the Jubilee ceremonies.

The two statues were made from copper beaten over a wooden core and completed with several parts (since lost) such as the king's crown, the uraeus serpent on Merenra's forehead, and the skirts worn by both men. All that remains to give us an idea of the extraordinary polychrome effect of the complete figures are the gold leaf on their toe-nails and the eyes inlaid with limestone and obsidian. (M.S.C.)

RELIEF OF A CONTEST BETWEEN FISHERMEN

PAINTED LIMESTONE; LENGTH 145 CM
SAQQARA, UNKNOWN TOMB
FIFTH DYNASTY 2465-2323 BC)

ROOM 32

The scene is a highly realistic portrayal of a contest between fishermen in their boats. The practice of fights with no holds barred between opposing teams was quite common during the Old Kingdom and the earliest example can be seen in the shrine of Meresankh III, the wife of Khufu, at Giza. The aim of the contest was to force the opponents into the water.

It was a hand-to-hand affair or perhaps fought using long staffs with a forked end. The inscriptions on the upper section of this particular fight scene reflect different moments of the bout: "Crack his skull open!", "Break his back!" and "But how? He's fallen on the ground!" (M.S.C.)

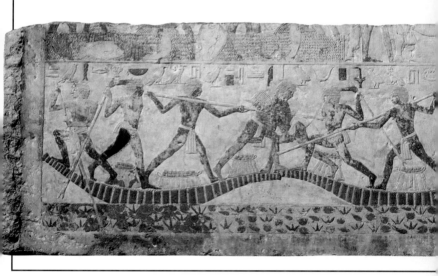

SMALL STATUE OF KHUFU

IVORY; HEIGHT 7.5 CM
ABYDOS; EXCAVATION BY W.M.FLINDERS PETRIE (1903)
FOURTH DYNASTY, REIGN OF KHUFU (2551-2528 BC)

ROOM 37

The face of the builder of the Great Pyramid at Giza, Khufu (Cheops), is only known to posterity from this small ivory statue found at the temple of Osiris at Abydos.

Archaeological remains from his reign are also scarce. A stela and a graffito found respectively north-west of Toshka and in the Wadi Maghara are evidence of the exploitation of the country's mineral resources, for the Nubian desert was rich in diorite and carnelian, while the mines in Sinai had provided Egypt with copper, malachite, and turquoise since much more ancient times.

Egypt did not remember Khufu with kindness: the reputation of the monarch described wise and devout Snefru, his father, and the other pharaohs of the Fifth Dynasty. The political motivation for the writing of the tales was to exalt the virtues of the Heliopolitan dynasty by painting Khufu black; however, Khufu's poor reputation is widely believed to have been true to life.

And yet, leaving Khufu's true nature to one side, construction of his massive and grandiose funerary of an enormous slice of the country's wealth.

The small size of this statue seems the posthumous retaliation of its subject's foolish ambition. He holds a sceptre in the form of a flail in his hand and wears the crown of

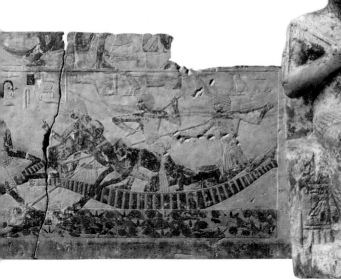

by Herodotus as cruel and blasphemous is confirmed in a collection of stories from the Middle Kingdom, known as the Westcar Papyrus, that describe the pharaoh as a proud and evil ruler, the very opposite of the exemplary image of the pyramid at Giza would have been inconceivable if he had not been a ruler with a strong and authoritarian personality, able to mobilize huge numbers of men and quantities of materials, not to mention avail himself Lower Egypt on his head. The name of the pharaoh is the abbreviation of Knum-khuefui, "Khnum protects me," which is just legible on the right side of the throne inside the archaic *serekh*. (M.S.C.)

THE GRAVE GOODS OF QUEEN HETEPHERES

Hetepheres was the wife of the first Fourth-Dynasty pharaoh, Snefru, and mother of their famous son Khufu. Her tomb was originally at Dahshur next to that of her husband, but after an early, though only partial, violation of the tomb, Khufu moved it near his pyramid at Giza. It was discovered there by the American archaeologist George Reisner with its splendid grave goods intact, but the beautiful alabaster sarcophagus was unfortunately empty.

The grave goods of Hetepheres are extremely refined examples of the taste and magnificence of the royal tombs during the Old Kingdom. (M.S.C.)

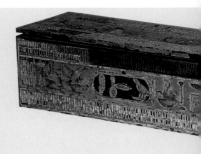

THE BED
WOOD AND GOLD LEAF
LENGTH 178 CM, WIDTH 97 CM,
HEIGHT 21.5 – 35.5 CM
GIZA, TOMB OF HETEPHERES I
EXCAVATION BY G. REISNER (1925)
FOURTH DYNASTY, REIGN OF SNEFRU
(2575-2551 BC)

ROOM 37

Beds in ancient Egypt did not have a bedhead, but a panel of wood mounted on the end by the feet. Two copper lined wooden tenons fit into copper lined cavities in the frame and held it fast. The foot of the bed was the only part that was decorated. The inner surface bears a carved motif of alternating fringes and rosettes painted blue-green and black in the colors that were repeated on all the objects in the tomb.

The lion's feet point towards the head of the bed; they are bound with thin leather thongs to the side bars which are finished with elements in

CANOPY HOLDER
CARVED GILDED WOOD
HEIGHT 18.5 CM, LENGTH 157.5 CM, WIDTH 21.5 CM
GIZA, TOMB OF HETEPHERES I
EXCAVATION BY G. REISNER (1925)
FOURTH DYNASTY, REIGN OF SNEFRU (2575-2551 BC)

ROOM 37

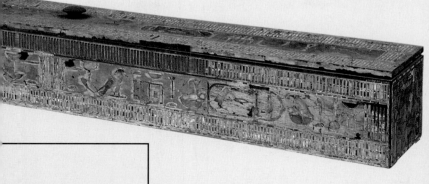

When the canopy was discovered, the wooden planks of the container had practically all turned to dust but the inlaid decoration had remained intact and its constituent elements were still distributed in their original positions. Patient reconstruction work of the façades has meant we are now able to appreciate the complete object. The long sides bear an inscription divided into two mirror image parts by the figures of Nekhbet, the god-vulture.
(M.S.C.)

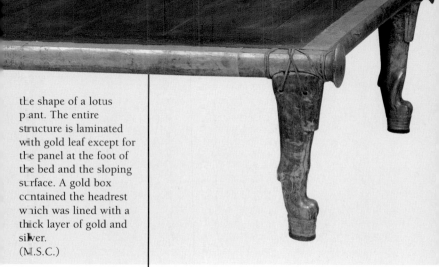

the shape of a lotus plant. The entire structure is laminated with gold leaf except for the panel at the foot of the bed and the sloping surface. A gold box contained the headrest which was lined with a thick layer of gold and silver.
(M.S.C.)

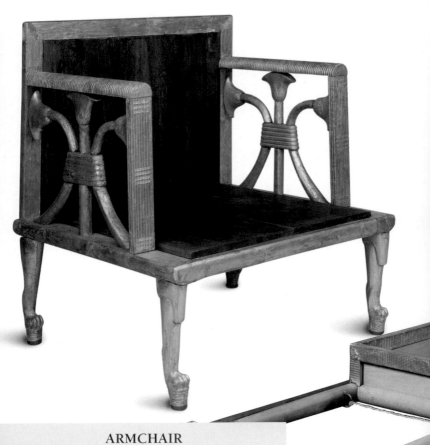

ARMCHAIR
WOOD AND GOLD LEAF
HEIGHT 79.5 CM, WIDTH 71 CM
GIZA, TOMB OF HETEPHERES I
EXCAVATION BY G. REISNER (1925)
FOURTH DYNASTY, REIGN OF SNEFRU (2575-2551 BC)

ROOM 37

The furniture in Hetepheres' tomb included two exquisitely made armchairs of similar style. The more important of the two was decorated with colorful inlays of the falcon Horus and the standards of the goddess Neith; unfortunately it has deteriorated irredeemably and only an approximate reconstruction has been possible. Somewhat better preserved is this gold-leaf seat in which the unpainted wooden panels have been added in recent times. The armrests have a discreet decoration of bound papyrus rods which help to lighten the simple geometry of the structure. The seat is made more comfortable by the slight inclination of the horizontal panel. (M.S.C.)

SEDAN CHAIR

WOOD AND GOLD LEAF
SEAT: HEIGHT 52 CM, WIDTH 52-53.5 CM, LENGTH 99 CM
POLES: LENGTH 99 CM
GIZA, TOMB OF HETEPHERES I
EXCAVATION BY G. REISNER (1925)
FOURTH DYNASTY, REIGN OF SNEFRU (2575-2551 BC)

ROOM 37

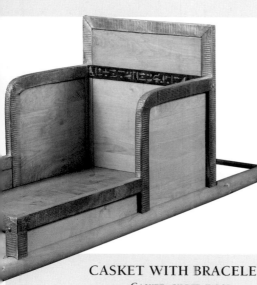

It is known that sedan chairs were used in Egypt from the First Dynasty, but the only example to have survived to the modern day is that of Queen Hetepheres. Here too, the joints are created with leather thongs or tenons lined with copper. On the front side of the backrest, at the height of the armrests, an ebony strip is inscribed as follows in gold hieroglyphs: "Mother of the King of Upper and Lower Egypt, daughter of Horus, charged with the affairs of the Imat, she for whom every word has been created, the daughter of the god, Hetepheres." On the back side the same inscription appears.

The entire structure is edged with gold decorated with geometrical patterns in relief. For the queen's greater comfort, the horizontal seat could be extended to allow her to stretch out her legs. (M.S.C.)

CASKET WITH BRACELETS

CASKET: GILDED WOOD
HEIGHT 21.8 CM, LENGTH 41.9 CM, WIDTH 33.7 CM
BRACELETS: ENGRAVED SILVER WITH CARNELIAN, LAPIS LAZULI,
AND TURQUOISE; DIAMETER 9-11 CM
GIZA, TOMB OF HETEPHERES I; EXCAVATION BY G. REISNER (1925)
FOURTH DYNASTY, REIGN OF SNEFRU (2575-2551 BC)

ROOM 37

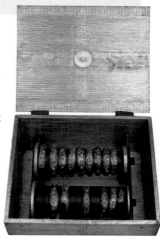

The only items of jewelry belonging to Queen Hetepheres to have escaped the notice of the tomb robbers were these lovely silver bracelets made from a single plate of curved metal open on the inside. The chromatic effects of the semi-precious stones set in the surface using the *champlevé* technique successfully reproduce the vivacity of four butterflies with their wings open. There were originally twenty bracelets in two rows of ten inserted in the two central cylinders of the casket.

The inscriptions "Box containing bracelets" and "Mother of the King of Upper and Lower Egypt Hetepheres" appear on either side of the knob on the lid; then, written in ink, the word "Bracelets." (M.S.C)

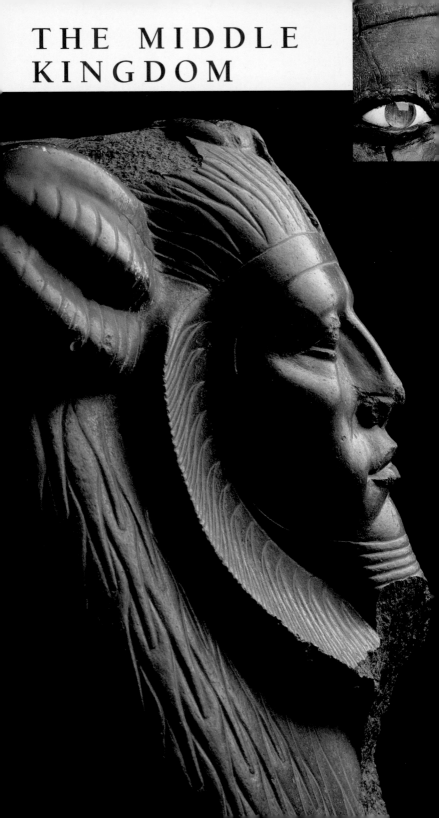

THE MIDDLE
KINGDOM

"... But a king will rise in the south, Ameni, justified ... He will receive the white crown and will wear the red crown ... Rejoice, men of his time! The Asiatics will fall from the fear that he inspires, the Libyans will fall before his flame ... the uraeus on his forehead will pacify his enemies ... Order will return, iniquitous disorder will be driven out. He who shall see and follow the king, rejoice! ..." (from the Prophecy of Neferty).

This is how one of the best-known works of ancient Egyptian literature ends, celebrating the advent of Amenemhat I (Ameni in the text), the first sovereign of the Twelfth Dynasty, and with him the return to order and a strong centralized power after the upsets of the First Intermediate Period.

Actually, Egypt had been re-unified under a single king by Mentuhotep II (end of the Eleventh Dynasty) with Thebes selected as the new political and religious capital of the country and the pharaohs' burial place.

The large painted sandstone statue of Amenemhat I found in 1900 in the "Gate of the Horse" in his funerary temple at Deir al-Bahari is the celebration of a dynamic king, "the living Horus" on earth and "Osiris" after death, dressed in Jubilee garments as proof of an eternally reinvigorated power. Amenemhat was already recognized in antiquity as the founder of a new stage of the Egyptian monarchy in the same way that Menes and Ahmose were respectively founders of the Old and New Kingdoms; as such, all three were represented in the Ramesseum for the procession of the festival of the god Min.

At the start of the Twelfth Dynasty, Amenemhat I oversaw a phase of the "rebirth" of Egypt, a complete renewal following a phase of break up, similar to the period when Tutankhamun returned the capital and religion to Thebes after the Amarnian "heresy," and to phases under Sety I and Rameses IX at the end of the New Kingdom.

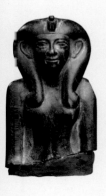

CHAPTER 3
GROUND FLOOR

92 SPHINX OF AMENEMHAT III
Gray granite
Twelfth Dynasty,
Reign of
Amenemhat III
(1842-1794 BC)

93 BUST OF A QUEEN
Serpentine; Height
cm 12; Elephantine;
Twelfth Dynasty,
Reign of
Amenemhat III
(1842-1794 BC)

ITINERARY THROUGH ROOMS
32, 26, 21, 22, 16, 11, HALL

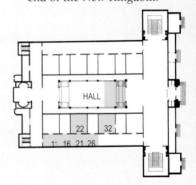

Watching the situation in the Delta carefully and bearing in mind possible incursions on the northern borders, Amenemhat I decided to move the political capital north from Thebes to Itji-Tauy, i.e. "(she who) grasps the Two Lands," and emphasized the policy of force required by the kings of the Thirteenth Dynasty to restore order. "I went down to Elephantine and back into the Delta, then, after examining the borders of the country, I inspected the interior. I travelled to the furthest limits of the fortifications with my powerful arm and my marvels ... the Nile respected me in all the plains. No-one suffered hunger or thirst during my reign..." (from the Instruction of Amenemhat I to his son Senusret). The new capital may have been placed where modern al-Lisht is today, about 30 miles south of Cairo in a strategic position for total control of the country and where both Amenemhat I and his son chose to be buried.

To be associated with a glorious past was a desire reflected in the architecture of their funerary complexes which were inspired by those of the pharaohs from the end of the Old Kingdom. Excavation near the pyramid of Senusret I – one of the most active builders in the Middle Kingdom – has unearthed a series of identical statues of the king and Osiriad pillars that commemorate the size and power of a state solidly in the hands of its king. Intense building can also be seen at Karnak where the temple of Amun-Ra became one of the most important sanctuaries of Egypt. The reliefs in the "White Chapel" of Senusret I (found disassembled in the third pylon and today reassembled in the outdoor museum at Karnak) are some of the most magnificent in all of Egyptian art.

The Twelfth Dynasty was a time of great activity and renewal reflected both inside and outside the country, for example, large areas of Fayum oasis were drained as part of a political plan to ensure wealth and well-being, and fortifications were built in Nubia following its conquest by the great warrior king, Senusret III, to ensure Egyptian control in an area that was economically and strategically important. The famous hymn in Senusret III's honour describes him as a dyke that holds back the river, a wall that protects, as shelter for the fearful, and as a mountain against the wind. It begins with a eulogy that highlights his abilities to protect and increase the borders of Egypt: "Greetings to you, ... you who protect the country, expand its borders, embrace the

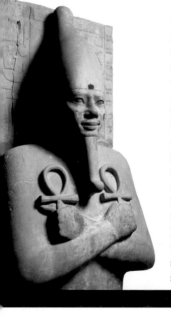

94 OSIRIAN PILLAR OF SENUSRET I
Painted limestone
Height 470 CM
Karnak; Twelfth Dynasty,
Reign of Senusret I
(1964-1929 BC)

95 STATUE OF MENTUHOTEP II
Painted sandstone
Height 138 CM
Deir al-Bahari
Eleventh Dynasty,
Reign of Mentuhotep II
(2065-2014 BC)

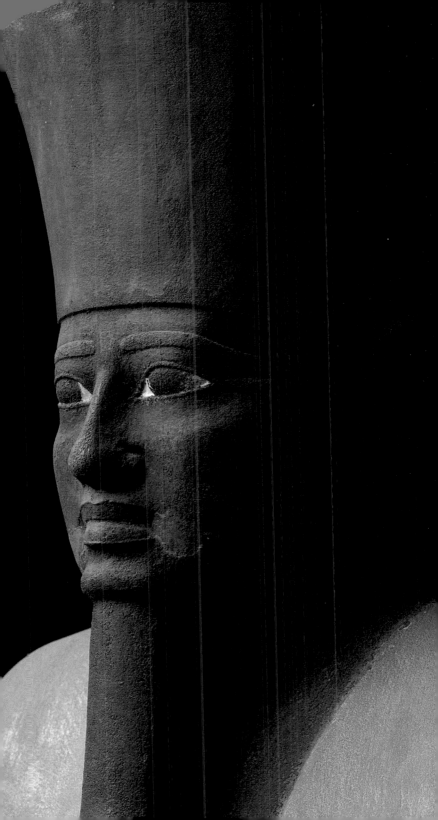

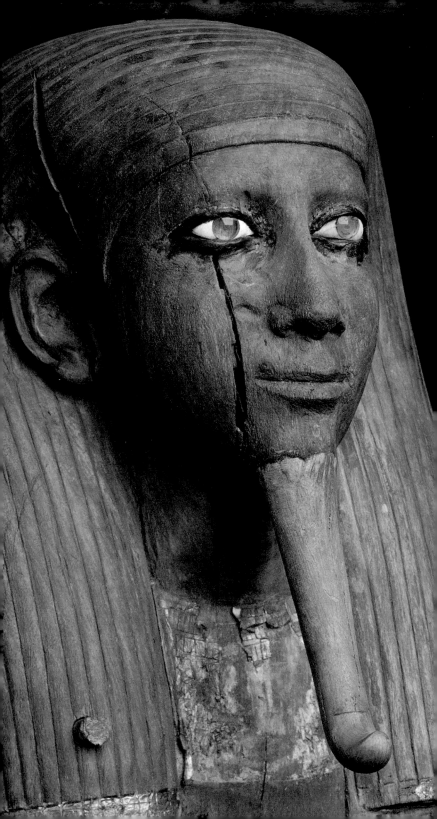

Two Lands with your arms, support foreign countries on your shoulders, massacre the Nine Archers (an expression that means Egypt's enemies) ... the only young man who fights for its borders ..." (from the Hymn to Senusret III). The king was responsible for important alterations in the temple at Karnak where the pharaohs asked for approval from Amun-Ra for their political plans and for work that had been carried out.

In the courtyard of the "Cachette" near the seventh pylon, and in French excavations near the fourth pylon three colossal and majestic statues of Senusret III made from pink granite were found that were all masterpieces of the art of the late Middle Kingdom. During the reigns of Senusret III and his son Amenemhat III, Egypt enjoyed a period of great splendor with control solidly held by the king against any attempts by individual nomarchs to intrude; the strong and decisive characters of these two pharaohs were reflected in the faces of royal statuary.

The reign of Amenemhat III, the last great ruler of the Middle Kingdom, was a period of absolutism and monarchical glory well matched by the construction of an enormous funerary complex at Hawara, in Fayum, known in antiquity as the "Labyrinth" for its extraordinary and massive size: "The pyramids likewise surpass description and are severally equal to a number of the greatest works of the Greeks, but the labyrinth surpasses the pyramids" (Herodotus, II, 148). The king chose to be buried in the pyramid of Hawara in an area where he had been especially busy, to the extent that he was deified in many sites of the area during the Ptolemaic era. A cenotaph was built at Dahshur near the burial places of his

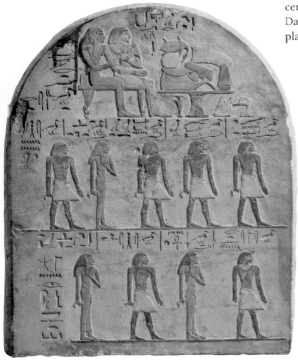

96 Statue of the KA of Auibra-Hor
Wood, gold leaf and semiprecious stones; Height 170 CM
Dashur, Funerary complex of Amenemhat III
Thirteenth Dynasty, Reign of Auibra-Hor (18th-first half 17th century BC)

97 Stela of Ibi
Painted limestone
Height 49 CM, width 38 CM; Abydos;
Middle Kingdom (2065-1650 BC)

predecessors, Amenemhat II and Senusret III; it was called the "black pyramid" because of its basalt *pyramidion* that contrasted with the lining of white limestone from Tura that covered surrounded with a thick lion's mane and large protruding ears that clearly celebrated Amenemhat as already being associated with the gods. An interpretation of this statue made in antiquity and taken by another pharaoh. This singular experiment was probably part of Amenemhat III's political propaganda with the aim of commemorating himself as a strong and capable monarch responsible for

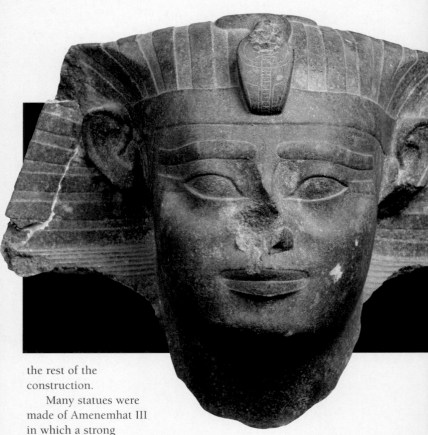

the rest of the construction.

Many statues were made of Amenemhat III in which a strong attempt was made to characterize the individual, as had been seen in statuary of his father, Senusret III. In particular, an unusual portrait of Amenemhat III can be seen in seven granite sphinxes made at Tanis in which the face of the king was justifies its being imitated during later ages. A statuary group of the sovereign made from gray granite, in which the king was represented as the two Niles side by side in a personification of fertility and regeneration of nature, was later moved to Tanis the ordered functioning of the cosmos and the guarantor of established order.

The end of the Middle Kingdom was lost in the list of many Twelfth-Dynasty kings who were collectively unable to protect the borders of the country and maintain internal order.

The phase known as the Second Intermediate Period opens a new historical era that is difficult to understand in which the "Shepherd Kings" made themselves "pharaohs" and the country was once again divided under a number of different masters: "It happened that the country of Egypt suffered in misery and there was no one Lord like there used to be the king. It happened that the king Seqenenra was master of the City of the South. The misery was in the city of the Asiatics and the Prince Apopi was in Avari ..." (from The Dispute between Apopi and Seqenenra).

The most important religious aspect to emerge in the Middle Kingdom is seen in the stelae raised in Abydos. Abydos was the religious center associated with Osiris and a large number of private funerary stelae were left there to permit the deceased to participate symbolically in the annual celebration of the resurrection of the god. A pilgrimage to the sacred city of Abydos became an essential deed to achieve eternal life after death. During the Old Kingdom, it had been the pharaoh that gave dignitaries their

tombs (thought to be "houses of eternal life") and interceded with the god on the functionary's behalf, as only he had access to the divine world after death but could make it available to those who were buried in the lee of the pyramids. The crisis of central power suffered at the end of the third millennium led to the king no longer being recognized as the guarantor of the destiny of his subjects beyond the tomb and, consequently, to a new

way of ensuring eternal life. The slow and gradual "democratization" of religion was a phenomenon that influenced all levels of the culture of ancient Egypt. The absence of data relating to terrestrial religion as clear as those relating to funerary religion should not, however, sidetrack research. It is crises in central power that initiates experimentation with new forms of expression that become established during phases of greater political stability. Interpretation of the Middle Kingdom in this light should not neglect close analysis of the First Intermediate Period which is only considered "obscure" by convention. (A.A.)

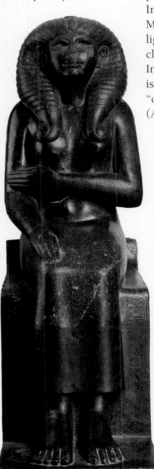

98 HEAD OF A SPHINX OF SENUSRET I Gray granite; Height 38 CM; Karnak, Temple of Amun-Ra, "Cachette" court; Excavation by G. Legrain (1904); Twelfth Dynasty, Reign of Senusret I (1964-1929 BC)

99 STATUE OF QUEEN NOFRET Black granite; Height 165 CM; Tanis; Head and chest found in 1860-1861; Excavation by A. Mariette; lower part found in 1904; Twelfth Dynasty; Reign of Senusret II (1898-1881 BC)

STELA OF A GENERAL
PAINTED LIMESTONE
HEIGHT 80 CM, WIDTH 55 CM
NAGA AL-DEIR
TWELFTH DYNASTY (1994-1781 BC)

ROOM 32

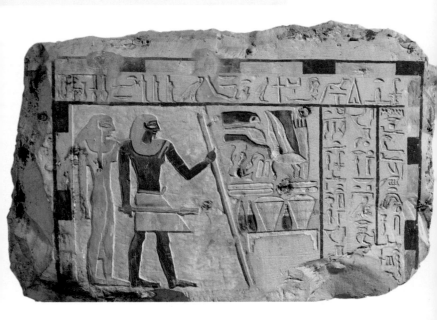

Naga in northern Upper Egypt was the location of a number of necropolises from the Predynastic Period until the Middle Kingdom. It was a large funerary area connected to This, the city that was eclipsed by the religious center of Abydos at the start of the second millennium BC.

This stela shows signs of a provincial origin and is damaged on the bottom half with the consequent loss of the deceased's name. He is shown standing, holding a long staff and the *sekhem* scepter in his hands, and accompanied by his wife who stands behind hi[m] The horizontal inscription contains the standard funerary offering formula to the god Anubis on beh[alf] of the "venerable" decease[d,] one of whose titles, gener[al,] is given at the bottom of the vertical column in the center. (A.A.)

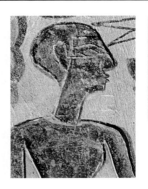

STELA WITH V-SHAPED CORNICE
PAINTED LIMESTONE; HEIGHT 56 CM
PURCHASED IN LUXOR IN 1889
PERHAPS LATE MIDDLE KINGDOM
(SECOND HALF OF THE SECOND MILLENNIUM BC)

ROOM 32

The stela has a monumental facade with a rounded painted molding topped by a V-shaped cornice with polychrome ribbing. The arrangement of the figures and objects in the three, rather disordered, registers suggests the stela was made during the late Middle Kingdom.

The upper register contains a horizontal three-line hieroglyphic inscription painted in yellow ocher divided by lines of varying thickness. The text begins with the typical offerings formula to the "great god" Osiris but is interrupted in the middle of the third line, implying the work was carried out hurriedly. The central part of the stela is filled with scenes of the funeral meal in which a small figure on the right (we only see half a body) holds out a container of either water or wine to the deceased who is accompanied by his wife. The husband wears a skirt that reaches to his ankles and holds a long staff in his left hand, while his wife rests her arm over her husband's shoulder. The different sizes of the two figures and the different planes they stand on make the scene somewhat

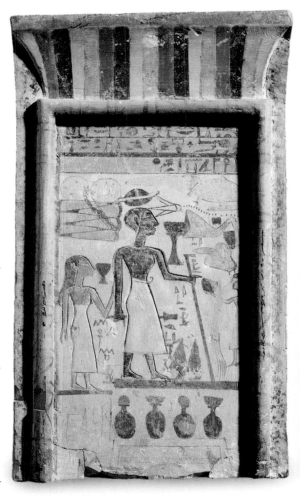

disorganized. The arrangement of the funerary offerings that fill all the spaces around the couple is also rather chaotic.

The sense of confusion is further increased by the decoration on the right of the lower part of the stela in which four pots with lids stand on a low table. (A.A.)

STATUE OF MENTUHOTEP II

PAINTED SANDSTONE; HEIGHT 138 CM
DEIR AL BAHARI, FUNERARY TEMPLE OF MENTUHOTEP II
DISCOVERED BY H. CARTER (1900)
ELEVENTH DYNASTY
REIGN OF MENTUHOTEP II (2065-2014 BC)

ROOM 26

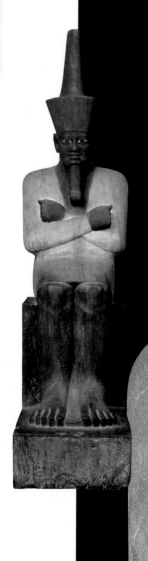

In 1900, the horse on which Howard Carter, future discoverer of the tomb of Tutankhamun, was riding tripped and accidentally revealed the entrance to an underground corridor that is known today as Bab al-Hosan (Door of the Horse). The corridor led to a funerary chamber in which this imposing statue of Mentuhotep II was found wrapped in a linen cloth.

The hypogeum was discovered inside a court of the funerary temple that the monarch had constructed in the natural rocky amphitheater of Deir al-Bahari; it was probably built as his cenotaph and would have been used for ritual and religious purposes.

This monarch, who reunified Egypt following the difficult First Intermediate Period, is shown life-size in a solid polychrome sculpture that emanates a sense of power and majestic dignity. Seated on a cubic throne, he wears the red crown of Lower Egypt and the short white cloak worn at the Jubilee ceremony that periodically renewed his power. The wide, fleshy face wears the false beard with the curved tip that characterized dead and divinized pharaohs, while the large eyes show extraordinary vivacity in the pupils highlighted by the bright white surround.

The massive and relatively unfinished body of Mentuhotep is painted black probably in an allusion to the identification of the dead king with the god Osiris, lord of the Afterlife, who is shown in the standard position with his arms crossed on his chest.

The barely modeled legs and arms of the statue are disproportionate to the rest of the body and show traces of the Theban sculptural tradition that was still marked by elements typical of late Old Kingdom statuary. (S.E.)

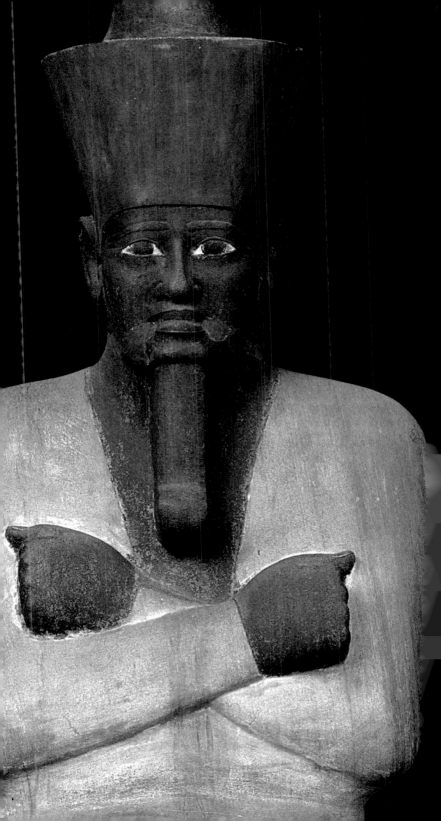

PILLAR OF SENUSRET I

PAINTED LIMESTONE
HEIGHT 434 CM, LENGTH 95 CM
KARNAK, TEMPLE OF AMUN-RA, COURT OF THE CACHETTE
EXCAVATION BY G. LEGRAIN (1903-1904)
TWELFTH DYNASTY, REIGN OF SENUSRET I (1964-1929 BC)

ROOM 21

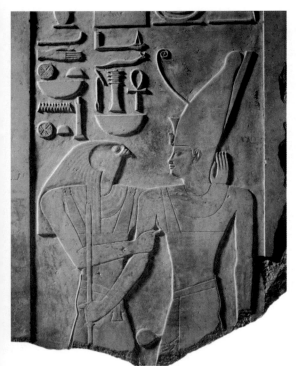

A secret store beneath the courtyard in front of the seventh pylon of the temple of Amun-Ra at Karnak was found, in the early 1900's, to contain hundreds of statues of pharaohs, deities, private individuals, and architectural elements covering an arc of time from the Eleventh Dynasty to the Ptolemaic Period. Among the works amassed in this large underground deposit was a pillar finely decorated with reliefs on four sides. It had been ordered by Senusret I, the great monarch who extended the borders of Egypt and embellished its magnificent monuments.

Each side of the pillar shows the pharaoh embraced by a different god on an equal footing. In each of the four scenes, Senusret I wears different clothes, from a tunic to a simple skirt, and is adorned by various headdresses that symbolize his royalty: the *nemes*, the red crown of Lower Egypt, and the double crown of unified Egypt. The gods with whom he is shown are Horus of Edfu, with a falcon head, Atum of Heliopolis, wearing the double crown, Amun of Thebes, with his typical crown formed by two long plumes, and Ptah of Memphis, who wears a tight cap on his head and is shown inside a temple.

The elegant hieroglyphs are arranged in columns around thei figures and list their names and titles; they also wish long life, stability, and power to the king whose name is represented in the cartouches.

As this pillar demonstrates, relief art during the Twelfth Dynasty – and particularly under Senusret I – reached an extraordinary level of formal purity and elegance of style that was rarely equaled throughout ancient Egypt's long history. (S.E.)

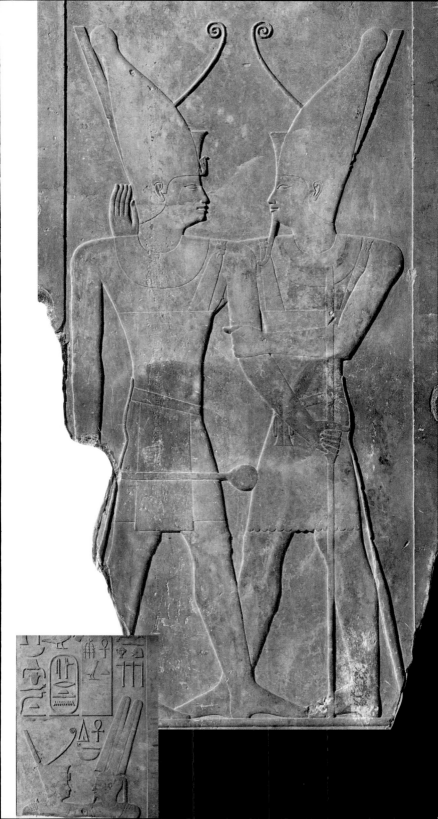

STATUE OF VIZIER ANKHU'S FATHER

GRAY GRANITE, HEIGHT 115 CM
KARNAK, TEMPLE OF AMUN-RA
LATE TWELFTH – EARLY THIRTEENTH DYNASTY
(SECOND HALF OF THE SECOND MILLENNIUM BC)

ROOM 21

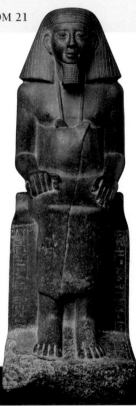

The statue shows a man who had the privilege of having his statue placed inside the great Temple of Amun-Ra at Karnak. From the time of the Middle Kingdom, it was not unusual for private citizens to obtain permission to place their images as offerings inside temples in order to benefit from eternal divine protection.

The figure is seated on a low throne with his hands resting on his legs. The rather stereotyped rounded face bears a composed expression and is framed by a thick striped wig that widens as it falls onto the shoulders. A beard decorated with a square motif hangs from his chin. His body is covered by a long piece of fabric with top strips crossed over the chest and supported by a cord that passes behind the neck. The clothing is typical of a vizier and suggests that this figure had this high political position towards the end of the Twelfth Dynasty.

The surface of the throne is adorned with two columns of hieroglyphs that contain the *hetep-di-nesu* offerings formula to ensure the deceased with eternal provisions of all things in the Afterlife. (S.E.)

FUNERARY STELA OF AMENEMHAT

PAINTED LIMESTONE; HEIGHT 30 CM, WIDTH 50 CM
ASSASIF (TT R4); EXCAVATION BY THE
METROPOLITAN MUSEUM OF ART (1915-1916)
ELEVENTH DYNASTY (2135-1994 BC)

ROOM 21

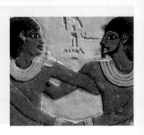

This limestone slab, with its original bright colors preserved, shows a funereal banqueting scene at which a whole family is present. A father, mother, and a son named Antef are seated on a long bench with lion's feet and are immortalized in a moment of intimacy and affection as they hug one another. A table covered with offerings of meat and vegetables separates the family from a female figure identified by the hieroglyphic inscription as Ipy, the daughter-in-law of the deceased.

The flesh of the two women is typically painted in pale colors, and they both wear a long white garment open over one breast, and necklaces, bracelets, and anklets. The two men, with darker flesh tones, wear a white skirt, a necklace, and bracelets. The father is identified by a black beard that grows thinner as it mounts his cheeks.

The horizontal hieroglyphic inscription forms an invocation to Osiris to provide supplies of food to the "venerable" couple, Amenemhat and his wife, I. (S.E.)

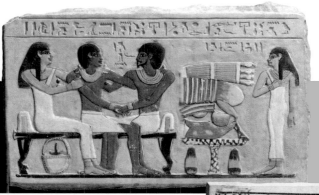

STELA OF NIT-PTAH
PAINTED LIMESTONE; HEIGHT 23 CM, WIDTH 30 CM; ASSASIF; EXCAVATION BY THE METROPOLITAN MUSEUM OF ART (1915-1916); END OF THE MIDDLE KINGDOM; (MID-SECOND MILLENNIUM BC)

ROOM 21

The stela comes from the Theban necropolis of Assasif and depicts four members of a family. Two male figures alternate with two females to create a pleasing chromatic contrast as a result of the different colors used for the flesh of the men (red) and the women (pale yellow).

The head of the family, Nit-Ptah, appears on the right dressed in a white skirt. He wears a wide necklace and holds a cane and a staff in his hands.

The figure that follows is probably his wife, "Seni, daughter of Tai," who wears a diamond-patterned dress, decorated with colored beads, that leaves one breast uncovered. She is adorned by a thin necklace, bracelets, and anklets and sniffs at an open lotus flower while holding a bud in her right hand. The two figures at the end are identified in the inscriptions as Seni's children. Antef is shown in the same position as his father, while Ded can be differentiated from her mother by her green dress.

The inscription over the figures invokes the god Ptah-Sokaris to provide offerings for the various ka of the members of the family. (S.E.)

FUNERARY STELA OF DEDUSOBEK

PAINTED LIMESTONE
HEIGHT 28.5 CM, WIDTH 18.5 CM
ABYDOS, NORTHERN NECROPOLIS
MIDDLE KINGDOM (2065-1650 BC)

ROOM 21

This stela is dominated by the figure of Upuaut, "he who opens the ways" in the Afterlife. It shows a family scene created with simple, schematic

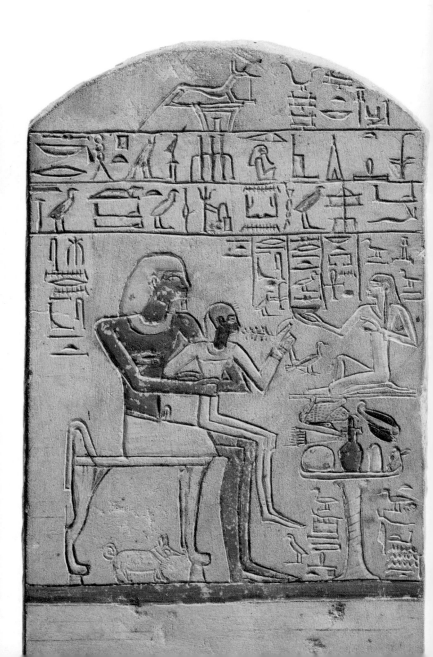

lines in a fresh and free composition. A young girl sits on her father's knee in front of a table of offerings while smelling a flower; she appears surrounded by her playing companions: the dog beneath the seat and a bird in front of her. The woman sitting that is holding a cup bears the title "Lady of the house" and is named Ankh-ser.

The barely drafted inscription contains the customary formula of offerings on behalf of the deceased. (S.E.)

STATUE OF AMENEMHAT III

YELLOW LIMESTONE; HEIGHT 160 CM; HAWARA
ELEVENTH DYNASTY,
REIGN OF AMENEMHAT III (1842-1794 BC)

ROOM 21

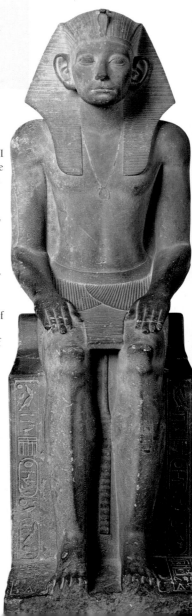

A fragmentary limestone statue of Amenemhat III seated on his throne was found in the funerary temple of the pharaoh at Hawara, cited by Strabo as the famous "Labyrinth." The sculpture was supposed to adorn the large building probably built to celebrate the *Sed* festival in which the pharaoh's power was believed to be renewed. This image of Amenemhat lacks the vigor and muscular strength in other statues of the king as his physique is less robust. but the idealized lines of his face give life to a portrait that emanates a sense of absolute imperturbability.

His gaze is fixed and severe, his torso barely modeled, and the rest of his body has been created with rigid, schematic forms. The pharaoh sits with his hands resting on a striped skirt and his throne is reminiscent of several similar statues of Senusret I found at Lisht. The sides of the throne are decorated in the same manner with the *sema-tawy* (heraldic emblem of the unification of the Two Egypts) flanked by two images of the Nile god Hapi standing in front of the symbols of the north and south of the country, a papyrus plant and a lotus plant. (S.E.)

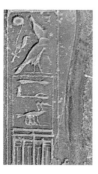

STELA OF NEMTYEMHAT

PAINTED LIMESTONE
HEIGHT 57 CM, WIDTH 23 CM
ABYDOS
MIDDLE KINGDOM (2065-1650 BC)

ROOM 21

Abydos, in northern Upper Egypt, became the most important religious center at the start of the Middle Kingdom. Osiris, identified with the local god Khentiamentiu, was the city's principal deity and he was even believed to have been buried here. Abydos was the site of important mystery ceremonies, a theatrical representation of the myth of Osiris, that were believed necessary for the god to be reborn and, with him, all the dead as well. The mysteries were celebrated at different periods and culminated in the resurrection of the god. A stela found in this sacred place recorded the benefits enjoyed by those who had participated, or who had magically been allowed to participate although they had not been present.

This stela belonged to Nemtyemhat, a functionary of Mentuhotep II, whose many titles included head of the priest-readers of the king's funerary complex. The central part of the stela bears a typical image of the deceased seated at an offerings table, accompanied by his wife. The upper section has two texts placed symmetrically on either side of a vertical line: the left side is the standard funerary offering to the god Osiris-Khentiamentiu and to all the gods of Abydos so that the deceased might be present at important local festivals, including that of the Haker, during which all the dead buried in the necropolis were called to appear with Osiris before the judgement of the gods. The text also hopes that Nemtyemhat will receive a place on the sacred bark.

The funerary offering to Osiris and to Khentiamentiu on the right side of the vertical line prays that the deceased may be allowed to participate in Osiris' procession and take part in the necropolis festivals with the other followers of the god.

An "invocation to the living" in front of a symbolic representation of the tomb of Nemtyemhat on the bottom section of the stela requests that the deceased's name might be kept alive for ever. (A.A.)

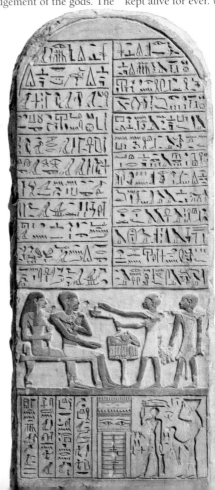

STATUE OF SENUSRET I

LIMESTONE; HEIGHT 200 CM
AL-LISHT, FUNERARY TEMPLE OF SENUSRET I
EXCAVATION BY THE FRENCH INSTITUTE
OF ORIENTAL ARCHAEOLOGY (1894)
TWELFTH DYNASTY, REIGN OF SENUSRET I (1964-1929 BC)

ROOM 22

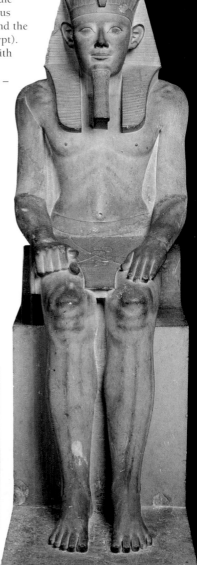

Ten similar statues showing the pharaoh seated on a solid cubic throne were found hidden near the funerary temple of Senusret I at Lisht. The white limestone sculptures were carved to adorn the complex but were never placed in the temple, perhaps because of alterations to the decoration plans.

The king has been given a serene expression on his well-proportioned and youthful face. The whole stylized figure still demonstrates the artistic traditions of the Old Kingdom, with a rigid and schematic representation of the figure's musculature that accentuates the pharaoh's impression of strength. Senusret wears the *nemes* headdress and a clinging skirt that is striped on some of the ten statues. The uraeus serpent on the forehead and the false beard are both symbols of royalty. The pharaoh's hands rest on his legs, a piece of fabric in one while the other lies palm downwards.

The solid throne is decorated on its sides with reliefs of the *sema-tauy* motif that

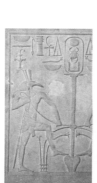

represents the unification of the Two Lands of Egypt. These are flanked by two personifications of the Nile god and by symbols of heraldic plants: the papyrus (Lower Egypt) and the lotus (Upper Egypt). The cartouche with the king's coronation name – Kheperkara – crowns the composition while other hieroglyphs bear the names and epithets of the gods represented.

The double image of the Nile god seen on the thrones of five of the statues is replaced on the others by the image of Horus and Set (emblems of North and South Egypt) and a cartouche with the king's birth name: Senusret. (S.E.)

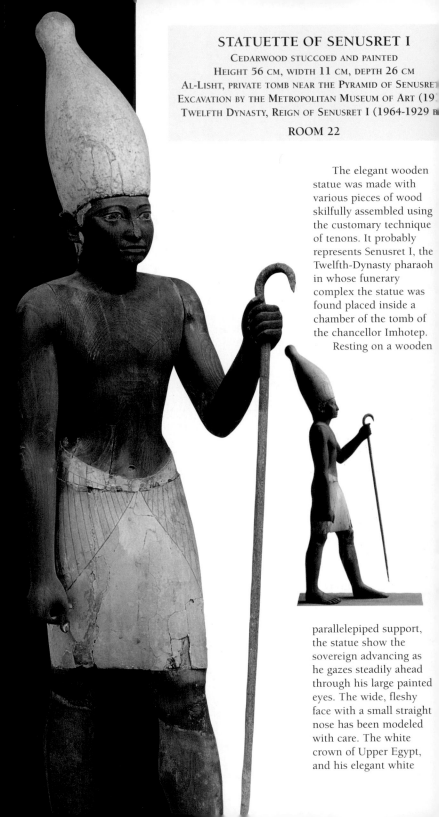

STATUETTE OF SENUSRET I

CEDARWOOD STUCCOED AND PAINTED
HEIGHT 56 CM, WIDTH 11 CM, DEPTH 26 CM
AL-LISHT, PRIVATE TOMB NEAR THE PYRAMID OF SENUSRET
EXCAVATION BY THE METROPOLITAN MUSEUM OF ART (19
TWELFTH DYNASTY, REIGN OF SENUSRET I (1964-1929 BI

ROOM 22

The elegant wooden statue was made with various pieces of wood skilfully assembled using the customary technique of tenons. It probably represents Senusret I, the Twelfth-Dynasty pharaoh in whose funerary complex the statue was found placed inside a chamber of the tomb of the chancellor Imhotep.

Resting on a wooden parallelepiped support, the statue show the sovereign advancing as he gazes steadily ahead through his large painted eyes. The wide, fleshy face with a small straight nose has been modeled with care. The white crown of Upper Egypt, and his elegant white skirt pleated with yellow raised slightly on his hips, create a strong chromatic contrast with the rest of the dark painted body. The veins in the wood have been used to emphasize the solid muscularity of the torso, the arms, and the bone structure of the knees.

The pharaoh grips a long staff with a curved end in his left hand: this is the *heqa* scepter, a symbol of royalty. The other hand probably held the *sekhem* scepter, an emblem of power, but it has been lost. The absence of the uraeus serpent that usually appeared on the forehead of pharaohs and gods, has suggested that the statue might represent not a particular sovereign, but be itself a symbol of royalty.

The room in Imhotep's tomb also contained a similar statue showing the sovereign wearing the red crown of Lower Egypt (today in the Metropolitan Museum of New York), a model of a boat, and a *naos* of Anubis, all carved from wood.

It is probable that the wooden statues of the sovereign were carried in procession during religious ceremonies and festivals. (S.E.)

NAOS OF NAKHT

PAINTED LIMESTONE
HEIGHT 38 CM
ABYDOS (1881)
MIDDLE KINGDOM (2065-1650 BC)

ROOM 22

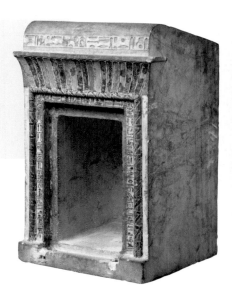

The *naos* held a cube statue of the owner identified by its inscription as the "guardian of the chamber" Nakht. The inside floor of the *naos* is higher at the back to bring more attention to the statue. The *naos* was closed by a double wooden door (ost). The door frame is adorned all around with a hieroglyphic inscription and a bull. The roof is decorated with an Egyptian style molding topped by an inscription that reads left to right stating that Nakht was "venerable at Ptah-Sokari".

This *naos* was one of a group of objects found in the North Necropolis, outside the temple of Osiris. This may suggest that there was a "processional way" that passed the west gate of the temple along which stood private funeral shrines that allowed their owners to participate in the Osirian mysteries The shrines – in some instances connected to a tomb or cenotaph – were the location of stelae, offering tables, and statues of various figures of a single family. Structures of this type, very popular between the reigns of Senusret I and Amenemhat II, and between those of Senusret III and Amenemhat III, can be considered a private version of the magnificent royal cenotaphs at Abydos. (A.A.)

OSIRIAN PILLARS OF SENUSRET I

PAINTED LIMESTONE
HEIGHT 180 CM
AL-LISHT, PYRAMID COMPLEX OF SENUSRET I (1895)
TWELFTH DYNASTY, REIGN OF SENUSRET I (1964-1929 BC)

ROOM 22

Senusret I's pyramid was identified at al-Lisht by G. Maspero in 1882; initial excavation in the area was directed by J.E. Gautier and G. Jéquier and later continued by the Metropolitan Museum of New York between 1906-34. Located 28 miles south of Cairo, al-Lisht is the site of the funerary complexes of the first two pharaohs of the Twelfth Dynasty (Amenemhat I and his son Senusret I) which were built a mile apart.

The design of the complex of Senusret (based on that of the Sixth-Dynasty Pepy II) fostered a revival of the traditions of the Old Kingdom with a temple placed lower, a covered ramp with decorated walls, a funerary temple in the shadow of the east side of the pyramid, and a small pyramid in the south-east corner of the enclosure wall. Much of the structure of Senusret's pyramid and funerary temple remains, but very little of the lower temple. A flat-roofed corridor at the top of

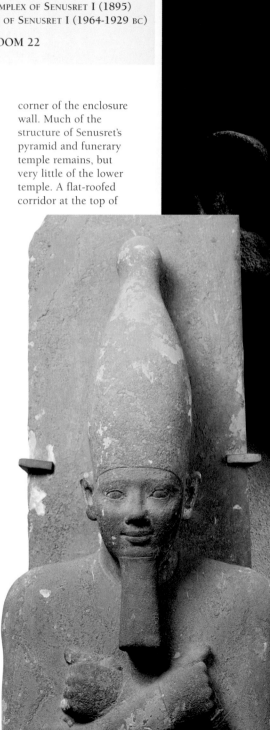

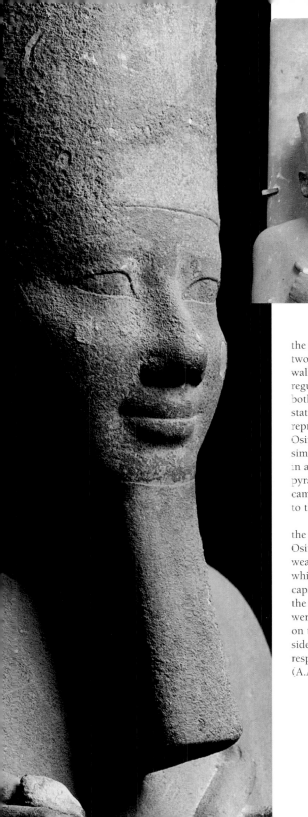

the ramp connected the
two temples, and its
walls had recesses at
regular intervals on
both sides that held
statues of the king
represented as an
Osirian pillar. Other
similar statues, found
in a trench near the
pyramid, probably
came from the entrance
to the funerary temple.

The two pillars in
the photograph depict
Osiris as a mummy
wearing the red and
white crowns in his
capacity as the "Lord of
the Two Lands"; they
were probably placed
on the south and north
sides of the corridor
respectively.
(A.A.)

STATUARY GROUP WITH SOBEKHOTEP

BLACK GRANITE; HEIGHT 35 CM, WIDTH 32 CM
KIMAN FARES, FAYUM (1911)
TWELFTH DYNASTY (1994-1781 BC)

ROOM 22

This small group is typical of a common artistic model in the Middle Kingdom in which small sculptures of families were carved rather rough-hewn in hard stone such as

other types of art were renewed by changing political circumstances.

This sculpture comes from the capital of Fayum province, Medinet al-Fayum (near present day Kiman Fares) that was

"venerable" man accompanied by four women in the sculpture was named Sobekhotep; starting on the left, we see his wife, his materna aunt, his mother and his maternal grandmother. The hieroglyphic inscriptions below the feet of the women give the name of each and he relationship to Sobekhotep. None of the figures has been given any particular characteristic features. (A.A.)

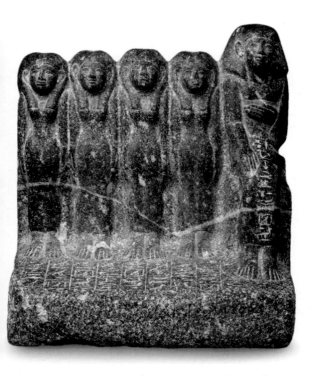

granite. Two results of the political vicissitudes of the First Intermediate Period were that private individuals became more confident with art and stylistic developments in private statuary, and

known to the Greeks as Crocodilopolis and later named Arsinoe in honor of the wife of Ptolemy III. Like all of the oasis, the city flourished under the pharaohs of the Twelfth Dynasty. The

STATUE OF THE MAJORDOMO SAKAHERKA

QUARZITE; HEIGHT 62 CM
KARNAK, TEMPLE OF AMUN-RA
LATE TWELFTH – EARLY OF THE THIRTEENTH DYNASTY
(SECOND HALF OF THE SECOND MILLENNIUM BC)

ROOM 22

Private statuary during the Middle Kingdom above all produced smaller sculptures than the great monuments of the previous epoch. The tendency of functionaries and dignitaries during the later period was to adorn their tombs with small statues of themselves made from semi-precious stone. These could be placed as offerings in temples where they would consequently enjoy for eternity the benefits accorded the gods during daily worship. The statue of Sakaherka, a majordomo who lived at the end of the Twelfth Dynasty, was placed as an offering in the great temple at Karnak.

The owner is seated on a solid throne with his hands placed on his legs as he gazes in front of him. The volumes of the warm-toned yellow quartzite sculpture are subdued and well-balanced. The headdress follows the custom of the era with a rounded surface that follows the shape of the

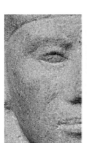

head. The features of Sakaherka's face have been strongly emphasized to create an individual portrait of the man. His body is wrapped in a skirt fixed around his stomach and featuring a column of hieroglyphs that states the name of the majordomo. (S.E.)

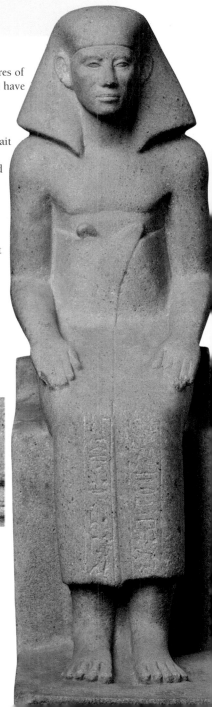

STATUE OF UKH-HOTEP AND HIS FAMILY

GRANITE
HEIGHT 37 CM, WIDTH 30 CM; MEIR
TWELFTH DYNASTY, REIGN OF SENUSRET III (1881-1842 BC)

ROOM 22

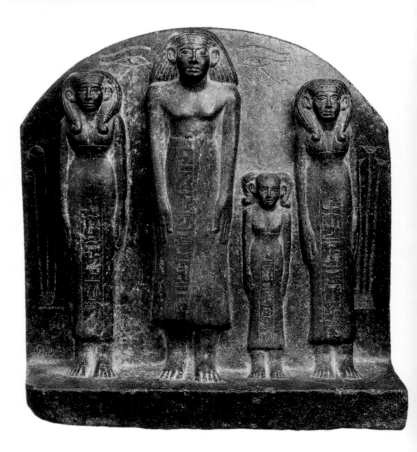

This small family group immortalized in granite represents a fairly common funeral monument in Egypt. One of the nomarchs of Middle Egypt, Ukh-hotep, is shown in the center of the stela flanked by his two wives and a daughter. The four figures are portrayed standing in line with features that are typical of great royal sculpture of the Middle Kingdom. Their unrefined faces are framed by heavy wigs and large earrings. The hairstyles of the wives end in tight curls on their shoulders in a fashion that was born in the royal court and spread among common women. The girl is shown with a typical hairstyle of a child but her clothing is a miniature copy of that worn by the two wives. Ukh-hotep wears a long skirt while the two women wear a clinging dress with double shoulder-straps. A column of hieroglyphs is engraved on each of their clothes that specifies the names and functions of each member of the family. Ukh-hotep is defined as "head of the priests of Hathor," the goddess worshipped in his *nome*.

The bodies of the four figures are long and thin and their arms, hanging down by their sides, are disproportionately sized to the height of each figure. Their feet, on the other hand, are large and solid as was typical of the heavy features seen in sculptural compositions of this period.

The group is bounded on each side by the images of two heraldic plants in Egypt, the papyrus and the lotus flower, while the entire composition is crowned by two *udjat* eyes that have a magical power.

The stela was found in the tomb of the nomarch at Meir which was the burial place of the governors of the fourteenth *nome* of Upper Egypt.
(S.E.)

STATUE OF A GODDESS
Limestone; Height 162 cm
Abydos, Temple of Osiris
Excavation by W.M. Flinders Petrie (1902)
Uncertain date

ROOM 22

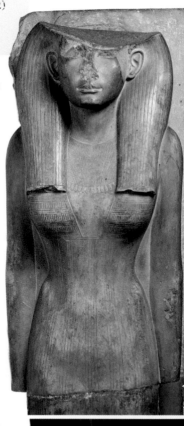

The site of Abydos was excavated by the Egypt Exploration Fund under the direction of Sir Flinders Petrie in the late nineteenth and early twentieth centuries. The digs of 1902 in particular examined various areas including the temple of Osiris where a number of sculptures were unearthed. This damaged statue of a woman was found with fragments of three other statues, all sculpted in limestone. Careful restoration distinguished two standing figures and two seated, of which only one of each type could be reconstructed.

Petrie dated them all to the Thirtieth Dynasty basing his judgement on the cartouche of Nectanebus on the pedestal of one of the seated figures, however, exact dating of this particular statue is uncertain as the docile modeling would suggest an earlier age. The elegant woman wears a simple, three-part, striped wig that leaves her ears uncovered. She has a splendid, finely carved mouth that immediately pulls the attention of the observer to her face although her nose and ears have been lost. The curves of her body can be seen below her long, tight fitting tunic, and her round breasts covered by wide straps confer her with a sensuality that is accentuated by the large necklace that adorns her open neckline.
(A.A.)

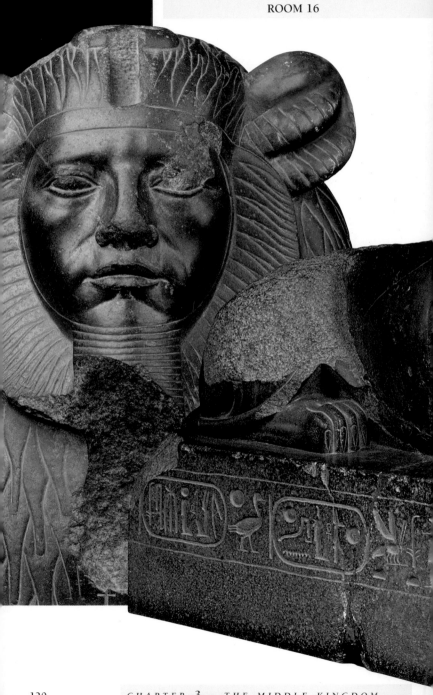

SPHINX OF AMENEMHAT III
Gray granite; Height 150 cm, length 236 cm
Tanis, Excavation by A. Mariette (1863)
Twelfth Dynasty
Reign of Amenemhat III (1842-1794 bc)

ROOM 16

It was in Tanis, the new capital of Egypt during the Twenty-first-Twenty-second Dynasties, that seven granite sphinxes of Amenemhat III were found. They evoke the superhuman power of the king and emphasize his savage appearance.

The austere and vigorous face of the pharaoh is characterized by features that were typical of royal portraiture, with prominent cheekbones, a protuberant mouth, and deeply furrowed cheeks that create strong effects of chiaroscuro.

A massive lionine mane from which large feral ears project substitutes the traditional regal *nemes* headdress and increases the sense of majesty of the entire figure. The uraeus serpent and false beard – standard symbols of divine regality – are also present.

The statues rest on a tall and solid base decorated with the cartouches of several sovereigns who, over the centuries, usurped the group of sphinxes, fascinated by their beauty: they are the Hyksos king Nehesy, Rameses II and Merenptah of the Ninth Dynasty, and Psusennes I of the Twenty-first Dynasty. It was Psusennes who placed the statues at Tanis where they were found, but it is probable that they were originally carved to decorate the temple of the goddess Bastet at Bubastis. (S.E.)

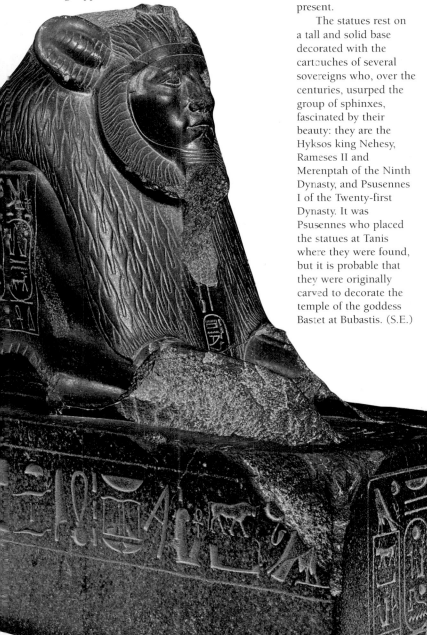

DOUBLE STATUE OF AMENEMHAT III AS THE NILE GOD

GRAY GRANITE; HEIGHT 160 CM
TANIS; TWELFTH DYNASTY
REIGN OF AMENEMHAT III (1842-1794 BC)

ROOM 16

This original sculpture from the reign of Amenemhat III represents two male figures making abundant offerings of fish, birds and aquatic plants. The double figure of the pharaoh includes two elements that bring to mind primordial deities: the heavy wig divided into large braids and the wide beard marked by parallel lines. Despite being damaged, the two faces are clearly portraits of Amenemhat III who emanates a sense of austere aggressiveness.

The bodies of the two bearers are an extraordinary example of modeling, with their powerful build visible even through their clinging, finely pleated skirts. The attempt at absolute symmetry forms a stylistic novelty never seen in prior sculptures of male figures. The two figures are shown in perfect balance with one of them advancing with the right leg rather than the left as was the custom.

The heavy tribute of gifts brings the balance of the composition forward and makes the two porters bend towards the massive block of granite historiated with elegant representations of river flora and fauna that allow us to identify the two figures with the Nile god. The river of Egypt, the bringer of nourishment and life, is portrayed with the semblances of Amenemhat III in an allegorical composition that associates the king with the concepts of fertility and abundance.

The hieroglyphic inscriptions on the front and back of the sculpture were added by Psusennes I, a pharaoh of the Twenty-first Dynasty whose cartouches are also to be seen, when he had the sculpture taken to Tanis, the new capital and burial place of several sovereigns from his epoch.
(S.E.)

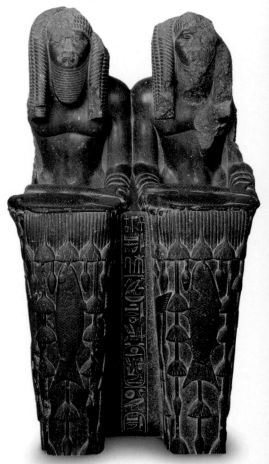

STATUE OF AMENEMHAT III

BLACK GRANITE; HEIGHT 90 CM
KARNAK, TEMPLE OF AMUN-RA, COURT OF THE CACHETTE
EXCAVATION BY G. LEGRAIN (1903-1904)
TWELFTH DYNASTY, REIGN OF AMENEMHAT III (1842-1794 BC)

ROOM 16

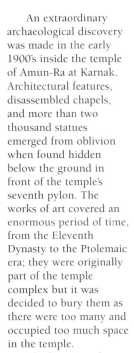

An extraordinary archaeological discovery was made in the early 1900's inside the temple of Amun-Ra at Karnak. Architectural features, disassembled chapels, and more than two thousand statues emerged from oblivion when found hidden below the ground in front of the temple's seventh pylon. The works of art covered an enormous period of time, from the Eleventh Dynasty to the Ptolemaic era; they were originally part of the temple complex but it was decided to bury them as there were too many and occupied too much space in the temple.

The large trench contained systematic arrangements of statues of private individuals, gods, and sovereigns, some of which were of the pharaoh Amenemhat III as a devotee. The king is identified by the style of the portrayal: he is standing, with his arms at his sides and his hands resting on his skirt. He wears the striped *nemes* headdress with the uraeus serpent on the forehead, and his large ears emerge from the sides. Although the face does not have the strongly emphasized features of other portraits of Amenemhat III, the statue was given individual traits that show the king to be middle-aged and with a serious, hieratic expression. The youthful torso is flanked by scarcely modeled arms that rest on his rigid triangular skirt in accordance with the portrayal of a ruler praying before his god. The surface of the skirt is marked by a geometric pattern around the waist that continues vertically down to where two cobras are shown in profile as a symbol of power. The statue has not survived undamaged, but the upper part of the legs show that the pharaoh was advancing in the traditional pose. (S.E.)

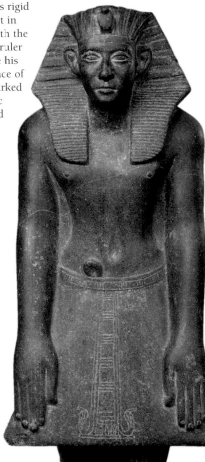

STATUE OF AMENEMHAT III

BLACK GRANITE; HEIGHT 100 CM
FAYUM, CROCODILOPOLIS (MIT FARÈS)
DISCOVERED IN 1862
TWELFTH DYNASTY, REIGN OF AMENEMHAT III
(1842-1794 BC)

ROOM 16

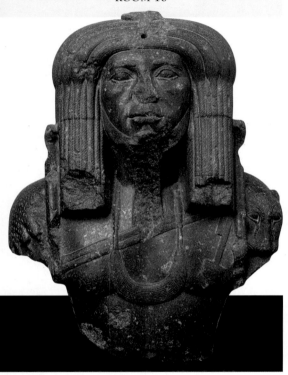

The area of Fayum, largely drained by Amenemhat III, was chosen by the king as his burial place where he built a pyramid and a large funerary complex celebrated in classical sources as the "Labyrinth."

The torso of a sculpture of the king portrayed with the semblances of a primordial priest was discovered in the ancient capital of Fayum, called Crocodilopolis by the Greeks. The face of the monarch is framed by a bulky and unusual haircut, seemingly Archaic in style, that falls heavily onto his shoulders in braids; traces of the missing uraeus serpent remain on his forehead. Nor has the false beard survived, but finely engraved indications of a real beard can be seen on the pharaoh's chin.

Amenemhat III's features are clearly marked and give life to a highly individualistic portrait quite unlike the idealized models of the ruler. The cheekbones protrude, the eyelids are heavy, the curves of the mouth evident, and the deep lines that indicate his advanced age express a sense of deep tension. Some observers have found in this statue an allegorical representation of the ancient institution of the monarchy rather than a realistic image of the pharaoh.

Amenemhat wears a leopard skin – indicated by a paw and the head on the king's shoulders – which is held in place by a double ribbon that crosses his chest diagonally. The upper parts of two divine insignia in the form of a falcon, held in his hand, can be seen on either side of the king's hair. This series of attributes refers to his function as a priest, traditionally held by each sovereign in his role as an intermediary between men and the gods.

(S.E.)

124

STATUE OF THE *KA* OF AUIBRA-HOR

WOOD, GOLD LEAF AND SEMI-PRECIOUS STONES
HEIGHT OF THE STATUE 170 CM
HEIGHT OF THE NAOS 207 CM
DASHUR, FUNERARY COMPLEX OF AMENEMHAT III
THIRTEENTH DYNASTY, REIGN OF AUIBRA-HOR
(18TH-FIRST HALF OF THE 17TH CENTURY BC)

ROOM 11

The ancient Egyptians believed that each individual was composed of five elements of immaterial nature: shadow, the *akh* (the spiritual form assumed by the gods and the dead), the *ba* (bringer of power and an emblem of each individual's personality), a name (the identifier of each person), and the *ka* (the vital strength in each individual).

To ensure the life of the deceased would continue after death, it was necessary to supply food and drink to the *ka* which went on living in the mummified body and that took possession of it every now and then to assimilate the essence of the offerings left in the tomb.

The statues placed in the burial chamber personified the vital force of the deceased and as such constituted a physical support for the *ka*. This was the function of the elegant wooden statue of the pharaoh Auibra-Hor, on whose head two open arms

were shown to represent the hieroglyph used to indicate the *ka*. The face, framed by a three-part lined wig, has been endowed with extraordinary animation by the deep and luminous encrusted eyes made from rock crystal, quartz, and bronze. The divine beard with the curved tip is the only sign of regality that has survived. The figure is completely naked and its surface bears traces of a necklace, a belt, and a skirt. The hands would originally have clasped a scepter and a staff. The arms, the ends of the feet, and the left leg were carved separately and then assembled with the rest of the body by tenons. A few traces of gold leaf are still visible which indicates that certain parts of the figures were originally covered with the precious metal.

The statue was

found inside a small wooden naos near the pyramid of Amenemhat III.
(S.E.)

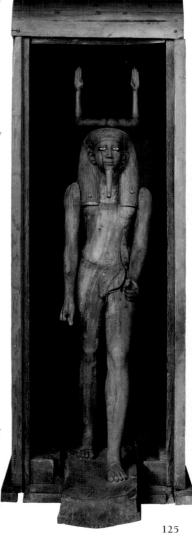

125

PYRAMIDION OF THE PYRAMID OF AMENEMHAT III

BASALT; HEIGHT 140 CM, WIDTH AT THE BASE 185 CM
DAHSHUR; TWELFTH DYNASTY, REIGN OF AMENEMHAT III
(1842-1794 BC)

HALL

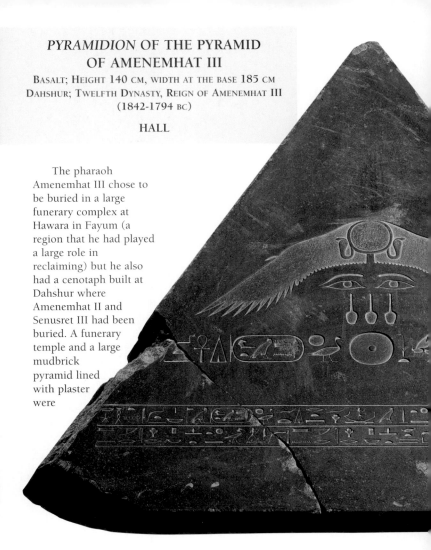

The pharaoh Amenemhat III chose to be buried in a large funerary complex at Hawara in Fayum (a region that he had played a large role in reclaiming) but he also had a cenotaph built at Dahshur where Amenemhat II and Senusret III had been buried. A funerary temple and a large mudbrick pyramid lined with plaster were constructed with the latter crowned by an elegant basalt *pyramidion* that formed the tip of the structure.

The hard stone monument is dark in color to create a strong polychrome contrast with the rest of the pyramid's surface. It is decorated with images and hieroglyphic inscriptions in exquisite basreliefs on the smooth surfaces. A winged sun disk flanked by two uraeus serpents dominates the composition on the east side that faced the rising sun. Two eyes are shown between the long wings positioned above the large hieroglyphs that refer to the beauty of the sun god Ra. The sun was assimilated to the heavenly god and shone upon the *pyramidion* each day as was indicated in the inscription below.

The name of the pharaoh, Amenemhat, and the phrase "son of Ra" are given in one cartouche while the other contains the name "Nimaatra" and the title "king of Upper and Lower Egypt." Both cartouches are followed by wishes for eternal life for the sovereign. (S.E.)

STATUE OF SENUSRET III

PINK GRANITE; ACTUAL HEIGHT 315 CM
KARNAK, TEMPLE OF AMUN-RA,
COURT OF THE CACHETTE; EXCAVATION BY G. LEGRAIN
1900 AND 1903; TWELFTH DYNASTY,
REIGN OF SENUSRET III (1881-1842 BC)

HALL

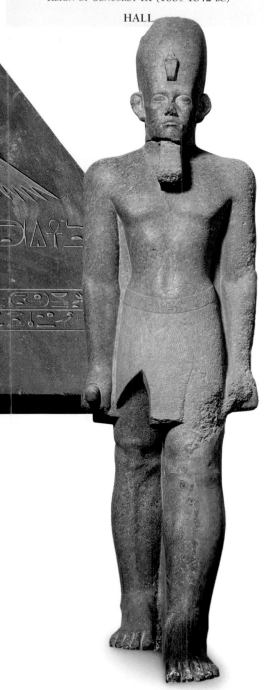

The colossus was found in the courtyard of the Cachette at Karnak on two occasions. Excavation by Legrain in 1900 unearthed two headless statues made from pink granite that were identified as being of Senusret III by the inscription on the rear support. It was only in 1903 that the respective heads were found bearing the Horus name of the king engraved on the rear support; the two complete statues were then put back together. The statues are identical: they show the king standing with his left leg advanced and wearing a *shendyt* skirt and false beard. The statue in the photograph wears the white crown with the uraeus serpent, while the other has the red crown to symbolize the pharaoh as the "Lord of the Two Lands.' The head is a masterpiece of classical art in its portrayal of the absolute power of an active and determined ruler.

The discovery in the Cachette of many monuments from the Middle Kingdom has shed light on the most ancient phases of the temple of Amun-Ra before it developed into Egypt's most important sanctuary during the New Kingdom.

The great conqueror of Nubia, Senusret III, left many traces of himself at Karnak, such as a huge pink granite head (81 centimetres) very similar to this example that was discovered in 1970 by a French excavation team. (A.A.)

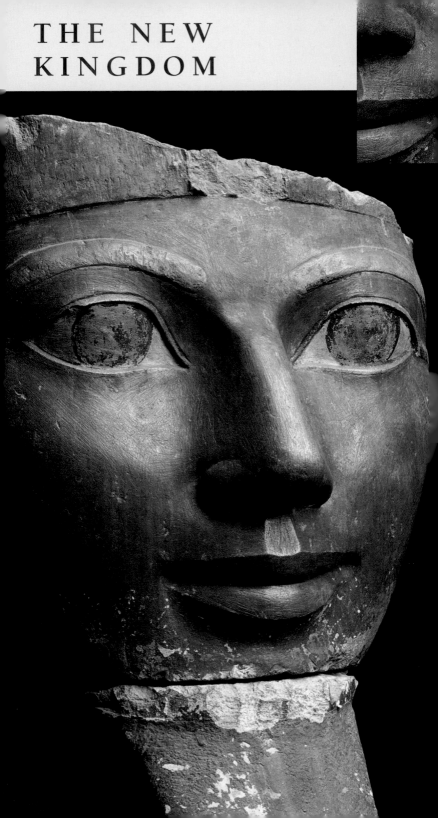

THE BEGINNING OF THE XVIII DYNASTY

The period of Egyptian history known as the New Kingdom was unquestionably one of the most flourishing politically and artistically. This was the era of Thutmosis III, Queen Hatshepsut, and the famous Rameses II. The faces of some of these extraordinary men and women can still be guessed in those of the mummies discovered in the *cachette* at Deir al-Bahari in 1881; this was a hidden store used by the Theban priests of the Twenty-first Dynasty to preserve the royal bodies from the abuse of tomb robbers. A similar hiding place found in the tomb of Amenhotep II in 1898 also contained the bodies of many kings in addition to that of Amenhotep himself.

The new historical phase began with the resurgence of some of the Theban dynasty against the invaders from the Near East, the Hyksos, who threatened to extend the power they had established in the Nile Delta across the rest of the country. The reconquest of Egypt began with the last king of the Seventeenth Dynasty, Kamose, but was only completed during the reigns of the first kings of the next dynasty, Ahmose and Amenhotep I, who took the chance to extend Egyptian power over the Hyksos' homeland, plus over Palestine and Kush, the Hyksos' allies during their 100-year dominion over Egypt. It is evident that the first pharaohs of the Eighteenth Dynasty were warrior kings permanently ready for battle and that they kept nearby peoples like the Mitannian and the Hittites worried. This background was even institutionalized in the art of the period with the kings of the New Kingdom nearly always shown in battle with emphasis placed on their physical force, and courage as the protectors of Egypt. The practice of military sports such as archery, hunting, and horse-riding were upheld above all by Amenhotep II and his successors following

CHAPTER 4
GROUND FLOOR

128 HEAD OF HATSHEPSUT
Painted limestone;
Height 61 CM;
Eighteenth Dynasty,
Reign of Hatshepsut
(1479-1458 BC)

129 AMENHOTEP II WITH
MERETSEGER
Granite; Height 125 CM;
Eighteenth Dynasty,
Reign of Amenhotep II
(1428-1397 BC)

ITINERARY THROUGH
ROOMS 12, 11, 7, 8, 3, 13,
HALL, 9, 10, 15, 14, 20, 25

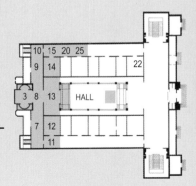

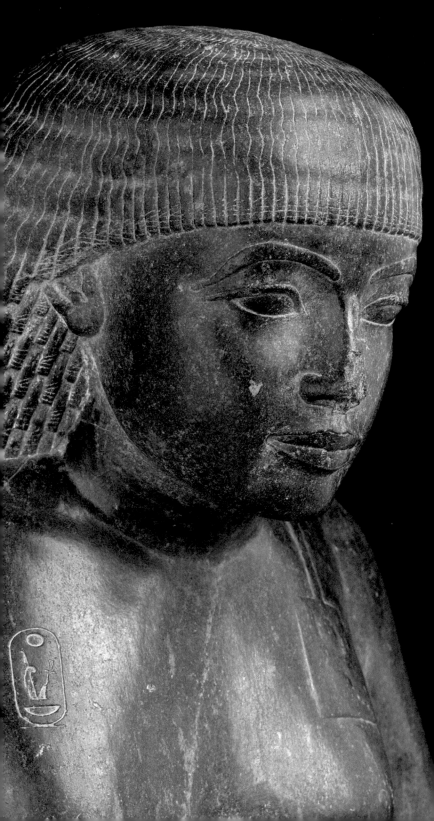

Asiatic influences that reached Egypt via Syria and Palestine. The importance of the military element is also reflected in the fact that members of the army assumed increasing political and economic power and that, from the Nineteenth Dynasty on, retired soldiers that had achieved particular distinction were rewarded with landed property on a hereditary basis. The Near Eastern influence was also felt during the New Kingdom in religion with the diffusion of the Syrian cults of Astarte and Reshef, and in technology with the importation of raw materials such as tin, copper, and silver.

Royal power in the New Kingdom also involved the figure of the pharaoh's principal wife (the "Great Royal Bride") who was nominated the "God's Wife of Amun," the only wife who was allowed to produce an heir to the throne. The basis for this role lay in mythology as the kings of this period believed they were Amun's sons; the corollary of this was the emergence of belief in the sovereign's divine birth, a concept that was depicted on the southern arcade of the second terrace in the "funerary" temple of Hatshepsut at Deir al-Bahari.

She was certainly a key figure in the New Kingdom; she took the reins of government as regent to Thutmosis III but continued to reign for 22 years. However, after her death, Thutmosis III gained his revenge by systematically cancelling her name and image. It was Hatshepsut that built the first of the "temples of the millions of years" on the west bank at Thebes that was dedicated to the cult of the monarch while she was alive and to her *ka* after her death.

The originality of the temple plan and decoration can be seen in the "temples of the millions of years" of her successors Amenhotep III, Ay, Rameses II, and Rameses III.

These were not simply funerary temples (R. Stadelmann. 1985, 706-711) although they were sited in the zone in Thebes dedicated to the cult of the deceased. The *Djeser-djeseru*, "The most sacred of the sacred (temples)" stood in the lee of the cliff on the hill of Deir al-Bahari and followed the schema already used by the Eleventh-Dynasty king Mentuhotep II for his temple that stands in the same area. The architect of Hatshepsut's temple was her counsellor, Senenmut, who was also tutor to

Princess Neferura.

Hatshepsut had no great military adventures but sent an important trading expedition to the land of Punt on the Red Sea to exchange Egyptian goods with highly prized local items such as incense (for ceremonial uses), ebony, and short-horn oxen. Illustrations of this event and the king and queen of Punt can be seen on the walls of the south arcade on the second terrace of Hatshepsut's temple. Military activity restarted when Thutmosis III was eventually able to reign independently after his aunt's death (1458 BC ca).

Thutmosis III was obliged to deal with a revolt by Asiatic princes and led 17 military campaigns before being able to control the situation. He had the record of his campaigns, in particular his clash with the Mitannian, inscribed in his *Annals* in the temple of Amun-Ra at Karnak and commemorated his victories in Syria in the same temple. He brought back a great deal of booty

130 AMENHOTEP, SON OF HAPU
Granite rock; Height 128 CM; Karnak, Temple of Amun Ra, Excavation by G. Legrain (1901); Eighteenth Dynasty, Reign of Amenhotep III (1387-1350 BC)

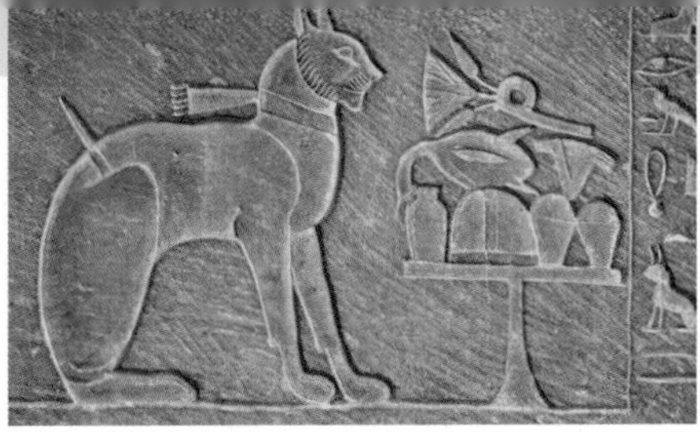

and examples of flora and fauna during these campaigns which he had illustrated in a "botanical garden" to the east of the "festival room" (*Akhmenu*) in his temple. It is Thutmosis's temple that represents the religious and ideological manifesto of the pharaohs of the New Kingdom in that all of them contributed to

contributions were a red granite shrine that contained the sacred bark used during processions of the divine statue, an offering shrine

on the western facade, and the erection of two pink granite obelisks in front of the fifth pylon where a hypostyle room built by Thutmosis I had previously existed.

Thutmosis III made alterations to all the works contributed by Hatshepsut in an attempt to eradicate her memory: he enclosed the two obelisks in sandstone containers so that only the tips were visible and connected the

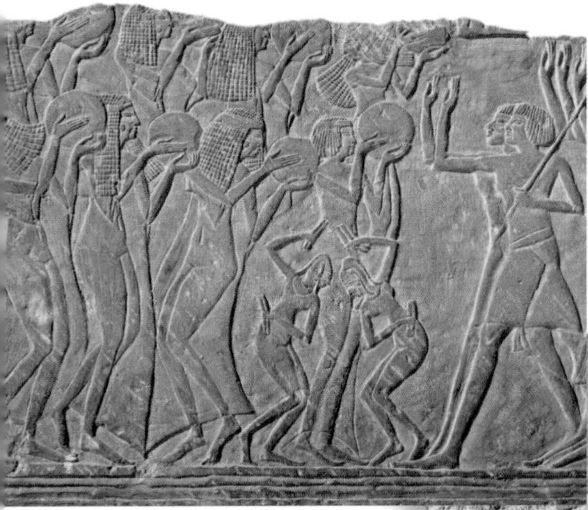

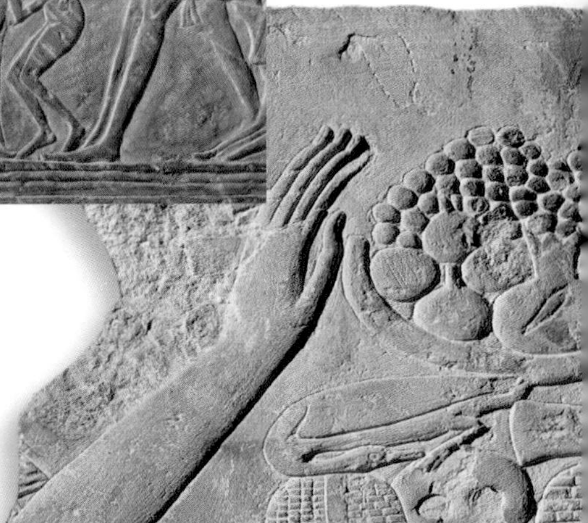

its structure, even if with only small modifications. Originally, the temple was dedicated to the local god, Montu, and was probably built during the Old Kingdom. The earliest certain archaeological evidence of the temple dates from the reign of Antef II, the third king of the Eleventh Dynasty. It covers three areas: the temple of Montu, the temple of Amun-Ra, and the temple of Mut. Hatshepsut's

132 top
SARCOPHAGUS OF
PRINCE THUTMOSIS'S
CAT; Limestone;
Height 64 CM;

Mit Rahina;
Eighteenth Dynasty,
Reign of
Amenhotep III
(1387-1350 BC)

containers to the fifth pylon. To the east of the sixth pylon, Thutmosis III built the *Akh-menu*, a hypostyle room sustained by 32 pillars on whose south face the *Text of Youth* describes his enthronement that took place following an oracle from Amun-Ra. His royal titles were inscribed on the architraves in a series which, from the Middle Kingdom on, was to include five for all the kings: the name of Horus, that of the Two Ladies (the two goddesses Uadjet and Nekhbet), that of "Horus of the Gold," the name of the king of Upper and Lower Egypt, and the name of the Son of Ra. He had himself portrayed making offerings to his predecessors at the entrance to the "festival room," in the *Chamber of Ancestors*.

Among Thutmosis III's successors was Amenhotep III, the son of Thutmosis IV and one of his concubines. Amenhotep III married Tiy, the daughter of Yuya, the commander of the chariot troops who played an important political role at the end of Tutankhamun's reign. Amenhotep maintained peaceful relationships with all the Mediterranean countries and his name was found documented in Crete, Mycenae, Anatolia, Babylon, and Assur. He was one of the greatest builders in Egyptian history: Sedeinga, Kawa, Elephantine, Wadi es-Sebua, and Aniba, among other temples, as well as additions to the temples at Karnak and Luxor. He too had a "temple of the millions of years" built on Thebes west bank and a palace at Malkata. During his reign, due to Oriental influence, the traditional canons of pharaonic art loosened, allowing Egyptian art to gain new sophistication and making him a precursor of some elements of Amarnian art. (M.T.)

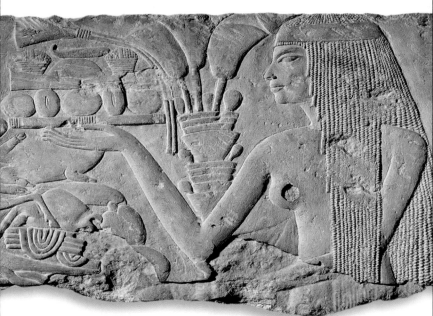

132 bottom RELIEF
WITH JUBILEE SCENE
Limestone; Height
51 cm; Saqqara;

Excavation by
A. Mariette;
Nineteenth Dynasty
(1291-1185 BC)

132-133
RELIEF DEPICTING AN
OFFERING SCENE
Limestone; Height

36 cm, length
75 cm; Saqqara;
Eighteenth Dynasty
(1550-1291 BC)

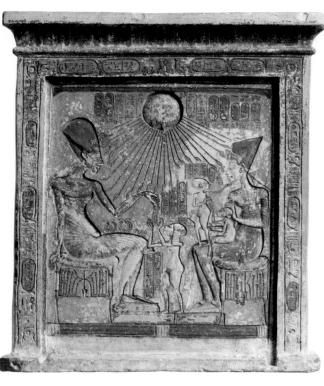

132 STELA WITH
THE ROYAL FAMILY
OF AMARNA
Painted limestone
Height 44 CM, width
39 CM; Tell al-
Amarna; Excavation
by L. Borchardt
(1912); Eighteenth
Dynasty; Reign of
Akhenaten (1346-
1333 BC)

133 HEAD
OF A QUEEN
Quartzite
Height 18 CM
Memphis, Palace of
Merenptah;
Excavation by the
University of
Pennsylvania
(1915); Eighteenth
Dynasty; Reign of
Akhenaten (1346-
1333 BC)

THE AMARNA PERIOD

It was during the reign of Amenhotep IV (1346-1350 BC) that the natural process of political and religious reform that had been carried out with some conviction since the times of Hatshepsut came to its conclusion.

In an attempt to restore absolute authority to the sacred figure of the pharaoh by reproposing the principal dogmas of the religious doctrine of Heliopolis, the "reformer" king soon came into conflict

with the most conservative body of the establishment, that which was linked to the Theban priesthood of the god Amun. Amenhotep IV's political action was based on courageous and positive decisions, but they were unsuited to the majority of the Egyptian people as his doctrine was restricted to a limited circle, though it made explicit claims of universalism. The "monotheism" championed by Amenhotep IV recognized Ra (Aten)

as the sole god while simultaneously raising the pharaoh to a position of special importance as the god's indispensable guarantor.

Following the early death of his elder brother, Thutmosis, and a probable period of co-regency with his father, Amenhotep III, the young prince ascended the throne. He married Nefertiti, who was to have been Thutmose's queen and whose background remains a source of debate. Documents – some of which were later "retouched" – show that at the start of his reign, Amenhotep IV showed respect and devotion to the other gods but this tolerance soon gave way to a more focused worship. During his early years as pharaoh, Amenhotep had a series of sacred buildings constructed dedicated to the new god, Aten (the visible manifestation of the sun god Ra) in the places that were traditionally linked to Montu, the ancient god of the Theban district: these were Ermonti, Medamud, Tod, and Karnak. It is reasonable to think that the choice of these sites was made in support of the priesthood of Montu and in direct opposition to the priesthood of Amun, the national and dynastic god that had replaced the ancient local beliefs since the Middle Kingdom despite the origins of the god not being Theban.

Co-existence with the powerful priesthood of Amun became increasingly difficult and around the sixth year of his reign, Amenhotep decided to leave the city on a permanent basis. He transferred his residence and court to a suitable place roughly halfway between Memphis and Thebes (modern Tell al-Amarna) that he renamed *Akhet-Aten* ("the Horizon of Aten"). In the lovely

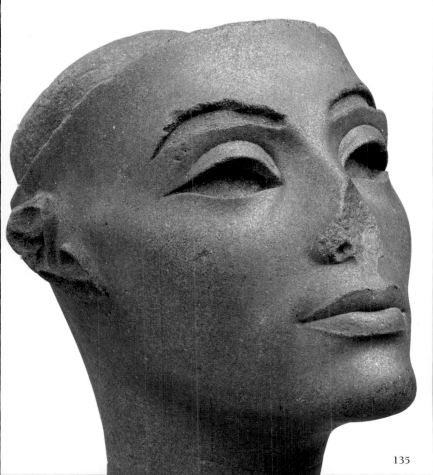

natural setting enclosed by the Nile and the desert mountains behind, a new capital was built from nothing on a well-organized and regular plan and with high-quality residential quarters. Here, the king changed his name from Amenhotep (meaning "Amun is satisfied") to *Akh-en-Aten* ("light of Aten") to emphasize his fundamental relationship with his god and in consequence definitively announcing his abandonment of Amun. Akhenaten also swore "never to leave the boundaries of the city" and began his rule of splendid isolation from political machinations in their widest sense, including relations with powers in the Near East, concentrating only on matters associated with religion.

Recent discoveries of diplomatic correspondence in the archives of Tell al-Amarna (the "Amarna Letters") have strengthened the hypothesis that the cause of the king's damaging inertia in foreign policy was a significant and reciprocal lack of understanding between powers.

Seeing that his reforms had failed towards the end of his reign, it seems Akhenaten attempted a reconciliation with Thebes and the priesthood of Amun but his death impeded any opportunity of compromise. His enigmatic co-regent, Smenkhkare, only reigned briefly before

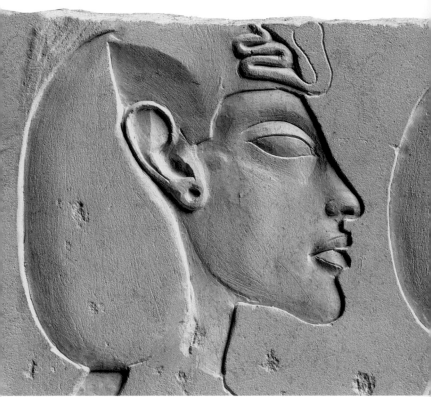

his premature death and the pharaoh's death, left the throne open to the nine-year old *Tut-ankh-aten* who changed his name to *Tut-ankh-amun* and returned to Thebes, closing the chapter of Tell al-Amarna for ever. The city fell into

134-135 MODEL FOR SCULPTURE WITH TWO PORTRAITS OF A KING Limestone; Height 23 CM, width 31 CM; Tell al-Amarna; Excavation by Pendlebury (1932-1933); Eighteenth Dynasty; Reign of Akhenaten (1346-1333 BC)

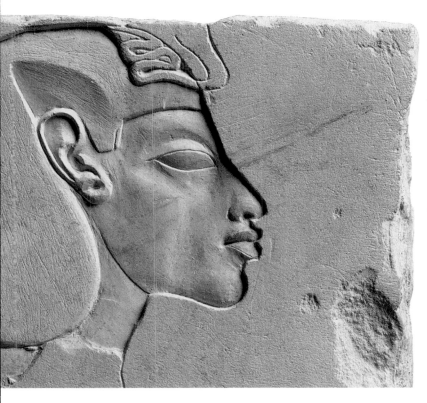

oblivion and remained forgotten until archaeological excavation at the end of the nineteenth century began to throw light on the period. And thus, the faint and almost erased memory of Akhenaten returned to general attention after having been damned as "the criminal Akhet-Aten," condemned without appeal to *damnatio memoriae*, and removed from all official lists of the kings of Egypt. (A.B.)

THE RAMESSIDS' PERIOD

Following the Amarna Period with its many repercussions on the political, artistic, and literary fields, the first sovereigns of the Nineteenth Dynasty enjoyed greater authority within the country but were obliged to confront international situations that were often difficult. The art of the Horemheb from the Delta, the new dynasty started with a ruler who ascended the throne with the name Rameses I. He moved the capital to Memphis where it remained until Rameses II established himself at Pi-Rameses, also in the north of Egypt. The decision to move the capital from Memphis to Pi-Rameses probably sprang from his rule than the others. He restarted military campaigns against the north-eastern countries that culminated in the battle of Qadesh and a peace treaty with the Hittites during the fifth year of his reign. The treaty was written out in Egyptian and Accadian and was the first peace treaty in history. The artistic emphasis during the

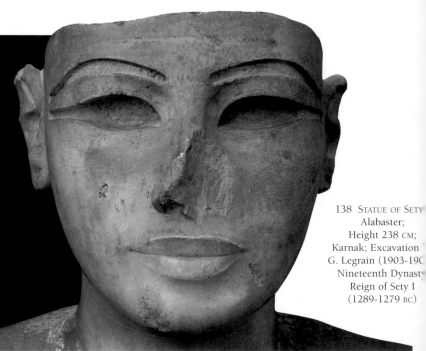

138 STATUE OF SETY
Alabaster;
Height 238 CM;
Karnak; Excavation
G. Legrain (1903-190
Nineteenth Dynast
Reign of Sety I
(1289-1279 BC)

Eighteenth and Nineteenth Dynasties was characterized by the same awareness of volumes and elegance of line as had been seen in Amarna, especially during Sety I's reign.

Founded by a fellow-soldier of the need to defend the north from Libyan attacks and to resume trading with the East. Rameses II is the most celebrated of the Nineteenth-Dynasty pharaohs and without doubt left far greater architectural evidence of reigns of Rameses II and, to a lesser extent, his successors was focused on the glorification of the pharaoh and soon led to his divinization during his lifetime.

After the death of Rameses II, the

religious authority of the pharaoh began to decline progressively along with his political and military prestige. A series of problems in the dynastic succession occurred as, for example, in the case of Tausret, a queen who was first co-regent and then outright sovereign, and the plot hatched by courtiers and harem officials against Rameses III.

Economic problems were added under the Twelfth Dynasty as demonstrated by the reduction in building during the reigns of Rameses III, IX, and XI. At the time this dynasty died out, there was rising inflation and increases in the price of cereals caused by insufficient flooding of the Nile and by a reduction in the size of the available workforce. Evidence exists of dishonesty and corruption in the harvest and redistribution of foodstuffs, particularly during the reigns of Rameses III, IV, and V, as well as strikes by workers at Deir al-Medina caused by delays in payments. Deir al-Medina was the village on the west bank of the Nile inhabited by workers in the royal tombs in the Valley of the Kings

during the period from Amenhotep I to Rameses III. Excavation of the site has revealed temples, houses and the necropolis plus a great many religious and administrative papyruses, a number of flat limestone blocks – *ostraka* – used for jotting down notes and for rough sketches. (M.T.)

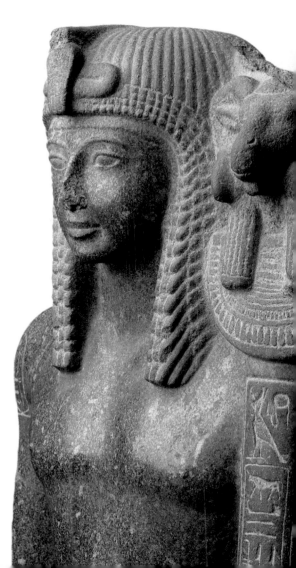

139 STATUE
OF RAMESES III
Granite rock;
Height 140 CM; Karnak;
Excavation by G.
Legrain (1905);
Twentieth Dynasty,
Reign of Rameses III
(1184-1153 BC)

STELA OF NEFERMENU

Painted limestone; Height 37 cm, width 23.5 cm
Abydos
New Kingdom (1550-1070 bc)

ROOM 12

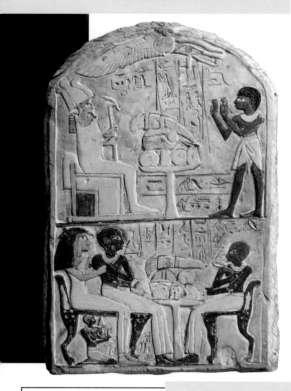

The first register of this stela shows Osiris seated on a throne wearing the *atef* crown and wrapped in white bandages that contrast with his green hands and face. There is a table of offerings in front of him and a man on the other side adoring the god. The second register depicts a couple on a lion's foot seat with a small child underneath, an offerings table in the center and a man sitting on a similar seat on the right. The man in the first register is the owner of the stela, referred to as the "servant" Nefermenu, and, in the second register, are the "servant" Hor, his wife Meshor, and their son Ty. The man standing is only referred to as Tit or Teti, and has no title.
(M.T.)

STELA OF NEBAMUN

Painted limestone; Height 34.5 cm, width 23.5 cm
Exact provenance unknown but probably Theban
New Kingdom (1550-1070 bc)

ROOM 12

The right side of the first register of the stela shows a man and a woman sitting on a lion's foot seat; the man wears a short curly wig and a large collar, and sniffs at a lotus flower. The woman holds the man's arm with her right hand and has her other arm round his chest.

To the right of the scene, a woman holds a young boy by the hand as a man in front of her hands three lotus flowers to the deceased. The religious symbolism of the lotus flower was linked to the fact that each morning the flower rises to the surface of the water and opens, then, each evening, it closes and sinks beneath the surface once more. For the ancient Egyptians, the lotus flower became an image of regeneration and the symbol of the creation of life from the primordial waters, and as such it was a frequent motif in the figurative arts (for example, see the head of Tutankhamun that emerges from the lotus flower (JE 60723).

The deceased is shown sitting on a lion's foot seat as he sniffs a lotus flower in his left hand and holds a piece of cloth in his right. He wears a short curly wig, a short skirt and a necklace made up of several loops. There are four fumigation vases in front of him on a table. On the right of the scene, a man holds a container of liquid for libation purposes in his right hand and grasps a goose by the wings with the left hand. He too wears a short wig and a large necklace, but has a longer transparent skirt covered by a short one. An offerings formula to Osiris in the three line text is expressed on behalf of Sheri (whose titles are not given) by his son who has the honorific title "Divine Father".
(M.T.)

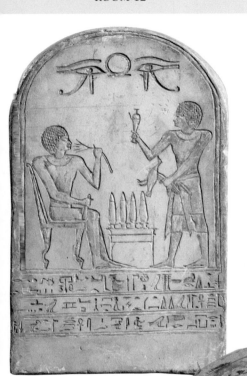

The texts on the stela contain the names of the figures shown and a prayer that Osiris will concede funerary offerings for the *ka* of the deceased for eternity. Nebamun, the owner of the stela, was the supervisor of the servants in the temple of Amun and is portrayed with his wife Ahmose and their children, the scribe Baki and the *wab* priest of Knum, named Knumaes, and his daughter Nubneferet.
(M.T.)

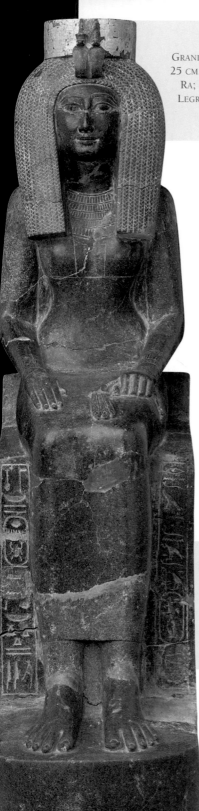

STATUE OF ASET

GRANITIC ROCK, GOLD LEAF; HEIGHT 98.5 CM, WID
25 CM, LENGTH 52.5 CM; KARNAK, TEMPLE OF AMU
RA; COURT OF THE CACHETTE; EXCAVATION BY G.
LEGRAIN (1904); EIGHTEENTH DYNASTY, REIGN OI
THUTMOSIS III (1479-1425 BC)

ROOM 12

Thutmosis dedicated the statue to his mother as is specified on the inscription on the sides of Aset's seat. Originally, several parts of the sculpture were covered with gold leaf besides that on the cylindrical headdress. Aset wears an elaborate three-part wig with two uraeus serpents on her forehead, one of which wears the white crown and the other the red crown. She also wears several items of jewellery including a *usekh* necklace and two wide bracelets. Her tunic is held by two straps that cover her breasts. Her right hand is placed flat on her thigh and the left holds a sceptre in the shape of a lotus flower. (M.T.)

STATUE OF THUTMOSIS IV WITH HIS MOTHER TIA

GRANITIC ROCK; H. 115 CM, W. 69 CM
KARNAK, TEMPLE OF AMUN-RA
EIGHTEENTH DYNASTY, REIGN OF
THUTMOSIS IV (1397-1387 BC)

ROOM 12

The couple sit on a wide seat with a bare backrest. Each has one arm around the waist of the other and their free hand resting on their thigh; the king's hand holds the *ankh* symbol and the queen's is open with the palm downward. Thutmosis IV wears a short curly wig with the royal uraeus serpent, and a *shendyt* skirt with his name inscribed on the buckle. A symbol of royalty, a bull's tail, hangs from the skirt. The king's feet rest on the "Nine Arches" that represent the

enemies of Egypt defeated by royal power. Tia, his mother, wears a long, three-part wig and uraeus crowned with the body of a vulture. which was an attribute of the mother of the heir to the throne. She wears many bracelets, a wide, six-string necklace, and a long tight-fitting tunic decorated with two rosettes on her breasts.

The faces of both

characters are full with delicate features, slightly squashed noses, and jutting eyebrows.

A column of hieroglyphs on either side of the couple cites their names and titles. Tia is referred to as "voice justified" which indicates that she had already died before the statue was sculpted.

(M.T.)

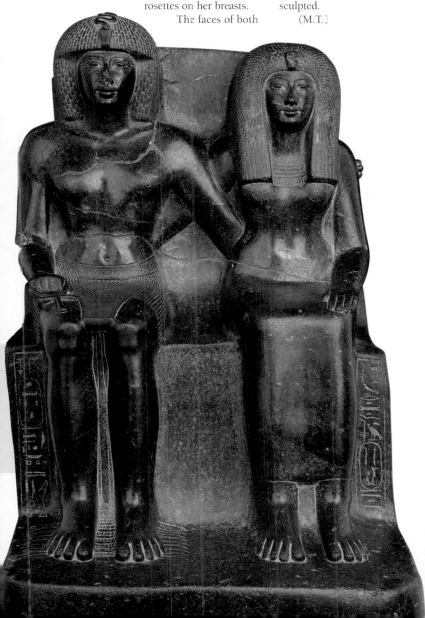

STATUE OF AMENHOTEP II WITH MERETSEGER

GRANITIC ROCK; HEIGHT 125 CM; KARNAK
EIGHTEENTH DYNASTY, REIGN OF AMENHOTEP II
(1428-1397 BC)

ROOM 12

The sovereign is portrayed stamping on the Nine Arches as he advances. Bare-chested, he wears the white crown with the uraeus serpent on his head and a straight skirt decorated with a band with two uraeus serpents. The cartouche with the name Amenhotep II is inscribed on the buckle of his skirt. Behind him, the Theban goddess Meretseger in the form of a cobra coils around him and protects him. The goddess wears a headdress with the horns and sun disk typical of Hathor. At the rear, her body forms coils that are in turn wrapped by papyrus stems. This detail and the pose of the goddess as she protects the king are both similar to elements seen in the statue of Amenhotep II with the goddess Hathor found in the shrine dedicated to her in Thutmosis III's temple at Deir al-Bahari.

The cult of Meretseger, whose name means "she who loves silence," is known of in the Valley of the Kings on the west bank at Thebes from the New Kingdom, where she was worshipped by the men who worked on the royal necropolis. But her popularity was at its greatest during the Ramessid Period in the community of Deir al-Medina. Meretseger was identified with the peak that dominates the necropolis on the west bank and therefore she played an important role in funerary beliefs. Her principal places of worship were the partly rock-cut temple on the route towards the Valley of the Kings, the small temples at the foot of the peak she was identified with, and some small shrines at Deir al-Medina near the Temple of Hathor. (M.T.)

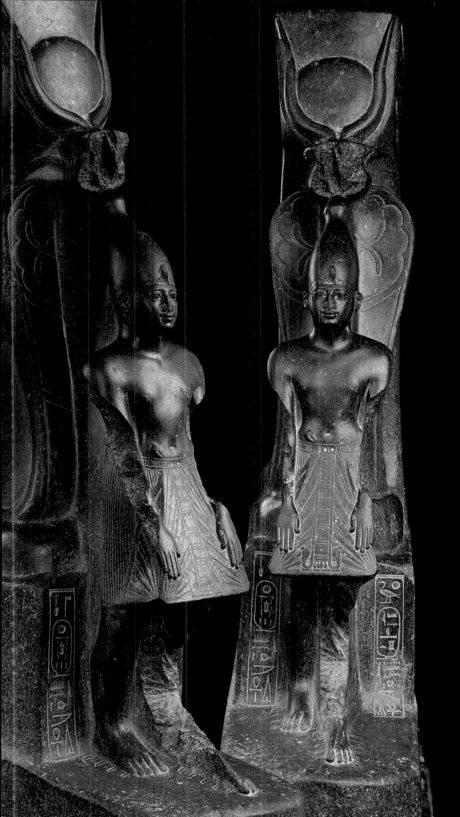

STATUE OF SENENMUT WITH NEFERURA

DIORITE; HEIGHT 60 CM
KARNAK, COURT OF THE CACHETTE, TEMPLE OF AMUN-RA
EXCAVATION BY G. LEGRAIN (1904); EIGHTEENTH DYNASTY
REIGN OF HATSHEPSUT (1479-1458 BC)

ROOM 12

Senenmut was the counsellor and architect of Queen Hatshepsut. Here he is portrayed holding Princess Neferura, to whom he was the tutor, on his lap. He is seated on a tall, four-sided seat with one leg bent to form a back-rest for the child who sits on his knees. Senenmut wears a short skirt and a long wig that leaves his ears visible. His right hand holds Neferura's knees while his left circles her shoulders. Most of the young girl's hair has been shaved off except for the long braid typical of children that falls onto her right shoulder. She wears the uraeus serpent on her forehead, sucks her finger and is covered with a cloak.

Senenmut's skirt is engraved with a column of hieroglyphs that give his name and title "Majordomo of Princess Neferura." Other titles are carved on the base, including "Superintendent of the granaries, the lands and the stock in the Dominion of Amun."

Being responsible for works of construction undertaken by the queen, Senenmut

oversaw the building of her temple at Deir al-Bahari; in this capacity, he had many portraits of himself added behind the doors of the shrines, so contravening the Egyptian tradition according to which little importance was given to the creator of the work.

Twenty five statues of him have survived, many of which are original and somewhat unconventional, like this example. Senenmut was honoured by Hatshepsut by being allowed to build two tombs, one at Qurna like many other functionaries of the New Kingdom, and one within the bounds of the temple at Deir al-Bahari in which there is a very famous example of a ceiling painted depicting the sky at night.
(M.T.)

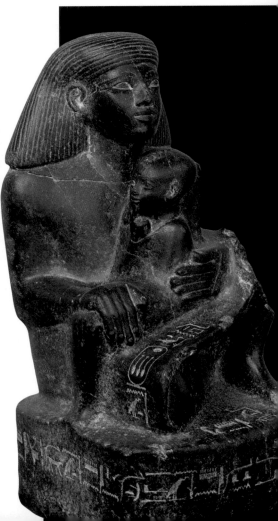

STATUE OF THUTMOSIS III SEATED
Diorite; Height 107 cm; Karnak, Temple of Amun-Ra; Excavation by G. Legrain (1907); Eighteenth Dynasty, Reign of Thutmosis III (1479-1425 bc)

ROOM 12

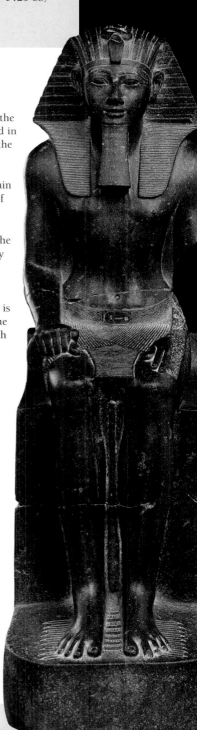

The statue was found in three parts broken at the hips and mid-way up the legs but the only parts missing are the head of the uraeus serpent and the left forearm. The first fingers of the left hand are still on the leg. With his chubby face and finely carved features, Thutmosis III is portrayed wearing the *nemes* headdress from which his ears protrude, the false beard, and a short *shendyt* skirt on which the cartouche with his coronation name, "Menkheperre," is carved on the buckle. His finely polished torso is nude. He crushes the Nine Arches below his feet, the symbol of Egypt's enemies.

The most complete inscription of his royal titles is given on the rear pillar, "The perfect god, lord of joy, son of Amun on his throne, Menkheperre, the King of Upper and Lower Egypt, beloved of Amun-Ra, endowed with eternal life" but the name of Amun was chiselled out during the reign of Amenhotep IV/Akhenaten.

A recent study by D. Laboury on the statues carved during the Thutmosid (1998: 241246) makes the deduction from Legrain's notes that the statue was not found in the *cachette*, but in the eastern chapel dedicated to Thutmosis III. Legrain does indeed speak of a seated statue of Thutmosis III, without specifying the excavation inventory number, that was found with an undamaged face of great beauty. As this is the only seated statue of Thutmosis III with an undamaged face found at Karnak, it must be the one identified as JE 39260. Moreover, Thutmosis III's chapel would not have been its original location as it did not fit into the decorative rationale of the room where it was found, which was used for worshipping and making offerings to a divine statue. not as a shrine for sculptures of the pharaoh. (M.T.)

STELA FOR TETISHERI

LIMESTONE; HEIGHT 225 CM, WIDTH 106.5 CM
ABYDOS; EXCAVATION BY THE EGYPT
EXPLORATION FUND (1903)
EIGHTEENTH DYNASTY
REIGN OF AHMES (1550-1525 BC)

ROOM 12

Seventeen lines of text remain legible on this arched stela, the rest have been lost. The pharaoh Ahmose is shown on the upper section in a mirror image on both left and right as he makes offerings to his maternal grandmother Tetisheri. His image on the right wears the double crown of Upper and Lower Egypt with the uraeus serpent, has the right arm bent in a position that in hieroglyphic form means the act of speaking, and holds a long staff and pear-shaped club in his left hand. In the scene on the left, he wears the white crown of Upper Egypt and the uraeus and holds some staves. In this case, his right arm is held towards the queen. In both scenes he wears a wide collar and the *shendyt* skirt from which the bull's tail hangs.

Tetisheri is seated and wears a headdress in the form of a vulture topped by two plumes; this was a customary distinction for the mother of the heir to the throne from the start of the Eighteenth Dynasty. She also wears a necklace and a tight-fitting tunic held by two shoulder straps, and holds a lotus flower in her left hand. In one of the two scenes, she holds the flower to her chest with her other arm bent while in the other, she

holds it on one knee with her opposite arm stretched out.

The head of the stela refers to the creation of the offerings for Tetisheri's shrine in Abydos where the stela was found by Petrie between the cliff

and the cultivated land. It also mentions the temple and pyramid that Ahmose intended to build for his grandmother in the necropolis at Abydos that have since been identified as the temple on the terrace and the cenotaph near the cliff. A town and a small cemetery for the workers who built the pyramid and for those in charge of the cult of Tetisheri have been found to the north and south of these two monuments. (M.T.)

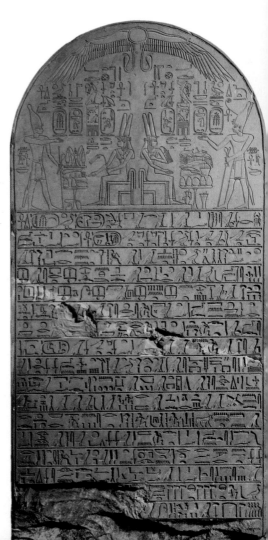

148

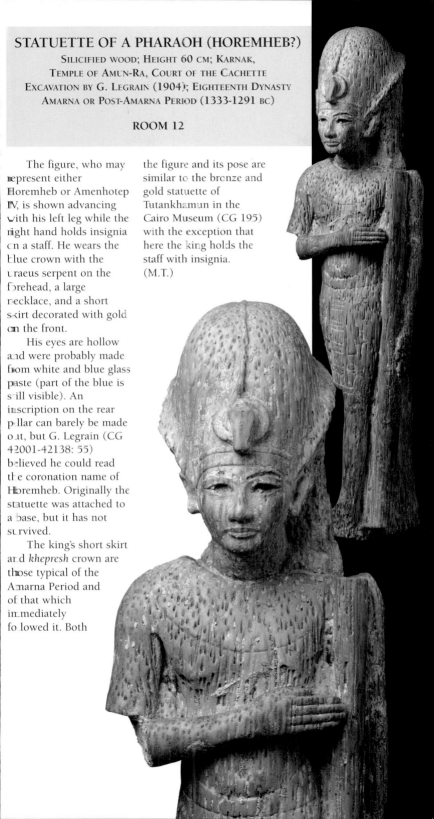

STATUETTE OF A PHARAOH (HOREMHEB?)

SILICIFIED WOOD; HEIGHT 60 CM; KARNAK,
TEMPLE OF AMUN-RA, COURT OF THE CACHETTE
EXCAVATION BY G. LEGRAIN (1904); EIGHTEENTH DYNASTY
AMARNA OR POST-AMARNA PERIOD (1333-1291 BC)

ROOM 12

The figure, who may represent either Horemheb or Amenhotep IV, is shown advancing with his left leg while the right hand holds insignia on a staff. He wears the blue crown with the uraeus serpent on the forehead, a large necklace, and a short skirt decorated with gold on the front.

His eyes are hollow and were probably made from white and blue glass paste (part of the blue is still visible). An inscription on the rear pillar can barely be made out, but G. Legrain (CG 42001-42138: 55) believed he could read the coronation name of Horemheb. Originally the statuette was attached to a base, but it has not survived.

The king's short skirt and *khepresh* crown are those typical of the Amarna Period and of that which immediately followed it. Both the figure and its pose are similar to the bronze and gold statuette of Tutankhamun in the Cairo Museum (CG 195) with the exception that here the king holds the staff with insignia. (M.T.)

STATUE OF HATHOR WITH AMENHOTEP II

PAINTED SANDSTONE; HEIGHT 225 CM,
LENGTH 227 CM,
DEIR AL-BAHARI, TEMPLE OF THUTMOSIS III
EXCAVATION BY THE EGYPT EXPLORATION FUND (1906)
EIGHTEENTH DYNASTY, REIGN OF THUTMOSIS III (1479-
1425 BC) - REIGN OF AMENHOTEP II (1428-1397 BC)

ROOM 12

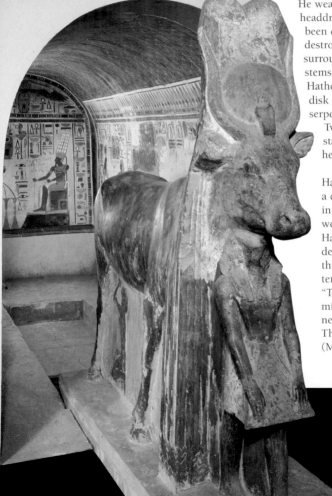

This statue of Hathor in the form of a cow bears the cartouche of Amenhotep II on its neck. It reproduces the same scene as the one shown on the walls of the shrine: the cow both protects the adult king who stands below her neck, and suckles the child-king who is shown crouching on the left of the sculpture.

The king wears a short skirt, has his left leg advanced, and his open hands resting on the skirt. He wears the *nemes* headdress, but his face has been completely destroyed. The cow is surrounded by papyrus stems and wears the Hathoric horns with sun disk and a uraeus serpent on her forehead. Two tall plumes stand up from her headdress.

The cult of Hathor in the form of a cow was widespread in the mountains of western Thebes. Hatshepsut had also dedicated a temple to this goddess in the temenos of her "Temple of the millions of years" next to that of Thutmosis III. (M.T.)

SHRINE DEDICATED TO HATHOR BY THUTMOSIS III

PAINTED SANDSTONE; HEIGHT 225 CM, WIDTH 157 CM
LENGTH 404 CM; DEIR AL-BAHARI, TEMPLE OF THUTMOSIS III
EXCAVATION BY THE EGYPT EXPLORATION FUND (1906)
EIGHTEENTH DYNASTY, REIGN OF THUTMOSIS III (1479-
1425 BC) - REIGN OF AMENHOTEP II (1428-1397 BC)

ROOM 12

The shrine and statue were found by chance by E. Naville under the detritus between the temples of Mentuhotep and Hatshepsut at Deir al-Bahari. The original coloring on both has been perfectly conserved. The shrine was built by Thutmosis III who is shown on the left wall with his wife Meritra as he consecrates offerings to Hathor. The goddess is depicted as a cow who both protects and suckles the king. On the same wall, the pharaoh appears before Hathor, shown this time as a woman wearing the characteristic headdress of two horns and a sun disk.

The same scene is represented on the right wall with the difference that the king is accompanied by two princesses rather than the queen. On the back wall, Thutmosis III pours libations and burns incense before Amun-Ra. The scene is surmounted by a frieze of plumes – called *khakher* – and the ceiling is decorated by a starry blue sky.

The name Hathor means "estate of Horus" and her hieroglyph depicts a falcon in a house. The meaning is still controversial, due to lack of knowledge about allusions to her original name. Hathor was closely associated with the sky and it was the concept of the sky represented as a cow, popular in the Delta, that gave Hathor her bovine form. Popular as a funerary goddess in this form, tomb decorations showed that the deceased aspired to become one of the "retinue of Hathor" as the goddess, like the setting sun that was part of her entourage, would protect the deceased from the powers of darkness. (M.T.)

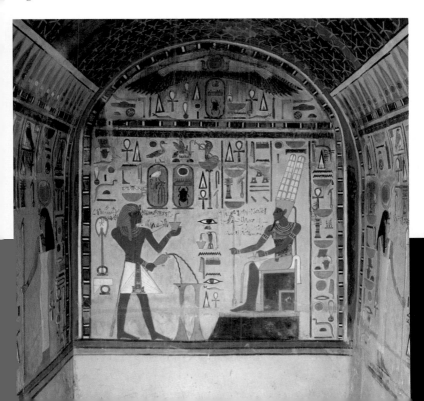

HEAD OF STATUE OF AMENHOTEP III

CLAY LINED WITH STUCCO AND PAINTED; HEIGHT 38 CM
KARNAK, TEMPLE OF AMUN-RA, COURT OF THE CACHETTE
EXCAVATION BY G. LEGRAIN (1906); EIGHTEENTH
DYNASTY, REIGN OF AMENHOTEP III (1387-1350 BC)

ROOM 12

In many aspects, this image of Amenhotep III anticipates the traits of the art of Amarna that came into vogue with the accession to the throne of Amenhotep's successor, Akhenaten. The pharaoh has had himself portrayed with the features of a young boy, a round and full face, almond-shaped eyes, and highly curved eyebrows. The nose is both small and squashed, and the fleshy and well delineated mouth is marked by two small lines at the side. These features determine the statue belonged to the "second group" of

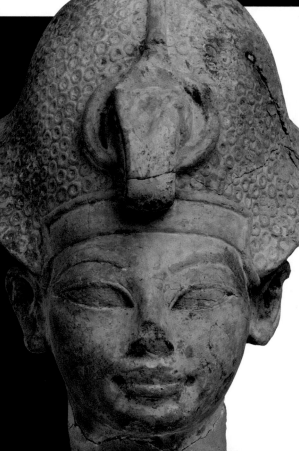

portraits of Amenhotep III from the last years of his reign. The trait of representing the eyes as long slits emphasised by sculpted or painted make-up also carried on into the next reign.

Amenhotep wears the blue crown decorated with concentric circles that was characteristic of battle images. This crown denotes action and was worn by the pharaoh when he led his troops in times of war, but also during religious ceremonies in the temple. The uraeus serpent appears on the front and its coils continue on the back of the crown. (M.T.)

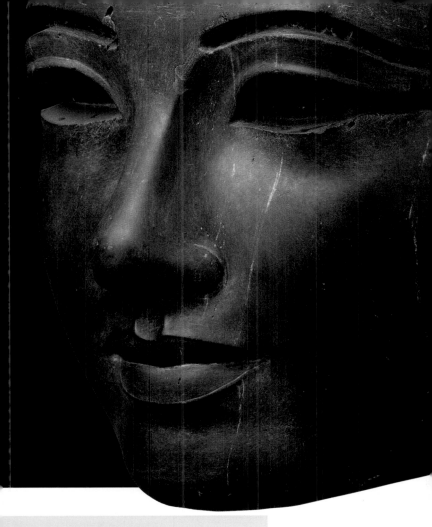

HEAD OF STATUE OF A WOMAN

OBSIDIAN; HEIGHT 20 CM, WIDTH 15 CM
ARNAK, TEMPLE OF AMUN-RA, COURT OF THE CACHETTE
CAVATION BY G. LEGRAIN (1905); EIGHTEENTH DYNASTY
(SECOND HALF OF THE 14TH CENTURY BC)

ROOM 12

The complete statue was made in separate parts and held together by tenons, remains of which can be seen on the back of the head. Although only parts of the woman's face remain, it is clear that her features were very fine, suggesting that the sculpture was carved during the most mature artistic phase of the Eighteenth Dynasty. Her eyes and eyebrows are hollow and this indicates that they were filled with various materials, for example, glass paste. The quality of the craftsmanship and the work itself are even more admirable if one considers that obsidian is an extremely hard stone; it is of volcanic origin and not found in Egypt so would have been imported from Ethiopia or central-southern Arabia, probably via the Red Sea (De Putter-Karlshausen, 1992: 111-113).

(M.T.)

STATUES OF AMENHOTEP
SON OF HAPU

GRANITIC ROCK; STATUE ON THE LEFT: HEIGHT 117 CM
WIDTH 70 CM; STATUE ON THE RIGHT: HEIGHT 128 CM
KARNAK, TEMPLE OF AMUN-RA, COURT OF THE CACHETTE
EXCAVATION BY G. LEGRAIN (1913); EIGHTEENTH
DYNASTY, REIGN OF AMENHOTEP III (1387-1350 BC)

ROOM 12

Amenhotep, Hapu's son, was one of the most important functionaries during Amenhotep III's reign and so favoured that the king allowed him a funerary temple in Medinet Habu.

Of modest birth, he rose in the social scale until he became the pharaoh's right hand man, the royal scribe, and the supervisor of all the king's works. The many statues of Amenhotep are of two types: portraits of him as a young or old man. Both types were based on the models of the Middle Kingdom.

The young Amenhotep (to the right) is shown as a scribe intent on his work; his face is made in the typical manner of the reign of Amenhotep III but the body is a copy of a statue of one of his illustrious predecessors, the royal architect and vizier Mentuhotep, who lived during the reign of Senusret I. The text on the unrolled papyrus informs us that Amenhotep had the honor of overseeing the quarrying, production, transportation, and erection of the Colossi of Memnon that stand in front of the funerary temple of Amenhotep III. The inscription is an invitation to the faithful in the temple of Karnak to pray to Amenhotep who, on the explicit wish of Nebmaatra (Amenhotep III), would intervene on their behalf with the god Amun.

The inscription on the statue to the left states that Amenhotep is shown as a man of eighty years of age. (M.S.C.)

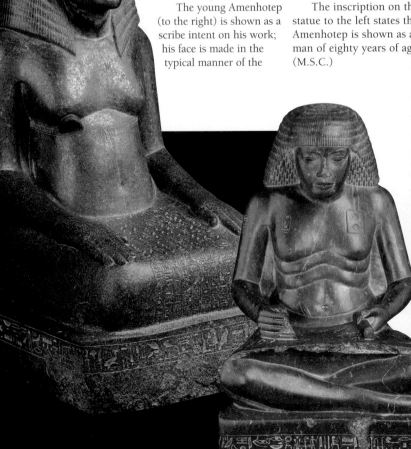

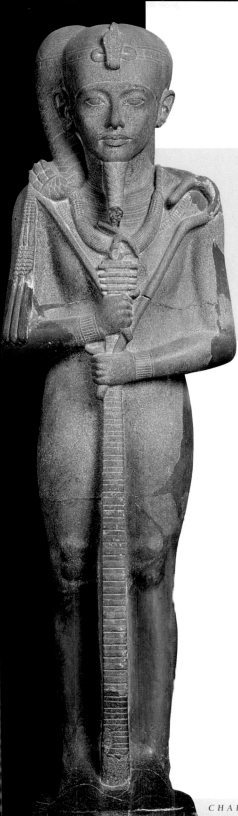

STATUE OF THE GOD KHONSU AS TUTANKHAMUN

GRANITIC ROCK
HEIGHT 252 CM
KARNAK, TEMPLE OF AMUN RA
EXCAVATION BY G. LEGRAIN
(1904); EIGHTEENTH DYNASTY,
REIGN OF TUTANKHAMUN
(1333-1323 BC)

ROOM 12

This sculpture shows King Tutankhamun wearing a cap, wrapped in a sheath, and with the attributes of the god Khonsu (the scourge and the curved sceptre in his hands, and the necklace and counterpoise on his shoulders). Khonsu was represented as a young boy with a braid of hair on one side emerging from the cap and with a uraeus serpent on the forehead.

The statue comes from Khonsu's temple at Karnak where a sanctuary had been dedicated to him since the Middle Kingdom. He was worshipped as a child and as a member of the Theban triad with Amun and Mut.
(M T.)

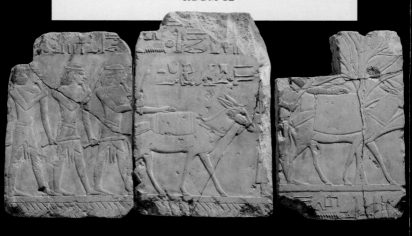

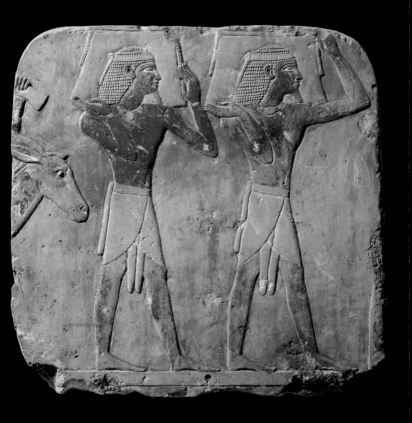

The two reliefs come from the south portico on the second terrace in the Temple of Hatshepsut at Deir al-Bahari. They were part of a series of scenes that give a detailed description of a trading expedition made during the ninth year of Hatshepsut's reign to Punt, a region probably on the Somalian coast.

The bottom scene shows the king of Punt, Parehu, with his wife Ati. The man is very thin, has a pointed beard, and wears a necklace and a short skirt with two tassels and a dagger in the waistband. He wears a cap and holds what looks like a staff in his right hand but the relief is partially damaged. He is followed by his wife who is depicted as being extremely fat with an excessive curvature of the spine, and rolls of fat on her arms, legs and torso. She has long hair behind her ears held in place by a band on her forehead and her facial features are very distinct. She wears a sleeveless dress, a necklace of flat disks, and anklets on both legs. The portrait reveals characteristics of caricature, but has encouraged experts to believe that Ati was affected by steatopygia, a physical condition that results in an abnormal accumulation of fat in and behind the hips and thighs.

The couple is followed by several men carrying some of the products of Punt: incense, myrrh, ivory, ebony, gold, malachite, and electrum. Trading between the two countries is documented as early as the Old Kingdom but these are the first artistic images of the contacts.

The other relief shows some servants urging a donkey to move that the inscription suggests is to carry the wife of the lord of Punt. (M.T.)

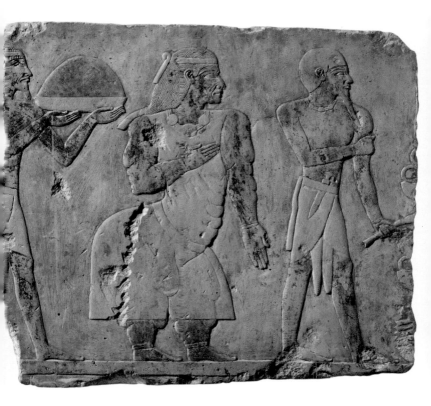

SENNEFER AND HIS WIFE SENAY

GRANITIC ROCK; HEIGHT 120 CM; KARNAK, TEMPLE OF AMUN-
RA, COURT OF THE CACHETTE; EXCAVATION BY G. LEGRAIN
(1903); EIGHTEETH DYNASTY, REIGN OF AMENHOTEP II
(1428-1397 BC) - REIGN OF THUTMOSIS IV (1397-1387 BC)

ROOM 12

This work is significant from a number of viewpoints: it portrays Sennefer, one of the most important figures from the reign of Amenhotep II, who was the mayor of Thebes and responsible for the tributes in grain paid to the Temple of Amun, and his wife Senay, the royal wet nurse; it is also one of the few items of Egyptian art to bear the name of its artists: on the left side of the seat a vertical inscription bears the names of the sculptors Amenmes and Djed-Khonsu; and finally, it is a superb piece of art.

Sennefer is shown sitting on the same seat as Senay with his left arm around her waist. He wears a heavy, curly wig from which his ears protrude; his face is round with elegant features. He is shown as being middle-aged with rolls of fat around his chest that were used to symbolize well-being and prosperity. Around his neck he wears the insignia of the "gold of the reward," a recognition awarded by the pharaoh for services rendered, and a pendant in the form of a double heart which may be a symbol of his position as mayor. However, the highest honour bestowed upon him was that of being allowed to place this double statue, similar to contemporary royal portraits, in the temple at Karnak which meant he could participate in the offerings and prayers of visitors to the temple. In addition to all this, Sennefer was the owner of one of the loveliest tombs in Thebes, no. 96, which is famous for the painting of a vine plant on the ceiling. Senay wears a braided wig that falls onto her shoulders, and a long tunic held by two shoulder straps.

A daughter of the couple, Mutnofret, is shown between the legs of her parents on the front and on the right side of the seat; her sister Nefertari is depicted on the left side. Two cartouches with the name of Amenhotep II are inscribed on the right shoulder of Sennefer and an offerings' formula for the *ka* of the couple can be seen on their clothes. (M.T.)

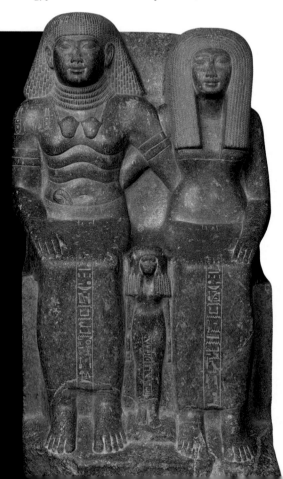

STATUETTE OF LADY IBENTINA

PAINTED WOOD; HEIGHT OF THE STATUETTE 31.8 CM
HEIGHT OF THE NAOS 62 CM, WIDTH 26.5 CM; DEIR AL-
EDINA, TOMB OF SATNEM (NO. 1379); EXCAVATION BY B.
BRUYÈRE (1933-34); EIGHTEENTH DYNASTY, REIGN OF
HATSHEPSUT OR THUTMOSIS III (1490-1450 BC)

ROOM 12

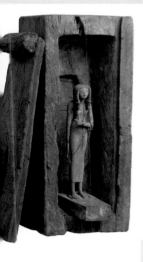

This statuette of Ibentina was one of a pair with the sycamore statuette of her husband, Satnem, that can now be seen in the Louvre. The statues were found in the Satnem's tomb.

The lady is portrayed standing with one arm down her body and the other folded in front of her; both her arms and legs are long and slender.

She wears a three-part wig with braids held in place by two ribbons. Her features are very delicate with a slim nose, a well-delineated mouth, and almond-shaped eyes. Ibentina wears a long, tight-fitting tunic, two bracelets on her wrists, and a small necklace made of faïence that links her left arm to her body. The statue was once lined with stucco and painted and placed in a *naos* closed by a sliding lid. An offerings' formula dedicated to Osiris, the lord of Abydos and Busiri, was inscribed around the base. (M.T.)

SPHINX OF THUTMOSIS III

GRANITIC ROCK; HEIGHT 21 CM, WIDTH 21 CM
LENGTH 61 CM; KARNAK, TEMPLE OF AMUN-RA, COURT
OF THE CACHETTE; EXCAVATION BY G. LEGRAIN (1905)
EIGHTEENTH DYNASTY
REIGN OF THUTMOSIS III (1479-1425 BC)

ROOM 12

The sovereign is shown in this sculpture as a sphinx wearing the *nemes* headdress crowned by a uraeus serpent. He wears the false beard and has the following inscription engraved on his chest: "The perfect god, the lord of the Two Lands, Menkheperra" (Menkheperre was Thutmosis III's coronation name). The statues of this pharaoh are distinguished by their high artistic quality and so many of them have survived that we are familiar with his iconography: he has a slightly curved nose, vaguely almond-shaped eyes with a deep line carved in the stone, projecting eyebrows and a quiet wide smile. (M.T.)

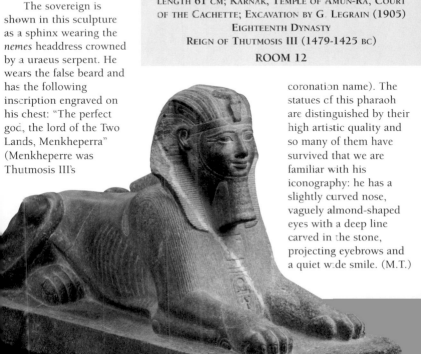

STATUE OF ISIS SEATED

GRANITIC ROCK; HEIGHT CM 176; ITALIAN EXCAVATION
AT ANTINOE; EIGHTEENTH DYNASTY, REIGN OF
AMENHOTEP III (1387-1350) - NINETEENTH DYNASTY
REIGN OF RAMESES II (1297-1212 BC)

ROOM 11

This statue, from Antinoe, can be dated to the reign of Amenhotep III. It was usurped by Rameses II who placed his cartouches at the sides of the goddess' feet.

Isis sits on a low-backed seat which prolongates into a base. She wears a smooth, three-part wig that leaves her ears uncovered, she has heavily made up eyes, a full mouth, and her eyebrows are very evident. Her cheekbones are very high, her chin small. She wears a broad pectoral around her neck and a tight-fitting tunic; her hands are closed around a *was* sceptre. (M.T.)

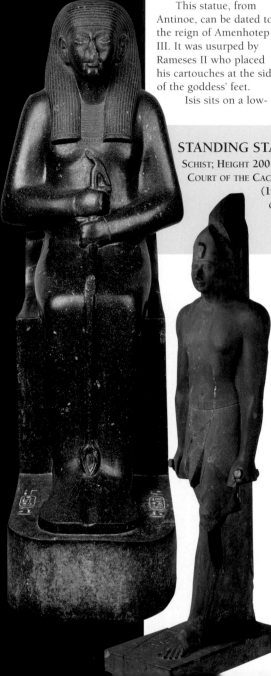

STANDING STATUE OF THUTMOSIS

SCHIST; HEIGHT 200 CM; KARNAK, TEMPLE OF AMUN-R
COURT OF THE CACHETTE; EXCAVATION BY G. LEGRAIN
(1904); EIGHTEENTH DYNASTY, REIG
OF THUTMOSIS III (1479-1425 BC)

ROOM 11

Thutmosis III advance with his left leg in the customary pose. He wears the white crown of Upper Egypt with the uraeus serpent on the front and a short skirt and belt with h coronation name engraved on the buckle. His facial features are similar to thos on other statues of this pharaoh: a slightly curved nose, almond-shaped eyes outlined with kohl, the heavily incised cut in the stone, jutting eyebrows, and lips in a serene smile. He holds two *mekes* sceptres, the symbol of royalty, in his hands and stands on the Nine Arches engraved in the stone that represent the enemies of Egypt.

The rear support on which the sculpture rests bears no inscription but th

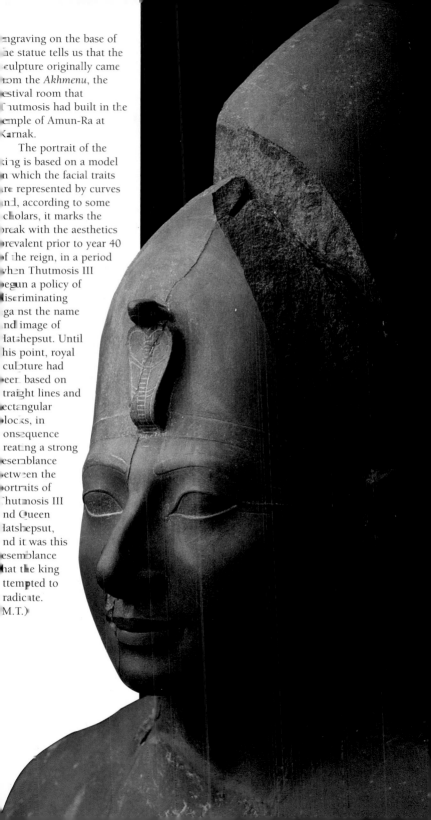

ngraving on the base of
the statue tells us that the
sculpture originally came
from the *Akhmenu*, the
festival room that
Thutmosis had built in the
Temple of Amun-Ra at
Karnak.

The portrait of the
king is based on a model
in which the facial traits
are represented by curves
and, according to some
scholars, it marks the
break with the aesthetics
prevalent prior to year 40
of the reign, in a period
when Thutmosis III
began a policy of
discriminating
against the name
and image of
Hatshepsut. Until
this point, royal
sculpture had
been based on
straight lines and
rectangular
blocks, in
consequence
creating a strong
resemblance
between the
portraits of
Thutmosis III
and Queen
Hatshepsut,
and it was this
resemblance
that the king
attempted to
eradicate.
(M.T.)

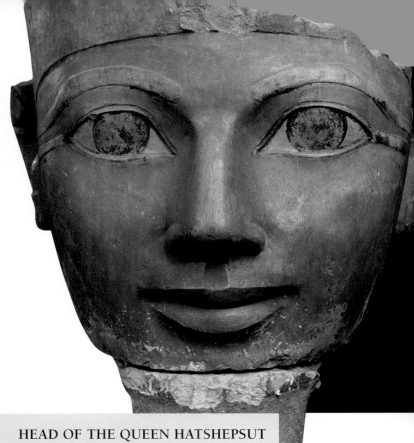

The head belonged to a colossal statue of Hatshepsut found in the portico of the third terrace of her temple at Deir al-Bahari. The queen is portrayed as Osiris with male attributes (the beard and red crown) yet the features of her face are graceful and feminine. The nose is straight and slender, the mouth small, and her long eyes are accentuated by black eyebrows and lines of kohl that reach around to the temples. The skin of her face is painted red in a convention that was generally used in Egyptian art to distinguish men from women (whose skin was painted a pale color). The divine essence of the pharaoh is endorsed by the blue false beard which was an attribute of gods and divinized kings. The queen probably wore the red crown of Lower Egypt with the white crown above to form the double crown; the pillar was probably on the north side of the third terrace where all the statues wore the double crown whereas those on the south side wore only the white crown of Upper Egypt.

Hatshepsut acted as regent for Thutmosis III and hung on to this post

for twenty-one years. As tradition did not allow women to be crowned as pharaoh, she assumed the male title "King of Upper and Lower Egypt" and was portrayed in statuary with male attributes.
(M.T.)

SPHINX OF HATSHEPSUT

PAINTED PLASTER; HEIGHT 62 CM; DEIR AL-BAHARI, TEMPLE OF HATSHEPSUT; EXCAVATION BY THE METROPOLITAN MUSEUM OF ART (1928-29) EIGHTEENTH DYNASTY, REIGN OF HATSHEPSUT (1479-1458 BC)
ROOM 11

This small sphinx comes from a pair on the first access ramp to the temple of Hatshepsut at Deir al-Bahari. The second sphinx is displayed in the Metropolitan Museum of New York but is in rather poor condition. The originality of the statue lies in the fact that, rather than simply substitute the lion's head with a human head, the artist has replaced only the muzzle of the animal with the face of the queen and so emphasized her feline character. This type of sphinx refers back to the characteristics of sphinxes portrayed at the end of the Twelfth Dynasty, like those of Amenemhat II found at Tanis and today held in the Egyptian Museum in Cairo. Hatshepsut's face is framed by a stylized mane and distinguished by typical elements of portraiture of the queen: almond-shaped eyes with highly curved eyebrows, a slim nose, and a small, smiling mouth. She wears a large, square false beard that has an inscription beneath with the name of the queen, "Maatkara, beloved by Amun and endowed with life for eternity."

The temple at Deir al-Bahari was designed and built by the queen's architect and counsellor, Senenmut, who had a second tomb built for himself in front of the sanctuary in addition to one in Qurna. The design of Hatshepsut's temple was largely inspired by the more ancient temple of Montuhotep II that stands slightly to the north. It comprises three terraces dug out of the rock, and two shrines, one dedicated to Hathor and the other to Anubis, and a solar temple on the third terrace.
(M.T.)

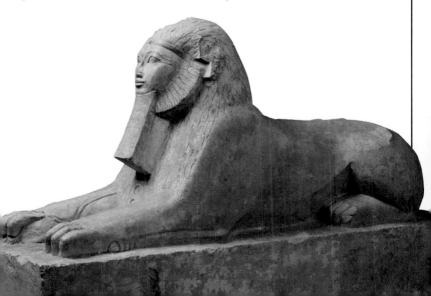

FRAGMENT OF A RELIEF SHOWING SCENES OF JOY

Limestone; Height 51 cm, length 105 cm
Saqqara, material taken from the Serapeum
Excavation by A. Mariette (1859)
Nineteenth Dynasty (1291-1185 bc)

ROOM 7

The relief shows a joy scene in typical post-Amarna style. It comes from one of the many tombs of Ramesside functionaries found at Saqqara, some of which were only discovered recently, for example, those of Tia and Imeneminet, both of whom were

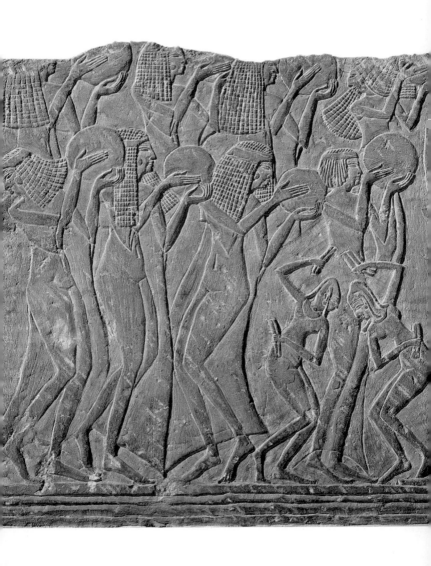

functionaries of the Ramesseum, the "Temple of the Millions of Years" built by Rameses II at l.c. western Thebes.

The scene on the left hand side is of a group of musicians followed by two young girls who tap sticks in rhythm and dance to the music. The music is to welcome a procession of eight men who have their arms raised in joy; the first two wear short wigs and skirts and one of them carries a long staff in his left hand. The second group is composed of three men with shaved heads and long pleated skirts, while those in the third group wear long wigs and garments with long, pleated sleeves.

Two inscriptions give the names and titles of the two figures: "the servant Aanakht" and "the scribe Imenkau." (M.T.)

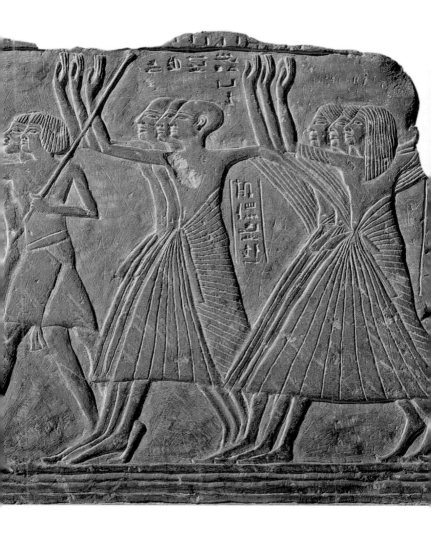

SARCOPHAGUS IN TOMB 55
VALLEY OF THE KINGS

WOOD, GOLD LEAF, AND GLASS PASTE; LENGTH 185 CM
VALLEY OF THE KINGS; EXCAVATION BY T.M. DAVIS (1907)
EIGHTEENTH DYNASTY, REIGN OF AKHENATEN (1350-1333 BC)

ROOM 8

Many doubts remain about the sarcophagus found in Tomb 55 in the Valley of the Kings. It was probably prepared for a woman – perhaps Queen Tiy, the wife of Amenhotep III – but the presence of the uraeus serpent and false beard and planned presence of other insignia of royalty such as the scepter and flail (not present today) suggest that it was altered to take the body of a pharaoh.

The body found in the sarcophagus was first thought to have been that of a woman, but in fact belonged to a young man who died at around the age of twenty-five. This was Smenkhkara, the co-regent and successor to Akhenaten who died prematurely, perhaps even before the "heretical pharaoh."

Why was Smenkhkara buried in Thebes? A number of signs indicate an attempt at reconciliation between the monarchy and the Theban priesthood of Amun and perhaps even a return of Smenkhkara himself, as is indicated by the presence of his funerary temple on the plain of west Thebes. The cartouches on the sarcophagus have been carefully erased and the face, uncommonly framed by a wig in place of the nemes headdress, was left unrecognisable by the removal of the gold leaf that served as a funerary mask. All the grave goods found in Tomb 55 were manufactured during the Amarna Period but it is still difficult to identify the occupant of the tomb. There were even claims that it is the body of Akhenaten himself but this hypothesis was almost immediately rejected by experts although we know nothing of the fate of this reformer monarch. The only circumstantial evidence we have is that the king was not buried in the tomb prepared for the entire royal family in a valley in Tell al-Amarna, which was almost certainly used exclusively by Maketaten, one of the daughters of Akhenaten and Nefertiti, who died young.
(A.B.)

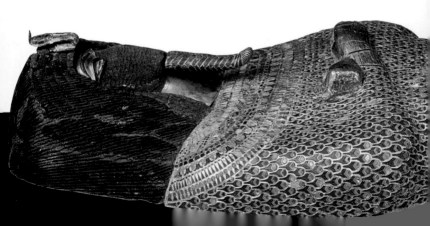

Comparison of this lifelike portrait or mold in the form of a mask with similar models in Berlin, has enabled scholars to reconstruct the creative process of the artist-sculptor step by step. The forceful modeling of this face is not just the factual portrait of a man at the court of Amarna but also a description of a unique culture. It is the product of a mature art that brought new vigour to inflexible artistic standards and which both maintained and advanced the traditions of sacred art.
(A.B.)

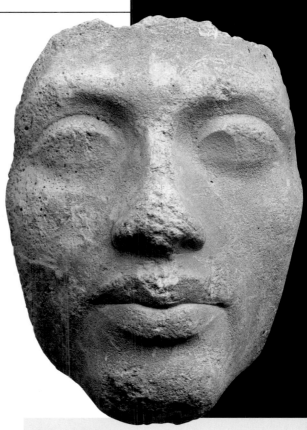

AMARNA-PERIOD MASK
PLASTER; HEIGHT 17 CM
TELL al-AMARNA; EXCAVATION BY THE EGYPT
EXPLORATION SOCIETY (1932-1933)
EIGHTEENTH DYNASTY
REIGN OF AKHENATEN (1350-1333 BC)

ROOM 3

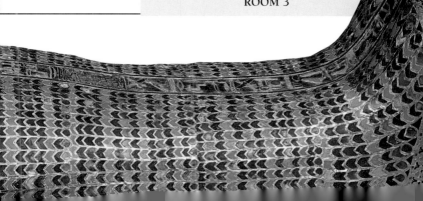

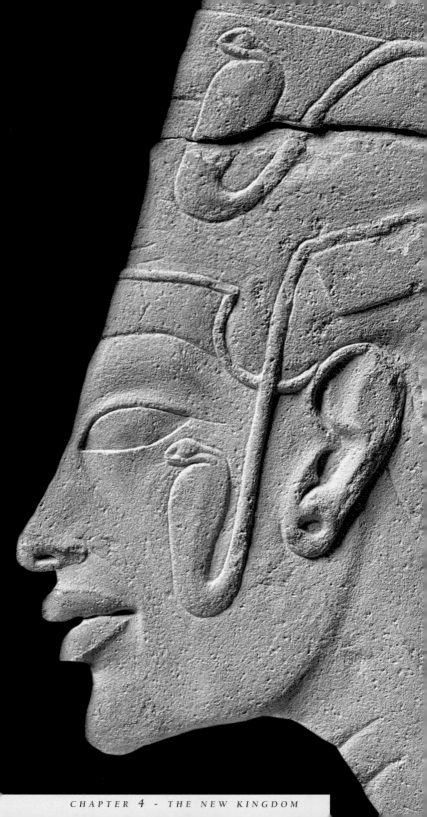

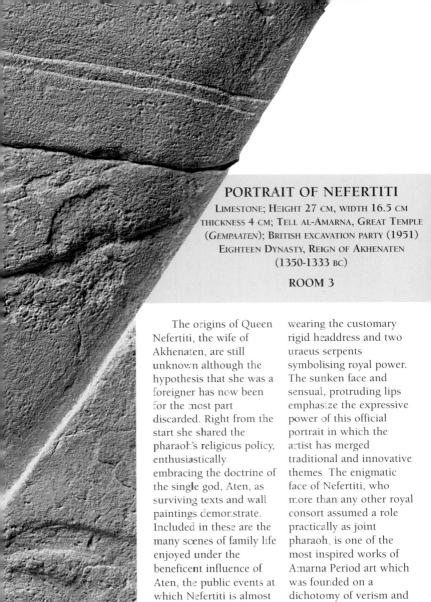

PORTRAIT OF NEFERTITI

LIMESTONE; HEIGHT 27 CM, WIDTH 16.5 CM
THICKNESS 4 CM; TELL AL-AMARNA, GREAT TEMPLE
(*GEMPAATEN*); BRITISH EXCAVATION PARTY (1951)
EIGHTEEN DYNASTY, REIGN OF AKHENATEN
(1350-1333 BC)

ROOM 3

The origins of Queen Nefertiti, the wife of Akhenaten, are still unknown although the hypothesis that she was a foreigner has now been for the most part discarded. Right from the start she shared the pharaoh's religious policy, enthusiastically embracing the doctrine of the single god, Aten, as surviving texts and wall paintings demonstrate. Included in these are the many scenes of family life enjoyed under the beneficent influence of Aten, the public events at which Nefertiti is almost always shown at the king's side, or when she is depicted alone or celebrating religious rites in adoration of Aten.

The limestone relief, almost certainly a sculptor's model, represents Nefertiti wearing the customary rigid headdress and two uraeus serpents symbolising royal power. The sunken face and sensual, protruding lips emphasize the expressive power of this official portrait in which the artist has merged traditional and innovative themes. The enigmatic face of Nefertiti, who more than any other royal consort assumed a role practically as joint pharaoh, is one of the most inspired works of Amarna Period art which was founded on a dichotomy of verism and stylistic exaggeration.

The rear side of the slab displays another illustration: it is of a figure kneeling in adoration but no information is available on the figure's identity. (A.B.)

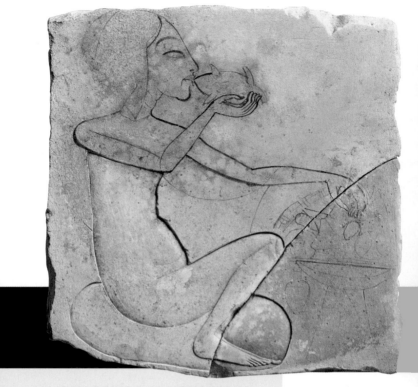

AMARNA PERIOD ARTIST'S STUDY

Limestone; Height 23.5 cm, width 22.3 cm
Tell Al-Amarna; Excavation by the Egypt
Exploration Society (1924); Eighteenth Dynasty
Reign of Akhenaten (1350-1333 bc)

ROOM 3

This artist's study is an extraordinary example of freedom of artistic expression. It was found at Tell al-Amarna and is concrete proof of the technical skill and creativity Egyptian painters and sculptors were capable of when liberated from the shackles of the rigid standards of sacred art. During the Amarna Period, the breaking of the traditional rules that had always governed iconography and proportions of the figures allowed the creation of non-conventional works such as this one of a naked girl perhaps biting into a roast duck. Displaying all the typical requisites of Amarna style, the young girl is portrayed with a long head and swollen belly as was customary for members of the royal family (she is probably a princess) and is shown busy eating which had not previously been considered a suitably dignified activity for an official portrait. Until the time of Amarna, and even after the short reign of Akhenaten, no one ever had himself portrayed directly eating food, particularly if he belonged to the restricted circle of the court. The many wall scenes of the deceased called to take possession of the "funerary meal" from the earliest dynasties and on stelae from different epochs were symbolic representations of daily life portrayed for practical purposes in the Afterlife and therefore endowed with magical qualities. This example, however, breaks the long established tradition that permitted depiction of the moments before or after a meal and portrays an act that is common to all, yet which is "revolutionary" for ancient Egyptian society. (A.B.)

ACCADIAN TABLET

CLAY; HEIGHT 13 CM, WIDTH 8 CM
TELL AL-AMARNA, ARCHIVE OF THE ROYAL PALACE
GERMAN EXCAVATION PARTY (1890)
EIGHTEENTH DYNASTY, REIGN OF AKHENATEN (1350-1333 BC)

ROOM 3

The appearance on the antiques market at the end of the 19th century of a series of clay tablets written in Accadian alerted scholars to the existence of an archaeological site of major importance for the understanding of the history of Egypt and the Near East. The tablets contained diplomatic correspondence in both cuneiform writing and the Accadian language that was kept in the archive of the palace in the city of Akhetaten ("Horizon of the Aten") that was built by Akhenaten and is today known by the Arabic name of Tell al-Amarna.

The discovery of these priceless tablets allowed the development of international relations between the Egyptian court with the kings and princes of the Near East to be reconstructed, and also led to the discovery of the city founded by the reforming king almost halfway between Memphis and Thebes.

The wealth of information provided by the tablets of Tell al-Amarna is unique given that they clarify the relationships between the great and small powers of the time and inform us of the political conniving practised to support some against others. The tablets also reveal the many incomprehensions and reciprocal distrust sometimes generated by uninhibited use of the diplomatic language of the period, Accadian.

This tablet refers to the negotiations between the king of Babylon, Kadashman-Enlil, and Amenhotep III regarding the pharoah's request to take a Babylonian princess as his wife. The reply, seemingly provisional and somewhat specious, accuses Amenhotep of sending too few gifts and of behaving in an unfriendly fashion towards the king of Babylon.

(A.B.)

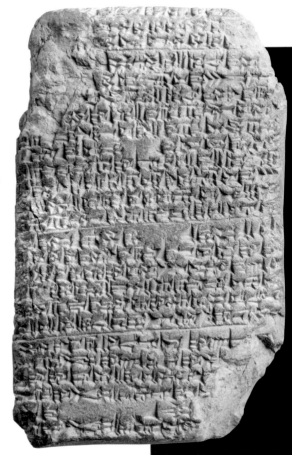

COLOSSUS OF AMENHOTEP IV

SANDSTONE; HEIGHT 239 CM; KARNAK
TEMPLE OF ATEN; EXCAVATION BY H. CHEVRIER (1926)
EIGHTEENTH DYNASTY, REIGN OF AKHENATEN
(1350-1333 BC)

ROOM 3

These colossal statues of Amenhotep IV come from one of the temples built by the young king and dedicated to Aten before he transferred his capital from Thebes to Tell al-Amarna, next to the Temple of Amun-Ra at Karnak. At the beginning of his reign when he still tolerated cults to other gods, Amenhotep IV had several sacred buildings raised around Thebes, in particular in the areas sacred to the ancient god Montu in the district of Thebes: at Medamud, Tod, Ermonti, and Karnak. His intention of conflict with the priesthood of Amun, dominant in Thebes, was evident.

The colossi found at Karnak are among the most conspicuous items from the Theban phase of the reign of Akhenaten. The colossi rest against pillars in the courtyards of the temples depicting the pharaoh standing with his arms folded and hands gripping the flail and *heqa* scepter, a symbol of royal authority.

His wrists and arms bear the "didactic name" of the Aten: the programmatic name of the sun god stated in the doctrine championed by Akhenaten himself: "Long live Ra-Harakhti, who rejoices on the horizon in his quality as light that is in the Aten."

The face of the king seems sunken, his eyes narrowed, and his chin long, imbuing the statue with an emotional tension that was typical of the early phase of Amarna art. The two plumes over the king's head (the statue on the right) are the symbol of the god Shu; the statue on the left wears the double crown of the Two Lands. Of the various and very similar colossal statues of Akhenaten found at Karnak, one shows a naked, "sexless" version of the king, which is thought by some experts to represent the king as the "mother and father" of his people, and by others as simply being an unfinished statue. (A.B.)

COLOSSUS OF AMENHOTEP IV

SANDSTONE; HEIGHT 185 CM
KARNAK, TEMPLE OF ATEN
EXCAVATION BY H. CHEVRIER (1926)
EIGHTEENTH DYNASTY, REIGN
OF AKHENATEN (1350-1333 BC)

ROOM 3

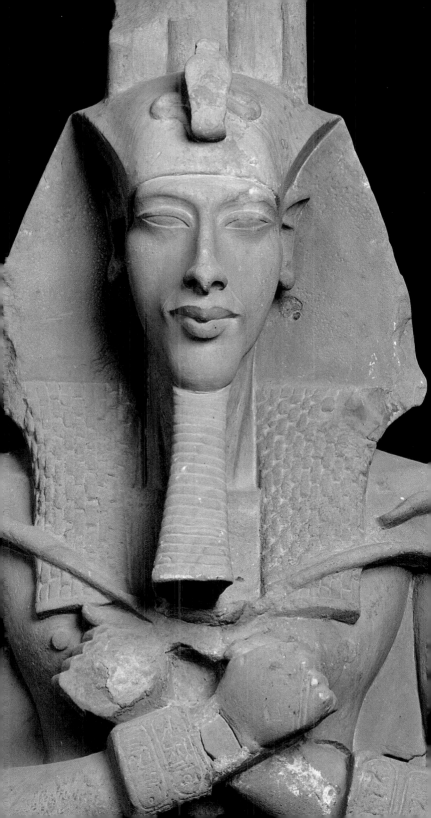

FRAGMENT OF PAVING FROM TELL AL-AMARNA

PAINTED PLASTER; HEIGHT 101 CM, WIDTH 160 CM
TELL AL-AMARNA, SOUTH PALACE (*MARU-ATEN*)
EXCAVATION BY A. BARSANTI (1896); EIGHTEENTH
DYNASTY, REIGN OF AKHENATEN (1350-1333 BC)

ROOM 3

A number of fragments of paving decorated with high quality paintings of plants and animals come from the South

social hierarchy.

The symbolism of aquatic plants and papyrus as being the first forms of life in the Egyptian version of the

of primeval disorder and thus triumph over death.

In the New Kingdom, the symbolism of victory over the dark forces of chaos became more widespread and is seen in the famous portrayals of Ankhesenamun (the wife of Tutankhamun) clutching wild ducks on the outer walls of the gilded shrine found in the tomb of her husband in the Valley of the Kings. In Amarna, this

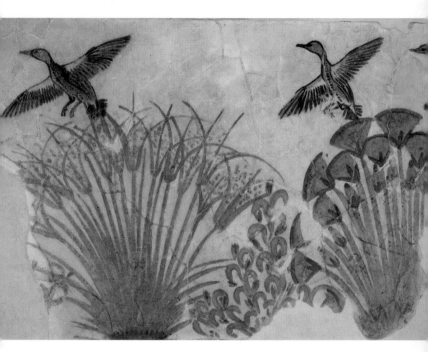

Palace in Tell al-Amarna, one of the secondary residences of the royal family. Here, the theme of wild ducks in the marshes achieved some of its most successful expressions and spread from the court residences to become popular at lower levels in the

Creation had been known since the earliest stages of Egyptian culture, when the depiction of hunting scenes with the harpoon or throwing sticks (a sort of boomerang) in tomb paintings meant that the occupant of the tomb would magically defeat the negative forces

symbolic interpretation was overlaid with the simple and touching description of the miraculous apparition of life in all its aspects and celebrated in the Hymn to Aten, the apotheosis of the natural philosophy championed by Akhenaten.
(A.B.)

ALTAR

PAINTED LIMESTONE; HEIGHT 98 CM, WIDTH 118 CM
TELL AL-AMARNA, HOUSE OF PANEHSY; EXCAVATION BY THE
EGYPT EXPLORATION SOCIETY (1926-1927)
EIGHTEENTH DYNASTY, REIGN OF AKHENATEN (1350-1333 BC)

ROOM 3

Articles testifying the cult of the royal family have often been found in the private houses at Amarna. The royal family had been believed since ancient times to be intermediaries in the relationship between the gods and the common people. This example is a household altar in the form of a shrine; the brick structure in front of it has both a decorative and devotional function and resembles the pylons of temples built around a cella. The walls of the two wings of the pylon are symmetrically decorated with scenes of Akhenaten,

Nefertiti, and their eldest daughter, Meritaten, adoring and making offerings to the god Aten. The king, with his swollen belly, wears the blue crown (khepresh) on his customarily exaggerated head and the queen a tall blue tiara crown and a long transparent tunic. Aten radiates his benefits of life and energy to the royal couple which were indispensable to ensure the continued existence of all that had been created.

Traces of brightly colored paint can still be made out on the recently restored monument. The

cartouches bearing the "didactic name of the Aten" (i.e. the name given by Akhenaten to his god) are applied below the molding of the pylons and on the sides of the entrance portal whereby the pharaoh is permitting the god the royal prerogative of seeing his own name in the royal cartouche. Two versions of the "name of Aten" are known; this one is the more recent: "May Ra live who appears in the Horizon of the Aten as a visible manifestation (shadow) that reaches like Aten." (A.B.)

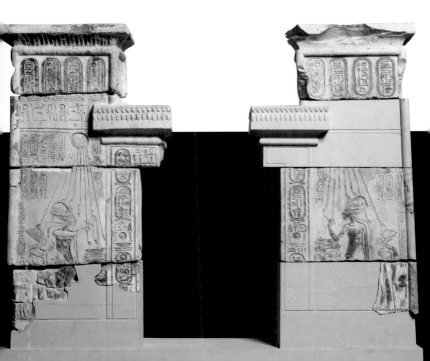

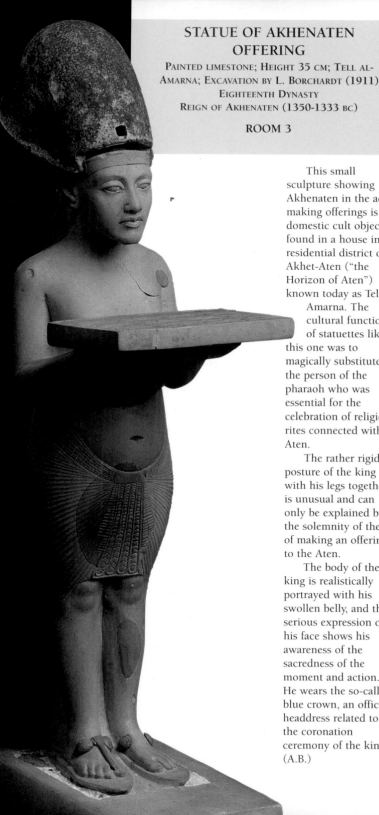

STATUE OF AKHENATEN OFFERING

Painted limestone; Height 35 cm; Tell al-Amarna; Excavation by L. Borchardt (1911)
Eighteenth Dynasty
Reign of Akhenaten (1350-1333 bc)

ROOM 3

This small sculpture showing Akhenaten in the act of making offerings is a domestic cult object found in a house in the residential district of Akhet-Aten ("the Horizon of Aten") known today as Tell al-Amarna. The cultural function of statuettes like this one was to magically substitute the person of the pharaoh who was essential for the celebration of religious rites connected with Aten.

The rather rigid posture of the king with his legs together is unusual and can only be explained by the solemnity of the act of making an offering to the Aten.

The body of the king is realistically portrayed with his swollen belly, and the serious expression on his face shows his awareness of the sacredness of the moment and action. He wears the so-called blue crown, an official headdress related to the coronation ceremony of the king. (A.B.)

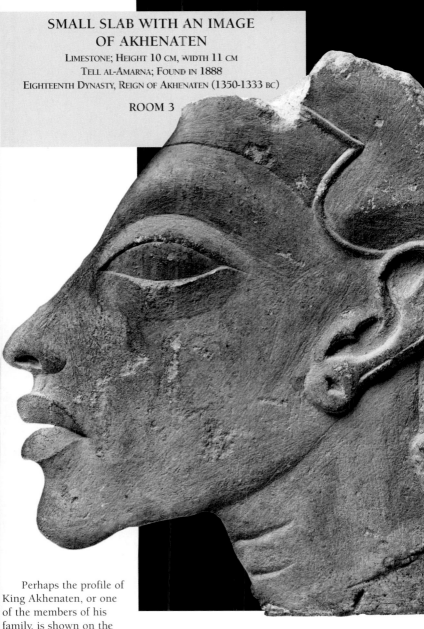

SMALL SLAB WITH AN IMAGE
OF AKHENATEN

LIMESTONE; HEIGHT 10 CM, WIDTH 11 CM
TELL AL-AMARNA; FOUND IN 1888
EIGHTEENTH DYNASTY, REIGN OF AKHENATEN (1350-1333 BC)

ROOM 3

Perhaps the profile of King Akhenaten, or one of the members of his family, is shown on the small limestone slab with the characteristic physical exaggerations seen in much of Amarna art. It is not clear if the decision to have himself portrayed in this manner was the result of personal physical deformities or was dictated by a desire to have his ideology represented artistically. The mystical inspiration attained by images such as this one still surprises the modern observer and raises many questions regarding the earthly and spiritual life of the monarch who has rightly been called "the first individual in history" in his capacity as the author of reforms to the ancient state religion in favor of monotheism.

(A.B.)

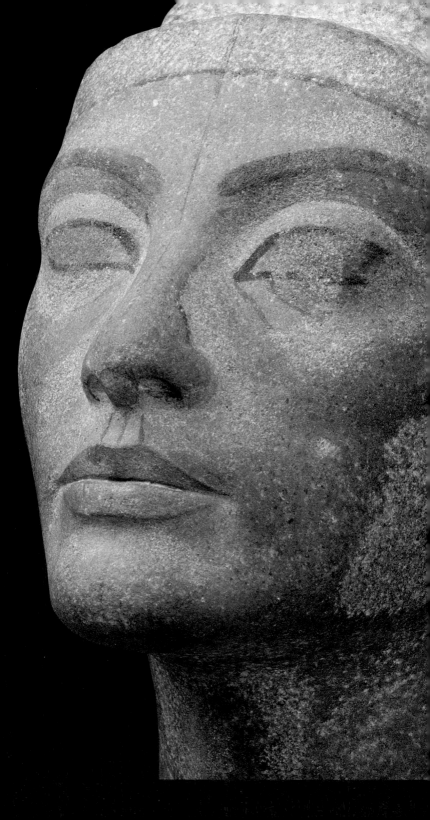

INCOMPLETE HEAD OF NEFERTITI

DARK QUARTZITE; HEIGHT 35.5 CM
TELL AL-AMARNA, WORKSHOP OF A SCULPTOR
EXCAVATION BY THE EGYPT EXPLORATION SOCIETY (1932)
EIGHTEENTH DYNASTY, REIGN OF AKHENATEN (1350-1333 BC)

ROOM 3

This head is unquestionably the loveliest of the portraits of Queen Nefertiti, the wife of Akhenaten. It belonged to a statue made of several parts that were assembled to form a whole. The refined sensitivity displayed by this masterpiece emphasizes the elegance and spirituality of a woman of power and legendary fascination.

Little is known of her background but the suggestion that she was of foreign parentage is no longer generally supported by scholars who now believe she was fully Egyptian. The importance of her role at court is indisputable and is attested by the many images of her with her husband at Thebes and Amarna, often with their children, in intimate scenes or during official worship of the Aten. She even achieved the distinction of having herself portrayed alone in a temple or private shrine officiating a religious ceremony, an act that had always been the prerogative of the pharaoh. Perhaps it was this "exaggerated" display of the royal couple that led to the subsequent rejection of Akhenaten's religious reforms.

The simplicity of the features is accentuated by the stone and the impenetrable pride of the queen's gaze; despite remaining unfinished, the veiled eyes underline the appeal of this woman who was fated to disappear mysteriously from history. Relegated to a secondary role – perhaps in self-exile in a palace to the north of Amarna – she was quickly replaced by Kiya of whom we also know very little, and, at a certain moment in time, all mention of Nefertiti ceased.

(A.B.)

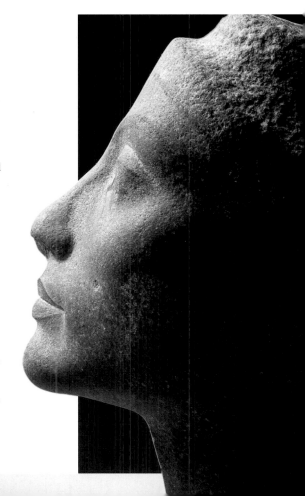

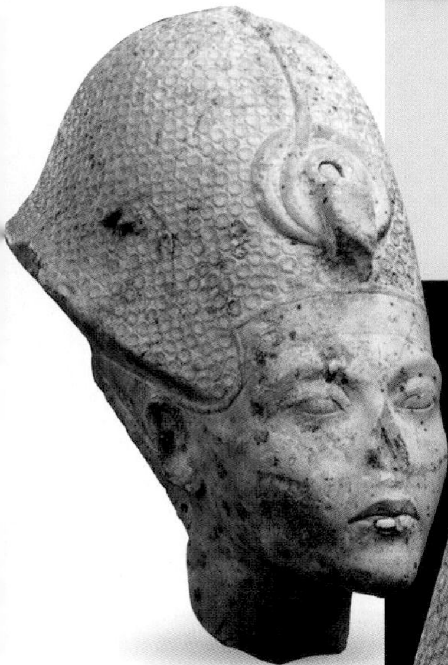

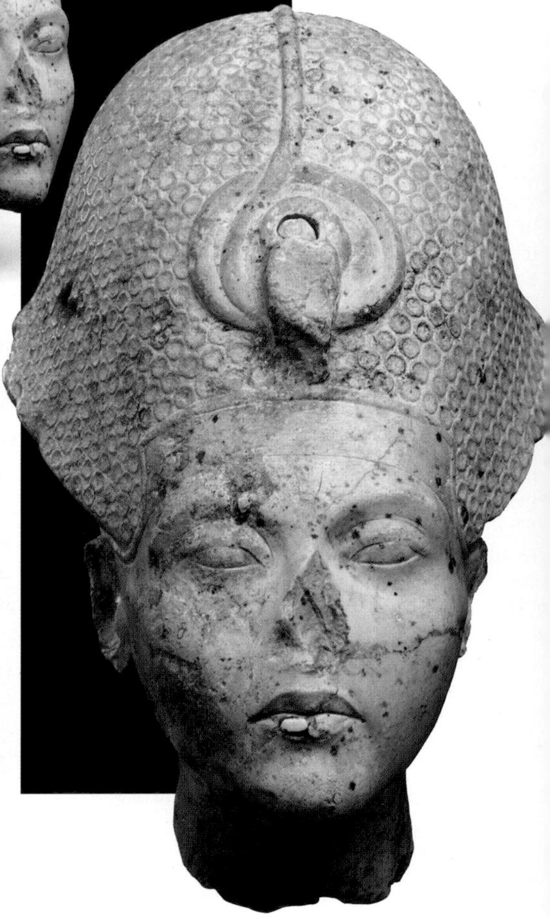

HEAD OF AKHENATEN
LIMESTONE; HEIGHT 24.5 CM
TELL AL-AMARNA
EIGHTEENTH DYNASTY
REIGN OF AKHENATEN (1350-1333 BC)

ROOM 3

This fine head of Akhenaten was found at Amarna during construction of a road for the visit of King Fu'ad of Egypt. It belongs to the most classical style of Amarna art, remote from the expressionism that characterized much of Theban production during the early years of his reign. His serene but firm expression, marked by a spiritual tension, resembles the superb bust in Paris, perhaps the most beautiful and meaningful image of Amenhotep IV-Akhenaten to have survived. The king's preference for the blue crown (*khepresh*) – an ideal form to suit the elongated depiction of his head – is here confirmed. A column at the back might have existed between this and its matching statue, as in the example in the Louvre. The head was given to King Fu'ad but was passed to the Cairo Museum shortly before his death.

The composed elegance and haughtiness of Ahkenaten's expression betray the iron will of a man who is often judged but perhaps never completely understood.

(A.B.)

The statue is unfinished but clearly of high artistic quality. It represents Akhenaten holding one of his daughters on his knee, perhaps the first-born Meritaten, but a more recent suggestion is that the female figure is Kiya, the pharaoh's second wife. The king sits on a stool wearing a short-sleeved tunic and the blue crown (*khepresh*) while the girl wears an ill-defined wig and has her head turned affectionately towards the pharaoh. Intimate scenes of life at court like this one are very much a feature of Amarna art and seem to reflect the doctrine championed by the pharaoh of "living in accordance with Maat," i.e. adhering to factual truth. Thus, a simple statue like this both portrays a moment of common love and represents a cultural program of great innovative force. (A.B.)

STATUE OF AKHENATEN WITH ONE OF HIS DAUGHTERS
Limestone; Height 39.5 cm; width 16 cm
Tell al-Amarna, workshop of a sculptor
Excavation by L. Borchardt (1912)
Eighteenth Dynasty
Reign of Akhenaten (1350-1333 bc)

ROOM 3

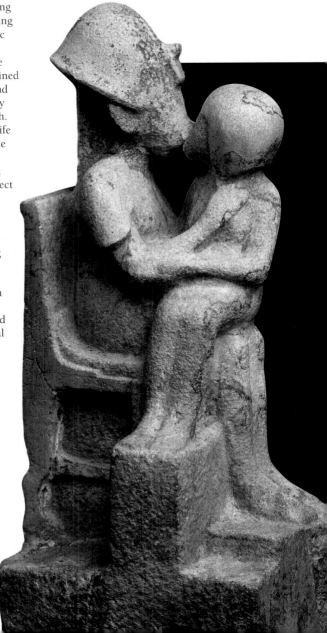

This canopic vase of praiseworthy artistic quality was found with three others – one of which is in the Metropolitan Museum in New York – in the mysterious and unfinished Tomb 55 in the Valley of the Kings. This imposing burial place was free of all decoration and inscriptions but held grave goods and a sarcophagus containing a mummy that were stylistically typical of the Amarna Period. The sarcophagus was made for a woman but was

AMARNA-PERIOD CANOPIC VASE

ALABASTER; HEIGHT 38.8 CM; THEBES
VALLEY OF THE KINGS (TOMB 55); EXCAVATION
BY T.M. DAVIS (1907); EIGHTEENTH DYNASTY
REIGN OF AKHENATEN (1350-1333 BC)

ROOM 3

used to hold the body, as has been scientifically proven as an almost certainty, of Smenkhkara, Akhenaten's young co-regent, who died young and who was buried in Thebes. The canopic vases were originally made for Meritaten, the eldest of Akhenaten and Nefertiti's six daughters and who married Smenkhkara, but were then used for Smenkhkara himself.

The facial features on the lid of the canopic vases are claimed by some to be of Meritaten and by others of Kiya (the woman who replaced Nefertiti at Akhenaten's side during the last years of his reign) and are a splendid example of Amarna art exported to Thebes. The collar that covers the figure's shoulders, the elaborate wig and uraeus serpent carved on the forehead, and the glass, quartz, and obsidian encrustations of the eyes and eyebrows reveal that the figure is of the very highest rank. (A.B.)

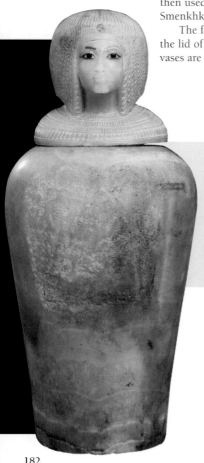

SLAB SHOWING A SCENE OF WORSHIP OF THE ATEN

PAINTED LIMESTONE; HEIGHT 53 CM,
WIDTH 48 CM DEPTH 8 CM; TELL AL-AMARNA,
ROYAL TOMB; EXCAVATION IN 1891
EIGHTEENTH DYNASTY,
REIGN OF AKHENATEN (1350-1333 BC)

ROOM 3

The conventional scene of adoration of the Aten by the royal couple, Akhenaten and Nefertiti, and some of their daughters (in this case Meritaten and Maketaten, the eldest two) is taken from a painted limestone slab

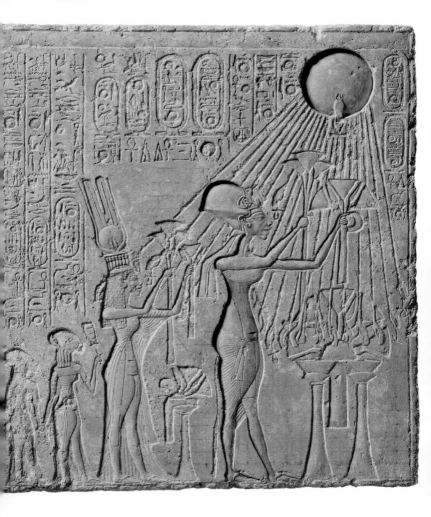

found in the ruins of the tomb of the royal family in Amarna. The placement of the work in the tomb is not clear but it was probably only used for the second daughter, Maketaten, who died young in childbirth as is touchingly shown on the reliefs that are still visible in the tomb.

King Akhenaten, whose physical deformities were artistically inspired according to some scholars, is shown here with Nefertiti who performs the same act of adoration and offering to the Aten. The god is represented as a sun disk with beneficent rays that dominates the scene; the cartouches give the name of the king and the didactic name of the Aten.

The constant presence of the royal couple as an intermediary between the sun god and the rest of the populace may lie at the origin of the Egyptian people's rejection of the new "vision of the world," more generally considered as a philosophy of nature.

Elements of the image are typical of the art at the start of Akhenaten's reign, for example, the treatment of the faces which are of high artistic quality though hardly realistic.
(A.B.)

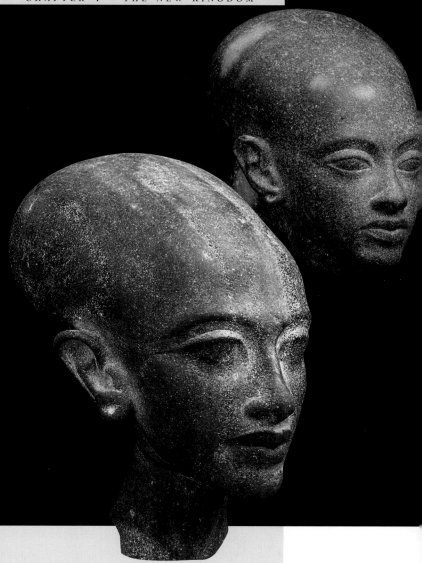

HEADS OF PRINCESSES
QUARTZITE
1) HEIGHT 25 CM; 2) HEIGHT 14 CM; 3) HEIGHT 21 CM
TELL AL AMARNA
LABORATORY OF THUTUROSE
EXCAVATION BY L. BORCHARDT (1912)
EIGHTEENTH DYNASTY
REIGN OF AKHENATEN
(1350-1333 BC)

ROOM 3

Characteristic of the
new artistic ideas that
flourished during the age
of Amarna, the young
daughters of Akhenaten
and Nefertiti were often
portrayed in family scenes
What strikes the observer
when viewing the heads
found in the workshop of
the chief sculptor,
Thuturose, in Tell al-
Amarna, is the deformity
of the skulls which were

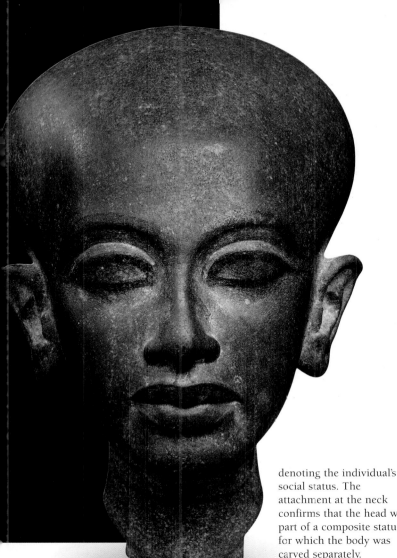

denoting the individual's social status. The attachment at the neck confirms that the head was part of a composite statue for which the body was carved separately.

The head on the left may represent Meritaten, the king's eldest daughter. The join at the neck suggests that the head was to be joined to a torso, sculpted separately, as part of a composite statue.

The other two heads are smaller than the previous one and are less discerning in the expression though the features are delicately carved.

(A.B.)

unnaturally lengthened although suffering from dolichocephalism. The hypothesis that the deformity was congenital is supported by the fact that other members of the family, including Akhenaten, had similar skulls, but it is not in itself sufficient to explain what seems to be an artistic choice. Contrasting with the often overdone mannerism of the previous epoch, the Amarna artist opted to base his work on the conceptual and artistic realism enforced by Akhenaten as dogma and high profile ethics.

The girls have large, heavily made up eyes, fleshy lips, and ears that stick out, as the norm in portraiture of this type was to blend individual features with elements

STELA OF MERENPTAH'S VICTORY
GRANITIC ROCK; H. 318 CM, W. 163 CM, T. 31 CM; THEBES
"TEMPLE OF THE MILLIONS OF YEARS" OF MERENPTAH
EXCAVATION BY W.M.F. PETRIE (1896); NINETEENTH
DYNASTY, REIGN OF MERENPTAH (1212-1202 BC)

ROOM 13

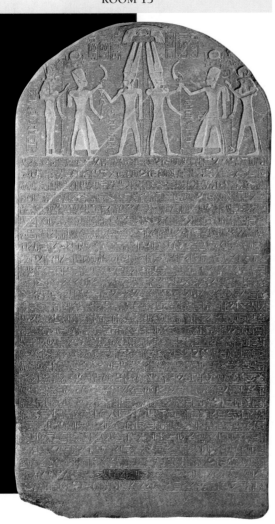

Indo-European migrations. They included the Libu, Meshuesh, and other Indo-European peoples from Anatolia and the islands of the Aegean. The text on the stela refers to the reaction of the Egyptians to the concerted attack of these peoples that ended with the slaughter of 6,000 enemies and the capture of 9,000 prisoners of war, but the clash wasn't definitive: 20 years later, Merenptah's successor, Rameses III, fought the Sea Peoples.

The stela also goes by the name of the "Stela of Israel" as it contains the only known reference to Israel in Egyptian sources: the name is listed with Gezer, Canaan, Yenoam, and Syria as having also been defeated by Merenptah but in fact the king had not undertaken any military action in Asia and these names might have been only cited as a deterrent against those countries. "Israel," however, does not refer to a place, in the text, but is used to refer to a people.

The lunette in the stela contains two engraved scenes beside one another. In both, the pharaoh is wearing ceremonial dress and offers Amun-Ra the reaping hook that symbolizes victory and the scepters of royalty; the difference between the scenes is that in the first Merenptah is followed by the goddess Mut and in the other by the god Khonsu. Both were members of the Theban triad of gods with Amun-Ra.
(M.T.)

The stela comes from the temple Merenptah had built in western Thebes using materials taken when he destroyed the temple of Amenhotep III. The new temple was built to celebrate the king's victory in the fifth year of his reign against the invasion of the coalition between the Libyan people and "Sea Peoples." This was the name given by the Egyptians to the peoples that arrived from across the Mediterranean who were pushed south by

COLOSSAL STATUARY
GROUP OF AMENHOTEP III

Limestone; Height 700 cm; Thebes, Medinet Habu
Excavation by A. Mariette (1859); Eighteenth
Dynasty, Reign of Amenhotep III (1387-1350 bc)

HALL

This statuary group iginally stood in the mple of Amenhotep III west Thebes but the mple was destroyed by erenptah in order to ild his own. All that was t were the two cnumental statues at the les of the pylon known the "Colossi of mnon." The statue was und in pieces at Medinet bu from where it was en to the Cairo seum and reassembled.

It shows the pharaoh th Queen Tiy at his e, and their ughters, Henuttaneb, ebetah, and another hose name has been st. The princesses e shown on a aller scale standing fore the throne. The yal couple had four ughters in all, the o mentioned and tamun and Isis who ere often shown in tues and reliefs.

Queen Tiy was also gularly represented side her husband in ulptures, on stelae, d in tomb and temple liefs. This fact denotes r importance in the e of the country and was with Tiy that the le of the pharaoh's nsort, the "Great yal Bride," assumed eater political portance than that

of the pharaoh's mother. Elements denoting her divine character, in addition to that of the king, appear in her iconography for the first time, for example, the cow's horns and sun disk on her head (the attributes of the goddess Hathor). Tiy was also the first queen to whom a

temple was consecrated, at Sedeinga between the second and third cataracts (this example was to be followed by Rameses II who built a temple to Nefertari at Abu Simbel).

The queen is depicted wearing a heavy three-part wig with a royal uraeus serpent and a modius on which Hathor's symbols must have appeared once. She wears a long, clinging garment, rests her left hand on her thigh with the palm open, and circles the waist of the king with her right arm in a sign of affection.

(M.T.)

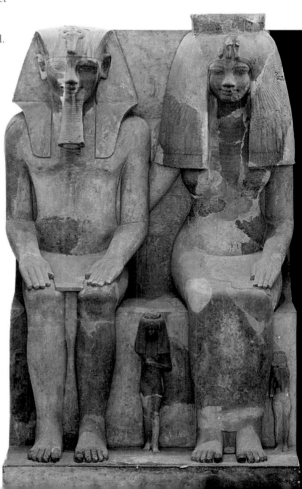

NAOS OF RAMESES II

PINK QUARTZITE; HEIGHT 156 CM, LENGTH 271 CM
WIDTH 190 CM; TANIS, TEMPLE OF AMUN-RA
EXCAVATION BY W.M.F. PETRIE (1904); NINETEETH
DYNASTY, REIGN OF RAMESES II (1279-1212 BC)

HALL

This *naos* was found as part of a pair with another also held in the Cairo Museum (CG 70004). It was dedicated by Rameses II to the solar deities Ra-Harakhti, Atum, and Khepri and it was for this reason that it was carved in pink quartzite as the stone was associated with the solar cult. It stood in the great temple of Amun-Ra in Tanis between the second and fourth obelisk.

Three images show the pharaoh making offerings to each of the deities. He wears the blue crown before both Ra-Harakhti and Khepri and the double crown of Upper and Lower Egypt before Atum. He wears a *shendyt* skirt and carries different offerings in his hands: two round containers, two loaves of bread, and two small cups. Ra-Harakhti is portrayed with the body of a man and the head of a falcon with a sun disk; Atum has a human head and body and wears a composed crown; Khepri also has a human head and body but wears a *nemes* crowned with a sun disk. The inscriptions around the images list Rameses' titles and various formulas of good omen.

Those buildings built Tanis prior to the Twenty-first Dynasty, like this one were reused for new constructions as no building works that exist the Temple of Amun-Ra were carried out before th reign of Psusennes I (104 994 BC). It is probable tha the original site of the *nao* was Pi-Rameses, the capit during the Ramessid Perio that stood close to Tanis. (M.T.)

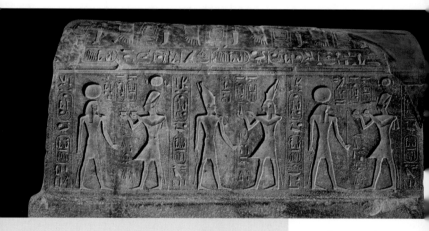

HATSHEPSUT'S FIRST SARCOPHAGUS

SILICIFIED SANDSTONE; LID: LENGTH 199 CM, WIDTH 73
CM, HEIGHT 90 CM; THEBES, WADI SIQQAT TAKA AL-
ZEIDE, TOMB OF HATSHEPSUT; EXCAVATION BY H.
CARTER (1916); EIGHTEENTH DYNASTY, REIGN OF
HATSHEPSUT (1479-1458 BC)

HALL

Hatshepsut had two tombs built for her, one at Deir al-Bahari when she was still "the royal bride" and had not yet become regent and the other in the Valley of the Kings with the royal name of Maatkara. Chronologically, this was the first of three sarcophaguses that were made. Another, made for the queen to be buried in Maatkara, was then transformed for Thutmosi I and is now displayed in the Museum of Fine Arts i Boston. The third is also i Cairo Museum (JE 47032) and was made to bury her in as the 'king.'

The tomb the sarcophagus was found in does not seem to have eve eld a body as the only bjects in it, besides the arcophagus, were ragments of clay vases. he sarcophagus itself is nscribed with the titles of Iatshepsut before her

ascent to the throne: 'daughter of the king, sister of the king, wife of the god, great wife of the king.' The upper surface of the lid is decorated with a cartouche in

which the goddess Nut is shown with her arms raised. A formula from the *Texts of the Pyramids*, common in the Eighteenth Dynasty, no. 777, is engraved in front of Nut and the words in favor of the deceased at the sides of the lid: Nut's words are on the right, Geb's on the left, Nephthys' at the end above the head, and Isis' below the feet. Two *udjat* eyes are shown between two columns of hieroglyphs. (M.T.)

THIRD SARCOPHAGUS OF HATSHEPSUT

RED SANDSTONE; LID: LENGTH 245
M, WIDTH 87 CM, HEIGHT 100 CM
THEBES, VALLEY OF THE KINGS,
TOMB OF HATSHEPSUT
EXCAVATION BY H. CARTER (1905)
EIGHTEENTH DYNASTY, REIGN OF
HATSHEPSUT (1479-1458 BC)

HALL

The sarcophagus is decorated with shallow relief figures of gods and the protective spirits of the deceased between columns of hieroglyphs. On the left side are two *udjat* eyes, the symbol of perfection and renewal. The end where the queen's head was to lie is rounded and the edge of the entire lid is decorated with a pattern in the form of a cartouche. The large stone container was built to hold three other anthropoid sarcophaguses

made from wood: sadly, those have not survived but we have the example of the wooden inner containers from the tomb of Tutankhamun. The base of this sarcophagus shows Isis crouching on the hieroglyph for gold and holding the *shen* circle that represents protection. Nephthys is in a similar position on the other side. Each goddess bears the hieroglyph representing her name on her head; in the case of Isis it is a seat

(*aset*) and in that of Nephthys it is a basket (*neb*) crowned by a stylized palace (*hut*). They both wear a wig with the uraeus serpent on the front.

The titles on the longer sides of the sarcophagus define Hatshepsut as "King of Upper and Lower Egypt" and as the "Daughter of Ra"; usually, however, she is given the masculine form of the titles. (M.T.)

SARCOPHAGUS OF MERENPTAH
REUSED FOR PSUSENNES I
PINK GRANITE; LENGTH 240 CM, WIDTH 120 CM, HEIGHT 89 CM
TANIS, TOMB OF PSUSENNES I; EXCAVATION BY P. MONTET (1940)
NINETEENTH DYNASTY, REIGN OF MERENPTAH (1212-1202 BC) -
TWENTY-FIRST DYNASTY, REIGN OF PSUSENNES I (1045-994 BC)

HALL

The sarcophagus was found in the tomb of Psusennes I in the walls of the temple of Amun-Ra at Tanis, but it is adorned with the cartouche of Merenptah, for whom it was evidently made. At the time of its reuse, almost all the cartouches of the Nineteenth-Dynasty pharaoh were chiselled off and substituted by those of Psusennes I, but this one remained which enables it to be dated to the Ramessid when it would have been buried in the Valley of the Kings.

The sarcophagus contained two mummy-shaped sarcophaguses, one made from black granite

(JE 85911) and the other made from silver and gold (JE 85917). The lid was decorated with the figure of the king in the form of a mummy wearing the false beard of royalty and holding the symbols of Osiris, the *heqa* scepter, the *neheh* scourge in his hands, and the false beard. The interior of the sarcophagus contains an image of Nut, the representation of night, with her arms stretched upwards. The outer sides are decorated with scenes of divinities associated with the world after death and related inscriptions. The lower register depicts a facade of a palace similar to the facades of Archaic sacred buildings. The inner surfaces, however, are

lined with figures of gods and goddesses and images of jewels, weapons, clothe and sandals.

Psusennes I's tomb wa one of a group belonging to the rulers of the Twent first and Twenty-second Dynasties that were foun almost intact at Tanis and he was not the only one c these pharaohs to reuse funerary materials from previous rulers: Takelot II made use of a sarcophagu originally produced durin the Middle Kingdom, Amenemopis used a sarcophagus lid made fro blocks from the Old Kingdom, and Sheshonq I had his sarcophagus carve out of a Thirteenth-Dynasty architrave. (M.T.)

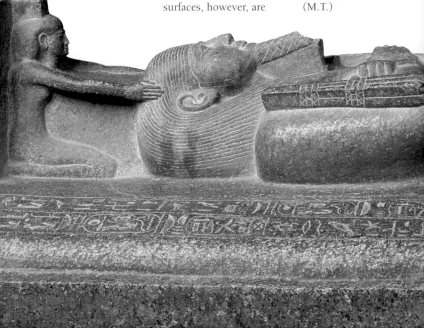

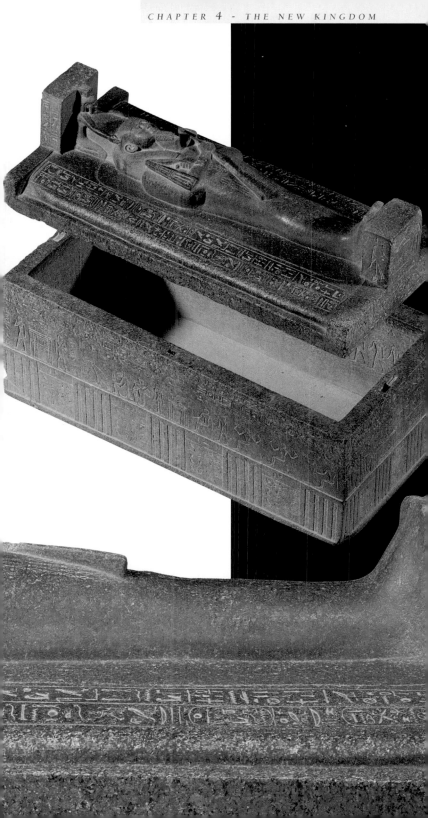

PHARAOH WITH THE OSIRIAN TRIAD

GRANITIC ROCK; HEIGHT 139 CM, WIDTH 116 CM
ABYDOS; EIGHTEENTH DYNASTY (1550-1291 BC)

ROOM 9

The statue bears no inscription nor any name of the king who is represented with the triad of Osiris, Isis, and Horus. The four are seated on a bench seat with a rounded base and side slab. Osiris is in his characteristic pose with two sceptres on his chest and the *atef* crown on his head. He wears a false beard and, like the other deities, four strings of pearls around his neck. Isis wears a tight-fitting dress supported by two braces, and a three-part wig with the cow's horns and sun disk of Hathor on top and a uraeus serpent on the front. Her right hand rests on her leg and holds the *ankh* sign while her left arm passes behind the shoulders of Osiris beside her. The nameless pharaoh to the left of Osiris wears the *nemes* headdress with the royal uraeus serpent. He too wears a wide necklace of five strings of pearls and the short *shendyt* skirt that leaves his chest bare. The face of the deity next to the king has been removed but logic tells us that this is Horus, the remaining figure of the Osiriac triad. Horus also wears a *shendyt* skirt, a three-part wig and a badly damaged headdress. He holds the *ankh* sign in his left hand and has his right arm around the waist of the pharaoh. Both Horus and the pharaoh bear animal's tails, a symbol of royal archaic clothing.

The slightly projecting eyes and full cheeks of the four figures are typical of Eighteenth-Dynasty sculpture but the flat pleats of the king's *nemes* are a characteristic of the end of that period. (M.T.)

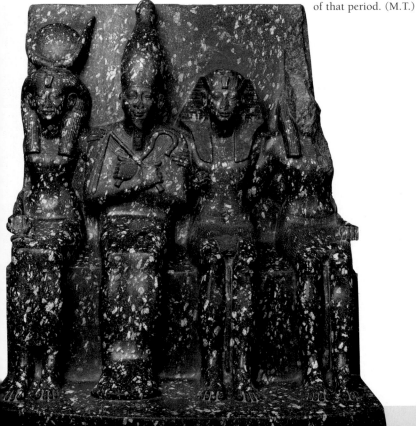

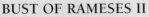

BUST OF RAMESES II

GRANITIC ROCK
HEIGHT 80 CM, WIDTH 70 CM
TANIS; NINETEENTH DYNASTY, REIGN
OF RAMESES II (1279-1212 BC)

ROOM 9

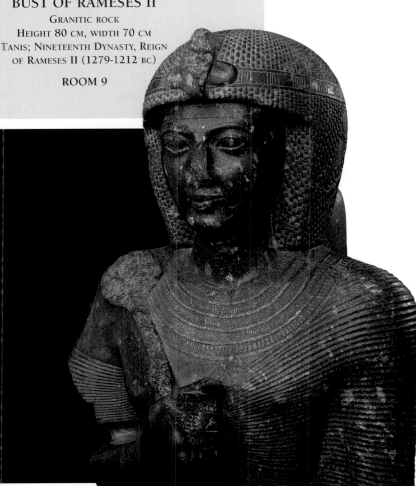

The bust comes from a seated statue of the famous pharaoh. He is portrayed with a short wig held in place by a band with a uraeus serpent. Although his nose is missing, it can be seen that the king is represented as a young man with a round face, jutting eyebrows, rather narrow eyes, and a calm smile on his mouth with the ends of lips slightly raised. Rameses wears a wide necklace made from many strings of pearls and a pleated garment with long, wide sleeves. What remains of his left arm lies by his body while his right arm is folded across his chest gripping the *heqa*, the hook-shaped scepter that was a symbol of royalty. The pharaoh's wrist is adorned with a bracelet decorated with the eye of Horus, the *udjat*, a symbol of good health and divine perfection. Several details of the statue, such as the pleated garment and short wig, repeat motifs that were previously fashionable in regal sculpture in the Eighteenth Dynasty (1550-1291 BC).

The overall impression given by this statue is a sumptuousness that suitably becomes the figure of one of Egypt's most famous pharaohs. (M.T.)

BUST OF MERENPTAH

GRANITIC ROCK; HEIGHT 91 CM, WIDTH 58 CM; THEBES,
"TEMPLE OF THE MILLIONS OF YEARS" OF MERENPTAH
EXCAVATION BY W.M.F. PETRIE (1896); NINETEENTH
DYNASTY, REIGN OF MERENPTAH (1212-1202 BC)

ROOM 10

This bust comes from a seated statue of the pharaoh Merenptah, the thirteenth child and successor of Rameses II. The idealized portrait shows the sovereign in the bloom of his youth (though in fact we know that he did not ascend the throne until he was at least fifty years of age). He wears a large necklace partially covered by the *nemes* headdress that consists of three pieces of striped fabric, one of which hangs down the back of the head and the other two that fall onto the shoulders and the upper part of the chest.

The uraeus serpent is positioned on his forehead and he wears the false beard, a symbol of divinity. His eyes are narrow and hidden below heavy eyelids and double eyebrows; he has a thin nose, large ears, and a rather wide mouth.

Two of the five royal names of Merenptah are inscribed on his shoulders: The Lord of the Two Lands, The sacred ram of Ra, beloved of Amun" and "The Lord of Diadems, The beloved of Ptah who is satisfied with justice." (M.T.)

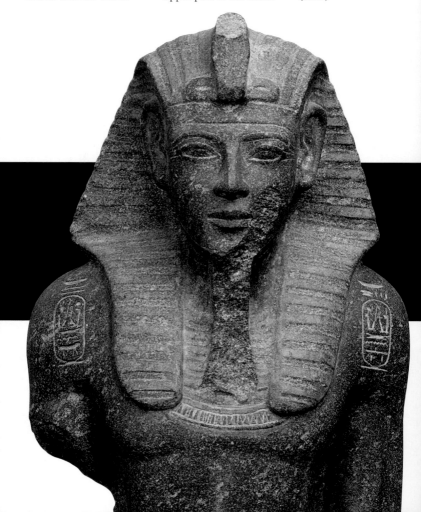

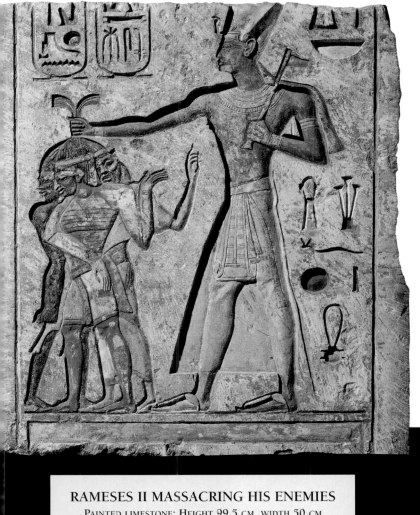

RAMESES II MASSACRING HIS ENEMIES

PAINTED LIMESTONE; HEIGHT 99.5 CM, WIDTH 50 CM
MIT RAHINA; PURCHASED BY THE MUSEUM (1917)
NINETEENTH DYNASTY, REIGN OF RAMESES II (1279-1212 BC)

ROOM 10

The theme of the pharaoh massacring his enemies was an ancient one and can be seen in royal images since the Protodynastic Period, for example the Narmer Tablet. In this example, Rameses II wears an elaborate garment, the blue crown, and sandals, and holds three prisoners by their hair. In his right hand he grips an axe with which he is about to strike his prisoners. The facial features and hair styles of the three men indicate that they belong to three different peoples: the Nubians, the Libyans, and the Syrians. The block was reused in one of Merenptah's buildings. (M.T.)

COLOSSAL STATUE OF TUTANKHAMUN

PAINTED QUARTZITE; HEIGHT 285 CM, WIDTH 73 CM
MEDINET HABU, "TEMPLE OF THE MILLIONS OF YEARS"
OF AY AND HOREMHEB; EXCAVATION BY THE ORIENTAL
INSTITUTE OF CHICAGO (1931); EIGHTEENTH DYNASTY
REIGN OF TUTANKHAMUN (1333-1323 BC)

ROOM 10

The pharaoh is depicted in the customary pose of advancing with his left leg. He wears the double crown (of which only the base remains) and the *nemes* headdress still faintly colored yellow and blue. His arms, legs, crown, part of the rear support, *nemes*, and right shoulder are all fragmentary but traces of polychromy can still be made out on the king's face.

Tutankhamun wears the royal uraeus serpent on his forehead (only partially conserved), the false beard on his chin, a pleated skirt (the *shendyt*), and a large seven-string necklace. A dagger with a falcon's head is inserted in his skirt, and a cartouche in the center of his waistband bears the name of Horemheb. The statue is attributed to Tutankhamun by stylistic motifs but it was appropriated by his immediate successor, Ay, who substituted his cartouche with that of the boy king and transferred it to his own "Temple of the Millions of Years." The next occupant of the throne, Horemheb, himself took possession both of the statue and the temple. Dating of the statue to the reign of Tutankhamun is certain as it displays many characteristics that were typical of the period of Amarna art: the slightly swollen stomach, the narrow eyes edged by a thick line, and the fleshy lips.

The statue was found in the transversal hypostyle room in the Temple of Ay where it stood on the south side of the far door. It was matched by a similar statue on the north side. (M.T.)

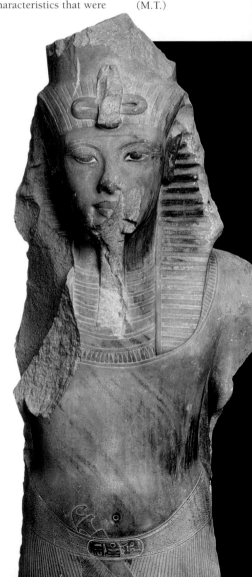

STATUE OF RAMESES II AS A CHILD AND THE GOD HORUN

GRANITIC ROCK AND LIMESTONE (FACE
OF THE FALCON); H. 231 CM; TANIS;
EXCAVATION BY P. MONTET (1934);
NINETEENTH DYNASTY. REIGN OF
RAMESES II (1279-1212 BC)

ROOM 10

The statue represents Rameses II as a child sitting naked and raising a finger to his mouth. This detail and the plait of hair that falls onto his right shoulder represent the iconography of children in Egyptian art. He wears a cap with the royal uraeus serpent topped by a sun disk and holds a rush in his right hand. This set of elements forms a puzzle that represents the name of the king himself: the sun disk is read as Ra, the boy as *mes* and the rush as *su* that together read *Ra-mes-su*, the name of the pharaoh.

The boy sits under the protection of the god Horun, a god from the mountains of Lebanon that had strong warlike connotations. Horun is shown in a stylized manner in the form of a falcon. What is unusual is the fact that the god's face was added at a later time, indeed, it was found separate from the statue in a building that was probably a restoration workshop where the statue was being repaired. The head of the falcon may have been damaged during transportation to Tanis as originally it stood in Giza where the cult of Harmakhis-Horun was particularly widespread. The worship of Horun was probably introduced into Egypt by prisoners of war and workers that Thutmosis III had brought back from his military campaigns in the Middle East to work on the necropolis at Memphis. Since the middle of the Eighteenth Dynasty, Horun was associated with the god Harmakhis ("Horus of the Horizon"), which was a local manifestation of the royal and heavenly deity personified by the imposing Sphinx of Giza.
(M.T.)

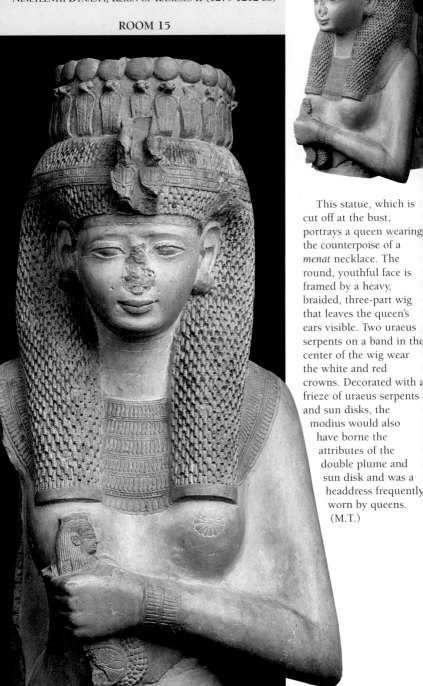

BUST OF QUEEN MERIT-AMUN

PAINTED LIMESTONE; HEIGHT 75 CM, WIDTH 44 CM, DEPTH 44 CM
WEST THEBES, RAMESSEUM, TEMPLE OF MERIT-AMUN
EXCAVATION BY W.M. FLINDERS PETRIE (1896)
NINETEENTH DYNASTY, REIGN OF RAMESES II (1279-1212 BC)

ROOM 15

This statue, which is cut off at the bust, portrays a queen wearing the counterpoise of a *menat* necklace. The round, youthful face is framed by a heavy, braided, three-part wig that leaves the queen's ears visible. Two uraeus serpents on a band in the center of the wig wear the white and red crowns. Decorated with a frieze of uraeus serpents and sun disks, the modius would also have borne the attributes of the double plume and sun disk and was a headdress frequently worn by queens. (M.T.)

STELA OF BAY

PAINTED LIMESTONE; HEIGHT 24.5 CM, WIDTH 14 CM
DEIR AL-MEDINA, *TEMENOS* IN THE TEMPLE OF HATHOR
EXCAVATION BY E. BARAIZE (1912)
NINETEENTH-TWENTIETH DYNASTIES (1291-1075 BC)

ROOM 15

This stela was dedicated by Bay to the god-ram Amun and comes from the workers' village of Deir al-Medina. It still retains its vivid colors, in particular the three pairs of ears painted blue, yellow, and green on the left side. These represent the ears of the god that "listens to prayers." This form of Amun was one that the more modest social classes worshipped during the New Kingdom when cults of personal worship grew alongside the official cults practised in the temples and at court.

The owner of the stela was a worker in the village and was portrayed on the left side of it; he kneels with his hands raised in an act of adoration separated from the divine ears of the god by a vertical line. The inscription above Bay says "Adoration of Amun-Ra by his servant in the Place of Truth, Bay." The name "Place of Truth" refers to the royal tomb.

Two rams with the plumes of Amun, a sun disk, and a uraeus serpent on their heads are shown in the upper part of the stela and each animal bears the inscription "Amun-Ra, the perfect ram." A jug on a small table is shown between them.
(M.T.)

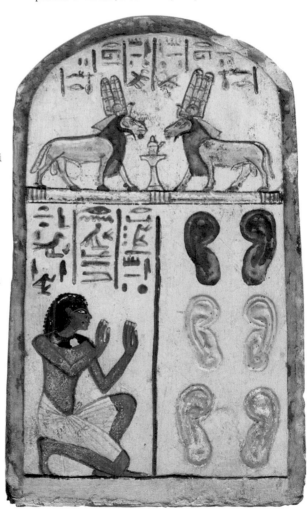

Rameses III was portrayed here as the standard bearer of the god Amun-Ra. As he marches, his left arm is held against the sacred staff of Amun topped by the head of a ram, the animal that is sacred to this god. The king wears a pleated skirt adorned with a row of five uraeus serpents with sun disks on their heads suspended from the head of a wild cat. Rameses wears a wig that covers his ears and has the royal uraeus serpent on the

STATUE OF RAMESES III STANDIN●
GRANITIC ROCK; HEIGHT 140 CM;
KARNAK, TEMPLE OF AMUN-RA, COURT OF THE CACHET
EXCAVATION BY G. LEGRAIN (1905); TWENTIETH
DYNASTY, REIGN OF RAMESES III (1184-1153 BC)

ROOM 15

front. His face is regular with delicate features that contrasts with the muscularity of his upper body. A different name of Rameses III is engraved on each arm; one of the other names of his royal protocol can be seen on

the waistband of his skirt and two more on his staff: the name of Horus is "the powerful bull whose royalt is great"; the Two Ladies: "of the many jubilees like Tatenen"; the king of Uppe and Lower Egypt: "Usermaatre Meryamun"; and the Son of Ra, lord of the crowns: "Rameses, prince of Heliopolis." The only one missing is Rameses' name as Horus.

Placed at the entrance to the temple, the function of this statue was to replace the king during religious processions when he was absent, on which occasion it was the responsibility of the high priest to carry the royal insignia.

Rameses III was the las great pharaoh of the New Kingdom and died during palace conspiracy as has been discussed by P. Harris I. The text on the statue describes Rameses' religiou devoutness and the many donations he made to the most important temples in the country. Artistic inspiration during his reign was based on that of Rameses II whom Rameses III consciously attempted t emulate: he too built a temple in west Thebes, at Medinet Habu, that was inspired by the Ramesseum the "Temple of the Million of Years" built by his predecessor.   (M.T.)

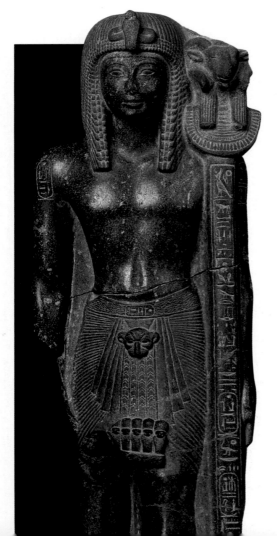

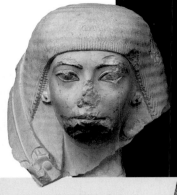

STATUETTES OF
NAKHTMIN AND HIS WIFE

LIMESTONE; HEIGHT: NAKHTMIN 34 CM
WIFE 85 CM; PROVENANCE UNKNOWN
PURCHASED IN 1897; END OF THE
EIGHTEENTH DYNASTY (SECOND HALF OF
THE 14TH CENTURY BC)

ROOM 15

The two statues were originally part of a group that was supported by a rear pillar with a rounded tip. Nakhtmin's almond eyes and youthful face are framed by a long curly wig, his ears are pierced and the folds of his neck are marked by two engraved lines. A fragment of the fan that the functionary carried and which indicated Nakhtmin's high social rank can still be seen on the right.

His wife is dressed in a pleated garment that shows off her figure and she wears a heavy wig over her refined face. Her eyes are also almond-shaped and made up with a black line like her eyebrows, and her lips still bear some of the original red paint. The wig is formed by long curls that end in tightly knitted tassels. She wears a six-string necklace around her neck and a diadem on her forehead decorated with lotuses that unite in the front in a bunch of three flowers; she holds a counterpoise of a necklace in her left hand.

The style of the two sculptures suggests they were carved during the post-Amarna Period. An inscription on the back of the statue of Nakhtmin's wife gives her husband's titles: prince, royal scribe, supreme commander, and, perhaps, viceroy of Kush. The epithet "son of the king, of his body" tells us that Nakhtmin was a member of the royal family. His name is combined with that of the god Min and indicates he was from Akhmin, the same city that the last pharaoh of the Eighteenth Dynasty, Ay, came from and to whom he may have been related.

The faces of the two statues were deliberately damaged, perhaps during the Christian era. The nose, mouth, and hands were chiselled off to prevent the statues from breathing in a superstitious act that was reminiscent of pharaonic Egypt.
(M.T.)

The stela belonged to a vizier and governor of the City (Thebes) named either Rahotep or Parahotep. There were two viziers with this name during the reign of Rameses II: one was buried at Sedment, a village in the southern part of Fayum, and the other was originally from Abydos, though some experts, like W. Helck (1958: 317), consider them to have been the same person. If that were the case, the following three objects belonging to him remain: a naophorous granite statue with the image of the god Ptah, and two canopic vases, one in the British Museum and the other in

STELA OF RAHOTEP
GRANITE; HEIGHT 157 CM
SAQQARA, SOUTH-WEST OF THE MONASTERY
OF APA GEREMIA; NINETEENTH DYNASTY
REIGN OF RAMESES II (1279-1212)

ROOM 15

the Royal Museums in Brussels. These objects and the stela all come from the same zone of the necropolis at Saqqara which suggests, along with a few remains of an architectural construction, that his tomb was built here.

The stela is decorated with a scene in the upper register in which Rahotep is shown adoring Osiris. He wears the vizier's costume of a wide tunic supported with braces, and has the shaved head of a priest. He holds a fan in his left hand as a sign that he bore the honorific court title Fan-holder on the right of the king. Behind the mummy image of Osiris there is another deity (Apis) with the head of a bull and a sun disk on his head. The ten lines of hieroglyphs praise the gods of the necropolis in Memphis, Ptah and Anubis, so that they might look kindly upon the *ka* of the deceased.
(M.T.)

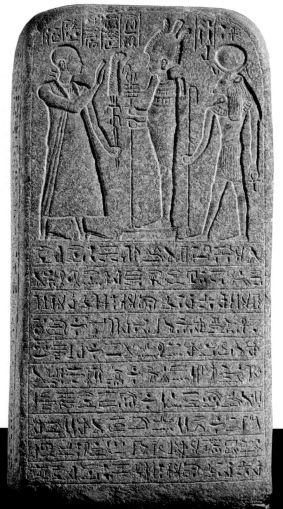

STATUE OF SETY I

ALABASTER; HEIGHT 238 CM
KARNAK, TEMPLE OF AMUN-RA, COURT OF THE CACHETTE
EXCAVATION BY G. LEGRAIN (1903-04)
NINETEENTH DYNASTY, REIGN OF SETY I (1289-1279 BC)

ROOM 14

The extent to which this statue was carved in the stylistic traditions of the end of the Eighteenth Dynasty leads one to think that Sety I may have appropriated it for his own use and had his own cartouches engraved on it. The idealized face, the extended almond-shaped eyes, and the full mouth are all elements to be seen in post-Amarna statuary.

The statue is created from different materials: the head and bust are sculpted in a compact alabaster, the legs and hands are in a veined stone, and the clothes and other missing parts would probably have been made in another stone. Sety I probably wore the blue crown (in yet another material) while his eyes were most likely inlaid with limestone and obsidian. The eyebrows, also missing, may well have been carved from another material, perhaps lapis lazuli. There is a large hole under the chin that was used to add the false beard of royalty, and the pharaoh's *shendyt* skirt was lined with gold leaf and decorated with an animal protome on the front. The statue was disassembled and stored in the Cachette at Karnak. (M.T.)

COLUMN OF THUTMOSIS IV
APPROPRIATED BY RAMESES II
Painted sandstone; Height 162 cm, diameter 96 cm
Elephantine; Eighteenth Dynasty, Reign
of Thutmosis IV (1397-1387 bc) and Nineteenth
Dynasty, Reign of Rameses II (1279-1212 bc)
ROOM 14

The column originally was part of a building constructed by Thutmosis IV whose royal protocol is inscribed and painted in yellow on one of the facades. Later, Rameses II added his own image and titles but without erasing those of his predecessor. Finally, during the reign of Emperor Trajan (98-117 AD), the column was divided into three parts and reused in the foundations of a Roman building.

The relief decoration still retains its bright colors. Rameses II is shown with a falcon on his head grasping the *shen* circle, the symbol of royal power, in its claws. The pharaoh offers flowers in the temple in ceremonial dress with a short skirt and a transparent upper garment of which we clearly see the right sleeve. He is adorned with a wide necklace with torques decoration and the blue crown with the royal uraeus on the front. He holds a bunch of flowers in his right hand and three lotus flowers in his left with the stems wrapped around his hand. The king's titles as King of Upper and Lower Egypt and Son of Ra are inscribed below the right open wing of the falcon and his coronation name *"User-maat-Ra Setep-en-Ra"* is inscribed on the waistband of his skirt. (M.T.)

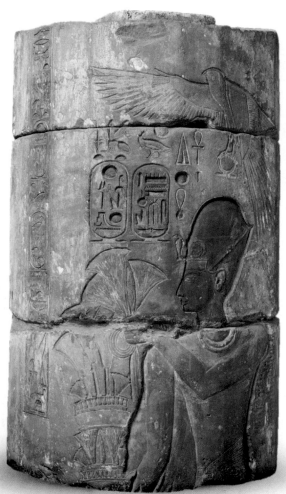

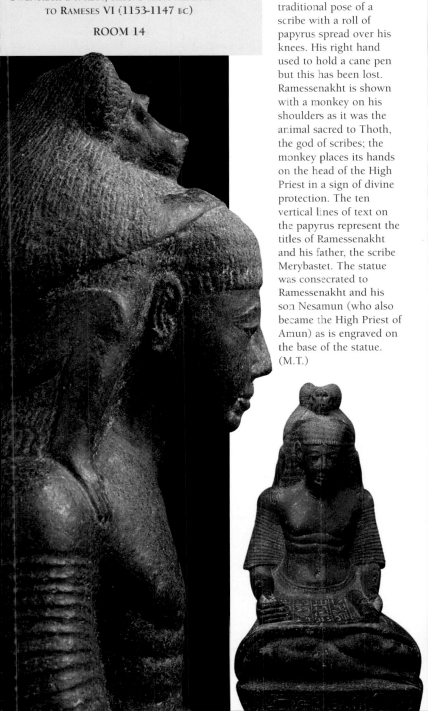

RAMESSENAKHT SEATED AS A SCRIBE

GRANITIC STONE; HEIGHT 75 CM, WIDTH 43 CM; KARNAK
TEMPLE OF AMUN-RA, COURT OF THE CACHETTE
EXCAVATION BY G. LEGRAIN (1904)
TWENTIETH DYNASTY, REIGNS FROM RAMESES IV
TO RAMESES VI (1153-1147 BC)

ROOM 14

Ramessenakht was the High Priest of Amun during the second half of the Twentieth Dynasty and is shown here in the traditional pose of a scribe with a roll of papyrus spread over his knees. His right hand used to hold a cane pen but this has been lost. Ramessenakht is shown with a monkey on his shoulders as it was the animal sacred to Thoth, the god of scribes; the monkey places its hands on the head of the High Priest in a sign of divine protection. The ten vertical lines of text on the papyrus represent the titles of Ramessenakht and his father, the scribe Merybastet. The statue was consecrated to Ramessenakht and his son Nesamun (who also became the High Priest of Amun) as is engraved on the base of the statue. (M.T.)

STATUE OF TJAY
AND HIS WIFE NAIA

Limestone; Height 90 cm; Saqqara; Excavation by
A. Mariette (1862); New Kingdom (1550-1070 bc)

ROOM 14

Tjay and Naia sit on the same high-backed seat. The man rests his right hand face up on his knee and has his left hand closed in a fist placed on his thigh. The woman has her left hand face up on her knee and holds her right arm around the waist of her husband. Osiris enthroned beneath a canopy is portrayed on the backrest between the couple and on the lower part of the seat there is a couple sitting opposite one another smelling lotus flowers. The rear of the seat is decorated with the carving of a seated man holding a piece of cloth and a *sekhem* staff in his left hand and a lotus flower in his right.

Hieroglyphic texts are inscribed on Tjay's skirt, on the base where the couple rest their feet, above the image of Osiris, and on the figures on the rear of the backrest. They all contain offering formulas to Ra-Harakhti and Ptah-Sokari in favor of the *ka* of the couple. (M.T.)

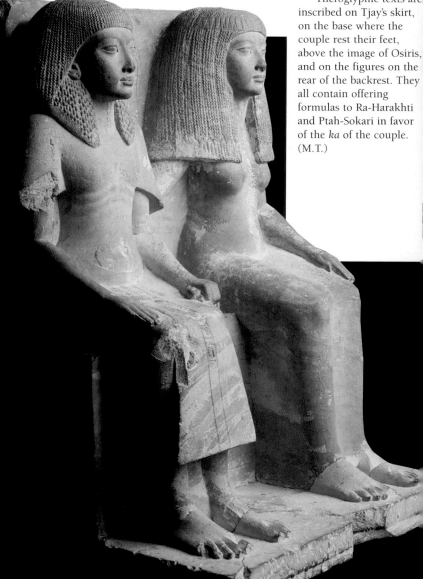

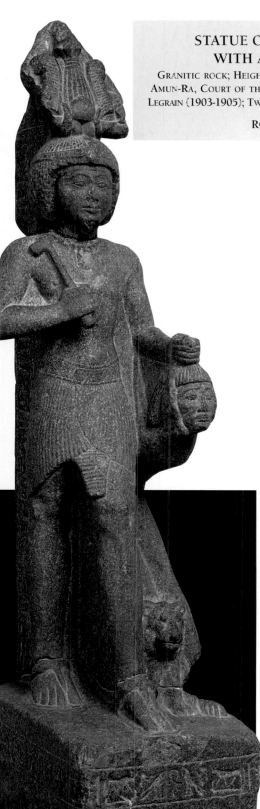

STATUE OF RAMESES VI WITH A PRISONER

GRANITIC ROCK; HEIGHT 74 CM; KARNAK, TEMPLE OF AMUN-RA, COURT OF THE CACHETTE; EXCAVATION BY G. LEGRAIN (1903-1905); TWENTIETH DYNASTY (1187-1075 BC)

ROOM 14

Rameses VI advances with his left leg in the standard pose of Egyptian male statuary, holding an axe in his right hand and a Libyan by the hair with his left. A lion can be seen between the legs of the Libyan. The king wears a pleated skirt with a wide belt and a pair of sandals on his feet. The prisoner has medium long hair with a long curl on the right side and he wears earrings. This right leg is covered by a long skirt but his left is bare.

Rameses' complete list of titles is inscribed on the rear support. The columns on the sides of the support give formulas that declare his devotion to Amun-Ra and to Hapi while two lines of text on the base provide further royal titles in parallel.

The statue was found in three pieces and reassembled. The original colors with which it was painted can be seen on Rameses' skirt and the mane of the lion. (M.T.)

The origin of this relief is unknown. It depicts three rows of prisoners, some with scarred faces, who are being held by the hair by the pharaoh about to hit them with his club. The prisoner shown face on in the last row at the bottom wears a two-string necklace with a pendant in the form of a fly. All of them have short curly hair and African features.

The depiction of the pharaoh triumphing over his enemies is a common scene in the iconography of the New Kingdom, for example, there is a similar but gigantic scene on the south wall of the seventh pylon at the temple of Amun-Ra at Karnak in which Thutmosis III is shown grasping a group of Asiatics by the hair. The other side of the pylon shows his triumph over the peoples who lived to the south of Egypt.

This relief is on a much smaller scale but it is probable that, as the guardian god of the kingdom, the god Amun-Ra would have been portrayed on the other side of the relief in analogy to the scenes at Karnak.
(M.T.)

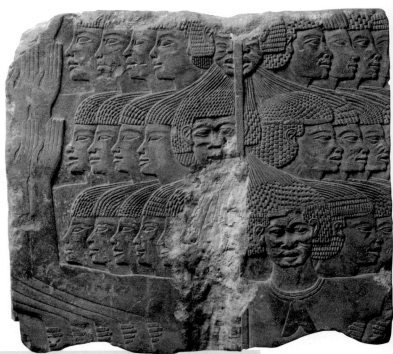

STATUE OF A STANDARD BEARER

GREEN BRECCIA; HEIGHT 48 CM; KARNAK, TEMPLE OF
AMUN-RA, COURT OF THE CACHETTE; EXCAVATION BY G.
LEGRAIN (1903-1904); END OF THE EIGHTEENTH
DYNASTY (14TH CENTURY BC) AND TWENTY-SECOND
DYNASTY, REIGN OF SHESHONQ II (890 BC)

ROOM 20

Stylistically, this statue dates from the end of the Eighteenth or the start of the Nineteenth Dynasties, and it bears the following inscription: "The High Priest of Amun-Ra, king of the ods, supreme commander of the army, Prince Sheshonq, justified, son of the Lord of the Two Lands, Osorkon Meryamun."

It was, therefore, used by Prince Sheshonq, the son of Osorkon I during the Twenty-second Dynasty (kings of Libyan origin). Sheshonq, the High Priest of Amun, would have reigned after his father but died before him and was buried at Tanis, which was still the political capital of the country.

The statue shows Sheshonq with all his insignia, in particular, the standard of a female deity with a wig, uraeus serpent, and a modius with the cow's horns and sun disk of Hathor. It would therefore seem to be the goddess Hathor but it might also represent Isis who had assumed many iconographic characteristics of Hathor by the end of the Eighteenth Dynasty. It is surprising that the statue bears the effigy of Amun-Ra with the *was* scepter on its chest and the effigy of Osiris on the skirt and it is probable that the two figures date from the time of the statue's reuse during the Libyan Twenty-second Dynasty. (M.T.)

STATUE OF SETY I AS A STANDARD BEARER

GRAYWACKE; HEIGHT 22 CM; ABYDOS; NINETEENTH DYNASTY, REIGN OF SETY I (1289-1279 BC)

ROOM 25

The statue, which shows the king walking with his arms by his sides, displays instances of Amarna style, in particular the modeling of the heavily pleated garment and the wavy braids of the wig with the uraeus serpent. In contrast, the facial features of the pharaoh suggest characteristics of the statuary produced during the reigns of the four Thutmoses, for example, the slightly aquiline nose and the straight line of the mouth. Part of the sculpture was a standard with the emblem of a deity but that has been lost and cannot now be identified. The statue comes from Abydos where Sety I had a temple and cenotaph built in honor of Osiris. (M.T.)

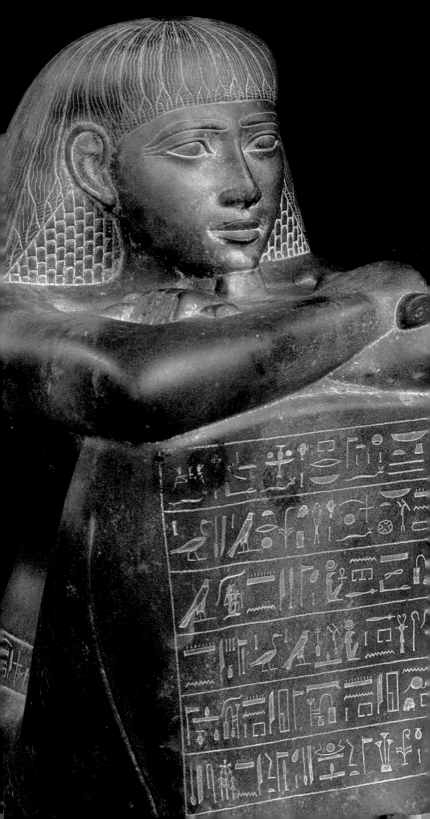

THE THIRD
INTERMEDIATE PERIOD
AND THE LATE PERIOD

The Third Intermediate Period conventionally began with the close of the New Kingdom at the end of the Twentieth Dynasty though signs of political and military crisis had been present during the reigns of the last three Rameses'. During the reign of Rameses XI, a civil war broke out led by the pharaoh on the one hand and the High Priest of Amun, Amenhotep, on the other; the war was brought to an end by the intervention of the royal prince of Cush, Panehesy, who ended up governing all of the area of Thebes. The foreign troops of Mishuesh and Libu participated in great numbers and then probably settled full-time in the Delta. In the nineteenth year of his reign, Rameses XI proclaimed the beginning of a new era, "Year 1 of the Rebirth," with which he wanted to inaugurate a new program of order and reorganization of the state.

However, it was at this same time that the star of Herihor, a military man perhaps of Libyan origin, began to rise. He succeeded in accumulating a number of important positions and appropriating royal prerogatives to the extent that he had his name inscribed in royal cartouches. This political shift occurred in tandem with an ideological change in the conception of the state that had begun in the Nineteenth Dynasty

CHAPTER 5
GROUND FLOOR

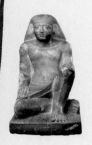

ITINERARY THROUGH ROOMS
20, 25, 24, 30, 40, 44, 45

210 CUBE STATUE
OF HOR,
ON OF ANKHKHONSU
chist; Height 51 CM
Karnak, Temple of
Amun-Ra, Court of
the Cachette;
Excavation by G.
Legrain (1904);
wenty-fifth Dynasty
(775-653 BC)

211 STATUE OF
PETIAMONNEBNESUTTAUY
Limestone;
Karnak,
Temple of Amun-Ra,
Court of the Cachette;
Excavation by G.
Legrain (1904);
Twenty-second
Dynasty
(945-718 BC)

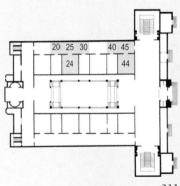

(1291-1185 BC) and which ended with the installation of a theocracy in the south of the country in which the gods of the Theban triad – Amun-Ra, Mut, and Khonsu – governed through the decisions made by their oracles. An illuminating text, *The report of Unamun*, in the 2nd Golenischeff papyrus, illustrates the weakness of the Egyptian monarchy during this period. The papyrus is dated to the Twenty-second Dynasty but refers to the events of the Twenty-first Dynasty and was written as a historical novel describing the adventures of a Theban functionary sent by Herihor to Lebanon with the aim of obtaining wood to build the sacred bark of Amun. The story reveals not just the little prestige that Egypt was held in beyond its borders but also the circumstances in which a certain Smendes governed the north of the country from Tanis as an administrator or regent of Lower Egypt, while the name of the pharaoh is not mentioned at all. In fact, the royal residence was moved from Pi-Rameses to Tanis at the start of the Twenty-first Dynasty (1075-945 BC) due to a series of natural and human factors.

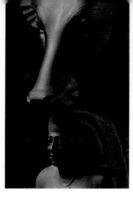

Meanwhile, the post of High Priest of Amun in Thebes had first passed to Piankh, then his son Pinedjem whose wife, Henuttauy, held the position of "Worshipper of Hathor." At the start of the Eighteenth Dynasty, the position of "God's Wife of Amun" had been instated and was first held by Queen Ahmes-Nefertari, the wife of Ahmes (1550-1525 BC). This function was initially purely honorific but had begun to play a political role by the start of the Twenty-first Dynasty.

Smendes' successor was Neferkara but he only reigned for a brief period before the ascent to the throne of Psusennes I, the son of the High Priest Pinedjem and Henuttauy, who thus reunited in a single person and single dynasty the royal personage and the most important religious function in Egypt. Psusennes was the first king to build his tomb in the sacred area of the Temple of Amun in

Tanis where secondary tombs held the mummies of his vizier, Undjebauendjed, and the pharaoh Amenemope (Psusennes' successor). Amenemope occupied a twin chamber to that of Psusennes that had originally been built for Psusennes' wife, Mutnedjemet, but she was buried elsewhere.

The internal struggles for priestly privileges of land and money, and the greed of the Libyan military contingents represented constant destabilizing forces for the Tanite Dynasty though the royal political decline of the period was not matched by a waning of artistic standards. It is true that following the construction of the Temple of Amun at Tanis by Psusennes I (much of which was built using materials from Pi-Rameses) building was curbed both in Tanis and Thebes until the era of the Libyan kings; however, the so-called "minor" arts such as jewelry, bronzework and pottery, besides painting and sculpture, continued to flourish.

The provincial areas of the kingdom had by now slipped out of the control both of the monarchs in Tanis and of the priests in Thebes

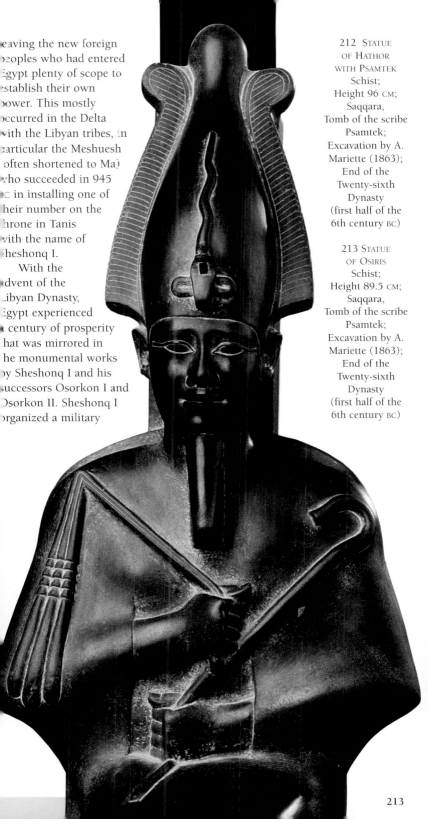

eaving the new foreign peoples who had entered Egypt plenty of scope to establish their own power. This mostly occurred in the Delta with the Libyan tribes, in particular the Meshuesh often shortened to Ma) who succeeded in 945 BC in installing one of their number on the throne in Tanis with the name of Sheshonq I.

With the advent of the Libyan Dynasty, Egypt experienced a century of prosperity that was mirrored in the monumental works by Sheshonq I and his successors Osorkon I and Osorkon II. Sheshonq I organized a military

212 STATUE OF HATHOR WITH PSAMTEK
Schist;
Height 96 CM;
Saqqara,
Tomb of the scribe Psamtek;
Excavation by A. Mariette (1863);
End of the Twenty-sixth Dynasty
(first half of the 6th century BC)

213 STATUE OF OSIRIS
Schist;
Height 89.5 CM;
Saqqara,
Tomb of the scribe Psamtek;
Excavation by A. Mariette (1863);
End of the Twenty-sixth Dynasty
(first half of the 6th century BC)

213

campaign against the Jewish kingdoms in Palestine in order to stem their growing power. The expedition was successful and resulted in a large booty of gold for the Egyptian treasury. Egyptian control was also re-established in Nubia which further enriched the coffers of the state.

For the first time since the reign of Rameses III, works to enlarge the Temple of Amun in Karnak were undertaken: two new colonnades known as the "Bubastite Portico" were built and their decoration begun.

The capital was moved to Bubastis – the city of the goddess Bastet – situated on the middle course of the Pelusiac branch of the Nile and embellished with new monuments. Osorkon I started a program of beautifying the city with the construction of monumental portals and colonnades with Hathoric capitals. The custom of placing royal tombs within the boundaries of sanctuaries continued in the Twenty-second Dynasty: the son of Osorkon I, Sheshonq II, was buried in the enclosure walls of the sanctuary of Amun-Ra at Tanis and the

Theban king, Harsiesi, who was co-regent with Osorkon II, was buried in the enclosure walls of the temple in Medinet-Habu.

The period during the end of the Twenty-second Dynasty and the start of the Twenty-fifth Dynasty was another epoch in the political splintering of Egypt. The country was divided into many more smaller princedoms of which Memphis and another one in the south of the country that had been known since the Middle Kingdom stand out. Around 713 BC, the third sovereign of the Twenty-fifth Dynasty and "Ethiopian" Dynasty, Piankhy, once again united Egypt. In 664 BC, an attempt at resistance by the Ethiopians against attacks by Assyria resulted in the sacking of the city of Thebes by Assurbanipal. This was a traumatic event for the Egyptians as the city of Amun had

remained unconquered for centuries.

Soon after these events, Psamtek I, the fourth king of the Twenty-sixth Dynasty "Saite" Dynasty (664-525 BC) and the puppet king of the Assyrians, succeeded in turning the situation in his favour and asserting himself in Memphis, Heracleopolis, and Thebes. Sais then became the capital of Egypt and its goddess, Neith, the principal deity. With regard to art, refined metal statuary took on great importance during the Twenty-second Dynasty and Twenty-third Dynasties, based on skilful use of various types of bronze, and encrustation with gold and silver. A resurgence of ancient models in statuary and reliefs had begun even before the "Saite Renaissance," in particular those from the Old, Middle, and New Kingdoms. Royal entitlements were also linked with the traditions of the greatest of ancient Egyptian epochs at the start of the 8th century BC. The Ethiopian kings promoted study of the ancient sacred scriptures and a return to classical religious tradition. Two

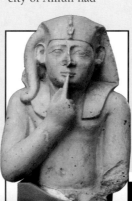

contemporaneous trends were seen in statuary: the traditional, austere productions of cube statues with faces that were often idealized, and the more realistic development that reproduced the facial features and robust physiques of the Cushite kings and functionaries.

One of the private functionaries to distinguish himself during the period of transition of the Twenty-fifth Dynasty to Twenty-seventh Dynasty was the Fourth Prophet of Amun and governor of Thebes, Montuemhat, who played an important political role in the period following the sack of Thebes and who was quick to recognize the authority of Psamtek I on his ascent to power. Montuemhat had many statues made of himself, portraying him both with the forms that were typical of the New Kingdom and in a more realistic style. Like other of his fellow nobles, he had a magnificent, large, and complex tomb built for himself, in Asasif near Thebes, with a brick pylon and an open courtyard that preceded a series of underground chambers supported by pillars.
(M.T.)

214 BUST OF THE STATUE OF PSAMTEK
Limestone;
Height 14 cm;
Twenty-sixth Dynasty,
Reign of Psamtek II
(595-589 BC)

215 LOW RELIEF OF HORHOTEP
Limestone;
Height 126 cm;
Tell al-Farain (Buto);
Excavation by H. Gauthier (1920)
Thirtieth Dynasty
(380-342 BC)

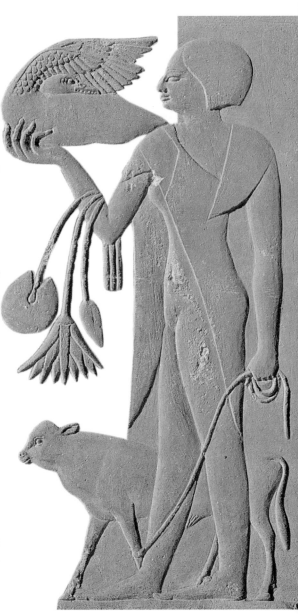

STATUE OF OSORKON III

Painted limestone; Height 18 cm
Karnak, Temple of Amun-Ra Court of the Cachette
Excavation by G. Legrain (1904-1905)
Twenty-third Dynasty
Reign of Osorkon III (788-760 bc)

ROOM 20

This small statue was found in pieces in the Cachette in the Temple at Karnak. It portrays the pharaoh Osorkon III as he pushes Amun's sacred boat. Despite being

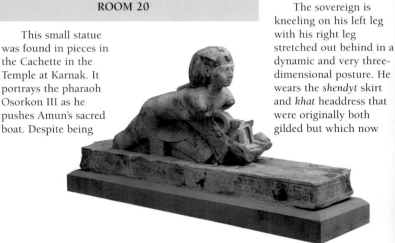

Osorkon II, king of the Twenty-second Dynasty, and who can only be distinguished by the epithet "son of Isis" instead of Osorkon II's "son of Bastet."

The sovereign is kneeling on his left leg with his right leg stretched out behind in a dynamic and very three-dimensional posture. He wears the *shendyt* skirt and *khat* headdress that were originally both gilded but which now

only partial – the oars and stern of the boat are missing – the remaining sections are sufficient for an understanding of the complete statue. The sovereign is identified by an inscription along the edge of the base on which the figure rests; he is the King of Upper and Lower Egypt, *Usermaatra Setepenamun*, the Son of

Ra *Osorkon Meryumon*, king of the Twenty-third Dynasty. During this period there were different successions of kings at Thebes, Hermopolis, Heracleopolis, and Tanis, and in some cases, the various rulers even had the same royal names!

This was the case of Osorkon III who had the same royal names as

have no more than a reddish tinge.

The sculpture was probably a royal votive offering to commemorate the gift of a portable boat to the god or the launching of a boat to carry the statue of Amun-Ra to Luxor to celebrate the "Beautiful Festival of the Valley."
(M.T.)

NAOPHOROUS STATUE OF PSAMTEKSANEITH

Scist; Height 44.5 cm
Mit Rahina (Memphis)
Twenty-seventh Dynasty (6th-5th century bc)

ROOM 25

A naophorous statue shows a *naos* (shrine) containing the image of a god held in front of a

functionary or a priest who may be either kneeling or standing. This type of statue

appeared during the Nineteenth Dynasty but gained in popularity during the Twenty-first.

The figure in this statue is Psamteksaneith, the "superintendent of all the king's works made from silver or gold," in other words, he was

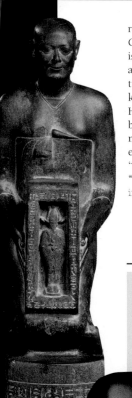

responsible for the Crown Jewels. His head is shaved and he wears a Persian V-necked tunic with a long wrap knotted at his chest. His head and face have been so carefully modelled that they have elicited the comments "schematic realism" and "start of true portraiture in the Late Period"

(Bothmer 1960: 78). The man's eyelids are heavy, his eyes ringed with bags, his cheeks marked by deep lines, and his cheekbones sunken. He has a slight smile on his thin lips.

The base, the rear support, and all four of the front edges of the *naos* are inscribed. (M.T.)

BLOCK STATUE OF AHMES
BASALT; HEIGHT 70 CM, WIDTH 30 CM
KARNAK, TEMPLE OF AMUN-RA, COURT OF THE CACHETTE
EXCAVATION BY G. LEGRAIN (1904)
TWENTY-SIXTH DYNASTY (664-5255 BC)

ROOM 25

The figure sculpted in the polished basalt is Ahmes, the priest of Amun, son of Pakharkhonsu. The front of Ahmes cloak is engraved and another line of text is found on the base of the statue. The figure wears a piece of cloth over his shoulders and a slight smile marks the idealized features of his face.

Block statues like this were often placed in the enclosure walls of a temple with the text of an "appeal to the living" or the biography of the figure portrayed. An "appeal to the living" was a plea from the deceased to those who passed before it to recite the offerings formula on the statue and not to let his name be forgotten. (M.T.)

217

STATUE OF MONTUEMHAT
AND HIS SON NESPTAH

GRANITIC ROCK; HEIGHT 34 CM; KARNAK; TEMPLE OF
AMUN-RA, COURT OF THE CACHETTE; EXCAVATION BY G.
LEGRAIN (1904); END OF THE FIFTEENTH – START OF THE
SIXTEENTH DYNASTY (MID-7TH CENTURY BC)

ROOM 25

Only the upper section of the damaged statue remains: it shows the Fourth Prophet of Amun, Montuemhat, with his son Nesptah on a stela. Their smiling faces have been sculpted rather conventionally with bulging

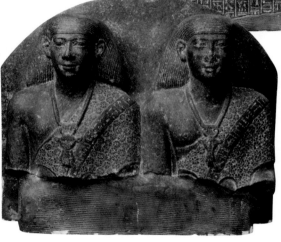

eyes below thick eyebrows. The two figures wear striped wigs and leopards' skins which were a form of clothing typical of the priesthood. Both father and son have the *bat* insignia of Hathor around their neck in which the cow's horns take the shape of a lyre. The band of text that starts at their left shoulders gives their names and titles. The sun disk and two uraeus serpents are carved at the top of the stela.

On the front of the slab,

two symmetrical scenes are crowned by the sun disk flanked by two uraeus serpents: on one side Montuemhat makes offerings to Amun, Ra-Harakhti, and Atum; on the other Nesptah makes offerings to Isis, Osiris, and Montuemhat, his father. Hieroglyphs in the lower section describe the scene giving the names of the gods and other individuals. The "Sait formula" (an invocation to the god of the city to protect the *ka* of

the deceased) is given twice on the edge of the stela, once each on behalf of Montuemhat and Nesptah.

Although Montuemhat was a rich and powerful man, we know little about him. He was active under Taharqa (690-664 BC), the sixth king of the Twenty-fifth Dynasty, and was the *sharru* of Thebes (an Assyrian term that corresponded to the Egyptian *iri-pat haty-a*, "prince and governor of a *nome*") during the Assyrian dominion (671-663 BC ca). Montuemhat ended his career during the reign of pharaoh Psamtek I (664-610 BC). His family numbered many dignitaries whose responsibilities lay in the temples of Amun and Montu.
(M.T.)

HEAD OF SHABAKA

PINK GRANITE; HEIGHT 97 CM
KARNAK
TWENTY-FIFTH DYNASTY
REIGN OF SHABAKA (713-698 BC)

ROOM 25

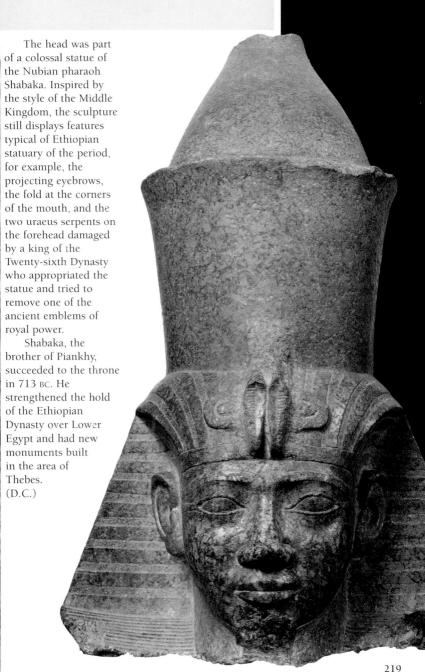

The head was part of a colossal statue of the Nubian pharaoh Shabaka. Inspired by the style of the Middle Kingdom, the sculpture still displays features typical of Ethiopian statuary of the period, for example, the projecting eyebrows, the fold at the corners of the mouth, and the two uraeus serpents on the forehead damaged by a king of the Twenty-sixth Dynasty who appropriated the statue and tried to remove one of the ancient emblems of royal power.

Shabaka, the brother of Piankhy, succeeded to the throne in 713 BC. He strengthened the hold of the Ethiopian Dynasty over Lower Egypt and had new monuments built in the area of Thebes.
(D.C.)

BAS-RELIEF OF HORHOTEP
LIMESTONE; HEIGHT 126 CM
TELL AL-FARAIN (BUTO)
EXCAVATION BY H. GAUTHIER (1920)
THIRTIETH DYNASTY (380-342 BC)

ROOM 24

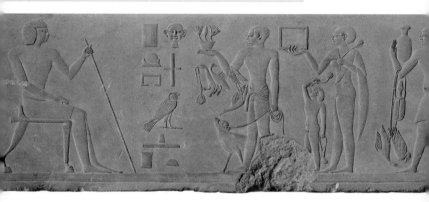

The relief is topped by a rounded molding and depicts a procession bearing offerings towards Horhotep, the priest of Buto and the main figure in the scene. Horhotep is shown seated on a lion's paw seat holding a long staff in his left hand and wearing a short wig and skirt. Both his pose and clothing are typical of the iconography of the functionaries of the Old Kingdom. The hieroglyphic inscription in front of Horhotep contains his name and titles. The bearers have been illustrated individually and are separated by figures of children waving flowers or of lambs with their heads raised. The men and women in the procession have round wigs and wear either a short skirt, a draped cloak, or just a loincloth. They all carry offerings of either birds, cows, pigs, jars, boxes, flowers, or baskets of fruit.

The theme of bearers of offerings was a return to motifs from the Old Kingdom taken up during the Late Period, but the interpretation of artists during the Thirtieth Dynasty was very different. The bodies of the human figures are rounder and they are arranged with empty spaces between them.

The size and rounded molding of the relief meant that it and similar reliefs were long considered an architectural element but, in fact, they are too thin for that function and so are now thought to have been the decoration on the outer walls of a type of tomb that was common above all in the Delta during the Saite Period. In this type of tomb the shrine acted as a crypt to protect the mummy from damp and it was here that the reliefs were probably fixed to the upper part of the walls.
(M.T.)

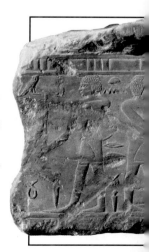

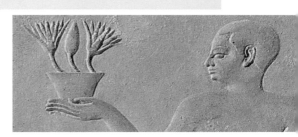

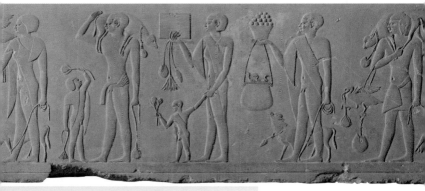

BAS-RELIEF OF
NEFERSESHEM-PSAMTEK

LIMESTONE; HEIGHT 30 CM, WIDTH 134 CM
MIT RAHINA; EXCAVATION BY A. MARIETTE (1860)
THIRTIETH DYNASTY (380-342 BC)

ROOM 24

Topped by a molding with a molding with bull decorations, this low relief comes from the tomb of Neferseshem-Psammetichus, the scribe of the divine book.

A functionary (perhaps the linen superintendent) appears to be closing one of the two chests while another presents two cups. The scene is symmetrically presented on the other side, but in that scene another functionary is opening the chest. The relief continues to the left with a fragmentary scene in which we see only a man with his arms stretched out in front. All the figures wear a short wig and skirt. Both their clothing and postures are typical of Old Kingdom iconography as was characteristic of the art of the Late Period. (M.T.)

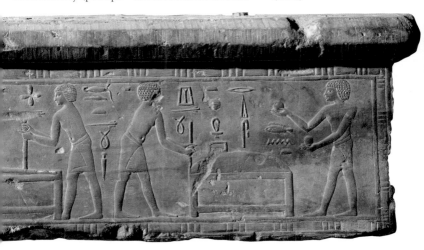

STATUE OF ISIS
STATUE OF HATHOR WITH PSAMTEK
STATUE OF OSIRIS

ISIS: SCHIST, HEIGHT 90 CM, WIDTH 20 CM
HATHOR: SCHIST, HEIGHT 96 CM, WIDTH 29 CM
OSIRIS: SCHIST, HEIGHT 89.5 CM, WIDTH 28 CM
SAQQARA, TOMB OF THE SCRIBE PSAMTEK
EXCAVATION BY A. MARIETTE (1863)
END OF THE TWENTY-SIXTH DYNASTY (FIRST HALF OF THE 6TH CENTURY BC)

ROOM 24

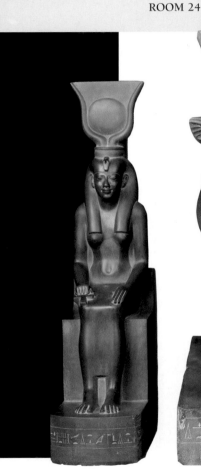
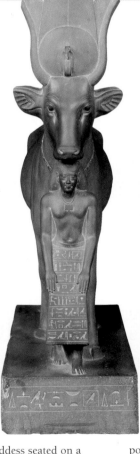

These three statues are all sculpted from the same material and in the same style. They come from the tomb of Psamtek, the chief scribe, superintendent of the seals and governor of the palace at Saqqara. The statue of Isis shows the goddess seated on a throne of which she originally was the personification; she has a round face, delicate features, and a smooth, three-part wig that falls onto her shoulders leaving her ears visible. Her features are subtly portrayed with her eyes just shown in relief and her mouth wearing a slight smile. The goddess wears a narrow tunic that reaches her ankles and her hands rest face down on her thighs, the left empty but the right holding an *ankh* sign. A central uraeus serpent appears on her forehead and she wears a modius with the attributes of Hathor: two horns and a sun disk. During this era, Isis was frequently assimilated to Hathor. An inscription on the base of the statue is of the offerings formula dedicated from Psamtek to Isis.

The statue of Hathor protecting Psamtek is based on the style of New Kingdom royal statuary: see, for

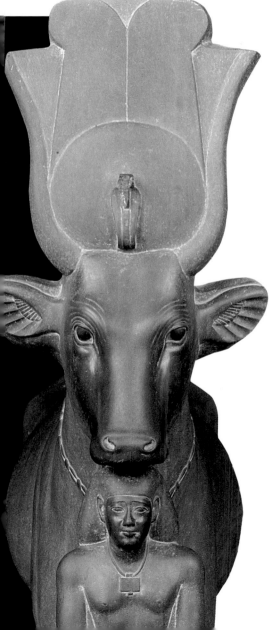

example, the statue of Hathor with Amenhotep II that was found in the Hathoric shrine of Thutmosis III at Deir al-Bahari. The goddess wears a necklace with a *menat* counterpoise and the crown consisting of the cow's horns with a sun disk, a solar uraeus serpent, and two plumes in the center. Psamtek is shown standing in the praying position below the muzzle of the animal with his hands flat on his long straight skirt. He wears a wig that leaves his ears uncovered and a necklace from which the symbol of his profession, a seal, hangs. The inscriptions on his skirt give his titles and name while those on the base of the statue contain a formula addressed to Hathor.

Osiris is represented as a mummy seated on a throne and wearing the beard of the gods. Only his hands emerge from the bandages and with these he holds the *heqa* scepter and *neheh* flail. He wears the *atef* crown which comprises the crown of Upper Egypt and two plumes at the sides, and the coils of a uraeus serpent are wound on his forehead. As with the other two statues, the base has a formula of prayer addressed to the god in the statue. (M.T.)

223

STATUE OF THE VIZIER HOR
BASALT; HEIGHT 96 CM
KARNAK, TEMPLE OF AMUN-RA, COURT OF THE CACHETTE
EXCAVATION BY G. LEGRAIN (1904)
TWENTY-SECOND DYNASTY (945-718 BC)

ROOM 24

The vizier is shown seated with one leg bent up against his chest and the other resting on the ground in a pose that had been rarely seen before. He has a shaved head, delicate features, rounded cheeks, and a small mouth. His skirt is held up by a large belt that is inscribed with details of his life including the titles of himself and his father, the priest Iuatjek. The torso and other parts of the statue are less carefully carved: his arms, pelvis, and legs are too large for his head and the upper chest is somewhat conventional.

The text on the base of the statue is an offering formula to Amun-Ra who has allowed Hor to erect a statue of himself in the god's temple. The inscription also refers to the king's appointment of Hor as vizier while he was still Superintendent of the Treasury of the Temple of Amun. The name of the king is not specified in the inscription but we know that Hor's father was named Iuatjek and was of Libyan origin, and this suggests the period of

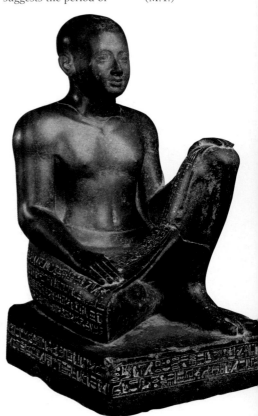

the Twenty-second Dynasty, a hypothesis that is supported by the style and the pose of the figure. There were two viziers during the Twenty-second Dynasty in Upper Egypt, one is referred to during Year 14 of the Reign of Takelot I and the other is cited in a document during Year 8 of Sheshonq III.
(M.T.)

BUST OF A STATUE OF MONTUEMHAT
GRANITIC ROCK; HEIGHT 50 CM
KARNAK, TEMPLE OF MUT
EXCAVATION BY BENSON-GOURLAY (1897)
LATE TWENTY-FIFTH –
EARLY TWENTY-SIXTH DYNASTY
(MID-7TH CENTURY BC)

ROOM 24

This fragment of statue has been identifie as Montuemhat by experts on the basis of analysis of the style of t figure and the sequence of the titles but in actua fact the name of the Fourth Prophet of Amu

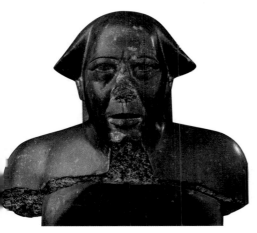

does not appear. The statue is broken below the shoulders. It is of an old man, with a lined face, protruding cheekbones, and straight eyebrows, who gazes ahead. The beard attachment below his chin has also been broken. He is mostly bald but has hair at each side of his head that hides half of his ears. According to J.J. Clère (1995: 153-157), the statue was originally of a man kneeling with a sistrum (the Hathoric emblem) held in front of him by his left hand while he was moving his right hand towards his mouth. This was a standard pose for statues of functionaries during the New Kingdom who were described by the appellation as "the bald one of Hathor" which is seen in the text on this bust.

The damaged text of six vertical lines on the rear support allows us to deduce that the statue was dedicated to Hathor (known as "The Golden One") who was often assimilated to Mut, especially during the Ethiopian epoch. The statue was found in the enclosure walls of the Temple of Mut at Karnak. (M.T.)

STATUE OF MONTUEMHAT
GRANITIC ROCK; HEIGHT 137 CM
KARNAK, TEMPLE OF AMUN-RA, COURT OF THE CACHETTE
EXCAVATION BY G. LEGRAIN (1904)
LATE TWENTY-FIFTH –
EARLY OF THE TWENTY-SIXTH DYNASTY
(MID-7TH CENTURY BC)

ROOM 24

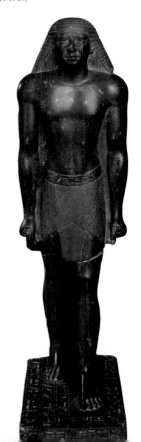

Montuemhat, the Fourth Prophet of Amun, Prince of Thebes and Governor of Upper Egypt, is one of the best known individuals from ancient Egypt owing to the many statues that have been found of him, to his tomb in the area of the Temple of Hatshepsut at Deir al-Bahari, and to the many epigraphs that describe him. He is shown in this example with his left leg forward and his arms down by his sides in the traditional pose of the Old Kingdom. He wears a wig which shows the curls of a second wig worn beneath.

His body is muscular, powerful but utterly conventional unlike the face which is heavily lined. The waistband of his skirt is inscribed with his titles and the name Montuemhat, while the rear support and the base of the statue are engraved with biographical notes, an offering formula, an "Appeal to the living" and the "Saite formula." (M.T.)

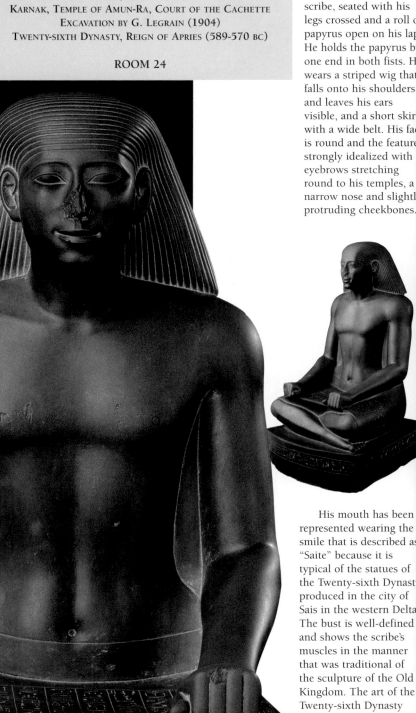

STATUE OF THE VIZIER NESPAQASHUTY

Schist; Height 78 cm
Karnak, Temple of Amun-Ra, Court of the Cachette
Excavation by G. Legrain (1904)
Twenty-sixth Dynasty, Reign of Apries (589-570 BC)

ROOM 24

Nespaqashuty is shown in the pose of a scribe, seated with his legs crossed and a roll of papyrus open on his lap. He holds the papyrus by one end in both fists. He wears a striped wig that falls onto his shoulders and leaves his ears visible, and a short skirt with a wide belt. His face is round and the features strongly idealized with eyebrows stretching round to his temples, a narrow nose and slightly protruding cheekbones.

His mouth has been represented wearing the smile that is described as "Saite" because it is typical of the statues of the Twenty-sixth Dynasty produced in the city of Sais in the western Delta. The bust is well-defined and shows the scribe's muscles in the manner that was traditional of the sculpture of the Old Kingdom. The art of the Twenty-sixth Dynasty was informed by a return to the artistic models of more ancient periods to contrast with the trends of the dynasties and foreign dominions that had preceded this dynasty. The papyrus is inscribed with a text in vertical lines, and the base with a line of hieroglyphics giving the name and titles of the figure.

Nespaqashuty was buried in a large tomb (TT 312) in Thebes with wall paintings illustrating a pilgrimage to Abydos (the location of the cult of Osiris) and the burial ceremony. He was the son of another vizier of Upper Egypt, Nespamedu, who was cited at the city of This during the age of the Fourth Prophet of Amun, Montuemhat.
(M.T.)

STATUE OF AHMES, SON OF NESBANEBDJED

SCHISTE; HEIGHT 95 CM; KARNAK, TEMPLE OF AMUN-RA COURT OF THE CACHETTE; EXCAVATION BY G. LEGRAIN (1904); END OF THE THIRTIETH DYNASTY – START OF THE PTOLEMAIC PERIOD (SECOND HALF OF THE 4TH CENTURY BC)

ROOM 24

The statue portrays Ahmes advancing with his left leg forward and his arms down by his sides; his figure is supported by a slab behind that has a pointed top. His head is shaven and the eyes in his oval face are outlined with make-up. His eyebrows are shown slightly in relief and his small mouth is well-formed but his nose is damaged.

The priest wears a *shendyt* skirt with a waistband that bears his names and titles.

The rear support and the space between his legs are also covered with inscriptions and figures. A scene engraved between the legs of the statue on the right shows Ahmes' eldest son, Nesbanebdjed (his grandfather's namesake), and the one on the left is of Ahmes kneeling above a text containing an "appeal to the living." The rectangular tip on the back of the slab is decorated with two scenes: Ahmes kneels before Osiris on the left, and before Amun on the right.
(M.T.)

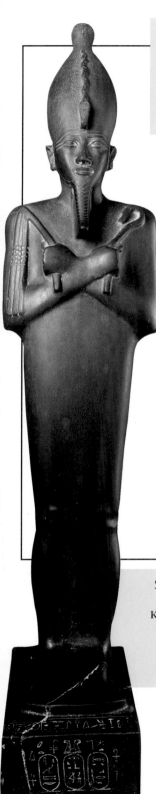

STATUE OF OSIRIS
BASALT; HEIGHT 150 CM
BASE: LENGTH 43 CM, WIDTH 24.5 CM
MEDINET HABU, IN FRONT OF THE GREAT TEMPLE
DISCOVERED IN 1895
TWENTY-SIXTH DYNASTY, REIGN OF PSAMTEK I (664-62⁵

ROOM 24

The statue was found close to the Temple of Rameses III at Medinet Habu. It shows Osiris wearing the white crown and a uraeus serpent, a typical element of the iconography of Osiris during the Late Period. The god is portrayed as a mummy with his arms folded, the *heqa* scepter in his left hand, the *nekhekh* flail in his right, and wearing the beard of the gods. The figure stands on a base bearing the names of Queen Nitocris and King Psamtek I. Osiris was worshipped equally at Busiris and Abydos where Sety I dedicated a cenotaph to the god, the *Osirion*.

Originally Osiris was a god of nature but he developed into the king of the underworld after the reign of Geb, one of the first mythical kings of Egypt. The god's element are land and water but he was not associated with any animals. He was usually painted green, to allude to his role as the god of nature, or black, like the mud of the Nile. Osiris was at the center of sacred festivals held during the month of Khoiak between the end of the annual flood and the sowing season. The festivals comprised both public and private ceremonies which were distinguished by whether the statue of the god left the temple on the sacred bark or not. Their purpose was to recreate the scene of the death and resurrection of the god. (M.T.)

STATUE OF THE GODDESS TAWERET
SCHIST; HEIGHT 96 CM, WIDTH 38 CM
KARNAK, NORTHERN SECTION OF THE TEMPLE OF AMUN-RA
CONFISCATED DURING SECRET EXCAVATIONS
BY A. MARIETTE IN 1874
TWENTY-SIXTH DYNASTY (664-525 BC)

ROOM 24

The statue represents the goddess Taweret (a Greek version of the Egyptian name Ta-uret, "The Great Goddess") who was associated with fertility and the hippopotamus. She is portrayed as a hybrid creature with the head of a hippopotamus, human arms, drooping breasts, a round belly and a lion's feet instead of legs. She rests her front paws on two supports in the form of the *sa* sign, a symbol of protection. She wears a striped, three-part wig and a cylindrical modius that used to support the crown of Hathor with cow's horns, a sun disk and a plume in the center. On the back, the wig reaches down to her feet in the form of a scaly tail like crocodile skin.

The upper side of the base and the rear support are inscribed with texts that say the statue was dedicated to Taweret and to Reret by Pabasa, the superintendent of the priests and the majordomo of God's Wife of Amun, Nitocri, daughter of King Psamtek I. Pabasa prays that the goddesses will protect the property that Nitocri received when she succeeded Shepenupet in her position.

Reret was another deity linked to the protection of unborn children and to fertility, and was often portrayed as a goddess-hippopotamus and assimilated to Taweret. She, on the other hand, was often assimilated to Hathor or Isis in her role as a wet nurse.

The statue was found in a limestone *naos* decorated with the scenes of Taweret receiving sistrums from Niteeri and with seven other goddesses holding tambourines. The seven goddesses are the seven Hathors: celestial cows that give life and fertility.

The perfect condition of the statue is explained by the fact that the *naos* was still sealed when it was discovered.
(M.T.)

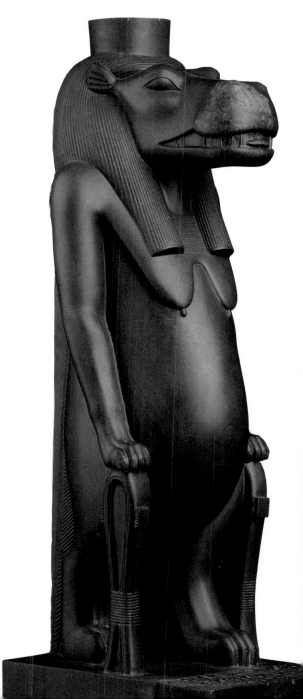

STATUE OF THE SCRIBE PETAMENHOTEP

QUARTZITE; HEIGHT 74 CM
KARNAK, TEMPLE OF AMUN-RA, COURT OF THE CACHETTE
EXCAVATION BY G. LEGRAIN (1904)
EARLY TWENTY-SIXTH DYNASTY
(SECOND HALF OF THE 7TH CENTURY BC)

ROOM 24

The priest-reader Petamenhotep is shown in this statue in the typical pose of a scribe with his legs crossed and a roll of papyrus open on his lap. He holds the papyrus with his left hand while his right hand used to hold a stylus (lost).

The pose was typical of statues of scribes produced during the Old Kingdom on which, undoubtedly, this statue was based. Even the short hairstyle of the scribe resembles that of ancient models although the most common type was with a flared wig. The papyrus is inscribed with Petamenhotep's name and titles and the base is also engraved with various texts. (M.T.)

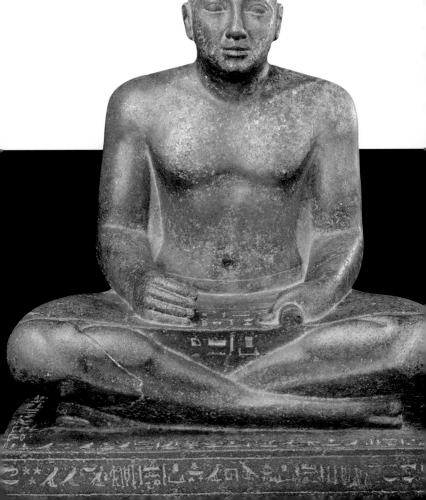

BLOCK STATUE OF HOR

GRANITIC ROCK; HEIGHT 109 CM
KARNAK, TEMPLE OF AMUN-RA
COURTYARD OF THE CACHETTE
EXCAVATION BY G. LEGRAIN (1904)
TWENTY-THIRD DYNASTY, REIGN OF PETUBASTIS (820-795 BC)

ROOM 30

Hor – the secretary of araoh Petubastis I – is rtrayed crouching with arms folded on his ees beneath his cloak. A graphical inscription d the images of Ra-rakhti and Osiris appear the front of the cloak. r's carefully modelled d wears a striped wig t does not cover his s and the features of his e are idealized.

Block statues appeared Egypt during the Middle ngdom but they became ticularly widespread during the Eighteenth Dynasty. They depict a figure with crossed legs and arms folded resting on the legs. The body is covered with a cloak from which only the hands and feet emerge. The surface of the statue was used for inscriptions that usually gave the biography of the individual or an "appeal to the living." Block statues were made for functionaries who had made a pilgrimage to the main temple of Osiris at Abydos. (M.T.)

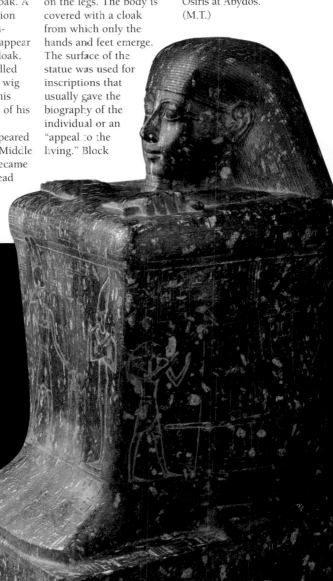

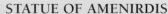

STATUE OF AMENIRDIS

ALABASTER; BASE MADE FROM BASALT; HEIGHT 170 CM
THEBES, TEMPLE OF KARNAK
FOUND BY A. MARIETTE IN 1858
THIRD INTERMEDIATE PERIOD, TWENTY-FIFTH DYNASTY
REIGN OF SHABAKA (713-698 BC)

ROOM 30

A strong monarchy developed in southern Nubia in the city of Napata near the fourth cataract at the end of the 9th century BC. The first king whose name has come down to us was Alara who reigned for about 20 years and died, presumably, around 765 BC. His successor Kashta conquered northern Nubia and began the unstoppable expansion of the Ethiopian Dynasty into southern Egypt. Kashta's son, Piankhy, came to the throne in 745 BC and soon took control of Thebes where he ensured that Shepenupet I, the daughter of the Libyan king Osorkon III, adopted his sister Amenirdis in the political and religious position as the "God's Wife of Amun" before he continued his march north.

Amenirdis held this position for a long time and later adopted the daughter of Piankhy, Shepenupet II, who succeeded her around 700 BC. The "God's Wives" (priestesses of Amun of royal lineage) governed the city of Thebes from the second half of the 11th century

BC right up until the Persian conquest. The held spiritual and temporal powers and spent their lives in the temple of Amun at Karnak where they dedicated themselves the cult of the god and to the administration the temple's treasures. Like the king, their names were enclosed cartouches and the succession of their powers and position w governed by adoption

This statue shows Amenirdis with the traditional insignia and clothing of the "God's Wives"; she holds a floral scepter in her le hand and wears a long tight-fitting tunic and heavy three-part wig t has two uraeus serpen on the front and is topped by the body of vulture (the emblem o Mut, the consort of Amun).

Mariette was particularly struck by the figure of Amenirdi when he found this sculpture, and, being a composer of opera librettos, suggested the plot for Giuseppe Verc Aida with Amenirdis a the basis for the character of Queen Amneris.
(D.C.)

STELA OF PIANKHY
GREY GRANITE; HEIGHT 180 CM, WIDTH 184 CM,
THICKNESS 43 CM; GEBEL BARKAL, TEMPLE OF AMUN
FOUND IN 1862; THIRD INTERMEDIATE PERIOD
WENTY-FIFTH DYNASTY, REIGN OF PIANKHY (745-713 BC)

ROOM 30

This monumental stela was engraved with a description of the victorious military campaign led by the Nubian king, Piankhy (or Piye) against Tefnakht, the king of Sais, and his local allies. Piankhy succeeded in controlling the whole of the Nile valley after continuing the expansion north of his predecessors, Alara and Kashta. After taking Memphis and accepting the submission of other important centers in Upper and Lower Egypt, Piankhy returned to Napata, the Nubian capital close to the fourth cataract of the Nile, and began to expand and embellish the great temple of Amun at Gebel Barkal where the stela was found in 1862. The king wished to erect this monument in the house of the god that directed his glorious deeds: "Amun of Napata has let me govern the entire country" was written on another stela found in the same temple.

The style of the account is reminiscent of the epic tone and propaganda characteristic of celebratory texts of the kings of the New Kingdom, such as the epic poem of the battle of Qadesh and the stela of Merenptah. (D.C.)

233

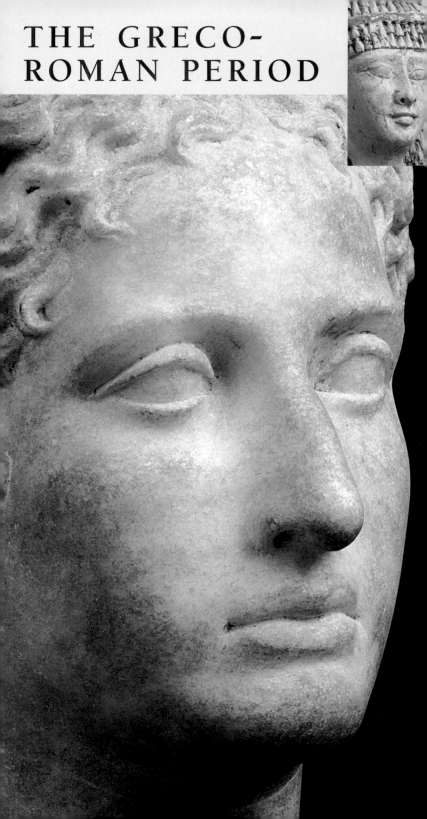

Having defeated the Persian army led by Darius at Issus, Alexander the Great entered Egypt in 332 BC where he was welcomed by the inhabitants as a liberator. After being crowned pharaoh at Memphis, he demonstrated his respect for the ancient gods by attending the oracle of Amun in Siwa oasis in full accord with the universalistic spirit he had learned from his extraordinary teacher, the Greek philosopher Aristotle.

During his brief stay in Egypt, Alexander encouraged the founding of a new city on the Delta coast: Alexandria was destined to become prosperous and populous, an influential center of Hellenistic culture throughout the Mediterranean.

On Alexander's death, one of his generals, Ptolemy, to whom the country had been entrusted, took possession of Egypt, first with the title of satrap, then, in 305 BC, as king. After a series of clashes between Alexander's successors, the *Diadochoi*, the division of the empire became definitive in 301 BC: the Seleucids reigned in Syria, the Lagids (from Lagus, Ptolemy's father) in Egypt. the Antigonids in Greece and Macedonia, and the Attalids in Pergamum.

Ptolemy and his descendants (overall there were sixteen rulers who were all crowned with the same name) governed Egypt for 270 years. They presented themselves to the inhabitants as pharaohs but never lost their identity as Hellenes in their dealings abroad, thus bestowing an unusual dual nature on the country. As a result of their decrees being drawn up in both Greek and Egyptian, J.-F. Champollion was able to decipher hieroglyphic script following the discovery of a bilingual edict, today known as the Rosetta Stone, that Ptolemy V had promulgated in 196 BC.

The two artistic traditions, Hellenistic and Egyptian, long retained their distinct identities

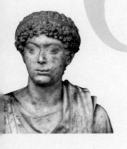

CHAPTER 6
GROUND FLOOR

234 HEAD
OF A WOMAN
Marble;
Height 35 CM;
Greco-Roman
Period
(332 BC - 313 AD)

235 HEAD
OF A WOMAN
Marble; Height 65 CM;
Found at San (Edgar);
Greco-Roman
Period
(332 BC - 313 AD)

ITINERARY THROUGH ROOMS
25, 34, 35, 50, 49

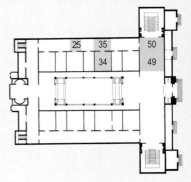

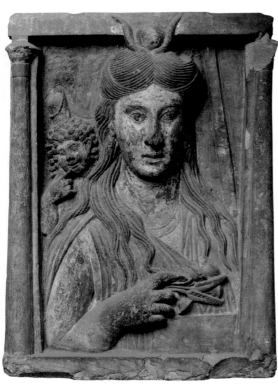

236 BUST-PORTRAIT OF A WOMAN
Marble;
Height 61 CM;
Kom Abu Billo
(Therenuthis);
Roman Era
(140-150 AD)

(the deceased bull Apis assimilated to Osiris) with the attributes of Zeus, Hades, and Asclepius.

The Greeks, fascinated by the complex Egyptian religious world, reinterpreted and assimilated the ancient gods with their own to form Amun-Zeus, Horus-Apollo, and Thoth-Hermes. Occasionally associated with different Hellenic goddesses (Demeter, Aphrodite, and Tyche), Isis was represented by iconography inspired by Greek and Greek-Egyptian models and became worshipped throughout all of the ancient world. Bes, the dwarf god who had exis from the most ancient o times, and Harpocrates, boy version of Horus, w the most venerated deiti in popular religion.

With regard to the construction or enlargement of temples, pure Egyptian style and even the ancient funera traditions were maintaine though reinterpreted: mummies were bound with white and brown bandages in order to for diamond shaped pattern and then covered with a material made from papyrus and cloth that w pressed and lined with stucco (*cartonnage*). Thi was then decorated with images from Egyptian iconography but often using new, untraditional color combinations.

Wall decorations whi reflect a mixture of style were painted in tombs o Egyptian typology, for example, the tomb of Petrosiris at Tuna al-Geb that was built at the star of the Ptolemaic era.

The Lagids brought t country a period of grea prosperity but in the 2n century BC slow political and economic decline se in, accompanied by soci revolts and dynastic strife Romans took advantage this weakness in 30 BC when Octavian conquere Egypt and turned it into prefecture bringing an e to the Nile Valley's independence for good and turning Egypt into

and never achieved a coherent combined expression despite frequent reciprocal influences.

The ancient gods were kept but new syncretistic cults were also created. In the attempt to integrate the ancient pharaonic creed with Greek religious traditions, a new god, Serapis, was introduced who combined the characteristics of the Memphite god Osorapis

Rome's granary." Slowly the redistribution of wealth within the country that had characterized the rule of the Ptolemies came to a halt. The members of the most wealthy classes were forced to assume burdensome responsibilities in extremely expensive public posts that ended by ruining them and thus generally weakening the country as a whole. Greek and Latin became the only official languages.

The Roman emperors had classical images of themselves distributed throughout the country while pharaonic customs and activities became increasingly rare. Private portraiture had appeared by the end of the Ptolemaic era but became popular under the Romans, inspired by Greco-Roman models.

Another characteristic of the first centuries AD was the production of funerary portraits on encausted wooden tablets (a technique using hot wax) that prevalently took place in the oasis of Fayum. The portraits were placed over the face of the deceased in a small opening in the sarcophagus to substitute the traditional funerary mask.

The Roman emperors ordered restoration and

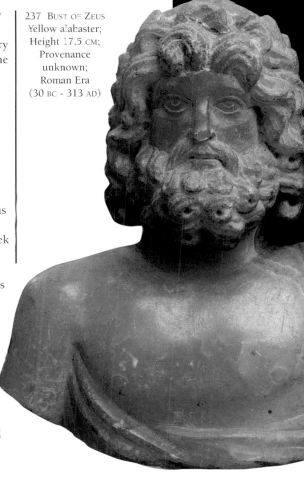

237 BUST OF ZEUS
Yellow alabaster;
Height 17.5 CM;
Provenance
unknown;
Roman Era
(30 BC - 313 AD)

expansion works of the great sanctuaries in the Nile Valley (the Temple of Hathor at Dendera, the Temple of Isis at Philae, etc.) but classical architecture buildings were also built.

Egyptian cults rapidly spread to Rome and throughout the Latin world, with those of Isis and Serapis springing up everywhere; the emperor Commodus was even a priest of Isis.

In 380, Theodosius decreed that Christianity was the only state religion and in 395 the Roman empire was divided in two with Egypt belonging to the Eastern Empire under Byzantium. The temples were transformed into churches, the ancient furnishings destroyed, and the millenary images of the ancient gods chiselled away. The last hieroglyphic inscription was made in 394 on the island of Philae. (D.C.)

STATUE OF A PTOLEMAIC QUEEN

Limestone; Height 47.5 cm
Karnak, Temple of Amun-Ra, Court of the Cachette; Excavation by G. Legrain (1904)
Ptolemaic Period (305-30 bc)

ROOM 25

This limestone statue still bears traces of the paint with which it was covered. Unlike sculptures in hard stone, those in soft stone were often painted though the range of colors was very basic: the wig and details of the face were black, the garments white, men's skin was red and women's yellow, and any jewelry was painted gold.

The statue is of a female figure with her left leg advanced in the customary position of Egyptian statuary. The right arm is held rigidly down by her side while the left is bent below her breast with her

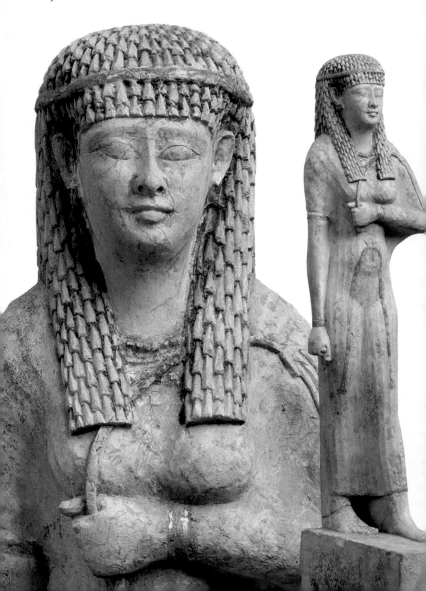

hand closed around a floral scepter, a typical attribute of queens. Her face is framed by a three-part wig tied with a red band. She wears a long pleated tunic that shows the curves of her body, and a red bow above her waist.

In the absence of inscriptions (the columns of the base should have been engraved with hieroglyphs but they were never carved), the figure cannot be identified precisely, however, she might have been a Ptolemaic queen from the first half of the 3rd century BC. (D.C.)

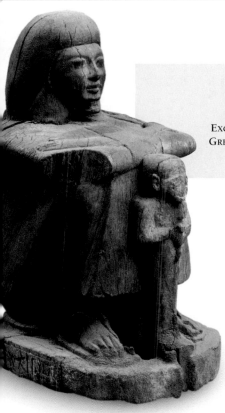

CUBE STATUE
WOOD; HEIGHT 18.7 CM
SAQQARA
EXCAVATION BY W. EMERY (1964-1967)
GRECO-ROMAN PERIOD (332 BC-313 AD)

ROOM 25

knees of the individual.

From the Ramessid Period on, it became common to sculpt a small deity on the front of the statue who in this case is Ptah, the god of Memphis worshipped as the creator of the world and the patron god of artisans. Ptah is portrayed in his standard iconography in a style that is close to that of archaic statuary: the head is portrayed in a perfunctory manner and he appears to be wrapped in a sort of sheath from which only his hands and head emerge. (D.C.)

This small wooden statue is of a man seated on the ground with his legs bent against his chest. His round head emerges from, and contrasts with, the solid block of the body below.

This unusual work is a cube statue, a typology seen from the Middle Kingdom until the Late Period. The figures portrayed in cube statues were usually middle-ranking functionaries whose titles and responsibilities were often inscribed on the base, rear support, and

PORTRAIT OF PANEMERIT
BASALT
HEIGHT 30 CM
TANIS
EXCAVATION BY A. MARIETTE (1861)
END OF THE PTOLEMAIC PERIOD (80-50 BC)

ROOM 34

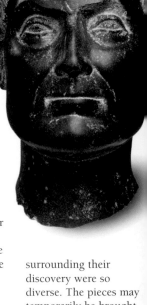

This basalt head was found by Mariette at Tanis in 1861. It portrays a man with a squarish head who is no longer young. Deep lines mark his chin and cheeks, and his eyebrows (which we understand were raised despite the stone being damaged) suggest a thoughtful gaze into the distance.

The head was part of a statue whose bust was found by Montet in 1937 and is now displayed in the Louvre. Probably the entire figure had one leg advanced in the customary position of Egyptian male statuary.

His left hand (lost) held an image of the god Horus who is shown on the chest in relief; the right hand, partially damaged, was raised in an act of adoration.

The hieroglyphic inscription on the pillar behind identifies the figure as Panemerit, the governor of Tanis at the time of the last Ptolemaic kings.

It is not rare for fragments of statues or reliefs to be displayed in different museums as the circumstances surrounding their discovery were so diverse. The pieces may temporarily be brought together for special occasions such as exhibitions.

(D.C.)

STELA OF AN INTERPETER OF DREAMS
PAINTED LIMESTONE
HEIGHT 35 CM, WIDTH 25 CM
SAQQARA
FOUND IN 1877
PTOLEMAIC PERIOD (END OF THE 3RD CENTURY BC)

ROOM 34

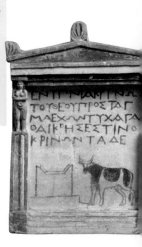

This stela comes from the Serapeum, a complex of religious buildings constructed in the Late Dynastic Period near the catacombs of the Apis bulls at Saqqara.

It was found near buildings used to welcome pilgrims. The form of a small Greek temple was commonly used for funerary stelae but in this case the inscription and the presence of holes on the back suggest it was used as insignia.

The Greek text is written in black on five lines and contains the words of a Cretan who declares that he interprets dreams. Probably this mystic found his customers among the faithful who slept between the walls of the temple waiting for dreams sent by the god.

The Apis bull is shown below the writing in front of an altar that stands on a plinth. The frame is created in high relief. The base has four steps that seem to lead to the painted scene. The sides are in the form of two pillars topped by naked female figures with their arms crossed. The triangular roof (the pediment of the temple) is decorated with palmettes at the corners. (D.C.)

PORTRAIT OF SEVERUS ALEXANDER
WHITE MARBLE; HEIGHT 23 CM
LUXOR
ROMAN PERIOD, REIGN OF SEVERUS ALEXANDER (222-235 AD)

ROOM 34

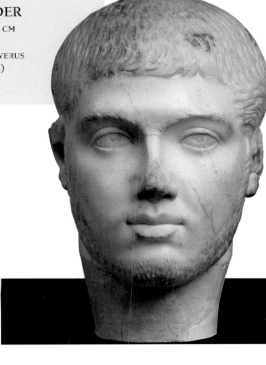

The Ptolemaic rulers presented themselves to the Egyptian people as pharaohs, therefore their portraits were frequently produced using ancient iconographic canons. Portraits in traditional costume and poses made during the Roman dominion were rare. Roman emperors championed the divulgation of effigies in pure classical style throughout Egypt and all subjected territories. Official portraiture developed from the need to diffuse an ideal image but was, somewhat unexpectedly, distinguished by an emphasis on true likeness.

This head was carved from white marble, an imported material which the Egyptians rarely made use of. Comparison with images on coins has identified the figure with that of Severus Alexander. The small locks of hair and the short beard were carefully sculpted; the mouth is shown in a barely perceptible smile. The stucco neck was the result of a clumsy attempt at restoration.

Painted by senatorial historiography as an ideal prince, Severus Alexander reigned from 222-235 AD and was killed on the Germanic front during a military revolt. (D.C.)

FUNERARY STELA

LIMESTONE
HEIGHT 43 CM, WIDTH 24 CM
PROBABLY FROM ALEXANDRIA
PTOLEMAIC PERIOD (150 BC CIRCA)

ROOM 34

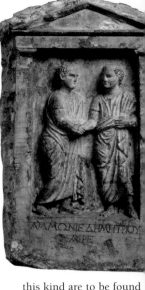

A large number of funerary stelae in pure Greek style produced during the Ptolemaic Period have been found mainly in and around Alexandria. This example has the typical form of a small temple created by two pillars and a triangular pediment. Two men in high relief shake hands in the hollow area below the pediment. The stout man on the right seems separated from the background as he solicitously greets his companion who faces us frontally with his head turned and a small smile on his face.

A two-line inscription in Greek letters below says: "Ammonius, son of Demetrius, farewell!" The deceased is probably the figure on the left and the other man perhaps a member of the family who dedicated this small funeral monument. Traces of the original paint can still be seen on the pediment, the pillars, and the two figures.

Previous works of this kind are to be found in Greek funerary stelae though the two artistic traditions used different materials; the Greeks used marble whilst the Egyptians used limestone, as marble had to be imported. (D.C.)

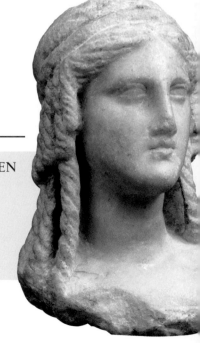

HEAD OF A PTOLEMAIC QUEEN ASSIMILATED TO ISIS

MARBLE; HEIGHT 19 CM
THMUIS (TELL TIMAI)
PTOLEMAIC PERIOD
(LATE 3RD – EARLY 2ND CENTURY BC)

ROOM 34

This head was found in Tell Timai (the ancient Thmuis), a locality in the Delta. It shows a woman with a pronounced chin, an elegant hairstyle of ringlets, and a diadem that was typical of a queen. She wears a metallic ornament on her head, perhaps the sun disk between two cow's horns, that was a divine attribute and seen on other heads with a similar hairstyle.

The woman is probably a Ptolemaic queen assimilated with Isis. Comparison with images on coins suggests that she was Berenice II, the sister and wife of Ptolemy III Evergetes. (D.C.)

STATUE OF HOR

BLACK BASALT
HEIGHT 83 CM
ALEXANDRIA
END OF THE PTOLEMAIC PERIOD (40 BC CIRCA)

ROOM 34

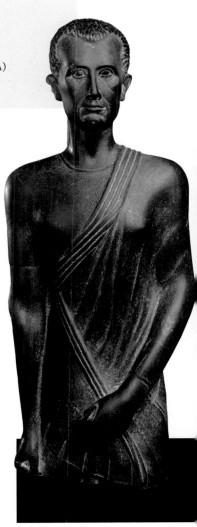

Various sculptural portraits of private individuals were made during the Late Ptolemaic Period, generally in hard black or green stone such as schist or basalt. These are particular items characterized by the introduction of Greco-Roman features into traditional pharaonic iconography.

This life-size sculpture is missing the lower section that in all probability portrayed the entire figure of a man standing with his left leg forward in the customary pose of Egyptian male statuary. The right arm stretches rigidly down his side while the left is folded over the stomach and clutches a flap of his cloak in an unusual position that is not part of the traditional schema.

The man has a long face, a wide forehead, and deep lines on his cheeks, chin, and at the corners of his mouth. He wears a tunic and a fringed cloak in Persian style thrown over his left shoulder. The support pillar behind the figure was a typical element of classical Egyptian statuary; it is inscribed with a small scene and hieroglyphs that tell us that the figure is a priest of the god Thoth, and that his name is Hor, son of Hor. (D.C.)

PAINTING WITH MYTHOLOGICAL SCENES OF OEDIPUS

PAINTED PLASTER
HEIGHT 98 CM, WIDTH 239 CM
TUNA AL-GEBEL
ROMAN PERIOD (30 BC-313 AD)

ROOM 34

This painting comes from the Greco-Roman necropolis of Tuna al-Gebel, a large archaeological site to the west of Hermopolis in

and presented him to the king of Corinth who brought Oedipus up as his own son.

As an adult, Oedipus learned of the fearful

three?" (man), whereupon the Sphinx killed herself. Oedipus was made king of the city and received the hand of Jocasta in marriage unaware that she was his mother. When he learned the truth, he blinded himself and Jocasta hanged herself.

This painting shows the episodes that are central to the myth: the solving of the riddle and the killing of Laius, with

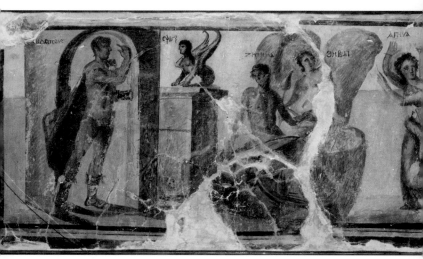

Upper Egypt. The scenes in the paintings show several episodes from the famous myth of Oedipus, son of Jocasta and Laius, the king of Thebes (the Greek, not Egyptian, city).

An oracle predicted that Laius would die by the hand of his son who would then marry his own mother so, in order to prevent the ill-omened prophecy from occurring, Laius abandoned the newborn Oedipus on Mount Cithaeron. A shepherd who found the baby, took pity on him

prophecy that he would kill his father and marry his mother, so he left Corinth and those whom he believed to be his parents. On the road to Thebes, Oedipus met his real father, Laius, and unaware of his identity, he killed him during a struggle. Once he reached Thebes, Oedipus freed the region of the Sphinx after answering the famous riddle, "What is it that has voice, in the morning walks on four feet, at midday on two, and in the evening on

all the figures identified in Greek. Oedipus is shown before the sphinx on the left. The third and fourth figures respectively symbolize "Riddle" and "Thebes". On the right, Oedipus stabs Laius in the neck with his sword in the presence of an allegorical figure, a female dancer identified by the caption as "Ignorance."

The rather poorly executed painting was probably a Roman copy of a Greek original.
(D.C.)

FUNERARY STELA OF NIKO

LIMESTONE
HEIGHT 69 CM, WIDTH 53 CM
ALEXANDRIA; PTOLEMAIC PERIOD
(FIRST HALF OF THE 3RD CENTURY BC)

ROOM 34

This limestone funerary stela in pure Greek style was found in Alexandria. It is in the form of a small temple with two pillars and a pediment (not survived) that rest on a thick base.

The high relief scene is of a female figure seated on the right who wears a long tunic and a cloak that covers her head and part of her body. Her head is slightly bowed and rests on her right hand; her other hand raises a flap of her mantle to reveal her foot resting on a low stool. In front of her, a servant, who is much smaller in size to emphasize her secondary importance, hands her mistress a lyre. The scene is dominated by the seated figure that represents the deceased to whom the stela is dedicated. The Greek inscription on the base tells us that the woman was Niko, the daughter of Timon.

The models that inspired this work were Greek funerary stelae that were usually made from marble. The Egyptians preferred to use limestone rather than marble as the latter had to be imported.
(D.C.)

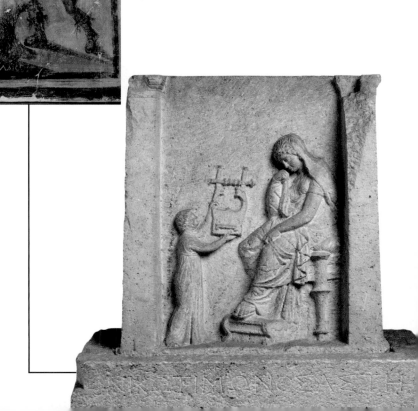

STELE DEDICATED BY PTOLEMY V TO THE BULL BUCHIS

LIMESTONE PAINTED AND GILDED
HEIGHT 72 CM, WIDTH 50 CM
ARMANT, *BUCHEUM*
EXCAVATION BY THE EGYPT EXPLORATION SOCIETY (1929-1930)
PTOLEMAIC PERIOD
REIGN OF PTOLEMY V EPIPHANES (205-180 BC)

ROOM 34

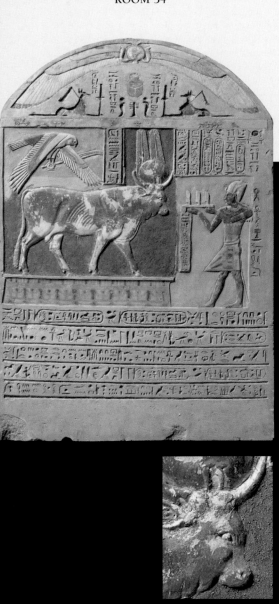

This stela comes from the *Bucheum*, the cemetery of the sacred bulls of Armant (ancient Iuni) on the west bank of the Nile in Upper Egypt. The cult of the bull Buchis, sacred to the war god Montu, took place at Armant from the Thirtieth Dynasty on.

The images and the hieroglyphic texts are engraved on the stela on three registers. In the arch at the top a scarab, the emblem of Osiris, is shown on a *djed* pillar flanked by two uraeus serpents. Two lateral images show Anubis with a dog's body and the whole scene is dominated by a winged sun disk.

The central register, bounded by the hieroglyph of the sky, shows Buchis with a gilded body and a sun disk with two plumes between his horns; the disk and plumes are attributes of Montu, the god of war. King Ptolemy V, dressed according to pharaonic custom, offers the bull the *sekhet*, the symbol of the fields. The god Montu is represented above the bull in the form of a falcon. The hieroglyphs show the names of the pharaoh, his wife Cleopatra, the god Montu and the bull Buchis.

The inscription in the lower register contains Ptolemy's and Cleopatra's dedication to the sacred bull that was born in year 11 of the king's reign, and died in year 25.
(D.C.)

HEAD OF ALEXANDER THE GREAT

WHITE ALABASTER
HEIGHT 10 CM
AL-YAUTA, WEST OF BIRKET QURUN
PTOLEMAIC PERIOD (332 - 30 BC)

ROOM 34

This alabaster head is all that remains of a statuette. The youthful face is a somewhat idealized portrait of Alexander the Great. The emperor has been given long thick curls held in place by a band that was an emblem of royalty and frequently represented in portraits of the Macedon. An ornament of some kind, probably a crown, was inserted in the hole that can be seen on top of the head. It was common in Hellenistic statuary to adorn stone sculptures with decorative elements or emblems, often made of metal, as can be seen in certain representations of Isis in which she wears the typical headdress of cow's horns and a sun disk.

The stylistic and iconographic characteristics of the head mark it as being part of the large production of images of the emperor created during the Ptolemaic Period but, without further evidence, it is not possible to date it more precisely.

Alexander received his early education at the hands of an exceptional teacher, the Greek philosopher Aristotle, and ascended the throne in 336 BC. During the 13 years that

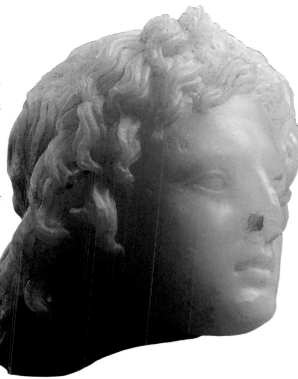

followed, his extraordinary military achievements defeated the Persian empire and took him as far as India. He died unexpectedly in Babylon at the age of 33 following which his

legend grew quickly and he became the first person in history to receive the nickname "the Great."

When he reached in Egypt in 332 BC, he was welcomed by the inhabitants as a liberator and was crowned pharaoh in Memphis. He made a pilgrimage to the temple of the god Amun in the Siwa oasis and then founded the city of Alexandria on

the Delta coast. He continued his journey east leaving the government of Egypt in the hands of his general Ptolemy who became king in 305 BC.
(D.C.)

MALE HEAD

PLASTER; HEIGHT 23 CM
PROVENANCE UNKNOWN
ROMAN PERIOD (LATE 1ST -
EARLY 2ND CENTURY AD)

ROOM 34

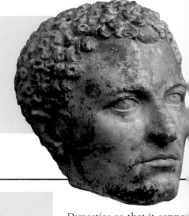

HEAD OF A KING

BLACK GRANITE
HEIGHT 46 CM
PURCHASED IN 1888 AT TELL AL-RUBA
PROBABLE DATE: TWENTY-NINTH DYNASTY (399-380 BC)

ROOM 34

This black granite head was purchased in 1888 in the Delta locality of Tell al-Ruba, the ancient Mendes. The sovereign is shown wearing the blue crown (khepresh) and the uraeus serpent, the emblem of royalty.

As the statue was a purchase and has no inscriptions, there are no objective data to aid precise dating, however, the most accredited hypothesis considers the statue to have been produced during the Twenty-ninth Dynasty.

The idealization of the features and the smile on the closed lips are typical of the Saite epoch (Twenty-sixth Dynasty) but certain details, such as the long eyes and carefully carved eyebrows, are distinctive elements of the sculptures from a slightly later age. The "double eight" motif created by the spirals of the uraeus serpents was only seen between the Twenty-sixth and Twenty-ninth Dynasties so that it cannot have been produced later. Since the head comes from Mendes, the city of origin of the rulers of the Twenty-ninth Dynasty, it may well be a portrait of one of these pharaohs who governed Egypt for roughly 20 years under the constant threat of the Persians.

(D.C.)

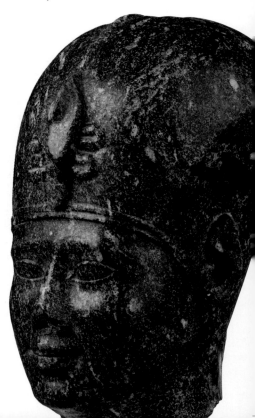

This male head is an example of the portraiture of private individuals that began to appear during the Ptolemaic Period and had a major boost during the Roman Era. The features of the young man have been carefully represented. The lean face with high cheekbones has a severe expression; his lips are thin, the slightly aquiline nose has a large tip, and the depth of the eye-sockets is emphasized by the projected eyebrows. The short curls of his hair have only received perfunctory treatment.

The portrait is made from plaster and was probably a preparation for a larger version. (D.C.)

STATUETTE OF A KNEELING SOVEREIGN
BRONZE
HEIGHT 26 CM
SAQQARA; EXCAVATION BY W. EMERY (1968-1970)
LATE PERIOD (664-332 BC)

ROOM 35

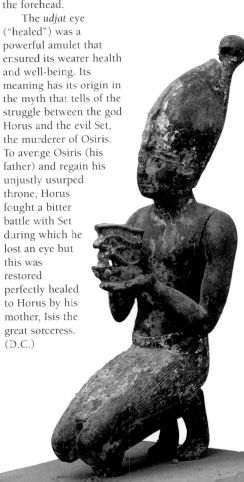

Bronze statuettes became very popular during the Late Period and many examples have been discovered in the votive stores of the great temples. They were made using the lost wax technique but it is not possible to date them with precision.

Despite turning green due to the natural process of oxidation, this statue still bears traces of its original gilding. It shows a kneeling sovereign offering an *udjat* eye of Horus that rests on the hieroglyph *neb*. The king wears a simple white pleated skirt and the white crown of Upper Egypt with the uraeus serpent, an emblem of royalty, on the forehead.

The *udjat* eye ("healed") was a powerful amulet that ensured its wearer health and well-being. Its meaning has its origin in the myth that tells of the struggle between the god Horus and the evil Set, the murderer of Osiris. To avenge Osiris (his father) and regain his unjustly usurped throne, Horus fought a bitter battle with Set during which he lost an eye but this was restored perfectly healed to Horus by his mother, Isis the great sorceress. (D.C.)

FEMALE HEAD
Marble
Height 73 cm
Provenance unknown
Probable date: Roman Period (30 bc - 313 ad)

ROOM 50

This female head belonged to a colossal statue that has not survived. Given the slight distension of the right side of the neck, it seems probable that the head was turned slightly to the left. The face has a full oval shape, the lips are small and protruding, and the nose has a rather wide bridge that continues into the area of the eyebrows. The right ear is pierced for earrings, a custom that was common during pharaonic times.

The marble used by the Egyptian sculptors from the Ptolemaic Period on was mostly imported.

(D.C.)

BUST-PORTRAIT OF A WOMAN
Marble
Height 61 cm
Kom Abu Billo (Terenuthis)
Roman Period (140-150 ad)

ROOM 50

The bust was found at Kom Abu Billo (the ancient Terenuthis), a locality in the Delta that was also the site of a temple dedicated to Hathor and a large necropolis with tombs spanning the period from the Old Kingdom to the Roman Period.

This bust shows a middle-aged woman with a long slender nose and a deeply lined chin. The elegant hairstyle in braids and curls has been carefully modeled to indicate a person of high rank.

It has been suggested that the woman in question was the mother of Marcus Aurelius but no conclusions can be drawn in the absence of further data. (D.C.)

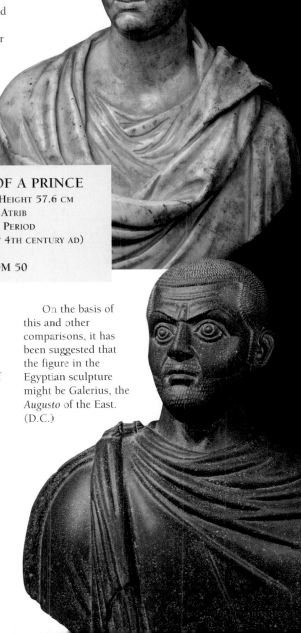

PORTRAIT OF A PRINCE
RED PORPHYRY; HEIGHT 57.6 CM
TELL ATRIB
ROMAN PERIOD
(LATE 3RD - EARLY 4TH CENTURY AD)

ROOM 50

This portrait of a prince was carved in red porphyry, a stone that was much appreciated by the Romans. The rigidity of the figure is typical of official portraiture at the start of the 4th century AD.

The work shares certain characteristics with a porphyry sculptural group of the Tetrarchs (the two *Cesari* and two *Augusti* created in Diocletian's division of power) located on the outside of St. Mark's church in Venice.

On the basis of this and other comparisons, it has been suggested that the figure in the Egyptian sculpture might be Galerius, the *Augusto* of the East. (D.C.)

STATUE OF A PTOLEMAIC KING

GRANITE
HEIGHT 280 CM
KARNAK
END OF THE PTOLEMAIC PERIOD (1ST CENTURY BC)

ROOM 50

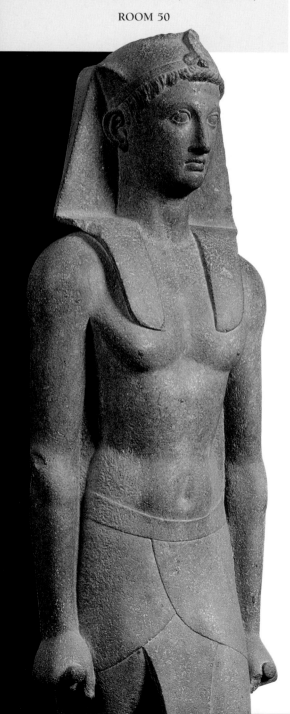

The standing figure with his left leg advanced and arms rigidly held down by his sides is portrayed in the traditional pose of Egyptian male statuary.

He wears a simple skirt and the *nemes*, a striped linen head-covering often worn by pharaohs instead of the crown. The uraeus serpent on the front is a symbol of royalty. This is probably a Ptolemaic king although if the lack of inscription makes identification and dating difficult. While the figure's pose and costume are typical of pharaonic art, the rendition of the features on the long face and the carefully carved locks of hair that escape from the *nemes* are indicative of a Hellenistic influence.

The dynasty of Ptolemaic sovereigns from Macedonia presented themselves to the Egyptian people as pharaohs with the result that their portraits were often made in accordance with ancient iconographic canons though elements of Greek inspiration were also often present. Works exhibiting characteristics of both cultures are not rare from this period, although both artistic traditions continued to maintain their individuality.
(D.C.)

SARCOPHAGUS OF PETOSIRIS

WOOD AND COLORED GLASS PASTE; HEIGHT 195 CM
TUNA AL-GEBEL, TOMB OF PETOSIRIS
EXCAVATION BY THE ANTIQUITIES SERVICE (1920)
START OF THE PTOLEMAIC PERIOD
(2ND HALF OF THE 4TH CENTURY BC)

ROOM 49

Hermopolis was the capital of the fifteenth *nome* of Upper Egypt. It was the principal center of worship of the moon god Thoth, the inventor of hieroglyphics and patron of scribes.

Almost no trace remains of the temple dedicated to the god though two rows of columns in the atrium were still visible until the Napoleonic era.

In the large archaeological site of Tuna al-Gebel, a short distance from Hermopolis, there is a necropolis with tombs dating from the Greco-Roman Period. Of these, the family tomb of Petosiris stands out for its original structure and interesting wall decorations. This important Hermopolitan figure lived at the start of the Ptolemaic Period and had many important religious functions including that of being the high priest of Thoth.

The tomb is in the shape of a temple; it has a colonnade and a chapel above ground while its funerary chambers are below ground. The traditional Egyptian themes in the relief decorations of the colonnade are imbued with a Greek influence, thus creating the mixed style characteristic of this period.

Classical religious scenes in the chapel are accompanied by a series of hieroglyphic texts known as the "Biography of Petosiris" that contains various maxims referring to the transitoriness of life and worldly goods.

The tomb was raided in antiquity but the two wooden sarcophaguses of Petosiris were left (empty) inside a stone sarcophagus. The example in the photograph is the innermost of the three and is decorated with a five-column inscription topped by the sign of the starry vault. The hieroglyphs are finely inlaid with colored glass paste and give the name and titles of the owner besides Chapter 42 of the *Book of the Dead*. (D.C.)

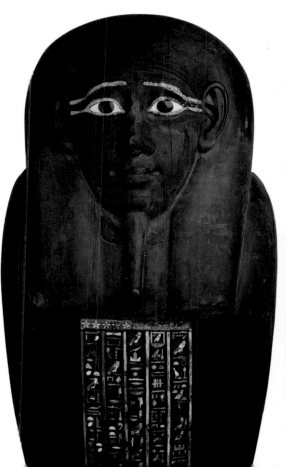

FIRST FLOOR

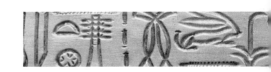

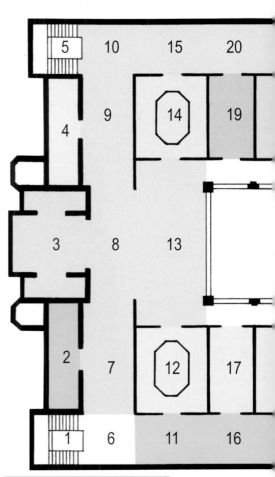

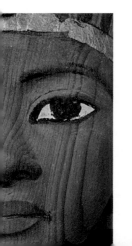

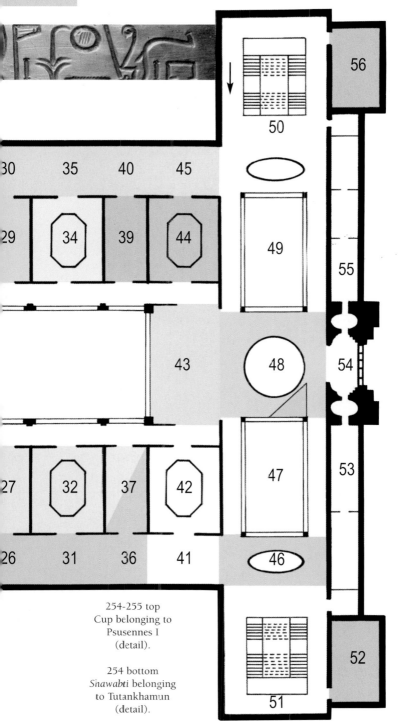

56

50

30   35   40   45

29   34   39   44   49   55

43   48   54

47   53

27   32   37   42

26   31   36   41   46

254-255 top
Cup belonging to
Psusennes I
(detail).

254 bottom
Snawabti belonging
to Tutankhamun
(detail).

52

51

TUTANKHAMUN

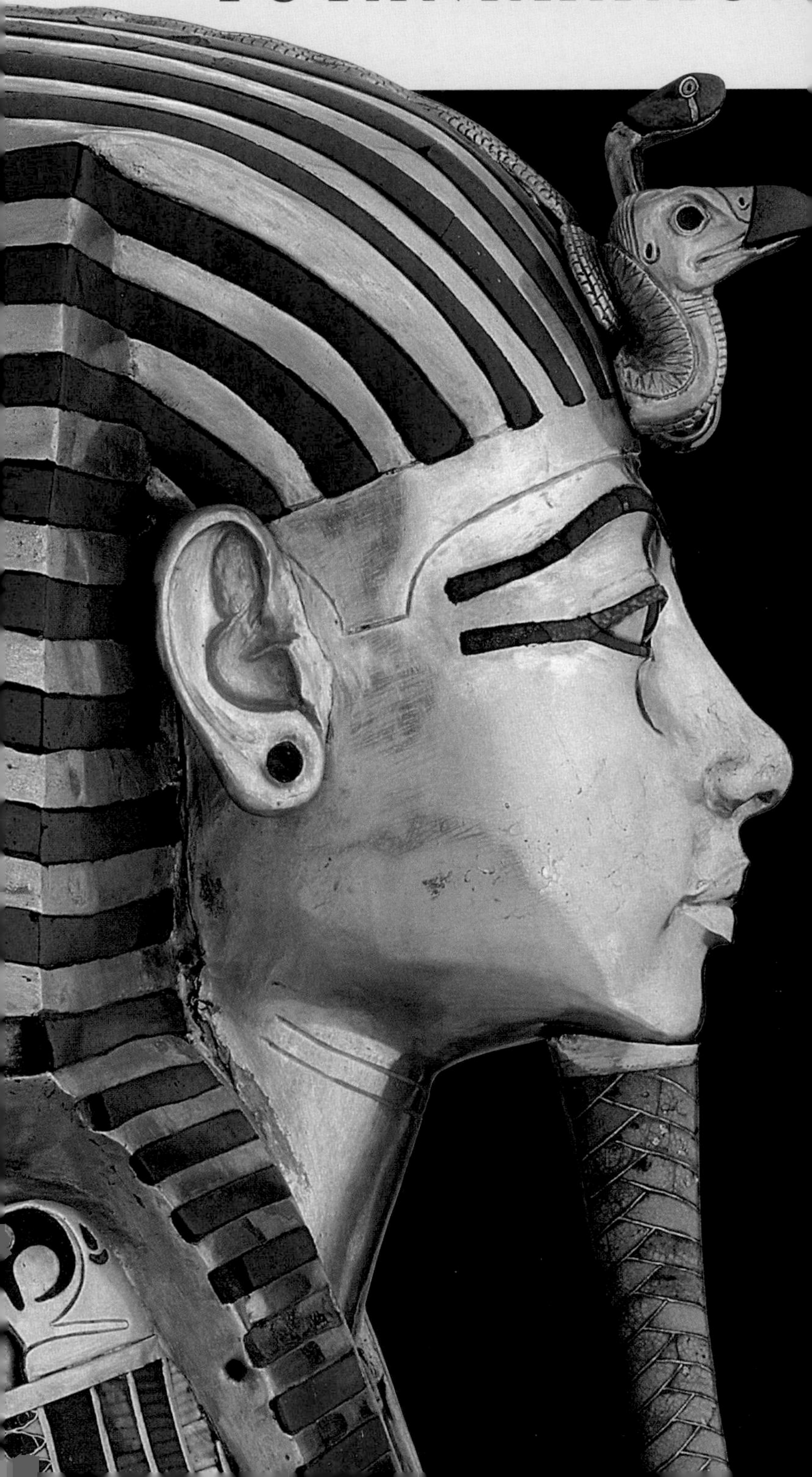

The religious beliefs of the Egyptians prescribed that the dead were to be buried with a set of personal and ritual objects that they would need in the world beyond the tomb. A number of jewels and amulets were placed between the bandages of the mummy for reasons of protection. The tombs of the dead were often the receptacles of priceless treasures and inevitably became the targets of thieves from ancient times, nor did the precautions taken by the authorities to put a stop to the long sequence of raids that devastated the necropolises throughout Egypt from the end of the Old Kingdom have any positive result, especially during periods of political and social instability. Consequently, it is extremely rare to find tombs and their grave goods intact, in particular the last resting places of the pharaohs, which were repeatedly broken into over the millennia. It was, therefore, a sensation when. in 1922, Howard Carter discovered the tomb of Tutankhamun, the only royal tomb from the New Kingdom to have survived practically intact. The quality of manufacture of the astonishing set of funerary goods belonged to the young pharaoh still continues to amaze; they were manufactured with a profusion of precious materials that can only give a vague idea of the extraordinary treasures, now lost forever, that the tombs of the great pharaohs buried in the Valley of the Kings must have contained.

Following the exceptional discovery, the figure of Tutankhamun roused understandable curiosity and inspired accounts that were often fantastic. In truth, we know only a little about this ruler – whom Carter defined "elusive" – whose reign took place during the last phase of the Amarna Period, one of the most fascinating in Egyptian history.

CHAPTER 7
FIRST FLOOR

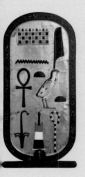

256 GOLD MASK OF
TUTANKHAMUN
Height 54 CM,
weight 11 KG

257 CARTOUCHE-
SHAPED CASKET
Wood,
ebony and ivory;
Length 64.5 CM

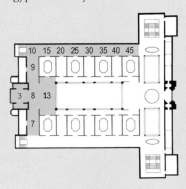

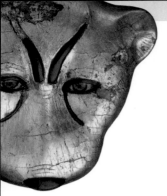

reign of Akhenaten. As a sign of reconciliation with the offended clergy of Amun (the process had already begun during the reign of Smenkhkara), Tutankhaten changed his name to

Tutankhaten ("living image of Aten", this was his original name) ascended the throne around 1333 BC on the death of Smenkhkara, the mysterious successor to Akhenaten. Given our present knowledge, it is impossible to establish the closeness of the relationship of the young king with the family of the "heretical pharaoh" though in all probability he was raised and educated at the court of Amarna and became pharaoh at the age of eight. The right of succession was legitimized by his marriage to the young Ankhesenpaaten ("she lives for Aten") who was the daughter of Akhenaten and Nefertiti. The young bride and groom reigned under the guidance of the army general, Horemheb and the "Father of the gods", Ay, formerly "head of the pharaoh's stables" during the

Tutankhamun and Ankhesenpaaten altered hers to Ankhesenamun.

The desert city of Amarna was abandoned and the court transferred to Memphis since the resentment against the king was more bitter at Thebes – the previous capital – than elsewhere. Guided by the regent Ay, Tutankhamun issued an

edict that reinstated the traditional cults; he also restored divine images that had been damaged and gave back the goods that had been confiscated from the temples.

He died, probably unexpectedly, after only nine years reign. Examination of the mummy shows that he was about eighteen years of age when he died but there is no certain knowledge of the cause of his death although there have been various conjectures: a brain tumour, pulmonary disease, and even murder as an autopsy in 1968 showed that the boy king had suffered a wound to the head at some stage.

Tutankhamun died without an heir and his young wife sent a disquieting message to the king of the Hittites, Suppiluliuma: "… my husband is dead and I have been told you have adult sons. Send me one, I will make him my consort and he shall reign over Egypt …".

After various doubts, Suppiliuma sent one of his sons but he was probably killed in an ambush before he reached Egypt.

Succession was handed to Ay and all trace of Ankhesenamun is lost.

Shrewdly, General Horemheb – who took power after Ay – destroyed Tutankhamun's name from Egyptian monuments as the young king had been linked to the family of the heretical pharaoh and was in some way the last representative of the Amarna Period. Buried in oblivion for three thousand years, the boy pharaoh became unexpectedly famous in 1922 when his tomb was discovered by two

Englishmen, the archaeologist Howard Carter and his sponsor Lord Carnarvon, who followed the excavations with enthusiasm.

Carter's adventure began in 1891 when his extraordinary drawing skill resulted in his being invited to the Nile valley by the Egypt Exploration Fund at the age of only eighteen to draw the scenes and inscriptions painted on the walls in the tombs. Working beside great archaeologists, he soon became absorbed by Egyptology and compensated for a lack of academic education by close observation (a fundamental requisite) and his experience in the field. He became Inspector General of Antiquities in Upper Egypt

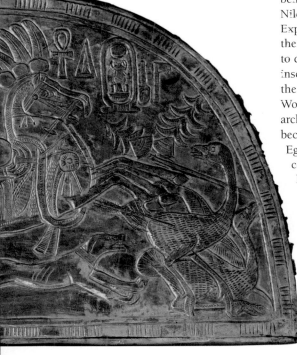

258 HEAD
OF A LEOPARD
Gilded wood
Height 16.5 CM

258-259 OSTRICH-
FEATHER FAN
Wood and gold leaf
Length 105.5 cm,
width of the plate
18.5 CM

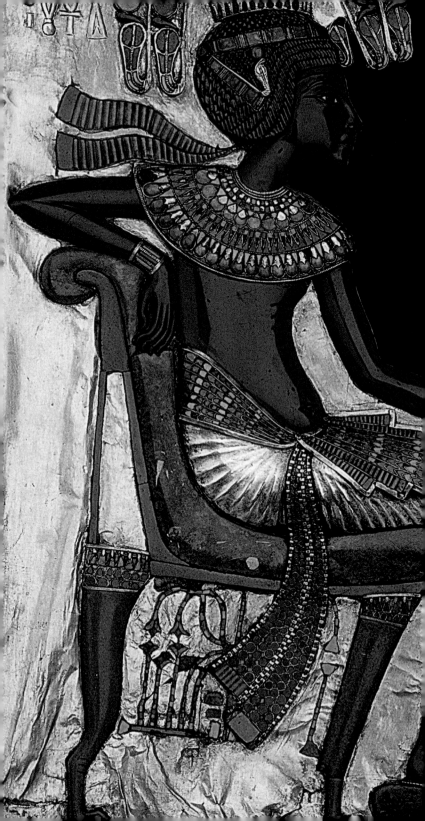

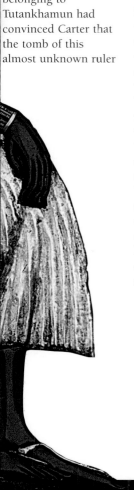

between 1899-1905 and for a short period led digs in the Valley of the Kings inspired by the desire to discover a royal tomb intact.

Various vicissitudes prevented him from undertaking systematic research for over ten years until 1917 when he could collaborate with Lord Carnarvon. The discovery during earlier years of fragments of objects belonging to Tutankhamun had convinced Carter that the tomb of this almost unknown ruler might be discovered. On November 4, 1922, after five long years of fruitless search, the patience and determination of the English archaeologist was finally rewarded: digging beneath the huts of workers near the entrance to the tomb of Rameses VI, a door was revealed that led down to an antechamber from which a small annexe opened out. Next came the funerary chamber and connected to that was the room referred to by Carter as the "Treasure Room." The tomb had escaped the violent looting that devastated the Valley of the Kings during the Twentieth and Twenty-first Dynasties, perhaps thanks to a violent thunderstorm that hid every trace of the entrance, but it had been broken into during ancient times, probably shortly after the burial of the king. The thieves had entered the antechamber, the annexe, and the Treasure Room but only the outermost of the four shrines that almost completely filled the burial chamber itself had been opened. Consequently, the mummy of the pharaoh was intact. The tomb raiders had stolen the valuable ointments and easily removed objects made from gold but left the rest in confusion. The administrators of the necropolis had tidied up the ante-chamber to some extent but left the annexe in a deplorable state.

The walls of the burial chamber show various scenes, including the funeral procession and the ceremony of the Opening of the Mouth presided over by Ay, Tutankhamun's successor.

The complex operations of removing and cataloging the many objects took Carter about ten years. Lord Carnarvon died on April 5, 1923 just a few months after the discovery.
(D.C.)

260 THRONE OF
TUTANKHAMUN (DETAIL)
Wood, gold leaf, silver,
glass paste;
Height 102 CM

STATUE OF THE *KA* OF TUTANKHAMUN

WOOD PAINTED WITH SHINY BLACK RESIN AND GILDED, BRONZE
HEIGHT 192 CM, LENGTH 98 CM, WIDTH 53.3 CM

ROOM 45

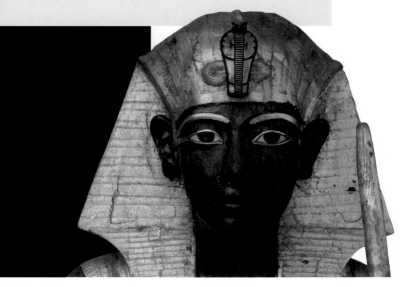

These two life-size statues of Tutankhamun stood facing one another on either side of the burial chamber. They are almost identical but differ slightly in the headdress and the inscriptions of the skirt. Originally they were wrapped in sheets of linen, traces of which were found when the tomb was opened.

One of the statues wears a "bag-like" wig known as *khat*, the other the *nemes*, the striped headdress with two flaps that hang down on the chest and another at the back. Both statues display a gilded bronze uraeus serpent on the forehead and clasp a club and a stick.

The pleated skirt known as a *shendyt* bears a vertical inscription on the trapezoidal cloth on the front that is different on each of the two statues. The birth name of the king is given on the statue with the *nemes*: "Tutankhamun, forever alive like Ra each day." The buckle on the belt of the other statue gives the king's coronation name Nebkheperura and the inscription "The perfect god filled with glory, a king to be proud of, the royal *ka* of Horakhty, Osiris, and Lord of the Two Lands, Nebkheperura, justified."

The *ka* – a fundamental component of the person, together with the *ba* (an animated manifestation of the deceased) and the *akh* (the transfigured spirit) – is a sort of vital force that keeps the individual alive both on earth and in the Afterlife.

The *ka* needs a physical support to survive, i.e. a mummified body. The "statues of the *ka*" averted destruction of the body by providing the soul with an incorruptible resting place.

The color of the skin assimilates the king to the god Osiris whose face is black – the color of deities of the Afterlife – or green like plant life to symbolize the eternal cycle of death and resurrection.
(D.C.)

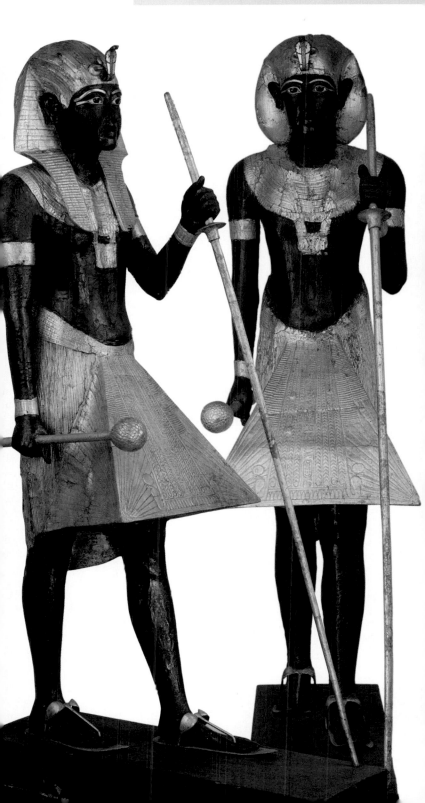

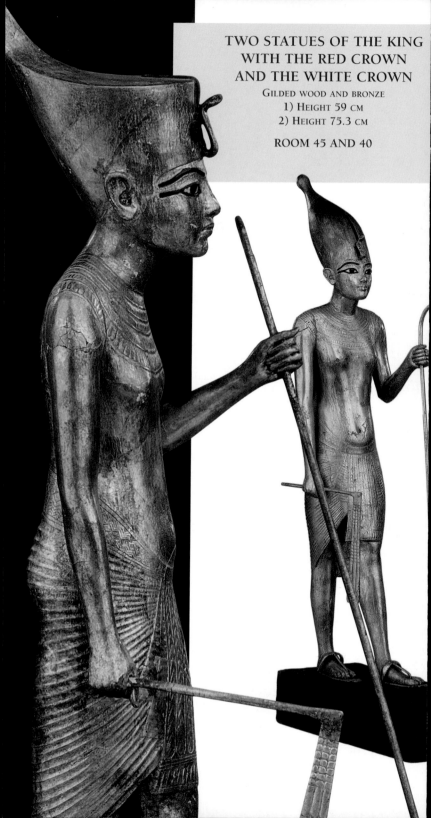

TWO STATUES OF THE KING
WITH THE RED CROWN
AND THE WHITE CROWN
GILDED WOOD AND BRONZE
1) HEIGHT 59 CM
2) HEIGHT 75.3 CM

ROOM 45 AND 40

Twenty-two black cabinets set along the south wall of the Treasure Room held a series of wooden statues, some of which portrayed the king, others various gods. Linen shrouds from the third year of Akhenaten's reign were wrapped around the bodies of the statues leaving only their faces visible, and the images of the gods were decorated with garlands of flowers on their foreheads.

Three of the statues were covered with tar but all the others were lined with gold leaf over plaster and placed on black rectangular pedestals. Those in the photograph portray Tutankhamun wearing the crowns of Upper Egypt (white) and Lower Egypt (red). No actual crown has ever been found and so knowledge of them is due purely to representations of this kind.

The red cap – a flat helmet with an attachment at the back – was probably made of copper, while the tall white tiara was made from a softer material, perhaps leather. Sometimes the pharaoh would wear both crowns together to symbolize his sovereignty over unified Egypt.

The depiction of the figures with the outstretched neck, swollen belly and low hips was clearly influenced by the art of the Amarna Period. (D.C.)

VOTIVE SHIELD
GILDED WOOD
HEIGHT 88 CM, WIDTH 55 CM

ROOM 45

Eight shields were found in the annexe of the antechamber, four of which were made of perforated and gilded wood that could not have been used for personal defence; Carter considered them to be purely ceremonial in purpose.

The shield illustrated is decorated with the traditional theme of the triumph of the pharaoh over the enemies of Egypt. Tutankhamun brandishes his sword as he grabs the tails of two lions that symbolize the enemies. Behind him, the guardian deity of Upper Egypt, the goddess-vulture Nekhbet, stands on a papyrus plant, the emblem of Lower Egypt. The three-column inscription compares the strength of the king in killing wild beasts to that of the Theban god Montu.

The scene is dominated by the winged sun disk. A desert landscape with three hills on the lower register forms the hieroglyphic symbol for foreign countries.

Images of the pharaoh defeating his enemies (sometimes symbolized by desert animals and marsh birds) are common. Foreign enemies of Egypt belonged to the kingdom of disorder and chaos and, inasmuch as it was the pharaoh's role to guarantee cosmic order, it was his duty to take action against them. (D.C.)

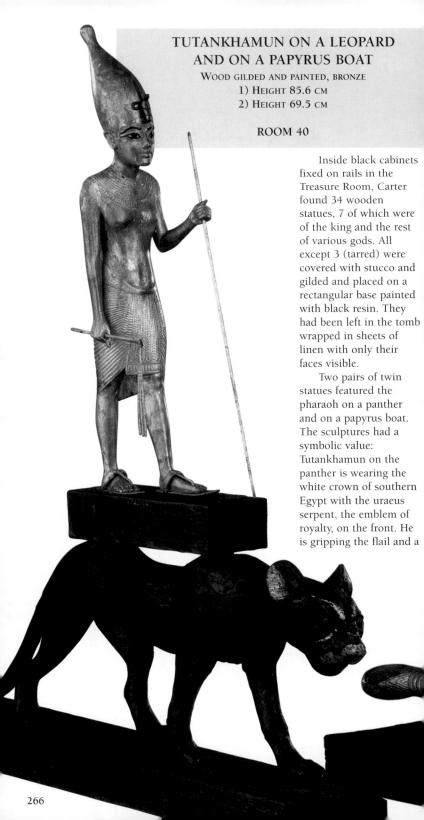

Inside black cabinets fixed on rails in the Treasure Room, Carter found 34 wooden statues, 7 of which were of the king and the rest of various gods. All except 3 (tarred) were covered with stucco and gilded and placed on a rectangular base painted with black resin. They had been left in the tomb wrapped in sheets of linen with only their faces visible.

Two pairs of twin statues featured the pharaoh on a panther and on a papyrus boat. The sculptures had a symbolic value: Tutankhamun on the panther is wearing the white crown of southern Egypt with the uraeus serpent, the emblem of royalty, on the front. He is gripping the flail and a

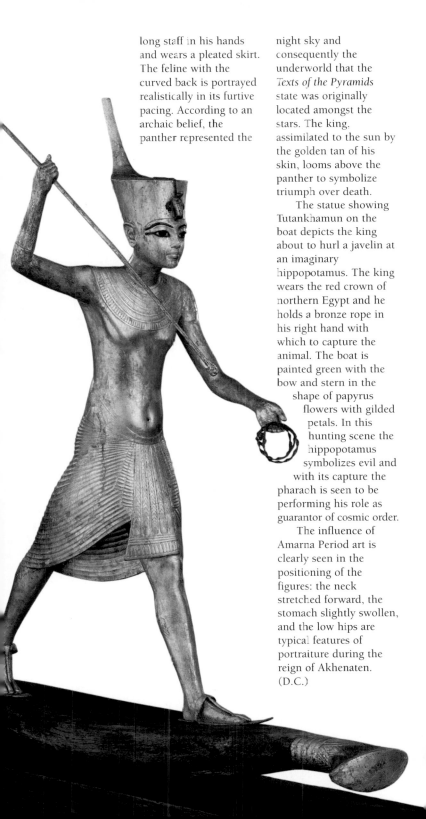

long staff in his hands and wears a pleated skirt. The feline with the curved back is portrayed realistically in its furtive pacing. According to an archaic belief, the panther represented the night sky and consequently the underworld that the *Texts of the Pyramids* state was originally located amongst the stars. The king, assimilated to the sun by the golden tan of his skin, looms above the panther to symbolize triumph over death.

The statue showing Tutankhamun on the boat depicts the king about to hurl a javelin at an imaginary hippopotamus. The king wears the red crown of northern Egypt and he holds a bronze rope in his right hand with which to capture the animal. The boat is painted green with the bow and stern in the shape of papyrus flowers with gilded petals. In this hunting scene the hippopotamus symbolizes evil and with its capture the pharaoh is seen to be performing his role as guarantor of cosmic order.

The influence of Amarna Period art is clearly seen in the positioning of the figures: the neck stretched forward, the stomach slightly swollen, and the low hips are typical features of portraiture during the reign of Akhenaten. (D.C.)

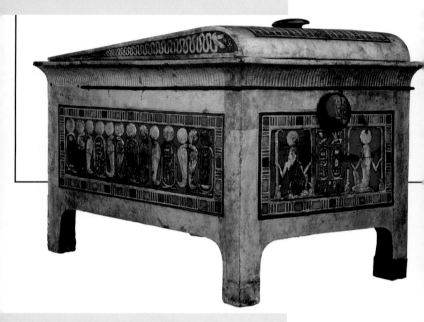

SMALL SARCOPHAGUS WITH A COVER
WOOD LINED WITH GOLD
SARCOPHAGUS: LENGTH 78 CM, WIDTH 26.5
COVER: LENGTH 74 CM

ROOM 40

In the Treasure Room Carter found a small wooden sarcophagus covered with a coat of black resin that contained a second sarcophagus lined with gold leaf on plaster. This contained a third sarcophagus made simply of wood beside which lay a small statue of Tutankhamun made from solid gold. A fourth and innermost sarcophagus held a lock of hair belonging to Queen Tiy.

A great quantity of ointments had been poured between the two outer sarcophaguses but have solidified over the millennia effectively glueing the bottoms of the two cases together to such a degree that they can no longer be separated. The cover of the second sarcophagus – shown in the photograph – portrays Tutankhamun in the traditional pose of the god Osiris with his body bound like a mummy and his arms crossed on his chest. The king is wearing the *nemes*, the striped linen headdress that often substituted the crown. Two goddesses in the form of vultures flank the bust of the king with their wings outspread as a sign of protection.

The column of hieroglyphs engraved on the lower part of the body is an invocation by Tutankhamun to Nut, the goddess of the sky: "Nut, my mother, lay down on me, make me one of your eternal stars that I may never die." (D.C.)

The chest was found with others heaped in disorder in the antechamber of the tomb. The design of the lid was inspired by the form of the primitive temples of Upper Egypt. It was held closed by a string tied to knobs on the cover and the body of the chest.

The beauty of the casket is created by the lovely dichromatic decoration of gold and faïence. On the long sides, five cartouches flanked by uraeus serpents, each with a sun disk, alternately bear the king's coronation and birth names. The short sides are also decorated with the king's cartouches that lie between the two figures of the "spirits of the millions of years." (D.C.)

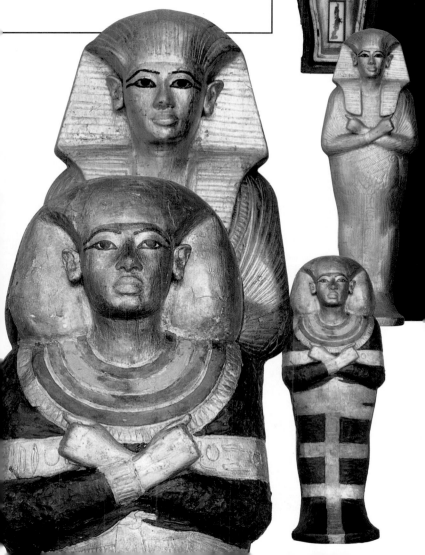

CASKET

WOOD COATED WITH STUCCO AND PAINTED
HEIGHT 44 CM, LENGTH 61 CM, WIDTH 43 CM

ROOM 40

This chest was found in the antechamber to the tomb. Carter was especial struck by the quality of the painting and declared it to be one of the most valuab objects found in the tomb. The decoration is symmetrical on either side and represents the traditional theme of victory over Egypt's enemies; as Egyptian beliefs defined foreigners as inhabitants of the kingdom of chaos, the pharaoh claimed the right to intervene militarily against anyone who compromised the univers order of which he was the guarantor.

On the longer sides of the chest, the pharaoh is shown on his chariot drawn by magnificently harnessed horses. As was

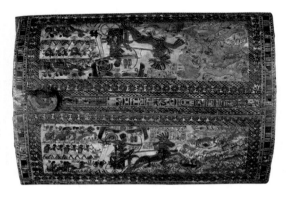

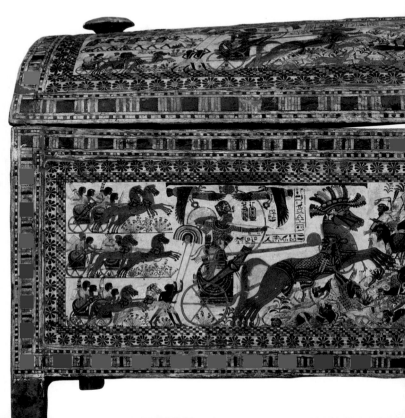

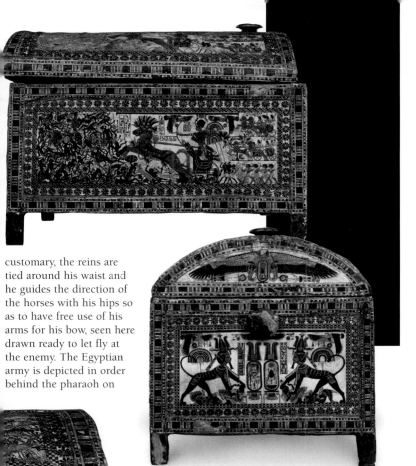

customary, the reins are tied around his waist and he guides the direction of the horses with his hips so as to have free use of his arms for his bow, seen here drawn ready to let fly at the enemy. The Egyptian army is depicted in order behind the pharaoh on three rows while the enemies (Syrians on one side and Nubians on the other) are shown in a chaotic and confused mass of chariots, soldiers, and horses.

On the short sides, Tutankhamun is portrayed as a sphinx trampling his northern and southern enemies. Another version of the triumphal theme is found on the lid of the chest which is decorated with two hunting scenes in the desert: the sovereign on his chariot shoots arrows into wild animals symbolizing Egypt's enemies.

The chest contained a number of objects: three pairs of gold sandals, one of papyrus plant, a gilded headrest, embroidered garments decorated with gold appliqués, necklaces, belts, and shoes. Carter had great difficulty in dealing with these items as they risked being damaged as soon as they were touched; to empty the chest required three weeks of work.
(D.C.)

SHAWABTY WITH THE RED CROWN
SHAWABTY WITH THE WHITE CROWN

GILDED WOOD AND BRONZE
1) HEIGHT 63 CM
2) HEIGHT 61.5 CM

ROOM 40

The two *shawabty* show the king wearing different crowns: the red crown of Lower Egypt and the white one of Upper Egypt. The red crown was a flat cap with an attached piece behind and was probably made of copper; the white crown was a tall tiara and was made from a soft material, perhaps leather.

Sometimes the pharaohs wore the "double crown" – *pshent* – with one worn over the top of the other to signify the ruler's sovereignty over unified Egypt.

The statue wearing the red cap with the uraeus serpent on the front holds the royal insignia of the scepter and flail; the other displays both the uraeus serpent and the vulture but the flail has been lost.
(D.C.)

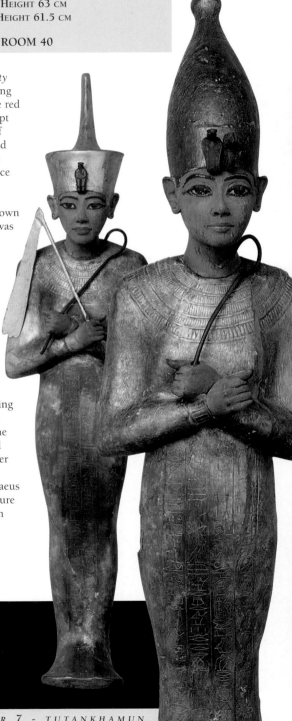
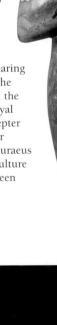

SHAWABTY WITH NUBIAN WIGS
SHAWABTY WITH TWO FLAILS
1) WOOD, GOLD AND BRONZE; HEIGHT 54 CM
2) WOOD AND GOLD; HEIGHT 52 CM

ROOM 40

These two funerary statuettes are wearing a short curly wig in Nubian style that was reserved for use by the royal family, both men and women. The first has the emblems of royal power, a uraeus serpent and vulture, on the front but the royal insignia, the scepter and flail, that the statue probably held in its hands were not found.

Oddly, the second is clutching two gilded bronze flails instead of a flail and a scepter; the absence of the scepter is unusual.

Chapter 6 of the *Book of the Dead* is engraved in four columns of hieroglyphs on both *shawabty*.
(D.C.)

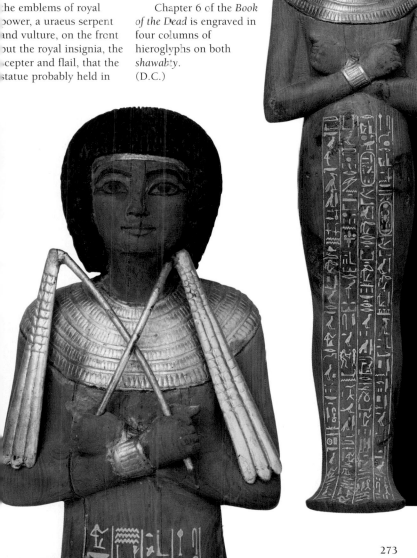

273

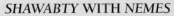

SHAWABTY WITH NEMES
WOOD, GOLD LEAF, BRONZE
HEIGHT 48 CM

ROOM 40

The *shawabty*
depicting Tutankhamun
all portray the king
with a young face but
differ in certain
details, for example,
the hairstyle or
headdress he is
wearing. This
statuette shows the
king with the
nemes, a linen
headdress of blue
and white stripes that
the pharaoh often wore
instead of the crown.
His hands are crossed
on his chest and hold
the *heqa* scepter and
flail.

A six-column
inscription on the
lower part of the statue
recounts Chapter 6 of
the *Book of the Dead* in
a custom that began to
establish itself during
the Eighteenth Dynasty.
(D.C.)

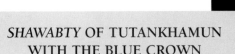

SHAWABTY OF TUTANKHAMUN
WITH THE BLUE CROWN
GILDED CEDAR WOOD
HEIGHT 48 CM

ROOM 40

Shawabty were funerary statues that formed an important element of grave goods from the Middle Kingdom on. In ancient Egyptian, the word *shawabty* meant "he who responds" for it was the duty of these statuettes to respond to Osiris' appeal and work in place of the deceased in the fields of the Afterlife. For this reason, they were usually created gripping farming implements in their hands.

The number of *shawabty* varied from epoch to epoch and according to the social status of the deceased: Tutankhamun had 413 of which 365 (the number of days in the year) were workers divided into groups of 10, 36 were of foremen and 12 of overseers (one per month).

Some of the statuettes of Tutankhamun wear the crown and hold royal insignia. The *shawabty* of Tutankhamun illustrated shows the king wearing the blue crown that was similar to a helmet. His body is in the traditional pose of Osiris, bound like a mummy with his arms crossed on his chest and holding the scepter and gold flail.

Two columns of hieroglyphs give a short version of Chapter 6 of the *Book of the Dead*. There is a dedication from an army general, Minnakht, engraved below the feet of the statue; functionaries used to donate a *shawabty* to their king as by so doing they could offer him their services in the Afterlife. (D.C.)

SHAWABTY WITH NUBIAN WIG
Gilded wood and bronze
Height 54 cm

ROOM 40

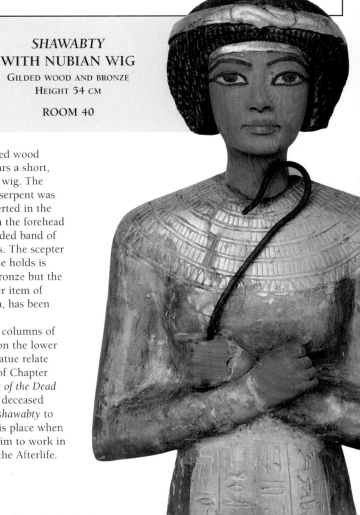

This gilded wood *shawabty* wears a short, Nubian-style wig. The royal uraeus serpent was probably inserted in the small hole on the forehead below the gilded band of the headdress. The scepter that the statue holds is made from bronze but the flail, the other item of royal insignia, has been lost.

The four columns of hieroglyphs on the lower part of the statue relate the formula of Chapter 6 of the *Book of the Dead* in which the deceased requests his *shawabty* to respond in his place when Osiris calls him to work in the fields of the Afterlife. (D.C.)

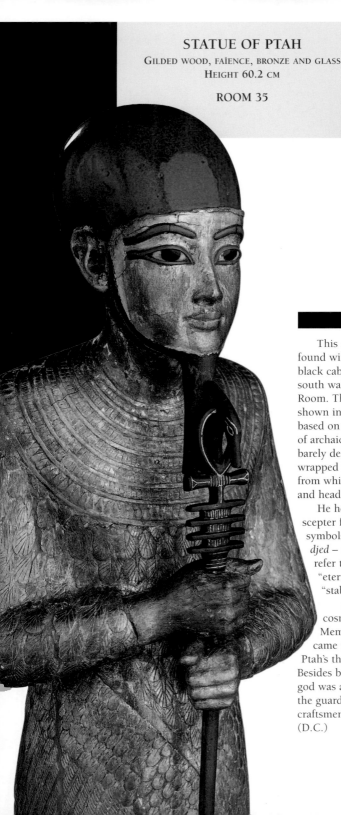

STATUE OF PTAH

GILDED WOOD, FAÏENCE, BRONZE AND GLASS
HEIGHT 60.2 CM

ROOM 35

This statuette was found with others in the black cabinets set along t south wall of the Treasure Room. The god Ptah is shown in his typical imag based on the stylistic norr of archaic statuary with h barely defined body wrapped in a sort of shea from which only his hand and head emerge.

He holds a composite scepter formed by three symbols – *was*, *ankh*, ar *djed* – that respectively refer to "power," "eternal life," and "stability."

According to the cosmogony of Memphis, the world came into being throu Ptah's thought and word Besides being a creator, th god was also worshipped the guardian deity of craftsmen.
(D.C.)

TWO FAÏENCE *SHAWABTY*

FAÏENCE
1) HEIGHT 30 CM
2) HEIGHT 30 CM

ROOM 35

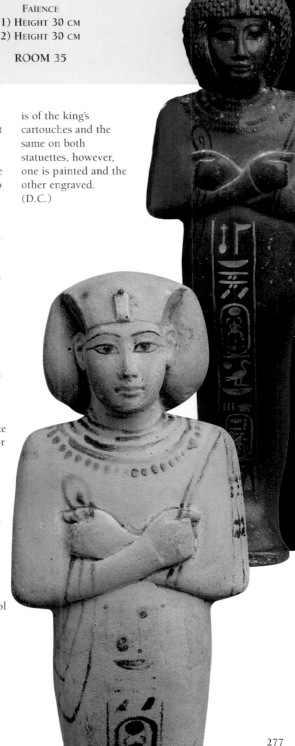

The *shawabty* of Tutankhamun were kept in special chests found in the Treasure Room and in the annexe of the antechamber. These two faïence statuettes lay with others made of the same material in one of the caskets found in the annexe.

Faïence products – mostly plate for table or toilet use – were made using mixes of quartz-based sand which were pressed into molds and later coated with green, turquoise, or blue glass pastes. The articles thus produced were a sort of cheaper version of the objects carved from semi-precious stones like lapis lazuli, turquoise, or feldspar. Faïence was used during the New Kingdom also in the production of funerary statuettes.

These two *shawabty* represented overseers and, with the other ten, monitored the work of the 36 teams of workers. The overseers hold the flail, the symbol of power, and a folded piece of material that was probably used to clean their hands.

The inscription is of the king's cartouches and the same on both statuettes, however, one is painted and the other engraved. (D.C.)

277

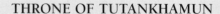

THRONE OF TUTANKHAMUN
Wood, gold leaf, silver, glass paste
and semi-precious stones
Height 102 cm, length 54 cm, width 60 cm

ROOM 35

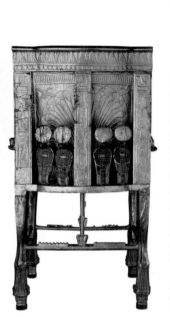

Beneath one of the large funerary beds in the antechamber of the tomb, Carter found a wooden throne entirely lined with gold. The magnificence of the decoration created with inlays of silver, semi-precious stones, and colored glass paste prompted the archaeologist to declare this the most beautiful object ever found in Egypt until that time.

The feet of the throne are in the form of a lion's feet; two winged serpents

form the armrests, wearing the double crown of Upper and Lower Egypt and spreading their wings a a sign of protection ove the cartouches of the king; and two lions' heads adorn the front section of the seat.

The backrest is decorated with a very beautiful scene: Tutankhamun is seated on a padded throne wit an arm resting on the back and his feet on a stool. He is wearing an elaborate crown, a large collar, and a pleated skirt. Ankhesenamun stands in front of him and with her right hand spreads an ointment on his shoulder from a pot she holds in the other hand. She wears a long tunic and large collar and, on her head, a diadem of cobras topped by cow horns which enclose two plumes and a sun disk. The garments of the couple are made from silver. A necklace rests on a high table behind the queen. The Aten (sun disk) spreads its beneficent rays that terminate in tiny hands over the young couple.

The cartouches give the names of the two figures in their original Amarnian form: Tutankhaten and Ankhesenpaaten, as well as in their later form.

The presence of the Aten in the decoration dates the throne to the first years of Tutankhamun's reign. The substitution of Amun for Aten in the cartouches probably occurred at a later time after the return to the orthodox worship of Amun.

The scenes from the private life of the royal family are typical of the Amarna Period. (D.C.)

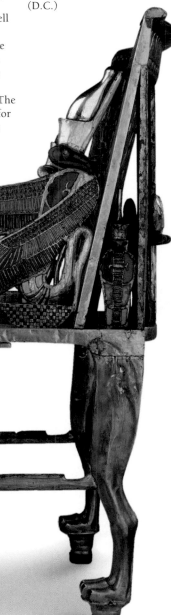

SHRINE FOR STATUE

Gilded wood and silver
Height 50.5 cm, length 48 cm
width 30.7 cm

ROOM 35

This wooden shrine was found in the tomb's antechamber. The walls are crowned by a moulding and the convex roof that slopes away towards the back to resemble the Predynastic temples of southern Egypt. It is entirely covered with gold leaf and rests on a sled lined with silver.

The shrine contained a royal statuette, probably

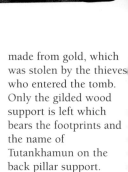

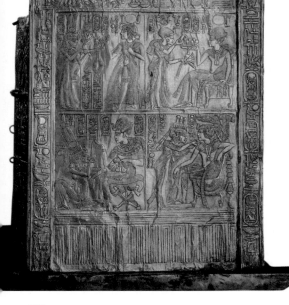

made from gold, which was stolen by the thieves who entered the tomb. Only the gilded wood support is left which bears the footprints and the name of Tutankhamun on the back pillar support.

Rich decoration covers the surfaces of the shrine. The pharaoh and his young bride are shown on the walls and doors in square portraits. In the two on the right wall, Tutankhamun is shown hunting birds in the marshes

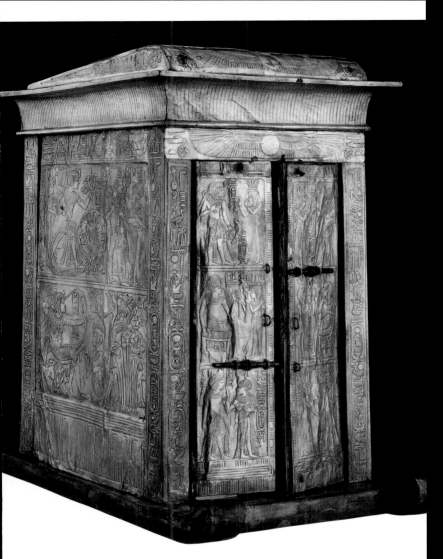

accompanied by
Ankhesenamun; on the
opposite side, the
enthroned sovereign
receives various objects
from the queen and pours
a liquid on her hands as
she crouches before him.
Other scenes of offerings
are shown on the rear
wall and door. The use of
images of royal family life
was inherited from
Amarna Period art and
the poses and behaviour

of the individuals seem
natural and intimate, yet
it is the symbology in
these scenes that
prevails; for example, in
the scenes of offerings, it
is the fundamental role
of the queen that is being
celebrated for it is she
who maintains the links
between the sky and the
earth and provides the
king with the energy
necessary for the
permanent regeneration

of life and royal power.
Ankhesenamun offers her
husband lotus flowers,
menat necklaces (symbols
of rebirth), and sistrums
the sounds of which ward
off evil.

The hunting scenes,
on the other hand,
celebrate the triumph of
order, of which the king
was guarantor, over
chaos, symbolized by the
marsh birds.
(D.C.)

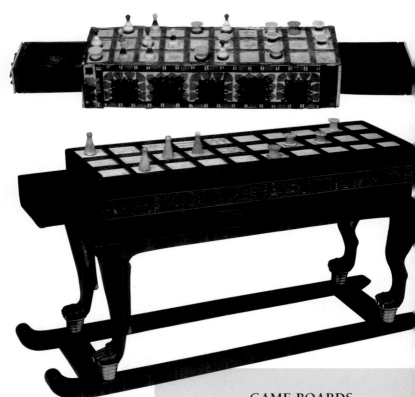

GAME BOARDS

1) WOOD, GOLD AND IVORY
HEIGHT 5.8, LENGTH 27.5 CM, WIDTH 9 CM

2) EBONY, GOLD AND IVORY
GAMES BOARD: HEIGHT 8.1 CM, LENGTH 46 CM
WIDTH 16 CM
SUPPORT: HEIGHT 20.2 CM, LENGTH 55 CM

ROOM 35

Table games were very much appreciated in ancient Egypt with the most popular being *senet*. The game was for two people and played on a rectangular board with the upper surface divided into thirty squares; probably the game consisted of moving tokens around the board in accordance with the throw of small battens that corresponded to our modern dice. The lower surface of the board was used for playing the "twenty-square game."

Tutankhamun had four *senet* boards of which the largest was the most lavish. The squares were inlaid with ivory and the board itself rests on a small frame with supports in the form of lions' paws and fitted with runners. The drawer on the short side was found empty and removed from its housing and, as the tokens were missing, it is supposed that they were made from a valuable material and stolen by the tomb thieves. The tokens shown in the picture belonged to other, less magnificent, boards.

During the New Kingdom, *senet* took on a magical-religious value and in the introductory formula in Chapter 17 of the *Book of the Dead*, it was considered essential that the deceased played a game against an invisible opponent to ensure his own survival. (D.C.)

Carter found a series of small chests in the Treasure Room that held items of jewelry and other valuable objects. Their contents had attracted the attention of the thieves who had grabbed some and left the rest in disarray.

This casket is unusual for its cartouche form. It is made from conifer wood with ebony edging to the supports. The name of Tutankhamun is given on the cover in hieroglyphs of ebony and ivory. The inscriptions carved on the chest and painted blue list the king's titles and attributes. (D.C.)

CASKET IN THE FORM OF A CARTOUCHE

Conifer wood, ebony and ivory; Length 64.5 cm; width 29.8 cm; Height 31.7 cm

ROOM 30

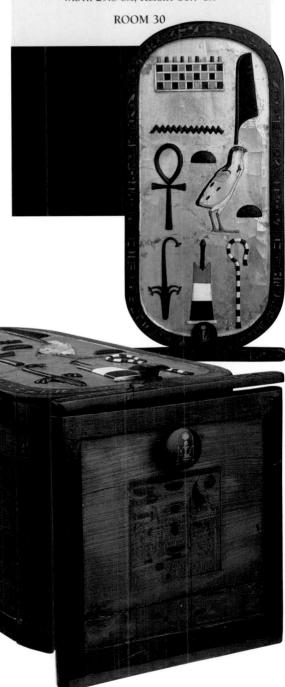

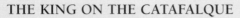

THE KING ON THE CATAFALQUE

WOOD
LENGTH 42.2 CM
WIDTH 12 CM

ROOM 30

This statuette of the king lying on the catafalque was found in a rectangular chest in the Treasure Room. The object was carefully wrapped in a linen cloth with several miniature agricultural tools similar to those belonging to the *shawabty* – the funerary statuettes of the king's assistants found in the tomb. The presence of these tools prompted Carter to consider there was a link between the small wooden sculpture and the funerary statuettes.

Tutankhamun lies on a catafalque decorated with two lions' heads; he wears the *nemes* headdress with a gilded uraeus serpent on the forehead. The body is in the traditional pose of Osiris, bound like a mummy and with his arms crossed over his chest. A falcon and a bird with a human head protect the sides and torso of the king with their open wings. The falcon is Horus, the god of the sky and royalty, while the bird with the human head represents the *ba*, the animated manifestation of the deceased.

The columns of hieroglyphs engraved on the body are an invocation by Tutankhamun to the goddess of the sky, Nut, whereas the inscription on the sides of the catafalque contains a dedication to by Maya, Tutankhamun's scribe and superintendent of the treasure. Maya also gave Tutankhamun a *shawabty*.
(D.C.)

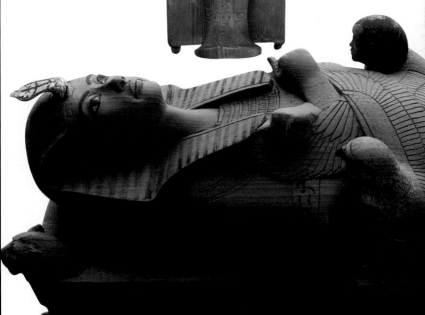

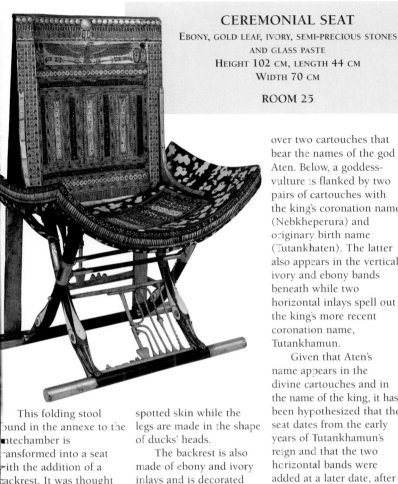

CEREMONIAL SEAT

EBONY, GOLD LEAF, IVORY, SEMI-PRECIOUS STONES
AND GLASS PASTE
HEIGHT 102 CM, LENGTH 44 CM
WIDTH 70 CM

ROOM 25

This folding stool found in the annexe to the antechamber is transformed into a seat with the addition of a backrest. It was thought by Carter to be a "ceremonial seat." It is made of ebony with irregularly shaped ivory inlays in imitation of a spotted skin while the legs are made in the shape of ducks' heads.

The backrest is also made of ebony and ivory inlays and is decorated with semi-precious stones, glass paste and gold leaf. In the center at the top there is a frieze of uraeus serpents and a sun disk over two cartouches that bear the names of the god Aten. Below, a goddess-vulture is flanked by two pairs of cartouches with the king's coronation name (Nebkheperura) and originary birth name (Tutankhaten). The latter also appears in the vertical ivory and ebony bands beneath while two horizontal inlays spell out the king's more recent coronation name, Tutankhamun.

Given that Aten's name appears in the divine cartouches and in the name of the king, it has been hypothesized that the seat dates from the early years of Tutankhamun's reign and that the two horizontal bands were added at a later date, after the Amarna Period had come to an end and maybe following intentional damage.
(D.C.)

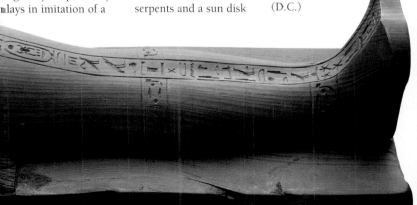

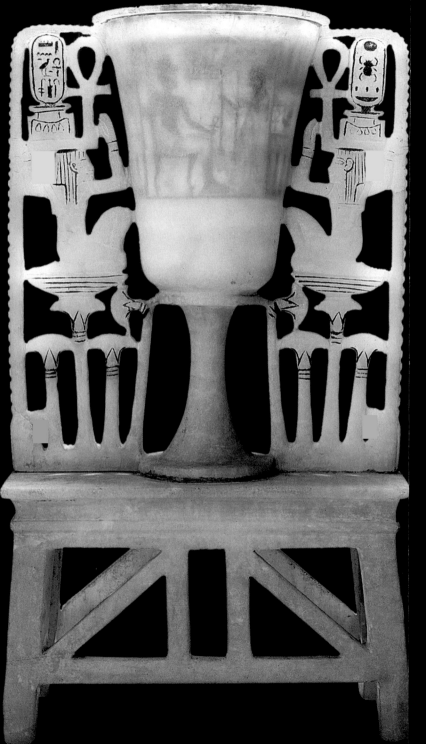

LAMP IN THE FORM OF A CUP

ALABASTER
HEIGHT 51.4 CM, WIDTH 28.8 CM

ROOM 20

This original alabaster oil lamp was found in the burial chamber. The cup, made in the form of an open lotus flower, is flanked by two ornamentations in which the god of the infinite, Heh, kneels on papyrus plants with his arms raised and holds a palm branch that frames the scene.

When the lamp is lit, a transparent colored scene is created with Tutankhamun and his wife on one side and the kings' cartouches on the other. The effect is created when the wick is lit and scenes painted on a smaller cup inside the lamp become visible. (D.C.)

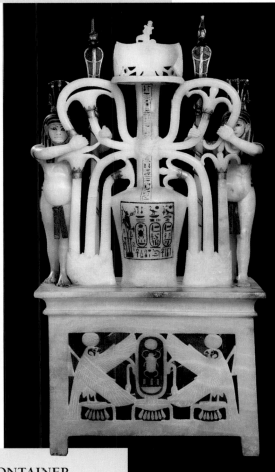

PERFUME CONTAINER

ALABASTER
HEIGHT 70 CM
WIDTH 36.8 CM

ROOM 20

This elaborate container was used to hold perfumed oils and ointments and was found in the burial chamber between the first and second shrines.

The container is in the form of the hieroglyph *sema* meaning "union". The two figures at the sides, representing the god of the Nile, knot the heraldic plants of Upper and Lower Egypt to the pot. The overall composition reproduces the emblem meaning "the union of the Two Lands" often seen on the throne in statues of the pharaohs. (D.C.)

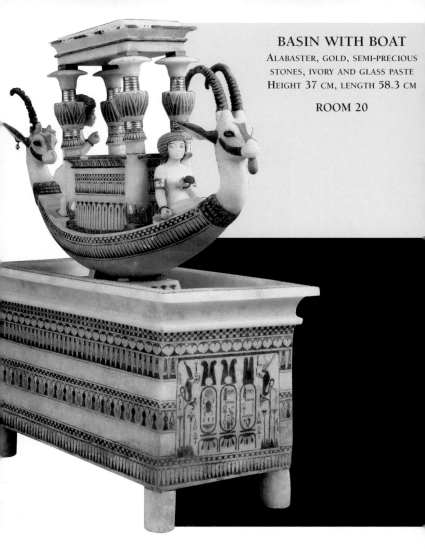

BASIN WITH BOAT

Alabaster, gold, semi-precious
stones, ivory and glass paste
Height 37 cm, length 58.3 cm

ROOM 20

This unusual
alabaster object was
found by Carter among
the grave goods heaped
haphazardly in the
annexe to the tomb. It is
a boat fixed to a pedestal
placed in a rectangular
basin. The bow and stern
of the boat are finished
with antelope heads with
real horns.

Richly decorated
columns with capitals in
the shape of lotus flowers
and papyrus support a
canopy in the center of

the boat. The sides of the
canopy are closed by
walls that reach half-way
up the columns. A naked
young girl crouches in
the bow holding a lotus
flower in her hand and a
realistically portrayed
female dwarf, also naked,
is at the wheel of the
boat.

The rectangular basin
is decorated with
geometric and floral
motifs in gold and glass
paste. Aligned with the
bow of the boat on the

short side of the basin,
three cartouches bear the
names of the king and
queen flanked by two
small uraeus serpents.

Carter hypothesized
that this original
sculpture was a very
refined table piece as,
when he found it, it was
adorned with garlands of
flowers and fruit. The
basin was in all
probability filled with
water so that the boat
appeared to float.
(D.C.)

CUP IN THE FORM OF A LOTUS FLOWER

ALABASTER
HEIGHT 18.3 CM

ROOM 20

This alabaster drinking cup was found at the entrance to the tomb. It was carved in the form of an open lotus flower surrounded by smaller blooms and flowers that form the handles and which are crowned by the figure of the god Heh.

Tutankhamun's cartouches are shown on one side of the cup while the inscription on the rim is a moving message to the young king: "May your *ka* live for ever, may you, who love Thebes, spend millions of years with your face to the north wind, and may your eyes see joy."

The hieroglyphs are carved and inlaid with blue pigment.
(D.C.)

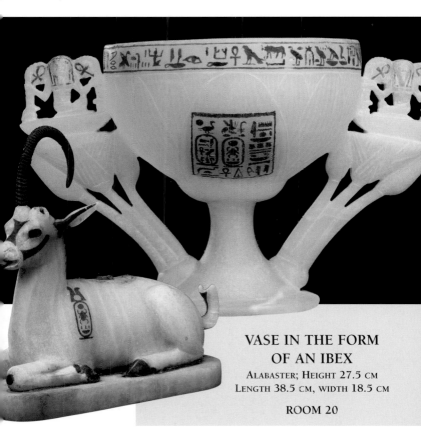

VASE IN THE FORM OF AN IBEX

ALABASTER; HEIGHT 27.5 CM
LENGTH 38.5 CM, WIDTH 18.5 CM

ROOM 20

This alabaster vase in the form of an ibex was found in the annexe of the antechamber with other containers made from the same material which were used to contain ointments.

The mouth of the vase was fixed to the back of the animal but was broken. The horn (only one remains) is real; the eyes, made from inlays of bronze and glass paste, are particularly expressive and the painted ivory tongue that protrudes from the lips realistically suggests the animal is bleating.

The unusual container is an excellent indication of the creative freedom of Egyptian artists when they were not bound by the complex regal symbolism of the funerary cult.
(D.C.)

A miniature fleet of eighteen model boats was found in the Treasure Room and other boats of the same type were found in the annexe to the antechamber. The boats were used by the king on his journey beyond the grave and consequently were all facing west to indicate the direction of travel.

The boat in the photograph is fitted with sails and shrouds and has a central cabin and a housing at either end decorated with images of a bull and a sphinx. This type of boat was used to make pilgrimages to the holy city of Abydos, the center of the cult of the god Osiris.

The other models are of boats designed for specific purposes: rafts

for transportation of goods, 'sun' boats for Tutankhamun's daily journey across the sky with the sun god Ra, canoes for hunting hippopotami and birds in the marshes of the Underworld, and boats for arrival at the "double land of happiness," a paradisiacal land rich in vegetation, rivers, and streams.

The purpose of the fleet was to enable the pharaoh to face any type of celestial navigation adequately.
(D.C.)

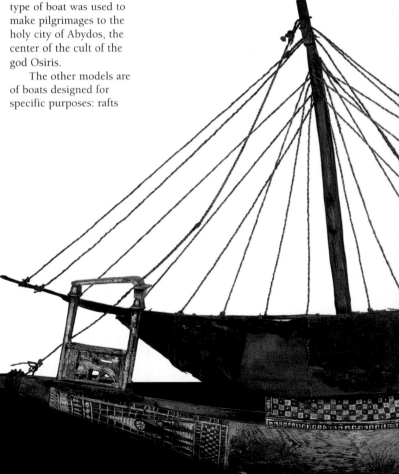

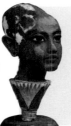

Carter found this unusual sculpture in the debris that cluttered the access corridor at the entrance to the tomb. That was probably not its original location and it has been suggested that the tomb robbers may have dropped it for one reason or another in their exit which could well have been a hasty one.

The creator of this small masterpiece has shown the head of the boy pharaoh emerging from a lotus flower with its petals open. The blue painted base represents the water on which the flower grows.

The lotus, both white and blue versions, was very common in Egypt. The form of the flowers and buds was used as an architectural element in the capitals of columns and as an ornamental motif in various contexts.

HEAD OF TUTANKHAMUN EMERGING FROM A LOTUS FLOWER

WOOD LINED WITH STUCCO AND PAINTED
HEIGHT 30 CM

ROOM 20

The strong symbolic value attributed by the ancient Egyptians to the lotus is derived from the characteristic of the flower to close its petals and sink below the water at dusk only to emerge at dawn and open its petals towards the east to greet the rising sun. The emerging lotus is the symbol of the sun that is also regenerated each morning following its nightly journey to the regions of the underworld.

Certain chapters of the *Book of the Dead* (chapters 77-88) contain the formulas that allow the deceased to take on different forms to move more easily

through the world beyond the grave; the formula in Chapter 81 allows death to transform itself into a lotus flower and the illustration that accompanies it shows the head of a man emerging from the lotus. With this transformation, the deceased hopes to acquire the capability of regeneration symbolized by the plant. Analogously, the small sculpture found in the tomb has the purpose of wishing the sovereign a destiny of perpetual rebirth.
(D.C.)

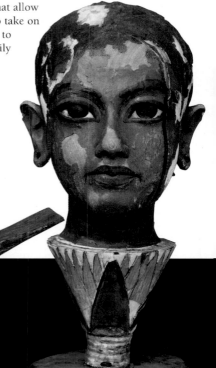

CEREMONIAL CHARIOT
Wood, gold, semi-precious stones and glass paste
Width of the body 105 cm, depth 46 cm,
diameter of the wheels 90 cm,
length of the shaft 216 cm,
Overall length 250 cm, height 118 cm

ROOM 13

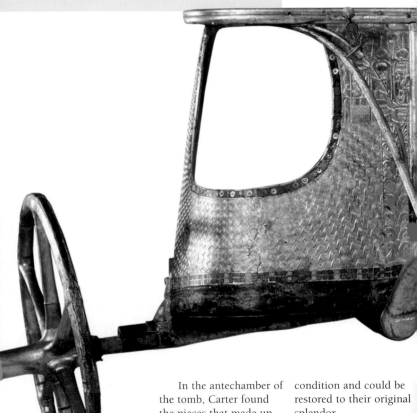

In the antechamber of the tomb, Carter found the pieces that made up four large chariots heaped in disorder along the east wall. The vehicles had been disassembled during the burial because they were too large to be wheeled through the narrow entrance corridor.

The disorder of the pieces was the work of tomb robbers who had moved everything around in their search for easily removable pieces of gold. Despite this treatment, the chariots were in good condition and could be restored to their original splendor.

This magnificent display chariot is made from wood lined with gold. The external decoration of the body is made up of small spiral motifs with a column of lilies in the center topped by the king's cartouches. The internal decoration is on three rows: Tutankhamun's cartouches are repeated at the top, the heraldic emblem of the union of Upper and Lower Egypt is displayed

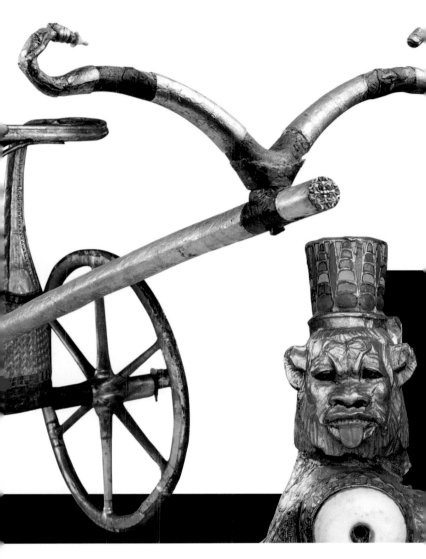

in the center, and the king is shown in the form of a sphinx trampling his prisoners at the bottom.

The floor of the chariot is formed by intertwined bands of hide covered by skins and linen matting, and the rims of the wheels were originally lined with leather. The yoke was joined to the shaft and decorated with the images of two prisoners at the ends.

The war chariot was introduced by the Hyksos during the Second Intermediate Period; during the New Kingdom, the chariot division was the most prestigious in the Egyptian army and charioteers reached the highest levels of the military hierarchy. Each chariot carried two soldiers: the driver and a fighter.

The pharaoh, on the other hand, drove his chariot alone at the head of his troops. The reins were tied to his waist and he guided the direction of the chariot with his hips so as to manage his bow and arrows with freedom.

The use of the chariot in civil life never became widespread.

(D.C.)

293

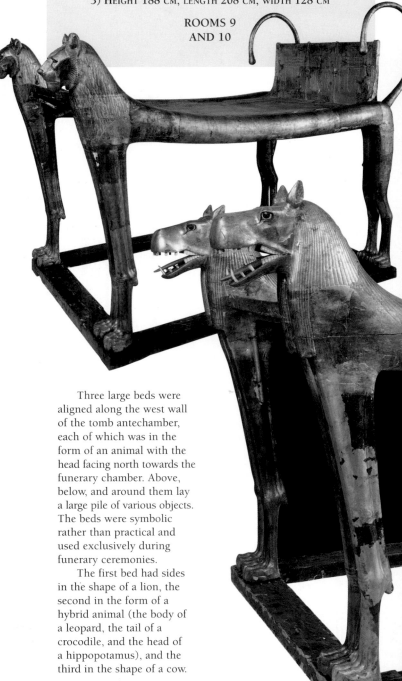

FUNERARY BEDS
WOOD LINED WITH STUCCO AND PAINTED, GOLD LEAF, GLASS PASTE
AND SEMI-PRECIOUS STONES
1) HEIGHT 156 CM, LENGTH 181 CM, WIDTH 91 CM
2) HEIGHT 134 CM, LENGTH 236 CM, WIDTH 126 CM
3) HEIGHT 188 CM, LENGTH 208 CM, WIDTH 128 CM

ROOMS 9
AND 10

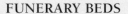

Three large beds were aligned along the west wall of the tomb antechamber, each of which was in the form of an animal with the head facing north towards the funerary chamber. Above, below, and around them lay a large pile of various objects. The beds were symbolic rather than practical and used exclusively during funerary ceremonies.

The first bed had sides in the shape of a lion, the second in the form of a hybrid animal (the body of a leopard, the tail of a crocodile, and the head of a hippopotamus), and the third in the shape of a cow.

The cow (with leopard spots that imitated the stars in the night sky) is *Mehet-Uret*, "the great flood," and represented the first being to emerge from Nun, the "Primordial Waters"; the hybrid animal is Ammut, the "devourer of cadavers," who appears in the scene of the weighing of souls in the *Book of the Dead* but the hybrid animal (with the appearance of a sow) was also a form of Nut, the sky that swallows the deceased at dusk and gives birth to him regenerated once more in the morning.

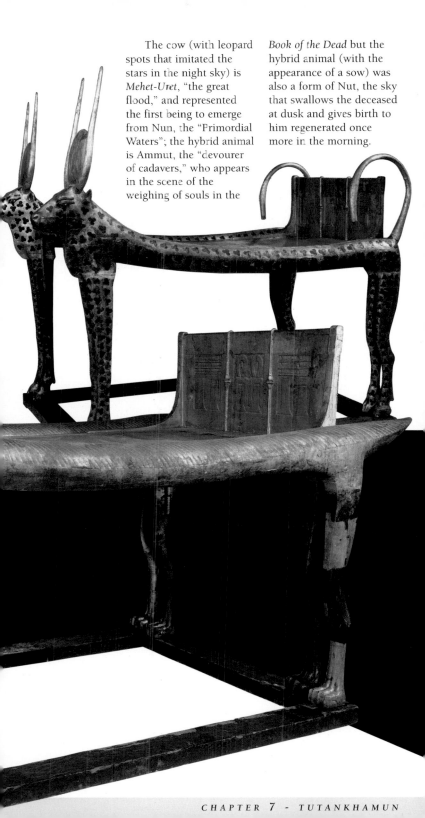

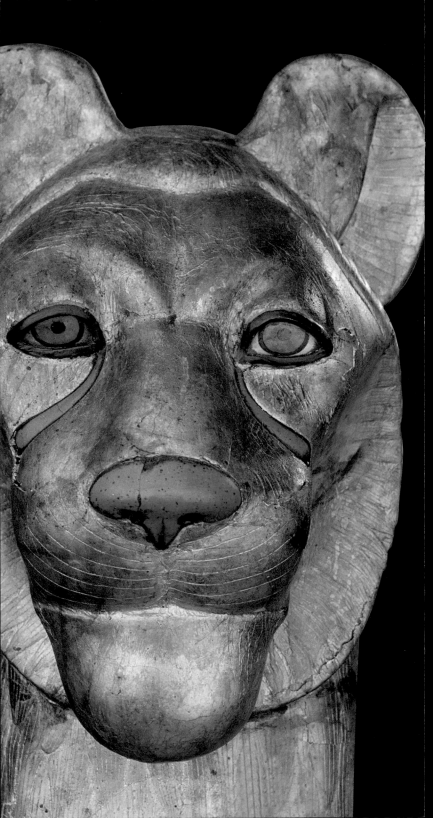

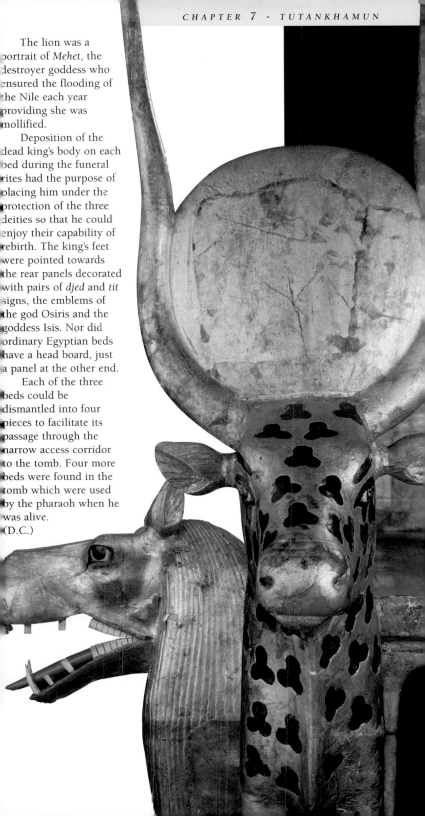

The lion was a portrait of *Mehet*, the destroyer goddess who ensured the flooding of the Nile each year providing she was mollified.

Deposition of the dead king's body on each bed during the funeral rites had the purpose of placing him under the protection of the three deities so that he could enjoy their capability of rebirth. The king's feet were pointed towards the rear panels decorated with pairs of *djed* and *tit* signs, the emblems of the god Osiris and the goddess Isis. Nor did ordinary Egyptian beds have a head board, just a panel at the other end.

Each of the three beds could be dismantled into four pieces to facilitate its passage through the narrow access corridor to the tomb. Four more beds were found in the tomb which were used by the pharaoh when he was alive.
(D.C.)

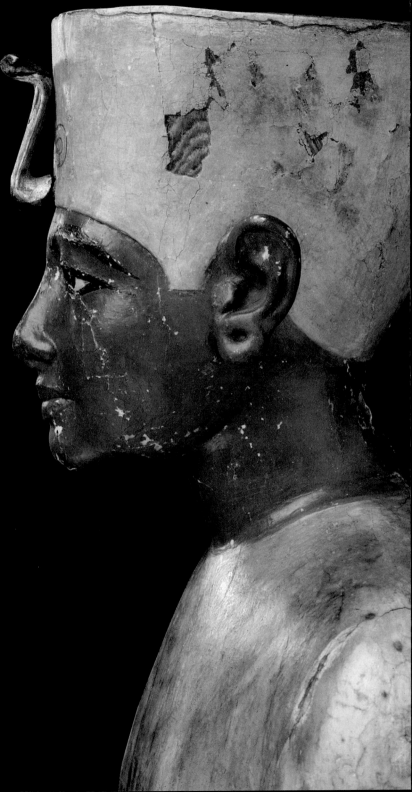

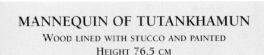

MANNEQUIN OF TUTANKHAMUN
Wood lined with stucco and painted
Height 76.5 cm

ROOM 9

This unusual life-size wooden statue without arms or legs was found in the antechamber of the tomb half hidden by an overturned carriage. Legs and arms are missing, the latter being neatly cut at armpit level. It was probably a mannequin used by tailors to fit the pharaoh's clothes.

The figure wears a low yellow head-covering with a gilded uraeus serpent on the forehead. The face of the sovereign is painted dark red which was the color traditionally used by the ancient Egyptians for male flesh.

The earlobes are pierced so earrings could be worn. Earrings were introduced by the Hyksos during the Second Intermediate Period and were worn by Egyptian women and men although it seems that males wore them only until adolescence. No representations have been found of adult men wearing this type of jewelry although their ears were always pierced from the reign of Akhenaten onwards.

The modeling of the face, the fleshy lips, and the pointed chin display clear influences of Amarna Period art. (D.C.)

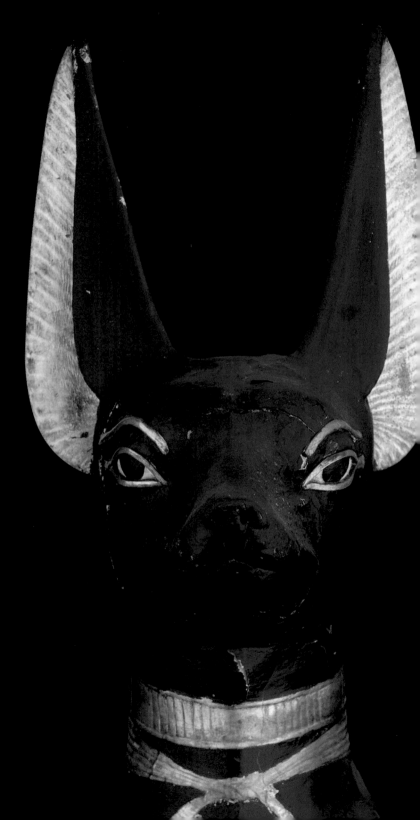

PORTABLE SIMULACRUM OF ANUBIS

WOOD LINED WITH STUCCO AND TAR, GOLD LEAF,
SILVER, GOLD, QUARTZ AND OBSIDIAN
HEIGHT 118 CM, LENGTH 270 CM
WIDTH 52 CM

ROOM 9

This statue of Anubis was fixed on the sliding cover of a casket in the form of a shrine; the shrine rested on a litter which was used to carry the image of the god in processions. The statue was found at the entrance to the Treasure Room with its nose turned towards the funerary chamber, probably so that its threatening appearance would frighten any intruders. When it was found, it was wrapped in a linen cloth dated to the seventh year of the reign of Akhenaten with only the head left uncovered. A finer piece of cloth, a scarf and a garland of lotus and lily flowers encircled the statue's neck. Between the front paws there was a scribe's ivory tablet that had belonged to Meritaten, one of the six daughters of Akhenaten and Nefertiti.

The statue is made from wood lined with stucco and tar. The inside of the ears, the bands around the neck, the edging of the eyes and the eyebrows are all rendered in gold; the eyes are made from calcite and obsidian and the fingernails from silver.

The shrine casket is decorated with two rows of alternating pairs of *djed* and *tit* signs, the symbols associated with Osiris and Isis. Inside there were amulets made from faïence, two alabaster vases, and eight breast plates. Thieves had undoubtedly rummaged through the casket as the objects, originally packaged and placed in compartments, were found heaped in disorder.

Anubis was represented as a black dog or in a hybrid form with the head of a dog and the body of a man. He was the lord of the necropolis and oversaw embalming rites; he was also responsible for guiding the dead to the Underworld and presenting them before Osiris for the weighing of the soul.

During the funerary ceremonies, the role of the god was interpreted by a priest who wore the mask of a jackal.
(D.C.)

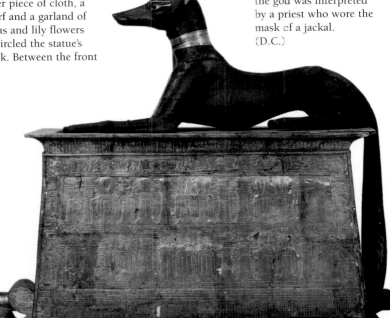

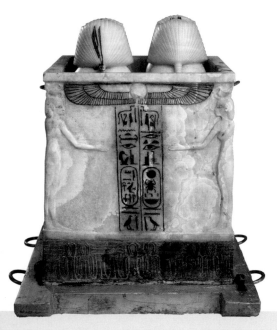

CONTAINER FOR CANOPIC VASES
ALABASTER, GOLD LEAF
HEIGHT 85.5 CM, LENGTH 54 CM, WIDTH 54 CM

ROOM 9

A shrine made from alabaster – a stone that the Egyptians quarried in the caves at Hatnub in Middle Egypt – lay inside the monumental shrine made of gilded wood found in the Treasure Room. The form of the alabaster shrine resembles the model of Predynastic temples in southern Egypt. It is fixed to a gilded wooden sled that was supposed to facilitate movement of the object. The inside of the shrine is divided into four compartments that held the solid gold sarcophaguses that contained Tutankhamun's internal organs. The compartments are closed by alabaster lids that bear the image of the king; his face is framed by the *nemes* headdress while a

ulture and a uraeus
serpent, the emblems of
royal power, appear on
his forehead.

Relief images of Isis,
Nephthys, Neith, and
Selket – identified by
the hieroglyphic marks
on their heads – appear
on the corners of the
shrine with their arms
open to protect the
body parts of the
pharaoh. The
inscriptions engraved
on the sides of the
shrine are the formulas
intoned by the
goddesses to further
protect Tutankhamun.

The base of the
shrine is covered with
thin gold leaf
decorated with a line
of *djed* and *tit*
symbols in
alternating pairs;
these are the emblems
associated with Osiris
and his consort Isis
respectively.
(D.C.)

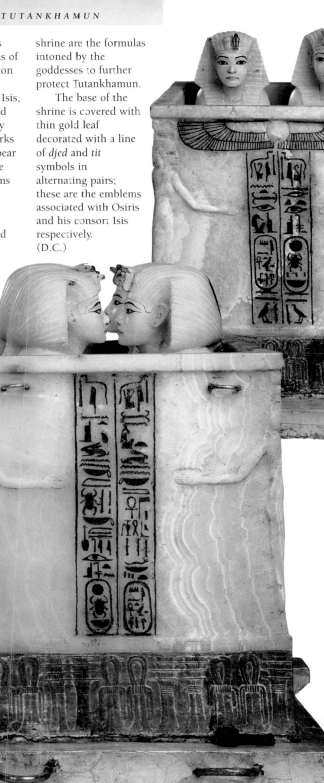

SHRINE FOR CANOPIC VASES

Wood lined with stucco and gilded, glass paste
Height 198 cm, length 153 cm
Width 122 cm

ROOM 9

This impressive shrine
for canopic vases was found
in the Treasure Room with
an alabaster container inside.
The container held four
miniature sarcophaguses
which contained the internal
organs of the king. The
shrine, fixed onto a sled, has
a canopy formed by four
corner pillars that hold up a
roof crowned with a frieze of
uraeus serpents and the sun

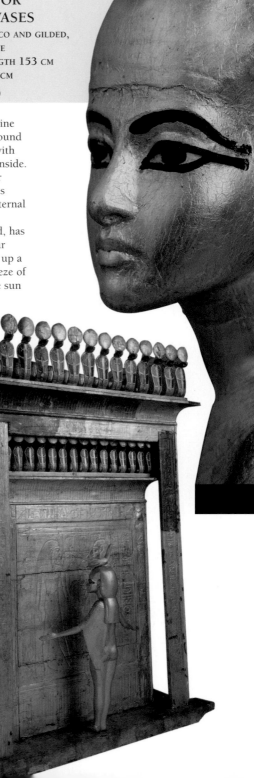

disk, while a second frieze is on the roof of the shrine itself. The inscriptions on the pillars give the names and titles of the pharaoh.

Four goddesses with open arms watch over the organs of the sovereign. They are identified by the hieroglyphs on their heads and on the low reliefs of the sanctuary walls. Each goddess faces and is associated with one of the four children of Horus whose duty was to preserve the king's organs the goddess Isis watches over the liver with Imset, Nephthys the lungs with Hapi, Neith the stomach with Duamutef, and Selket the intestines with Qebehsenuf.

Characteristics typical of the art of Amarna can be seen in the slight rotation of the statues' heads (compared to the frontal tradition of Egyptian statuary), the long neck stretching forwards and the naturalistic modeling of the bodies. (D.C.)

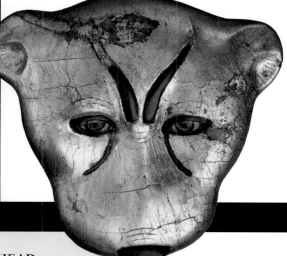

LEOPARD HEAD
GILDED WOOD, QUARTZ AND GLASS PASTE
HEIGHT 16.5 CM

ROOM 8

This leopard head adorned a garment that imitated the animal's skin with the use of silver stars. The use of stars in place of spots can be traced back to the archaic conception of a leopard as a symbolic representation of the sky.

The leopard skin was the distinctive attribute of the *sem* priest who was charged with revitalizing the mummified body of the pharaoh in the ritual known as the "Opening of the mouth." If the deceased was his predecessor, the new pharaoh would supervise the ceremony dressed as a *sem* priest.

The tomb also contained other leopard heads and various fragments of hides. (D.C.)

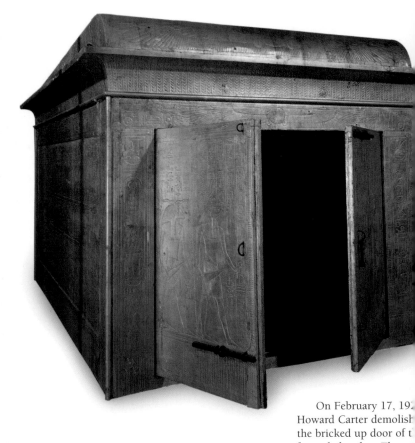

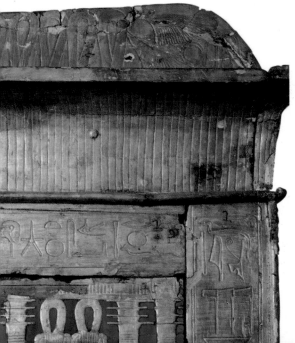

On February 17, 19.
Howard Carter demolish
the bricked up door of t
funeral chamber. The ro
was almost completely
filled with a massive shr
which turned out to be
only the outer example
total of four which lay in
one another and protect
the sarcophaguses of the
king. The shrines are ma
of heavy oak panels 6 cm
thick lined with gold lea
on plaster. The difficult
task of dismantling the
shrines took 84 days.
Fortunately the tomb
robbers had only opened
the doors to the first shr
and the seals to the othe
three had remained inta

The form of the shri
was symbolic: the first
probably represented the
pavilion in which the ki

THE FOUR SHRINES
GILDED WOOD, FAÏENCE
1) HEIGHT 275 CM, LENGTH 508 CM
WIDTH 328 CM
2) HEIGHT 225 CM, LENGTH 374 CM
WIDTH 235 CM
3) HEIGHT 215 CM, LENGTH 340 CM
WIDTH 192 CM
4) HEIGHT 190 CM, LENGTH 290 CM
WIDTH 148 CM

ROOM 8

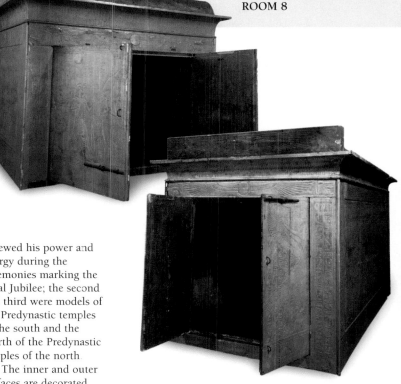

renewed his power and energy during the ceremonies marking the royal Jubilee; the second and third were models of the Predynastic temples of the south and the fourth of the Predynastic temples of the north.

The inner and outer surfaces are decorated with religious texts and scenes. The external panels of the first shrine are inlaid with blue faïence and bear alternate pairs of *djed* and *tit* signs, the emblems associated with Osiris and Isis. Passages from the *Book of the Dead* and the *Book of the Heavenly Cow* are cited on the inside of the panel, the latter being a funerary text that deals with one of the popular myths of the solar cycle.

The wooden structure of the second shrine was covered by a linen drape and decorated with scenes and texts taken from the *Book of the Dead*.

The outer sides of the third shrine bear extracts from the *Book of Amduat*, the account of the journey of the sun through the underworld during the twelve hours of the night.

On the walls of the fourth shrine are religious scenes and Chapter 17 of the *Book of the Dead*, while the doors and the extreme end depict the goddesses Isis and Nephthys stretching out their winged arms in a sign of protection. Various objects were placed in the spaces between the shrine walls. (D.C.)

TUTANKHAMUN'S HORN

SILVER, GOLD, WOOD
LENGTH 58.2 CM

ROOM 8

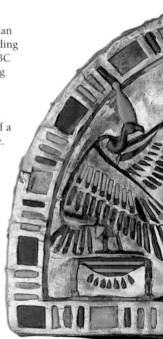

Horns (*sheneb*) were mostly used in the military, often with drums during parades or to assemble the soldiers. The first representations of horns to our knowledge date from the start of the New Kingdom, and the only actual horns to have survived to the modern day were the two found in the tomb of Tutankhamun, one in silver and one in bronze. The object in the Louvre that was once believed to be a horn was in fact a censer as has recently been demonstrated.

The silver example shown here consists of a tube and a flare originally decorated with a finely engraved lotus flower, the emblem of regeneration. At a later date, a small silver band depicting Amun-Ra and Ra-Harakhty before the god Ptah was added.

The plaque contains hieroglyphs giving the names and epithets of the three deities and above this are the cartouches of the pharaoh. The mouthpiece and the decorative band at the tip of the flare are made of gold. Both horns have a wooden core, probably to prevent dents.

In spring 1939, an extraordinary recording was made for the BBC (British Broadcasting Corporation) of the sounds of the two ancient instruments with the insertion of a modern mouthpiece. The musician involved was a trumpeter with the British army, James Tappern, who obtained the notes C, G, and C an octave higher, but the silver horn suffered serious damage.

It seems that the instruments had also been blown six years before by Professor Kirby of the University of Johannesburg without the use of a modern mouthpiece; this required a very strong air pressure and the notes were particularly difficult to sound. (D.C.)

FAN

GILDED WOOD AND MULTICOLORED GLASS PASTE
LENGTH 125 CM

ROOM 8

This fan was found together with many other things in the annexe. It is formed by a long staff shaped like a lotus flower at the top and by a flat section on which ostrich plumes were attached at the edge.

The stems of some of the plumes were still visible when the tomb was opened but they were so delicate that they did not survive.

The flat section is decorated with inlays of multicolored glass paste with an image of the king's cartouches in the center crowned by two sun disks and the hieroglyph that signifies the sky. On either side of the cartouches, two deities in the form of vultures hold the emblems of power (uas) and eternity (shen) between their open wings as a sign of protection. The birds are wearing the white crown of Upper Egypt and the red crown of Lower Egypt and rest, like the two cartouches, on the hieroglyph representing gold, the metal of the gods which, because of its quality of inalterability, was also a symbol of eternal life.

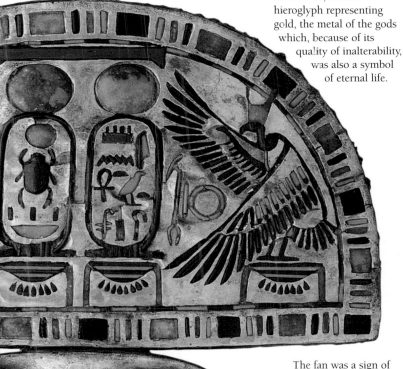

The fan was a sign of regality and carried in processions behind the pharaoh to protect him from the sun; several were also fixed to the sides of the throne. The position of "His Majesty's fan bearer" was one of the most sought after in the royal court.
(D.C.)

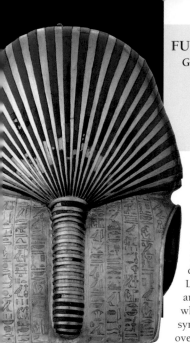

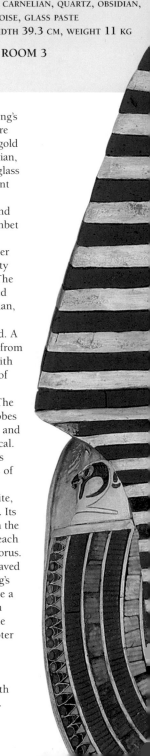

This splendid solid gold mask protected the head, shoulders, and upper chest of Tutankhamun's mummy. The youthful and graceful facial features form an idealized portrait of the king. The slightly elongated face, the almond-shaped eyes with their curved eyebrows, and the fleshy lips are some of the typical features portrayed during the reign of Akhenaten.

Tutankhamun is wearing the *nemes*, a white and blue striped linen headdress pulled close around the head, fixed over the forehead, with two flaps at the side and an attachment at the rear. The horizontal bands are formed using blue glass paste which imitate lapis lazuli. The *nemes* was reserved for the sovereign, often replacing the crown.

The figures of a vulture and a uraeus serpent can

be seen on the king's forehead. They are made from solid gold inlaid with carnelian, lapis lazuli, and glass paste and represent the two guardian deities of Upper and Lower Egypt, Nekhbet and Uadjet, which when shown together symbolize sovereignty over unified Egypt. The king's eyes, reproduced with quartz and obsidian, have the corners eyes realistically painted red. A long false beard made from gold and glass paste with the curved tip typical of the gods hangs from Tutankhamun's chin. The ears have perforated lobes in the Amarna fashion and are slightly asymmetrical. The large *usekh* collar is formed by twelve rows of beads made from lapis lazuli, quartz, amazonite, and colored glass paste. Its ends have two clasps in the form of falcon heads, each the image of the god Horus.

Hieroglyphics engraved in columns on the king's back and shoulders cite a magical formula which came to be a part of the *Book of the Dead* (chapter 151b) during the New Kingdom. It invokes various deities whose limbs are identified with those of the dead king.
(D.C.)

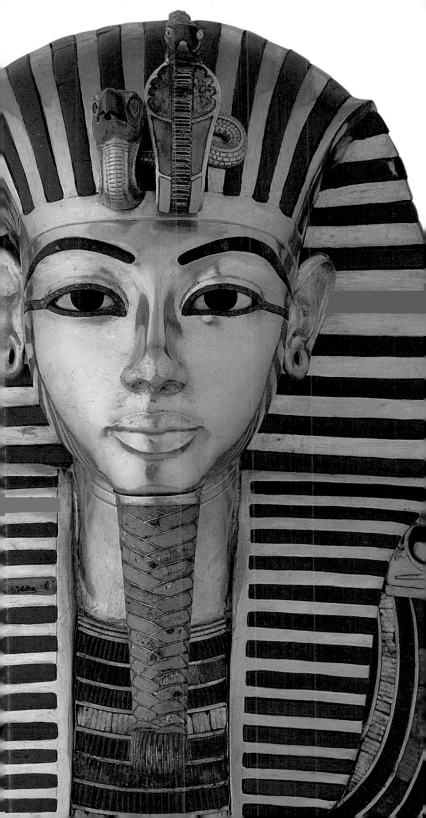

DOUBLE BALSAM HOLDER

GOLD, SILVER, SEMI-PRECIOUS STONES, GLASS PASTE
HEIGHT 16 CM
WIDTH 8.8 CM
DEPTH 4.3 CM

ROOM 3

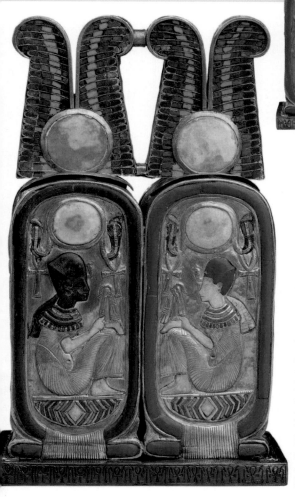

cartouches, the pharaoh is shown crouching on the hieroglyph *heb* which means "celebration"; he wears a long pleated garment and holds the royal scepter and flail. Above, two uraeus serpents emerge from a sun disk from each of which hangs the sign of bounty and felicity, the *ankh*.

The scene on the opposite sides is similar but with two minor differences: on one side the king has a long plait hanging down on one side of his head (typical of young princes) while on the other side he wears the blue crown; and his arms are crossed on his chest on one side and resting on his knees on the other.

The primordial god of the infinite, Heh, is portrayed on the other two sides of the container; on his head he bears the hieroglyph *neb*, a scarab and the sun disk to reproduce the pharaoh's coronation name, Nebkheperura.
(D.C.)

This original container in the shape of a double cartouche was used to contain ointments. The base is made from silver, the containers from gold inlaid with colored glass paste, and the lid is made in the form of two pairs of plumes with a sun disk united by two gold pieces that lie above the double balsam holder. The surfaces are richly decorated with symbolic images that celebrate the eternity of the kingdom and the life of the king.

In both the

312

GOLD STATUETTE OF THE CROUCHING PHARAOH

GOLD AND GLASS PASTE
HEIGHT 5.4 CM
LENGTH OF THE CHAIN 54 CM

ROOM 3

Carter found a wooden sarcophagus about 80 CM long covered with a layer of black resin lying on the chests that contained the *shawabty* in the Treasure Room. A second sarcophagus inside was lined with plaster and gold leaf and contained a third one, of simple wood. This solid gold statuette lay beside the third sarcophagus wrapped in linen. A fourth sarcophagus, the innermost and only 10 CM long, bore the name of Queen Tiy, the consort of Amenhotep III, and contained a lock of her hair wrapped in linen.

The statuette is a pendant for a necklace. The ends of the chain are tied with two strips of linen which were used to tie the ornament around the neck. The king wears the blue crown with the uraeus serpent on the front, grips the scepter and flail in his right hand, and his neck is adorned with a string of glass paste beads.

Carter believed the pharaoh illustrated was Amenhotep III, the father of Akhenaten, and that his image, carefully placed in the small sarcophaguses with the hair of his wife, would have been buried with Tutankhamun as a family memento. The hypothesis is an attractive one although no data exist to support identification of the statuette. (D.C.)

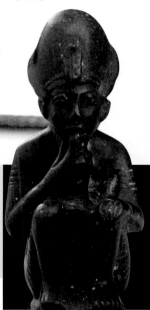

STATUETTE OF THE PHARAOH

GLASS PASTE
HEIGHT 5.8 CM

ROOM 3

This small statue was found in a casket in the antechamber of the tomb and depicts Tutankhamun as "Horus the Child." The pharaoh, wearing the *khepresh*, the blue crown, is squatting with a finger in his mouth. This childlike gesture was the traditional characterization of Horus the Child, the son of Isis and Osiris who spent his childhood hidden with his mother in the papyrus beds of the Delta to escape the ire of the evil god Seth, the murderer of his father. When Horus became an adult, he won back the throne that had been unjustly usurped from him and transmitted power to the pharaoh, his earthly incarnation. (D.C.)

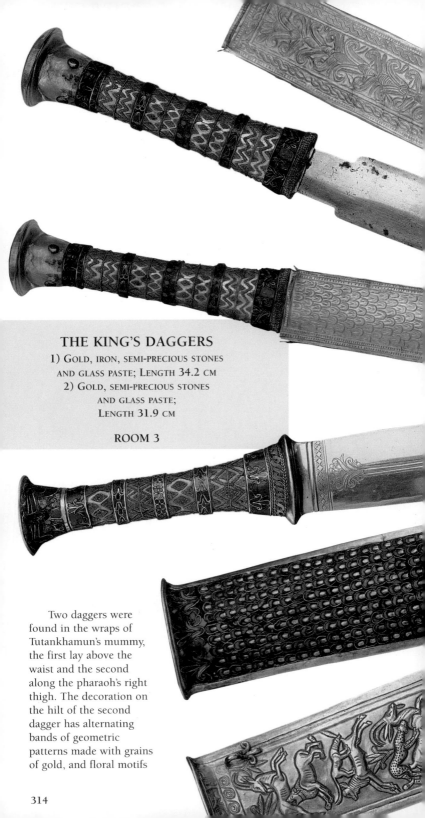

THE KING'S DAGGERS

1) GOLD, IRON, SEMI-PRECIOUS STONES
AND GLASS PASTE; LENGTH 34.2 CM
2) GOLD, SEMI-PRECIOUS STONES
AND GLASS PASTE;
LENGTH 31.9 CM

ROOM 3

Two daggers were
found in the wraps of
Tutankhamun's mummy,
the first lay above the
waist and the second
along the pharaoh's right
thigh. The decoration on
the hilt of the second
dagger has alternating
bands of geometric
patterns made with grains
of gold, and floral motifs

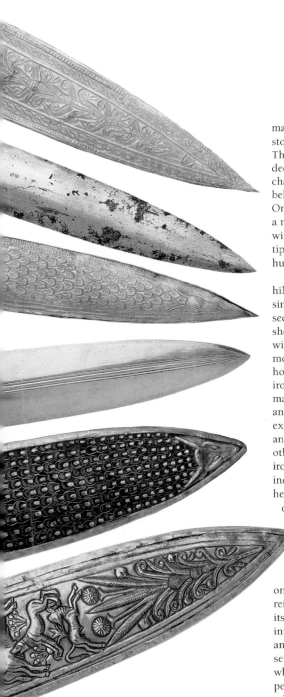

made from inlays of stones and glass paste. The solid gold blade is decorated with two chased lines in the center below a palmette design. One side of the sheath has a motif of small plumes with a fox's head at the tip, and the other a hunting scene.

The decoration on the hilt of the first dagger is similar to that of the second and the gold sheath is also decorated with floral and plume motifs. The blade, however, was made from iron which was a rare material in Egypt as the ancient Egyptians almost exclusively used copper and bronze. Carter found other objects made from iron in the tomb, including an amulet and a headrest among the wraps of the mummy's shroud, and sixteen models of tools in the Treasure Room.

Use of iron in Egypt was sporadic and is only attested from the reign of Tutankhamun on; its use was probably introduced by the Hittites, an Indo-European people settled in Anatolia, with whom the Egyptians had permanently bad relations.

(D.C.)

315

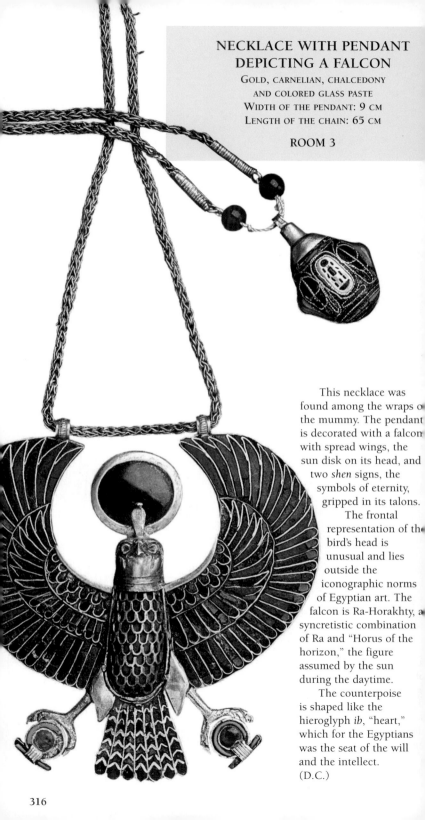

NECKLACE WITH PENDANT
DEPICTING A FALCON
GOLD, CARNELIAN, CHALCEDONY
AND COLORED GLASS PASTE
WIDTH OF THE PENDANT: **9** CM
LENGTH OF THE CHAIN: **65** CM

ROOM 3

This necklace was found among the wraps of the mummy. The pendant is decorated with a falcon with spread wings, the sun disk on its head, and two *shen* signs, the symbols of eternity, gripped in its talons.

The frontal representation of the bird's head is unusual and lies outside the iconographic norms of Egyptian art. The falcon is Ra-Horakhty, a syncretistic combination of Ra and "Horus of the horizon," the figure assumed by the sun during the daytime.

The counterpoise is shaped like the hieroglyph *ib*, "heart," which for the Egyptians was the seat of the will and the intellect. (D.C.)

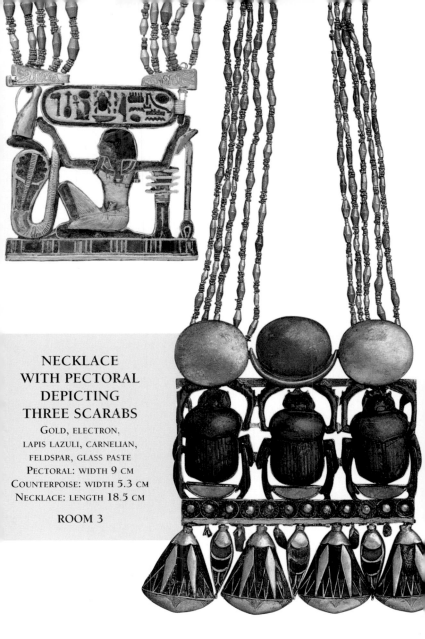

NECKLACE WITH PECTORAL DEPICTING THREE SCARABS

GOLD, ELECTRON,
LAPIS LAZULI, CARNELIAN,
FELDSPAR, GLASS PASTE
PECTORAL: WIDTH 9 CM
COUNTERPOISE: WIDTH 5.3 CM
NECKLACE: LENGTH 18.5 CM

ROOM 3

This necklace was found among the wraps of the mummy. The pectoral is formed by three lapis lazuli scarabs, each resting on the hieroglyph *neb* meaning "lord, owner." The central scarab holds the moon crescent and the moon disk both made in electron while the other two support the sun disk made from gold.

The lower section of the pectoral is composed of flowers and lotus blooms. The counterpoise is united to the pendant by strings of glass paste and gold beads and represents Heh, the god of infinite space, who carries on his head the cartouche with the name of the pharaoh accompanied by the epithet, "Good god, chosen by Amun-Ra." (D.C.)

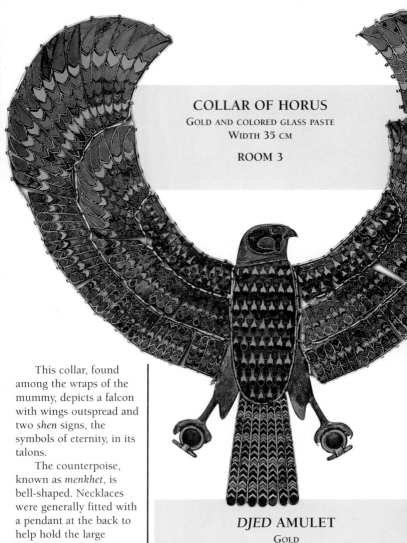

COLLAR OF HORUS
GOLD AND COLORED GLASS PASTE
WIDTH 35 CM

ROOM 3

DJED AMULET
GOLD
HEIGHT 9 CM

ROOM 3

This collar, found among the wraps of the mummy, depicts a falcon with wings outspread and two *shen* signs, the symbols of eternity, in its talons.

The counterpoise, known as *menkhet*, is bell-shaped. Necklaces were generally fitted with a pendant at the back to help hold the large pendants stable on the chest and to distribute the ornament's weight.

The falcon is Horus, the god of the sky and royalty, of whom the pharaoh was the earthly manifestation.

The *Book of the Dead* tells us that it was important to place these collars of Horus on the body of the deceased as they were considered powerful apotropaic amulets.
(D.C.)

Carter found numerous jewels and amulets among the wraps of the linen shroud around Tutankhamun's mummy, some of which were worn by the pharaoh during his life, some purely for funerary use. This *djed* pillar was one of the twenty amulets arranged on the king's neck in six

layers separated by the sheets of linen.

The origins of *djed* were ancient: the first known representations a from the First Dynasty b it became a symbol of th god Osiris around the beginning of the New Kingdom. Some experts have identified the pilla with the spinal column

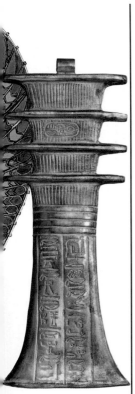

PLAQUE SHOWING THE KING ON HIS CHARIOT
GOLD
HEIGHT 6.2 CM, LENGTH 8.5 CM

ROOM 3

Several sheets of perforated gold were found in the antechamber but their function still remains a source of conjecture. It has been hypothesized that they were plaques used to decorate the chariots but it is more probable that they were used as belt buckles or as decorative elements on ceremonial garments.

The sheet illustrated here shows Tutankhamun on a chariot drawn by magnificently harnessed horses preceded by two prisoners in chains, an Asian and a Nubian. The guardian deities of Upper and Lower Egypt, Nekhbet and Uadjet, protect the pharaoh with their wings outspread: the vulture, Nekhbet, places the sign of eternal life on Tutankhamun while the winged cobra, Uadjet, holds the cartouche of the name of the king.

Lower down on the sheet, the heraldic emblem of the union of Upper and Lower Egypt is shown and enhanced by the presence of two prisoners on their knees.

The overall image is another version of the theme of the triumph of the king over his enemies: Tutankhamun parades victorious on his chariot with prisoners in chains after once more winning a battle that has enabled him to maintain order and harmony in the universe (*maat*).

(D.C.)

siris on the basis of the sociation seen in many nerary and religious texts etween the *djed* and the od's spine. Others onsider it to have been a tylized representation of a eaf of plant stalks as the ed was connected to the orld of vegetation and its cles of regeneration by s own destiny of death nd resurrection.

The amulets were laced on the king's ummy to protect him on s journey beyond the mb and their powers ere strengthened by the ddition of magical rmulas.

The two columns of ieroglyphs engraved on e *djed* are an extract from hapter 155 of the *Book of e Dead*.

).C.)

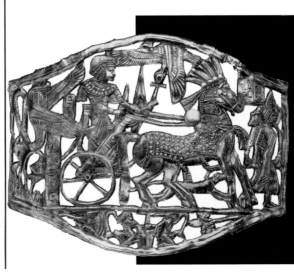

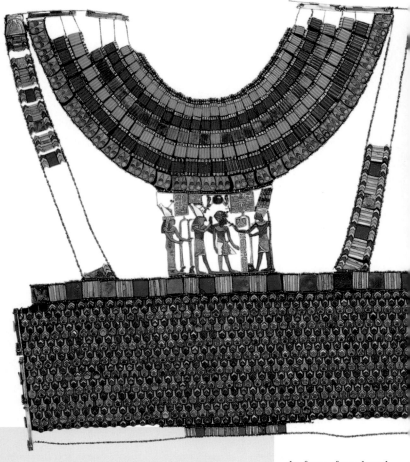

TUTANKHAMUN'S CORSLET
GOLD, GLASS PASTE, IVORY, SEMI-PRECIOUS STONES
HEIGHT 40 CM, LENGTH 85 CM

ROOM 3

Carter found the fragments of this corslet in various places around the antechamber of the tomb; some were contained in three small chests and a small gilded wooden shrine, while others lay on the ground in the antechamber and the corridor. The precious object was probably damaged by thieves as they rummaged through the chests looking for easily removable objects of value. The painstaking restoration of the corslet took Carter and his associates a long time.

The pharaoh wore the corslet during state ceremonies. Made of several parts, the two rectangular bands that circled the torso were decorated with a motif of small plumes made of colored glass paste. They were joined by straps in the form of two broad collars made from rows of gold and glass paste beads. Two pendants were joined to the collars: the front one portrays Amun-Ra on the left offering Tutankhamun palm branch (the symbol of time) and the sign of eternal life (the *ankh*). The sovereign wears the blue crown and is accompanied by the god Atum and the goddess Iusaas, his consort. The scene is dominated by a sun disk made from carnelian from which two cobras emerge. The figures are made from gold with inlays of semi-precious stones, ivory, and glass paste.

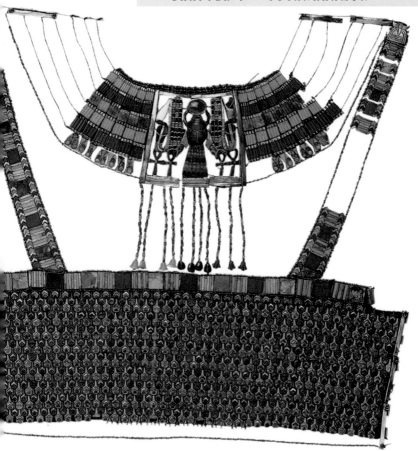

The pendant on the upper part is inserted in the center of the collar and shows a scarab with a sun disk set in the body of a falcon. This hybrid animal that symbolizes the sun holds two *ankh* signs in its talons and is flanked by two cobras with the crowns of Upper and Lower Egypt from which two other *ankh* signs hang. Although royal corslets were known of from wall paintings and decorations, a complete one had never been found before the discovery of Tutankhamun's tomb. (J.C.)

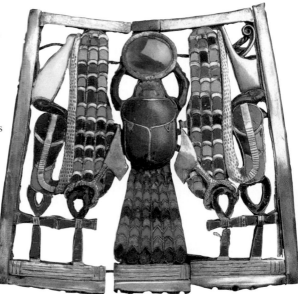

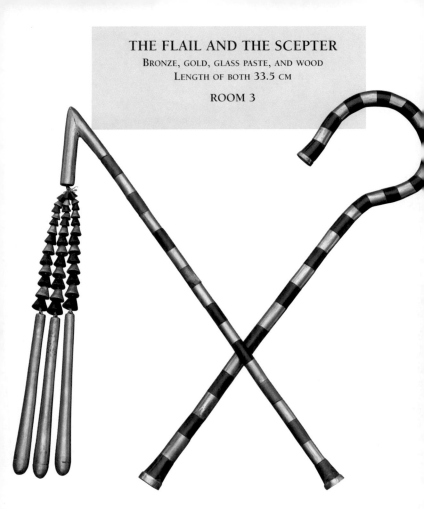

The flail and the scepter are ancient royal insignia. Various hypotheses have been put forward on the nature and significance of these emblems: the flail may represent a fly-swatter or could be a stylized version of the hieroglyph *mes* ("generate") to emphasize the sovereign's quality as a giver of life. The scepter, on the other hand, seems to be a reproduction of an archaic shepherd's staff.

The two examples in the photograph were made using the same technique: a bronze frame covered with alternating cylinders of gold and blue glass paste. As they are of the same length, it has been suggested that they were a pair although they were found in different locations in the tomb. The sovereigns held these representations of power during the ceremonies of the coronation and the *Sed* festival, a complex ritual of renewal of the king's power.

The cartouches engraved on the base of the flail bear the name of the king in its original Amarnian form (Tutankhaten); this implies that the young ruler held these two insignia when he was crowned at Amarna, the capital founded by his predecessor Akhenaten.

As lord of the Underworld, Osiris inherited these attributes from the king. (D.C.)

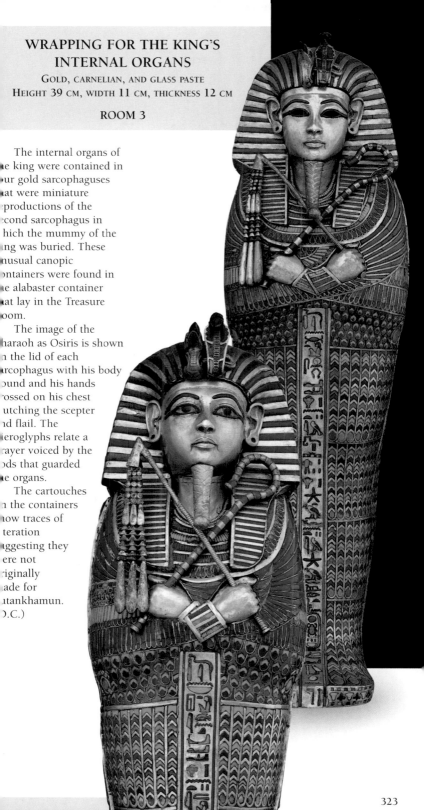

WRAPPING FOR THE KING'S INTERNAL ORGANS

Gold, carnelian, and glass paste
Height 39 cm, width 11 cm, thickness 12 cm

ROOM 3

The internal organs of
the king were contained in
four gold sarcophaguses
that were miniature
reproductions of the
second sarcophagus in
which the mummy of the
king was buried. These
unusual canopic
containers were found in
the alabaster container
that lay in the Treasure
Room.

The image of the
pharaoh as Osiris is shown
on the lid of each
sarcophagus with his body
bound and his hands
crossed on his chest
clutching the scepter
and flail. The
hieroglyphs relate a
prayer voiced by the
gods that guarded
the organs.

The cartouches
on the containers
show traces of
alteration
suggesting they
were not
originally
made for
Tutankhamun.
(D.C.)

323

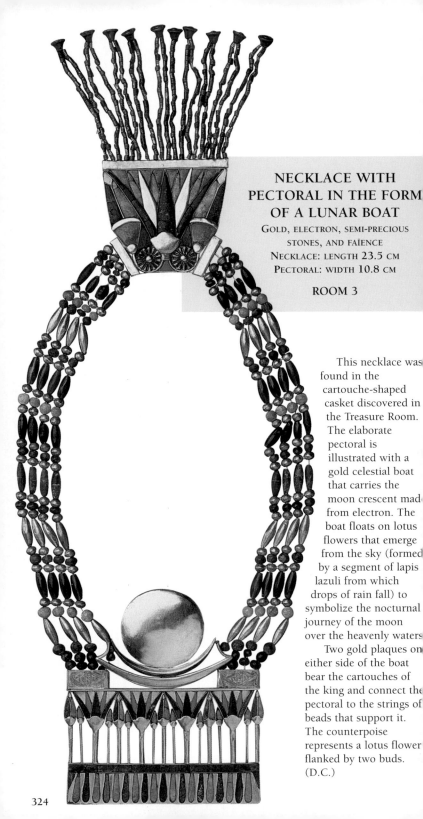

NECKLACE WITH PECTORAL IN THE FORM OF A LUNAR BOAT

GOLD, ELECTRON, SEMI-PRECIOUS STONES, AND FAÏENCE
NECKLACE: LENGTH 23.5 CM
PECTORAL: WIDTH 10.8 CM

ROOM 3

This necklace was found in the cartouche-shaped casket discovered in the Treasure Room. The elaborate pectoral is illustrated with a gold celestial boat that carries the moon crescent made from electron. The boat floats on lotus flowers that emerge from the sky (formed by a segment of lapis lazuli from which drops of rain fall) to symbolize the nocturnal journey of the moon over the heavenly waters.

Two gold plaques on either side of the boat bear the cartouches of the king and connect the pectoral to the strings of beads that support it. The counterpoise represents a lotus flower flanked by two buds. (D.C.)

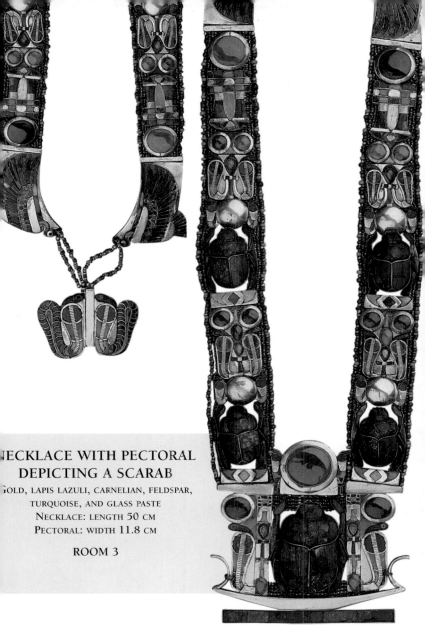

NECKLACE WITH PECTORAL DEPICTING A SCARAB

GOLD, LAPIS LAZULI, CARNELIAN, FELDSPAR,
TURQUOISE, AND GLASS PASTE
NECKLACE: LENGTH 50 CM
PECTORAL: WIDTH 11.8 CM

ROOM 3

The pendant on this charming necklace is made up of a gold celestial boat in the center of which a large lapis lazuli scarab supports the sun rising on the horizon. The scarab, identified by Egyptians with the god Khepri, i.e. the morning sun, is flanked by two uraeus serpents and three signs: *djed*, "stability," *ankh*, "eternal life," and *nefer*, "beauty."

The bands of the necklace are decorated with slight variations of the elements on the pectoral and are terminated by two vultures connected by four strings of beads to the small counterpoise in the form of two uraeus serpents. (D.C.)

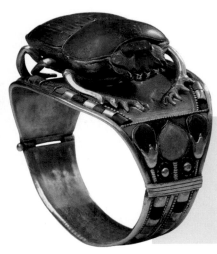

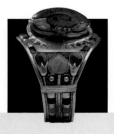

BRACELET WITH SCARAB

GOLD, LAPIS LAZULI, CARNELIAN, TURQUOISE
AND QUARTZ
DIAMETER 5.4 CM

ROOM 3

This bracelet was found with two others of similar manufacture in the cartouche-shaped casket found in the Treasure Room. As it shows signs of wear, it is probable that it was worn by the king, perhaps, given its small size, when he was a child.

It is formed by two semi-circles connected by a hinge and a fastener; the belly of the scarab on the upper half is decorated with gold and its back inlaid with lapis lazuli. Scarabs were identified with Khepri, a god that incarnated the rising sun, and were therefore symbols of eternal rebirth. (D.C.)

COUNTERPOISE DEPICTING THE GOD HEH

GOLD, CALCITE, CARNELIAN, GLASS PASTE
HEIGHT 6.9 CM
WIDTH 8.2 CM

ROOM 3

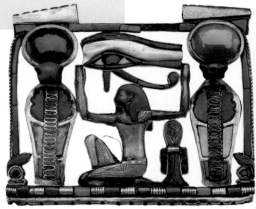

The necklace to which this counterpoise belonged was not found. In the center there is Heh, the divine manifestation of infinite space, who bears the eye of Horus on his head, an amulet that guarantees its wearer good health and well-being. The god is flanked by two uraeus serpents and has a *tit* sign, the emblem associated with Isis, behind him.

The scene is encircled by two palm branches, the symbol of time; each branch rests on a tadpole (the hieroglyph that means hundreds of thousands) which is in turn placed on the symbol of eternity, *shen*.

The purpose of the elaborate illustration is to wish the sovereign a long reign. (D.C.)

PECTORAL WITH A WINGED SCARAB

GOLD, SILVER, SEMI-PRECIOUS STONES, AND GLASS PASTE
WIDTH 14.5 CM
HEIGHT 14.9 CM

ROOM 3

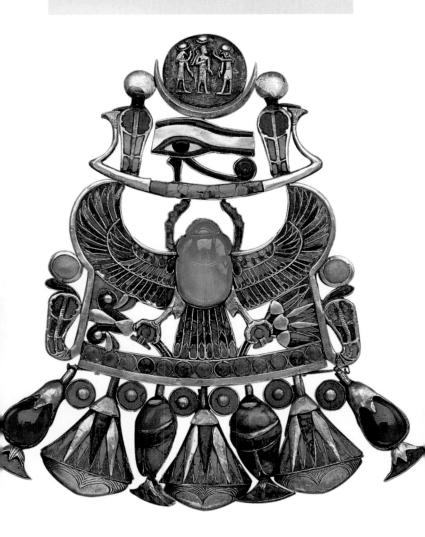

The center of this intricate pectoral is adorned with a green chalcedony scarab set in the body of a falcon: it symbolizes the sun. The front paws and tip of the tail of this composite creature support a celestial boat containing the left eye of Horus – the emblem of the moon – crowned by a silver moon disk with a crescent in gold. The pharaoh is depicted in the disk flanked by the moon god Thoth and by the sun god Ra-Horakhty in a protective pose.

Flowers and buds of papyrus and lotus plants, the emblems of Upper and Lower Egypt, form the base of the pectoral.
(D.C.)

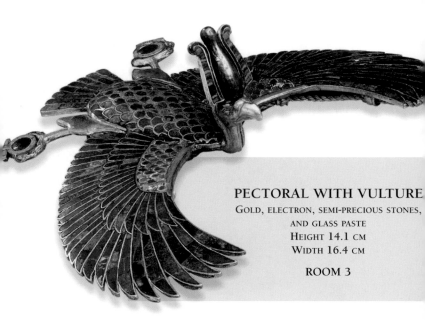

PECTORAL WITH VULTURE

GOLD, ELECTRON, SEMI-PRECIOUS STONES,
AND GLASS PASTE
HEIGHT 14.1 CM
WIDTH 16.4 CM

ROOM 3

The richly worked gold pectoral with inlaid stones represents the goddess-vulture Nekhbet, the protective deity of southern Egypt. The bird's head is generally shown in profile in accordance with traditional iconography, but in this case is seen face on. The back of the article bears a finely chased decoration that repeats the design formed with semi-precious stones on the front.

Carter found this unusual object inside a box in the Treasure Room.
(D.C.)

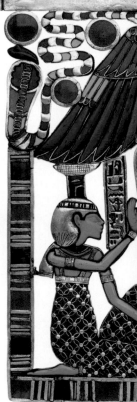

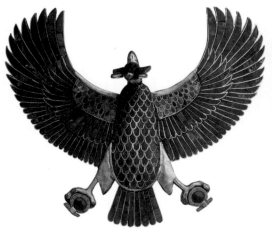

PECTORAL DEPICTING A SCARAB WITH ISIS AND NEPHTHYS

GOLD, SEMI-PRECIOUS STONES, AND MULTICOLORED GLASS PASTE
HEIGHT 16.5 CM, WIDTH 24.4 CM

ROOM 3

The portable shrine of Anubis contained eight pectorals, none of which was decorated with necklaces or counterpoises, suggesting they were most likely produced exclusively for funerary purposes.

The complex decoration of this pectoral centers on the large funerary scarab – known as the "scarab of the heart" – made from green semi-precious stone. It holds up the cartouches of the king and is flanked by the two goddesses Isis and Nephthys (identified by the hieroglyphs on their heads) who hold their arms open as a sign of protection. The scarab was found in the cartouche-shaped casket and placed in its original position on the pectoral following

careful examination of the text carved on its obverse. The inscription bears a passage from Chapter 30B of the *Book of the Dead* in which the deceased urges his heart to testify in his favor at the weighing of his soul before Osiris.

The formula uttered by the two kneeling goddesses in which Isis and Nephthys invoke the sun god Ra on behalf of Tutankhamun's heart is contained in the columns of hieroglyphs on the pectoral. The consistency of the two texts and the matching dimensions of the scarab and pectoral were the factors that favored its replacement. (D.C.)

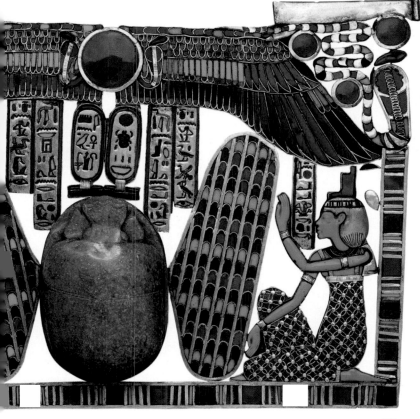

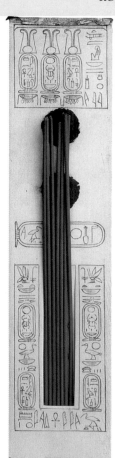

SCRIBE'S TABLET
IVORY
WIDTH 4.7 CM
LENGTH 30.3 CM

ROOM 3

The contents of a number of chests found along the north wall of the Treasure Room had been ransacked by the thieves in their feverish search for valuable objects. A set of scribe's equipment containing two tablets, a pen holder, a papyrus sleeker, and an ivory cup had been thrown haphazardly into a casket that was originally made to hold gold cosmetics' containers.

The possession of a scribe's set was very important for the deceased as he could then make use of the capabilities of the lunar god Thoth, the inventor of hieroglyphs. Numerous votive tablets made especially for the grave goods were found in the annexe to the antechamber and the two tablets found in the casket were probably used by the sovereign while he was alive.

One was made from wood covered with gold, the other (shown in the photograph) was made of ivory and bears the king's cartouches which say that Tutankhamun is "loved by Atum, Amun-Ra, and Thoth."

The two cakes of red and black ink, obtained from smoke-black and natural ocher, had been partially used, perhaps by Tutankhamun himself. The brushes were made from slender rushes chewed at one end.
(D.C.)

PECTORAL DEPICTING NUT
GOLD, CARNELIAN, AND MULTICOLORED GLASS PASTE
HEIGHT 12.6 CM, WIDTH 14.3 CM

ROOM 3

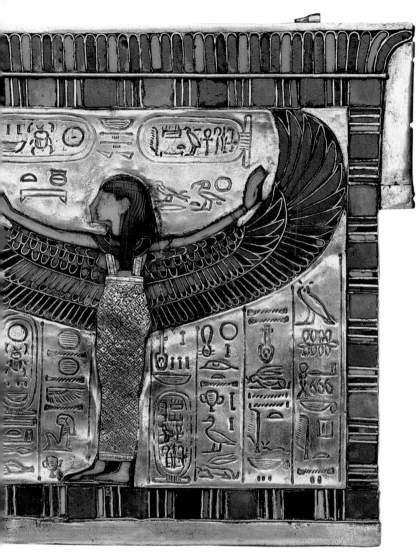

The portable shrine on which the statue of Anubis stood contained eight pectorals, none of which were attached to necklaces or counterpoises. It is most likely that the pectorals were produced exclusively for funerary purposes. The pectoral in the photograph shows the goddess Nut bearing the king's cartouches with her wings and arms outspread.

The eight columns of hieroglyphs engraved on the lower part represent some of the formulas uttered by the goddess to protect Tutankhamun. The scene is encircled by a geometric frame made from inlays of carnelian and glass paste and is crowned by a frieze of palm frond motifs.

Nut was an ancient deity who represented the heavenly vault. She is often depicted as a woman arched over the earth, with her hands in the west and feet in the east, to protect the human world below. Each evening, Nut would swallow the sun to give birth to it from her womb the following morning.

It has been suggested that this pectoral was not made originally for Tutankhamun as the coronation and birth names of the king on the cartouches seem to have been written over the names of another sovereign. (D.C.)

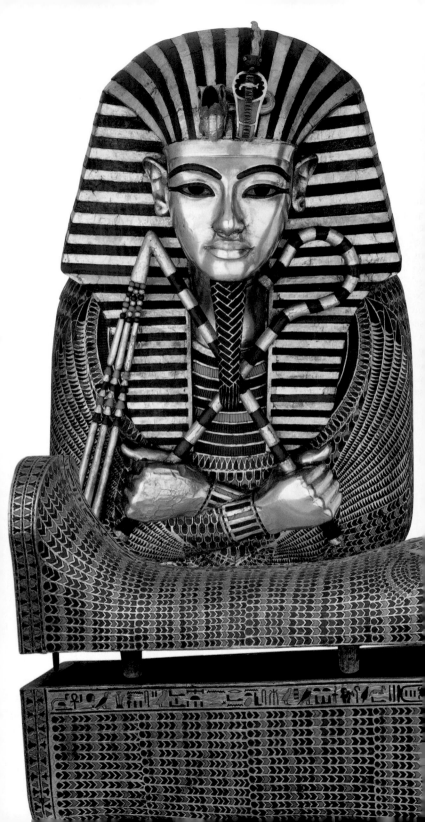

SECOND GILDED SARCOPHAGUS

GILDED WOOD, SEMI-PRECIOUS STONES, AND GLASS PASTE
LENGTH 204 CM
HEIGHT 78.5 CM MAX., WIDTH 68 CM MAX.

ROOM 3

Once the four large shrines were removed and the heavy lid of the quartz sarcophagus lifted, Carter found himself looking at a sarcophagus in gilded wood decorated with the images of the goddesses Isis and Nephthys with wings outspread. Inside was a second coffin wrapped in a linen shroud on which garlands of olive leaves, lotus flowers, and lilies were placed. This sarcophagus was lined with gold leaf and richly inlaid with semi-precious stones and colored glass paste. The pharaoh is shown in the traditional pose of the god Osiris with his hands crossed on his chest while holding the scepter and flail.

The king wears the *nemes* headdress with the uraeus serpent and the vulture on the front while his chin is adorned with the curved false beard typical of the gods. The goddesses Nekhbet (the vulture) and Uadjet (the winged cobra) protect the body of the pharaoh between their open wings. The surface of the sarcophagus is covered by a decorative motif of small plumes called *rishi*.

It has been suggested that the coffin was not originally built for Tutankhamun as the facial features of the king do not correspond to those of the other images found in the tomb. (D.C.)

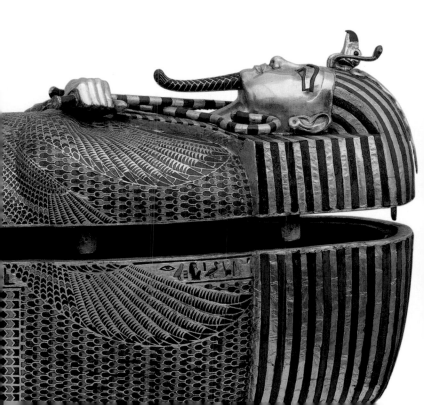

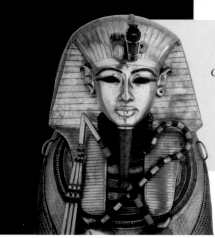

TUTANKHAMUN'S INNER SARCOPHAGUS

GOLD, SEMI-PRECIOUS STONES, AND GLASS PAST

HEIGHT 51 CM
LENGTH 187 CM
WIDTH 51.3 CM
WEIGHT 110.4 KG

ROOM 3

In order to reach Tutankhamun's mummy, after having dismantled the four gilded wood shrines that took up nearly all of the funerary chamber, Carter still had to open a rectangular quartzite sarcophagus, two more made of gilded wood, and finally the splendid solid gold sarcophagus illustrated here.

Embellished with inlaid semi-precious stones and glass paste, it depicts the mummified pharaoh in the traditional pose of the god Osiris with his arms crossed on his chest and the royal scepter or flail in his hands. The king wears the *nemes* headdress adorned with the vulture and uraeus serpent. The inlays of the eyes have not been conserved as they were damaged by solidification of the plentiful ointments poure onto the coffin during the burial rites. The eyelids and eyebrows are made of blue glass paste; the curve beard typical of the gods hangs from the chin.

The chest is adorned with a large collar while a jewel formed by two rows of small gold and faïence disks is fixed at the neck. Broad bracelets of inlaid

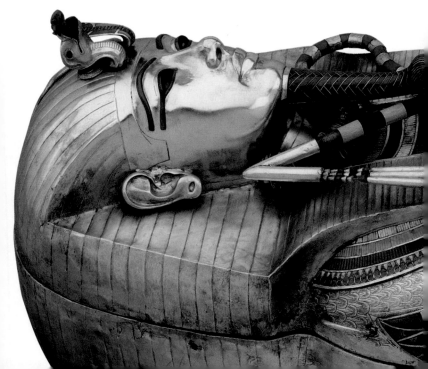

...ones cover the wrists.

The goddesses Nekhbet and Uadjet in the form of a vulture and winged cobra surround the bust of the king in a sign of protection. They are, respectively, the guardian goddesses of Upper and Lower Egypt, and their image repeated on the king's forehead symbolizes his power over the unified country. Their wings are inlaid with stones and glass paste and they hold the *shen* sign, the symbol of eternity, in their talons. Further down, Isis and Nephthys protect the king with their arms and wings spread. On the two columns of hieroglyphs is the formula recited by the two goddesses.

Isis kneels with her wings spread below the king's feet and a long hieroglyph is engraved on the edges of the case. (D.C.)

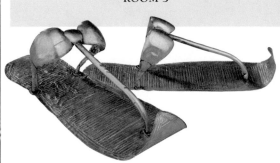

GOLD SANDALS
GOLD
LENGTH 29.5 CM

ROOM 3

Footwear in common use was generally made from papyrus, rushes or, more rarely, leather. These gold sandals, found at the feet of the mummy, have striated soles in imitation of plant fibres but it is probable that they were made specially for the burial as the sovereign would have worn more comfortable shoes. Carter found a number of sandals in the tomb, some of simple design, others more complicated.

Egyptians always carried sandals with them but walked barefoot and wore them only on special occasions. One of the positions at court was that of the "bearer of the royal sandals." (D.C.)

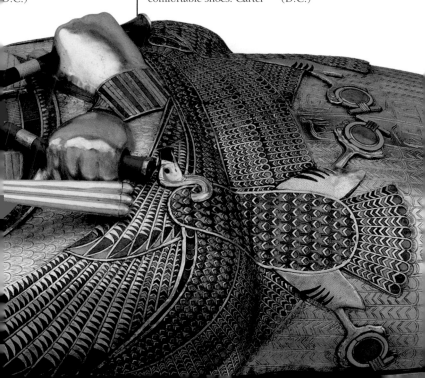

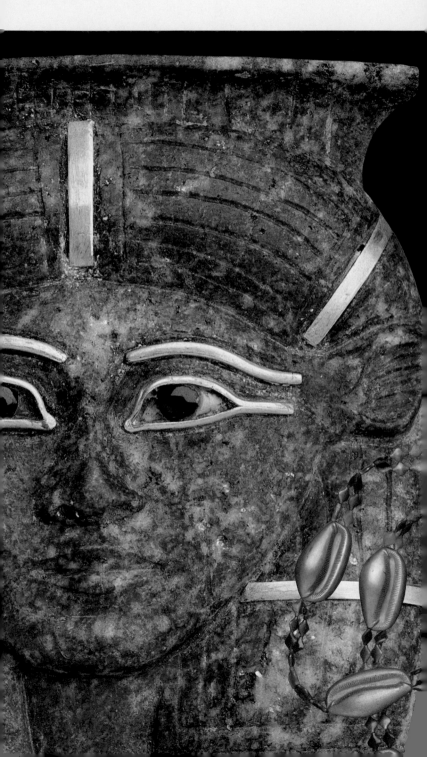

Despite the passing of thousands of years, the elegant forms and intense chromatic contrasts that emphasize the complex symbolism of the jewelry of ancient Egypt continue to fascinate and amaze. The treasures that have been handed down to us represent only a tiny part of the ceaseless work of the goldsmiths during the pharaonic age.

Whoever could afford a tomb, however modest, was buried with his or her jewelry, some placed on the body of the deceased, others in special containers. Thieves, attracted from ancient times by the wealth contained in the tombs, did not hesitate to profane the mummies to steal the jewels.

The splendid objects now seen in museums were found in the few tombs that remained intact or in hiding places that managed to escape the attention of the thieves.

Jewelry from the Old Kingdom is rare, but the few examples found display an extraordinary mastery of the working of gold and semi-precious stones. There are many objects, on the other hand, that demonstrate the creative skill of the jewelers of the Middle Kingdom: Jacques de Morgan discovered the treasures of the princesses, Sathathor and Mereret, hidden below the floor of their plundered tombs during excavations at Dahshur at the end of the 19th century and he found the four intact tombs belonging to Khnumit, Ita, Ita-Uret, and Sathathormerit that also contained superb sets of jewels.

The jewelry belonging to Princess Sathathoriunet was discovered at al-Lahun in 1914 while two other digs – in 1955 at Hawara (the Egyptian Antiquities Service) and in 1994 at Dahshur (Metropolitan Museum of Art) – brought to light the unentered tombs of Princess Neferuptah

CHAPTER 8
FIRST FLOOR

336 PENDANT IN THE FORM OF THE HEAD OF HATHOR; Gold and lapis lazuli; H. 5.5 CM, W. 5.3 CM; Mit Rahina (Memphis), Tomb of Sheshonq; Excavation by A. Badawy (1942); Twenty-second Dynasty, Reign of Osorkon II (883-850 BC)

336-337 BELT OF SATHATHOR Gold and semi-precious stones; L. 70 CM; Dashur; Twelfth Dynasty, Reign of Senusret III (1881-1842 BC)

ITINERARY IN ROOM 4

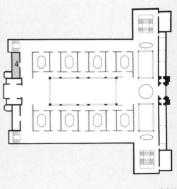

and Queen Uret, shedding new light on the jewelry belonging to female members of the royal family during the Twelfth Dynasty.

It was usual for jewels placed among the wraps of the mummy to be made specially for the burial, whereas those jewels placed in caskets were ornaments that the deceased had used during earthly life; this distinction is not always easy to make, however, as those jewels worn habitually could also be adapted to funerary use.

Jewelry production during the New Kingdom is attested by several sets of grave goods including that of Queen Ahhotep and the famous treasure of Tutankhamun; the works of gold and silver found in the necropolis of Tanis, on the other hand, are evidence of the technical and artistic skills of the jewelers during the Third Intermediate Period. Temples too held large quantities of precious objects donated as votive offerings, for instance, the finds at Tell Basta and the jewels from the Roman Period discovered at Dush.

Jewels had mainly a protective function. Precise magical and symbolic characteristics were attributed to stones and precious metals so that the design and choice

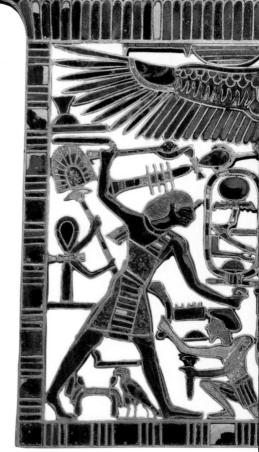

of gems and colors in an amulet, for example, could not be separated from its ritual use, symbolic value, or apotropaic power. Red carnelian (mined in the eastern desert) represented blood and life; turquoise (mined in Sinai) symbolized the slender shoots of spring; lapis lazuli (imported from Afghanistan) signified water and the clear depths of the sky. Gold, incorruptible and shining like the sun, belonged to the world of

the gods who had golden limbs and locks of lapis lazuli, accordingly the two precious materials were often associated in jewelry.

The Egyptians possessed immense deposits of gold that were mined and melted into large rings, then worked with great skill. The mines were operated by groups of army soldiers and prisoners of war. The gold was of excellent quality but was still contaminated by various

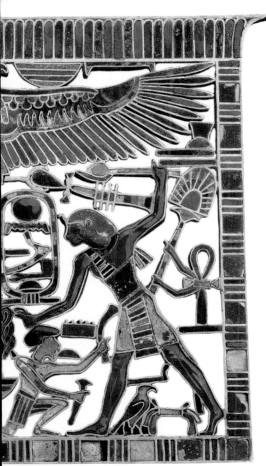

however, that reached the highest level of skill was the cutting and setting of semi-precious stones in a specially designed grid, made from gold. Often colored glass paste was used in place of stones as it was easier to work, cheaper, and gave off a color and light equal to that of gems. Precious stones remained unknown to the Nile Valley until the arrival of the Romans. Craftsmen could create a particular type of welding using resins and copper carbonate that gave great precision in the manufacture of joints which remained invisible to the naked eye.

Ornaments were made for the various parts of the body for men and women. Both wore diadems, hair-bands, earrings, simple chains with pendants, large collars with strings of beads, pectorals, bracelets, rings, and belts, though anklets were only worn by women.
(D.C.)

impurities such as copper, iron, or silver that altered the luminous color of the metal over time. Sometimes silver was mixed with gold in a ratio of 1:5 to make the natural alloy electron, a pale silver-colored metal which was produced artificially from the New Kingdom on and often associated with the moon. Pure silver was mostly imported from Asia and was considered to be a variety of gold.

The jewelers used very simple tools: a precious metal was melted in a terracotta crucible placed over the brazier and the heat increased by a stream of air blown through a rush reed fitted with a clay tip. The metal was then either poured into molds or hammered into sheets using smoothed stone tools. Sheets of gold were embossed and chased to produce well detailed designs and low reliefs.

The technique,

338-339 NECKLACE IN THE NAME OF AMENEMHAT III
Gold and semi-precious stones; Height of pectoral 7.9 CM Dashur; Twelfth Dynasty, Reign of Amenemhat III (1842-1794 BC)

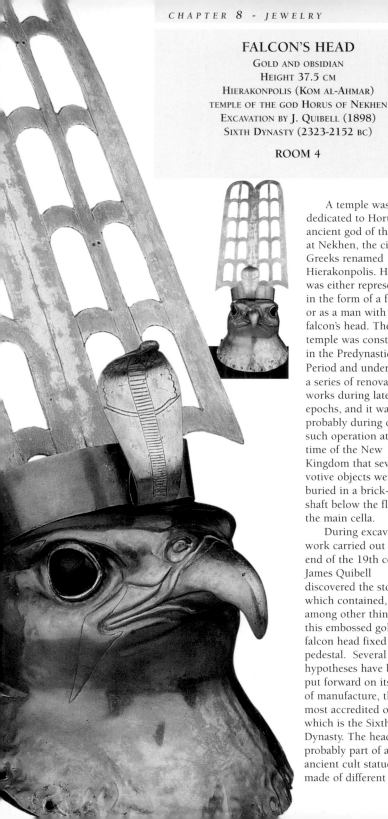

FALCON'S HEAD
GOLD AND OBSIDIAN
HEIGHT 37.5 CM
HIERAKONPOLIS (KOM AL-AHMAR)
TEMPLE OF THE GOD HORUS OF NEKHEN
EXCAVATION BY J. QUIBELL (1898)
SIXTH DYNASTY (2323-2152 BC)

ROOM 4

A temple was dedicated to Horus, the ancient god of the sky, at Nekhen, the city the Greeks renamed Hierakonpolis. Horus was either represented in the form of a falcon or as a man with a falcon's head. The temple was constructed in the Predynastic Period and underwent a series of renovation works during later epochs, and it was probably during one such operation at the time of the New Kingdom that several votive objects were buried in a brick-lined shaft below the floor of the main cella.

During excavation work carried out at the end of the 19th century, James Quibell discovered the store which contained, among other things, this embossed gold falcon head fixed to a pedestal. Several hypotheses have been put forward on its date of manufacture, the most accredited of which is the Sixth Dynasty. The head was probably part of an ancient cult statue made of different materials. The body, perhaps of wood, has not survived but it was fixed to the head with copper strips and nails.

An image of the king was added in front of the statue at a later date to underline the close link between the god and his terrestrial manifestation. The headdress – formed by a gold band adorned with a uraeus serpent and topped by two plumes – was also added later, in all probability during the Eighteenth Dynasty shortly before the statue was replaced. Despite the stylization of some features, this splendid head is a very realistic depiction of the features of a falcon and the eyes, in particular, are extraordinarily expressive. (D.C.)

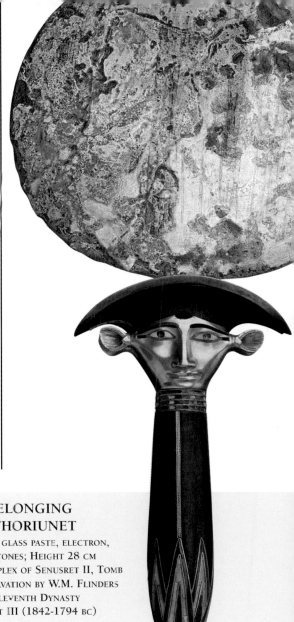

MIRROR BELONGING TO SATHATHORIUNET

SILVER, GOLD, OBSIDIAN, GLASS PASTE, ELECTRON, AND SEMI-PRECIOUS STONES; HEIGHT 28 CM
AL-LAHUN, FUNERARY COMPLEX OF SENUSRET II, TOMB OF SATHATHORIUNET, EXCAVATION BY W.M. FLINDERS PETRIE (1914), ELEVENTH DYNASTY
REIGN OF AMENEMHAT III (1842-1794 BC)

ROOM 4

The tomb of Sathathoriunet, one of the daughters of Senusret II, was robbed in ancient times but several items of jewelry hidden in a space in the wall escaped the thieves' notice. This refined mirror is a superb example of the skills of the jewelers of the Middle Kingdom. The reflective surface is a disk made of silver and the obsidian handle inlaid with semi-precious stones is shaped like a papyrus stem; both sides of the handle are decorated with the face of Hathor with cow's ears. Sometimes represented in the form of a cow, Hathor was the goddess of joy and love. (D.C.)

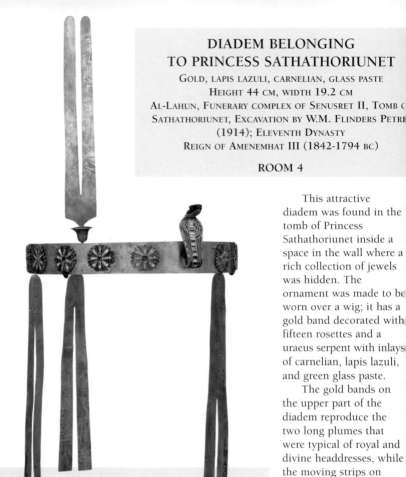

DIADEM BELONGING TO PRINCESS SATHATHORIUNET

GOLD, LAPIS LAZULI, CARNELIAN, GLASS PASTE
HEIGHT 44 CM, WIDTH 19.2 CM
AL-LAHUN, FUNERARY COMPLEX OF SENUSRET II, TOMB (
SATHATHORIUNET, EXCAVATION BY W.M. FLINDERS PETRI
(1914); ELEVENTH DYNASTY
REIGN OF AMENEMHAT III (1842-1794 BC)

ROOM 4

This attractive diadem was found in the tomb of Princess Sathathoriunet inside a space in the wall where a rich collection of jewels was hidden. The ornament was made to be worn over a wig; it has a gold band decorated with fifteen rosettes and a uraeus serpent with inlays of carnelian, lapis lazuli, and green glass paste.

The gold bands on the upper part of the diadem reproduce the two long plumes that were typical of royal and divine headdresses, while the moving strips on either side of the face and at the back of the neck resemble the ornamental ribbons that were often applied to floral garlands. (D.C.)

URAEUS SERPENT OF SENUSRET II

GOLD, LAPIS LAZULI, CARNELIAN, AMAZONITE; HEIGHT 6.7 CM, WIDTH 3 CM; AL-LAHUN, PYRAMID OF SENUSRET II EXCAVATION BY W.M. FLINDERS PETRIE (1920); TWELFTH DYNASTY
REIGN OF SENUSRET II (1897-1878 BC)

ROOM 4

The term "uraeus" is derived from the Greek transcription of the Egyptian *iaret*, i.e. the cobra with the swollen stomach ready to strike.

An emblem of royalty, the reptile was applied to crowns to protect the king from evil with its poison. One legend says that it was the eye of Ra transformed into a serpent, but it was also believed that it was the form taken by Uadjet, the guardian deity of Lower Egypt. This gold uraeus serpent inlaid with precious stones was found among the rubble in the pyramid of Senusret II and had probably been dropped by the thieves. (D.C.)

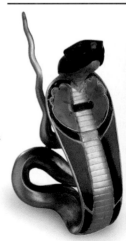

BRACELETS FROM THE TOMB OF DJER

GOLD, TURQUOISE, LAPIS LAZULI AND AMETHYST
LENGTH VARIES BETWEEN 10.2 AND 15.6 CM
ABYDOS, TOMB OF DJER;
EXCAVATION BY W.M. FLINDERS PETRIE (1901)
FIRST DYNASTY, REIGN OF DJER (2920-2770 BC)

ROOM 4

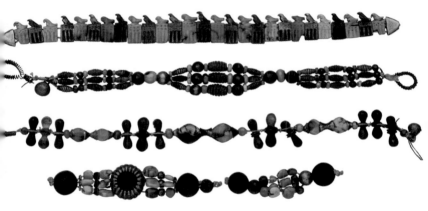

The tombs of all the pharaohs of the First Dynasty were discovered in Abydos, the ancient religious center of southern Egypt. The superstructures have not survived but it is thought that they were smooth-sided parallelepiped buildings made with adobe bricks in the *mastaba* or "bench" style.

tablets made from wood, bone, and ivory, and these four bracelets found in the tomb of Djer, one of the first pharaohs of the Thinite Dynasty. The ornaments were on a mummified forearm found in a crack in the wall. The presence of parts of the mummy around the tomb was not unusual; they resulted

rectangular space representing the courtyard. The *serekh* contains the first and most ancient of the five names of the pharaoh, the "name of Horus," which identified the king with the god of the sky represented in the form of a falcon.

The other three bracelets are composed of gold, turquoise, amethyst,

The hypogean rooms had a central burial chamber surrounded by a number of rooms used to store the grave goods.

The dig led by Flinders Petrie at the start of the 20th century brought to light a series of small objects including several clay seals, fragments of stone vases,

from the brutal actions of thieves as they ripped the bodies apart in their search for jewels and valuable objects.

The first bracelet is formed by alternate gold and turquoise plaques engraved with the god-falcon Horus on the *serekh*, the archaic royal palace, topped by a

and lapis lazuli beads in various shapes arranged in fantastic figures that draw attention to the central part of the ornaments.

The use of turquoise, mined in Sinai, and lapis lazuli, from central Asia, is evidence of the extensive trading links that existed in ancient times.
(D.C.)

343

BELT BELONGING TO PRINCE PTAHSHEPSES

GOLD, CARNELIAN, OBSIDIAN, AND TURQUOISE
BELT: LENGTH 90 CM, HEIGHT 4.5 CM, WEIGHT 148 GR
BUCKLE: LENGTH 10 CM, HEIGHT 4.5 CM; SAQQARA, LOWER TEMPLE
OF UNAS, SARCOPHAGUS OF PTAHSHEPSES; FOUND IN 1944
PROBABLY SIXTH DYNASTY (2323-2152 BC)

ROOM 4

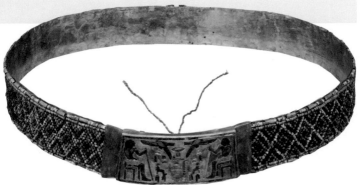

During research in the Valley Temple of Unas at Saqqara in 1944, a schist sarcophagus was found that contained the mummy of Prince Ptahshepses but copious infiltration of water had caused the almost total decomposition of the body. The belt, which had originally been placed between the bandages of the mummy, was in poor condition. It was covered with melted wax to hold the various elements in place and then taken to Cairo Museum where it underwent restoration.

It is composed of a thin band of gold on which beads were fixed to form a geometric pattern of diamonds and triangles. The buckle is also made from gold leaf and is decorated with inlays and chasing. The figure of the prince is shown seated on both sides with a long staff in his right hand, dominated by two falcons, representing Horus, with their wings outspread and the *shen* symbols of eternity in their claws. The hieroglyphs list the titles and the name of the prince. Ptahshepses was the "son of the king" who is not identified but probably a pharaoh of the Sixth Dynasty. (D.C.)

SHELL SHAPED CONTAINER

GOLD; LENGTH 5.3 CM; SAQQARA
FUNERARY COMPLEX OF SEKHEMKHET
EXCAVATION BY THE EGYPTIAN ANTIQUITIES
SERVICE (1950)
THIRD DYNASTY, REIGN OF SEKHEMKHET
(2611-2630 BC)

ROOM 4

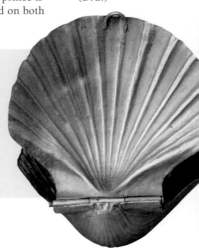

This original cosmetics container in the shape of a scallop was found in the pyramidal complex of the pharaoh Sekhemkhet which was built on the model of his predecessor Djoser. For the ancient Egyptians, the plant and animal worlds were an inexhaustible source of decorative themes, particularly in the design of small, everyday objects. Oils, ointments, and powders used as cosmetics were kept in elaborate containers of various shapes and materials.

This shell was made from pure gold and is one of the most outstanding examples to have survived to the modern day; its simplicity is evidence of the refinement and skill of the ancient goldsmiths. (M.S.C.)

GOLD VESSELS
OF QUEEN HETEPHERES I

GOLD; CUP WITH SPOUT: HEIGHT 5.2 CM, DIAMETER 8.5 CM; SMALL CUPS: HEIGHT 2.4 CM, DIAMETERS 8.2 CM AND 8 CM; GIZA, TOMB OF HETEPHERES I EXCAVATION BY G. REISNER (1925) FOURTH DYNASTY, REIGN OF SNEFRU (2575-2551 BC)

ROOM 4

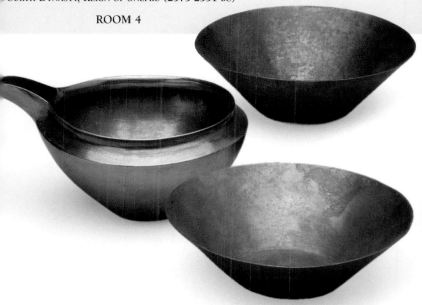

These valuable gold containers were found in the grave goods of Queen Hetepheres together with other alabaster vases and other items made from inlaid gilded wood. The elegance of the forms is evidence of the taste of the era for simple, linear objects which, in this case, were the skilful work of court craftsmen. The three containers were cast from a very pure alloy and worked into a single gold leaf. It would anachronistic to define the clean lines of this style as "modern" but the clear fondness of gentle but fundamental lines is very close to our own aesthetic tastes. (M.S.C.)

BELT BELONGING
TO PRINCESS SATHATHOR

GOLD, LAPIS LAZULI, CARNELIAN, AND FELDSPAR
LENGTH 70 CM; DAHSHUR, FUNERARY COMPLEX
OF SENUSRET III, TOMB OF PRINCESS SATHATHOR
EXCAVATION BY J. DE MORGAN (1894); TWELFTH
DYNASTY, REIGN OF SENUSRET III (1881-1842 BC)

ROOM 4

The thieves that robbed the tomb of Princess Sathathor did not find the jewels hidden beneath the floor. The caskets containing the precious items were only discovered by archaeologists at the end of the 19th century.

This belt, at first thought to be a necklace, alternates gold shells with double rows of carnelian, lapis lazuli, and feldspar beads. The ingenious fastening operates by sliding together two halves of a shell at the ends of the belt to form a single shell identical in appearance to the others. (D.C.)

GIRDLE BELONGING
TO PRINCESS MERERET

GOLD AND AMETHYST; LENGTH 60 CM
DASHUR, FUNERARY COMPLEX OF SENUSRET III
TOMB OF PRINCESS MERERET; EXCAVATION
BY J. DE MORGAN (1894); TWELFTH DYNASTY
REIGN OF SENUSRET III (1881-1842 BC)

ROOM 4

The use of girdles as a woman's ornament was widespread in Egypt from the Middle Kingdom and wall paintings often show naked girls clad only with small chains formed by alternating beads and amulets around their hips. This example comes from the grave goods of Princess Mereret and formed a pair with an anklet, also made from gold and amethyst. The panthers' heads had a protective function and were analogous to the talon pendants on the ankle ornaments. (D.C.)

NECKLACE WITH PECTORAL BEARING THE NAME OF SENUSRET II

GOLD, CARNELIAN, TURQUOISE, AND LAPIS LAZULI
HEIGHT: PECTORAL 4.9 CM; DAHSHUR, FUNERARY
COMPLEX OF SENUSRET III, TOMB OF PRINCESS SATHATHOR
EXCAVATION BY J. DE MORGAN (1894); TWELFTH
DYNASTY, REIGN OF SENUSRET II (1900-1881 BC)

ROOM 4

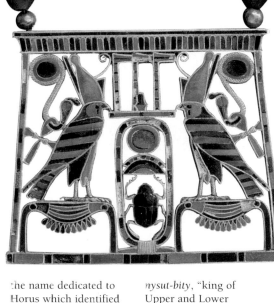

Fragments of numerous jewels were found in a hiding place in the tomb of Sathathor, one of the daughters of Senusret II, but painstaking reconstruction was able to restore them to their original splendor.

This necklace is fixed to a gold pectoral inlaid with lapis lazuli, turquoise, and carnelian. Two of the five names of Senusret II are given inside a frame in the form of a sanctuary; these are flanked by two falcons wearing the double crown of Egypt placed above the hieroglyph for gold. A uraeus serpent circles a sun disk behind each bird with the *ankh* sign of eternity hanging from its coils. The falcon represents the god Horus whose earthly manifestation was the pharaoh; the title "Gold Horus" was one of the many assigned to the king.

The pharaoh's complete list of titles – established definitively during the Middle Kingdom – was formed by five names: the first and most ancient was

the name dedicated to Horus which identified the king with the god of the sky with the form of a falcon; the second was *nebty*, "the Two Ladies," through which the sovereign identified himself with the guardian goddesses of Upper and Lower Egypt, Nekhbet and Uadjet; the third name was the rather obscure "Gold Horus" (being incorruptible, gold symbolized the body of the god); the fourth name was assumed by the pharaoh on his coronation and was preceded by the title

nysut-bity, "king of Upper and Lower Egypt"; it was enclosed in a cartouche, as was the pharaoh's fifth name, his birth name, which was linked to the title *sa-Ra*, "son of Ra."

Senusret II's name "Gold Horus" (*hetep-netjeru*, "the gods are peace") is inscribed in the cartouche that also gives the king's coronation name (*Khakheperra*) between the two falcons on the upper part of the pectoral. This necklace was probably a gift from Senusret to his daughter. (D.C.)

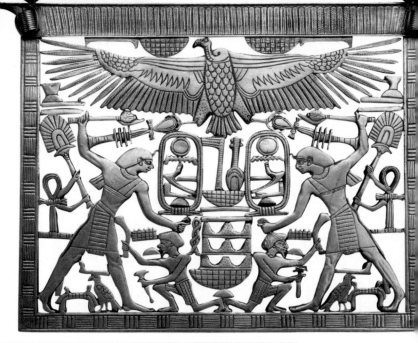

NECKLACE WITH PECTORAL IN THE NAME OF AMENEMHAT III

GOLD, CARNELIAN, TURQUOISE, AND LAPIS LAZULI
HEIGHT OF THE PECTORAL 7.9 CM, WIDTH 10.5 CM
DASHUR, FUNERARY COMPLEX OF SENUSRET III
TOMB OF PRINCESS MERERET
EXCAVATION BY J. DE MORGAN (1894)
TWELFTH DYNASTY, REIGN OF AMENEMHAT III (1842-1794 BC)

ROOM 4

This item of jewelry came from the grave goods belonging to Princess Mereret, a daughter of Senusret III. The simple necklace is attached to an ornate pectoral with a border in the form of a temple. The complex representation is based on the classic theme, dear to the Egyptians, of the pharaoh defeating foreign enemies. The cartouches of Mereret's brother, Amenemhat III, are shown in the center with the traditional attribution, "The perfect god, the lord of the two lands and of all foreign countries." The sovereign is shown on either side brandishing a war club as he grasps the hair of a kneeling enemy identified in the hieroglyphs as an Asiatic Bedouin.

The scene takes place beneath the image of the goddess-vulture Nekhbet, guardian deity of southern Egypt, with wings spread as a sign of protection and the signs of *ankh* ("eternal life") and *djed* ("stability") clutched in her talons. The hieroglyphs on either side of her head and plumes describe her as the "Lady of the sky sovereign of the two lands." Two personified *ankh* signs support the fan (an emblem of royalty) that is often shown behind the king.

The necklace was present from Amenemhat III to his sister; pectorals decorated with themes from official iconography were customary gifts from kings to members of the royal family. Representations of the pharaoh crushing his enemies are frequent in wide variety of contexts, ranging from small items of jewelry like this to huge reliefs on temple walls.

The high quality decoration of this pectoral includes inlays on the front and chasing on the back.

(D.C.)

NECKLACE WITH PECTORAL BEARING THE NAME OF SENUSRET III

Gold, carnelian, turquoise, lapis lazuli, and amethyst
Height 6.1 cm, width 8.6 cm; Dahshur, Funerary complex
of Senusret III, Tomb of Princess Mereret
Excavation by J. de Morgan (1894)
Twelfth Dynasty, Reign of Senusret III (1881-1842 bc)

ROOM 4

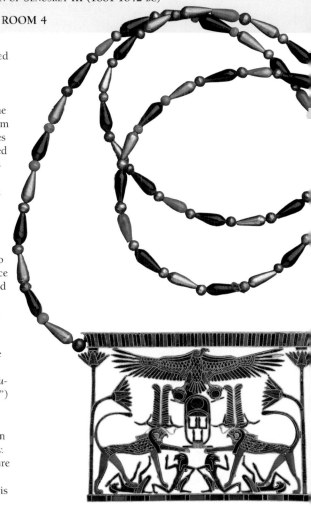

The thieves that robbed the tomb of Mereret, the daughter of Senusret III, could not find the jewels buried below the floor. The baskets that contained them were discovered by Jacques de Morgan when he carried out a series of excavations at the end of the 19th century at Dahshur, about 5 miles south of Cairo.

This piece of jewelry bearing the name of Senusret III was probably a gift from the pharaoh to his daughter. The necklace is formed by a row of gold beads and semi-precious stones. The gold pectoral is inlaid with lapis lazuli, turquoise, carnelian, and amethyst and displays the cartouche with the king's coronation name (Kha-kau-ra, "The ka of Ra appear") in the center. This is flanked by two sphinxes with falcons' heads shown about to strike the enemy. Above, the goddess-vulture Nekhbet (the guardian deity of southern Egypt) is shown with her wings spread as a sign of protection and gripping two shen signs in her talons.

The falcon-headed sphinxes symbolize the pharaoh, identified with the gods Atum, and Horus and who are represented respectively as a lion and a falcon. The headdress, with long plumes mounted on a double pair of cow and ram's horns, also has a uraeus serpent as seen on sovereigns and deities.

Decoration of the pectoral is based on the traditional theme of the king defeating the enemies of Egypt. Foreign peoples belonged to the realm of disorder and it was the king's duty to eliminate any threat to the universal order he was the guarantor of.

The scene frame is in the form of a sanctuary in which the walls are replaced by lotus plants. (D.C.)

Like necklaces and bracelets, anklets were a common ornament popular with Egyptian women. This example belonged to the grave goods of Princess Mereret and was found hidden in her tomb with other jewels. It consists of two rows of small beads made from gold and amethyst and has two pendants in the form of a talon. It was fastened by gold clasps decorated with a braided motif.

Wall paintings often depict dancers wearing anklets with talon-shaped pendants that were considered to protect their wearer. (D.C.)

ANKLET BELONGING TO PRINCESS MERERET

GOLD AND AMETHYST; LENGTH 34 CM; DAHSHUR, FUNERARY COMPLEX OF SENUSRET III, TOMB OF PRINCESS MERERET; EXCAVATION BY J. DE MORGAN (1894); TWELFTH DYNASTY, REIGN OF SENUSRET III (1881-1842 BC)

ROOM 4

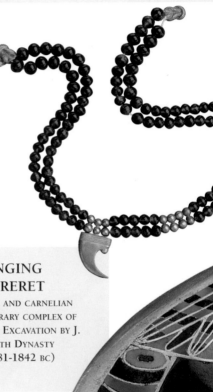

PENDANT BELONGING TO PRINCESS MERERET

GOLD, TURQUOISE, LAPIS LAZULI, AND CARNELIAN HEIGHT 4.6 CM; DAHSHUR, FUNERARY COMPLEX OF SENUSRET III, TOMB OF MERERET; EXCAVATION BY J. DE MORGAN (1894); TWELFTH DYNASTY REIGN OF SENUSRET III (1881-1842 BC)

ROOM 4

The tomb belonging to Princess Mereret, entered and robbed during antiquity, still held an outstanding collection of jewels hidden below the floor that remained unnoticed by the thieves.

This small gold pendant was made to imitate polished mother-of-pearl and is enhanced by sophisticated inlays of semi-precious stones.

A central nucleus of carnelian is surrounded by a stylized garland of flowers made from turquoise and lapis lazuli; the garland develops out of a lotus flower, the emblem of regeneration, in the upper part of the ornament.
(D.C.)

BRACELETS BELONGING TO QUEEN URET

GOLD, TURQUOISE, LAPIS LAZULI, CARNELIAN
LENGTH CIRCA 15 CM; DAHSHUR, FUNERARY COMPLEX OF
SENUSRET III, TOMB OF QUEEN URET; EXCAVATION BY THE
METROPOLITAN MUSEUM OF ART (1994-1995); TWELFTH
DYNASTY, PERIOD FROM THE REIGN OF AMENEMHAT II TO
THAT OF SENUSRET III (1932-1842 BC)

ROOM 4

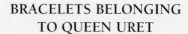

Bracelets were common ornaments and worn by both women and men. These, found with a number of other items of jewelry in a small space in the wall of the tomb of Queen Uret, the mother of Senusret III, are formed by two rows of beads made from gold, turquoise, carnelian, and lapis lazuli. The two parts of the clasp slide together to close and are decorated by a braided motif. The two small gold lions in the center of the bracelets symbolize the figure of the pharaoh and probably also had a protective function.
(D.C.)

351

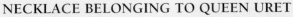

NECKLACE BELONGING TO QUEEN URET

GOLD, TURQUOISE, LAPIS LAZULI, CARNELIAN; NECKLACE: LENGTH
62.9 CM ; PECTORAL: HEIGHT 1.7 CM, WIDTH 1.7 CM
DAHSHUR, FUNERARY COMPLEX OF SENUSRET III, TOMB OF QUEEN
URET; EXCAVATION BY THE METROPOLITAN MUSEUM OF ART (1994-
1995); TWELFTH DYNASTY, PERIOD FROM THE REIGN OF
AMENEMHAT II TO THAT OF SENUSRET III (1932-1842 BC)

ROOM 4

This necklace belonging to Queen Uret is made of drop-shaped beads in gold, turquoise, carnelian, and lapis lazuli. The small pectoral is decorated with the hieroglyph of the heart, *ib*, enclosed in a frame in the shape of a temple formed by three other hieroglyphs: at the base there is *hetep*, "peace," and on the walls and roof there are two standards that indicate *netjer*, "god." The combination of these signs forms a brief phrase, "The hearts of the two gods are at peace," which referred to the reconciliation of the two rival gods, Horus and Seth, in the person of the pharaoh. (D.C.)

BELT BELONGING
TO QUEEN URET

GOLD, TURQUOISE, LAPIS LAZULI, CARNELIAN; LENGTH 84 CM
DAHSHUR, FUNERARY COMPLEX OF SENUSRET III, TOMB OF URE
EXCAVATION BY THE METROPOLITAN MUSEUM OF ART (1994-199
TWELFTH DYNASTY, PERIOD BETWEEN THE REIGNS OF AMENEMHA
AND SENUSRET III (1932-1842 BC)

ROOM 4

The belt was part of the grave goods found in the tomb of Queen Uret, the mother of pharaoh Sesostris III. It alternates double strings of beads of carnelian, turquoise, gold, and lapis lazuli with gold elements in the shape of cowry shells that were believed by the ancient Egyptians to be powerful amulets that increased female fertility.

This type of belt was very common in the Middle Kingdom and is seen in tomb paintings and "treasure hoards" of other princesses of the period.
(D.C.)

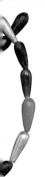

BRACELETS AND ANKLETS BELONGING TO QUEEN URET

GOLD, TURQUOISE, CARNELIAN, LAPIS LAZULI; BRACELETS: HEIGHT 4 CM, LENGTH 15.5 CM; ANKLETS: HEIGHT 3.8 CM, LENGTH 21.5 CM
DAHSHUR, FUNERARY COMPLEX OF SENUSRET III, TOMB OF QUEEN URET
EXCAVATION BY THE METROPOLITAN MUSEUM OF ART (1994-1995)
TWELFTH DYNASTY, PERIOD FROM THE REIGN OF AMENEMHAT II TO THAT
OF SENUSRET III (1932-1842 BC)

ROOM 4

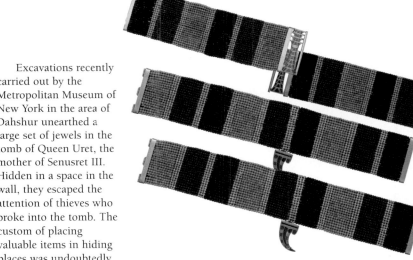

Excavations recently carried out by the Metropolitan Museum of New York in the area of Dahshur unearthed a large set of jewels in the tomb of Queen Uret, the mother of Senusret III. Hidden in a space in the wall, they escaped the attention of thieves who broke into the tomb. The custom of placing valuable items in hiding places was undoubtedly motivated by the fear that tombs would be robbed, a widespread practice even in antiquity.

Uret's treasure included bracelets, anklets, a necklace, a belt, and some scarabs. The examples shown here were made using grains of gold, turquoise, carnelian, and lapis lazuli to create a geometric pattern of alternating bands.

The fasteners of the bracelets are embellished with two inlaid *djed* pillars between the gold plaques. The *djed* – a hieroglyph meaning "stability" – is a very ancient amulet.

The anklets have two gold pendants inlaid with carnelian, turquoise, and lapis lazuli in the form of talons. Dancers in wall paintings are often shown wearing anklets fitted with talons which were believed to be imbued with the power of protection.
(D.C.)

353

JEWELS BELONGING TO PRINCESS KHNUMIT
GOLD DECORATED WITH GRANULES AND STRINGS
1) MEDALLION: DIAMETER 2.85 CM; 2) NECKLACE: LENGTH 28 CM
3) BUTTERFLY-SHAPED CLASP: WIDTH 2.7 CM; 4) STAR-SHAPED PENDANTS:
WIDTH 2.5 CM; 5) ORNAMENTS IN THE FORM OF SMALL BIRDS: HEIGHT 1 CM
DASHUR, FUNERARY COMPLEX OF AMENEMHAT II, TOMB OF KHNUMIT;
EXCAVATION BY J. DE MORGAN (1894); MIDDLE KINGDOM
TWELFTH DYNASTY, REIGN OF AMENEMHAT II (1932 - 1898 BC)

ROOM 4

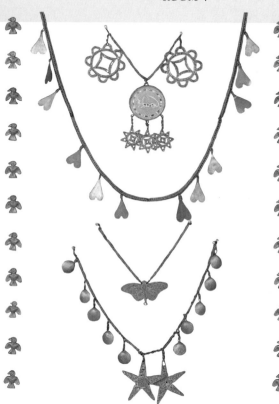

mounted on a gold frame decorated with small granules. Three eight-pointed stars hang from the lower edge while two rosettes are attached to the small chain that supports the medallion. In both cases, the decoration is derived from Syrian models.

The second necklace is adorned with a series of pendants of stylized bees, a motif that was to be seen in both the Aegean and the Nile Valley.

The third item is a delicate butterfly-shaped clasp made from thin gold leaf. The details of the body and wings are accurately recreated with the application of thread and granules of gold. The motif of a butterfly is characteristic of Minoan culture but was used by Egyptian jewelers from the Fourth Dynasty.

The fourth jewel is a series of pendants in the form of shells and two large five-pointed stars. The small gold birds seen to the sides of the necklaces are ornaments that adorned the princess head when threaded onto the braids of her hair. (D.C.)

These items of jewelry belonging to Princess Khnumit are characterized by the decorative technique of applied gold threads and granules that was very popular outside of Egypt, particularly in Syria and the area of the Aegean.

One hypothesis (Aldred, 1972) is that the jewels were given to Khnumit by a foreign prince, but they may also have been the work of immigrant goldsmiths or Egyptian jewelrs inspired by exotic styles.

The pendant at the top has a blue enamel plaque at the center bearing the image of a dappled heifer in a round border. The elegant miniature is covered by a thin layer of rock crystal and is

DIADEM BELONGING TO PRINCESS KHNUMIT

GOLD, SEMI-PRECIOUS STONES. AND GLASS PASTE
CIRCUMFERENCE 64 CM
DAHSHUR, FUNERARY COMPLEX OF AMENEMHAT II
TOMB OF KHNUMIT
EXCAVATION BY J. DE MORGAN (1894)
TWELFTH DYNASTY, REIGN OF AMENEMHAT II (1932-1898 BC)

ROOM 4

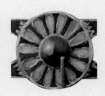

The tombs of princesses who lived during the Middle Kingdom were found to contain a number of elegant diadems shaped like elaborate garlands of flowers and made from gold and semi-precious stones.

This example came from the grave goods of Khnumit, one of the daughters of Amenemhat II. It is made up of a series of horizontal and vertical decorative elements made in gold with inlays of semi-precious stones and glass paste. Each horizontal element is composed of a rosette flanked by two bell-shaped flowers heavily inlaid with carnelian, turquoise, and lapis lazuli; this motif is repeated eight times and separated by an equal number of vertical elements of similar design.

The inside of the jewel is made from gold and engraved with a decoration that repeats the lines of the inlays. Two delicate ornaments were applied to the front and back of the diadem but they were found separate and in a poor state of repair. The first represents a tree branch and is formed by a small gold tube onto which gold leaves were fused alternating with small flowers created with semi-precious stones. The second ornament depicts the goddess-vulture Nekhbet with her wings outspread as a sign of protection and two *shen* signs of eternity gripped in her talons.

The diadem would have been worn by the princess during state ceremonies and combined with an elaborate hairstyle that usually included small gold cylinders applied to thick artificial plaits.

Princess Khnumit's tomb, violated by thieves, contained a outstanding collection of jewelry, some of which was placed between the wraps of the mummy's shroud, and some in the annexe to the funerary chamber. In addition to several necklaces and various bracelets, there was another exquisite diadem. (D.C.)

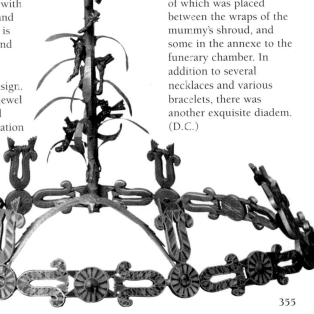

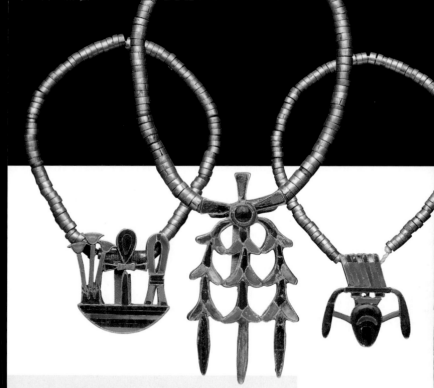

BRACELETS BELONGING TO PRINCESS KHNUMIT

GOLD, CARNELIAN, LAPIS LAZULI, AMAZONITE
HEIGHT OF FASTENERS 1.9 CM, 3.3 CM, 1.9 CM
DAHSHUR, FUNERARY COMPLEX OF AMENEMHAT II
TOMB OF PRINCESS KHNUMIT
EXCAVATION BY J. DE MORGAN (1894)
TWELFTH DYNASTY, REIGN OF AMENEMHAT II (1932-1898 BC)

ROOM 4

Princess Khnumit was buried at Dahshur near her father's pyramid (Amenemhat II). Her tomb contained a rich set of jewelry the pieces of which were found wrapped in the linen shroud of the mummy and beneath a small chest in the annexe to the burial chamber.

These three bracelets are composed of simple strings of gold beads that contrast with the elaborate fasteners whose purpose was not only decorative. The bracelets can, in fact, be "read": the fasteners were created in the shape of hieroglyphs to form a message of good omen. The first fastener is made up of four signs which are as follows, from right to left: a folded mat (*sa*, "protection"), the lace of a sandal (*ankh*, "eternal life"), a tuft of papyrus (*ha*, a particle that states the phrase is an exclamation), and a wicker basket (*neb*, "every"). The combination of these four hieroglyphs wishes Khnumit "All protection and life!"

The second represents a sign that symbolizes three animal skins knotted together that reads *mes*, i.e. "birth."

The third is created by the combination of two signs that respectively represent a section of the backbone and the heart and which together read *au-ib*, "joy."

Hieroglyphic writing used signs that represent plants, objects, people, and animals which could be employed as ideograms – their meaning being the same as their image – or as phonograms, indicating sounds, or as determinatives to add precision to the meaning of words.
(D.C.)

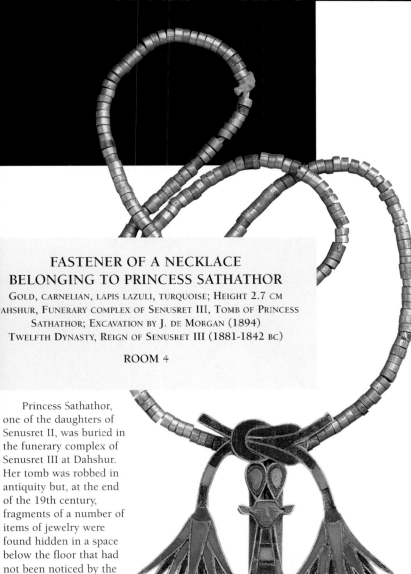

FASTENER OF A NECKLACE
BELONGING TO PRINCESS SATHATHOR

GOLD, CARNELIAN, LAPIS LAZULI, TURQUOISE; HEIGHT 2.7 CM
ɔAHSHUR, FUNERARY COMPLEX OF SENUSRET III, TOMB OF PRINCESS
SATHATHOR; EXCAVATION BY J. DE MORGAN (1894)
TWELFTH DYNASTY, REIGN OF SENUSRET III (1881-1842 BC)

ROOM 4

Princess Sathathor, one of the daughters of Senusret II, was buried in the funerary complex of Senusret III at Dahshur. Her tomb was robbed in antiquity but, at the end of the 19th century, fragments of a number of items of jewelry were found hidden in a space below the floor that had not been noticed by the thieves. Careful restoration succeeded in reconstructing the jewels after comparison with other examples from the same period.

This small clasp was made to fit a simple necklace of gold beads similar to the three bracelets found in the tomb of Princess Khnumit. It is made from gold and decorated with inlays of carnelian, turquoise, and lapis lazuli depicting two lotus flowers pointing downwards and the stems knotted. Beneath them there is a sort of sistrum with the human head and the ears and the horns of a cow; this is Bat, the goddess of the seventh *nome* of Upper Egypt, who was identified with Hathor from the New Kingdom on.

The lotus flower motif was often used on jewels but was not purely ornamental: for ancient Egyptians the plant was the symbol of eternal rebirth. (D.C.)

NECKLACE BELONGING TO PRINCESS KHNUMIT

GOLD, CARNELIAN, TURQUOISE, LAPIS LAZULI; WIDTH 35 CM
DAHSHUR, FUNERARY COMPLEX OF AMENEMHAT II
TOMB OF PRINCESS KHNUMIT
EXCAVATION BY J. DE MORGAN (1894)
TWELFTH DYNASTY, REIGN OF AMENEMHAT II (1932 - 1898 BC)

ROOM 4

Egyptian jewelry was more than purely decorative and often included symbols supposed to protect the wearer. The apotropaic function of this necklace found on the mummy of Princess Khnumit is clearly seen in the symmetrical repetition of a series of amulets on either side of a central composition. The symbols lie between two rows of gold beads that have a fastener in the form of a falcon's head at either end. The center of the object is decorated with the *ankh* sign meaning "eternal life" over the *hetep* sign that represents a table of offerings.

Another ten amulets are represented at the two sides: the *user* sign, "power"; the goddess-vulture Nekhbet and the goddess-cobra Uadjet, the respective guardian deities of Upper and Lower Egypt; a human head fetish with earrings and cows' horns that represents the goddess Bat, later to be assimilated to the sistrum decorated with the image of Hathor; the eye of Horus that ensured the wearer of well-being and health; the *khenem* pot, "union"; the *djed* pillar, "stability"; another *ankh* sign; the *sema* sign showing lungs and a trachea, "union"; and the bee, the symbol of Lower Egypt.

The amulets are made of gold inlaid with semi-precious stones on the front and chased on the back. (D.C.)

CLASPS OF BRACELETS BELONGING TO PRINCESS KHNUMIT

GOLD, TURQUOISE, LAPIS LAZULI, AND CARNELIAN
HEIGHT 3.9 CM; DAHSHUR, FUNERARY COMPLEX
OF AMENEMHAT II; TOMB OF PRINCESS KHNUMIT
EXCAVATION BY J. DE MORGAN 1894; TWELFTH DYNASTY
REIGN OF AMENEMHAT II (1932 – 1898 BC)

ROOM 4

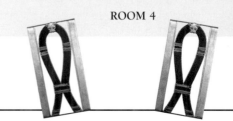

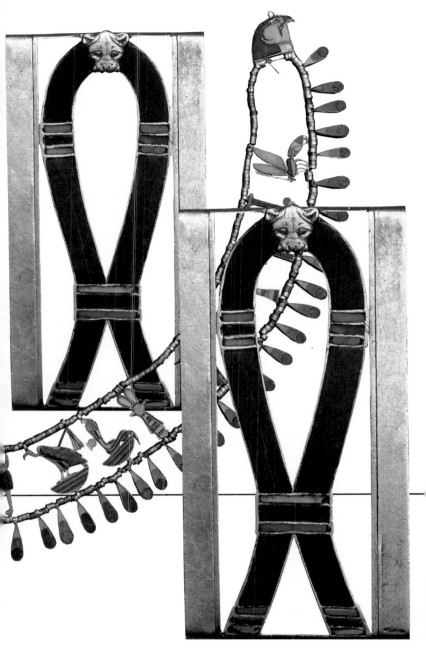

These clasps belonged to the grave goods of Princess Khnumit and were used to fasten two bracelets made from gold beads and semi-precious stones. A lapis lazuli amulet inlaid with three bands of turquoise and carnelian is represented on a gold leopard head between the two gold plaques. The amulet is the hieroglyph sa, the symbol of protection, which represents the folded reed mat used by shepherds to shelter from bad weather.

The backs of the two amulets are made from gold engraved to imitate the reeds of the mats tied by three strings.
(D.C.)

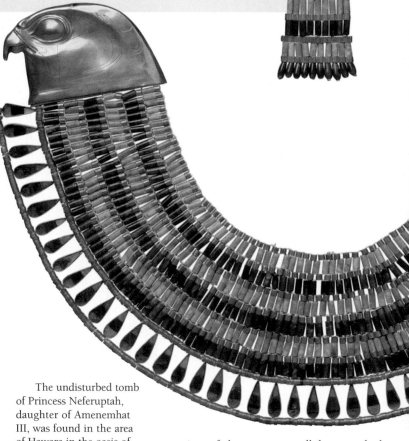

NECKLACE BELONGING TO PRINCESS NEFERUPTAH

GOLD, CARNELIAN, FELDSPAR, AND GLASS PASTE
LENGTH 36.5 CM, HEIGHT 10 CM
HAWARA, PYRAMID OF PRINCESS NEFERUPTAH
EXCAVATION BY J. DE MORGAN (1894)
TWELFTH DYNASTY, REIGN OF AMENEMHAT III (1842-1794 BC)

ROOM 4

The undisturbed tomb of Princess Neferuptah, daughter of Amenemhat III, was found in the area of Hawara in the oasis of Fayum. Infiltration of water had caused all organic materials to decompose, leaving only traces of the wooden coffin, the mummy, and its burial clothing inside the granite sarcophagus. Nor were the threads of various pieces of jewelry preserved: a long task of restoration and comparison of elements to other items from the same period were necessary to reassemble the articles.

This elegant collar, called *usekh* ("wide") by the Egyptians, was placed around the neck of the mummy. It consists of six strings of cylindrical beads of carnelian and feldspar with a motif of small drops on the lower edge. Two fasteners in the shape of falcons' heads are connected to a counterpoise by two strings of beads; the counterpoise is made in a shape similar to the collar.

Usekh collars were also considered to ward off evil spirits. (D.C.)

360

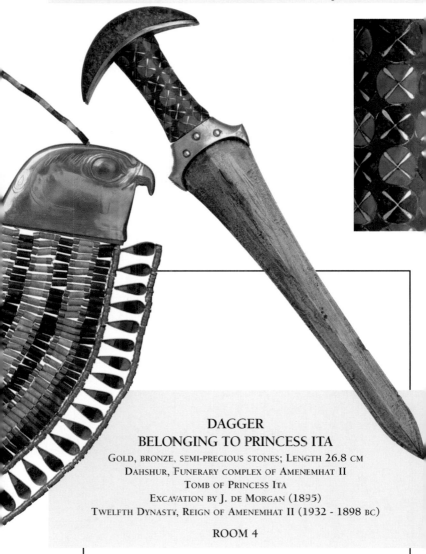

DAGGER
BELONGING TO PRINCESS ITA

GOLD, BRONZE, SEMI-PRECIOUS STONES; LENGTH 26.8 CM
DAHSHUR, FUNERARY COMPLEX OF AMENEMHAT II
TOMB OF PRINCESS ITA
EXCAVATION BY J. DE MORGAN (1895)
TWELFTH DYNASTY, REIGN OF AMENEMHAT II (1932 - 1898 BC)

ROOM 4

The undisturbed tomb of Princess Ita contained a precious collection of jewelry, most of which lay among the wraps of the mummy. The small hoard of treasure included bracelets, anklets, a necklace, a belt, and this refined dagger. The lapis lazuli pommel is shaped like a crescent moon while the grip is formed by a gold tube decorated with inlays of carnelian, lapis lazuli, and amazonite and is fixed to the bronze blade by three small gold nails.

It was probably a ceremonial object as it is not sufficiently strong to be used as a weapon. (D.C.)

BRACELETS BELONGING
TO QUEEN AHHOTEP

GOLD; OUTER DIAMETER 10.4 CM, INNER DIAMETER 7.4 CM
THEBES, TOMB OF QUEEN AHHOTEP AT DRA ABU AL-NAGA
EXCAVATION BY A. MARIETTE (1859)
EARLY EIGHTEENTH DYNASTY (1554-1529 BC)

ROOM 4

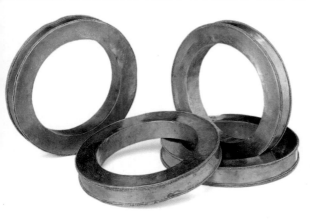

BRACELET BELONGING
TO QUEEN AHHOTEP

GOLD, CARNELIAN, LAPIS LAZULI, AND GREEN FELDSPAR
HEIGHT 8.2 CM, WIDTH 11 CM; THEBES
TOMB OF QUEEN AHHOTEP AT DRA ABU AL-NAGA
EXCAVATION BY A. MARIETTE (1859)
EARLY EIGHTEENTH DYNASTY (1554 - 1529 BC)

ROOM 4

Bracelets existed in Egypt from earliest history and were very popular; they were wor both on the wrist and t arm. These gold bands were found in the tomb of Queen Ahhotep in t Theban necropolis. The lid of the queen's gilded sarcophagus with *rishi* decorations (from the Arabic word meaning "plumed") and the treasure in the tomb clearly attest that the domination of the Hyks had not harmed Egypti goldsmiths' creativity.

These bracelets are all the same size. The large flat rings and squ recesses are formed fro thin leaves of gold and adorned by a braided motif – single on one si and doubled on the oth (D.C.)

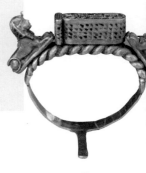

This bracelet, one of the grave goods belonging to Queen Ahhotep, was originally thought to be a crown as it was found among the mummy's hair. However, given its diameter, there are no doubts today that it was in fact worn on the arm, and, as it seems too large for the wrist, it may have been worn on the forearm.

It is a small ring half decorated with a plaited motif and half inlaid with lapis lazuli, carnelian, and feldspar in a frieze of alternating *djed* and *tit* signs (emblems associated with Osiris and Isis).

A particularly thick cartouche in the center bears the following inscription: "Son of Ra,

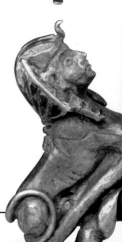

BRACELETS BELONGING TO QUEEN AHHOTEP

GOLD, LAPIS LAZULI, CARNELIAN, TURQUOISE; HEIGHT 3.6 CM, DIAMETER 5.4 CM; THEBES, DRA ABU AL-NAGA, TOMB OF QUEEN AHHOTEP; EXCAVATION BY A. MARIETTE (1859) EIGHTEENTH. DYNASTY, REIGN OF AHMES (1550-1525 BC)

These bracelets were part of the goods found in the tomb of Queen Ahhotep, the mother of Kames and Ahmes, the two rulers that liberated Egypt from the domination of the Hyksos. The decoration is created by series of minute beads of gold, turquoise, carnelian, and lapis lazuli mounted on gold threads and arranged to form a pattern of small triangles.

The clasps are engraved with hieroglyphs that can only be read when the two gold plaques are closed together: they form the cartouches of the queen's son, Ahmes, who founded the Eighteenth Dynasty. His coronation name, *Nebpehtyra*, is given on one, and his birth name, Ahmes, on the other. (D.C.)

Ahmes, who lives eternally and for ever." Ahmes, the son of Ahhotep, gave his mother a great many objects in recognition of her role in the war against the Hyksos.

Two small sphinxes symbolizing the king were applied on either side of the cartouche. The small inlaid gold bar that protrudes on the opposite side was worn on the inside of the arm, probably to prevent the armband being turned. (D.C.)

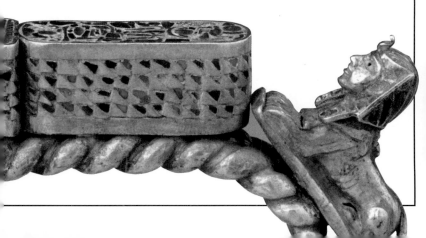

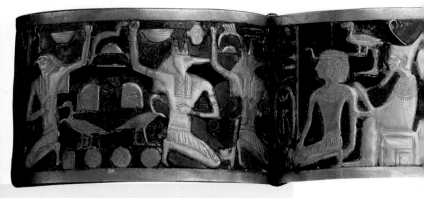

BRACELET BELONGING
TO QUEEN AHHOTEP

GOLD AND LAPIS LAZULI; HEIGHT 3.4 CM, DIAMETER 5.5 CM
THEBES, DRA ABU AL NAGA, TOMB OF QUEEN AHHOTEP
EXCAVATION BY A. MARIETTE (1859)
EIGHTEENTH DYNASTY, REIGN OF AHMES (1550 - 1525 BC)

ROOM 4

Most of the objects found in the tomb of Queen Ahhotep bear the names of her sons, Kames and Ahmes, the pharaohs that chased the Hyksos out of the country. The queen played a major role during the war of liberation as testified by the many objects that her sons donated to her grave goods. Some of those gifts were weapons, unusual for a woman's tomb.

This bracelet is formed by two semi-circles. Gold and lapis lazuli are the materials used to create its beautiful dichromatic decoration. A fan placed on the *shen* sign, the emblem of eternity, divides the right half into two parts with symmetrical scenes: Geb, the god of war who wears the red crown of Lower Egypt on one side and the double crown on the other, is seated on a throne with his hands resting in a sign of protection on the shoulder and arm of the king kneeling before him. The hieroglyphs give the name of the god and the cartouches of the king.

The other half of the bracelet is engraved with falcon and jackal-headed figures, the souls of Pe (Buto) and Nekhen (El Kab), the mythical ancestors of the rulers of Egypt before unification. (D.C.)

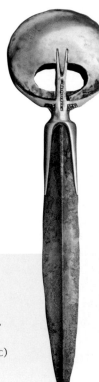

DAGGER BELONGING
TO QUEEN AHHOTEP

GOLD, SILVER, AND BRONZE
LENGTH 21.3 CM
THEBES, DRA ABU AL NAGA, TOMB OF QUEEN AHHOTEP
EXCAVATION BY A. MARIETTE (1859)
EIGHTEENTH DYNASTY, REIGN OF AHMES (1550 - 1525 BC)

ROOM 4

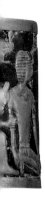

This dagger belonged to the grave goods of Queen Ahhotep. It has three parts. The bronze blade is slightly thicker in the center and still bears traces of its original gold leaf lining; the grip is formed by two convex silver plaques fixed around a wooden core; the fastening is made from gold and decorated with small grains of gold.

The archaeologist who discovered the knife, Auguste Mariette, believed it was used by gripping the unusual hilt in the palm of the hand with the blade passing between the forefinger and middle finger. (D.C.)

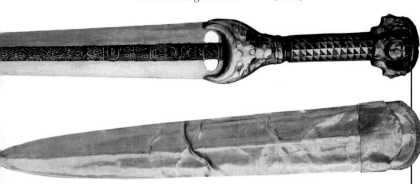

DAGGER BELONGING TO AHMES

GOLD, ELECTRON, NIELLO, SEMI-PRECIOUS STONES, AND WOOD; LENGTH 28.5 CM; THEBES, DRA ABU AL-NAGA; TOMB OF AHHOTEP; EXCAVATION BY A. MARIETTE (1859); EARLY EIGHTEENTH DYNASTY, REIGN OF AHMES (1554-1529 BC)

ROOM 4

Several ceremonial weapons belonging to Ahmes were found in the tomb of his mother, Queen Ahhotep, which he probably gave to her at the time of her burial. Ahmes was the first pharaoh of the Eighteenth Dynasty and was responsible for chasing the Hyksos out of Egypt. Ahhotep played an important role in the war of liberation as is demonstrated by the many ritual military objects found in her tomb.

This refined dagger is richly decorated. Both faces of the gold blade bear the two cartouches of the king followed by a floral motif which terminates at the tip on one side with a fox's head, and on the other with a hunting scene. Hieroglyphs and decorative elements are engraved on two bands of niello, a black substance obtained by the fusion of lead, copper, and sulphur.

The cedarwood grip is connected to the blade by two relief bulls' heads. It is covered with gold and densely inlaid with semi-precious stones (carnelian and lapis lazuli) and electron, an alloy of gold and silver; the pommel is formed by four female heads. The sheath was created by the fusion of two sheets of gold leaf but has no decoration. Its lack of display contrasts with the rich decoration of the dagger itself. (D.C.)

MODEL BOATS

1) Gold and silver, length 48 cm
2) Boat: gold and silver, length 43.3 cm
Chariot: wood and bronze, length 20 cm
Thebes, Dra Abu Al Naga, Tomb of Queen Ahhotep
Excavation by A. Mariette (1859)
Eighteenth Dynasty, Reign of Ahmes (1550 - 1525 bc)

ROOM 4

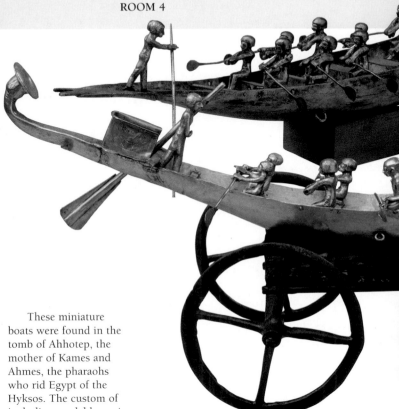

These miniature boats were found in the tomb of Ahhotep, the mother of Kames and Ahmes, the pharaohs who rid Egypt of the Hyksos. The custom of including model boats in grave goods began in very ancient times as they were the preferred method of transport in a country whose existence was dependent on the river Nile and thought to be essential to the deceased for his journeys in the Afterlife. The presence of the chariot, however, is a novelty as wheeled vehicles, unknown before the Second Intermediate Period, were introduced by the Hyksos.

The boat, made from gold, has the bow and stern shaped like a papyrus umbrella. The oarsmen are made from silver but the more important figures are in gold. One stands in the bow with his hand to his mouth as he gives orders to the crew. The helmsman is in the stern and the seat behind him bears the cartouche of Kames. A third figure is seated in the center of the boat.

The chariot is made from wood and has bronze wheels. When the tomb was discovered, the second model boat, made of silver, stood on top of the chariot; it is less intricate than the first and has only the oarsmen and the helmsman on board. (D.C.)

NECKLACE WITH PENDANTS IN THE FORM OF A FLY

GOLD
LENGTH OF THE CHAIN 59 CM
LENGTH OF THE PENDANTS 9 CM
THEBES, DRA ABU AL NAGA, TOMB OF QUEEN AHHOTEP
EXCAVATION BY A. MARIETTE (1859)
EIGHTEENTH DYNASTY, REIGN OF AHMES (1550 - 1525 BC)

ROOM 4

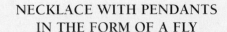

It was a custom for the pharaoh, the supreme commander of the army, to present his most courageous soldiers with a necklace with pendants in the form of flies as a reward for their valor on the battlefield.

This charming ornament was found in the tomb of Ahhotep with many other ceremonial military objects that had been offered to the queen by her sons, the pharaohs Kames and Ahmes.

The flies are made from very fine gold and are extremely stylised; they have smooth wings and chased bodies and are hung from short, finely linked chains that attach to the rings fixed between their protruding eyes.
(D.C.)

367

NECKLACE WITH PENDANT
IN THE FORM OF A SCARAB

Gold and lapis lazuli; Length of the chain 202 cm; Length of the scarab 3 cm
Thebes, Dra Abu Al Naga, Tomb of Queen Ahhotep
Excavation by A. Mariette (1859)
Eighteenth Dynasty, Reign of Ahmes (1550 - 1525 bc)

ROOM 4

This necklace was found in the tomb of Queen Ahhotep. The back of the small gold pendant in the shape of a scarab is inlaid with lapis lazuli. The thick six-link chain has a goose-eye clasp at either end engraved with the cartouches of Ahmes, the son of Queen Ahhotep and the first pharaoh of the Eighteenth Dynasty. In view of its considerable length, it is probable that the necklace was wound around the neck a number of times. The scarab was identified by Egyptians with Khepri, the god that incarnated the rising sun, and was considered a symbol of eternal rebirth and a powerful amulet. (D.C.)

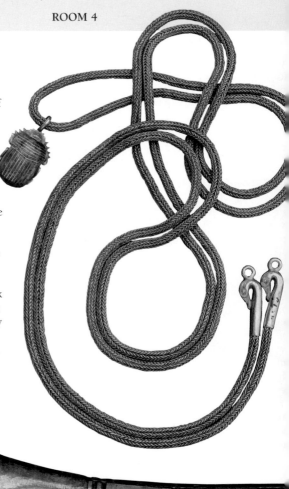

CEREMONIAL AXE OF KING AHMES

Wood, copper, gold, and semi-precious stones
Handle length 47.5 cm
Size of the blade: length 26.3 cm, width 6.7 cm
Thebes, Dra Abu Al Naga, Tomb of Queen Ahhotep
Excavation by A. Mariette (1859)
Eighteenth Dynasty, Reign of Ahmes (1550 - 1525 bc)

ROOM 4

This ceremonial axe belonged to Ahmes who led a victorious war against the Hyksos.

The handle is made from gilded cedarwood and bears an inscription with the king's titles, and the copper blade has three registers of inlaid

EARRING

Gold and glass paste; Diameter 3.9 cm, weight 17.8 gr
Saqqara, Tomb of Horemheb
Excavation by the Anglo-Dutch expedition directed by G.
Martin (1977); Eighteenth. Dynasty, probably during the
Reign of Akhenaten (1346-1333 bc)

ROOM 4

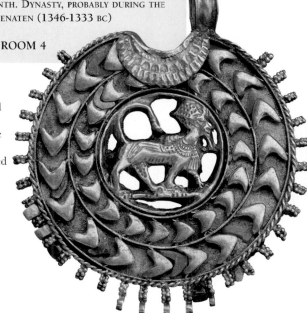

This earring was found in the tomb at Saqqara that the general Horemheb had built for himself before he became pharaoh. The solid gold jewel bears a finely chased image of a sovereign in the form of a sphinx wearing the blue crown adorned with a uraeus serpent, the false beard and a large *usekh* collar. Two circular bands decorated with a V motif in alternating gold and blue glass paste (only partly preserved) surround the sphinx. Cylindrical glass paste elements were originally applied between the small granulated rings on the rim of the earring of which the five lower ones were probably attachments for pendants. A sheet of gold leaf in the form of an *usekh* collar was fused to the top of the earring.

The earring was held in place by a small screw that passed through the ear lobe and attached to a ring on either side; in this case, only one of the two rings has survived.

As the profile of the sphinx resembles the image of Akhenaten, it is probable that the jewel was produced during his reign or during the first years of the Reign of his son-in-law, Tutankhamun.

A relief from the Tomb of Horemheb, now to be seen in Leida, shows Tutankhamun giving his general a similar earring. (D.C.)

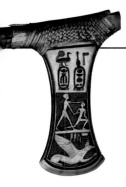

decoration on both sides. On one side are the king's cartouches at the top, a representation of Ahmes striking down his enemy in the center, and a winged sphinx symbolizing the pharaoh at the bottom.

On the other side at the top, the god of infinite

space. Heh, is holding two palm branches, the symbol of time; in the center, the guardian goddesses of Upper and Lower Egypt are depicted as a vulture and a cobra; and, in the bottom register, a sphinx lifts the head of an enemy. (D.C.)

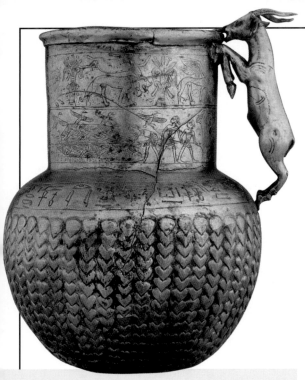

VASE WITH A HANDLE
IN THE FORM OF A GOAT
GOLD AND SILVER; HEIGHT 16.5 CM
TELL BASTA (BUBASTIS), TREASURE DISCOVERED IN 1906
NINETEENTH DYNASTY, REIGN OF RAMESES II (1279-1212 BC)

ROOM 4

Finds of gold and silver plate are rare as the metals were often melted down to produce other objects. This example was part of a hoard found in a sanctuary dedicated to the goddess Bastet.

The body of the vase is decorated with small drops placed on top of one another in columns. The inscription above this unusual motif gives a message of good omen to the owner of the vase, the cupbearer of King Atumentyneb. The hieroglyphs are arranged on either side of a scene in which a man is shown with his arms raised in adoration of the goddess.

The neck of the vase is decorated on two registers; the upper band bears a frieze of alternating floral and animal motifs, both real and imaginary. The orientalizing inspiration of the motif attests the cosmopolitanism of the period which, during the reigns of the various Rameses', was present throughout Egypt following increasingly frequent contacts with foreign peoples.

The lower band is decorated with typical Egyptian scenes of hunting and fishing. A small gold goat standing on its back legs forms the handle to this elegant vase.
(D.C.)

BRACELETS OF RAMESES II
GOLD AND LAPIS LAZULI
MAX. DIAMETER 7.2 CM
TELL BASTA (BUBASTIS), TREASURE DISCOVERED IN 1906
NINETEENTH DYNASTY, REIGN OF RAMESES II (1279-1212 BC)

ROOM 4

A quantity of jewels and gold and silver plate were unearthed during the construction of a railway at Tell Basta (the ancient *Per Bastet*), a district in the Delta. Only some of these are

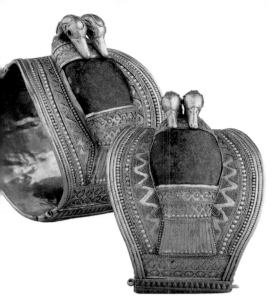

workers, probably belonged to the temple.

These rigid, solid gold bracelets are formed by two semi-circles connected by a hinge and a clip and have rich granule ornamentation in a series of geometric patterns. The upper part is decorated with the relief heads of two ducks with bent necks connected to a single body; the body is created with lapis lazuli while the creature's tail is decorated with small granules of gold. The cartouches of Rameses II are engraved next to the fastener.

It is most probable that the pharaoh himself offered these bracelets to the goddess Bastet. (D.C.)

now in the Egyptian Museum in Cairo, the rest are exhibited in New York and Berlin.

Per Bastet (the "Abode of Bastet") was the center of worship of the goddess Bastet who was depicted as a woman with a cat's head. The temple of the goddess was built during the Old Kingdom and enlarged by various sovereigns over the following epochs. The treasure, found quite by chance by the railway

---

SMALL CUP
GOLD
HEIGHT 9.4 CM
TELL BASTA (BUBASTIS), TREASURE DISCOVERED IN 1906
D OF THE NINETEENTH DYNASTY (EARLY 12TH CENTURY BC)

ROOM 4

Gold and silver plate was usually only produced in small sizes. This cup comes from the votive offerings in a temple of the goddess Bastet that were found by chance during the construction of a railway line at Tell Basta. The shape of the cup is that of an open lotus flower with rudimentary petals engraved on the surface.

The base of the cup is decorated with geometric patterns and bears the cartouche of Queen Tausert, the consort of Sety II.

The lotus flower was often a model used in the production of cups and was considered a symbol of eternal rebirth by the ancient Egyptians. (D.C.)

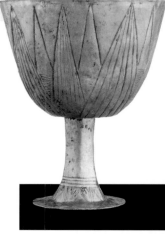

VASE WITH A HANDLE
IN THE FORM OF A COW

GOLD; HEIGHT 11.2 CM
TELL BASTA (BUBASTIS), TREASURE DISCOVERED IN 1906
NINETEENTH DYNASTY (1291-1185 BC)
REIGN OF RAMESES II (1279-1212 BC)

ROOM 4

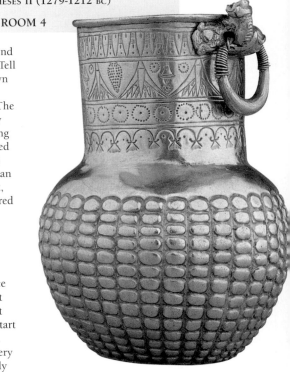

This vase was found with other objects at Tell Basta, the ancient town of *Per Bastet*, in the south-eastern Delta. The articles were probably part of a votive offering in the temple dedicated to Bastet, the goddess represented as a woman with the head of a cat, whose cult was centered in this locality.

The body of this charming vase is decorated with small embossed beads supposed to reproduce a pomegranate, a fruit introduced into Egypt from the East at the start of the New Kingdom. Pomegranates were very popular and frequently appeared in funerary offerings.

Floral motifs in four registers decorate the neck of the vase including, from the top, a frieze of lance-shaped leaves, a series of lotus flowers, bunches of grapes and small flowers, a row of stylized rosettes, and a garland of flowers. The handle is formed by a moving ring that passes through a bar fixed to the rim of the vase. The bar is decorated with a relief of a lying calf.

The use of precious gold and silver plate was limited to the royal court and their dimensions were usually small. (D.C.)

VASE

GOLD
HEIGHT 7.6 CM, DIAMETER OF THE NECK 3.6 CM
TELL BASTA (BUBASTIS), TREASURE DISCOVERED IN 1906
END OF THE NINETEENTH DYNASTY (EARLY 12TH CENTURY BC)

ROOM 4

This small vase was also part of the votive offerings in the temple dedicated to the goddess Bastet. The topmost decorative band is a frieze of lance-shaped leaves that point downwards, the middle

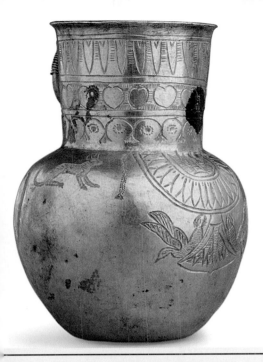

one a motif of large drops, and the bottom band a series of circles with stylized rosettes.

A ring-shaped handle is fixed below the rim by a small bar in which a stone is set. The body of the container is engraved with a garland of leaves in the form of a necklace from which a lotus flower hangs flanked by two birds with outspread wings. (D.C.)

SMALL DIADEM

GOLD; DIAMETER 17 CM
VALLEY OF THE KINGS, ANONYMOUS TOMB NO.56
EXCAVATION BY T. DAVIS (1908)
NINETEENTH DYNASTY, REIGN OF SETY II (1199-1193 BC)

ROOM 4

The rubble in an anonymous tomb in the Valley of the Kings was found to contain several items of jewelry that bear the names of Sety II and his consort Queen Tausert. The tomb was probably used as a

hiding place by the thieves who ransacked the tombs of the two sovereigns.

The presence of a small coffin suggests that some items had been made for a dead girl, perhaps a princess of the

royal couple. This tiny crown is made from a small gold ring with sixteen small roses attached whose petals were engraved with the names of Sety and Tausert. (D.C.)

EARRINGS IN THE NAME
OF RAMESES XI

Gold; Height 16 cm; Abydos, Kom al-Sultan
Excavation by A. Mariette (1859); Twentieth
Dynasty, Reign of Rameses XI (1099-1070 bc)

ROOM 4

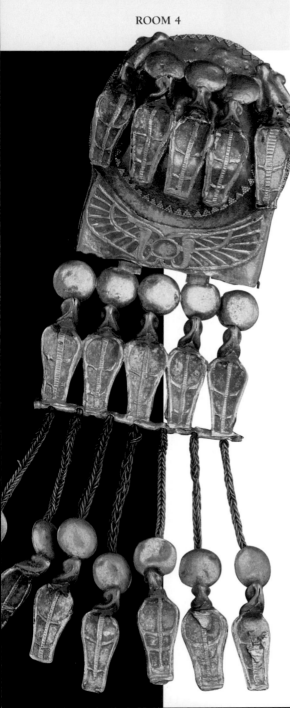

The earrings bear the engraved cartouches of Rameses XI and were found on the mummy of a woman, perhaps a member of the royal family, buried in a sarcophagus below the temple of Osiris at Abydos.

The articles are formed by a convex disk grooved along the edge and decorated by five uraeus serpents on the outer face; the three uraeus serpents in the middle bear a sun disk while the two outer examples wear a tiara with a long plume on either side.

Five other uraeus serpents are attached to the sheet of gold welded to the lower part of the disk and decorated with an image of the winged sun; the five serpents rest on a small bar from which hang seven pendants also in the shape of uraeus serpents. The cartouches of Rameses XI – the last ruler of the Twentieth Dynasty – are engraved on the inner face of the disk.

The uraeus serpent, a cobra with a swollen throat ready to strike, is the emblem of royal power and is seen on the foreheads of the pharaohs. In one legend, it is the eye of Ra transformed into a serpent, but it is also the form taken by Uadjet, the guardian goddess of Lower Egypt.
(D.C.)

EARRINGS BELONGING TO SETY II

GOLD; HEIGHT 13.5 CM
VALLEY OF THE KINGS, ANONYMOUS TOMB NO. 56
EXCAVATION BY T. DAVIS (1908)
NINETEENTH DYNASTY, REIGN OF SETY II (1199 - 1193 BC)

ROOM 4

These gold earrings were found with other precious objects belonging to Sety II and his queen, Tausert, in an anonymous tomb in the Valley of the Kings that was probably used by tomb robbers to

The cap and rosette were engraved with cartouches inscribed with the coronation and birth names of the pharaoh. The pendants are composed of two elements: a trapezoid

probably by the Hyksos, the Canaanite peoples who settled in Egypt during the Second Intermediate Period. Earrings were worn by both sexes although it appears that males only

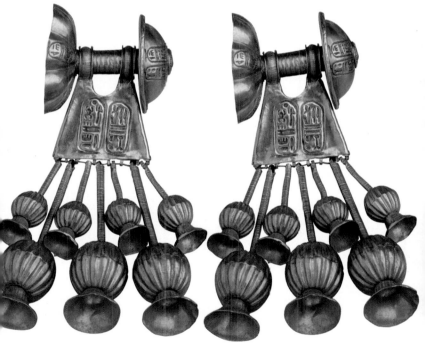

hide their booty.
The two large earrings were attached to the ears by inserting two small tubes welded to a rosette and a cap into the holes in the ear lobes, then engaging the two earrings together.

plaque also engraved with Sety II's cartouches and seven smaller pendants in the shape of lilies.
Earrings were introduced to the valley of the Nile at the start of the New Kingdom,

wore them until adolescence. Earrings are never seen in representations of adult men although ear lobes were always pierced from the period of Akhenaten on.
(D.C.)

BRACELETS BELONGING TO SETHI II

SILVER
MAXIMUM WIDTH 6.5 CM
VALLEY OF THE KINGS, ANONYMOUS TOMB NO. 56
EXCAVATION BY T. DAVIS (1908)
NINETEENTH DYNASTY, REIGN OF SETY II (1199 - 1193 BC)

ROOM 4

Bracelets were a common ornament worn by both women and men. These examples come from the Valley of the Kings and were found together with other items belonging to Sety II and his consort, Queen Tausert, in an anonymous tomb that was probably used as a hiding place by the thieves that had violated the couple's tomb.

The two silver jewels are of similar manufacture and composed of two parts united by a hinge and a fastener. The main part of the bracelet was worn on the outside of the wrist and is decorated with a scene showing Queen Tausert offering the pharaoh a vase and a flower. Sety is seated on a throne with his feet depicted as the paws of a lion; he holds a cup in his left hand and a palm leaf (a symbol of time) in his right. Above, cartouches appear bearing the name of Tausert, "Great Rroyal Bride," and the coronation and birth names of Sety II (*Userkheperura Sety*). The other part of the bracelet is decorated with five overlying bands with stylized floral motifs.

Silver, imported from the East, was called "the white metal" by the Egyptians and was considered a type of gold.
(D.C.)

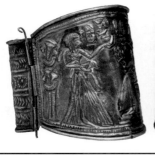 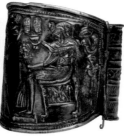

NECKLACE WITH PECTORAL

GILDED WOOD, AMBER, CARNELIAN, LAPIS LAZULI, AND GLASS
PASTE; HEIGHT 11 CM, WIDTH 12.2 CM; SHEIKH ABD AL-
QURNA, TOMB OF HATIAY; EXCAVATION BY G. DARESSY,
1896; NEW KINGDOM, EIGHTEENTH DYNASTY, START OF THE
REIGN OF AMENHOTEP IV-AKHENATEN (1350 - 1333 BC)

ROOM 4

This lovely jewel was found among the grave goods in the tomb of Hatiay, the scribe and superintendent of the granaries of the temple of Aten. The necklace is formed by three strings of beads made from colored glass paste; the wooden pectoral, lined with gold leaf, is in the shape of a temple. A large amber scarab is shown inside a geometric border and flanked by a *djed* pillar (on the left) made from lapis lazuli and glass paste, and a *tit* sign made from carnelian on the right. The scarab was identified by the Egyptians with Khepri, the god of the rising sun, and was considered a symbol of eternal rebirth as well as being a powerful amulet.

The *djed* sign was

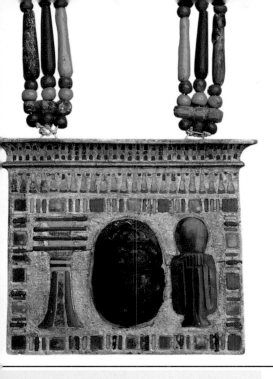

probably a stylized representation of a bunch of plant stems that signified "stability" and became the symbol most often associated with Osiris from the period of the New Kingdom onwards.

The *tit* sign was an emblem associated with Isis and may have represented the knot of the goddess' girdle (it is also known as an "Isis' knot") or a part of her body. It is usually painted red and is therefore in some way linked to blood.
(D.C.)

EARRINGS
GOLD AND PEARLS
LENGTH 11.5 CM
PURCHASED IN 1888
GRECO-ROMAN PERIOD (332 BC-313 AD)

ROOM 4

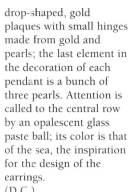

The use of earrings became common in Egypt during the New Kingdom following their introduction to the Nile Valley by the Hyksos. They were worn by women of all ages and by males probably just until adolescence.

The examples in the photograph are thought to have been produced during the Greco-Roman Period but it is not possible to date them more accurately. A simple open ring formed by a curved gold pin supports an elaborate pendant of notable size

and weight. The pendant is composed of two parts: a small plaque and three smaller pendants. The image on the plaque is of two dolphins whose tails touch as they dive into the water below. A gold thread with two pearls is positioned in the space between the dolphins and the water.

The long, smaller pendants consist of large,

drop-shaped, gold plaques with small hinges made from gold and pearls; the last element in the decoration of each pendant is a bunch of three pearls. Attention is called to the central row by an opalescent glass paste ball; its color is that of the sea, the inspiration for the design of the earrings.
(D.C.)

CUP

Silver; Height 9.2 cm
Max. diameter 11.4 cm
Tell al-Temai; Excavation by E. Brugsch
Ptolemaic Period (305-30 bc)

ROOM 4

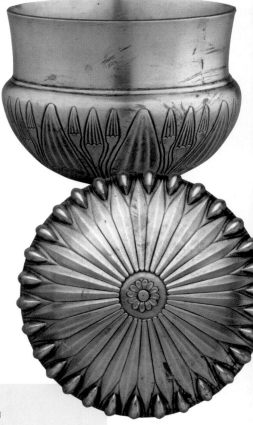

Like the patera, this container came from Tell al-Temai, the modern name for the ancient city of Thmuis that lay not far from Tanis. The decoration is very similar to that of Tanite vases and cups which indicates the popularity of the style in later ages.

The cup is quite deep, decorated on the outside of the base with the open corolla of a lotus flower and has a high smooth band for the mouthpiece.

The motif of the open flower was used during the Middle Kingdom and can be seen in the metal vases of the treasure of Tod. (M.T.)

PATERA

Silver; Height 3.2 cm
Max. diameter 11.4 cm
Tell al-Temai; Excavation by E. Brugsch
Ptolemaic Period (305-30 bc)

ROOM 4

The patera is engraved in the center with a 'navel' in the form of a small daisy.

It is surrounded by twenty-eight rays that act as petals separated by small ovules. Pateras decorated with ovules were known in the Near East, especially in Syria and Cyprus, but in this case the ovules are smaller than the Near Eastern version and are distributed along the outer rims of the container.

Also present are motifs seen in grave goods in Tanis, in particular on some cups found in the funerary goods of Undjebauendjed. (M.T.)

NECKLACE WITH PENDANTS

GOLD
DIAMETER 12.5 CM, WEIGHT 169 GR
FOUND AT DENDERA IN 1914
PTOLEMAIC EPOCH (305-30 BC)

ROOM 4

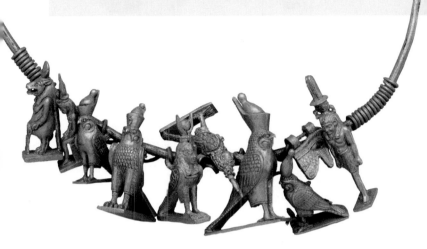

This heavy collar consists of a thick gold thread on which are hung ten pendants of different shapes measuring between 1.3 - 3.8 CM in height. A second thread has been passed through the rings and wrapped around the ones at the sides so that the pendants cannot move on the necklace. Starting from the left, the pendants represent:

1) the goddess Tueris, a popular deity in the form of a hippopotamus with lion's feet and the tail of a crocodile. She protected pregnant women and watched over births and weaning. Her cult was widespread in the Late Period;

2) the goddess Isis seated on a throne. Isis was the wife of Osiris, the mother of Horus, and an expert in the arts of magic. Starting in the Hellenistic period she was associated with the god Serapis who was introduced to Egypt by the Ptolemies;

3) a falcon, the image of Horus, the ancient god of the sky and royalty. He wears the white crown of Upper Egypt over the red one of Lower Egypt;

4) another falcon that once had decorated wings and a tail but the inlays are now missing;

5) a bird with a human head which represents the *ba*, the animated manifestation of the deceased. It wears a sun disk between cow's horns on its head;

6) another bird with a human head of the same size;

7) a falcon wearing a double crown;

8) another falcon wearing the white crown of Upper Egypt in the form of a tiara;

9) an *udjat* eye, the healed eye of Horus, a potent amulet that assured the wearer of good health and well-being;

10) an image of the god Nefertum, the personification of the lotus plant that rose from the primeval waters and from which life originated.

All the pendants except for the *udjat* eye were placed upon a thin base.

The necklace was held closed by two hooks created by bending the ends of the thread. (D.C.)

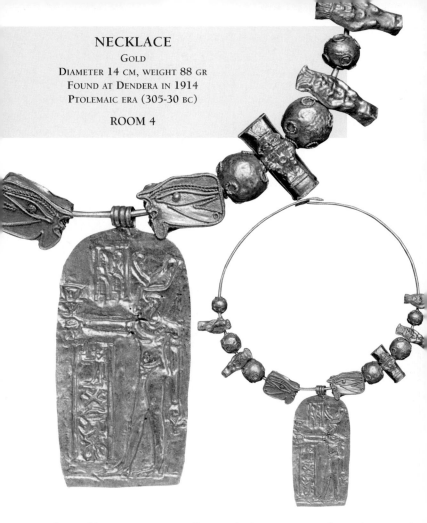

NECKLACE

GOLD
DIAMETER 14 CM, WEIGHT 88 GR
FOUND AT DENDERA IN 1914
PTOLEMAIC ERA (305-30 BC)

ROOM 4

This necklace is formed by a gold thread on which thirteen ornaments have been inserted; with seven on one side and six on the other, they flank a thin rectangular sheet of gold leaf with rounded upper corners suspended from a ring.

This pendant, which forms the central part of the jewel, is decorated with the image of the god *hor-pa-kherd* ("Horus the Child" known by the Greeks as Harpocrates) with the side plait

typically worn by boys. Usually portrayed with a finger in his mouth, in this case the god-child holds one arm down his side and the other stretched out in front of him. He holds an *ankh* sign and a sistrum (a musical instrument sacred to the goddess Hathor) and wears the double crown of Egypt (the red crown of Lower Egypt topped by the white one of Upper Egypt).

The objects that alternate on either side of the pendant are two *udjat*

eyes, five rather coarsely produced images of the god Bes, and six small orbs.

The *udjat* eye of Horus was a powerful amulet that assured its wearer of good health and well-being. Bes was a popular numen portrayed as a dwarf with bow legs and a protruding tongue. Grotesque in appearance, he was a beneficent spirit who watched over pregnant women, protected marriages, and warded off evil spirits. (D.C.)

GOLD BRACELET

GOLD;

DIAMETER 8 CM, WEIGHT 178 GR
FOUND AT TUKH AL GARAMUS (BUBASTIS)
IN 1905 PTOLEMAIC PERIOD (3RD CENTURY BC)

ROOM 4

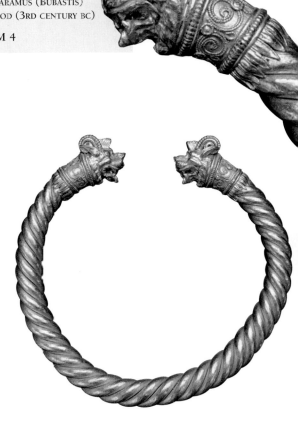

This bracelet was found in 1905 at Tukh al-Garamus (the ancient Bubastis) in the eastern Delta. It made a pair with another, slightly larger bracelet but of the same weight. Four tightly twisted, solid gold strands form the rigid ring of the ornament; two lion heads face one another and almost touch at either end of the ring. The two cats have long, pointed ears, a horned brow, a tall crest between their curved horns, and they show their fangs in a menacing manner. The neck of each lion is adorned with an elaborate collar decorated with a frieze of filigree volutes. A motif of small leaves traces a garland that masks the welding between the ring of the bracelet and the two heads. The various parts of the ornament (heads, horns, ears, collars, and ring) were all produced separately and fused together.

Although the bracelet was found in Egypt and dates from the start of the Ptolemaic era, it was clearly inspired by Persian art. During the two centuries that preceded the conquest of Egypt by Alexander the Great, the Achaemenid rulers who ruled the country imported typically Asiatic styles into jewelry and clothing, the influence of which was still being felt in the 3rd century BC.

This lovely bracelet may well have been the work of an immigrant Persian craftsman or of an Egyptian jeweler inspired by Achaemenid designs. Lion heads with curved horns are often found on earrings and necklaces. A bracelet similar to this one was found on the statue of Udjahorresne (a very learned doctor, priest, and functionary in the city of Sais who served the Persians) that can be seen in the Vatican Museums. (D.C.)

NECKLACE

GOLD, RED STONES
LENGTH 42 CM
GIFT OF KING FUAD I (1936)
GRECO-ROMAN PERIOD (332 BC-313 AD)

ROOM 4

Neck ornaments were used in Egypt from the most ancient times and were often given symbolic forms. The choice of stones was made on the basis of precise precepts that were linked to the apotropaic value of the ornament. During the Greco-Roman Period, jewels derived from pharaonic models were joined by designs that were purely decorative, like this example.

Typified by the contrast of the brilliant gold and shiny red light of the stones, the necklace has a simple woven pattern in the center and eight three-part pendants. (D.C.)

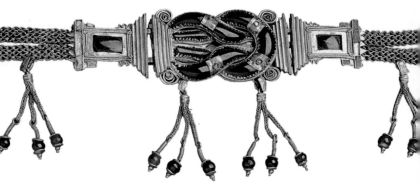

RING

GOLD
DIAMETER 2.3 CM
GIFT OF KING FUAD I (1936)
GRECO-ROMAN PERIOD (332 BC-313 AD)

ROOM 4

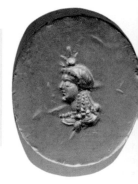

The origin and date of manufacture of the ring are unknown. The engraved decoration shows a head facing left with finely chased details of the face and hairstyle.

Rings were used by the Egyptians during the Old Kingdom as supports for scarab-shaped seals but new models spread during the Second Intermediate Period, probably imported from Asia, that placed emphasis on decoration and remained popular until the Late Period. (D.C.)

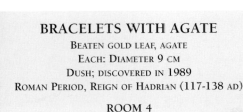

BRACELETS WITH AGATE

BEATEN GOLD LEAF, AGATE
EACH: DIAMETER 9 CM
DUSH; DISCOVERED IN 1989
ROMAN PERIOD, REIGN OF HADRIAN (117-138 AD)

ROOM 4

These elaborate bracelets were made from a simple sheet of beaten gold enhanced by a thick motif of vine leaves with an agate set in gold in the center. The stone is rectangular and black on the first bracelet, but oval and black, white, and red on the second.

These items of jewelry date from the second half of the 2nd century AD and were found in 1989 at Dush (ancient Kysis) in al-Kharga oasis. They were found with a diadem and pectoral in a sealed terracotta vase in a temple dedicated to Isis and Serapis built during the Roman Period. The diadem was from the same period and decorated in a similar manner and clearly accompanied the bracelets.

They were probably ritual ornaments worn by priests during ceremonies dedicated to Serapis whose image can be seen on the front of the crown. Serapis was a Greco-Egyptian god who united the characteristics of the Late Dynastic god Osorapis (the deceased bull Apis assimilated to Osiris and venerated in Memphis) with the attributes of Zeus, Hades, and Asclepius. His cult was introduced by the Ptolemaic pharaohs. (D.C.)

383

DIADEM WITH SERAPIS
BEATEN GOLD LEAF
DIADEM: DIAMETER 22 CM
PLAQUE: HEIGHT 12.5 CM, WIDTH 8.5 CM
DUSH; DISCOVERED IN 1989
ROMAN PERIOD, REIGN OF HADRIAN (117-138 AD)

ROOM 4

This diadem from Dush in the oasis of al-Kharga may have been a priestly ornament. It was found in a terracotta vase with two bracelets and a necklace in the area of the temple dedicated to Isis and Serapis.

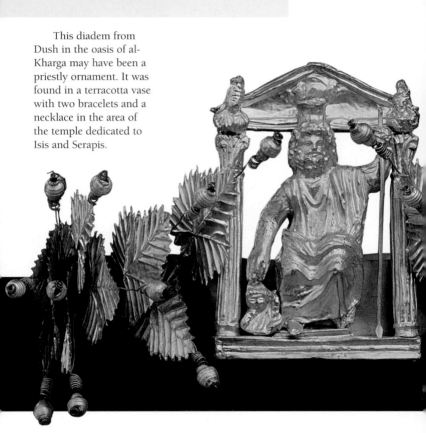

The crown is formed by a small ring adorned with gold leaves and small buds in imitation of a garland. The front is almost three centimetres bigger than the back and bears a plaque depicting Serapis in a small shrine. The god is seated on a throne and wears a chiton and a cloak; he has a thick curled beard and long thick hair on which a *kalathos* ("hamper," a symbol of fertility) is shown. He holds a lance in his left hand while his right rests on the bust of a god, probably Mithras. The image of the shrine is formed by two columns with Corinthian capitals, each of which bears a representation of the goddess Isis, and by a pediment decorated with a sun disk flanked by two uraeus serpents.

The cult of Serapis was instituted by the Ptolemies when the characteristics of the late dynastic Memphis god Osorapis (the dead bull Apis assimilated to Osiris) were united with the attributes of Zeus, Hades, and Asclepius. (D.C.)

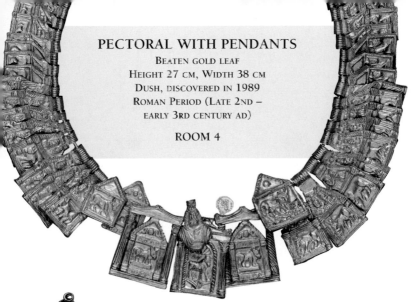

PECTORAL WITH PENDANTS

BEATEN GOLD LEAF
HEIGHT 27 CM, WIDTH 38 CM
DUSH, DISCOVERED IN 1989
ROMAN PERIOD (LATE 2ND –
EARLY 3RD CENTURY AD)

ROOM 4

Ritual ornaments closed in a sealed terracotta container were found in a temple dedicated to Isis and Serapis during the Roman age at Dush (ancient Kysis) in the oasis of al-Kharga.

This elaborate pectoral, made entirely of gold, is formed by a compact series of small plaques threaded onto a thick string through grooved cylindrical rings.

They are all decorated with representations of the bull Apis in a small sacrarium formed by two columns and a pediment with images of Isis and Serapis. It is probable that the plaques were "mass-produced" as votive offerings like the small medallion bearing the inscription "Faustina Augusta" on one side and the image of the goddess Cybele (assimilated to Isis) on the other. The center of the pectoral is formed by three pendants of larger size and a bust of Serapis with a thick, curly beard and flowing locks on which a *kalathos*, the symbol of fertility, is shown. The clasp is made in the shape of a snake's head.

Serapis was a Greco-Egyptian deity who combined the characteristics of the Memphite god Osarapis (the dead bull Apis assimilated to Osiris) and the attributes of Zeus, Hades, and Asclepius. His cult was associated with those of Isis and Harpocrates ("Horus the Child") and was introduced by the Ptolemaic kings in an attempt to integrate the ancient Egyptian belief with Greek religious traditions. The new god was widely worshipped by Greeks and Romans throughout the Mediterranean and further afield but the Egyptians remained tied to their old gods.

The most important temple dedicated to Serapis was built by Ptolemy III Evergetes in Alexandria where the god was identified with the serpent *Agathodàimon* during the Roman domination. (D.C.)

385

COLLAR BELONGING
TO PRINCESS NUBHOTEP

Gold and semi-precious stones; External diameter 32 cm
Dahshur, Tomb of Nubhotep-ta-khered
Excavation by J. de Morgan (1894-1895)
Thirteenth Dynasty, Reign of Hor (1781-1650 bc)

ROOM 4

Excavation work carried out at the end of the 19th century by Jacques de Morgan at Dahshur unearthed the funerary goods of several princesses from the Thirteenth Dynasty.

The many items of jewelry found between the bandages of the mummies or in small alcoves in the walls of the tombs aroused much wonder, as prior to these discoveries few jewels had been found in Egypt.

The finds threw new light on goldworking techniques and on the forms and complex symbolism of the ornaments.

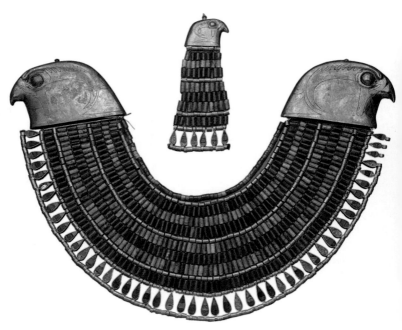

The necklace in the photograph belongs to the grave goods of Princess Nubhotep-ta-khered and was found in very poor condition on the mummy.

This type of collar was known as *usekh* ("wide") by the Egyptians and was the most popular form of necklace worn by both women and men. Princess Neferuptah, buried at Hauara (a site to the south of Dahshur in the oasis of Fayum) owned a collar that was almost identical. The collars were always attached to a counterpoise at the back (*menkhet*) that had the function of balancing the weight of the item across the shoulders.

Egyptians were especially skilled at manufacturing items of beaded jewelry; stones selected for their magical and symbolic values were cut to shape, perforated with

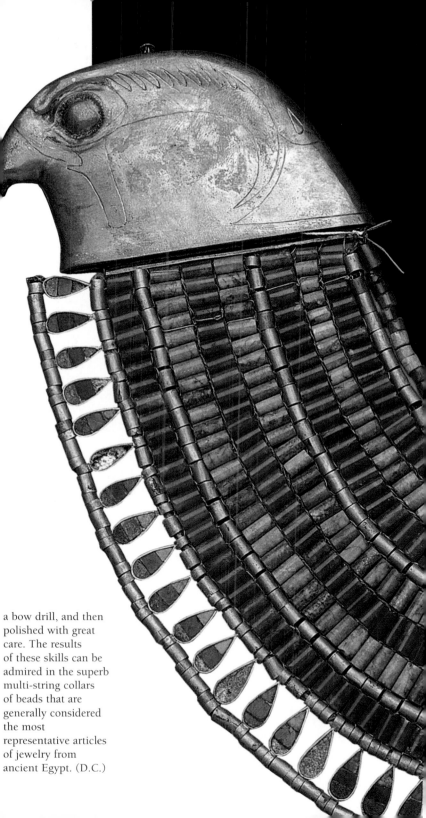

a bow drill, and then polished with great care. The results of these skills can be admired in the superb multi-string collars of beads that are generally considered the most representative articles of jewelry from ancient Egypt. (D.C.)

BRACELET BELONGING TO SHESHONQ II
GOLD AND LAPIS LAZULI
DIAMETER 7.7 CM
SEAL IN LAPIS LAZULI: LENGTH 2.8 CM, THICKNESS 1.7 CM
TANIS, TOMB III, ANTECHAMBER, GRAVE OF SHESHONQ II
EXCAVATION BY P. MONTET (1940)
BRACELET: TWENTY-SECOND DYNASTY (CIRCA 890 BC)
SEAL: AGADE ERA (CIRCA 2300 BC)

ROOM 4

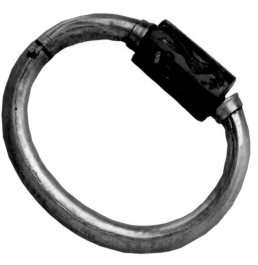

Sheshonq II, a pharaoh during the Twenty-second Dynasty, was buried in the royal necropolis situated in the enclosure of the temple dedicated to Amun-Ra at Tanis. This bracelet was part of his grave goods and was found with two others on the right wrist of the mummy.

The ornament consists of two parts connected by a hinge. It has a cylindrical Mesopotamian seal at its center made from lapis lazuli that dates from the end of the 3rd millennium BC, i.e. fifteen centuries before Sheshonq's era. The presence of an Akkadian seal on an Egyptian bracelet is evidence of a taste for the ancient and exotic that has rarely been seen in the Nile Valley.

The decoration shows aligned figures of mythical heroes and rampant animals. Two bearded figures in the center struggle with a lion: the first is dressed in a loincloth and the second, naked and with shaggy hair, grasps the lion by the mane from behind and brandishes a curved weapon. A third hero attacks a bull on which a lion-headed bird (today damaged) is probably sinking its fangs into the bull's rump.

The remaining section is divided into two registers; in the lower one, the god of waves (Enki or Ea) is shown dressed in a ruffled garment seated on the right with waves flowing out of his body and a figure praying before him. The upper register is divided into two parts: one is filled by a partially damaged inscription and the other by a seated figure, perhaps a god.

The cylindrical seal was rolled to allow the entire surface of the print to be used as a sort of signature on documents. The decoration on the seal dates the object to the richly archaistic production of the Reign of Sargon around 2300 BC. (D.C.)

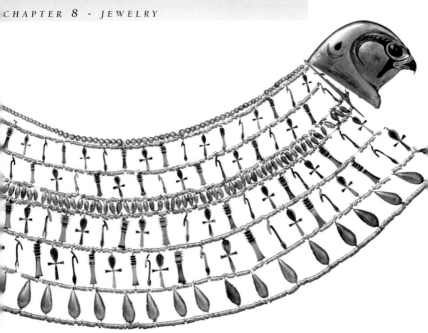

NECKLACE BELONGING TO PRINCESS KHNUMIT

GOLD, LAPIS LAZULI, TURQUOISE, CARNELIAN, GARNET, FELDSPAR
OVERALL DIMENSIONS: HEIGHT 3.8 CM, WIDTH 4.3 CM
DAHSHUR, FUNERARY COMPLEX OF AMENEMHAT II
TOMB OF PRINCESS KHNUMIT
EXCAVATION BY J. DE MORGAN (1894)
TWELFTH DYNASTY, REIGN OF AMENEMHAT II (1932-1898 BC)

ROOM 4

Many pieces of jewelry were found in the tomb of Princess Khnumit, one of the daughters of Amenemhat II. Some were placed on her body and others found heaped below a small chest in an annexe to the funerary chamber.

This elegant collar, known to the ancient Egyptians as *usekh*, was placed around the mummy's neck. It was found in pieces as the threads that held the many elements together had decomposed, but careful restoration has now returned the necklace to its original beauty.

The necklace is formed by six rows of pendants terminated by gold beads and has two fasteners at either end in the shape of a falcon's head.

The three hieroglyphic signs, *ankh*, *djed*, and *uas*, are made from gold inlaid with semi-precious stones and are repeated in order on four rows. In addition to their beauty, these signs were considered powerful amulets being symbols respectively of "eternal life," "stability," and "power."

Like other symbolic pieces of jewelry, *usekh* collars were placed among the linen wraps of the mummy to ward off evil from the deceased. (D.C.)

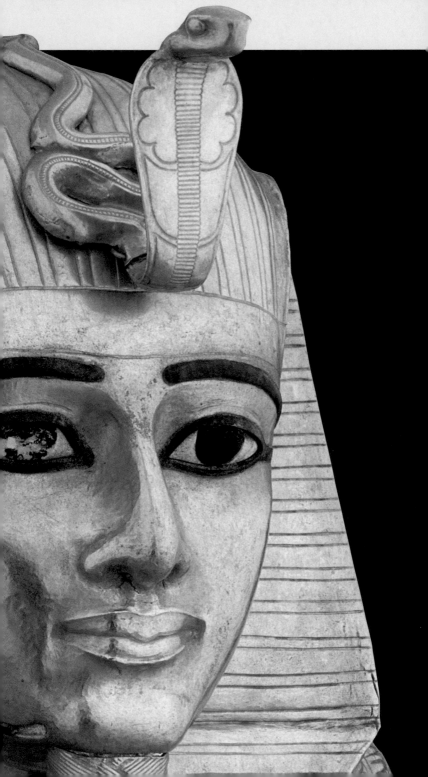

Tanis (modern-day San al-Hagar) lies on the east bank of a secondary branch of the Nile, roughly 80 miles north east of Cairo. The name Tanis was derived from the ancient Egyptian term *Tsa'ani* (of unclear meaning) that was passed down via the Copt name *Tjaani*, which was transmuted into the Arabic *San* to which the *al-Hagar* ("the stones") was added in reference to the monuments on the site which had long provided building materials.

The excavated site of Tanis, 290 acres, is formed by three sand hills. It was on and around them – called in Arabic the "sandy islands" (*geziret ramliyeh*) – that the city was built between the Twenty-first Dynasty (1075-945 BC) and the Roman Period (30 BC-313 AD). The great temple of Amun stood on one of these hills in the northern part of the site while the temple of Mut (called "of Anta" by P. Montet) was built in the north-west corner outside the sanctuary's enclosure walls. To the west of the site, the hills slope down to the river where the landing stage for Amun's sacred boat lay. The foundations of another temple have recently been discovered by the French Excavation Mission directed by P. Brissaud by another large "sandy island" known as Tulul al-Bed at the southern tip of the site. The construction was rebuilt several times during the Late Period (664-332 BC) but was destroyed during the Ptolemaic Period (305-30 BC). It was probably a sanctuary dedicated to Amenemope, a local form of the god Amun.

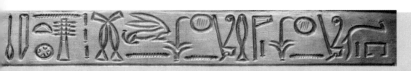

CHAPTER 9
FIRST FLOOR

The most intensively excavated area of the site is the Temple of Amun where Montet began systematic research in 1929. It was in the sacred walls that the foundation offerings of Siamun, Osorkon II, Apries, Nectanebus I, and other Lagid kings were discovered. The entire main axis of the great temple was dotted with monuments of Rameses II, such as

---

ITINERARY THROUGH ROOM 2

390
FUNERARY MASK
OF PSUSENNES I
Gold, lapis lazuli,
glass paste
Height 48 CM;

Tanis
Twenty-first
Dynasty,
Reign of
Psusennes I
(1045-994 BC)

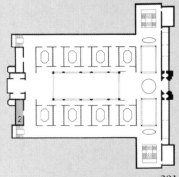

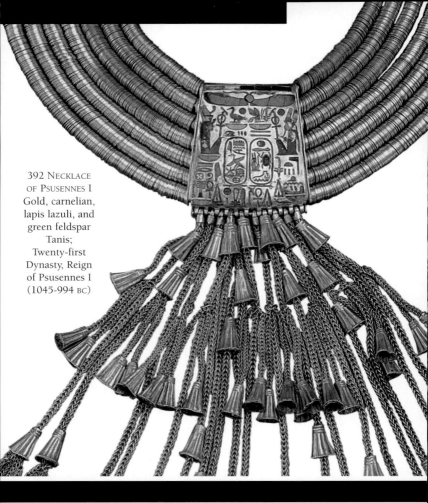

392 NECKLACE
OF PSUSENNES I
Gold, carnelian,
lapis lazuli, and
green feldspar
Tanis;
Twenty-first
Dynasty, Reign
of Psusennes I
(1045-994 BC)

the statuary group of
Hurun protecting the
king-child. In the center of
the temple, Montet found
a triad of Rameses II with
two deities and a colossus
sculpted during the Old
Kingdom that Rameses
had appropriated. Other
excavations have revealed
other elements inside the
walls: three temples – one
dedicated to Horus,
another to Khonsu, and
a temple of the East – and
a sacred lake.

Statues of Sekhmet,
Uadjet, and Anat (the

latter of Syrian origin)
that date from the reign
of Rameses II were
discovered in the temple
of Mut where they had
been placed during the
Ptolemaic Period.

Montet's most
dramatic find at Tanis
was made in 1939 with
the discovery of the
tombs of the pharaohs of
the Twenty-first and
Twenty-second Dynasties
that had no apparent
superstructure. The first
tomb to be found was
that of Osorkon II; it has

four chambers made fro[m]
limestone and adobe
bricks that were dug int[o]
the subsoil at the end of
long passageway. The
tomb had been robbed
and only contained an
empty granite sarcophag[us]
with no inscriptions.
Next, Montet found the
entrance and the
antechamber of a secon[d]
tomb which turned out [to]
be that of Psusennes I. I[t]
contained alabaster
recipients, *shawabty*, an[d]
a magnificent silver
sarcophagus with the hea[d]

of a falcon that belonged to Sheshonq II, the fourth pharaoh of the Twenty-second Dynasty. The mummy inside it was intact and still wore the jewelry with which it had been buried.

The following year, Montet continued his dig in the tomb of Psusennes I and could enter the burial chamber where he found the pink granite sarcophagus of the king. Inside was another granite sarcophagus and the silver, mummy-shaped one that held the body of the king with his gold funerary mask. In the tomb there were also the grave goods of Psusennes' general, Undjebauendjed, and King Amenemope who had been buried in the chamber originally meant for Queen Mutnedjemet. Psusennes

water jugs, and pateras made from precious metals that all revealed the fine taste and skills of the craftsmen of the age.

The abundant use of silver in the treasures of the kings of Tanis show that this metal was not rare and a status symbol as it had been during the New Kingdom and that, probably, the economic crisis that had struck the last reigns of the Ramessid pharaohs had run its course. In fact, the treasure of Tutankhamun – another of the rare examples of a more or less intact set of grave goods to have survived – included very few silver objects. The images in the tombs and temples show the use of some of these silver objects: the

advanced technical and artistic skills of the court jewelers. The items that stand out are the four *shebiu* necklaces and four pectorals in the form of winged scarabs that belonged to Psusennes I. The latter are all very similar but each is unique in the stones used, the engraved texts, and the decoration of the wings. The oldest pectorals of this sort to have been found were on Tutankhamun's mummy, but the pictures in the Theban tombs demonstrate that they had been used as early as the reign of Amenhotep III (1387-1350 BC).

There were six royal tombs at San al-Hagar, belonging to Psusenne I, Amenemope, Osorkon III, Sheshonq III, and two unidentified kings. (M.T)

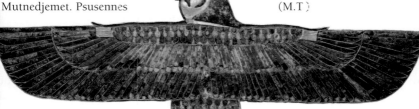

I had seized the two stone sarcophaguses for himself: the large pink granite one had belonged to King Merenptah and the second to a high functionary during the Ramessid Period. The combined grave goods of Psusennes I, Undjebauendjed and Amenemope contained no fewer than thirty containers, cups, jugs,

pateras were used to contain flowers and to cook birds sacrificed to the god while the jugs served to pour water during ceremonies.

The tomb of Psusennes I also contained a series of necklaces, bracelets, and exquisitely made rings of gold and semi-precious stones that indicate the

393 PENDANT OF
AMENEMOPE
Gold and colored
glass paste;
Width 37.5 CM
Tanis, Tomb of
Psusennes I, sepulcher
of Amenemope;
Excavation
by P. Montet (1940)
Twenty-first Dynasty,
Reign of Amenemope
(994-985 BC)

PLAQUE FOR THE MUMMY
OF PSUSENNES I
GOLD; HEIGHT 9.9 CM, WIDTH 16.6 CM
TANIS, TOMB OF PSUSENNES I, SEPULCHER OF PSUSENNES I
EXCAVATION BY P. MONTET (1940); TWENTY-FIRST DYNASTY
REIGN OF PSUSENNES I (1045-994 BC)

ROOM 2

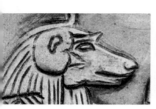

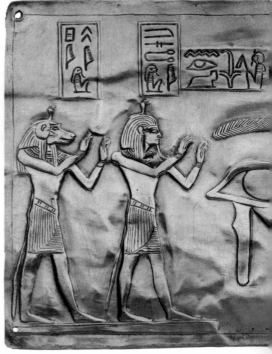

The mummification processes used by the ancient Egyptians are known to us through descriptions left by Herodotus (5th century BC) in Book II of his *Histories*. The longest and most costly procedure required removal of the internal organs from the body with the liver, lungs, intestines, and stomach being embalmed separately. The brain was extracted with a hook inserted through the nasal cavity while the other organs were removed through a cut made in the lower part of the stomach. Next the entire body was cleaned and filled with bandages soaked in mineral substances and the cut was sewn up and protected by a plaque.

The plaque was supposed to restore the body to its original state of strength as the wound was considered to be vulnerable and a possible entry point for negative forces. The plaque is decorated with the *udjat* eye, as the symbol was associated with the idea of physical wholeness and protection. The four sons of Horus – Imset, Hapi, Duamutuef, and Qebehsenuef – are shown at the sides of the eye with the royal cobra on their heads and their names engraved with a burin. They wear pleated skirts and *usekh* necklaces.

An inscription on the *udjat* eye says, "To the Osiris King Psusennes meryamun." The plaque has a small engraved molding with four holes in the corners to fix it to the bandages of the mummy. (M.T.)

394

ANKLET BELONGING TO PSUSENNES I

GOLD, LAPIS LAZULI, AND CARNELIAN
HEIGHT 5.5 CM, MAX. INTERNAL DIAMETER 6.6 CM
TANIS, TOMB OF PSUSENNES I, SEPULCHER OF PSUSENNES I
EXCAVATION BY P. MONTET (1940); TWENTY-FIRST DYNASTY
REIGN OF PSUSENNES I (1045-994 BC)

ROOM 2

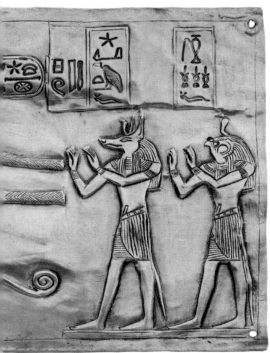

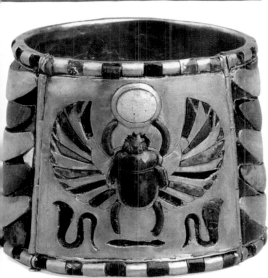

The anklet is shaped like a truncated cone and decorated in the central panel with a champlevé gold plaque depicting a winged scarab pushing a sun disk. Two uraeus serpents on either side of the scarab frame the hieroglyph *aa* to create a design that forms the hieroglyphic group representing the royal name of Psusennes I: Aakheperre.

The inside of the item is inscribed with a dedication by Smendes, who was the High Priest of Amun and the son of Menkheperre. Friezes on the lower and upper borders of the anklet are made from small beads of lapis lazuli and gold. In addition to the central plaque, the bracelet is made of three panels decorated with crescent moons alternately made of gold and lapis lazuli, and connected by hinges to the main section. (M.T.)

SWORD HILT

BRONZE AND GOLD LEAF
HEIGHT 16 CM
TANIS, TOMB OF PSUSENNES I, CRYPT OF PSUSENNES I
EXCAVATION BY P. MONTET (1940); TWENTY-FIRST
DYNASTY, REIGN OF PSUSENNES I (1045-994 BC)

ROOM 2

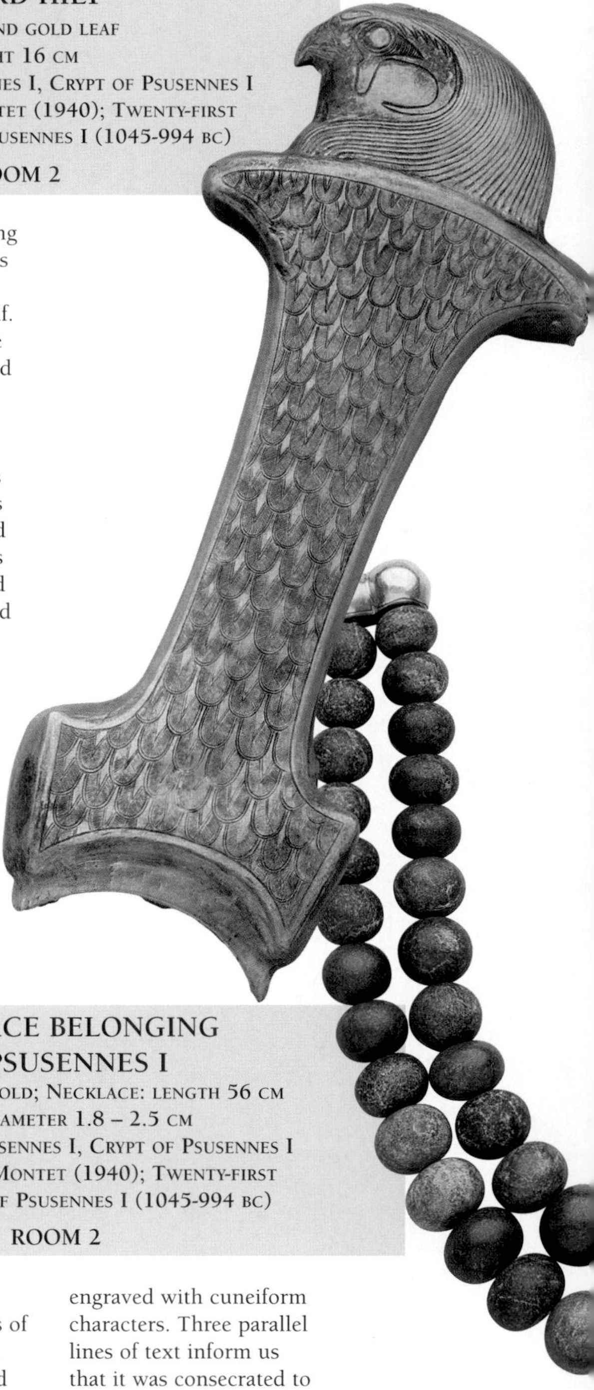

The grip belonging
to King Psusennes I is
made of bronze and
covered with gold leaf.
The pommel is in the
form of a falcon's head
and the inner part is
engraved with
decorations in
imitation of the bird's
plumage. The falcon's
head has been created
with great skill: it has
vertical stripes chased
in the metal, a hooked
beak and its eye is in
the form of an *udjat*
with a highly
emphasised eyebrow
and a stylized tear.
The *udjat* eye was
used to protect many
of the objects in the
treasure of Tanis.
(M.T)

NECKLACE BELONGING
TO PSUSENNES I

LAPIS LAZULI AND GOLD; NECKLACE: LENGTH 56 CM
BEADS: DIAMETER 1.8 – 2.5 CM
TANIS, TOMB OF PSUSENNES I, CRYPT OF PSUSENNES I
EXCAVATION BY P. MONTET (1940); TWENTY-FIRST
DYNASTY, REIGN OF PSUSENNES I (1045-994 BC)

ROOM 2

The necklace
comprises two strings of
round balls: two gold
ones in the center and
fifty-six made from lapis
lazuli of which one is

engraved with cuneiform
characters. Three parallel
lines of text inform us
that it was consecrated to
the gods of Assur by a
high Assyrian dignitary

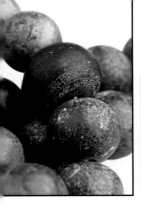

WATER JUG BELONGING
TO PSUSENNES I
GOLD; HEIGHT 38 CM
TANIS, TOMB OF PSUSENNES I, CRYPT OF PSUSENNES I
EXCAVATION BY P. MONTET (1940); TWENTY-FIRST
DYNASTY, REIGN OF PSUSENNES I (1045-994 BC)

ROOM 2

for the life of his oldest daughter.

Palaeographic and historical studies have enabled Assyriologists to date the bead to the 14th or 11th century BC but in either case it is not clear how the bead ended up in the possession of Psusennes I. The gold fastener is a small clasp decorated with a cartouche that bears the name of Psusennes I. (M.T.)

A water jug of similar shape for pouring water over the hands at mealtimes was found with its accompanying basin in the tomb of the architect Kha. It was dated to the New Kingdom when this sort of container was used. This one has a flat bottom, a rounded base, and a long flared neck. The spout is in the shape of a papyrus umbrel with finely chased leaves that are held together at the base by five ties.

The cartouches of Psusennes I are engraved on the jug and on the basin with the titles, "The King of Upper and Lower Egypt, Aakheperre Setepenamun, the Son of Ra, the Lord of the Crowns, Psusennes-Meryamun." (M.T.)

NECKLACE BELONGING
TO PSUSENNES I

GOLD AND SEMI-PRECIOUS STONES; PECTORAL HEIGHT 12 CM
TANIS, TOMB OF PSUSENNES I, CRYPT OF PSUSENNES I
EXCAVATION BY P. MONTET (1940); TWENTY-FIRST
DYNASTY, REIGN OF PSUSENNES I (1045-994 BC)

ROOM 2

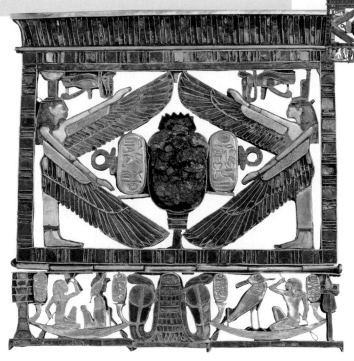

The pectoral consists of two parts joined by a hinge with the upper part showing Isis and Nephthys with wings outspread to protect a scarab on a *djed* pillar, the symbol of stability. There are *shen* rings at the sides of the scarab and cartouches give the royal names of Psusennes I. Engravings on the rear of the scarab resemble the insect's back. Each goddess bears the hieroglyph of her name on her head: the *aset*-seat for Isis and the *neb*-basket with the sign of the *hut*-building for Nephthys. The space between the wings of the goddesses and the upper frame is filled with *udjat* eyes, one for each side.

Two uraeus serpents and an upturned lotus flower in the lower section separate two boats; the king is depicted in the boat on the right with the *benu*-bird and with Osiris in the boat on the left. A *djed* pillar stands against the boat of the left and the *iabet*-standard signifying the East against the other. The pectoral is linked to a double chain formed by

twin gold beads and beads in other colors. The chain is fitted with a counterpoise in the form of an upturned lotus flower.

The jewelry found in the treasure at Tanis cannot rival that discovered in Tutankhamun's tomb, however, they show that even during the period of weakness of the central power (referred to as the Third Intermediate Period), the royal workshops still produced wonderful pieces of jewelry. (M.T.)

NECKLACE BELONGING TO PSUSENNES I

GOLD; RED AND GREEN JASPER; BLACK, RED, AND BLUE GLASS; GREEN FELDSPAR
CHAIN: LENGTH 42 CM; PENDANT: HEIGHT 10.5 CM
WIDTH 12.5 CM; SCARAB: HEIGHT 6.5 CM, WIDTH 4.5 CM
COUNTERPOISE: HEIGHT 4 CM, WIDTH 2.5 CM; TANIS, TOMB OF
PSUSENNES I, CRYPT OF PSUSENNES I; EXCAVATION BY P. MONTET (1940)
TWENTY-FIRST DYNASTY, REIGN OF PSUSENNES I (1045-994 BC)

ROOM 2

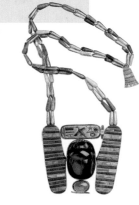

The pectoral shows a winged scarab and has a counterpoise in the shape of a lotus flower that hangs from a double string of gold beads and semi-precious stones. The scarab represents the rebirth of the sun but it carries the cartouche of the pharaoh Psusennes I between its front legs in place of the traditional solar ball, while its back legs hold the *shen* sign. The technique used to form the cartouche was cloisonné while the scarab's wings are set with horizontal bands of stones in alternating warm and cool colors. The underside of the scarab bears the text of Chapter 30 of the *Book of the Dead* in which the deceased beseeches his heart not to testify against him during the "weighing of the soul" before Osiris and the tribunal of 42 gods. The text reads, "Osiris-King Psusennes says, Oh my heart of my mother, my heart of my transformations, do not rise up in evidence against me, do not oppose me before the tribunal, show no hostility towards me before the guardians of the scale, because you are the soul of my body ..."

The rear face of the wings is embossed with the same pattern of horizontal lines seen on the front side. The pendant hangs from a double chain of beads made from gold and colored stones attached to a counterpoise in the shape of a lotus flower and known in Egyptian as *menkhet*.
(M.T.)

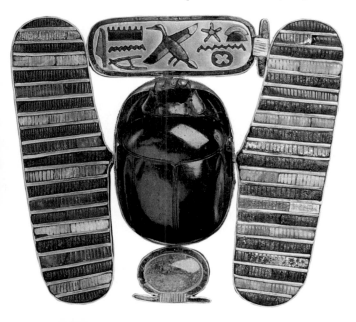

PECTORAL BELONGING TO PSUSENNES I

GOLD, CARNELIAN, LAPIS LAZULI, FELDSPAR, RED JASPER
HEIGHT 13.8 CM, WIDTH 13.5 CM, THICKNESS 0.7 CM
TANIS, TOMB OF PSUSENNES I, CRYPT OF PSUSENNES I
EXCAVATION BY P. MONTET (1940)
TWENTY-SECOND DYNASTY, REIGN OF PSUSENNES I (1045-994 BC)

ROOM 2

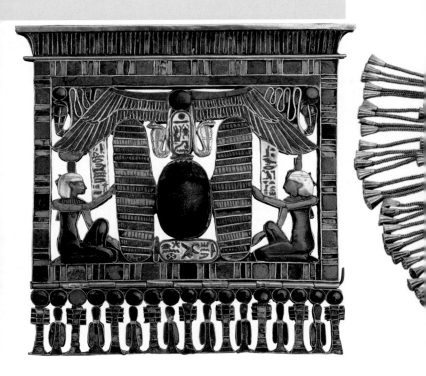

This is one of the four pectorals that adorned the mummy of Psusennes I. It was produced using the cloisonné technique and portrays a winged, lapis lazuli scarab surrounded by Isis and Nephthys. Small gold plaques in front of the two goddesses are inscribed with the words uttered by the pair in favour of Psusennes I. The wings of the scarab are inlaid with inscribed polychrome stones, and

the insect's head, which bears the cartouche with the pharaoh's coronation name, "Aakheperre Setepenamun," lies below a winged sun disk from which two uraeus serpents descend. The wings of the disk are decorated with two more tightly coiled uraeus serpents with the sun disk on their heads. Another cartouche with the name "Pasbakhaenniut Meryamun" lies behind the scarab and the entire scene lies within the

outline of a temple pylon.

Seventeen amulets, attached to the base by a hinge, alternately depict the *djed* pillar (emblem of Osiris) and the *tit* knot (linked to Isis). These symbols also lie beneath sun disks.

The pectoral is suspended from a double row of beads made from gold and semi-precious stones that has a counterpoise in the shape of a flower inlaid with colored stones. (M.T.)

NECKLACE OF PSUSENNES I

GOLD, CARNELIAN, LAPIS LAZULI AND GREEN FELDSPAR
CLASP: HEIGHT 6.2 CM
TANIS, TOMB OF PSUSENNES I, CRYPT OF PSUSENNES I
EXCAVATION BY P. MONTET (1940); TWENTY-FIRST
DYNASTY, REIGN OF PSUSENNES I (1045-994 BC)

ROOM 2

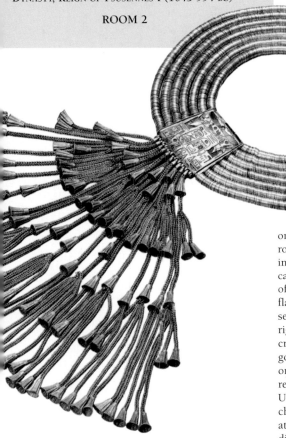

This necklace of seven heavy gold threads attached to a decorated gold plaque was found on the mummy of Psusennes I. The plaque is decorated with inlays of semi-precious stones in the form of a winged sun disk over two of Psusennes' cartouches that bear the names "Son of Ra" and "Ra of Upper and Lower Egypt" followed by the formula "endowed with life like Ra." The god Amun is represented to the right of the cartouches with two tall plumes on his head and holding the *ankh* and *was* scepters, respectively symbols of eternal life and power. To the left, the goddess Mut holds the same scepters in her hands and wears the double crown of Upper and Lower Egypt with the royal uraeus serpent on the front. Psusennes' royal names are inscribed in a single cartouche in the center of the rear of the plaque, flanked by two uraeus serpents. The one to the right wears the white crown and represents the goddess Nekhbet; the one on the left wears the red crown and represents Uadjit. A series of gold chains of variable length attached to the plaque is divided into four smaller chains each completed by a stylized lotus flower.

It was noted by M. Nelson (*Ramsès le Grand*: 306) that this type of necklace is common in images of divine boats, in particular that of Amun-Ra, where they adorn the stern and bow, and consequently they were more likely to be part of a temple's treasure than a set of grave goods. (M.T.)

The patera is in the shape of a hemisphere with the center marked by a gold nail and four other gold nails attached close together on the rim. A line of hieroglyphics in a cartouche on the other side proclaims, "Life to the perfect god, lord of the Two Lands, High Priest of Amun Psusennes."

Six of the twenty metal objects found in the tomb of Psusennes were placed against the sarcophagus. Another fourteen – including this patera – were grouped in various locations on the floor of the chamber between the *shawabty* and the south wall of the tomb.
(M.T.)

SILVER PATERA BELONGING TO PSUSENNES I

SILVER AND GOLD; DIAMETER 15.2 CM
TANIS, TOMB OF PSUSENNES I, CRYPT OF PSUSENNES I
EXCAVATION BY P. MONTET (1940); TWENTY-FIRST
DYNASTY, REIGN OF PSUSENNES I (1045-994 BC)

ROOM 2

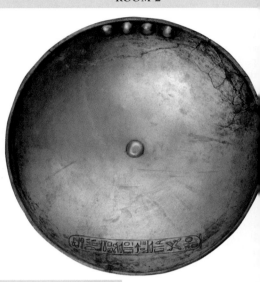

JUG WITH SPOUT BELONGING TO AMENEMOPE

SILVER; HEIGHT 12 CM, MAX. DIAMETER 11.5 CM
TANIS, TOMB OF PSUSENNES I, SEPULCHER OF AMENEMOPE
TWENTY-FIRST DYNASTY, REIGN OF AMENEMOPE
(CIRCA 990 BC)

ROOM 2

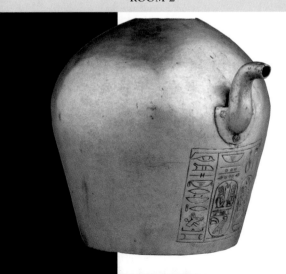

The shape of this jug is often seen in hieroglyphic texts in which it is called *nemset*. It was used in purification rites and in pouring libations for the gods. The bottom of the jug has been restored and the spout is held together with three rivets.

Below the spout is an inscription: "The perfect god, Usermaatra-Setepenra, the Lord of the Two Lands, Amenemope-Meryamun, loved by Osiris-Sokar, Lord of Rosetau." Sokar was a god who was often identified with Osiris, he was the lord of the necropolis known as Rosetau at Giza.
(M.T.)

CUP BELONGING TO UNDJEBAUENDJED

SILVER AND GOLD; DIAMETER 16 CM
TANIS, TOMB OF PSUSENNES I
SEPULCHER OF UNDJEBAUENDJED
EXCAVATION BY P. MONTET (1946)
TWENTY-FIRST DYNASTY, REIGN OF PSUSENNES I (1045-994 BC)

ROOM 2

The cup belonging to Undjebauendjed – the army general of the pharaoh Psusennes I – is decorated with a flower motif at a central point and a series of broken lines at the outermost circle. At one end, there is a gilded silver ring so that the cup could be hung. The object was found in an alcove of the royal tomb reserved for the grave goods of this official. The style and decoration are all similar to cup which was part of the same set of grave goods.
(M.T.)

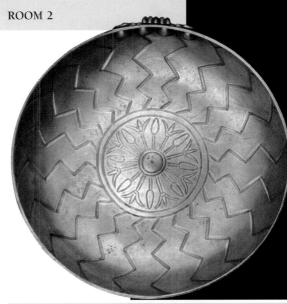

CUP BELONGING TO UNDJEBAUENDJED

SILVER; DIAMETER 16.5 CM
TANIS, TOMB OF PSUSENNES I, GRAVE OF UNDJEBAUENDJED
EXCAVATION BY P. MONTET (1946); TWENTY-FIRST DYNASTY,
REIGN OF PSUSENNES I (1045-994 BC)

ROOM 2

The cup belonged to Psusennes I's army general, Undjebauendjed, and was found in an alcove in the royal tomb reserved for the soldier's grave goods. These items are evidence of the very sophisticated taste and technical skill of the craftsmen of the period. The cup is chased on the inside with the image of a rosette with a gilded button at its center. The rosette is surrounded by a concentric circle of lotus flowers and then by an outer, zigzag edge. Gilded silver rings for hanging the cup are attached to one side.
(M.T.)

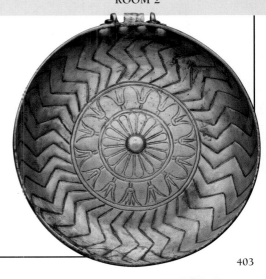

CUP BELONGING TO UNDJEBAUENDJED

Gold, silver, and glass paste
Diameter 184 cm
Tanis, Tomb of Psusennes I, Crypt of Psusennes I
Excavation by P. Montet (1946); Twenty-first Dynasty
Reign of Psusennes I (1045-994 BC)

ROOM 2

The cup is made from silver with an embossed section of gold leaf in the center. The inside of the cup is decorated in the form of a rosette with twelve gold petals encrusted with glass paste. At one end, a hook held by four rivets was used to hang the cup. The first ring outside of the rosette is decorated with two pairs of female swimmers in a pool facing one another. They are surrounded by the plant and animal life of the marshes including three ducks, fish, and birds with lotus flowers in their mouths. All the details of the composition have been created with great skill.

The outermost ring of the cup is inscribed with a dedication which runs, "The King of Upper and Lower Egypt, Aakheperre, chosen by Amun, the Son of Ra, Psusennes. Given as a gift by the king to the majordomo of Khonsu-at-Thebes-Neberhotep, the prophet of Khonsu, the general of the armies, the head of the pharaoh's archers, the director of the prophets of all the gods, the prophet Undjebauendjed justified, of the house of Osiris, lord of Mendes." (M.T.)

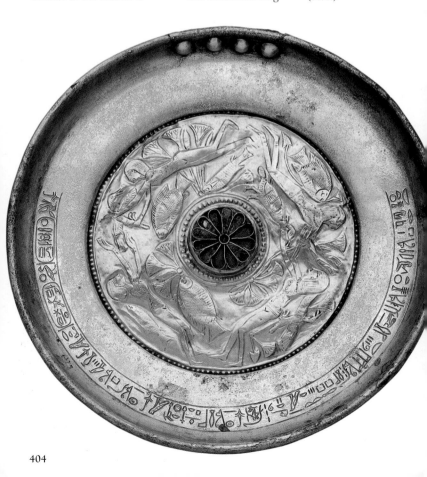

UP BELONGING TO UNDJEBAUENDJED

GOLD AND COLORED GLASS PASTE
DIAMETER 15.5 CM, HEIGHT 4.6 CM
NIS, TOMB OF PSUSENNES I, GRAVE OF UNDJEBAUENDJED
EXCAVATION BY P. MONTET (1946)
TWENTY-FIRST DYNASTY
REIGN OF PSUSENNES I (1045-994 BC)

ROOM 2

The cup is decorated in the center with a cloisonné polychrome glass paste flower from which 23 grooves radiate. In the opinion of P. Montet, its discoverer, the central pattern represents the union of the umbels of papyrus and lotus flowers and therefore forms the graphic transcription of the symbol of the union of Upper and Lower Egypt, the *sema-tauy*. Like the rest of the treasure found at Tanis, this cup has a side handle that allows it to be hung. In front of the handle, a short inscription states that the owner of the cup was "the agent of Khonsu, prophet of Khonsu, Undjebauendjed, justified."
(M.T.)

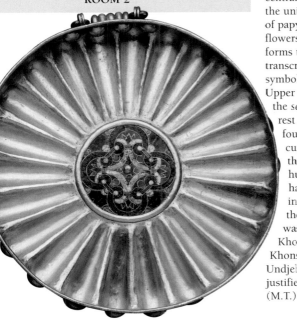

CUP BELONGING TO UNDJEBAUENDJED

GOLD AND ELECTRUM; DIAMETER 13.3 CM; HEIGHT 5.5CM
TANIS, TOMB OF PSUSENNES I, GRAVE OF UNDJEBAUENDJED
EXCAVATION BY P. MONTET (1946); TWENTY-FIRST
DYNASTY, REIGN OF PSUSENNES I (1045-994 BC)

ROOM 2

The cup is in the form of a flower whose petals are alternately made of gold and electron. An inscription on one of the gold petals contains the cartouche of Psusennes I and that of his wife, Mutnedjemet. Three signs are below the cartouches: a monkey that is moving his paw towards his mouth, a band of flowers, and the head of a lion that could represent the hieroglyphic group *ankh, udjat, seneb*, "life, strength, and health!", a well-wishing exclamation placed after the king's names. The inscription shows the favour which Undjebauendjed enjoyed.
(M.T.)

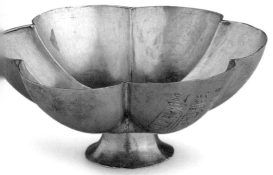

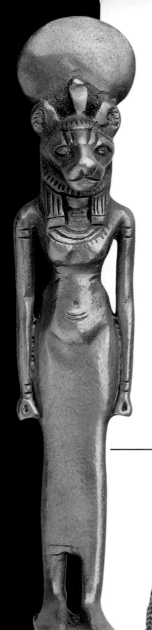

PENDANT BELONGING TO UNDJEBAUENDJED

GOLD; HEIGHT 7.2 CM
TANIS, TOMB OF PSUSENNES I, GRAVE OF UNDJEBAUENDJE
EXCAVATION BY P. MONTET (1946); TWENTY-FIRST DYNAST
REIGN OF PSUSENNES I (1045-994 BC)

ROOM 2

The pendant shows the goddess Sekhmet, with the body of a woman and the head of a lionness, below the sun disk and a uraeus serpent. She wears a long tight dress and has her hands down her sides. She also wears a neatly defined necklace. Two other figures of women with lion's heads were found in the tomb of Undjebauendjed with an inscription identifying them as Bastet as opposed to Sekhmet. Both belong to the group of lionness-goddesses and were assimilated to one another. The name Sekhmet means "the Powerful One"; she had the role of mother and guardian deity of the king. Sekhmet also protected Ra and was consequently also known as the "Eye of Ra." From the Middle Kingdom on, the aggressive and wild nature of the goddess became prevalent in religious texts with the result that her more peaceful aspect was identified with Bastet. (M.T.)

PENDANT DEPICTING ISIS

GOLD; PENDANT: HEIGHT 11 CM, WIDTH 2.2 CM
CHAIN: LENGTH 82 CM
TANIS, TOMB OF PSUSENNES I,
GRAVE OF UNDJEBAUENDJED; EXCAVATION BY
P. MONTET (1940); TWENTY-FIRST DYNASTY
REIGN OF PSUSENNES I (1045-994 BC)

ROOM 2

The pendant belonged to the army general, Undjebauendjed, who lived during the reign of Psusennes I. It shows a female deity with cow's horns and a sun disk that are symbols of the goddess Hathor. An inscription on the base names the goddess as "Isis, Mother of the God" who was increasingly portrayed with the iconographical elements of Hathor from the Third Intermediate Period on.

Like the items of jewelry found in the tomb of Tutankhamun, those discovered at Tanis form one of the rare homogeneous collections to have survived in the history of Egyptian jewelry. The purpose of the large number of pendants and pectorals was to assure the deceased would be reborn or – as in this case – to place him under the protection of a particular deity. (M.T.)

FUNERAL MASK OF UNDJEBAUENDJED

GOLD AND GLASS PASTE; HEIGHT 22 CM
TANIS, TOMB OF PSUSENNES I, GRAVE OF UNDJEBAUENDJED
EXCAVATION BY P. MONTET (1946)
TWENTY-FIRST DYNASTY
REIGN OF PSUSENNES I (1045-994 BC)

ROOM 2

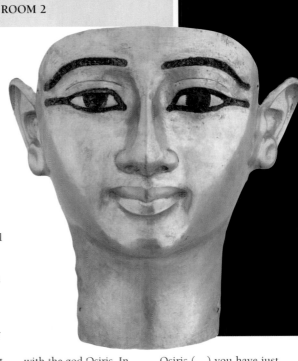

The mask that covered the face of Psusennes I's army general is covered by a thick layer of gold and was attached to the mummy by six small perforated splines. The eyes are cavities filled with colored glass paste – black for the pupil and white for the eyeball – as are the edging of the eyes and the eyebrows. The facial features are delicately portrayed and give an idealized representation of the dead general. Only the ears are asymmetrical with the left sticking out slightly further than the right.

Gold, being in direct contact with the mummy, was the last form of protection offered to the deceased. It was considered to be "the flesh of the gods" and by covering the dead body with the metal, the deceased was identified with the god Osiris. In addition to the funeral mask, finger and toe sheaths and sandals were also made from gold for the mummy and were present on Psusennes I himself.

The texts used in the funeral rites say: "O Osiris (...) you have just received your gold finger sheaths and your fingers are of pure gold, your fingers are of electron! The radiation of the sun reaches right down to you, you truly have the divine body of Osiris!" (M.T.)

PECTORAL OF AMENEMOPE

GOLD AND LAPIS LAZULI; HEIGHT 9.8 CM, WIDTH 10.6 CM
TANIS, TOMB OF PSUSENNES I, GRAVE OF AMENEMOPE
EXCAVATION BY P. MONTET (1940)
TWENTY-FIRST DYNASTY
REIGN OF AMENEMOPE (994-985 BC)

ROOM 2

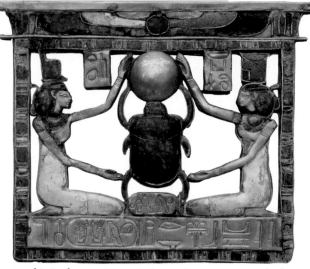

The pectoral is in the form of a shrine with two lateral pillars and a hollowed molding containing the winged sun disk. The *netjer nefer* epithet, "the perfect god" and the name of Amenemope in the cartouche are engraved in gold on the base where the two sister goddesses, Isis and Nephthys, kneel on the right and left respectively. They support a lapis lazuli scarab that holds a gold sun disk in its front feet and the king's cartouche between its back feet. A small gold plaque in front of each goddess states her name. Two rings on the upper edge of the molding were used to attach a chain on which the pectoral was hung.
(M.T.)

BRACELETS OF PSUSENNES I

GOLD, LAPIS LAZULI, CARNELIAN, GREEN FELDSPAR
HEIGHT 7 CM, MAX. DIAMETER 8 CM
TANIS, TOMB OF PSUSENNES I, CRYPT OF PSUSENNES I
EXCAVATION BY P. MONTET (1940)
TWENTY-FIRST DYNASTY
REIGN OF PSUSENNES I (1045-994 BC)

ROOM 2

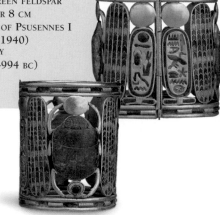

The two bracelets were manufactured using the cloisonné technique and depict the scarab with the sun disk between his front legs.

408

Psusennes' cartouches enclose the name of the Son of Ra, "Aakheperre Setepenra" and that of the King of Upper and Lower Egypt, "Pasebakhaenniut Meryamun." to identify the deceased. Scarabs and the *udjat* eye were the most popular forms of amulets to ward off evil from the time of the New Kingdom on. The wings of the scarab are set with stones of various colors but in a herring-bone pattern.

Bracelets and anklets were items of major importance for the protection of the mummy as the role of their patterns was to guarantee immortality to the deceased. In total, 26 bracelets and anklets were found on Psusennes' mummy, 10 on the right arm, 12 on the left, 2 above the knees, and 2 at the ankles.

(M.T.)

FUNERARY MASK OF AMENEMOPE

GOLD LEAF, BRONZE AND SEMI-PRECIOUS STONES
HEIGHT 30 CM
TANIS, TOMB OF PSUSENNES I, GRAVE OF AMENEMOPE
EXCAVATION BY P. MONTET (1940); TWENTY-FIRST DYNASTY
REIGN OF AMENEMOPE (993-985 BC)

ROOM 2

Amenemope was buried in a tomb chamber built by his predecessor, Psusennes I, where Mutnedjemet (Psusennes' wife and sister) was supposed to have been buried. The mask was part of Amenemope's wooden sarcophagus which has been lost. The king is shown wearing the *nemes* headdress with the uraeus serpent made from gold and blue, red, and light blue stones on the front. The pupils, eyebrows, the outline of the eyes, and the oval edging to the face on the mask are all made of bronze.

The treasure discovered at Tanis included three other pharaonic funerary masks belonging to Psusennes I, Sheshonq III, and general Undjebauendjed which can only be compared to the mask found in Tutankhamun's tomb for their superb craftsmanship and beauty. What impresses about Tutankhamun's mask is the sumptuousness of the materials used – highly polished solid gold, and encrustations of stones and polychrome glass paste – which contrast with the refined simplicity of the masks at Tanis. Another difference is that they have no inscriptions unlike some examples from the Middle Kingdom and Tutankhamun's on which Chapter 531 of the *Sarcophagus Texts* and Chapter 151b of the *Book of the Dead* were written.

(M.T.)

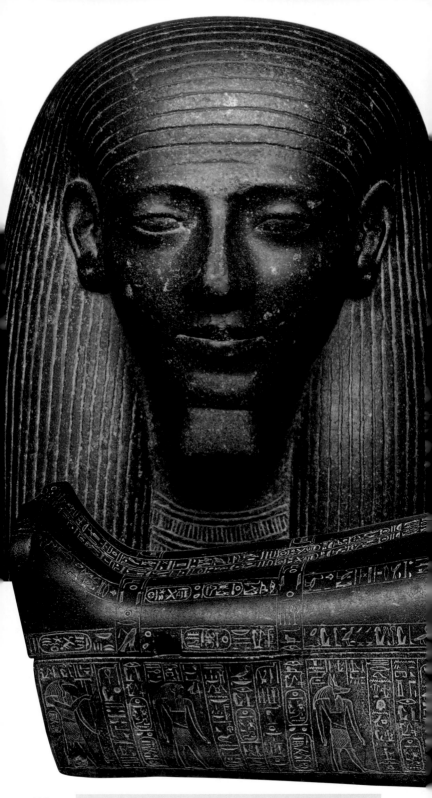

SARCOPHAGUS OF PSUSENNES I
GRANITIC ROCK
LENGTH 220 CM, WIDTH 65 CM, HEIGHT 80 CM
TANIS, TOMB OF PSUSENNES I, CRYPT OF PSUSENNES I
EXCAVATION BY P. MONTET (1940)
NINETEENTH DYNASTY (1291-1185 BC) AND TWENTY-
FIRST DYNASTY, REIGN OF PSUSENNES I (1045-994 BC)

ROOM 2

This is the outermost sarcophagus used by Psusennes I inside which lay the pink granite sarcophagus that Psusennes appropriated from the Nineteenth Dynasty pharaoh, Merenptah, and the silver sarcophagus made especially for Psusennes. The mummy of the deceased is represented on the lid with his arms folded, wearing a striped wig and a short false beard. Around his neck he has a large necklace comprising several strings and bracelets on his wrists. The goddess Nut with spread wings is represented on a level with the stomach, followed by a column of hieroglyphs and other vertical and horizontal texts that give the titles and cartouches of Psusennes I. The bottom half of the sarcophagus is decorated with various gods linked to the funerary cult such as Anubis and the four sons of Horus; the text spoken by each god to the deceased is given in a column of hieroglyphs before his image.

Like the pink granite sarcophagus, this one was also appropriated by Psusennes from another pharaoh for his own sepulcher. In certain points, the royal cartouches were inscribed with another name but they have been chiselled off. The stylistic features of the sarcophagus suggest an original date of the Nineteenth Dynasty and the lack of royal attributes on the figure indicates that it probably belonged to a private functionary. (M.T)

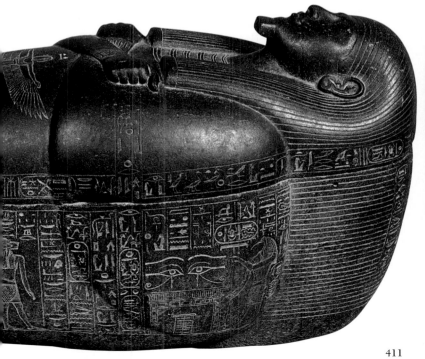

411

SARCOPHAGUS OF PSUSENNES I
Silver and gold; Length 185 cm
Tanis, Tomb of Psusennes I, Crypt of Psusennes I
Excavation by P. Montet (1940); Twenty-first
Dynasty, Reign of Psusennes I (1045-994 bc)

ROOM 2

This is the innermost, and therefore the most precious, of the three sarcophagi that contained the mummy of Psusennes I. One of the two outer ones was made from represented on the body of the sovereign, each of which clutches *shen* cartouches in its talons. The sarcophagus is wholly decorated with an engraved herring-bone

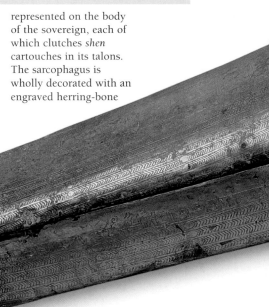

stone and dates from the reign of Merenptah: JE 87297 in Cairo Museum; the other is JE 85911 and also kept in the museum. On the lid, the pharaoh is shown in the form of a mummy with the *nemes* headdress, the uraeus serpent on the front, the false beard, and the scepters that represent Osiris held crossed on his chest. The uraeus and band around his forehead are made from gold and his eyes are encrusted with glass paste and made up with black lines.

Three birds with the head of a vulture, a ram, and a falcon are

pattern in which vertical columns of text contain prayers to the funerary gods on behalf of the deceased.

The goddesses Isis and Nephthys are shown at the feet of the sarcophagus on either side of a column of hieroglyphs that begins half-way up the side. The inside of the sarcophagus is decorated with the image of Nut standing on the symbol of gold, *nub*. The guardian goddesses of the deceased, Isis and Nephthys, are also depicted on the lower section; these two sisters watched over, mourned, and prepared the dead

Osiris for his rebirth and, according to Osiriac ritual, were believed to perform the same duties for human remains. This was even more strongly the case for a dead king's body who "became" Osiris after his death.

The sarcophagus contained the mummy of Psusennes I who still wore the funerary mask with which he was buried. The king built temples dedicated to Amun, Mut, and Khonsu at Tanis inside an enclosure wall of sun-baked bricks where his tomb also lies.
(M.T)

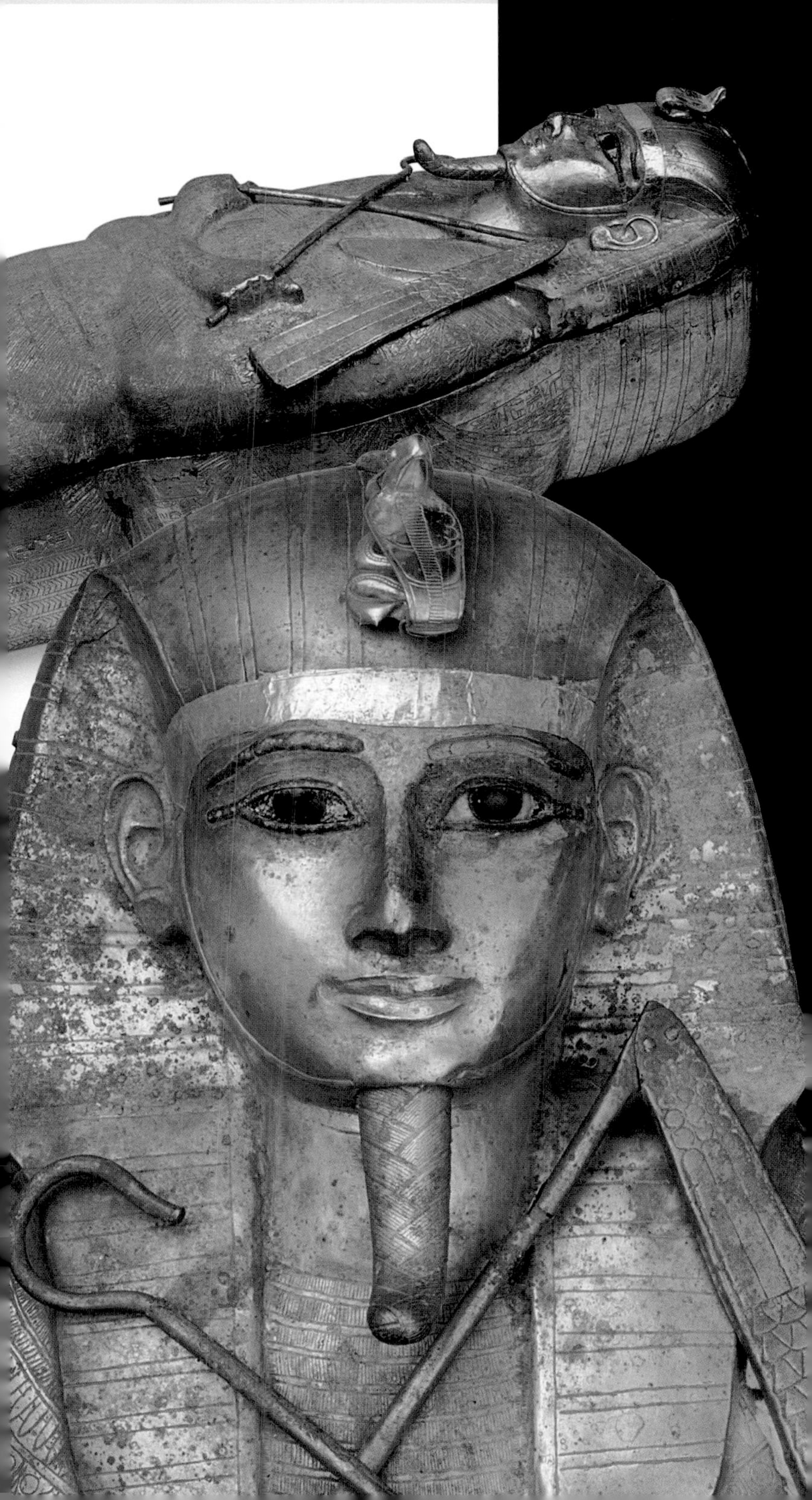

BASIN WITH HANDLES BELONGING TO PSUSENNES I

Gold; Height 17 cm, max. diameter 10.2 cm
Tanis, Tomb of Psusennes I, Crypt of Psusennes I
Excavation by P. Montet (1940); Twenty-first
Dynasty, Reign of Psusennes I (1045-994 bc)

ROOM 2

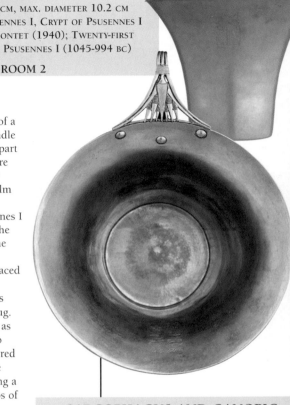

The flared, flat-bottomed basin resembles the shape of a lotus flower. The handle is formed by a three-part stem with the juncture with the lotus flower above and a small palm tree below. The cartouches of Psusennes I are engraved inside the container opposite the handle.

The basin was placed in the king's burial chamber where it was found with a water jug. The two made a pair as the basin was used to collect the water poured from the jug over the hands of diners during a banquet. In the tombs of private individuals during the New Kingdom, for example that of Nebamun, similar jugs were depicted inside the basin below the offerings table. It is probable that the objects were introduced to Egypt from the Near East as they are often shown in the hands of foreigners from the Aegean or Asia. (M.T.)

SARCOPHAGUS AND CANOPIC VASES OF SHESHONQ II

Silver; Length 190 cm
Tanis, Tomb of Psusennes I, grave of Sheshonq II
Excavation by P. Montet (1940); Twenty-second
Dynasty, Reign of Sheshonq II (890 bc circa)

ROOM 2

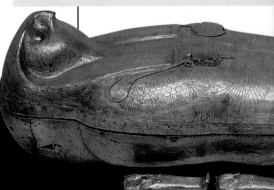

CEREMONIAL BRAZIER BELONGING TO RAMESES II

BRONZE; HEIGHT 24 CM, WIDTH 26.5 CM, LENGTH 33.5 CM
TANIS, TOMB OF PSUSENNES I, CRYPT OF PSUSENNES I
EXCAVATION BY P. MONTET (1940); NINETEENTH DYNASTY
REIGN OF RAMESES II (1279-1212 BC)

ROOM 2

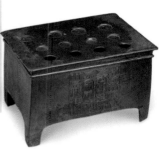

The brazier is in the shape of a box with four feet and a V-shaped edging on the top. The cartouches containing the royal names of Rameses II are inscribed on one side with a text that states that the object was made for the *sed* festival. This festival celebrated the renewal of royal power every four years and, Rameses II reigned for over 60 years, it would have been celebrated at least fourteen times. The inscription says that Rameses was a devotee of Ptah-Tatenen and, in particular, of Ra-Harakhti, the principal god of his capital Pi-Rameses.

The brazier could be used to make small offerings to the god or to burn perfumed resins.
(M.T.)

The tomb of Psusennes was found to contain the sepulchers and grave goods of other pharaohs from later periods, such as Sheshonq II, the third king of the Libyan Dynasty, whose silver sarcophagus and canopic vases were deposited in Psusennes' antechamber. The body and grave goods of Amenemope (Psusennes' successor) were also found here although a tomb had been built for him. Even Siamun, Psusennes II, and the army general, Undjebauendjed, were buried in separate bays in the tomb.

The commonest method of dealing with the internal organs from the Middle Kingdom on was to embalm them in canopic vases and only rarely, as in this case, were the organs placed in human-shaped containers. Both the falcon-headed sarcophagus and the four containers of Sheshonq II are made from silver. The containers themselves are miniature sarcophaguses in the image of the pharaoh with the nemes headdress, the royal uraeus serpent, the false beard, and heavily made-up eyes. The hands emerge from the mummy's bandages to hold the Osiriac scepters but these have been lost. A vertical inscription on the body identifies the four spirits, the sons of Horus, under whose protection the king's organs were placed: "Imset (Duamutef, Hapi, Qebehsenuf) of whom Sheshonq Meryamun is the son."

The hands on the outside of the falcon-headed sarcophagus are closed to hold the Osiriac scepters. The falcon's head probably identified the king with Osiris-Sokari, an underworld, funerary god in the Memphis necropolis. The lid is decorated with images of winged deities like Isis and Nephthys divided into two fields by a vertical inscription in the center. The four sons of Horus are shown facing one another in pairs in the lower section.
(M.T.)

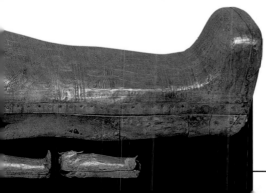

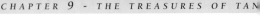

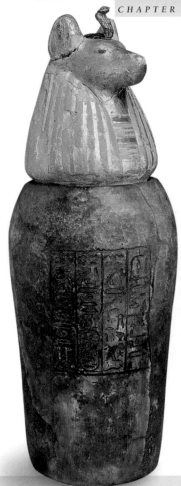

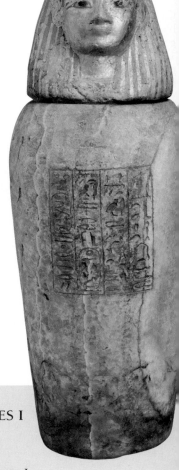

CANOPIC VASES OF PSUSENNES I

ALABASTER AND GOLD LEAF
1) HEIGHT CM 41; 2) HEIGHT CM 43
3) HEIGHT CM 39; 4) HEIGHT CM 38
TANIS, TOMB OF PSUSENNES I, CRYPT OF PSUSENNES I
EXCAVATION BY P. MONTET (1940); TWENTY-FIRST
DYNASTY, REIGN OF PSUSENNES I (1045-994 BC)

ROOM 2

Canopic vases were made to contain the mummified internal organs of the deceased. They were generally made from alabaster, calcite, or terracotta and had a lid in one of four possible forms: the head of either a human, a baboon, a falcon, or a jackal. They represent the four spirit sons of Horus – Amset, Hapi, Qebehsenuf, and Duamutef – who each presided over one of the organs: the liver was protected by Amset, the lungs by Hapi, the stomach by Duamutef, and the intestines by Qebehsenuf. These four were in turn watched over by the goddesses Isis, Nephthys, Neith, and Selkis. Canopic vases began to appear in funerary goods in the Middle Kingdom but it was only during the Ramessid that lids were produced portraying the four sons of Horus.

The vases belonging to Psusennes I had lids lined with a thin sheet of gold and blue glass paste. The four figures bear a gilded bronze uraeus serpent on their heads while the body of each vase is inscribed with an invocation in four columns that associate Isis and Amset with the vase with the human head, Nephthys and Hapi with the vase with the baboon's head, Neith and Duamutef with the vase with the jackal's head, and Selkis and Qebehsenuf with the vase with a falcon's head. The four vases were found placed in front of the granite sarcophagus with other objects from the set of grave goods: the skeleton of an animal in a wooden sarcophagus, an alabaster container with a handle, some alabaster *shawabty*, some bronze *shawabty*, and a number of small tools for the *shawabty* to use. (M.T.)

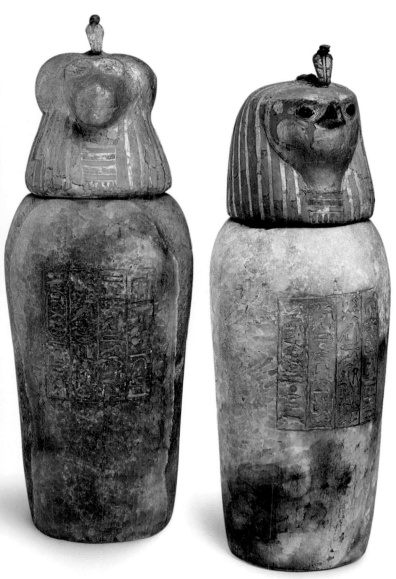

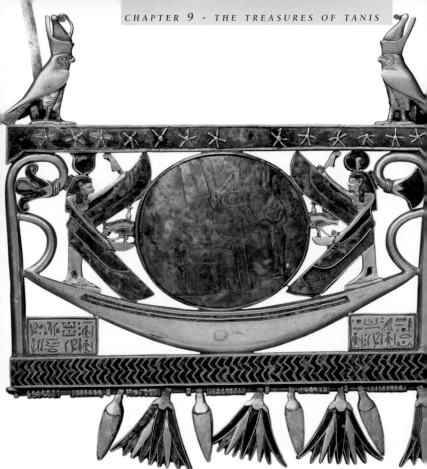

PECTORAL OF SHESHONQ I

GOLD, LAPIS LAZULI AND GLASS PASTE; HEIGHT 7.8 CM
TANIS, TOMB OF PSUSENNES I, GRAVE OF SHESHONQ II
EXCAVATION BY P. MONTET (1939); START OF THE
TWENTY-SECOND DYNASTY (10TH CENTURY BC)

ROOM 2

The inscriptions on the ends of the solar boat on this gold pendant encrusted with lapis lazuli and glass paste state that it belonged to Sheshonq, the son of Nimlot. This could have been Sheshonq I, the founder of the Twenty-second Dynasty, and therefore the pendant

would have been inherited by his son Sheshonq II in whose tomb it was found. The pectoral is decorated with the image of a solar boat navigating below the starry vault. A lapis lazuli solar disk is shown in the center of the boat with a representation of the

goddess Maat standing beside Amun-Ra-Harakhti. A goddess stands at each end of the solar bark: Hathor, wearing cow's horns and a red glass paste sun disk stands at the back, and Maat, with the sun disk and ostrich plume on her head, is at the front. The winged arms of the two goddesses are stretched out towards the sun disk, both holding a plume in one hand and a hieroglyph in the other composed of the *nefer* sign, the *udjat* eye, and the *neb* basket.

The wings, hair, and heavenly vault are all made from lapis lazuli, the latter being dotted with gold to signify the stars. The sky is supported at either side by the two heraldic plants of Upper and Lower Egypt made from gold and semi-precious stones, while upside down lotus flowers hang from a hinge at the bottom of the pendant. Two gold falcons stand in the corners above the sky and wear the double crown of Upper and Lower Egypt on their heads (M.T.)

PECTORAL BELONGING TO SHESHONQ II

GOLD, LAPIS LAZULI, PALE GREEN AND RED FAÏENCE
PENDANT: HEIGHT 7 CM, WIDTH 5 CM
TANIS, TOMB OF PSUSENNES I, GRAVE OF SHESHONQ II
EXCAVATION BY P. MONTET (1940)
TWENTY-SECOND DYNASTY, REIGNS OF SHESHONQ I (945-924 BC)
AND SHESHONQ II (890 BC CIRCA)

ROOM 2

Like the other pectorals found at Tanis, this one has a solar scarab at its center symbolizing the rebirth of the sovereign. The lapis lazuli scarab wears a gold sun disk on its head and is ringed by two uraeus serpents wearing the white crown and crossing a *shen* circle. Alternating closed and open papyrus flowers decorate the bottom of the pendant. The gold ribbon is attached to the back of the pectoral through three rings where the same decorations are to be seen except that the underside of the scarab is not flat but rounded and divided into segments.

The white crown on the uraeus serpents is an exceptional feature as other pectorals from Tanis and the treasure of Tutankhamun all wear either the double crown or the sun disk. This suggests that the white crown may be a reference to the royal name of Sheshonq I (the original owner) as king of Upper and Lower Egypt: *Hedjet* (the white crown)-*kheper* (the scarab)-*Ra* (the sun disk).
(M.T.)

FUNERARY SANDALS OF PSUSENNES I

GOLD; LENGTH 23.3 CM
TANIS, TOMB OF PSUSENNES I, CRYPT OF PSUSENNES I
EXCAVATION BY P. MONTET (1940)
TWENTY-FIRST DYNASTY
REIGN OF PSUSENNES I (1045-994 BC)

ROOM 2

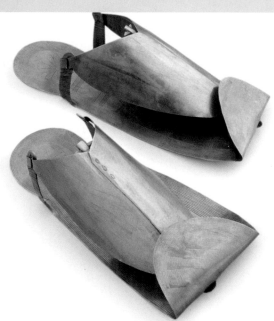

These ritual sandals were made symmetrically, each one consisting of a sole and two triangular sections fused together. The soles extend at the front and curve upwards.

The upper side of the soles is decorated with parallel lines that follow the shape, with the engraving of a sixteen petal rose at the heel, and with herring-bone patterns in the middle.

The sandals were placed on the feet of the mummy to ensure the pharaoh-Osiris would rise to join the gods. Given the value of the material, the sandals could not be used in life, although they were based faithfully on the leather sandals used during daily life.

Protection of the mummy was ensured by the placement in the burial chamber of accessories such as the "evisceration" plaque positioned on the cut made in the body to extract the internal organs; the canopic vases used to hold the deceased's embalmed organs; gold sheaths slipped over the mummy's fingers and toes to ensure eternal use of the limbs; the gold death mask that identified the deceased and gave him the same appearance as the gods (their flesh was gold); and the gold sandals in which the deceased was able to march triumphantly towards the world beyond the tomb.
(M.T.)

FUNERAL MASK OF SHESHONQ II

GOLD
HEIGHT 26 CM, WIDTH 23 CM
TANIS, TOMB OF PSUSENNES I, CRYPT OF PSUSENNES I
EXCAVATION BY P. MONTET (1939); TWENTY-FIRST DYNASTY
REIGN OF PSUSENNES I (1045-994 BC)

ROOM 2

The mask was found still on the pharaoh's mummy but seriously damaged. It was made from a thick sheet of embossed gold with hollow spaces for the eyes and eyebrows where glass paste was to have been inserted (as for example in the case of the army general, Undjebauendjed, JE

87753). The mask was fixed to the mummy by five small perforated tenons, three on the forehead and two just below the ears.

Few funerary masks have been found outside of Tanis but they include those belonging to Khaemuaset (a son of Rameses II), that of an Ethiopian queen from the 7th century BC, and those belonging to a number of Saite dignitaries. (M.T)

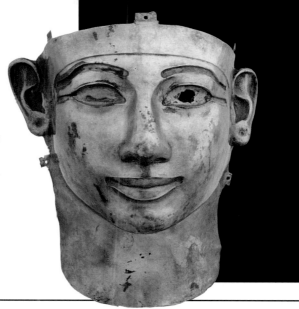

BRACELETS BELONGING TO SHESHONQ II

GOLD, LAPIS LAZULI, CARNELIAN, AND FAÏENCE
HEIGHT 4.6 CM, MAX. OUTER DIAMETER 7 CM
TANIS, TOMB OF PSUSENNES I, GRAVE OF SHESHONQ II
EXCAVATION BY P. MONTET (1939); TWENTY-SECOND
DYNASTY, REIGN OF SHESHONQ II (890 BC CIRCA)

ROOM 2

Archaeologists found seven bracelets on the mummy of Sheshonq II. Those with the *udjat* eye are a pair with the single difference: each one reproduces either the left or right eye. Besides indicating the Egyptians' penchant for symmetry allowed the deceased to reach eternity wearing the two eyes of the sun duly paired.

The image of the *udjat* eye appears on a background formed by a central square of pale lapis lazuli; the eyebrow and hanging scrolls are also made from lapis lazuli, but the pupil is made of black stone and the cornea of white faïence. The eye rests on a *neb* basket decoration with small squares of lapis lazuli, carnelian, and gold. The image was believed to protect the sovereign as it represented the healed eye in the myth of Horus and his uncle Seth. The myth says that Seth struck out the eye of Horus during a struggle and reduced it to pieces but that Thoth magically recomposed the eye which then became known as *udjat* or "healed eye." The *udjat* was one of the most widespread talismans in ancient Egypt and is even seen on a bracelet in the treasure of Tutankhamun. The *udjat* represents refound wholeness and the restoration of lost well-being.

Around the square with the eye, the bracelet is decorated with vertical bands of gold and lapis lazuli, and the edges with a strip of rectangles of inlaid lapis lazuli alternating with squares of carnelian. Inside, there are two engraved cartouches bearing the name of Sheshonq I, from whom Sheshonq II inherited many jewels. (M.T.)

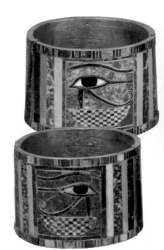

PECTORAL BELONGING TO SHESHONQ II

GOLD, SEMI-PRECIOUS STONES, AND GLASS PASTE
HEIGHT 15 CM, LENGTH OF CHAIN 75 CM
TANIS, TOMB OF PSUSENNES I, GRAVE OF SHESHONQ II
EXCAVATION BY P. MONTET (1940)
TWENTY-SECOND DYNASTY, REIGN OF SHESHONQ II (CIRCA 890 BC)

ROOM 2

Sheshonq II's mummy was found wearing this rectangular pectoral with a winged steatite scarab at its center. The scarab bears the king's cartouche on his head and another on his body. The goddesses Isis and her sister Nephthys kneel on either side with their arms held out to support the wings of the scarab below a winged gold disk with two uraeus serpents. The upper part of the outer border has a winged sun disk and a V-shaped decoration. The pectoral hangs on a gold ribbon chain attached to a small gold plaque in the shape of a lotus flower.
(M.T.)

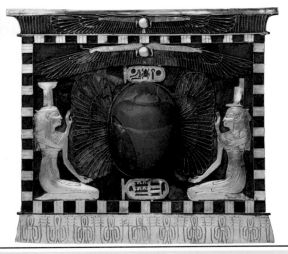

FUNERAL MASK OF PSUSENNES I

GOLD, LAPIS LAZULI, AND GLASS PASTE
MAX HEIGHT 48 CM, MAX. WIDTH 38 CM
TANIS, TOMB OF PSUSENNES I, CRYPT OF PSUSENNES I
EXCAVATION BY P. MONTET (1940); TWENTY-FIRST DYNASTY
REIGN OF PSUSENNES I (1045-994 BC)

ROOM 2

The magnificent funerary mask belonging to Psusennes I is one of the masterpieces of the treasure of Tanis. The king is portrayed with idealized features on a thin sheet of finely chased gold, the "flesh of the gods." The king wears the *nemes* headdress with the horizontal stripes clearly defined; he has a uraeus serpent on his forehead and a braided false beard that ends in a slight curve upwards. He also wears an *usekh* necklace with twelve strings of beads from which three wider bands decorated with drop-shaped and plant motifs hang. Black and white glass paste is used for his eyes and eyebrows and for the groove that encircles his face in imitation of the string with which the false beard was attached.
(M.T.)

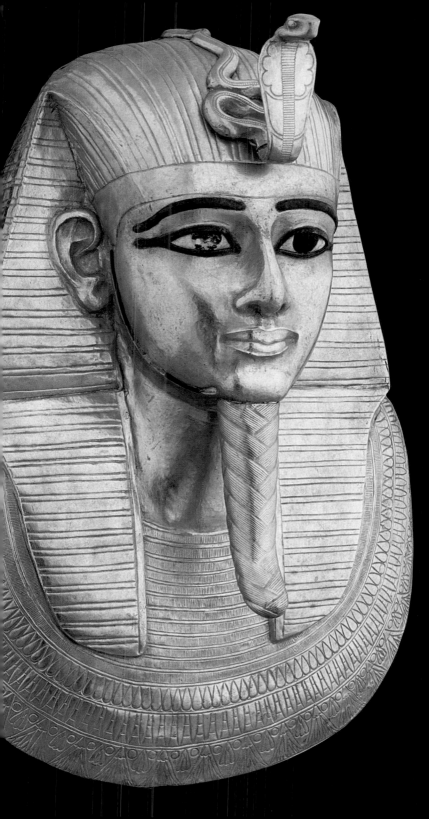

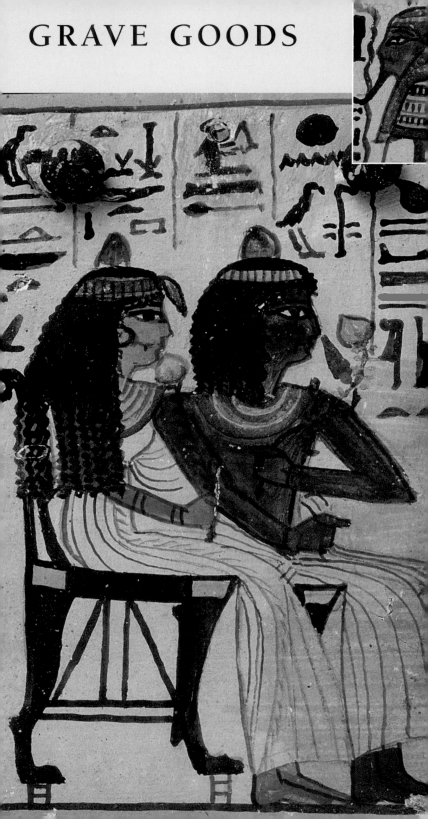

Most of our knowledge about daily life on the banks of the Nile in ancient Egypt comes from detailed wall paintings and sets of grave goods buried in tombs with the body of the deceased. The great care paid to the "eternal abodes" and the fact that they were built from non-perishable materials are clear statements that the tombs were built to preserve the body of the deceased, an indispensable requisite for life beyond the tomb.

The feelings that accompanied this enormous expenditure of energy were contradictory: the serenity depicted in the scenes and texts painted on the tomb walls contrasts with the anguish of some of the ancient texts: "…no-one comes from There, who might tell us of their state, inform us of their needs, calm our hearts until we too can go where they have gone…" (from the *Song of the Harpist*). The anxiety felt for the unknown did, however, result in the creation of the most beautiful works of Egyptian art, valuable treasures meant to last for eternity that were never used in earthly life which was as "transient as a breath of wind."

The discovery of entire sets of grave goods is a rare occurrence as they were mostly stolen in ancient times. The robberies themselves were an indispensable aid to the circulation of wealth that would otherwise have remained locked in the tombs for eternity. The high symbolic value of the reliefs and inscriptions compensated for the possible loss of the grave goods as the magical power attributed to words and images was able to perpetuate what was written and represented on the walls. The most traditional scene, in which the deceased is seated at a table of offerings of all kinds

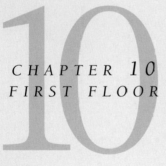

CHAPTER 10
FIRST FLOOR

424 *SHAWABTY*
HOLDER OF KHONSU
Wood; H. 35.6 CM;
Deir al-Medina
Nineteenth Dynasty,
Reign of Rameses II
(1279-1212 BC)

425 *SHAWABTY*
OF KHONSU
Limestone; H. 21 CM
Deir al-Medina,
Tomb of Sennedjem;
Nineteenth Dynasty,
Reign of Rameses II
(1279-1212 BC)

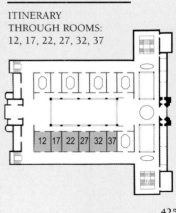

ITINERARY
THROUGH ROOMS:
12, 17, 22, 27, 32, 37

12 17 22 27 32 37

accompanied by the inscription that lists everything required for the sustenance of the individual during his future life, had the same validity as the baskets of food left inside the tomb.

The funerary cult assured the survival of the deceased. Funerary priests were appointed for this very reason; they were a sort of professional brotherhood that handed down their power and responsibilities from father to son. This is an extract from the Egyptian text, *The Teaching of Hergedef*: "...the house of the dead is needed for life. Try to acquire a property of fields irrigated by the annual flood. Choose a part of your field for the (funerary priest) which will receive the waters every year! It will be more useful to you than your own son and preferable to an [heir]!"

A contract was signed during life with the funerary priest whose duty was to see to the provision of a table of offerings and libations for the gods on a daily basis and during the festivals held in the necropolis.

In addition to the food and drink, a huge quantity of objects would be placed in the tomb, all of which were considered necessary to a respectable eternal life without hardship. The most precious item in the grave goods, the sarcophagus, was placed in the burial chamber – the internal and most protected room in the tomb –

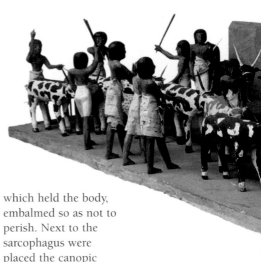

which held the body, embalmed so as not to perish. Next to the sarcophagus were placed the canopic vases, the four containers that held the dried internal organs of the deceased which were believed to be reunited with the body after death to allow it to perform its vital functions.

So that the deceased might overcome any dangers in the world beyond the tomb and survive the final divine judgement before he entered the Elysian Fields, the deceased was provided with the *Book of the Dead*, the book that contained the funerary texts and a series of magical formulas used in the dangerous journey to the Afterlife and eternal peace. The *Book of the Dead* was placed directly on the mummy or in special boxes decorated with divine funerary figures for protection.

Shawabty models assured the deceased an eternal life free from physical toil. The name *shawabty* comes from ancient Egyptian and literally means "he who responds" to the request of the deceased to work in the fields of the beyond (as described in Chapter 6 of the *Book of the Dead* and generally placed on the body of the deceased itself). The small statues were made from various materials and often were placed together in decorated boxes.

Care of the body was assured by the provision of ointments and perfumes kept in special containers but, being expensive raw materials, they were usually removed by

were the first articles to be stolen, including those placed directly in the wraps of the mummy even if it was necessary to remove the body from its shroud and sarcophagus.

especially to accompany the owner of the tomb on his most important journey.

Once the burial rituals were completed, the seals were applied to the tomb in a hopeless attempt to preserve its contents and to consecrate the deceased to the Afterlife definitively.
(A.A.)

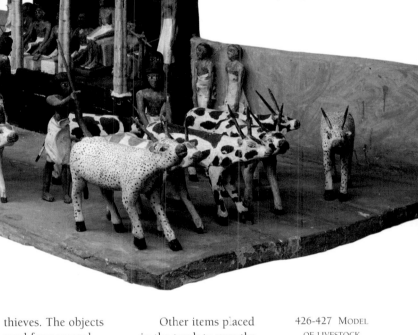

thieves. The objects used for personal *toilette* were usually of importance, sometimes masterpieces of the jeweler's art made from valuable materials. Precious jewels, generally not worn during earthly life, were added to accompany the deceased in a life filled with joy and happiness but, unfortunately, these

Other items placed in the tomb to ease the life of the deceased in the world beyond the grave were furniture, table objects, work tools, measuring instruments, vases, different sorts of containers, amulets, weapons, and games. Each element of the set of grave goods became an opportunity to create a work of art made

426-427 MODEL OF LIVESTOCK CENSUS
Wood
Length 173 CM
Deir al-Bahari;
Tomb of Meketra; Late Eleventh Dynasty-Early Twelfth Dynasty (late 3rd-early 2nd millennium BC)

ALABASTER POT OF HATSHEPSUT

ALABASTER; HEIGHT 33.5 CM; TELL AL-AMARNA
EIGHTEENTH DYNASTY
REIGN OF HATSHEPSUT (1479-1458 BC)

ROOM 12

A variety of vases were produced in ancient Egypt in both refined and unrefined materials. Many of them were found in tombs – like most of the examples in documents – as there they were protected physically and in favorable conditions of temperature and humidity.

Stone was freely available in the highlands of the desert and along the ridges that bordered the Nile Valley and the different varieties were generally used to hold oily or greasy substances. This example is made from calcite (mistakenly known as "Egyptian alabaster") which was one of the most common materials along with granite, diorite, quartzite, and basanite. The use of calcite was considered to add value to a vase and alabaster in particular would give an object a special luster.

This pot bears the double cartouche of Queen Hatshepsut, "the foremost of the nobles." The name of the king is often found engraved on pots, whether they were from the royal household or gifts to the pharaoh's functionaries as rewards, which confers each object with a certain gravity. (A.A.)

COW'S HEAD

PAINTED CEDARWOOD
HEIGHT 46 CM, MAX. WIDTH 45 CM
VALLEY OF THE KINGS; TOMB OF AMENHOTEP
EXCAVATION BY V. LORET (1898); EIGHTEENT
DYNASTY, REIGN OF AMENHOTEP II (1428-1397

ROOM 12

The head was part of the grave goods found in the tomb of pharaoh Amenhotep II that was discovered in 1898 by Victor Loret for the Egyptian Antiquities Service. The find was one of the most sensational discoveries in the Valley of the Kings as it brought to light seventeen other royal mummies stacked in two rooms to the side of the burial chamber. The body of Amenhotep II was found, still covered with flowers, in a yellow quartzite sarcophagus (probably not originally made for him) in the crypt.

Other funerary items contained in the tomb included fragments of a wooden chariot, statues of members of the royal family and gods, various articles of furniture, wooden models of boats, pots, fruit and flowers made from faïence, and items used for personal care and *shawabty* figures.

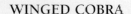

WINGED COBRA

PAINTED WOOD; HEIGHT 44 CM, LENGTH 65 CM, WIDTH
5 CM; VALLEY OF THE KINGS, TOMB OF AMENHOTEP II
(KV 35); EXCAVATION BY V. LORET (1898); EIGHTEENTH
DYNASTY, REIGN OF AMENHOTEP II (1428-1397 BC)

ROOM 12

A wooden cobra with a female head painted in bright colors and fixed to a double green and white base was one of the objects found among the grave goods of the pharaoh, Amenophis II. The sinuous body of the snake is transformed into a human to form a composite creature. The face, with black eyes, is framed by a blue wig and the chest is ornamented with a striped necklace.

The body is painted red and green on a yellow background. The wings, stretched forwards and fixed by tenons, are decorated with long blue feathers on a yellow background with touches of red paint at the tips.
(S.E.)

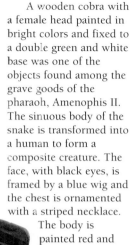

This head was carved from cedarwood imported from Lebanon. The animal has been given large horizontal ears, slightly curved horns, and large *udjat* eyes that identify the animal as the manifestation of a god.
(A.A.)

ANKH SIGN

FAÏENCE; HEIGHT 42 CM, WIDTH 21 CM
VALLEY OF THE KINGS, TOMB OF AMENHOTEP II
EXCAVATION BY V. LORET (1898); EIGHTEENTH
DYNASTY, REIGN OF AMENHOTEP II (1428-1397 BC)

ROOM 12

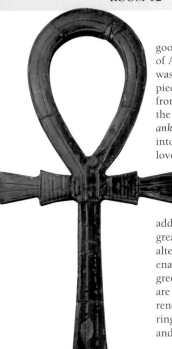

Among the grave goods found in the tomb of Amenhotep II, there was a turquoise colored piece of jewelry made from faïence representing the hieroglyph for life, *ankh*. Broken in antiquity into nine pieces, this lovely object has now been recomposed but still bears the marks on its surface. In addition, contact with a greasy material has altered the color of the enamel producing a greenish haze. Both faces are lightly engraved to render the surface of the ring, its horizontal arms and the leg of the *ankh* more vigorous. The poorly fired enamel contains some bubbles and slight cracking.

The sign of the *ankh* has been attributed with various meanings. The most commonly accepted considers it as the graphic representation of the upper part of a sandal with the ring at the top, in this case representing the tie that passes around the ankle. This hieroglyph is one of the most common on the monuments of ancient Egypt and was used to indicate "life, living"; it quickly took on a magical and apotropaic power. Similar pieces of jewelry were often placed in tombs to accompany the deceased on his journey to the Afterlife and to assure him of a safe existence for eternity.
(S.E.)

MIRROR WITH CASE

CASE: SYCAMORE AND IVORY; LENGTH 28 CM
MIRROR: BRONZE; L. 12.5 CM W. 11 CM
WEST THEBES, CACHETTE AT DEIR AL-
BAHARI (DVB 320); DISCOVERED BY
THE EGYPTIAN ANTIQUITIES SERVICE
(1881) TWENTY-FIRST DYNASTY,
PONTIFICATE AND REIGN OF PINUDJEM
I (END OF 2ND MILLENIUM BC)

ROOM 12

The sophisticated case containing a bronze mirror was found on the mummy of Queen Henuttauy, the wife of Pinudjem, the high priest of Amun-Ra, who lived during the Twenty-first Dynasty. The

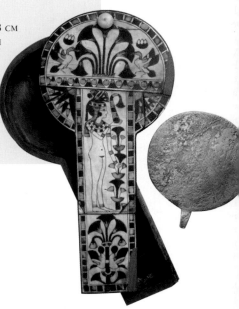

sarcophagus of the queen was placed with those of famous Egyptian pharaohs in the tomb of Inhapy, the consort of the pharaoh Ahmes. Her tomb was used to hide royal sarcophagi during an era when raids on the Theban necropolis were frequent.

The lid of the case is edged with a continuous geometric pattern and sumptuously decorated with inlays. The central panel shows a slender and naked young girl wearing jewelry and flowers on her head; she holds a branch with blossoms in one hand and a papyrus plant in the other. A stylized grove of papyrus plants with two ducks is represented beneath her feet. The same marshy setting is used in the circular part of the case where sheaves of papyrus are flanked by a pair of flying ducks and by nests filled with eggs. An ivory knob on the upper part of the lid was used to open the case. The original wooden handle of the bronze mirror has not survived.
(S.E.)

CASKET OF RAMESES IX

Wood and ivory; Height 21.5 cm, width 24 cm, length 22 cm; West Thebes, Cachette at Deir al-Bahari (DB 320); Official discovery by the Egyptian Antiquities Service (1881); Twentieth Dynasty Reign of Rameses IX (1126-1108 bc)

ROOM 12

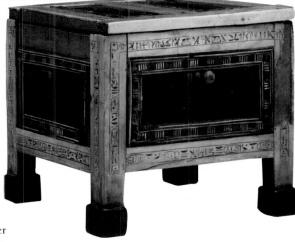

The box was found in 1881 by the Egyptian Antiquities Service in the Cachette at Deir al-Bahari (DB 320) which was the hiding place used to store the mummies of the royal families and high priests of Amun. In fact, the discovery was due to a well-known family of tomb-robbers who had placed a number of precious antiquities on the market, arousing the attention of the Egyptian authorities. The Cachette (DB 320) contained a number of other objects from the New Kingdom including a box made from sycamore that had belonged to Queen Hatshepsut.

This example is made of finely carved ivory with square feet that rest on a wooden base. The four sides each have a central panel made from wood edged with a frame of colored rectangles. A hieroglyphic inscription runs around the panel giving the full titles of pharaoh Rameses IX. The sliding lid is flat and decorated with two wooden rectangular panels like those on the sides. The box was closed by winding a string around a knob on the front of the box and attaching it to another knob (missing) on the lid.
(A.A.)

FUNERARY MASK FOR THE MUMMY OF A FOETUS

Cartonnage and gold leaf
Height 16 cm; Valley of the Kings (shaft 54)
Discovered by T.M. Davis (1907); Eighteenth Dynasty
Reign of Tutankhamun (1333-1323 bc)

ROOM 12

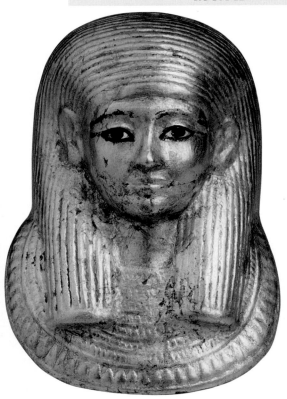

Discovered by Davis in 1907 inside shaft 54 in the Valley of the Kings, the small gilded *cartonnage* mask was originally made for one of the foetuses buried in the underground tomb of Tutankhamun but it was never used for that purpose. Its size is too small for the mummy for which it was meant, so it was instead placed in the entrance corridor to the tomb and, at a later time, moved to the shaft where it was found. The radiant, smiling face has exquisite childlike features framed by a three-part wig marked with parallel lines. The black pupils of the eyes are ringed with white within a black line that runs up to the temples parallel to the eyebrows. The chest is ornamented with a wide striped necklace with a drop-shaped motif that forms the edge of the mask.

The foetus for which the mask was made was found, with another foetus, inside a wooden box in the Treasure Room in Tutankhamun's tomb. Embalmed and buried in miniature mummy-shaped sarcophaguses, the two foetuses were perhaps the offspring of the young pharaoh and his wife Ankhesenamun.

The small mummy for which the gilded mask was made probably belonged to a female of between 7-9 months gestation who died at birth. Radiographic examinations tell us that the foetus suffered from certain congenital malformations, including spina bifida and scoliosis. The procedures used to mummify the foetus were the same as those practiced on adults; this is demonstrated by the cut made at the groin used to pass the bandages into the abdominal cavity. The wrapping of the foetus was very carefully performed with multiple layers of fabric and very fine linen.
(S.E.)

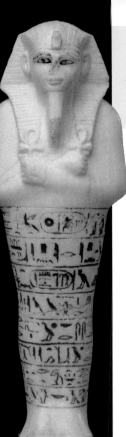

SHAWABTY OF AMENHOTEP II
ALABASTER; HEIGHT 22.5 CM
VALLEY OF THE KINGS; TOMB OF AMENHOTEP II
DISCOVERED BY V. LORET (1898); EIGHTEENTH DYNASTY,
REIGN OF AMENHOTEP II (1428-1397 BC)
ROOM 12

The statue was another of the grave goods found in the tomb of Amenhotep II (KV 35). This *shawabty* is made from dazzling white alabaster and has large, long eyes emphasized by black lines and eyebrows. The model represents a dead king wrapped in bandages with his arms crossed on his chest in the characteristic posture of male figures. The bandages cover all the body except for the hands that each hold an *ankh* symbol. The pharaoh wears the striped, rigid *nemes* headdress that falls onto his shoulders, and a false beard tied behind his ears: to complete the attributes of royalty, the uraeus serpent is fixed to his forehead.

The lower section of his body is completely covered with horizontal hieroglyphs, and the names of Amenhotep II can be read in the cartouches on the first and third lines. The text in the inscription is Chapter 6 of the *Book of the Dead* which asks the *shawabty* to work in place of the deceased in the world of the dead. An identical statue made from gray-green schist was found in the same tomb. (A.A.)

URAEUS SERPENT
BRONZE WITH GOLD ENCRUSTATIONS; HEIGHT 23 CM
VALLEY OF THE KINGS, TOMB 55 (KV 55)
EXCAVATION BY E.R. AYRTON ON BEHALF OF T.M. DAVIS (1907); EIGHTEENTH DYNASTY (1550-1075 BC)
ROOM 12

The uraeus serpent was part of the grave goods found in Tomb 55, the most debated of all the tombs found in the Valley of the Kings. The discovery was published in 1910 as being of the "Tomb of Queen Tiy" but that description is still unproven as is identification of the mummy found in a wooden sarcophagus.

One of the various hypotheses is that the tomb belonged to the "heretic" pharaoh Amenhotep IV (Akhenaten).

The uraeus in question is made from bronze and has gold encrustations that form the scales of the serpent. Two gilded cartouches below the head bear the name of Aten. (A.A.)

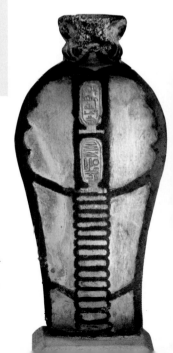

SHAWABTY BELONGING TO RAMESES VI
PAINTED WOOD; HEIGHT 26 CM
VALLEY OF THE KINGS
TWENTIETH DYNASTY, REIGN OF RAMESES VI (1143-1135 BC)

ROOM 12

The exact location in which this funerary statue was found is unknown, although it is established as having belonged to the tomb of Rameses VI (KV 9). The tomb originally also held the mummy of Rameses V who had begun its construction, but the two bodies were found hidden in the tomb of Amenhotep II (KV 35)

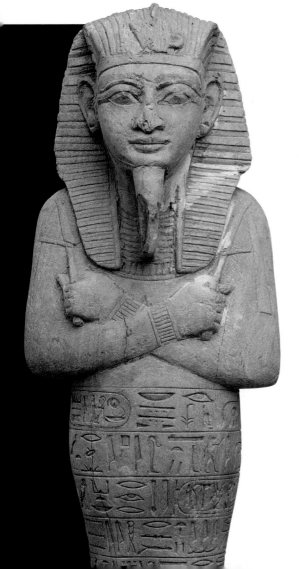

where they had been moved. Almost all the grave goods had been removed from tomb KV 9, leaving only parts of the innermost mummy-shaped sarcophagus of Rameses VI. A fragmentary text (the Mayer B papyrus) literally provides an account of the theft of the metal objects in the tomb by one of those involved.

Made from wood, the carefully carved details of the figure were highlighted by the use of color, some of which still remains. The pharaoh's round face is framed by the *nemes* headdress and the uraeus serpent, the false beard, and a broad necklace that covers his chest; the lower part of the mummy's legs, however, has been damaged. The only part of the body uncovered is the arms crossed on the chest and the hands that grasps two ploughs, a typical attribute of an *shawabty*.

As stated in Chapter 6 of the *Book of the Dead* engraved on the lower section of the figure's body, the *shawabty* was obliged to "answer" the call of the deceased and work in his place in the fields of the Afterlife. (A.A.)

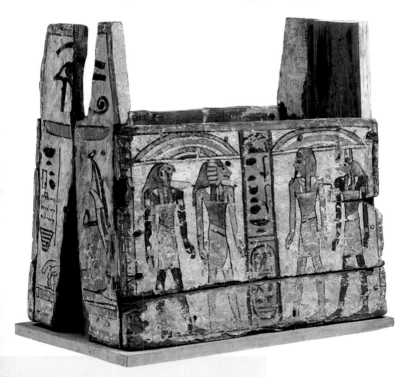

SHAWABTY CONTAINER OF HENUTTAUY

PAINTED WOOD; HEIGHT 58 CM, WIDTH 34 CM
CACHETTE AT DEIR AL-BAHARI (DB 320); OFFICIAL
DISCOVERY BY THE EGYPTIAN ANTIQUITIES SERVICE (1881)
TWENTY-FIRST DYNASTY (1075–945 BC)

ROOM 12

This *shawabty* case made from painted wood is richly decorated on all sides with images of the guardian deities from the afterlife who generally appear on grave goods: there are the four sons of Horus (standing), and the goddesses Isis and Nephthys kneeling on the shorter sides as they symbolically weep at the death bed of the god Osiris. The vertical inscription in the center of the long side gives the name of the "royal daughter, royal wife, Lady of the Two Lands, Osiris Henuttauy-devotee-of-Hathor."

Henuttauy was a very common name during the Third Intermediate Period and several women of standing with this name are known to have lived at that time. The Henuttauy in question was a queen, probably the daughter of King Smendes (1075–1049 BC), and wife of the High Priest Pinudjem I. It was owing to Pinudjem I and his great devotion that many of the royal mummies from the Valley of the Kings were preserved as, for fear of tomb robbers during that period of internal troubles

and economic crisis, Pinudjem had all the mummies transferred to a single tomb at Deir al-Bahari (DB 320). It was officially discovered in 1881, though in practice it had been found some years earlier by a well-known tomb robber, Abd al-Rassul Ahmed. It is still in doubt whether the mummies were moved directly to DB 320 or first stored in another tomb (WN A?) and then moved to DB 320 by the High Priest Pinudjem II (Twenty-second Dynasty).

The two side rooms in DB 320 contained over 3700 funerary statues and more than 20 boxes containing wooden *shawabty* lined with stucco and painted. Of these, one was of Henuttauy and another of her husband Pinudjem I. (A.A.)

SHAWABTY CONTAINER OF KHONSU

WOOD LINED WITH STUCCO AND PAINTED; HEIGHT 35.6 CM,
WIDTH 12.5 CM, LENGTH 20 CM; DEIR AL-MEDINA,
TOMB OF SENNEDJEM; EXCAVATION BY THE EGYPTIAN
ANTIQUITIES SERVICE (1886); NINETEENTH DYNASTY
REIGN OF RAMESES II (1279-1212 BC)

ROOM 17

The small funerary statues that were supposed to work in place of the deceased in the Afterlife were known as *shawabty* ("those who respond") as it was their duty to answer the summons when called by their master. The statues were placed inside wooden boxes with painted sides.

Khonsu was a "servant in the House of Truth" and lived and worked in Deir al-Medina which was the residential village for the builders and craftsmen that worked on the royal tombs in the Valley of the Kings.

Part of his grave goods consisted of a box made to hold *shawabty*. The double vault top is bordered by two vertical panels and the four sides are decorated with brightly painted scenes representing Khonsu alive and as a mummy. On one side, Khonsu is seated next to his wife, both of whom wear elegant everyday clothes and wigs crowned with a cone of perfumed wax. On the other side, the mummy of the deceased is being purified by his daughter Nakhtmut as part of the funerary ceremony. The standing mummy of Khonsu appears on both the short sides of the box. Short hieroglyphic inscriptions give the name and titles of the deceased and frame the scenes. (S.E.)

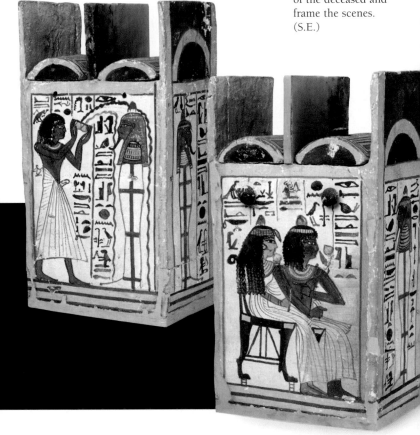

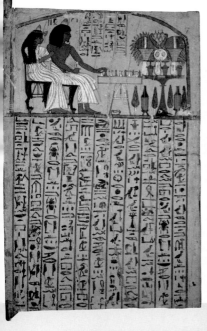

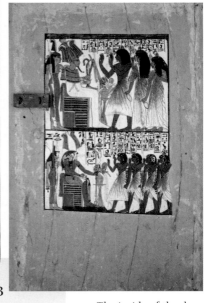

DOOR OF THE TOMB OF SENNEDJEM

WOOD LINED WITH STUCCO AND PAINTED
HEIGHT 135 CM, WIDTH 117 CM; DEIR AL-MEDINA
TOMB OF SENNEDJEM; EXCAVATION BY THE EGYPTIAN
ANTIQUITIES SERVICE (1886); NINETEENTH DYNASTY
REIGN OF RAMESES II (1279-1212 BC)

ROOM 17

During excavation work by G. Maspero in the rock necropolis of Deir al-Medina, he came across the untouched tomb of Sennedjem, one of the many craftsmen that worked on the construction of the magnificent royal underground tombs in the Valley of the Kings. Entrance to the burial chamber at the bottom of a shaft was closed off by this small wooden door that still bears the intact seal of the Theban necropolis. The seal displays the image of the god-jackal Anubis above nine prisoners. The warm colors and the themes of life beyond the tomb taken from the figurative images in the *Book of the Dead* elegantly unite the decoration of the burial chamber and the door.

The outside of the door shows Sennedjem with his wife and daughter adoring Osiris and the goddess Maat; the god is seated on the throne with the *atef* tiara, the royal scepters and the *uas* staff green like his face and hands to symbolize the power of Osiris over the eternal cycles of natural growth. In the lower scene, the deceased appears once more with his children as he pays homage to the syncretistic form of Ptah-Sokar-Osiris and to Isis.

The inside of the door shows Sennedjem and his wife Iyneferty seated below a pavilion of reeds. Both wear wigs crowned with a cone of aromatic grass and, in the woman's case, also by lotus buds whose divine perfume gave eternal life. Sennedjem is playing *senet*, a popular game that had strong symbolism in a funerary context: the deceased is betting the destiny of his spirit, if he wins, it will survive.

The scene ends with a table heaped with offerings and goods of all kinds for Sennedjem's sustenance.

A long inscription below gives extracts of the *Book of the Dead*. The first is a prayer to the gods of eternity not to close the door in the face of the deceased (Chapter 72) and the second sanctions the wish of the spirit to play *senet* in the Afterlife (Chapter 17).
(M.S.C.)

437

SARCOPHAGUS OF THE LADY ASET

WOOD COVERED WITH CLOTH, LINED WITH STUCCO AND
VARNISHED; HEIGHT 193.5 CM, WIDTH 47 CM, DEPTH
31.18 CM; DEIR AL-MEDINA, TOMB OF SENNEDJEM
EXCAVATION BY THE EGYPTIAN ANTIQUITIES SERVICE
(1886); NINETEENTH DYNASTY, REIGN OF RAMESES II
(1279-1212 BC)

ROOM 17

The intact tomb of the craftsman Sennedjem contained not just a valuable set of grave goods (now displayed in various museums around the world) but also the sarcophaguses of several members of his family.

Aset was the wife of Sennedjem's son, Khabekhent, who was also a craftsman and the owner of Tomb no.2 in the same necropolis. Aset had two anthropomorphic sarcophaguses: an outer one in the standard shape of a mummy, and the middle one – shown in the photograph – that housed an embalmed body protected by a full-length *plastron*. The layout of the decorations and choice of colors on this sarcophagus was decided by their relative contrasts.

Aset's body was wrapped in a pleated tunic of purest white linen and was represented as though she were still living, rather than as a mummy, following the naturalistic philosophy of the Amarna Period. Sprays of flowered ivy lay on the tunic bringing color and sinuous lines in harmony with the symmetry of the background.

The simplicity of the tunic contrasts with the opulence of the jewels that Aset wears on her fingers, arms, and ears. The large *usekh* necklace that covers her breasts, turning them into decorative elements, is especially splendid. The band of stylized plant motifs around the braided wig includes the lotus flower whose sweet perfume bestowed the gift of eternity.
(M.S.C.)

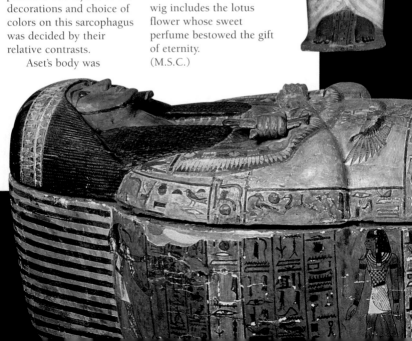

SARCOPHAGUS OF SENNEDJEM

WOOD LINED WITH STUCCO, PAINTED AND VARNISHED
HEIGHT 184.5 CM, MAX. WIDTH 50 CM, DEPTH 31 CM
DEIR AL-MEDINA, TOMB OF SENNEDJEM
EXCAVATION BY THE EGYPTIAN ANTIQUITIES SERVICE (1886)
NINETEENTH DYNASTY, REIGN OF RAMESES II (1279-1212 BC)

ROOM 17

Like all "servants in the Place of Truth" (the workers that worked on the tombs in the Valley of the Kings), Sennedjem was also buried in the necropolis next to the village of Deir al-Medina.

The photograph shows the outer of the two sarcophaguses in which he was buried. It is shaped like a tightly bandaged mummy who holds the *tit* and *djed* emblems in his hands, though the second has been damaged at the top.

Sennedjem's typical Ramessid wig is adorned by a band of pointed leaves and fruits and the protective figure of Nephthys who corresponds with Isis, below Sennedjem's feet. The *usekh* necklace that covers the deceased's chest is embellished with a parure with the image of the sacred blue lotus flower at either end. Below, the winged goddess of the sky, Nut, kneels at the start of the long central inscription that invokes her name. The squares created by the crossing of the bands are the setting for the symmetrical figures of Anubis on his shrine, a goddess on the *shen* ring, and the goddess of the sycamore tree who offers Sennedjem a drink. Kneeling with his hands outstretched to take the precious liquid, Sennedjem is portrayed with black hair on one side and white hair on the other (M.S.C.)

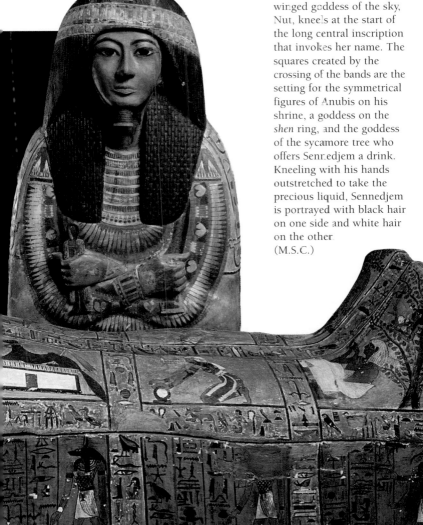

SARCOPHAGUS BELONGING TO KHONSU

WOOD LINED WITH STUCCO AND PAINTED
HEIGHT 125 CM, WIDTH 98 CM, LENGTH 262 CM
DEIR AL-MEDINA, TOMB OF SENNEDJEM EXCAVATION BY
THE EGYPTIAN ANTIQUITIES SERVICE (1886); NINETEENTH
DYNASTY, REIGN OF RAMESES II (1279-1212 BC)

ROOM 17

Deir el-Medina was the village inhabited by workers who built the funerary tombs and temples of the kings and queens of the New Kingdom. It was here that Maspero came across an unentered tomb in 1886 that had been built for Sennedjem (TT 1), one of the workers in the Valley of the Kings. The tomb contained twenty bodies of which nine were perfectly preserved inside their sarcophaguses. One of these was Khonsu, the son of Sennedjem, who was also a "servant in the Place of Truth," as the village was called in ancient times.

Khonsu's body lay inside two mummy-shaped sarcophaguses after being transported into the tomb on a sled in another sarcophagus (shown in the photograph) which was then left in a corner. This superb item is evidence of the ability of this small community to re-use themes and motifs that they employed on a daily basis in royal funerary complexes for their own use. The decoration revolves principally around the text of Chapter 17 of the *Book of the Dead* and the still brightly colored pictorial images relating to it. One scene in particular on one of the long sides of the sarcophagus shows Anubis preparing the body of the deceased-Osiris on his death bed, veiled by the god's wife, Isis, and her sister, Nephthys. Chapter 17 and its related illustrations cover the two longer sides of the sarcophagus while two pairs of guardian goddesses watch over the body on the shorter sides.
(A.A.)

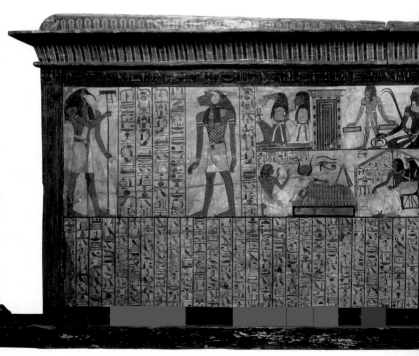

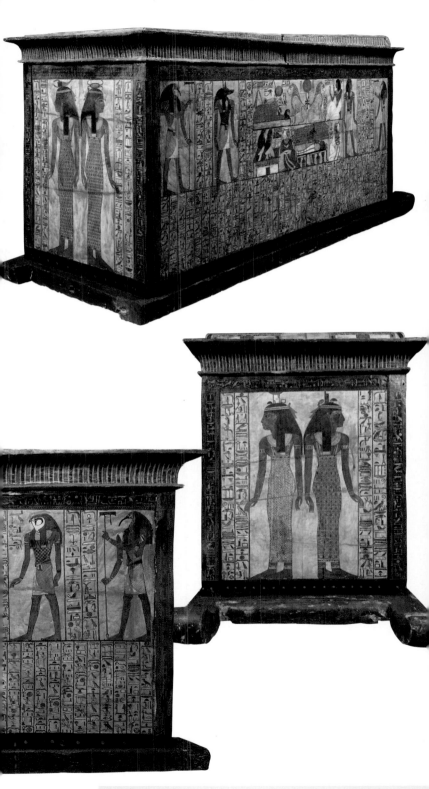

SHAWABTY OF AMENHOTEP

Painted limestone; Height 29 cm
West Thebes, Sheikh Abd al-Qurna
Excavation by the Metropolitan Museum
of Art (1936);
Eighteenth Dynasty (1550-1291 bc)

ROOM 22

The inscription on the central column of this little statue states that it belonged to the mummy of Amenhotep. The text of the column on the right – "from his brother Senu who keeps his name alive" – can be understood from the fact that the funerary cult of Amenhotep was entrusted to his brother who was responsible for keeping the memory of the pharaoh alive after his death.

The body of the *shawabty*, symbolically white, is wrapped in linen bandages from which only the hands crossed on the figure's chest emerge. The false beard and striped wig are blue.
(A.A.)

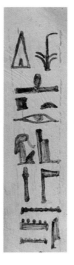

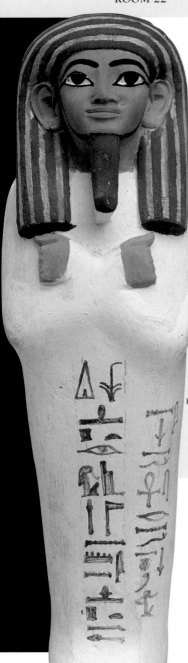

NAOS WITH FALCON

Wood lined with stucco and painted
height 69.5 cm, length 27 cm, width 26.5 cm
Provenance unknown
Roman Period (1st-2nd century ad)

ROOM 22

Since earliest Egyptian history the falcon was believed to be a sacred bird connected with the world of the gods. Horus, the son of Isis and Osiris, was the god whose effigy was in the form of a falcon but the bird was also identified with the deities Ra, Montu, and Sokar. As a sacred creature, the falcon was an object of worship throughout Egypt during the Late Period when it was customary to mummify falcons after their death and to bury them in specially reserved necropolises.

The wooden *naos* that was to hold the mummified body of the falcon has been given the form of a temple with a projecting cornice. The walls taper as they rise and are covered by differently colored designs in which

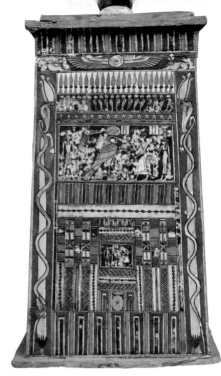

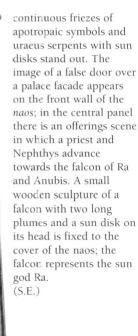

continuous friezes of apotropaic symbols and uraeus serpents with sun disks stand out. The image of a false door over a palace facade appears on the front wall of the *naos*; in the central panel there is an offerings scene in which a priest and Nephthys advance towards the falcon of Ra and Anubis. A small wooden sculpture of a falcon with two long plumes and a sun disk on its head is fixed to the cover of the *naos*; the falcon represents the sun god Ra.
(S.E.)

SCARAB

GLASS PASTE, WOOD, GOLD LEAF
LENGTH 11 CM, WIDTH 6.5 CM
PROVENANCE UNKNOWN
GRECO-ROMAN PERIOD (332 BC - 312 AC)

ROOM 22

This lovely glass paste scarab fixed to a gilded wooden base represents a dung beetle (*Scarabaeus sacer*) and was part of a category of jewels made from faïence, semi-precious stones, and glass paste that were very common in ancient Egypt because they were believed to ward off evil.

The female beetle, the behaviour of which the Egyptians used to study, uses her legs to roll a ball of dung in which she deposits her eggs. The creation of life within the tiny balls of dung was considered miraculous and the scarab was treated as the symbol of new life. The term used by the Egyptians to define the insect was *kheper*, similar in sound to the verb *kheperer*, "to be born, come into existence, become." Scarabs were also associated with Khepri, the sun god of the daytime, who was reborn each morning and crossed the sky in the form of a disk; this daily journey was considered analogous to the rolling of the dung-ball by the insect's legs.

Jewels in the form of a scarab bearing the name of a functionary or a sovereign were used from as early as the Middle Kingdom as seals to protect documents, amphoras, and bolts from being broken open. The court used to issue scarabs on special historical events to commemorate royal weddings, military victories, and inauguration ceremonies.

Egyptians made wide use of "heart scarabs" in a funerary context which were placed on the chest of the mummy. Their flat surface was decorated with a hieroglyphic inscription of Chapter 30 of the *Book of the Dead* in which the deceased entreated his heart not to testify against him during the gods' judgement of the individual (the "weighing of the soul"). (S.E.)

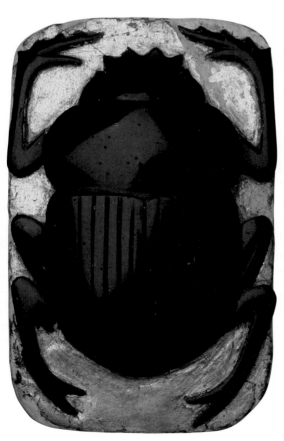

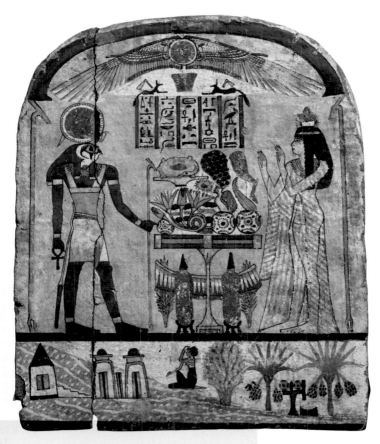

STELA OF DJEDDJEHUTYIUANKH

WOOD COVERED WITH STUCCO AND PAINTED
HEIGHT 27.6 CM, WIDTH 23 CM, THICKNESS 2.7 CM
DEIR EL-BAHARI
TWENTY-SECOND DYNASTY (945-718 BC)

ROOM 22

Some of the funerary stelae found in the necropolis of Thebes stand out for the originality of their contents, the fresh and lively style of the composition and for the colors that have maintained their original beauty. One of these stelae is divided into two panels decorated with completely different subjects. The lower section is decorated with an unusual landscape set among the mountains of the necropolis close to the desert. A woman in mourning tears her hair as she kneels before some buildings. one of which is a funeral chapel crowned by a pyramidion. Behind her stand a sycamore, two date palms, and a table loaded with offerings for the deceased. The upper, and larger, part of the stela is more conventional: the deceased, wrapped in a transparent garment, is shown before an offerings table as she pays homage to the god Ra-Horakhty. A winged sun disk above the scene is dominated by the heavenly vault, supported by *uas* scepters at the sides of the composition, and two jackals that symbolize the transition to the life beyond the grave. The brief hieroglyphic inscription above mentions the name of the owner of the stela.
(S.E.)

MODEL OF A LIVESTOCK CENSUS

Painted wood; Height 55 cm, width 72 cm
length 173 cm; Deir al-Bahari, Tomb of Meketra
Excavation by the Metropolitan Museum of Art
(1919-1920); Late Eleventh - early Twelfth
Dynasty, (late 3rd-early 2nd millennium bc)

ROOM 27

Narrative sculpture and lively, brightly colored scenes reach their apex in this model found in the tomb of Meketra in which

Meketra himself is taking a census of his animals. Men and animals move around in a space that represents the courtyard of a

country house. The gestures and poses of the figures, each performing his assigned task, infuse the composition with life and realism. The oxen are dappled different colors and file before a

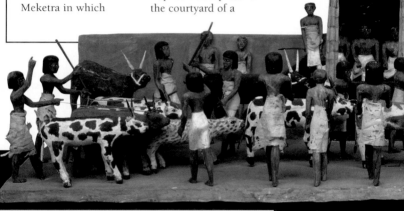

CANOPIC VASES OF INEPUHOTEP

Limestone and painted wood; Height 34 cm,
diameter 11 cm; Saqqara Necropolis to the
north of Teti's Pyramid; Excavation by the
Egyptian Antiquities Service (1914), Start of the
Twelfth Dynasty (start of the 2nd millennium bc)

ROOM 27

A Middle Kingdom tomb belonging to Inepuhotep and Usermut was discovered near the pyramid of the pharaoh Teti at Saqqara. Among the grave goods found in the double tomb were four canopic vases that held Inepuhotep's internal organs extracted during the embalming process. The vases were

placed in a wooden container that bears the name of the owner on the sides: Inepu.

The first canopic vases, made from limestone or wood, appeared during the Old Kingdom. They were closed with simple rounded caps that were developed into images of human heads around

the start of the First Intermediate Period; the human heads were associated with the four sons of Horus whose duty was to guard the four organs: Amset, Hapi, Duamutef, and Qebehsenuf were respectively the guardian spirits of the liver, lungs, stomach, and intestines. It was only toward the end of the Nineteenth Dynasty that each of the four canopic vases was given a top that reproduced the features of the corresponding god. Amset was the only one to retain a human head; Hapi was given the head of a baboon, colonnaded pavilion where Meketra, his son and four scribes are seated as they take a census of the animals on a papyrus stretched out on their knees. The overseer bows with respect before his master while other men stand around with long staffs in their hands ensuring everything happens correctly. The animals are pushed with sticks and led by ropes knotted around their horns. All the figures in the scene are bare-chested and wear a white skirt which, in some cases, is formed by a piece of cloth knotted at the waist. (S.E.)

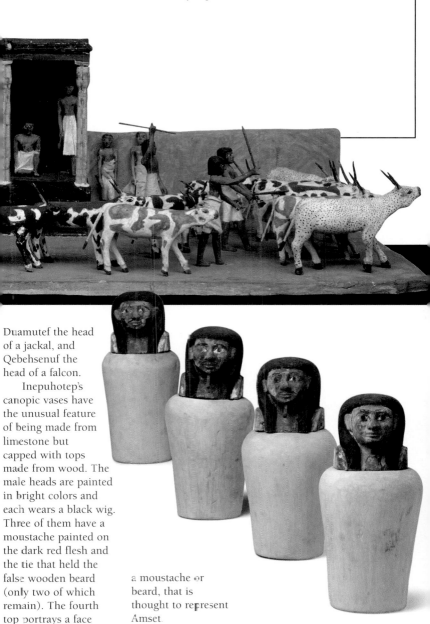

Duamutef the head of a jackal, and Qebehsenuf the head of a falcon.

Inepuhotep's canopic vases have the unusual feature of being made from limestone but capped with tops made from wood. The male heads are painted in bright colors and each wears a black wig. Three of them have a moustache painted on the dark red flesh and the tie that held the false wooden beard (only two of which remain). The fourth top portrays a face colored ocher, without a moustache or beard, that is thought to represent Amset. (S.E.)

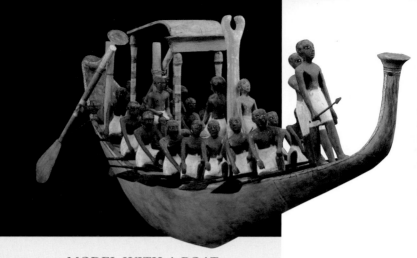

MODEL WITH A BOAT

PAINTED WOOD; HEIGHT 61 CM, WIDTH 25 CM,
LENGTH 139 CM; DEIR AL-BAHARI, TOMB OF MEKETRA
EXCAVATION BY THE METROPOLITAN MUSEUM OF ART
(1919-1920); LATE ELEVENTH - EARLY TWELFTH
DYNASTY, (LATE 3RD-EARLY 2ND MILLENNIUM BC)

ROOM 27

The many wooden models found in the tomb of chancellor Meketra represent scenes such as the inspection of animals, weavers' and carpenters' workshops, and boats sailing on the Nile. This curious and realistic miniature world was made to accompany the deceased on his journey beyond the tomb with the purpose of serving him in his daily needs in the Afterlife. It

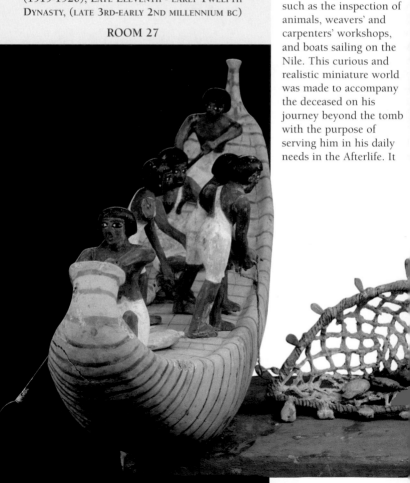

s an eloquent example of the concept of the "small world," a distinctive feature of the Far East endowed with a philosophical value that seems to have been prefigured in the culture of ancient Egypt. Some of the model boats were to be used for fishing, others to transport Meketra either alone or with members of his family.

The ends of one of the boats are shaped like papyrus flowers; it has a canopy supported by four columns and covered by a sloping roof, called per-ur, like the one on the ancient temple in Hierakonpolis. Meketra sits with dignity below the canopy. A row of oarsmen lines each side of the boat and two large paddles are fixed to poles near the stern. The faces of all the

figures have been given large painted eyes that emphasize the attempt to imbue the scene with realism.
(S.E.)

MODEL WITH A FISHING SCENE

PAINTED WOOD; HEIGHT 31.5 CM, WIDTH 62 CM, LENGTH 90 CM; DEIR AL-BAHARI, TOMB OF MEKETRA EXCAVATION BY THE METROPOLITAN MUSEUM OF NEW YORK (1919-1920); LATE ELEVENTH - EARLY TWELFTH DYNASTY, (LATE 3RD-EARLY 2ND MILLENNIUM BC)

ROOM 27

The *serdab* of Meketra's tomb contained twenty-five wooden models of men and women at various daily tasks typical of life along the Nile. One vivid and animated scene shows fishermen on board two green-hulled boats used on the river in ancient times; the boats are made from strips of rushes tied with cords. Two squatting oarsmen, one in the bow and one in the stern, propel the boats while other men, dressed in white trousers held up by a single brace that crosses the chest, are busy freeing fish from the net slung between the two boats. The net is weighed down at the sides by wooden weights and dragged with the aid of ropes held by the two sets of fishermen.

The bright polychrome scene is made vivid by the realism of the portrayals and faithfully reproduces an activity that took place daily on the Nile. Fish were an important element of the ancient Egyptian diet. The entire composition is fixed to a wooden board painted green.
(S.E.)

MODEL OF WEAVERS AT WORK

PAINTED WOOD; H. 25 CM, W. 42 CM, L. 93 CM; DEIR AL-
BAHARI, TOMB OF MEKETRA; EXCAVATION BY THE
METROPOLITAN MUSEUM OF ART (1919-1920)
LATE ELEVENTH - EARLY TWELFTH DYNASTY,
(LATE 3RD-EARLY 2ND MILLENNIUM BC)

ROOM 27

Weaving was one of Egyptian women's main activities. Use of the first, simple horizontal loom combined with an exceptional mastery of the required skills resulted in spinners and weavers producing a huge quantity of cloths that were turned into clothes, bed-linen, funerary shrouds, etc. Egyptian cloth was renowned for its high quality and, besides being used by the court of the pharaoh, it was exported to all countries in the Near East.

This spontaneous and realistic model shows the frenetic activity of a group of women at work weaving. The room, with the door half open, is dominated by the two looms resting on the floor around which the weavers are crouching. The weavers are shown at the moment that they roll the yarn around the spindles. All the women have been painted with dark skin, they have long black hair and wear white garments held up by a single shoulder strap that crosses the chest diagonally. The painted dress on some of the women is covered by a piece of cloth knotted roughly around their bodies.
(S.E.)

MODEL OF A HOUSE AND GARDEN

PAINTED WOOD; H. 43 CM, W. 40 CM, L. 87 CM
DEIR AL-BAHARI, TOMB OF MEKETRA; EXCAVATION BY THE
METROPOLITAN MUSEUM OF ART (1919-1920)
LATE ELEVENTH - EARLY TWELFTH DYNASTY,
(LATE 3RD-EARLY 2ND MILLENNIUM BC)

ROOM 27

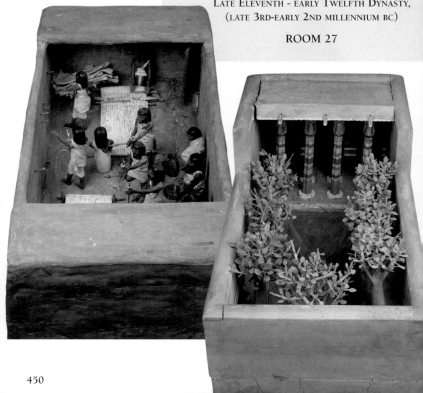

Sets of grave goods containing model houses representing the abodes of ancient Egyptians were common. Placed inside tombs to accompany the deceased to the Afterlife, the miniature models provide valuable information on how such buildings were constructed as, being made from perishable materials like adobe, wood, and rushes, none have survived to the modern day. The style and size of a house would vary depending on the social status of its owner. Modest houses of just a few rooms stood next to luxury two-floor constructions. Roofs were flat and covered with light materials thick enough to keep the sunlight out. Often the building was surrounded by an open area of greenery: a simple vegetable garden or perhaps a large garden with palms and sycamores around a small pool that helped to cool the area.

This model is of an opulent home with a portico supported by two rows of four polychrome columns decorated with lotus flower capitals. The colors are as bright as when they were painted even on the walls of the house. Motifs suggest ancient mattings made from vegetable fibers. The luxuriant garden outside the colonnade is embellished by seven realistic leafy sycamore trees planted around a central pool of water painted blue. The walls of the house and the wall of the garden use wooden panels to reproduce the mud bricks and dried straw used in reality. The vivid colors and precision of the details confer an extraordinary sense of realism on the model as a whole.

(S.E.)

CARPENTRY WORKSHOP

PAINTED WOOD; H. 26 CM, W. 52 CM, L. 93 CM;
DEIR AL-BAHARI, TOMB OF MEKETRA;
EXCAVATION BY THE METROPOLITAN MUSEUM
OF ART (1919-1920); LATE ELEVENTH -
EARLY TWELFTH DYNASTY,
(LATE 3RD-EARLY 2ND MILLENNIUM BC)

ROOM 27

This wooden model was found in the tomb of Meketra with other miniature representations of various activities.

The model depicts intense activity inside a carpentry workshop. Several woodworkers animate the scene: one saws a panel attached to a central pole, others smooth or put the final touches to panels already cut, and one creates the mortices necessary to assemble the pieces of wood with a hammer and chisel. A group of men are gathered around a fire in the corner of the room as they forge the worn surfaces of various tools.

The workshop also contains a large chest painted white that was closed with a cord and a clay seal when the object was discovered. The chest was found to contain the workers' spare tools: axes, blades, chisels, drills, and saws.

The workers – bald or wearing black wigs – are shown bare-chested and dressed in a simple white skirt.

(S.E.)

MODEL OF A SAILING BOAT

PAINTED WOOD; LENGTH 124 CM; DEIR AL-BAHARI
TOMB OF MEKETRA; EXCAVATION BY THE METROPOLITAN
MUSEUM OF ART (1919-1920); LATE ELEVENTH -
EARLY TWELFTH DYNASTY,
(LATE 3RD-EARLY 2ND MILLENNIUM BC)

ROOM 27

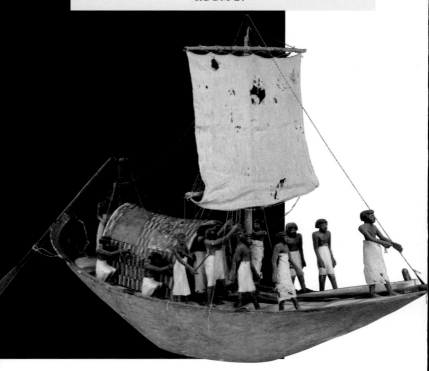

The tomb of Meketra, the chancellor of pharaohs Mentuhotep II and III, contained an extraordinary series of wooden models created to accompany the deceased in the Afterlife that was believed to be similar to terrestrial life in terms of requirements and rhythms. Around the end of the First Intermediate Period, wall paintings in tombs that had previously reproduced scenes of daily life began to be substituted by highly realistic miniature scenes almost childlike in their spontaneity. The models recreated scenes of war, navigation, and domestic and agricultural work with unusual faithfulness to detail.

The boat found in Meketra's tomb is filled with men at work dressed in a long white skirt, either painted or created using a piece of fabric similar to that used to make the sail. Another group of men is busy pulling on the ropes. The sailors perform their duties following the instructions of the bald-headed captain who gives his orders with a staff. The cabin was reserved for Meketra; it was covered with matting and decorated on the outside with painted shields. (S.E.)

FUNERARY MASK

WOOD LINED WITH STUCCO AND PAINTED
HEIGHT 50 CM
PROVENANCE UNKNOWN
MIDDLE KINGDOM (1994-1650 BC)

ROOM 27

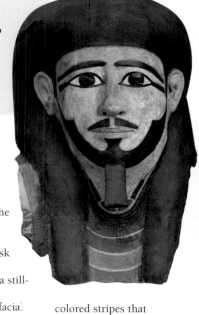

Funerary masks made from *cartonnage* (linen soaked in stucco and painted) began to appear in Egypt from the start of the First Intermediate Period. Manufactured to resemble the features of the deceased, they were placed on the mummies to perpetuate their identity. This mask from the Middle Kingdom shows a still-young man with brightly colored facial features. He wears a black wig and has both a beard and moustache. He wears a broad necklace with multi-colored stripes that has a thin chain at the top threaded with two pairs of red and black beads.
(S.E.)

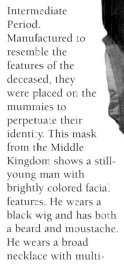

OFFERINGS' BEARER

PAINTED WOOD; HEIGHT 123 CM; DEIR AL-BAHARI
TOMB OF MEKETRA; EXCAVATION BY THE METROPOLITAN
MUSEUM OF ART (1919-1920); LATE ELEVENTH - EARLY
TWELFTH DYNASTY, (LATE 3RD-EARLY 2ND MILLENNIUM BC)

ROOM 27

This offerings' bearer found in the tomb of Meketra radiates a sense of sophistication and elegance that is rarely found in funerary models. The slim woman advances carrying a wicker basket that contains four wine containers on her head, and clutching a duck by the wings in her right hand. Her sinuous body is emphasized by a long, tight-fitting garment held up by two large shoulder pieces and adorned by polychrome beads. The bearer also wears jewelry: a necklace, bracelets, and anklets in alternating stripes the same colors as the rest of the sculpture.
(S.E.)

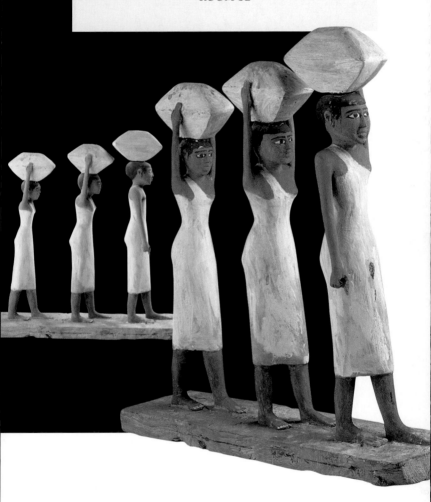

THREE BEARERS OF OFFERINGS

Painted wood; Height 59 cm, length 56 cm
Meir, Tomb of Niankhpepy the Black
Excavation by the
Egyptian Antiquities Service (1894)
Sixth Dynasty, Reign of Pepy I (2289-2255 bc)

ROOM 32

The three women are dressed in the same manner and balance large containers on their heads with their hands. The leader differs from the other two by the position of her arms and consequently breaks the symmetry of the three figures together. There was a purpose in representing three women as three was synonymous with the concept of "plural" to ancient Egyptians. The height of the bearers decreases from the leader to the woman at the back in an extraordinary use of perspective, either to give the idea of an approaching procession or t represent three separate moments of the advance of the same figure. (S.E.)

STATUE OF A MAN HOEING

Painted wood; Height 29 cm
**Meir, Tomb of Niankhpepy the Black; Excavation by
the Egyptian Antiquities Service (1894)**
Sixth Dynasty, Reign of Pepy I (2289-2255 bc)

ROOM 32

One of the most realistic of the small statues from the tomb of the governor, Niankhpepi "the Black," shows a man working in the fields with a hoe. The long slender figure of the man was created without too much attention being paid to details, but it is imbued with an extraordinary sense of movement. With his back bent, the man is shown driving the hoe into the muddy earth in which his feet are realistically sinking. The style and conception of the statue are removed from those of the previous era which were dominated by a rigid formalism that had little to do with reality.
(S.E.)

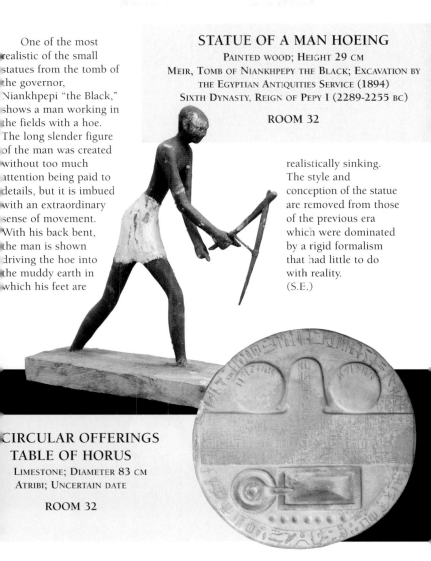

CIRCULAR OFFERINGS TABLE OF HORUS

Limestone; Diameter 83 cm
Atribi; Uncertain date

ROOM 32

The table is attributed to Horus, who was the Head Prophet of the god Khenty-Khety in the city of Atribi. The table is decorated in every part: the hieroglyph *hetep* ("offering") lies in the center with two loaves above and jug and basin for libations below. Above the horizontal sign *hetep* is the list of the offerings which, combined with the two loaves, the jug, and the upper part of the *hetep* sign, creates the funerary offerings formula for the *ka* of Horus. An inscription of all Horus' titles runs around the table edge.

The most interesting decoration is the strip that runs around the circumference of the table which contains four scenes in which the deceased is seated at the funeral table. Unfortunately, the poor condition of the object means that it is difficult to interpret the decoration but comparison with the table of Mentuemhat (CGT 22054 in Turin) may prove useful. The two are of the same typology, have same decoration on the upper surface, and share a detailed series of scenes and inscriptions. The dating of Horus' table is uncertain but comparison with that in Turin and other elements suggest it is from the Late Period.
(A.A.)

Many wooden or limestone models found in tombs from the Old Kingdom onwards represent men and women performing various tasks for the benefit of the deceased. The images of servants, once painted on tomb walls, were materialized in small, full relief, polychrome models which, though perfunctorily manufactured, were still endowed with a fair degree of realism. The production of this sort of tomb object evolved further

MODEL SHOWING THE PREPARATION OF BREAD AND BEER

PAINTED WOOD; HEIGHT 35 CM, LENGTH 53 CM
MEIR, TOMB OF NIANKHPEPY II THE BLACK
EXCAVATION BY THE EGYPTIAN ANTIQUITIES SERVICE (1894)
SIXTH DYNASTY, REIGN OF PEPY I (2289-2255 BC)

ROOM 32

MODEL OF A WOMAN STEEPING AND ANOTHER POKING A FIRE

PAINTED WOOD; LENGTH 60 CM; MEIR, TOMB OF NIANKHPEPY II THE BLACK; EXCAVATION BY THE EGYPTIAN ANTIQUITIES SERVICE (1894)
SIXTH DYNASTY, REIGN OF PEPY I (2289-2255 BC)

ROOM 32

during the First Intermediate Period when more complex and varied scenes appeared.

The preparation of bread and beer, both basic elements of the ancient Egyptian diet, was one of the commonest three-dimensional representations. Darkly colored men dressed in white skirts are shown stirring fermenting beer or preparing the flour or barley for bread. The bread mix consisted of flour, milk, and various ingredients to bestow flavor, and was placed in preheated terracotta containers to bake it. Beer was obtained by crumbling barley and, after briefly being cooked, by steeping it in sugared water. (S.E.)

MODEL OF A WOMAN
POKING THE FIRE

PAINTED WOOD; LENGTH 30.5 CM
MEIR, TOMB OF NIANKHPEPY II THE BLACK
EXCAVATION BY THE EGYPTIAN ANTIQUITIES SERVICE (1894)
SIXTH DYNASTY, REIGN OF PEPY I (2289-2255 BC)

ROOM 32

Niankhpepi (known as "the Black") was governor of the 14th *nome* of Upper Egypt at the time of the last pharaoh of the Sixth Dynasty, Pepy I.

Many models of servants busy in various activities were found in his hypogeum at Meir, including the image of a woman lighting a fire inside four disks which, in real life, were made from terracotta and used to protect the flames. The squatting man in the second model is cooking a duck on a spit while fanning the embers with a fan.
(S.E.)

MODEL OF A MAN
ROASTING A DUCK

PAINTED WOOD; HEIGHT 24 CM; MEIR, TOMB OF
NIANKHPEPY II THE BLACK; EXCAVATION BY THE
EGYPTIAN ANTIQUITIES SERVICE (1894); SIXTH
DYNASTY, REIGN OF PEPY I (2289-2255 BC)

ROOM 32

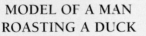

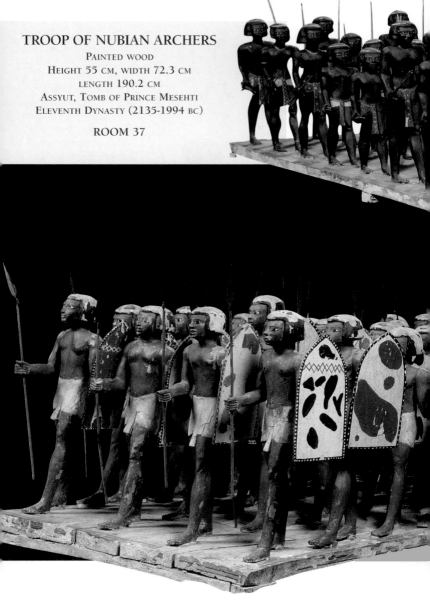

TROOP OF NUBIAN ARCHERS
PAINTED WOOD
HEIGHT 55 CM, WIDTH 72.3 CM
LENGTH 190.2 CM
ASSYUT, TOMB OF PRINCE MESEHTI
ELEVENTH DYNASTY (2135-1994 BC)

ROOM 37

Mesehti, the governor of the 13th *nome* of Upper Egypt, lived during the period of political instability that put the solidity of centralized power in crisis during the First Intermediate Period. It was a time of frequent disorder in which the nomarchs were usually surrounded by soldiers and, consequently, Mesehti wished to be accompanied on his journey to the Afterlife by the models of two bodies of troops on the march. His rock tomb was found to hold two wooden sculptures of Nubian archers and Egyptian lancers, each composed of ten rows of four soldiers.

The Nubians are

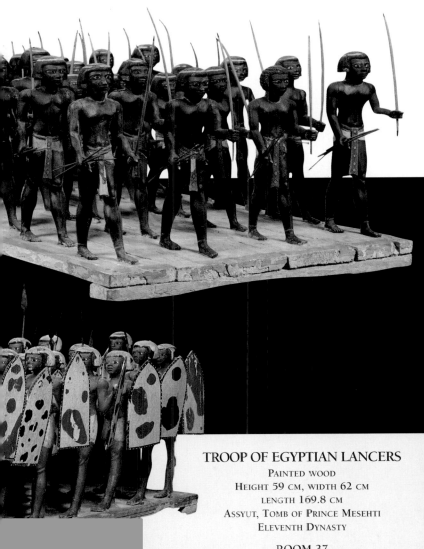

TROOP OF EGYPTIAN LANCERS

PAINTED WOOD
HEIGHT 59 CM, WIDTH 62 CM
LENGTH 169.8 CM
ASSYUT, TOMB OF PRINCE MESEHTI
ELEVENTH DYNASTY

ROOM 37

painted with very dark skin and wear a loincloth with a central flap decorated with green and red geometric motifs, and a white band in their hair. The Egyptians have lighter colored skin and wear a white skirt. Their faces are brought to life by large eyes with white irises.

The Nubians hold their bows in one hand and a bundle of arrows in the other, while the Egyptians have large decorated shields on their left arms and grip long lances in their right.

The soldiers are of different heights and give a realistic idea of an army on the move. (S.E.)

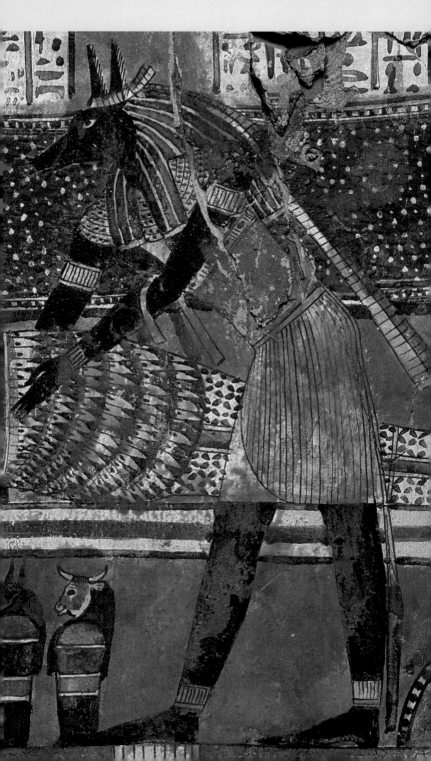

Sarcophaguses were endowed with a very high symbolic value besides providing physical protection for the body. Just like the tomb itself, the sarcophagus represented a magical microcosm that ensured eternal life to the deceased in the guise of the house of the Afterlife.

When decorated in the style of a "palace facade," the association was obvious; the lid was actually thought of as the sky, the bottom as the earth and the four sides as the four horizons. Inside, the body was laid with the head to the north and the face pointing to the east where the sun was reborn daily.

The east side of the sarcophagus at the height of the head was usually decorated with two large *udjat* eyes to symbolize the potential participation of the deceased in the solar cycle and to permit the deceased contact with the world of the living.

The concept of the body enclosed between the sky and earth in a coffin took the form of a return to the womb: the sarcophagus as womb was identified with the goddess Nut or Neith who protected the deceased for eternity, as was recited by the priest over the mummy during the liturgy that followed the embalming rites, "...I have enclosed you in the arms of your mother Nut!" (formula 44 of the *Sarcophagus Texts*) in an embrace that was necessary for rebirth after death.

The sarcophagus also ensured eternal life by transposing the grave goods onto its inner walls in the form of decorative friezes. The magical power of the decorations ensured the deceased of extensive provisions of food, drink, and

CHAPTER 11
FIRST FLOOR

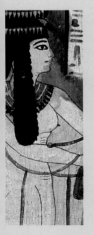

460 SARCOPHAGUS
OF DJEDHOREFANKH
Painted wood
Length 203 CM
West Thebes.
Gurna;
Start of Twenty-
second Dynasty,
Reign of
Sheshonq I
or Osorkon I
(circa 930-920 BC)

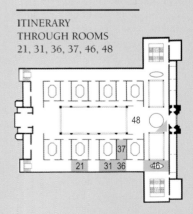

ITINERARY
THROUGH ROOMS
21, 31, 36, 37, 46, 48

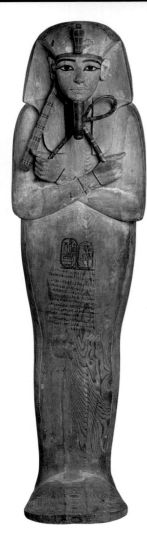

furnishings after death to provide a serene and comfortable existence. The development of the anthropomorphic (man-shaped) sarcophagus during the Twelfth Dynasty was a further elaboration of this concept in which the coffin substituted the body should the mummy inside be damaged or destroyed for any reason.

As a further precaution, the material "cartonnage" was used in place of the sarcophagus from the Third Intermediate Period on, as it could not be removed: if an attempt was made to tear it away, it would break.

Cartonnage, a costly material, was a wrapping placed around the mummy; it was made from layers of linen stuck together which were then lined with plaster and painted.

The sarcophagus proper was then closed over the mummy. Cartonnage never replaced the sarcophagus completely.

Documentation known conventionally as the *Sarcophagus Texts* was another development related to the sarcophagus. The texts were generally written out on the coffin but were also prepared on papyrus and tomb walls; although they were partly derived from the more ancient *Pyramid Texts*, they evolved out of religious speculation and a society undergoing enormous change.

Close analysis of the Texts reveals that they had a double function: they accompanied the deceased on his journey beyond the tomb and were used for recitation and the cult of the dead. Specially trained priests made use of the Texts on three different occasions: during the embalming ritual, the burial ritual, and the cult of the funerary chamber after the body

462 COVER OF RAMESES II'S SARCOPHAGUS
Wood; L. 206 CM; West Thebes, Tomb of Inhapi; Excavation by the Egyptian Antiquities Service (1881); Nineteenth Dynasty, Reign of Rameses II (1279-1212 BC)

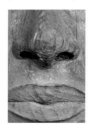

463 SARCOPHAGUS OF AHHOTEP
Wood lined with stucco, gold leaf, alabaster, and obsidian; length 212 CM; Dra Abu al-Naga, Tomb of Ahhotep; Excavation by the Egyptian Antiquities Service (1894); Eighteenth Dynasty, Reign of Ahmes (1550-1525 BC)

had been deposed. When taken together, some of the formulas seem to form a liturgy or series of liturgies that were fundamental to the proper burial of the deceased and his subsequent rebirth.

The complexity of funerary religion resulting from the anguish related to death and the unknown is evidence of the profound hope that ancient Egyptians bore for eternal life despite it taking place in a new dimension, in a world of "opposites" threatened by continual danger. (A.A.)

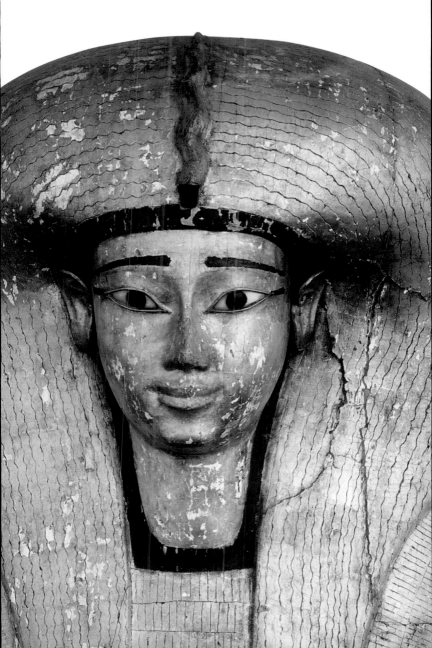

WOODEN SARCOPHAGUS

Sycamore decorated with polychrome terracotta
Height 94 cm, length 199 cm, width 57 cm
Saqqara, Serapeum
Greco-Roman Period (332 bc-313 ad)

ROOM 21

The sarcophagus is made from expensive sycamore with an elaborate series of decorations made from terracotta in a design that has not been seen elsewhere to the best of our knowledge. All four outer sides of the bottom have a grooved central section containing a terracotta cord. The upper edge of each side ends in a polychrome molding with a winding decoration bounded at the top by a pattern of gilded waves.

The lid makes this sarcophagus unique. The sides and upper section are hinged (see the small colored cylinders) with a pin that runs the length of the top. When the pin is removed, the two halves open outward like shutters. The hinges are locked on three sides of the tympan by three pateras decorated with a Medusa's head. The two tympans are each elaborately decorated: a painted terracotta Siren with soft, white flesh and two large green-blue wings lies on a light brown background decorated with floral motifs in gilded high relief. "… the birds of Egypt are still known by the name of siren …" (Luigi Vassalli). The lower part of the Siren's body has the long tail and feet of a bird of prey. The feet stand on falling leaves that seem to hang in the air like the Siren herself. (A.A.)

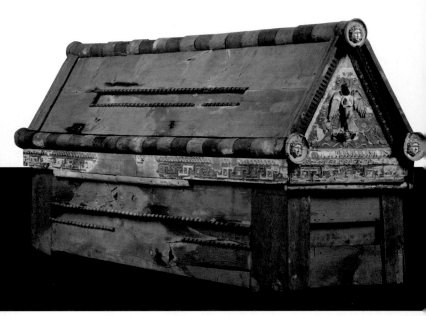

SARCOPHAGUS OF NEFERI

PAINTED WOOD
HEIGHT 104 CM, WIDTH 99 CM, LENGTH 265 CM
AL-BERSHA, TOMB OF NEFERI
EXCAVATION BY THE EGYPTIAN
ANTIQUITIES SERVICE (1897)
TWELFTH DYNASTY (1994-1781 BC)

ROOM 21

The sarcophagus comes from al-Bersha in Middle Egypt where the tombs of the Middle Kingdom nomarchs of the fifteenth *nome* of Upper Egypt were found. The necropolis excavated stretches over the sides of the mountains that border the valley. The tombs are of the shaft type with a (probably Neferi himself), some fragments of boats, alabaster canopic vases, and fragments of furniture. Wooden objects lay around the body. The photograph shows the outer sides. Below a band of small polychrome squares, a horizontal hieroglyphic inscription gives the traditional sarcophagus has two *udjat* eyes above the representation of the door of the tomb decorated with polychrome squares.

The inner decoration of the sarcophagus is the same on all four sides and is divided into three registers: the first has two horizontal bands of large hieroglyphs with the offerings formula

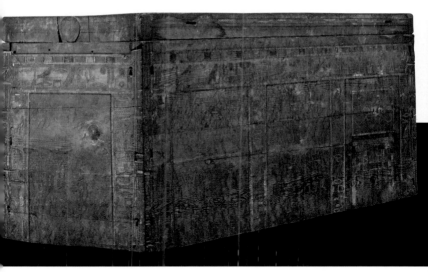

burial chamber at the end and are laid out on three levels. Many contained sets of grave goods, such as sarcophaguses, some of which still had the mummy.

This example comes from the tomb where Neferi was buried; the tomb held a double rectangular wooden sarcophagus that contained a male mummy funerary offerings formula on behalf of the "venerable" Neferi, while the two long and two short sides respectively have four and two columns of hieroglyphs that place the deceased under the protection of a number of deities.

As was customary, the outer eastern side of the to four pairs of gods – Nephthys and Nut, Isis and Tefnet, Anubis and Geb, Osiris and Thoth – in favor of the "venerable" Neferi; below are figures of objects from the grave goods with cursive hieroglyphic captions; and the third register has cursive hieroglyphs containing formulas from the *Sarcophagus Texts*. (A.A.)

DJEDHOREFANKH'S SARCOPHAGUS

PAINTED WOOD; LENGTH 203 CM, WIDTH 61 CM
WEST THEBES, GURNA
START OF THE TWENTY-SECOND DYNASTY, REIGN
OF SHESHONQ I OR OSORKON I (CIRCA 930-920 BC)

ROOM 31

Djedhorefankh, a superintendent of the altars in the temple of Amun-Ra at Karnak during the Twenty-second Dynasty, was buried in a multi-colored, mummy-shaped

and images of the mummy undergoing the last preparation treatments before burial.

The largest panel is seen on the lower section; it is crowned by a

restore use of the senses to the deceased so that he would be able to cope in the Afterlife.

On the back side of the sarcophagus of Djedhorefankh, a mirror-image scene is shown painted in vivid colors. Two deities, identified with the mummy-shaped god Ptah, are seated on thrones receiving offerings from a priest and priestess.

Ptah's body is adorned with necklaces and a net

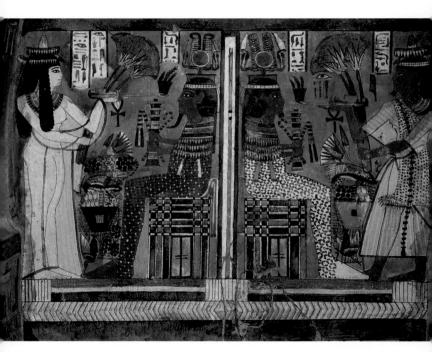

wooden sarcophagus that was found, uncovered, hidden near Thebes.

The inside of the sarcophagus of Djedhorefankh is completely covered with polychrome scenes divided into registers showing deities, funerary priests, figures making offerings, divine emblems,

continuous frieze of uraeus serpents and illustrates one of the most important moments in the funeral ceremony: the ritual of the Opening of the Mouth. The *sem* priest, wearing a leopard skin over his white garment, fumigates the mummy with incense. The ritual purpose was to

similar to the one usually placed over the mummies of the deceased.

The sarcophagus also has an elaborate decoration along the sides. One of these scenes shows the customary offering of gifts made by a priest to two gods. The god identified as Ptah is adorned by garlands and

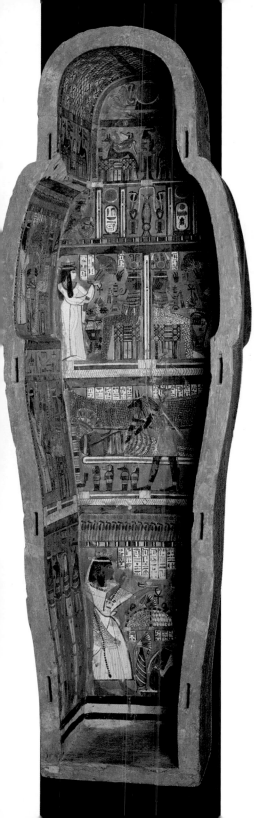

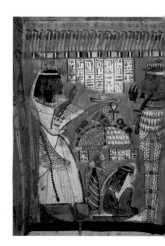

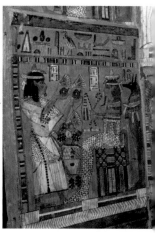

holds the symbols of
royalty, the scepter and
scourge, in his hands. The
figure of Anubis, the god
that presides over the
embalming rites, stands
behind him.

The scene below
shows the four sons of
Horus whose function
was to protect the internal
organs of the deceased:
Amset with the head of a
man, Duamutef with the
head of a jackal, Hapi with
the head of a baboon, and
Kebksenuf with the head
of a falcon.

(S.E.)

467

SARCOPHAGUS OF KHUY

Painted wood; Length 189 cm; Assyut, Tomb 8
Excavation by the French Institute
of Oriental Archaeology (1910)
Mid-Twelfth Dynasty (20th-19th century bc)

ROOM 37

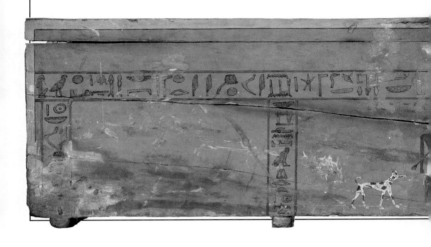

SARCOPHAGUS OF SENBI

Painted wood
Length 212 cm
Meir
Excavation by A. Kamal (1910)
Twelfth Dynasty (1994-1781 bc)

ROOM 37

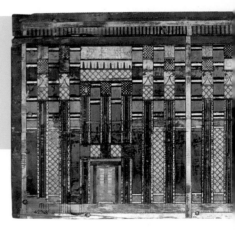

This sarcophagus was found at Meir, the necropolis of the ancient city of Cusae, the capital of the Sixteenth *nome* in Upper Egypt, but no trace of Cusae itself remains.

Meir contained several rock tombs dating from the Sixth to Eleventh Dynasties. The name Senbi is linked to several of the local nomarchs in the Middle Kingdom who

left splendid decorated tombs with many funerary goods. The picture shows the outer sides of one of the three sarcophaguses found side-by-side in the tomb, each of

The sarcophagus comes from Assyut which was the capital of the thirteenth *nome* of Upper Egypt and the departure point for the "forty day" caravan to Kharga oasis that continued to Sudan. The outer decoration of the coffin has a long horizontal inscription that runs all the way around with a standard funerary formula and two eyes on the eastern side allow the deceased to see.

Note the image of Khuy with his dog Iupu held on a leash. This animal, loved by Egyptians, often appears in the decorations below the seat of the occupant of the tomb. The mummy of a dog was found near the tomb of Amenhotep II in trench tomb KV 50 with the mummy of a monkey; these two animals were the favorites of the pharaoh and buried so that they could accompany him in the Afterlife. (A.A.)

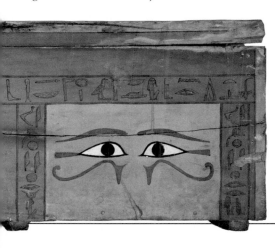

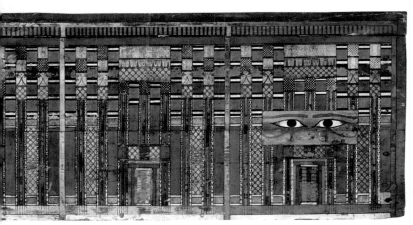

which belonged to a man named Senbi.

The surface is of the "palace facade" type, with a series of doorways adorned with square and rectangular pattern decorations imitating polychrome matting used on the walls of buildings.

Two large *udjat* eyes symbolically dominate the tomb's monumental entrance. (A.A.)

SARCOPHAGUS OF MAATKARA
CEDAR WOOD AND ACACIA PAINTED, GOLD LEAF
LENGTH 223 CM; WEST THEBES, CACHETTE OF
DEIR AL-BAHARI; OFFICIAL DISCOVERY BY THE
EGYPTIAN ANTIQUITIES SERVICE (1881)
TWENTY-FIRST DYNASTY, PONTIFICATE
AND REIGN OF PINUDJEM I
(END OF SECOND MILLENNIUM BC)

ROOM 46

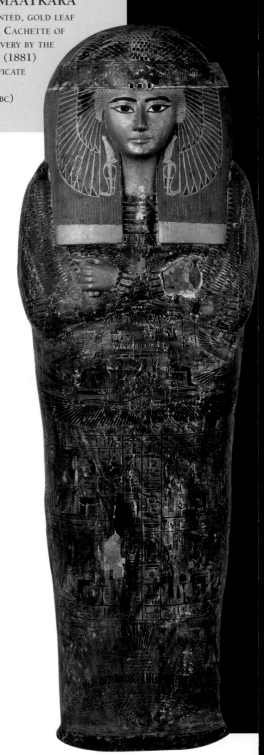

In addition to the sarcophaguses belonging to pharaohs and members of the high Theban priesthood, the cachette of Deir al-Bahari was also found to contain the large external sarcophagus of Maatkara, the daughter of Amun-Ra's supreme priest, Pinudjem I. Maatkara was invested with the title "God's Adorer of Amun" and was considered the consort of the god. The deceased is shown on the lid with her arms resting on her chest. She has a wide face lined with gold leaf that shows a mild expression and large, painted, almond-shaped eyes. The solid blue wig is covered by the image of a vulture with outspread wings edged with gold that end in images of a double cobra wearing the white crown of Upper Egypt.

Maatkara's torso is adorned with two necklaces over a pectoral containing the image of a scarab flanked by two seated gods. The rest of the surface of the sarcophagus is covered with polychrome scenes of the deceased rendering homage to various gods. The custom of filling every available space with decoration – known as *horror vacui* – is typical of this period.
(S.E.)

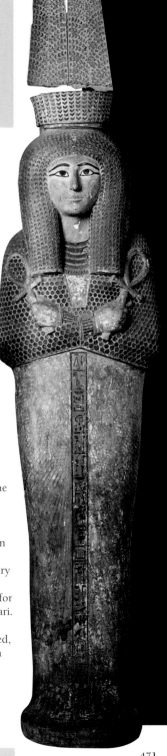

SARCOPHAGUS OF AHMES NEFERTARI

WOOD AND CLOTH; TOTAL LENGTH 378 CM
WEST THEBES, CACHETTE OF DEIR AL-BAHARI;
OFFICIAL DISCOVERY BY THE EGYPTIAN ANTIQUITIES
SERVICE (1881); EIGHTEENTH DYNASTY,
REIGN OF AHMES (1550-1525 BC)

ROOM 46

The enormous sarcophagus of Ahmes Nefertari was found in the Tomb of Inhapy, the consort of Ahmes, which was used as a hiding place to protect the sarcophaguses of pharaohs, members of the royal family, and high priests from tomb robbers during the Twenty-first Dynasty.

Ahmes Nefertari, the mother of Amenhotep I, was the first queen to be installed as "God's wife of Amun" and thereby became an object of worship in the area of Thebes at the start of the 1st millennium BC. Her mummy-shaped wooden sarcophagus was originally covered with gold leaf but this was removed by thieves in antiquity; the lining was replaced with an ocher paint during the restorations made when the sarcophagus was moved to its new location.

The face of the queen, with her large painted eyes, is enclosed by the image of a massive wig topped by a flared crown with two long plumes. The surface of the hair and the elaborate headdress is decorated by small depressions engraved in the wood filled with blue stucco. A similar decoration covers the bust of the deceased which seems to be wrapped round with a low narrow shawl. The hands crossed on the chest hold two large *ankh* signs, the symbol of life, and the wrists bear large striated bracelets similar to the necklace.

Long birds' feathers are shown on the rest of the surface of the sarcophagus to evoke the wings of the goddess Isis, in accordance with a Theban tradition that was common during the Second Intermediate Period.

A long column of hieroglyphs engraved in the center of the lid represents the customary formula, *hetep-di-nesu*, that invoked offerings for the *ka* of Ahmes Nefertari.

When the sarcophagus was opened, it was found to contain two mummies: one of Rameses III, and the other of an unknown woman.
(S.E.)

SARCOPHAGUS
OF QUEEN AHHOTEP

**WOOD LINED WITH STUCCO, GOLD LEAF
ALABASTER AND OBSIDIAN; LENGTH 212 CM
DRA ABU AL-NAGA, TOMB OF QUEEN
AHHOTEP; EXCAVATION BY THE EGYPTIAN
ANTIQUITIES SERVICE (1859); EIGHTEENTH
DYNASTY, REIGN OF AHMES (1550-1525 BC)**

ROOM 46

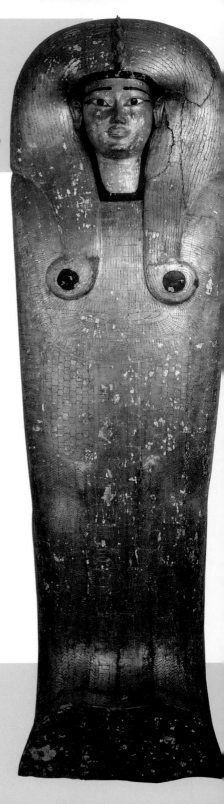

Ahhotep was the daughter of the pharaoh Seqenenra Taa I and his consort Tetisheri. She was married to her brother, Seqenenra Taa II, and from their union gave birth to two pharaohs, Kames and Ahmes, who reunified Egypt after chasing the Hyksos out of the country.

The queen's mummy was buried in the necropolis at Dra Abu al-Naga in an elegant, wooden, mummy-shaped sarcophagus of which only the lid covered with gold leaf has survived.

The image of Ahhotep wears a massive wig with a rounded border and marked by thin wavy incisions. The wig stops at the chest with two large curls around blue centers. The forehead would have been adorned with a uraeus serpent, perhaps made of gold, of which only the curling tail remains on the queen's hair. Her face has a serene expression; her idealized features are animated by large almond-shaped eyes made from encrusted alabaster and obsidian. Her eyebrows, the extension of the eyelids, and the outline of the face are emphasized with blue lines that give vitality to the figure. A necklace made from strings of pearls is reproduced on her chest and, above, a cobra and vulture are depicted, the emblems of the two guardian deities of Lower and Upper Egypt.

The mummified body of the queen has two sharp protrusions that suggest the bones of the legs; she is adorned with images of birds' feathers to imitate the wings of Isis that hold the body of the deceased in a protective embrace in an image that was typical of the Second Intermediate Period when this type of sarcophagus, known as *rishi* from the Arabic word meaning "plumed," became widespread in the Theban area.

The name of Ahhotep is written inside a cartouche in the column of hieroglyphs in the center of the lid. (S.E.)

SARCOPHAGUS OF AHMES MERITAMUN

Cedar wood; Length 313.5 cm, width 87 cm; Deir al-Bahari, rock tomb (TT 358); Excavation by the Egyptian Antiquities Service and the Metropolitan Museum of Art (1929); Eighteenh Dynasty Reign of Amenhotep I (1525-1540 bc)

ROOM 46

The refinement of form and stylistic elegance of the large wooden sarcophagus make this a symbolic sculptural monument of the Eighteenth Dynasty. It belonged to Queen Ahmes Meritamun whom some scholars believe to have been the wife of Amenhotep I, by others the wife of Amenhotep II. The deceased is shown with her arms crossed on her chest, and with a hieratic facial expression embellished by inlays of glass paste; she wears a magnificent wig decorated with small depressions painted blue. Beneath the necklace, the surface is covered with an engraved geometric pattern around the chest and arms that leaves only the hands untouched; these hold the two papyrus-shaped scepters that are the symbols of youth. The rest of the sarcophagus is decorated with long plumes carved in the wood in imitation of the wings of Isis that protected the body of the deceased. This type of decoration – known as *rishi* (from the Arabic word meaning "plumed") – became widespread in Thebes during the Second Intermediate Period. A column of hieroglyphs in the center of the lid, at one time inlaid with glass paste, represents the customary formula of offerings made on behalf of the queen. (S.E.)

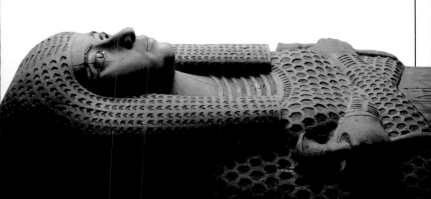

SARCOPHAGUS OF PAKHAR

PAINTED WOOD
HEIGHT 189 CM, WIDTH 59 CM
DEIR AL-BAHARI, CACHETTE AT BAB AL-GASUS
DISCOVERED BY G. DARESSY (1891)
MID-TWENTY-FIRST DYNASTY
(END OF ELEVENTH CENTURY BC)

ROOM 48

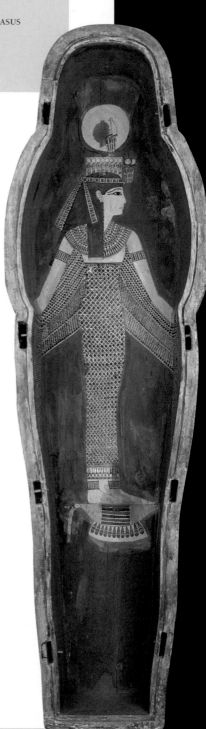

The sensational discovery of the Tomb of the "Horse Door" that allowed detailed study of the period of the Twenty-first Dynasty was officially made in 1891 in Deir al-Bahari. The tomb contained 153 sarcophaguses of the priests of Amun at Karnak from the pontificate of Menkheperre where they had either been buried or hidden following burial in other tombs. Like the example in the image, 101 were double sarcophaguses that, owing to their great number, the Egyptian government allowed to be distributed to museums around the world.

This example belonged to Pakhar, the "priest responsible for the burning of incense, he who opens the gates of the sky of Amun in Karnak…." As was customary during the Twenty-first Dynasty, a copy of the *Book of the Dead* had been placed between the mummy's legs. Typical of the period, Pakhar's sarcophaguses were richly decorated to make up for the lack of decoration in the tomb itself.
(A.A.)

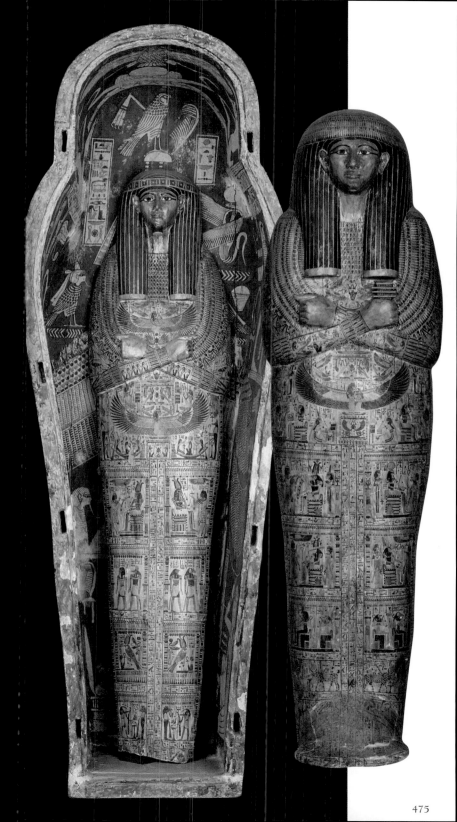

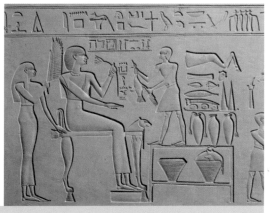

The princesses of the court of Mentuhotep II were buried in elegant limestone sarcophaguses near the temple of the pharaoh at Deir al-Bahari. For the first time, the sarcophaguses were decorated with scenes of everyday life, for example, the women surrounded by handmaidens and servants as they wait to receive body care treatment. The relief that covers the outside of the sides of the sarcophagus is simple in the rather inflexible stylistic canons of the Old Kingdom, but shows occasional elaborate details like the hairstyles created using curls carefully strung together, the many items

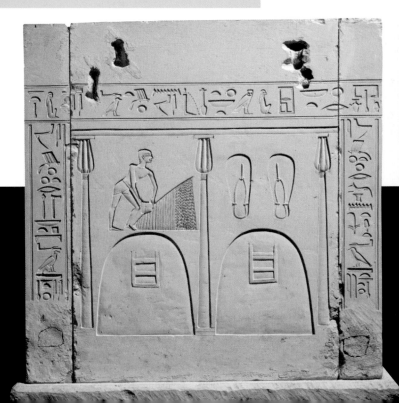

of jewelry worn and the furnishings worthy of a palace.

The shorter sides of the sarcophaguses, of the two princesses, Kauit and Ashayt, show grain storerooms supported by columns. Under the vigilant eye of the supervisor, the servants carry sacks of grain towards arched silos.

The scenes are framed by hieroglyphic texts that list the goods offered to the ladies and wish them eternal well-being. Short inscriptions by each figure state the words said by the servants to the noble ladies of the court. (S.E.)

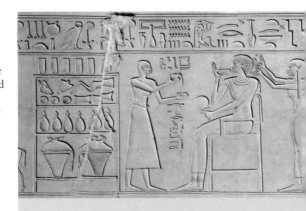

SARCOPHAGUS OF KAUIT (DETAIL)
LIMESTONE; HEIGHT CM 119; WIDTH CM 119
LENGTH CM 262; DEIR AL BAHARI, TEMPLE OF
MENTUHOTEP II; EXCAVATION BY THE EGYPT
EXPLORATION FUND (1903-1907); ELEVENTH DYNASTY
START OF REIGN OF MENTUHOTEP II
(MID-SECOND MILLENNIUM BC)

ROOM 48

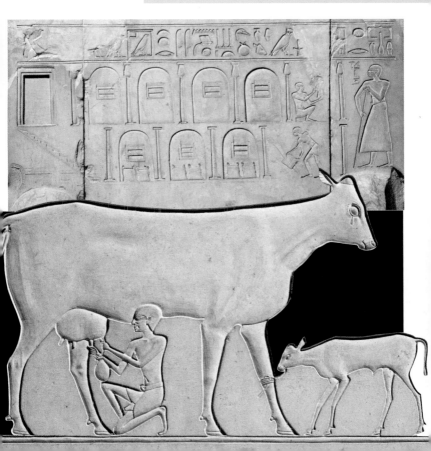

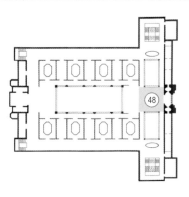

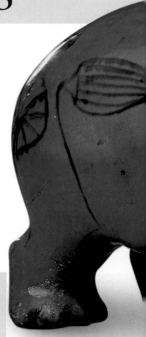

STATUETTE OF A HIPPOPOTAMUS
BLUE FAÏENCE; HEIGHT 11.5 CM, LENGTH 21.5 CM
THEBES, NECROPOLIS OF DRA ABU AL-NAGA
EXCAVATION BY A. MARIETTE (1860)
SECOND INTERMEDIATE PERIOD (1781-1550 BC)

DISPLAY CASE A

The statuette is of a blue hippopotamus painted with black decorative images of aquatic plants and birds that live on the Nile. The eyes, mouth and ears of the animal are also painted black.

This type of figurine is frequently found in tombs of the Middle Kingdom and Second Intermediate Period, but none have been found from the end of the Seventeenth dynasty onwards. In tombs, they were often associated with female images of fertility, known as "concubines." The hippopotamus is linked to the iconography of the Tausret, the goddess of fertility and guardian deity of childbirth. (M.T.)

STATUETTE OF HENUT-NAKHTU
WOOD, ORIGINALLY GILDED AND PAINTED; HEIGHT 22.2 CM
SAQQARA; EXCAVATION BY A. MARIETTE (1859)
NEW KINGDOM, END OF THE EIGHTEENTH DYNASTY
(CIRCA END OF THE 14TH CENTURY BC)

WINDOW B

The statuette is of a well-to-do lady from the end of the Eighteenth Dynasty named Henut-Nakhtu and reflects the artistic elements and female fashions of the period. She wears a magnificent curly wig held in place

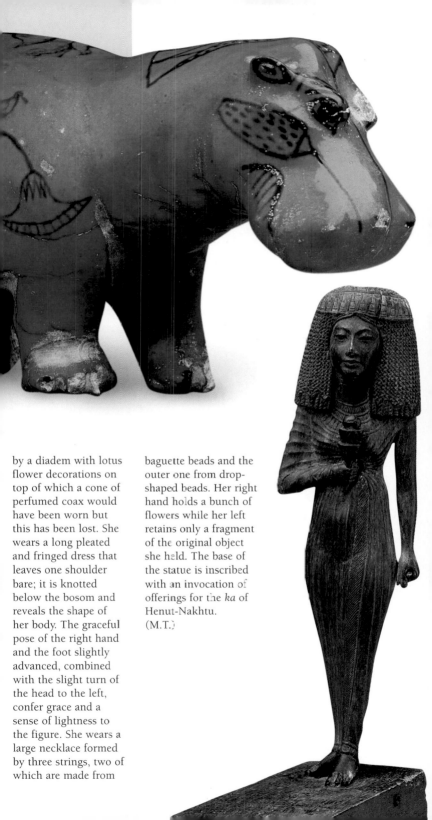

by a diadem with lotus flower decorations on top of which a cone of perfumed coax would have been worn but this has been lost. She wears a long pleated and fringed dress that leaves one shoulder bare; it is knotted below the bosom and reveals the shape of her body. The graceful pose of the right hand and the foot slightly advanced, combined with the slight turn of the head to the left, confer grace and a sense of lightness to the figure. She wears a large necklace formed by three strings, two of which are made from baguette beads and the outer one from drop-shaped beads. Her right hand holds a bunch of flowers while her left retains only a fragment of the original object she held. The base of the statue is inscribed with an invocation of offerings for the *ka* of Henut-Nakhtu. (M.T.)

The head is from a
small statue of Queen Tiy,
the wife of Amenhotep III,
that was found in the
Temple of Hathor at
Serabit al-Kadim. Hathor
was worshipped in this
temple since the Middle

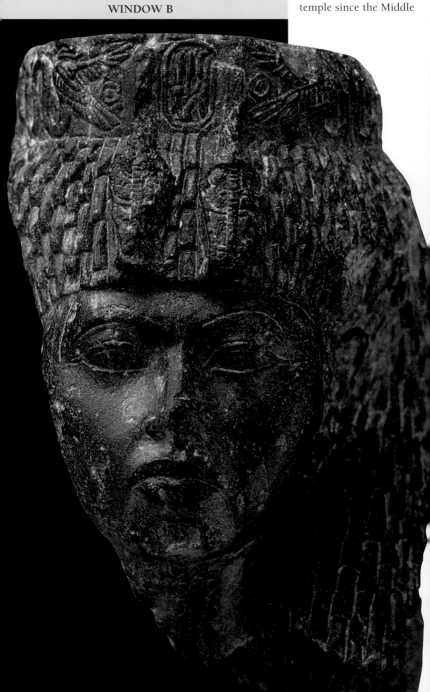

Kingdom and was known as the "Lady of Turquoise" as she protected the turquoise mines in the Sinai that the Egyptians had quarried since the Old Kingdom.

Teye wears a long curly wig that leaves her ears visible. A modius on the top of her wig at one time had two plumes attached, but now all that is seen are the two winged uraeus serpents whose coils wind down the sides of the diadem. The cartouche with the name of the queen lies between the two cobras. Two more uraeus serpents are represented on Tiy's forehead which wear the crowns of Upper and Lower Egypt. Her oval face has high cheekbones, almond-shaped eyes, curved eyebrows, and a mouth with slightly drooping corners that together give the statue a serious and detached air. It has been commented that there is "something haughty, if not actually disdainful, in this small, young, energetic face of a woman who is conscious of her rank and proud to have achieved it" (Corteggiani 1979: 96). This last comment refers to the fact that Tiy had become the "Royal Wife" of Amenhotep III although she was only the daughter of a cavalry officer, Yuya, who was destined to play an important political role at the end of the reign of Tutankhamun. In addition, Amenhotep III was not the son of a "Royal Wife" of Thutmosis IV but of one of his concubines. (M.T.)

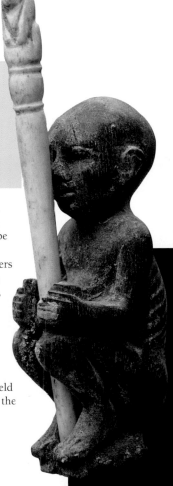

KOHL STICK HOLDER

**WOOD AND IVORY; HEIGHT OF STATUE 7 CM
OVERALL HEIGHT 9.5 CM; PROVENANCE UNKNOWN
PURCHASED IN 1914; NEW KINGDOM (1550-1070 BC)**

WINDOW B

This tiny statue is of bald man, probably Asiatic, squatting and holding a *kohl* stick that ends in the head of a falcon. Horizontal engravings on his back represent the vertebra to emphasize how skinny he is.

Kohl pots were known from the Middle Kingdom and were generally made from alabaster though sometimes from semi-precious stone or wood. The wide rim, narrow neck, and tube-shaped cavity were typical but they took on a new tube shape during the New Kingdom. The containers sometimes had a small stick made from wood, hematite, ivory, or, more rarely, bronze. As in this case, the holders were often in the form of an Asiatic servant, distinguished by a long skull, who held out the *kohl* tube with the stick inserted in the pot. (M.T.)

FIGURINES OF THREE DANCING DWARVES

Ivory; Height 7.8 cm, length 15.8 cm, width 4.5 cm
Lisht; Excavation by the Metropolitan
Museum of Art (1934)
Twelfth Dynasty (1994-1781)

WINDOW B

The three dancing dwarves were probably part of a toy found during excavation work by the Metropolitan Museum of Art (at the foot of a brick wall that closed the burial chamber of a girl named Hapi) at Lisht. The toy was formed by a perforated pulley base with the three figurines on top. Each dwarf stands on a small rectangular base, also perforated. A system of strings through the holes and around the pulley makes the figures "dance".

A fourth figure, in the Metropolitan Museum in New York, stood at the end of the base. He directed the group by clapping his hands to create the rhythm while he simultaneously flexed his knees. The three dancers wear only strips of fabric around their chests and necklaces made of large beads.

The figures have been produced with a certain degree of realism: their squat bodies, bowed legs, and faces are typical of a realistic artistic trend that materialized during the Middle Kingdom which was principally used in figurines of servants and common people in general.

Dancing in ancient Egypt had a ritual function in that it formed entertainment for the god during a religious festival, therefore this object may not be a simple toy but a cult object placed in a tomb.
(M.T.)

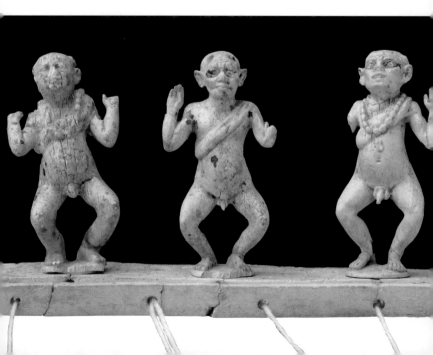

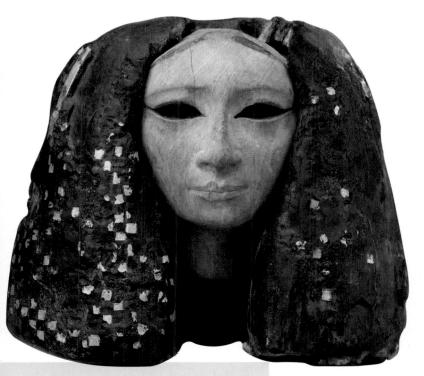

HEAD OF A STATUE OF A WOMAN

PAINTED WOOD WITH GILDING; HEIGHT 10.5 CM
LISHT, AREA OF THE PYRAMID OF AMENEMHAT I
XCAVATION BY THE METROPOLITAN MUSEUM OF ART (1907)
WELFTH DYNASTY, REIGN OF AMENEMHAT I (1994-1964 BC)

DISPLAY CASE B

This small head was part of a statue found at Lisht in the area of the Pyramid of Amenemhat I, a Twelfth-Dynasty king. It was part of a composite statue made from different materials, which was rare in Egypt during the Middle Kingdom. The head is made in two parts – the pale-colored face and black painted wig – held together by tenons. The large and long wig is adorned with square gilded inserts of which only some remain.

It is probable that the wig also had a diadem or a crown as the top is much thinner than the parts at the side. This would suggest that the head was of a princess or a queen, a hypothesis that is supported by the fineness of the carving and the ornamentation on the wig. The woman's hairline can be seen on her high forehead, she has eyebrows carved in relief, and her almond-shaped eyes at one time were set with glass paste. She has a straight nose and a serious expression on her mouth.

The body of the statue has been lost with only the arms being found by Winlock two years after the original dig. Lisht lay halfway between Dahshur and Maydum and was the capital of Egypt during the Middle Kingdom. There are two pyramids there, the earlier of which was built by Amenemhat I. The temple of the pyramid has been almost totally destroyed; it was built on a terrace cut out of the hill at a level lower than that of the pyramid. The building was modelled on the Theban temple of Nebhetepra Mentuhotep from the previous dynasty.

In addition to this statue, the temple of the pyramid also revealed the skull of a cow and models of vases that were part of the ritual deposit made in the foundations. (M.T.)

SHAWABTY AND THE MODEL OF A SARCOPHAGUS BELONGING TO AMENHOTEP KNOWN AS HUY

FAÏENCE; SARCOPHAGUS: HEIGHT 18 CM, WIDTH 8 CM
SHAWABTY: HEIGHT 13.8 CM
ABYDOS, PURCHASED IN 1950
EIGHTEENTH DYNASTY (1550-1075 BC)

WINDOW C

The Egyptian term *shawabty* comes from the verb *usheb* meaning "respond" in that the small statues were expected to "respond" to the request of the deceased to take his place should he be required to perform physical work in the fields of the Land beyond the Tomb.

The first *shawabty* were made from stone, wood, or faïence and were probably manufactured to replace the mummy if it should be damaged. During the Eighteenth Dynasty, royal *shawabty* appeared whereas

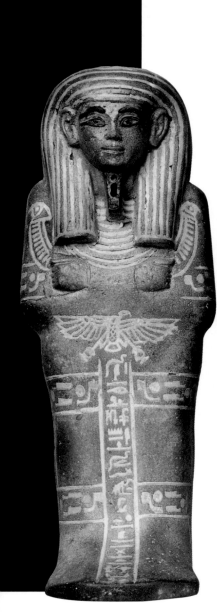

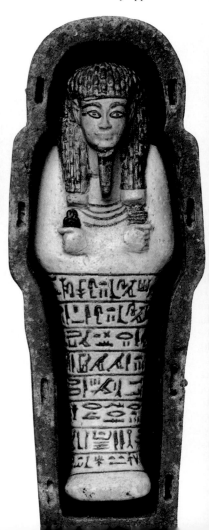

previously they had only existed in the tombs of functionaries. *Shawabty* in miniature sarcophaguses began to appear at the end of the Seventeenth Dynasty but were only made from wood.

This particular statue is made from white faïence with blue decorations and has a long curly wig and false beard. He holds the *sa* amulets that signify protection and the *djed* pillar ("stability") crossed on his chest.

Eight horizontal lines inscribed on his body give the traditional text of the *shawabty*, i.e. Chapter 6 of the *Book of the Dead*, with which the deceased ordered the statue to take his place when called to perform work. The formula first appeared on *shawabty* during the Twelfth Dynasty.

The small statue was found in a mummy-shaped sarcophagus whose lid was carved in the image of the deceased assimilated to Osiris; the figure wears a striped, three-part wig and has black lines to emphasize the eyes and beard. The sarcophagus itself has two lines of horizontal text intersected by one vertical line and pale decorations on a blue background. The lid was closed on the bottom half of the sarcophagus by a mortice and tenon.

The statuette and the sarcophagus belonged to a royal scribe named Amenhotep (known as Huy) who may have been the functionary with the same name who lived during the reign of Amenhotep III.
(M.T.)

VASE IN THE SHAPE OF A PAPYRUS UMBREL
FAÏENCE; HEIGHT 18 CM, WIDTH 8 CM
PROVENANCE UNKNOWN
NEW KINGDOM (1550-1070 BC)

WINDOW C

This liquid container made from blue faïence in the form of a cup is decorated on the outside by papyrus plants, birds, animals, and a man who lifts a duck in each hand. The circular base is missing. Many images of funeral banquets from the New Kingdom show kings or dignitaries serving themselves with containers such as this one. Cups or vases for libations of wine were often blue and decorated with black representations of pastoral scenes.

Faïence is a ceramic material made with quartzite and small quantities of silt and natron and was usually glazed in shiny blue or green created using natron, silt, and silicon. The ancient Egyptian term for faïence was *tjehenet* which means "shiny" and it was probably used to imitate certain semi-precious stones like turquoise or lapis lazuli. The black decoration on objects made from faïence was achieved using pigments obtained from manganese.

Papyrus, the emblem of Lower Egypt, grew in the thick marshes of the Delta and was believed to have been the first form of life to grow on the primordial hill of creation.
(M.T.)

CENSER IN THE SHAPE OF AN ARM

GILDED WOOD; LENGTH 55 CM
MEDINET DIMAI; EXCAVATED IN 1893
PTOLEMAIC PERIOD (END 4TH CENTURY BC)

WINDOW C

The censer is in the shape of an arm that holds a small container decorated with a uraeus serpent in which the incense was burned. A falcon's head is at the other end of the arm and a small container in the center is in the form of a cartouche.

Incense was burned in temples during religious ceremonies, in tombs during funerary rites, and was used to create perfumes for personal use. Images of exotic "incense trees" imported from the land of Punt can be seen in Hatshepsut's temple at Deir al-Bahari but aromatic substances often used in combination with

STATUETTE OF THUTMOSIS III

IVORY AND GOLD
HEIGHT 18 CM
PROVENANCE UNKNOWN
EIGHTEENTH DYNASTY, REIGN OF THUTMOSIS III
(1479-1425 BC)

WINDOW C

The statuette shows Thutmosis III advancing. His left arm lies down his side while the right is bent forward and probably held a weapon or staff one time. The pharaoh is wearing the white crown of Upper Egypt with a gold uraeus serpent, and a *shendyt* skirt knotted at the front. The statue stands on a base made of ivory and wood.

The elephant was already extinct in Egypt during the Dynastic Period so ivory was imported from other parts of Africa and eastern Asia. An inscription tells us that Thutmosis III boasted of having killed 120 elephants on an ivory-hunting expedition to Niy. Although we cannot be sure where Niy was exactly, it probably lay in the valley of the river Oronte. (M.T.)

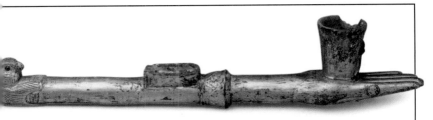

incense were also imported from Mediterranean countries.

A religious text from the New Kingdom known as the "Ritual of Amun" or "Ritual of the daily cult of the god" mentions the various ceremonies practised on the statue of Amun in the temple each day. Two were libation with water and fumigation with incense, both of which were performed to bring the god (or a dead man) back to life. Libation was believed to restore the necessary liquids to the body while the aim of fumigation was to return the senses to life. Incense was thought to be an emission from the body of Osiris.

(M.T.)

STATUETTE OF A HEDGEHOG
BLUE FAÏENCE
HEIGHT 5.3 CM, LENGTH 7 CM
NECROPOLIS IN THEBES
MIDDLE KINGDOM (2065-1650 BC)

WINDOW C

The statue is a faithful model of a hedgehog with a long nose, small eyes, and pointed ears, but the body is completely covered with spines in a rather representational manner. The animal is made from blue faïence and stands on an oval faïence base.

Images of hedgehogs were painted in tombs of the Old Kingdom as decoration on the bows of boats. It was also used in the production of small, animal-shaped perfume containers until the Roman Period (30 BC-313 AD). It is probable that hedgehogs were connected with the god of childbirth, Mut or Bes. (M.T.)

SHAWABTY BELONGING TO LIEUTENANT HAT

PAINTED LIMESTONE; HEIGHT 20.2 CM
TUNA AL-GEBEL, PURCHASED IN 1908
EIGHTEENTH DYNASTY, REIGN OF AMENHOTEP IV-
AKHENATEN (1346-1333 BC)

WINDOW C

This *shawabty* was found during secret digging in the necropolis at Tuna al-Gebel on the west bank of the Nile opposite Tell al-Amarna. It was here that Hat, a lieutenant in the chariot troops, probably had a tomb built. Some of the colors remain on this model made from yellow limestone and painted: the lips are red, the wig has traces of blue, and the eyes, eyebrows and the corners of the mouth are touched with black. The figure has pierced ears – a typical feature of the iconography of Amarna art – folded arms, holds a hoe in each hand, and a basket hangs over his left shoulder. *Shawabty* with farming implements such as hoes, sacks, and baskets that hang on the end of a stick began to appear during the Eighteenth Dynasty, however, during the Amarna era they were very rare, particularly in the tombs of private individuals, as the practices and beliefs based on Osiris had been abandoned. In some cases, though, traditional religion and the worship of the Aten were

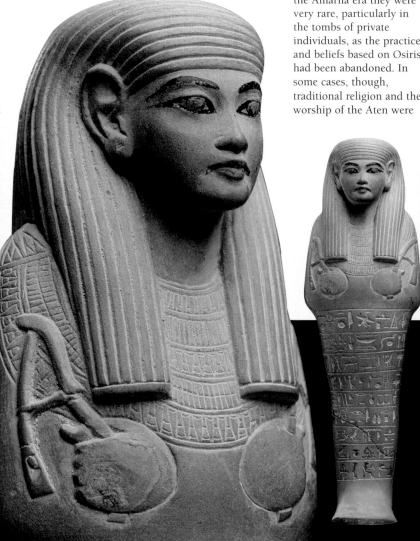

able to coexist without contradiction as is shown by a hymn to Aten on this statue next to passages from Chapter 6 of the *Book of the Dead* but without any reference to work in the Afterlife.

Nine lines of text were found on the mummy of Hat that contained a formula of offerings to Aten on behalf of the *ka* of the deceased. (M.T.)

SHAWABTY BELONGING TO PTAHMES

POLYCHROME FAÏENCE
HEIGHT 20 CM, WIDTH 6 CM
ABYDOS; EXCAVATION BY A. MARIETTE (1881)
EIGHTEENTH DYNASTY, REIGN OF AMENHOTEP III
(1387-1350 BC)

WINDOW C

This statue is of the vizier, mayor, and high priest in the Temple of Amun at Thebes, Ptahmes, who lived during the reign of Amenhotep III. The statue was found in the north section of the necropolis in Abydos where a number of functionaries had built chapels or cenotaphs since the Middle Kingdom to take advantage of the protection of Osiris who had his primary place of worship there. Their tombs, however, could be built elsewhere and Ptahmes was in fact buried in Thebes. In general, a stela or simply one or two *shawabty* were left in Abydos.

This *shawabty* is in the form of a tightly wrapped mummy with arms crossed on his chest and with the image of a vulture with open wings. The figure wears a large polychrome necklace around his neck and a three-part wig colored yellow and blue. His body is completely covered with twelve horizontal lines of hieroglyphs containing Chapter 6 of the *Book of the Dead*, and has one line of vertical text detailing the names and titles of the deceased.

The art of the New Kingdom reached its apex in the reign of Amenhotep III when the rigid stylistic traditions were abandoned at the start of the Eighteenth Dynasty and influences were felt from the Aegean and the Near East, as indicated by this very well-made *shawabty*. (M.T.)

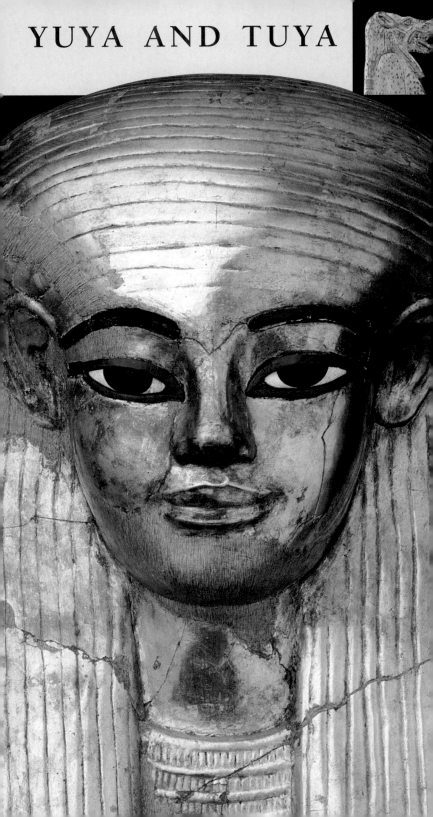

Yuya and Tuya were the parents of Tiy, the Great Royal Bride of Amenhotep III (Eighteeth Dynasty) and had the honor of being buried in the Valley of the Kings (KV 46). The Valley of the Kings was the royal Theban necropolis of the New Kingdom (Eighteeth-Twentieth Dynasties) and is known in Arabic as Wadi Biban al-Muluk, "the Valley of the Doors of the Kings"; it contains tombs tens of metres long dug out of the rock whose shape inspired the ancient Greeks to call them "syringes."

The Valley of the Kings does not only contain royal remains but also those of members of the royal family and important functionaries. These are characterized by the simplicity of the architecture: they are modest in size and without decoration, in design being nothing more than shaft tombs or with one or two descending corridors with steps that lead directly to the burial chamber. From the time of Rameses I (Nineteenth Dynasty), the wives and children of the pharaoh were buried in their own necropolis known as the Valley of the Queens – in Arabic, Wadi Biban al-Harim ("Valley of the Doors of the Women") – at the southern end of the Theban necropolis. The first queen to be buried there was Rameses I's own wife, the Great Royal Bride Sat-Ra.

With the financial backing of the American, Theodore M. Davis, it was possible for the Chief Inspector of the Antiquities Service of Upper Egypt, James E. Quibell, to open tomb no. 46 on February 5, 1905 which he found filled with sarcophaguses and grave goods up to the ceiling. A small flight of steps led into a first descending corridor, then a second descending corridor followed with steps that led into a rectangular burial chamber. The tomb was not pristine and it is thought that it had been entered on at least two occasions, perhaps three. All small objects

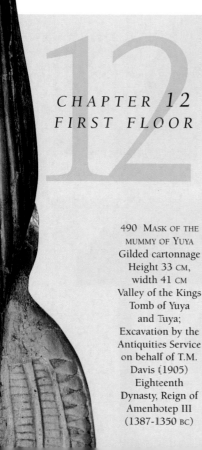

CHAPTER *12*
FIRST FLOOR

490 MASK OF THE MUMMY OF YUYA
Gilded cartonnage
Height 33 CM, width 41 CM
Valley of the Kings
Tomb of Yuya and Tuya;
Excavation by the Antiquities Service on behalf of T.M. Davis (1905)
Eighteenth Dynasty, Reign of Amenhotep III
(1387-1350 BC)

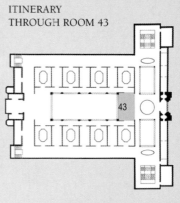

ITINERARY
THROUGH ROOM 43

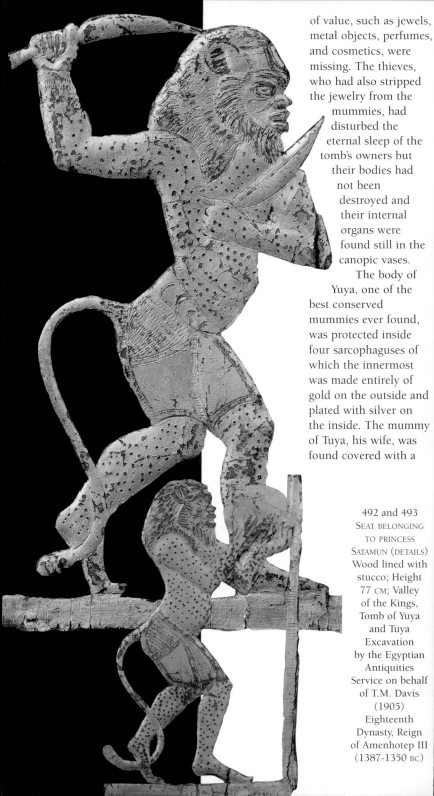

of value, such as jewels, metal objects, perfumes, and cosmetics, were missing. The thieves, who had also stripped the jewelry from the mummies, had disturbed the eternal sleep of the tomb's owners but their bodies had not been destroyed and their internal organs were found still in the canopic vases.

The body of Yuya, one of the best conserved mummies ever found, was protected inside four sarcophaguses of which the innermost was made entirely of gold on the outside and plated with silver on the inside. The mummy of Tuya, his wife, was found covered with a

492 and 493
SEAT BELONGING
TO PRINCESS
SATAMUN (DETAILS)
Wood lined with
stucco; Height
77 CM; Valley
of the Kings,
Tomb of Yuya
and Tuya
Excavation
by the Egyptian
Antiquities
Service on behalf
of T.M. Davis
(1905)
Eighteenth
Dynasty, Reign
of Amenhotep III
(1387-1350 BC)

sheet inside two anthropoid sarcophaguses as though someone had tried to tidy the tomb up. The different canopic vases and embalming techniques used suggest that the couple died at different times. Quite unusually, the internal organs of Tuya were wrapped in bandages to form a small mummy with the head covered by a small gilded stucco mask.

The grave goods of the couple numbered objects of different types, including *shawabty* and their boxes, various sandals, a mirror, amulets, a papyrus, different boxes, small seals, the neck of a sistrum, a wig in a box, staffs, the handle of a whip, and a great many vases with lids. In particular there was a splendid chariot with spiral and rosette decorations in gilded stucco that had survived in marvellous condition. The chariot was part of the set of grave goods belonging to Yuya, the commander of the chariot division of his son-in-law, Amenhotep III. In addition there were three superb, richly ornamented seats and three beds, one of which had panels decorated in silvered stucco. These were exceptional items that impressed their discoverers and the public highly with their individual elegance and magnificence as a set.

It was only a few years later, in 1922, that these items were completely overshadowed by the sensational discovery of Tutankhamun's tomb, the only royal tomb to be found with a practically complete set of grave goods. The splendor of the treasure in Tutankhamun's tomb continues to inspire dreams of what masterpieces must have been contained in the other, plundered, tombs bearing in mind the opulence and refinement of the goods that belonged to a boy-king who died at the age of just eighteen.
(A.A.)

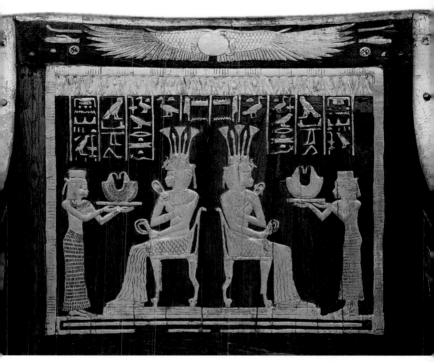

FUNERARY MASK BELONGING TO TUYA

LINEN AND STUCCO, GOLD LEAF, GLASS PASTE, ALABASTER
HEIGHT 40 CM; VALLEY OF THE KINGS, TOMB OF YUYA
AND TUYA; EXCAVATION BY THE EGYPTIAN ANTIQUITIES
SERVICE ON BEHALF OF T.M. DAVIS (1905); EIGHTEENTH
DYNASTY, REIGN OF AMENHOTEP III (1387-1350 BC)

ROOM 43

Tuya was the wife of Yuya and the mother of Queen Tiy, and she was buried with her husband in a tomb in the Valley of the Kings that contained a valuable set of grave goods. Their family relationship to the pharaoh Amenhotep III was certainly responsible for the superb objects produced to accompany them to the Afterlife.

Tuya's mummy was laid to rest in a magnificent, mummy-shaped sarcophagus of gilded wood placed inside two others, the outermost of which was carved to resemble a huge four-sided chest. The woman's mummified body was adorned, as was conventional, with a gilded linen and stucco mask whose purpose was to protect the head and perpetuate the features of the deceased as was stated in Chapter 151b of the *Book of the Dead*. The mask was originally covered with a thin dark veil that has still

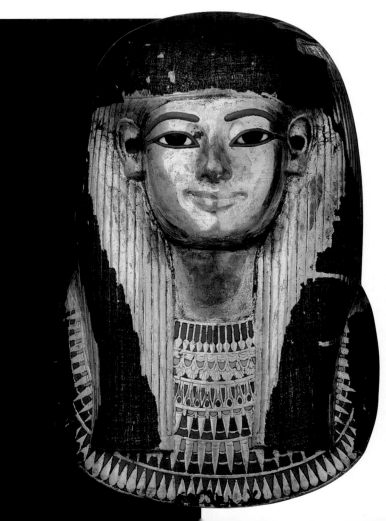

partially survived on the wig and necklace. The full and wide face of the mask is lit up by a faint smile and inlaid eyes; the edge and eyebrows are formed by blue glass paste in imitation of lapis lazuli; and the black glass paste pupils are set into white alabaster given a realistic touch of red paint in the corner.

The wig that frames the face and leaves the ears visible is marked by parallel stripes and circled by a floral band. A large, elegant necklace covers the mummy's chest in a custom that was mirrored on the sarcophaguses. The strings of the necklace are adorned by polychrome floral and

geometric patterns. The gilded sign, *nefer*, is repeated on the blue background around the neck followed by a design of palmettes and more stylized decorations. The row of drop-shaped motifs on the lower edge of the necklace forms the bottom of the mask. (S.E.)

STATUE OF THE *BA* OF YUYA

PAINTED LIMESTONE; HEIGHT 13.5 CM
VALLEY OF THE KINGS, TOMB OF YUYA AND
TUYA; EXCAVATION BY THE EGYPTIAN
ANTIQUITIES SERVICE ON BEHALF
OF T.M. DAVIS (1905); EIGHTEENTH
DYNASTY; REIGN OF AMENHOTEP III
(1387-1350 BC)

ROOM 43

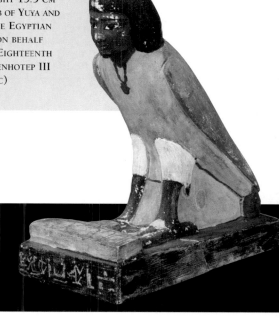

A hieroglyphic inscription on the base of the statue states that it represents the *ba* of Yuya and was part of the deceased's grave goods. Responsible for the many transformations of the deceased in the Afterlife, the *ba* was considered a mobile entity and has therefore been depicted as a bird with a human head, able to move freely on land, in the air, and in the underworld.

The Egyptian term *ba* has traditionally been translated as "spirit" but it refers to the potential of a being to take different forms whether part of the human or divine spheres. The union of the *ba* with the body was considered indispensable for the

deceased to survive in the Afterlife, and it was the preservation of the body by embalming that allowed the *ba* to be reunited with it for eternity. Chapter 89 of the *Book of the Dead* had to be recited over a bird with a human head placed on the chest of the deceased (it was supposed to be the voice

of the deceased speaking): "… may my *ba* come with me from wherever it may be … may my ba see my body, may it rest on my mummy, and may it not be destroyed or perish." Furthermore, Chapter 61 entreats that the *ba* might not be taken from the deceased in the Afterlife. (A.A.)

POTS

PAINTED WOOD; HEIGHT 20.5 CM (1); 14 CM (2); 19 CM (3)
VALLEY OF THE KINGS, TOMB OF YUYA AND TUYA
EXCAVATION BY THE EGYPTIAN ANTIQUITIES SERVICE
ON BEHALF OF T.M. DAVIS (1905); EIGHTEENTH DYNASTY
REIGN OF AMENHOTEP III (1387-1350 BC)

ROOM 43

The grave goods belonging to Yuya and Tuya contained a number of painted wooden pots that bore no inscription, decorated to imitate glass (left and top right) and stone (bottom right). The vases were first painted white and then, if to imitate glass, it was further painted blue; if it was painted to imitate stone, it was covered with small red squiggly brushstrokes. Some of the lids were decorated with a hieroglyph, which was a red cross with a white border and the

FOUR VASES IN THE NAME OF YUYA

PAINTED LIMESTONE; HEIGHT 25 CM, LENGTH 38 CM
VALLEY OF THE KINGS, TOMB OF YUYA AND TUYA
EXCAVATION BY THE EGYPTIAN ANTIQUITIES SERVICE
ON BEHALF OF T.M. DAVIS (1905); EIGHTEENTH DYNASTY
REIGN OF AMENHOTEP III (1387-1350 BC)

ROOM 43

spout that ends in the head of an ibex. The lids of the vases are decorated with the effigies of certain animals: the head of a calf dappled with black, a crouching ibex, a frog, and the head of a calf

Four false containers of an unusual design were placed in a corner of the chamber where Yuya and Tuya were buried. Fixed to a single wooden base, the vases were made from white limestone painted to imitate the more valuable material, alabaster. Although similar, the four containers are slightly different in form and decoration: three have handles in various styles and the fourth has a

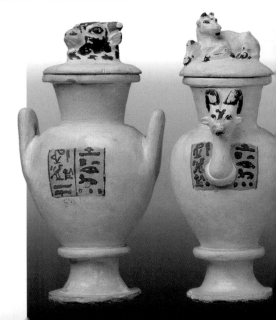

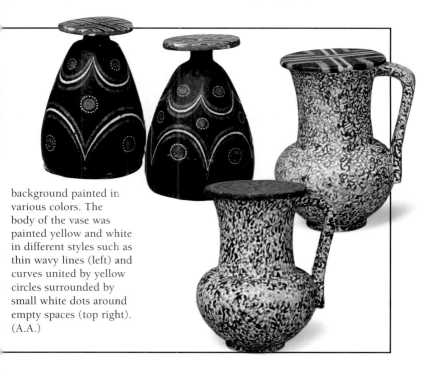

background painted in various colors. The body of the vase was painted yellow and white in different styles such as thin wavy lines (left) and curves united by yellow circles surrounded by small white dots around empty spaces (top right). (A.A.)

dappled with red.

The body of each vase bears a painted cursive hieroglyphic inscription on a yellow background with good wishes for "the Osiris Yuya justified" in a phrase commonly used with the dead. The "inside" of each container was carved out for just a few centimetres but the rest was left solid in imitation of real vases that held oils and ointments for the Afterlife. The ancient Egyptians believed that the presence of containers, even if imitations, magically guaranteed a supply of their hypothetical contents to the deceased during the Afterlife. (S.E)

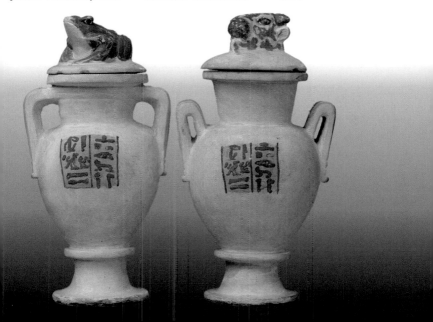

CHAIR BELONGING TO PRINCESS SATAMUN

WOOD LINED WITH STUCCO, GOLD LEAF, AND PLANT FIBERS
HEIGHT 77 CM; HEIGHT OF THE SEAT 34 CM
VALLEY OF THE KINGS, TOMB OF YUYA AND TUYA
EXCAVATION BY THE EGYPTIAN ANTIQUITIES SERVICE
ON BEHALF OF T.M. DAVIS (1905);
EIGHTEENTH DYNASTY
REIGN OF AMENHOTEP III (1387-1350 BC)

ROOM 43

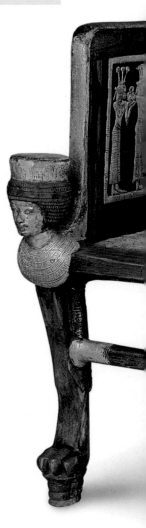

Princess Satamun was the daughter of Amenhotep III and Queen Tiy and the grand daughter of Yuya and Tuya. She placed this elegant wooden chair, that belonged to her personally, in the tomb of her grand parents as a funerary gift. The four legs were carved to imitate the muscular legs of a lion and the seat is formed by pieces of wood skilfully assembled using mortices, tenons, and bronze nails. The front section is decorated by models of the head and shoulders of two females whose face, neck, and crown were covered in gold leaf while the hair was left the natural color of the wood. The insides of the two high armrests are historiated with gilded panels that show a procession of four young girls with papyrus plants on their heads. The women carry trays filled with gold rings, "the gift of the foreign countries of the south," and advance towards the backrest where the procession ends. Here, two mirror images represent a young girl who hands a large necklace to a seated woman who is identified in the inscription above as "the daughter of the king, the great, his beloved Satamun." The princess wears a necklace, earrings, bracelets, and a wig tied with a ribbon and crowned by the image of a papyrus plant, the emblem of rebirth and fertility. She holds a sistrum and a *menat* necklace, the customary instruments used by female musicians in religious processions. Like the girls that pay her homage, Satamun also wears a long, pleated skirt.

The outside panels of the armrests show the figures of Bes and Toeris involved in a dance to the sound of tambourines to ward off evil spirits. The two gods were closely connected to the female world by the magical protection they bestowed on women in pregnancy and childbirth.
(S.E.)

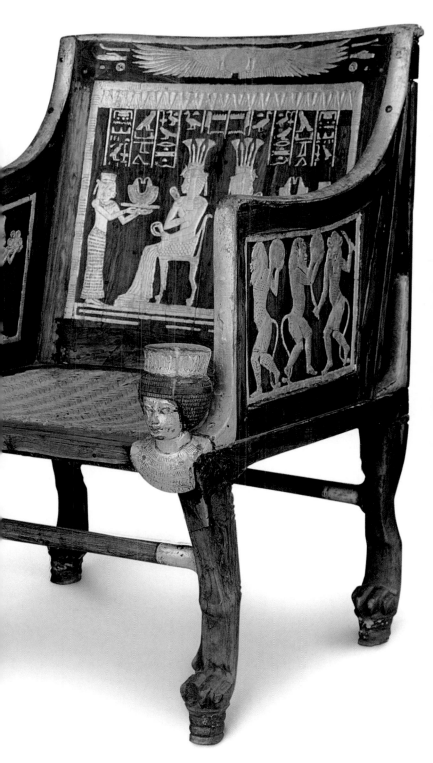

YUYA'S MUMMY-SHAPED SARCOPHAGUS

WOOD, GOLD AND SILVER LEAF, GLASS PASTE, ALABASTER, AND CARNELIAN
HEIGHT 59 CM, WIDTH 55 CM, LENGTH 204 CM
VALLEY OF THE KINGS, TOMB OF YUYA AND TUYA
EXCAVATION BY THE EGYPTIAN ANTIQUITIES SERVICE
ON BEHALF OF T.M. DAVIS (1905); EIGHTEENTH DYNASTY
REIGN OF AMENHOTEP III (1387-1350 BC)

ROOM 43

Yuya's mummy was found in the innermost sarcophagus – one of the most spectacular items in his grave goods – robbed of his jewelry and amulets. Thieves probably entered the tomb during the Reign of Rameses III, and idealized with full cheeks, a narrow mouth, and large eyes and eyebrows highlighted in blue glass paste. A colored necklace from shoulder to shoulder has two gold fasteners in the form of falcons' heads traditional guardian deities of the body – Thoth, Anubis, and the four sons of Horus – plus some hieroglyphic inscriptions. Nut appears once more on both the lower and upper parts of the inside of the

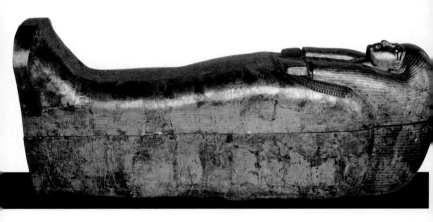

succeeded in removing the most valuable and easily carried items but may have been disturbed at work. The outer coffin is completely covered in gold leaf and adorned with glass paste inlays on the outside, while the inside is lined with silver leaf. The face of the deceased has been while the combination of colors on the protective vulture below the necklace brings sparkle to the ensemble. The goddess Nut with her arms raised covers the lower part of Yuya's body and the goddess Isis kneels below his feet. The outer walls are decorated with the sarcophagus. Chapter 166 of the *Book of the Dead* is engraved close to Nut's head pleading that the head might not separate from the body in the Afterlife as eternal life was only possible if all the parts of the body were preserved.
(A.A.)

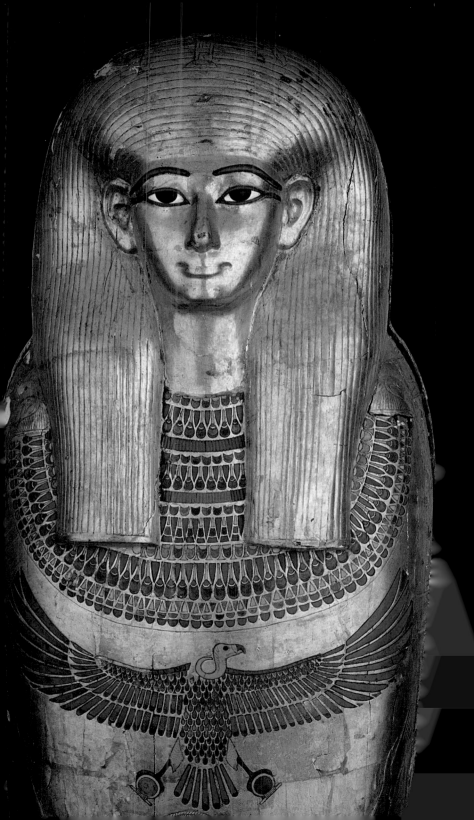

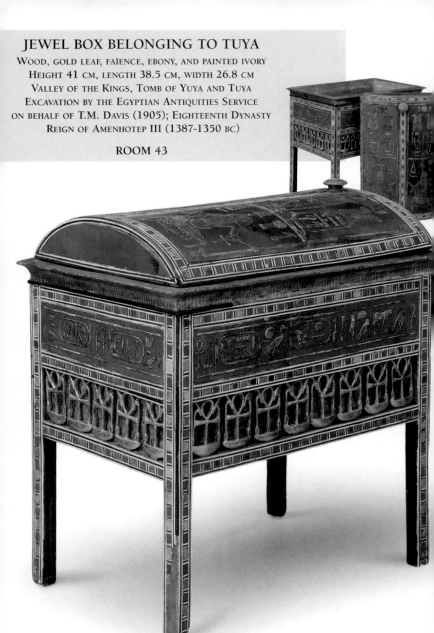

JEWEL BOX BELONGING TO TUYA

WOOD, GOLD LEAF, FAÏENCE, EBONY, AND PAINTED IVORY
HEIGHT 41 CM, LENGTH 38.5 CM, WIDTH 26.8 CM
VALLEY OF THE KINGS, TOMB OF YUYA AND TUYA
EXCAVATION BY THE EGYPTIAN ANTIQUITIES SERVICE
ON BEHALF OF T.M. DAVIS (1905); EIGHTEENTH DYNASTY
REIGN OF AMENHOTEP III (1387-1350 BC)

ROOM 43

This lovely jewel box was found in the tomb of Yuya and Tuya but its contents had been stolen by thieves in antiquity. The box is supported by long, slender legs decorated with squares of faïence and ivory painted pink. The same continuous pattern runs around the edges of the sides of the casket and its curved lid. The sides are divided into two equal parts by the geometric frieze with the upper section decorated by a hieroglyphic inscription of gilded wood that gives the cartouches of Amenhotep III and his consort, Tiy, the daughter of Yuya and Tuya. The lower section repeats three gilded hieroglyphs: *ankh*, *uas*, and *neb* that wish the owner of the casket eternal life and power.

The lid is divided into two mirror images of high relief inscriptions and images in gilded wood on a faïence surface. The upper part has two large cartouches that contain the throne name and the birth name of Amenhotep III beneath long plumes and a sun disk. The lower part shows Heh, the god of the millions of years, who kneels on the sign for gold, *nebu*. The god holds two long palm stems, the emblem of time and an augury for long life and a long reign.

The casket was held closed by a string wound around two knobs that were fixed on the lid and one of the sides. The names and attributes of the royal couple appear on all of the box without once mentioning the name of Tuya – whose jewels it held – which suggests that the casket was manufactured by court artisans for Tiy who then decided to place it in the tomb of her parents as a final gift.
(S.E.)

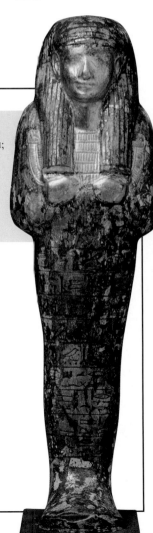

SHAWABTY BELONGING TO TUYA

Wood lined with stucco and gilded; Height 27.7 cm;
Valley of the Kings; Tomb of Yuya and Tuya
(KV 46); Excavation by the Egyptian Antiquities
Service on behalf of T.M. Davis (1905):
Eighteenth Dynasty, Reign of Amenhotep III
(1387-1350 bc)

ROOM 43

The tomb of Yuya and Tuya held a great number of *shawabty* of different manufacture, most of which belonged to the grave goods of the husband Yuya. This one, however, belonged to Tuya and is a fine example made from wood lined with stucco and gilded. The gold on the face, neck, and hands draws the attention together with the broad necklace held with two fasteners in the form of falcons' heads. The body of the *shawabty* is wrapped in bandages covered with an inscription in horizontal bands that cites the sixth chapter of the *Book of the Dead*.
(A.A.)

MAGICAL STATUE

PAINTED CEDARWOOD; HEIGHT 25.5 CM
VALLEY OF THE KINGS; TOMB OF YUYA AND TUYA
EXCAVATION BY THE EGYPTIAN ANTIQUITIES SERVICE
ON BEHALF OF T.M. DAVIS (1905)
EIGHTEENTH DYNASTY, REIGN OF AMENHOTEP III (1387-1350 BC)

ROOM 43

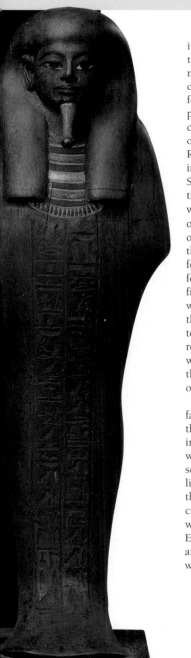

The hieroglyphic inscription reveals that the *shawabty* was a magical statue that came from one of the four magical bricks placed in the burial chamber. From the age of Thutmosis III to Rameses III (and only in a Sait tomb at Saqqara during later times), four niches were found in the walls of the burial chamber of eight pharaohs and three queens that formed the locations of four bricks on which figures and amulets were placed to protect the deceased. Only the tomb of Tutankhamun retained all four bricks, whereas the niches in the walls of all the other tombs were empty.

The figures-amulets faced the four points of the compass: the statue in the north-facing wall was a *shawabty*, the south-facing wall held a lit torch, the east wall the god Anubis crouching, and the west wall the *djed* pillar. Each of the four amulets was inscribed with a section of Chapter 151 of the *Book of the Dead*, which was the formula that described the purpose of the amulets as being to resist any of the enemies of the god Osiris in whatever form they might appear.

This example is an *shawabty* made from painted cedarwood. The figure wears a striped, three-part wig, a false beard, and a large necklace painted red, yellow, green, and dark blue. A hieroglyphic inscription in his bandages gives two sections of Chapter 151 in two columns engraved and painted blue. The right-hand column is the "Formula of the Flame" in abbreviated form; the one on the left is the "Formula of the *shawabty*," also in abbreviated form. It is probable that the *shawabty* protected both the west and north walls although no other amulets of this type exist to support this hypothesis. (A.A.)

SHAWABTY BELONGING TO TUYA

WOOD LINED WITH STUCCO AND GOLD LEAF; HEIGHT 27 CM
VALLEY OF THE KINGS; TOMB OF YUYA AND TUYA
EXCAVATION BY THE EGYPTIAN ANTIQUITIES SERVICE
ON BEHALF OF T.M. DAVIS (1905)
EIGHTEENTH DYNASTY, REIGN OF AMENHOTEP III (1387-1350 BC)

ROOM 43

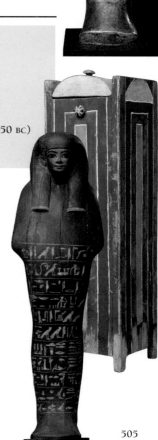

The statue comes from the grave goods belonging to Tuya, the mother of Tiy. Tuya was a high ranking woman in the royal harem who bore the title *"Chekeret-nesut"* which literally means "jewel of the king/she who adorns the king." The *shawabty* is made from wood and covered with a thin layer of stucco on which a layer of finely engraved gold leaf was applied. A large necklace over the bandages has two clasps in the form of falcons' heads. Below the *shawabty*'s hands, which are crossed over the chest there is the traditional formula of the *shawabty*, Chapter 6 from the *Book of the Dead*, in a nine line hieroglyphic inscription. (A.A.)

SHAWABTY BELONGING TO YUYA WITH ITS BOX

PAINTED WOOD; HEIGHT 29.8 CM
VALLEY OF THE KINGS; TOMB OF YUYA AND TUYA
EXCAVATION BY THE EGYPTIAN ANTIQUITIES SERVICE
ON BEHALF OF T.M. DAVIS (1905)
EIGHTEENTH DYNASTY, REIGN OF AMENHOTEP III (1387-1350 BC)

ROOM 43

The grave goods of the parents of Queen Tiy contained many *shawabty* statues with a box in the shape of a sentry box. This statue was one of Yuya's belongings and is made from painted wood. The bandaged body bears the text of the standard *shawabty* formula from the *Book of the Dead*.

The box has a knob on the upper part of the lid and one on the front, each in the form of a rose, around which a tie was wound to hold the box closed. The sides of the box are decorated with green, blue, and red vertical bands edged with white while the curved lid is painted yellow. (A.A.)

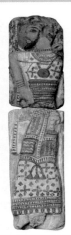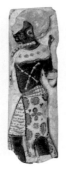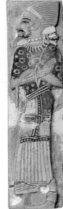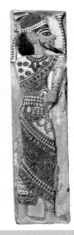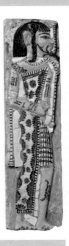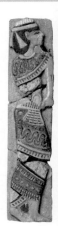

TILES WITH PICTURES OF PRISONERS
POLYCHROME FAÏENCE; MAX. HEIGHT 26 CM, MAX. WIDTH 7 CM
MEDINET HABU, PALACE OF RAMESES III
EXCAVATION BY THE EGYPTIAN ANTIQUITIES SERVICE (1910)
TWENTIETH DYNASTY, REIGN OF RAMESES III (1184-1153 BC)

ROOM 44

These faïence tiles come from the royal palace annexed to Rameses III's funerary temple at Medinet Habu. The brick building, today very damaged, comprized reception rooms, private apartments, and a "presentation balcony" that faced onto the first court of the temple from which the king would appear to his people and throw them money and gifts.

The tiles paved the floor near the window and are decorated with images of chained prisoners characterized by their typical attributes. The peoples that can be identified include, from the left of the display, a Shasu Bedouin, a Nubian, another Shasu Bedouin, a Syrian prince with a pointed beard, a Libyan with a side braid and tattoos, an Asiatic prisoner, a Hittite, recognizable by his lack of a beard and long hair thrown back, and two more prisoners (one Asiatic and one Libyan).

The second pharaoh of the Twentieth Dynasty, Rameses III had to deal with an invasion of Libyans into the western Delta in the fifth year of his reign and the attempted sea invasion of the Sea Peoples (Indo-Europeans from the Caucasus) in the eighth year, both of whom he defeated. These events are narrated in the splendid reliefs on the temple walls next to the traditional, symbolic scenes in which the king sacrifices his prisoners before the gods.

The theme of the defeated enemy is seen again on the palace floor which the pharaoh trod in ritual celebration of his victories over the foreigners. The tiles can be considered a variant of the Nine Arches that were crushed beneath the pharaoh's feet in statues to symbolize Egypt's total domination of its world.
(D.C.)

506

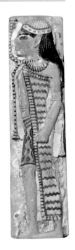

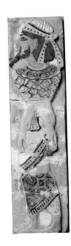

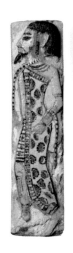

SISTRUM

BRONZE; HEIGHT 42.7 CM, MAX. WIDTH CM 49.5
PROVENANCE UNKNOWN
PROBABLY DATED FROM THE GRECO-ROMAN PERIOD
(332 BC-313 AD)

ROOM 44

Religious ceremonies in honour of Hathor – the goddess of joy, love, and music – were always accompanied by the jingling sounds of sistrums. These bells were shaken in rhythm by priestesses and musicians in order to ward off the forces of darkness and evil.

The sistrum in the image is in excellent condition and still retains traces of its original gilding. The handle bears a double image of the face of Hathor who can be recognized by her bovine ears and characteristic wig.

The sound of the sistrum was often combined with that of the *menat*, another type of jingling instrument made of rows of beads strung between two chains attached to a handle. (D.C.)

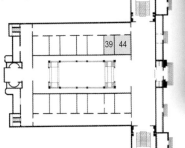

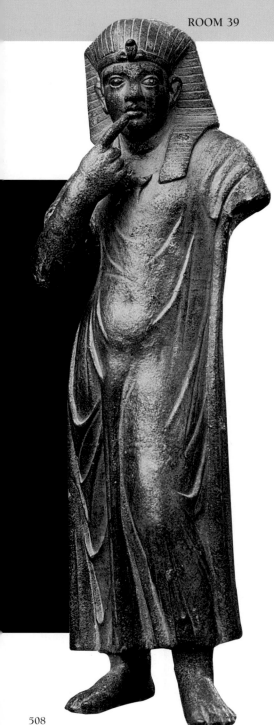

STATUETTE OF HARPOCRATES

BRONZE; HEIGHT 26.7 CM; GIFT OF KING FAROUK (1937)
PTOLEMAIC PERIOD (305-30 BC)

ROOM 39

This small statue is a good example of the religious syncretism that occurred during the Ptolemaic Period. The figure in question is the god Somtus ("he who reunites the two lands") – a form of Harpocrates ("Horus the Child") – who was assimilated to Herishef, the god-ram of Herakleopolis Magna who was associated with Heracles from the start of the Ptolemaic Period.

The god wears the *nemes* headdress and moves his finger to his mouth in a pose that was typical of Harpocrates. The join of the long braid on one side of the head can be seen close to the right ear but the braid itself has been lost. Comparison with other statues suggests that the god-child held a club in his left hand that rested on his shoulder.

The pose of the figure and the folds in the tunic are typically Greek but the *nemes* and uraeus serpent are traditional Egyptian attributes. The two artistic styles do not merge to form a coherent, unique aesthetic and in spite of the very many combinations of the two artistic traditions, they both continue their distinct identities throughout the Ptolemaic Period.
(D.C.)

STATUETTE OF ISIS-APHRODITE

TERRACOTTA
HEIGHT 31.5 CM
PROVENANCE UNKNOWN
GRECO-ROMAN PERIOD (305 BC- 313 AD)

ROOM 39

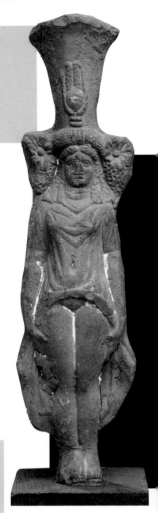

From the start of the Hellenistic Period, the fusion of the Greek and Egyptian pantheons produced new religious syncretisms based on similarities between various deities. One of these was a new form of Isis assimilated to the Greek goddess Aphrodite; her widespread popularity is indicated by hundreds of polychrome clay statuettes of the new goddess.

This example of the goddess lifting her garment emphasizes the erotic aspects of the figure that was in evident reference to the qualities of Aphrodite (the goddess of love) and to the Greek preference for opulent forms and exaggerated, sensual, womanly forms.

Her bud-like hair is crowned with flowers and a tall *calathos* with Isis' typical headdress: a sun disk with two plumes enclosed by cow's horns.
(D.C.)

STATUETTE OF ANUBIS

BRONZE
HEIGHT 14.8 CM. WIDTH 6.5 CM
PURCHASED FROM THE HUBER COLLECTION
ROMAN PERIOD (2ND CENTURY AD)

ROOM 39

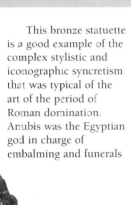

This bronze statuette is a good example of the complex stylistic and iconographic syncretism that was typical of the art of the period of Roman domination. Anubis was the Egyptian god in charge of embalming and funerals and is shown here in his characteristic form of a man with the head of a dog. Despite the double crown and pharaonic inspiration, the statue is clearly based on Roman models. The god wears a breast-plate and wears a cloak over one shoulder; he holds a patera in his right hand and is flanked by two barely modeled dogs.
(D.C.)

This glass vase was made using the technique of blowing introduced to Egypt at the end of the 1st century BC. Blown glass took several forms: cups, jugs, amphoras, and small flasks were manufactured for use at the table or to hold ointments and medicines. Some containers were decorated with ring or serpentine applications for ornamental reasons.

This example is a small transparent amphora decorated with strings of colored glass that were applied to the body while hot; the amphora is in turn fixed to a three-legged support. The rings that hang from the blue waves on the neck are made from gilded bronze but their color has been altered by oxidation.

Glass items have been found from the Dynastic Period made using the technique whereby the glass mass was modeled against a sand or earthen shape that was later removed. During the 3rd century BC, a different technique was used in which the craftsmen poured the molten glass into a mold and then worked on it.

The introduction of blowing in the 1st century BC gave a significant boost to the production of glass containers.
(D.C.)

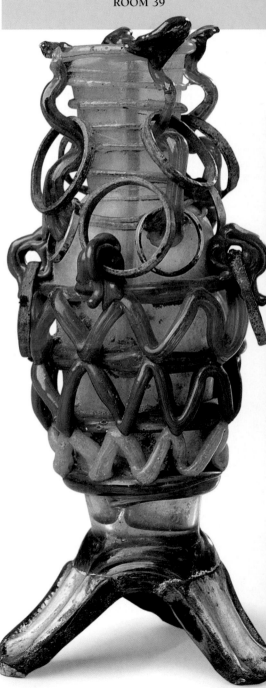

ORNAMENTAL VASE
GLASS, BRONZE, GOLD
HEIGHT 13 CM
PURCHASED; PROBABLY MADE IN FAYUM
ROMAN PERIOD, 2ND-3RD CENTURY AD

ROOM 39

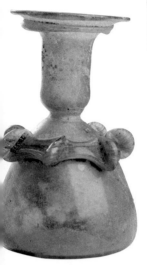

PHIAL
GLASS
HEIGHT 10.3 CM, WIDTH 6 CM
PROVENANCE UNKNOWN
GRECO-ROMAN PERIOD (332 BC-313 AD)

ROOM 39

This small, blown-glass phial was probably used to hold a perfume or ointment. The long neck with the narrow bottom ends with a broad, flat rim to enhance the fragrance and allow the owner to recognize its contents easily from its smell. A greenish glass paste ring roughly pleated to imitate a garland was a common form of decoration on small bottles, and the rather imprecise seal was supposed to prevent the liquid contents from dripping out onto the cosmetics shelves. (D.C.)

FAÏENCE VASE
FAÏENCE; HEIGHT 7.2 CM
ABYDOS
PTOLEMAIC PERIOD (2ND CENTURY BC)

ROOM 39

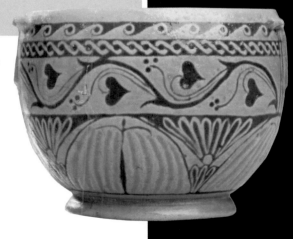

Containers and vessels made from faïence were usually only small in size and made from mixtures based on quartziferous sand that were molded, then lined with green, turquoise, and blue glass paste. The results shone with luminous color in a sort of economical version of the objects cut in semi-precious stones like lapis lazuli, feldspar, and turquoise.

This drinking cup from Abydos – the ancient religious center in southern Egypt – is decorated with geometric and floral patterns painted blue on a brilliant green background. (D.C.)

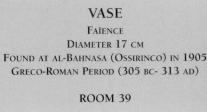

VASE

FAÏENCE
DIAMETER 17 CM
FOUND AT AL-BAHNASA (OSSIRINCO) IN 1905
GRECO-ROMAN PERIOD (305 BC- 313 AD)

ROOM 39

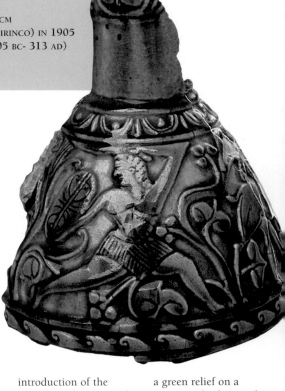

The vase comes from Ossirinco (the ancient Per-meged) which was a town in Middle Egypt that flourished during the Greco-Roman Period. The production of faïence vases and pots had existed in Egypt since earliest times but received a particular boost during the New Kingdom: cups, chalices, and bottles were the commonest items and were generally used to hold cosmetics or to serve food and drink at banquets and festivals. Decorations of flowers, papyruses, fish, boats, or young girl swimmers were both painted and produced in relief; the colors of the material (green, turquoise, or blue) lent themselves well to the depiction of aquatic subjects. The introduction of the blowing technique in the 1st century BC led to a substantial increase in the production of glass articles but items made from faïence continued to be popular.

This fragmentary example, decorated with a green relief on a turquoise background, is inspired by Greek models: the continuous frieze is framed by two moldings of an antelope, a sphinx, flowers, and a hero armed with a shield.
(D.C.)

VASE WITH RELIEF DECORATION

TERRACOTTA
HEIGHT 14 CM; MEMPHIS
PTOLEMAIC PERIOD (2ND-1ST CENTURY BC)

ROOM 39

A recent study has shown that the manufacture of clay plate with molded decorations, believed typical of the early centuries AD, in fact dates back to the Ptolemaic Period. Objects discovered of this nature, generally small in size, are adorned with patterns based on a mixture of Greek and Egyptian motifs.

This example is decorated in the center with alternating figures of Harpocrates (Horus the Child) and grooved columns with capitals in the shape of lotus flowers. The bottom section of the container is decorated with leaves in the shape of a cup and the upper part with geometric and stylized floral patterns. (D.C.)

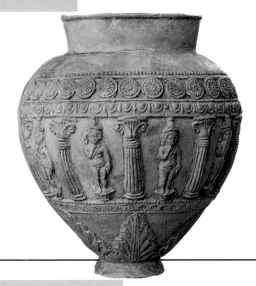

DECORATED FLASK
TERRACOTTA; HEIGHT 30.5 CM
PROVENANCE UNKNOWN
ROMAN PERIOD (4TH CENTURY AD)

ROOM 39

Terracotta plate had been extensive in the pharaonic and Ptolemaic periods but production received a huge stimulus when the Romans took control of Egypt. Widely differing shapes of vases have been found throughout the country, in necropolises, temple complexes, and residential areas. Large containers used to conserve foodstuffs and transport goods usually had smooth sides but small examples often had molded decorations. The range of figurative decoration is fairly varied and derived from models used in Greek and Roman art. Comparison with similar typologies indicates this flask was produced during the 4th century AD. The decoration covers the whole side of the container on two registers, featuring men and women dancing inside structures formed by columns and arches. Those on the upper register are small and barely outlined, probably in an attempt to create an effect of perspective accentuated by the squeezing of the figures together towards the rim. (D.C.)

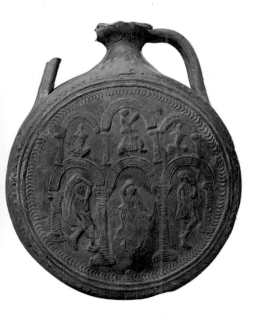

MALE FIGURE WITH GOATSKIN

TERRACOTTA
HEIGHT 8.5 CM
AREA OF THE DELTA
PTOLEMAIC PERIOD (305-30 BC)

ROOM 39

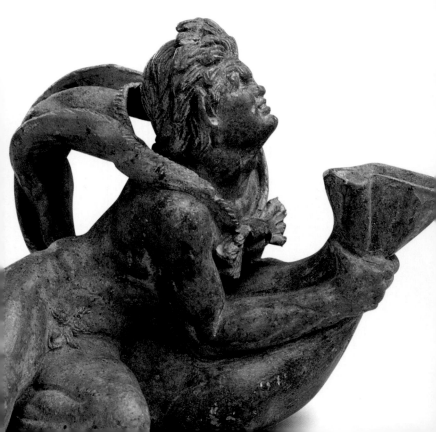

Production of small clay statues enjoyed a substantial boost from the 3rd century BC onwards. The best were made in Alexandria where large workshops used imported clay that was better than the Egyptian equivalent that contained many impurities. The range of iconographic elements was very varied and characterized by the imitation of models borrowed from Greek figure sculpture.

This example portrays a kneeling man leaning down to hold a goatskin; his hair is tousled by the wind and his cloak held in place by a knot around his neck. It has been suggested that the figure is Aeolus, the god and father of the winds, as this is a central feature of the composition and realistically evoked by the stance of the man.

Another hypothesis is that the figure is Dionysus, the god who crossed the river Idaspe by holding onto a goatskin filled with air. In another interpretation, the goatskin is filled with wine and the figure – with pointed ears – is a satyr.
(D.C.)

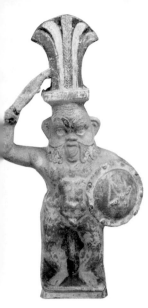

STATUETTE OF THE GOD BES

TERRACOTTA
HEIGHT 34 CM
PROVENANCE UNKNOWN
GRECO-ROMAN PERIOD (332 BC-313 AD)

ROOM 39

The small statue shows Bes wearing a headdress of tall ostrich feathers and brandishing a knife and shield. Bes was a popular deity of grotesque appearance, represented as a dwarf with a tongue that hung over his beard, bow legs and with the ears and tail of a wild cat.

His many functions included defending houses from evil spirits, protecting sleep by averting nightmares (he was often depicted on beds), assisting women in labor and children with the goddess-hippopotamus Tueris, and watching over personal hygiene and cosmetics.. He was also the god of dance and his image as he played a tambourine was tattooed on the legs of dancers.

Bes probably originated in central Africa and, though he appeared in Egypt in very ancient times, his cult only became widespread during the New Kingdom and reached its peak during the Greco-Roman period (he was one of the last pagan gods in Egypt before the arrival of Christianity).

This family god, the protector of Horus the Child, was assimilated to Harmakis (Horus of the horizon) and his fearsome appearance was given the role of guardian of the gates of the eastern horizon.
(D.C.)

TERRACOTTA ISIS-APHRODITE

TERRACOTTA; HEIGHT 29.5 CM
ABYDOS
ROMAN PERIOD

ROOM 39

This brightly painted clay statuette represents Aphrodite, the goddess of love, assimilated to Isis, the model of the faithful wife and affectionate mother. Her simple nudity is broken only by two ribbons that cross between her breasts and contrasts with her impressive hairstyle of long hair and a garland of flowers topped by a tall basket-shaped headdress known as a *calathos*.

Excavation in residential areas has discovered a huge number of clay images of Isis-Aphrodite, and marriage contracts show that these small statues were often included as part of the dowry of young brides.
(D.C.)

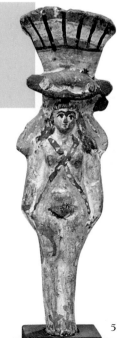

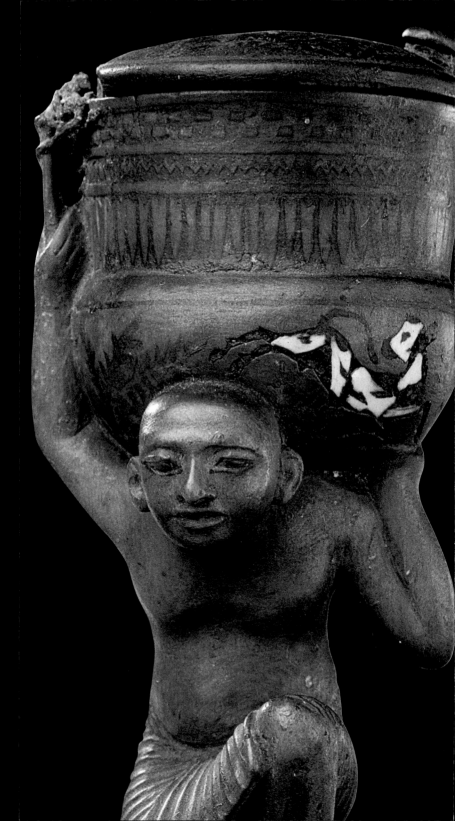

DAILY LIFE

Evidence left to us in the form of written documents, paintings on tomb walls, and objects that formed sets of grave goods provides sufficient information for us to have a wide understanding of daily life in ancient Egypt.

The most frequent scenes are of working in the fields: ploughing, seeding, reaping, and harvesting that busied men and beasts for most of the year. The raising of livestock to provide food – cattle, sheep, and fowl – was very widespread but there were other professions not linked to the cycles of nature such as construction, carpentry, pottery, jewelry, medicine, bureaucracy, and other specialized vocations for the carrying out of all kinds of services and production of goods.

At mealtimes, the Egyptians for the most part ate bread and drank beer that were both made at home using water and the flour of spelt or barley. The bread was made in different forms that probably corresponded to different tastes. Left-over soured pastry was used as a yeast and sweetmeats were prepared using honey, dates, carobs, and currants. Beer was made by fermenting bread cooked only on the outside, crumbled, and probably mixed with date juice. These basic foodstuffs were accompanied by various types of vegetables, fruits, and, on occasion, meat or fish. Wine, cider, and cow or goat's milk were also very popular.

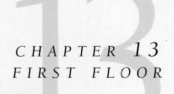

CHAPTER 13
FIRST FLOOR

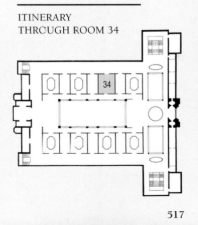

516 ANOINTMENT
HOLDER OF SIAMUN
Wood; Height 14 CM;
Eighteenth Dynasty,
Reign of Amenhotep III
(1387-1350 BC) - start of
reign Amenhotep IV-
Akhenaton
(1350-1333 BC)

517 KOHL HOLDER
Polychrome glass;
Height 9.4 CM, max.
diameter 3.8 CM; found
in 1897; Eighteenth
Dynasty
(1550-1291 BC)

ITINERARY
THROUGH ROOM 34

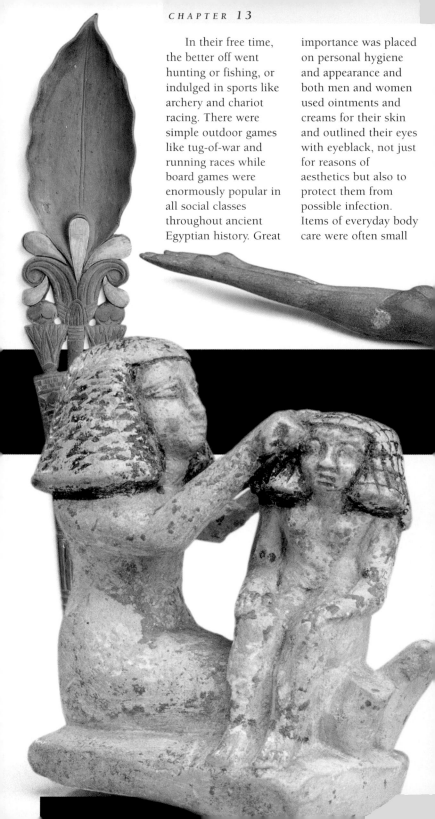

In their free time, the better off went hunting or fishing, or indulged in sports like archery and chariot racing. There were simple outdoor games like tug-of-war and running races while board games were enormously popular in all social classes throughout ancient Egyptian history. Great importance was placed on personal hygiene and appearance and both men and women used ointments and creams for their skin and outlined their eyes with eyeblack, not just for reasons of aesthetics but also to protect them from possible infection. Items of everyday body care were often small works of art and the production of combs, ointment containers, mirrors, and spoons for cosmetic powders were opportunities for craftsmen to express their creativity with works of great imagination far removed from official conventionality.

Hairstyles, especially of the women, were elaborate, often created with ribbons, floral garlands, and elegant pins. Wigs were usually made using real hair and differed in style from era to era.

Music played an important role in everyday life, contributing to social and private entertainment. With dance, it was an essential ingredient at

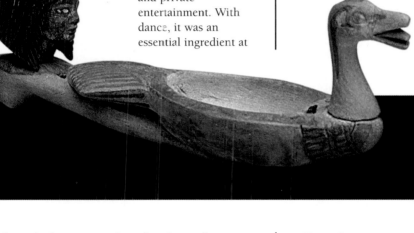

festivals, banquets, and family celebrations like weddings and births. Singing and chanting accompanied by percussion instruments were used in funeral processions to emphasize the sadness of the occasion. Musicians were also often used to provide rhythm and co-ordinate effort during work, for example, horn players and drummers signalled orders and marching rhythms in the military.

Despite the abundance of documentation of daily life, it is still difficult to reconstruct the domestic habits of the Egyptians, above all because the discoveries made of inhabited areas are rare and generally associated with particular contexts. Consequently, we are only able to make deductions based on the linking of separate elements and any attempt to draw these together remains firmly hypothetical.
(D.C.)

WOODEN FIGURINE OF A FEMALE

PAINTED WOOD, DRIED MUD; HEIGHT 23 CM
THEBES, ASASIF, TOMB NO. 816
EXCAVATION BY THE METROPOLITAN
MUSEUM OF ART (1920-1930)
MIDDLE KINGDOM, END OF THE
ELEVENTH DYNASTY (2050-1991 BC)

ROOM 34

The meaning of this figurine is not clear. It has been suggested that it was a toy, a sort of rattle in the form of a doll whose body was the handle and the dried mud hair the rattle but this interpretation is contradicted by the decoration that shows the naked breasts and intimate parts of the figure. It is more likely to be a wooden version of the "concubine of the deceased," a faïence figurine that was included in grave goods during the Middle Kingdom as a symbol of fertility and renewal.
(D.C.)

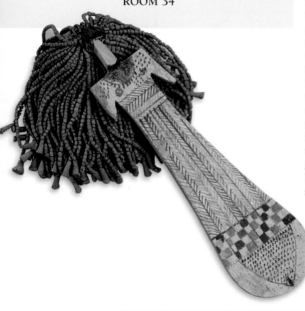

SENET BOARD

EBONY, BONE, AND FAÏENCE
LENGTH 26.5 CM, WIDTH 7.8 CM
DRA ABU AL-NAGA, TOMB OF HORAKHT
EXCAVATION BY L. VASSALLI (1862-1863)
END OF THE SEVENTEENTH DYNASTY (1650-1550 BC)

ROOM 34

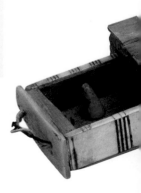

Senet was one of the favorite pastimes of the ancient Egyptians; the game was based on a rectangular board divided into thirty squares known in Egyptian as *peru*, "houses" and the pieces were moved in accordance with the fall of sticks thrown by the players. The oldest example was found in a tomb near Abydos and is from Pre-Dynastic times and the name of the game appeared for the first time in a list of objects on the walls of the tomb of Prince Rahotep (Fourth Dynasty).

Senet became very popular during the New Kingdom when it took on magical-religious overtones and became part of the funeral ritual. The latest known example of *senet* was in

This unusual object comprises six small sticks mounted on a base in the form of a Nile turtle that has its head raised and fins gathered below its shell. The shell has 23 holes which were all used to insert sticks. Of the 6 sticks remaining, the tops of 5 of them are decorated with the head of a dog and one with the head of a jackal.

At first the object was thought to be used for personal *toilette*, for example hair pins, but it is now realized that the sticks were used in a game that was very popular in ancient Egypt from the Middle Kingdom called the "game of the dog and the jackal." (D.C.)

GAME OF THE DOG AND JACKAL

WOOD
LENGTH OF THE SUPPORT: 5.5 CM
DRA ABU AL-NAGA
BASE: SIXTEENTH DYNASTY (1650-1550 BC)
PIECES: EIGHTEENTH DYNASTY,
REIGN OF AMENHOTEP III

ROOM 34

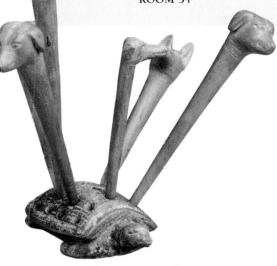

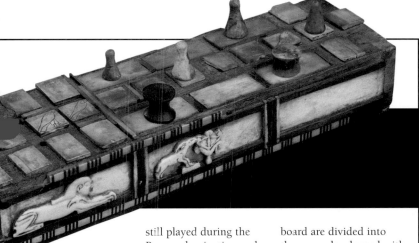

the tomb of Petosiris, the high priest of Thoth who lived at the beginning of the Ptolemaic Period. It seems that the game was still played during the Roman domination and even today a similar game exists in Egypt and Sudan.

Grave goods usually included at least a playing board and this fine quality example comes from the tomb of Horakht near Thebes. The sides of the board are divided into three panels adorned with bone representations of a sphinx and a goat. The pieces differ in shape and material: the conical ones are made from faïence and the bobbin shaped pieces are in ebony. (D.C.)

STATUETTE OF A HARPIST

PAINTED LIMESTONE
HEIGHT 18.5 CM
SHEIKH AL-FARAG
EXCAVATION BY G. REISNER (1913)
TWELFTH DYNASTY (1994-1781 BC)

ROOM 34

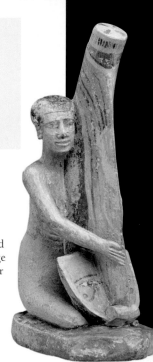

The small statue was found among the rubble that cluttered a small tomb dug in the rock at Sheikh al-Farag, a necropolis in Upper Egypt. It is of a kneeling harp player whose vacant gaze suggests that he is blind. The resonance box is adorned with *udjat* eyes, the emblem of health and well-being.

The harp (*benet* in Egyptian) was the favorite instrument of this people and was played by blind men and women. There were large versions but also smaller ones that could be carried over one's shoulder.
(D.C.)

DIAPHRAGM OF A DRUM

PAINTED PERGAMUM
DIAMETER 25 CM,
AKHMIM; LATE PERIOD (664-332 BC)

ROOM 34

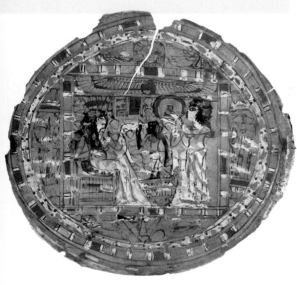

Many objects have been found at Akhmim, an area in Upper Egypt on the east bank of the Nile, but it is not always possible to document the circumstances of the discoveries. This diaphragm of a drum is certainly from the Late Period but the lack of data makes precise dating impossible.

It is a disk of well-preserved vellum with a painted scene inside a square frame.

There are three figures: on the left, Isis is seated on a cushion and throne and wears a long transparent tunic,

522

she is identified by the two columns of hieroglyphs beside her elaborate headdress that say "Isis, lady of the sky, sovereign of the gods"; in front of Isis there is a small figure with dark skin and behind him a musician who plays a drum. Above the scene there is a winged sun disk and, above the frame, the face of the goddess Hathor.

Drums (*kemkem* in Egyptian) could be round or square and were used in religious ceremonies and at funerals. They were formed by two skins stretched over a wooden frame. (D.C.)

UNGUENTARY BELONGING SIAMUN

PAINTED WOOD AND IVORY
HEIGHT 14 CM; THEBES, QURNA, TOMB OF HATIAY
EXCAVATION BY G. DARESSY (1896)
NEW KINGDOM, EIGHTEENTH DYNASTY,
START OF THE REIGN
OF AMENHOTEP IV-AKHENATEN
(1350-1333 BC)

ROOM 34

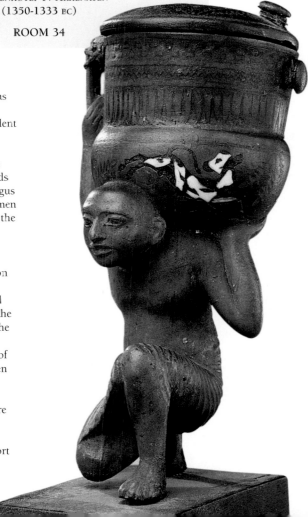

This unusual ointment container was found in the tomb of Hatiay, the superintendent of the granaries in the temple of Amun. The object comes from the small set of grave goods found in the sarcophagus of one of the three women in his family, Siamun, the "lady of the house."

The container resembles Syrian amphoras in decoration and shape, with its geometric and stylized floral decorations on the neck and a frieze on the handle that includes ivory representations of calves running between the trees.

The container is supported by the figure of a servant who is realistically portrayed suffering from the effort of lifting its weight. (D.C.)

HAIR PIN

IVORY

TOTAL LENGTH 14.5 CM, HEIGHT OF THE FIGURINE 3.9 CM
THEBES, ELEVENTH DYNASTY (2135-1994 BC)

ROOM 34

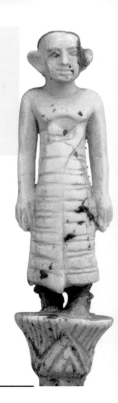

Long pins usually made of bone or ivory to hold hair in place had both a practical and ornamental function and were often included in grave goods.

This broken example was originally probably double its current length. It is formed by a stick shaped like a papyrus stem with the open flower supporting a small male figure. The man is standing with his left leg forward, his head is shaved, his ears stick out, and he wears a long tunic that leaves his chest bare. His face and garment have been carved in minute detail. (D.C.)

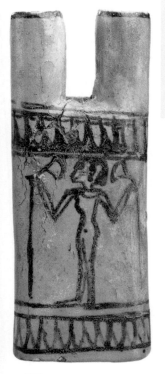

KOHL CONTAINER

FAÏENCE

HEIGHT 13 CM
ABYDOS
NEW KINGDOM (1550-1075 BC)

ROOM 34

Both men and women in ancient Egypt took a great deal of care in making up their eyes by tracing eyeblack with sticks around the rims. Eyeblack, also called kohl, was a thick black paste made by mixing eyeblack powder with grease and water. The treatment not only highlighted the beauty of the eyes but protected them from infection.

Kohl was contained in one or two tubes kept in elegant phials. This example is made of faïence and has two naked female figures painted in black on the surface. One holds two papyrus stems and the other a lotus flower, the emblems of youth and renewal. (D.C.)

MIRROR

BRONZE, WOOD, SILVER, AND, GLASS PASTE
HEIGHT 24.9 CM
DEIR AL-BAHARI:
EXCAVATION BY G. DARESSY (1891)
ELEVENTH DYNASTY (2135-1994 BC)

ROOM 34

The reflecting disk of this mirror is made of silver and the handle of wood with inlays of colored glass paste to imitate turquoise and carnelian; it is shaped like a papyrus stem and bears the image on both sides of the face of Hathor, the goddess of beauty, joy, and love.

The mirror was essential for applying make-up and was often present in grave goods. Its form is symbolic, with the disk representing the sun, the papyrus-shaped handle symbolizing youth, and Hathor granting the owner joy and eternal beauty. (D.C.)

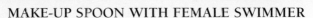

MAKE-UP SPOON WITH FEMALE SWIMMER

PAINTED WOOD
LENGTH 30.5 CM
FAYUM, GUROB
EXCAVATION BY W.M. FLINDERS PETRIE (1889)
EIGHTEENTH DYNASTY (1350 BC CIRCA)

ROOM 34

The excavations at Gurob have unearthed the remains of a village inhabited during the Eighteenth Dynasty. The high quality of life of the inhabitants is evidenced by the discovery of sophisticated objects for personal use and body-care.

This spoon in the form of a duck was used to hold make-up powders; the cover was formed by the wings of the bird but these have not survived.

A slender figure of a naked swimmer forms the handle of the container. The lovely object is an excellent example of the imagination and creative freedom of the craftsmen of the New Kingdom. (D.C.)

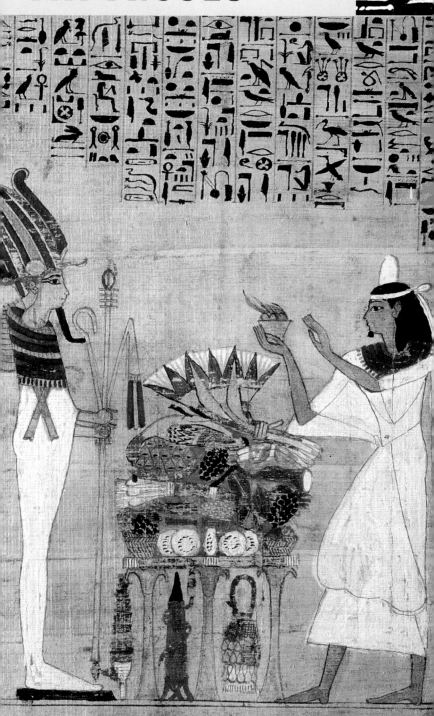

FUNERARY PAPYRUSES

Funerary books were written on tomb walls and sarcophaguses as well as on papyrus. Their purpose was to facilitate the journey of the deceased in the Afterlife by providing him with magic formulas to overcome dangers or difficulties and to indicate the direction to take.

The commonest funerary text on papyrus is undoubtedly the *Book of the Dead* which was also placed in the tombs of private individuals from the New Kingdom, either next to the sarcophagus or between the legs of the mummy. The *Book of the Dead* was a list of formulas derived partly from the *Sarcophagus Texts* of the Middle Kingdom that were written to accompany the deceased on his journey beyond the tomb.

Some books created by Theban theologians during the New Kingdom were reserved for use by the pharaoh and employed as wall decorations in the tombs of the Valley of the Kings. One of the best known is the *Book of the Amduat* which illustrated the passage of the god Ra through the underworld during the 12 hours of night. Shortened versions of these texts appeared on funerary papyruses of private individuals from the Twenty-first Dynasty.

OSTRAKA

Egyptians used small slabs of limestone when it was necessary to jot down notes, make calculations, create a list of names, do student exercises, and make sketches, whether humorous or for professional purposes. The word "*ostraka*" is taken from the Greek word for "fragment."

A great many *ostraka* have been found throughout Egypt, including some thousands in Deir al-Medina, the village inhabited during the New Kingdom by workers who built the tombs in the Valley of the Kings. *Ostraka* offer plenty of useful information about this small community that lasted for 450 years.
(D.C.)

CHAPTER 14
FIRST FLOOR

526 FUNERARY PAPYRUS OF THE HIGH PRIEST OF AMUN NESPERENNEBU Papyrus; Height 35 CM, length 300 CM Bab al-Gasus (Deir al-Bahari) Excavation by G. Daressy (1891), End of the Twenty-first Dynasty, (first half of the 10th century BC)

ITINERARY THROUGH ROOM 24

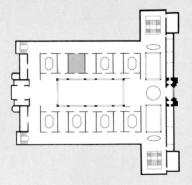

OSTRAKON WITH THE PLAN OF A ROYAL TOMB

PAINTED LIMESTONE; LENGTH 83.5 CM
EXCAVATION BY G. DARESSY (1889)
VALLEY OF THE KINGS, TOMB OF RAMESES IX
END OF THE TWENTIETH DYNASTY (11TH CENTURY BC)

ROOM 24

An *ostrakon* is a fragment of limestone or clay that was used as a cheap substitute for papyrus leaves to jot down notes or make sketches. This example was found among the rubble that cluttered the

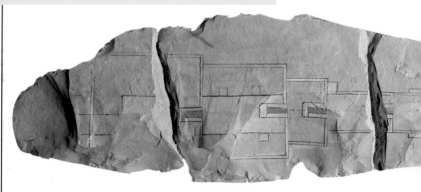

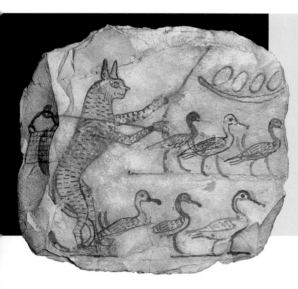

DECORATED *OSTRAKON*

LIMESTONE
HEIGHT 11 CM; WIDTH 11 CM
DEIR AL-MEDINA
EXCAVATION BY THE FRENCH INSTITUTE OF ORIENTAL ARCHAEOLOGY
LED BY B. BRUYÈRE (1934)
NINETEENTH-TWENTIETH DYNASTIES (1291-1075 BC)

ROOM 24

The illustration on this limestone fragment was probably an artistic exercise by a painter. The scene on two registers shows a cat leading six geese to food. The cat stands on its back legs with a bundle on its back and grips a staff to keep the geese in order. A nest with four eggs is drawn in the top right.

As in modern fables, the representation of animals indulging in human behaviour is used as a means to criticize and caricature particular customs, however, the purpose of this illustration is difficult to understand at a distance of over three thousand years.

(D.C.)

528

tomb of Rameses IX, one of the last pharaohs of the Twentieth Dynasty.

The surface is painted with the layout of Rameses' tomb. It is no more than a sketch and was almost certainly used by workers when the tomb was being built; the actual plans of the tomb would have been drawn up on papyrus.

The tomb opens with a stairway with a central ramp to facilitate conveyance of the heavy stone sarcophagus inside. Three corridors, one after the other, lead to the "waiting room" where purification ceremonies were carried out over the mummy.

The sovereign's chariot was placed in the large room with four pillars that followed, and the final room was where the pharaoh was laid to rest.

The illustrations of the doors in the plan have been shown face on as was customary in Egyptian design.
(D.C.)

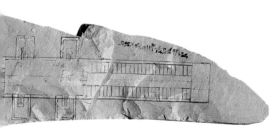

The limestone fragment (*ostrakon*) is painted on both sides. The scene on the front, probably an artistic exercise by an apprentice, shows two figures in military dress struggling as they grasp each other by the throat; it was first sketched out in red, then painted over in black with a few corrections, presumably made by the master.

The rear is decorated with an extremely realistic scene of two mice; one nibbles at a piece of fruit held in its front paws, the other is shown crouching with its fur bristling.
(D.C.)

DECORATED *OSTRAKON*
LIMESTONE; HEIGHT 28.5 CM, WIDTH 23.5 CM
THEBES, VALLEY OF THE KINGS, TOMB OF RAMESES VI
FOUND IN 1890
TWENTIETH DYNASTY
REIGN OF RAMESES VI (1143-1135 BC)

ROOM 24

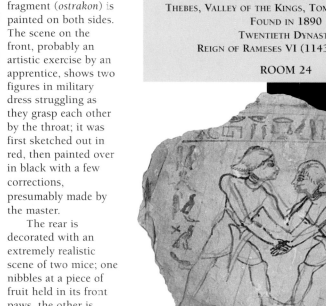

OSTRACON

LIMESTONE
HEIGHT 10.5 CM
DEIR AL-MEDINA; EXCAVATION BY B. BRUYÈRE (1934)
NINETEENTH-TWENTIETH DYNASTIES (1291-1075 BC)

ROOM 24

This unique *ostrakon* shows a naked lute player from above in an exceptional example of the ability of Egyptian artists to forget the traditional artistic models in favor of original and more daring interpretations. It is likely that this sketch was a creative outlet for a talent suffocated by the official aesthetic conventions that were rigorously faithful to the two dimensional, frontal view of reality. The beauty of the female body has stimulated the artist to explore new forms of expression and the woman is portrayed with deep sensuality: her long curly hair falls onto her shoulders and her free hand pulls a few rebellious locks away from her face in a gesture that seems to be happening right before our eyes.

Her body is slender, elegant and just veiled by a light, tight-fitting dress that leaves nothing to the imagination.

It is unsurprizing that this fragment comes from Deir al-Medina, the residential village of the artists and craftsmen who worked on the royal tombs of Biban al-Moluk. Many "unofficial" finds of daily life have been found here that chronicle aspects of the ordinary – and extraordinary – existence of skilful professionals who built and decorated the final resting places of their kings for generations. (M.S.C.)

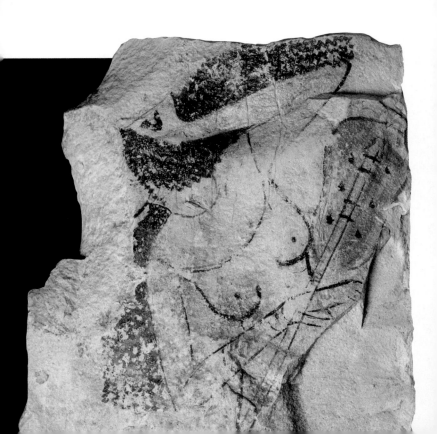

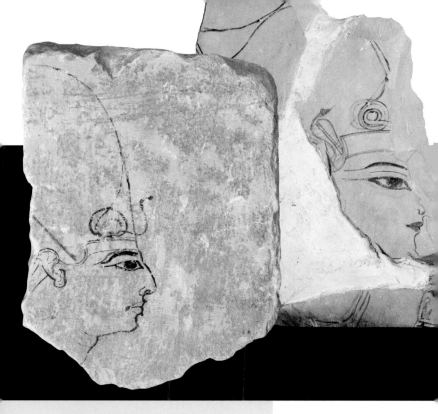

TWO *OSTRAKA* WITH IMAGES OF THE PHARAOH

1) Limestone; Height 18 cm
Saqqara, shaft to the south
of the Pyramid of Unas
Found in 1899; Undated
2) Limestone; Height 42 cm
Thebes, Valley of the Kings, Tomb of Rameses VI
Twentieth Dynasty
Reign of Rameses VI (1143-1135 bc)

ROOM 24

Egyptian artists always made a rough outline of their drawings on *ostraka* first. These two paintings represent the head of a pharaoh wearing the blue crown (*khepresh*) which was a leather cap adorned with small metal plaques frequently worn by the rulers of the New Kingdom.

The sketch on the first *ostrakon* has been drawn in black and shows a carefully rendered face and a uraeus serpent that has hardly been outlined.

The sketch on the second *ostrakon* was initially traced out in yellow ocher, then in diluted red ocher. The final design was painted using smoke-black and given touches of color with red on the lips and eyebrows and pale yellow on the chin and cheek. Although the stone has been damaged, the coils of a uraeus serpent can be made out on the pharaoh's forehead; the purpose of the uraeus was to protect the ruler from negative influences. Another uraeus was drawn with particular care on the side of the headdress. In the bottom right the remains of an inscription can be read, "Loved by Osiris."

The painters used brushes made from small reeds frayed at one end and natural pigments taken from ocher and minerals.

(D.C.)

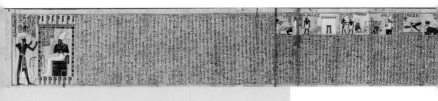

BOOK OF THE DEAD BELONGING TO PINUDJEM I

PAPYRUS; HEIGHT 37 CM, LENGTH 450 CM
WEST THEBES, TOMB OF QUEEN INHAPY; EXCAVATION
BY THE EGYPTIAN ANTIQUITIES SERVICE (1881); THIRD
INTERMEDIATE PERIOD; TWENTY-FIRST DYNASTY
PONTIFICATE AND REIGN OF PINUDJEM I (1060-1020 BC)
ROOM 24

At the start of the Third Intermediate Period southern Egypt was governed by the high priests of Amun. Pinudjem I did nothing more than confirm an already established situation when he decided to assume the title of Pharaoh during the second part of his long pontificate. His name is written in cartouches in this superb example of the *Book of the Dead* that was revealed during one of the most astonishing discoveries in the history of Egyptology when the mummies of some of the greatest pharaohs of the New Kingdom were found in 1881 at Deir al-Bahari, on the west bank of the Nile in front of Karnak. The mummies had been hidden by the priests of the Temple of Amun in the rock tomb of Queen Inhapy in an attempt to protect them from the repeated desecration of robbers of the royal tombs. A number of mummies of the priesthood in the Temple of Amun were found in the same tomb, one of whom was Pinudjem I, who had been placed in a sarcophagus that had belonged to Thutmosis I. He was found with his bandages partly unwrapped and a papyrus scroll containing some illustrated chapters of the *Book of the Dead* between his legs.

The first examples of this funerary text date from the end of the Seventeenth Dynasty. It contains a collection of magical-religious formulas written to accompany the deceased on his journey beyond the tomb.

Although it was originally destined to the king and his family, the *Book of the Dead* became popular also among well-to-do social classes.

Drawn up on papyrus and then rolled up, the *Book of the Dead* was placed in the sarcophagus either beneath the hands or between the legs of the mummy, or was sometimes deposited in a small alcove in the wall of the tomb. The text was written in black and red ink, included brightly colored illustrations, and was bounded above and below by horizontal colored lines. The papyruses were of varying sizes as the number of the formulas and illustrations differed depending on the customer's economic means. The chapters were not written in a particular order and it was only during the Twenty-sixth Dynasty that the sequence of 165 standard formulas was fixed; a further 30, only recently identified, were added later.

Egyptologists conventionally divided The *Book of the Dead* into five sections:

• The texts relating to the burial (1-30)

• The warding off of enemies and invocation of certain gods (31-63)

• The departure of the deceased from the tomb and his assumption of different forms to facilitate the journey through the Underworld (64-92)

• The crossing of the sky on the solar boat and arrival at the side of Osiris, the god of the dead (93-125)

• The description of the Afterlife (126-165).

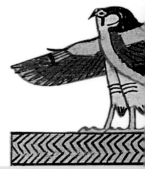

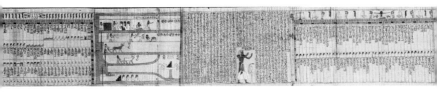

Chapter 125 is the crucial passage in the Book as it deals with the episode when the deceased must face a tribunal of forty-two gods presided over by Osiris. Anubis and Horus weigh the heart and Thoth records the result. If the result is negative, it is given to Ammut, a terrifying monster; if positive, the deceased will live for ever happily in the fertile land of the Afterlife. The illustration of this chapter frequently appears on the papyruses.

Pinudjem's Book contains Chapters 23, 72, 27, 30, 71, 141, 110, 125. The illustrations show Pinudjem adoring Osiris, the exit from the tomb, the weighing of his soul, Ra emerging from the primordial ocean with Mehet-uret (the Great Flood) and the ibis-headed Thoth, a series of gods divided into registers inside a *naos* frame below a frieze of plumes (the emblems of the goddess Maat), the fields of Iaru (the kingdom of the blessed in which the deceased is busy in agricultural activities), and the forty-two judges before two seated goddesses: Maat (Justice) and Maati (Double Justice). (D.C.)

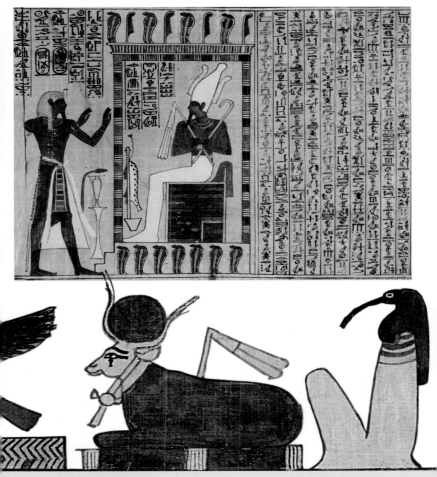

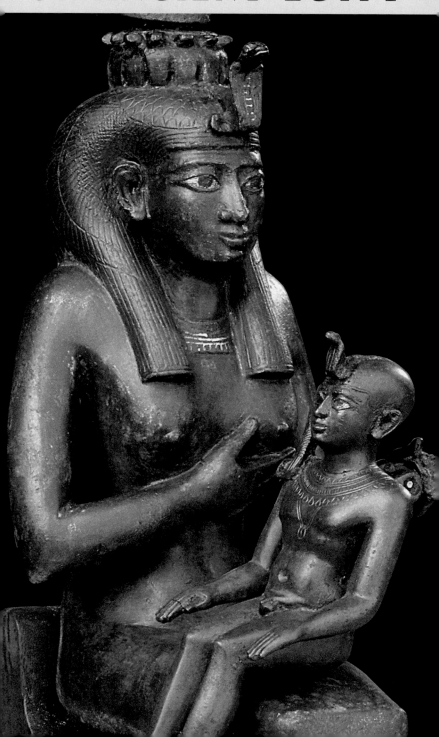

THE GODS
OF ANCIENT EGYPT

The world of the gods of ancient Egypt at first appears to be an unending list of names and forms that overlap and entwine to form every possible combination of human and animal figures. Herodotus' description of the Egyptians as "…religious to excess, far beyond any other race of man" (III, 37) accords well with the long parade of deities.

To understand such complex world, it is necessary to think in the way Egyptians did, to use a logic that allowed them quite happily to see a goddess represented as a woman, but also as a cow, a tree, a bird, or half-woman and half-animal. Egyptologists call it the logic of the "multiplicity of approaches," which allows a single entity (a god) to be defined through a variety of concepts, including opposites, each of which describes a different facet of that entity; only when these various concepts are combined and complement one another is a complete description of the initial entity given. In fact, this kind of logic was not restricted to just the religious world but was used in all expressions of Egyptian culture.

The cult of animals and the representation of deities as animals is the most unusual feature of the Egyptian pantheon: "The animals that exist in the country, whether domesticated or otherwise, are all regarded as sacred" (Herodotus, II, 65). Every village, city, or region had its own sacred animal that was associated with a particular divinity. It was not the animal itself that was worshipped but the divine power within it. A highly regarded or feared quality in an animal was believed to be divine, such as the courage of the lion and the strength of the bull, and this quality was considered so admired by the local god that it became one of the god's manifestations. The most well-known example is that of the bull Apis (sacred in Memphis) which

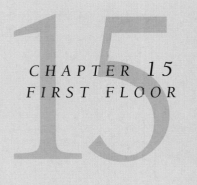

CHAPTER 15
FIRST FLOOR

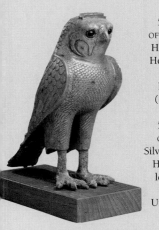

534 STATUE
OF ISIS SUCKLING
HORUS: Bronze
Height 46.5 CM
Karnak
Late Period
(664-332 BC)

535 STATUE
OF A FALCON
Silver with gilding
Height 19 CM,
length 24 CM
Dendera
Uncertain date

ITINERARY
THROUGH ROOM 19

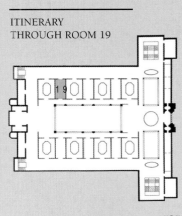

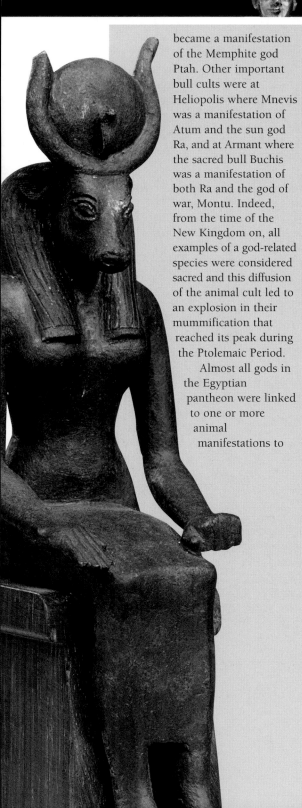

became a manifestation of the Memphite god Ptah. Other important bull cults were at Heliopolis where Mnevis was a manifestation of Atum and the sun god Ra, and at Armant where the sacred bull Buchis was a manifestation of both Ra and the god of war, Montu. Indeed, from the time of the New Kingdom on, all examples of a god-related species were considered sacred and this diffusion of the animal cult led to an explosion in their mummification that reached its peak during the Ptolemaic Period.

Almost all gods in the Egyptian pantheon were linked to one or more animal manifestations to better express their characters. The god Horus was a falcon, Thoth was an ibis and a baboon, Sobek a crocodile, Sekhmet a lioness, Hathor a cow, Anubis a jackal, and so on. They usually appeared in half-human and half-animal form.

Syncretistic divine forms reflect a further attempt to represent the gods in their multiple aspects; in these cases, a god would be characterized by the combined name of two or three divinities all of whom were equally present in the mystery of his being. These syncretistic forms were thought of as new divine forms that mirrored the continual transformation of the world. An example of this development can be seen in the phenomenon that Egyptologists call the "solarization" of religion: the solar cult was widespread in Egypt, enjoying particular popularity during the Fifth Dynasty, and it gave rise to new divine forms whose names indicated their mystical union with the sun god Ra: Sobek-Ra, Atum-Ra, Montu-Ra, Osiris-Ra, etc.

Gods behaved like humans, crying, laughing, eating, sleeping, making mistakes, arguing, losing their tempers, living in a hierarchical society and in families. Combinations of divine beings existed in complex structures, the best-known example being the Ennead at Heliopolis, a set of nine deities all born from the same god and united by blood relationships: the bisexual god Atum generated the couple Shu and Tefnet, whose union gave birth to Geb and Nut, who in turn gave birth to Osiris, Isis, Seth and Nephthys.

Every city worshipped its own god, though usually combined with two others to form a triad: mother, father, and child. Very often the local god passed local confines and became a regional or even a national divinity. This was the case with the Theban god, Amun, who evolved into a national and dynastic god during the New Kingdom. His temple was in Thebes, on the west bank at Karnak and was to become the most important in Egypt.

The god resided in his temple which was truly believed to the "abode of the god" on earth. The power of the god, his *ba*, descended from heaven and was incarnated in his statue (i.e. his terrestrial form) that lived protected inside the temple. A daily temple ritual served to maintain this mystical

union in a cycle of eternal consecration. Every morning when the sun rose, the priest performed a particular ritual on the statue as a result of which the *ba* of the god descended from heaven once more and entered the statue/body of the god. The god awoke on the new day, reborn for a new life, and with him the whole cosmos and all its creatures.

The temple was protected by walls to hide and preserve the mystery of the divinity. It could be approached and understood only by the pharaoh and the priesthood. The profane world was kept outside and only allowed to "see the god" during religious festivals when solemn processions accompanied the statue of the god outside the temple but enclosed in a shrine.

In parallel to the official world of the deity, which existed in the reliefs and complex rituals of the temple, a more "personal" manner of communicating with the divinity was practised that allowed the devotee to feel that the divinity was closer to his own world and his problems. The offerings made by the king to the god inside the temple had their counterpart in the votive offerings made by ordinary

citizens to the local god in a minor sanctuary. This dual level is indicative of the mystery and complexity of the divine figure: distant, transcendent, hidden and unreachable, yet alive and present on the earth, providing protection and a support to the needy. (A.A.)

536 STATUE
OF HATHOR
Bronze;
Height 21 CM
Gift from King
Fu'ad I (1936)
Probably Saite Era
(664-525 BC)

537 STATUE
OF OSIRIS
Bronze with gilding
Height 16.2 CM
Purchased in 1897
Uncertain date

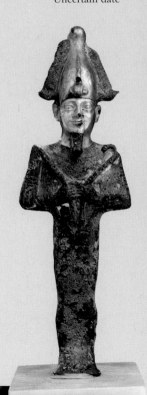

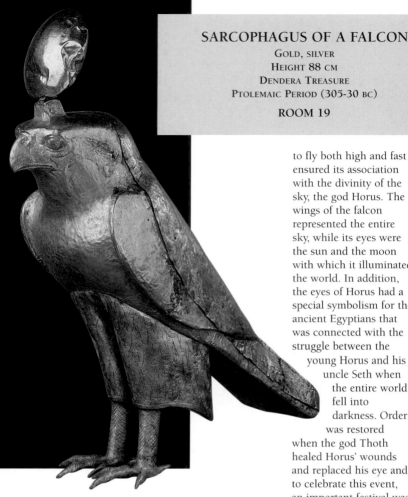

SARCOPHAGUS OF A FALCON
GOLD, SILVER
HEIGHT 88 CM
DENDERA TREASURE
PTOLEMAIC PERIOD (305-30 BC)

ROOM 19

to fly both high and fast ensured its association with the divinity of the sky, the god Horus. The wings of the falcon represented the entire sky, while its eyes were the sun and the moon with which it illuminated the world. In addition, the eyes of Horus had a special symbolism for the ancient Egyptians that was connected with the struggle between the young Horus and his uncle Seth when the entire world fell into darkness. Order was restored when the god Thoth healed Horus' wounds and replaced his eye and, to celebrate this event, an important festival was included in the Egyptian calendar. Horus' eye then became an amulet of protection both on earth and in the Afterlife, and a symbol of regeneration.

The mystery of Egyptian royalty was strongly linked to the god-falcon Horus: the coronation of the king was also a celebration of his divinity and marked his identification with Horus; on his death, the pharaoh flew "in heaven like a falcon" to enter the world of the gods. (A.A.)

This splendid item made from gold and silver attracts the attention of the museum visitor. The statue seems imbued with the mystery of the god-falcon who is represented with a large sun disk on his head, a proud gaze, and talons solidly set. The difference in color of the metals used for the body and feet gives the creature elegance and lightness. The body is split in two so that it can contain the mummified body of a real falcon; in other words, it is a sarcophagus in the shape of a falcon.

Embalming sacred animals became popular in the later eras to the extent that real and large necropolises were created for that very purpose, for example, the one around Saqqara that is still being excavated. The falcon is a bird of prey found in Egypt and, ever since earliest times, the size of its wingspan, the haughtiness of its expression, and its ability

Scarabs were one of the most important symbols in ancient Egyptian beliefs. There was a strong consonance between the word *kheperer*, meaning scarab, and *kheper* meaning "to become" or "enter existence." The god-scarab Khepri represented the sun that rose each morning (re-entering existence) thus ensuring the cycle of the eternal regeneration of the cosmos and all its creatures.

Closely connected to the solar cycle as it was in ancient Egypt, the scarab in consequence came to mean rebirth after death. In particular, the winged scarab was placed over the heart of the deceased and known as the "heart scarab." The Truth about each individual was contained in one's heart and it was the heart that was weighed on the scales during the judgement of the gods after death (Chapter 125 of the *Book of the Dead*). The "heart scarab" was endowed with the power of regeneration needed to overcome death and this was invoked by Chapter 30 of the *Book of the Dead* that contained the formula engraved on the lower surface of the insect: *"O my heart that I received from my mother … do not bear witness against me in the presence of the Universal Lord, …."*

The importance of the scarab is reflected in the precious and symbolic materials it was made from: gold, silver, and lapis lazuli. (A.A.)

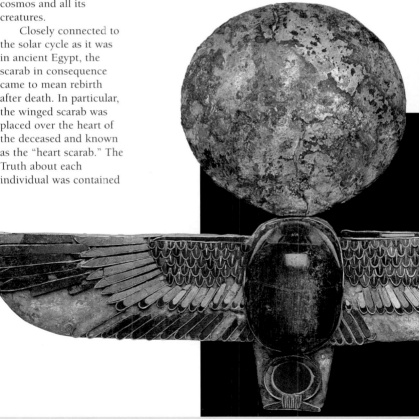

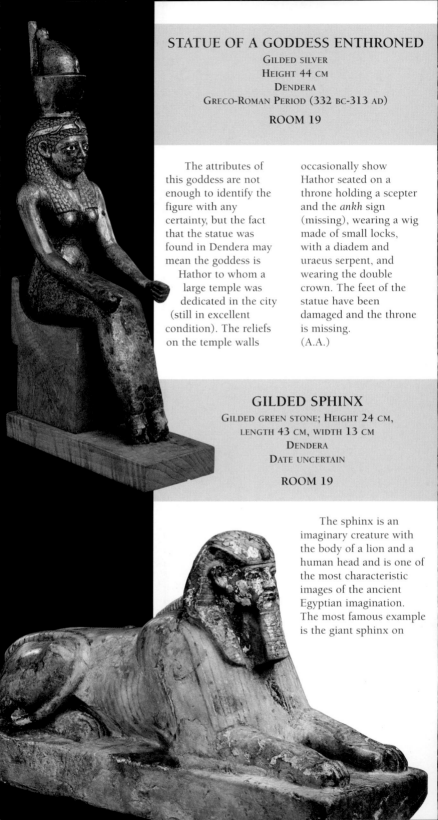

STATUE OF A GODDESS ENTHRONED
GILDED SILVER
HEIGHT 44 CM
DENDERA
GRECO-ROMAN PERIOD (332 BC-313 AD)

ROOM 19

The attributes of this goddess are not enough to identify the figure with any certainty, but the fact that the statue was found in Dendera may mean the goddess is Hathor to whom a large temple was dedicated in the city (still in excellent condition). The reliefs on the temple walls occasionally show Hathor seated on a throne holding a scepter and the *ankh* sign (missing), wearing a wig made of small locks, with a diadem and uraeus serpent, and wearing the double crown. The feet of the statue have been damaged and the throne is missing.
(A.A.)

GILDED SPHINX
GILDED GREEN STONE; HEIGHT 24 CM,
LENGTH 43 CM, WIDTH 13 CM
DENDERA
DATE UNCERTAIN

ROOM 19

The sphinx is an imaginary creature with the body of a lion and a human head and is one of the most characteristic images of the ancient Egyptian imagination. The most famous example is the giant sphinx on

Giza plateau carved with the face of the pharaoh Chephren that appears as a sort of guardian of the royal necropolis from the Fourth Dynasty. This example rests on an unmarked, smooth rectangular plinth. The lion's body is stretched sinuously with its long front legs stuck out in front and its tail curved across its right rear leg. The musculature of the animal is subtly suggested with thin engraved lines, some of which still contain the original gilt of the statue. The head is of a pharaoh who wears the royal nemes headdress, lined and stiff, that frames his face. The symbol of divinity and regality, the uraeus serpent, is shown on his forehead as a sign of protection and the large squarish false beard was tied behind the protruding ears. Some traces of the original gilt covering can still be seen. The absence of an inscription means the figure of the pharaoh cannot be identified. (A.A.)

STATUE OF OSIRIS
BRONZE ENCRUSTED WITH GOLD AND SILVER
HEIGHT 29.2 CM
SAQQARA, SERAPEUM
SIXTEENTH DYNASTY (664–525 BC)

ROOM 19

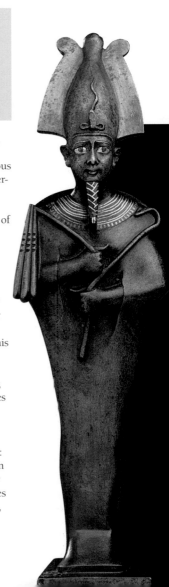

This statue standing on a plinth without inscription has the typical iconography of Osiris, the god of vegetation that dies and is born again in a cycle of eternal rebirth. Wrapped in his bandages with his arms crossed on his chest, the royal scepters in his hands, and wearing the false beard and the *atef* crown on his head, the god is the absolute master of the Afterlife, he who first defeated death to live once more in a new dimension beyond the grave. The color of the metal and the polished surface confer the figure with a sense of mystery that is increased by the large eyes encrusted with silver and golden highlights.

Osiris was one of the most important gods in the Egyptian pantheon and his exploits were well-known as a result of Plutarch's description that has survived. Osiris, the beloved lord of the earth, was killed and his body dismembered by his jealous brother Seth, but his sister-wife Isis and his sister Nephthys searched and found the scattered parts of his body and put them back together again, returning him to existence. The union of Osiris and Isis produced the god Horus who, after gaining his revenge over Seth and regaining his terrestrial throne, made his father Osiris lord of the kingdom of the dead.

In Egyptian theology, the myth of Osiris ensures the continuation of existence after death and implicitly supported the concept of the monarchy: the king became Horus in the coronation ceremony and Osiris during the rites of embalming and burial, indispensable to the continual renewal of the state and the universe. (A.A.)

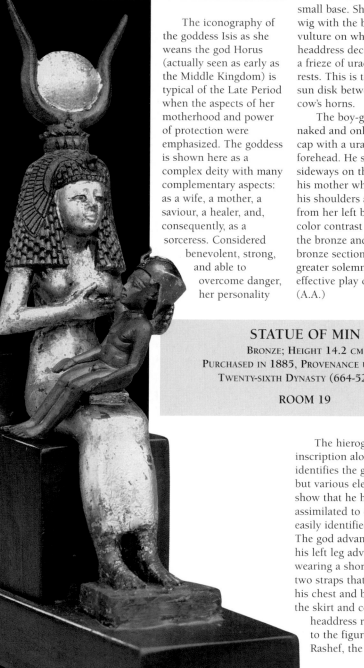

STATUE OF ISIS WEANING HORUS
Gilded bronze; Height 22.1 cm
Abu Sir; Late Period (664-332 bc)

ROOM 19

The iconography of the goddess Isis as she weans the god Horus (actually seen as early as the Middle Kingdom) is typical of the Late Period when the aspects of her motherhood and power of protection were emphasized. The goddess is shown here as a complex deity with many complementary aspects: as a wife, a mother, a saviour, a healer, and, consequently, as a sorceress. Considered benevolent, strong, and able to overcome danger, her personality certainly influenced the Hellenistic and Roman worlds.

In this statue, Isis is seated on a throne wrapped in a long tunic with her feet resting on a small base. She wears a wig with the body of a vulture on which a headdress decorated with a frieze of uraeus serpents rests. This is topped by a sun disk between two cow's horns.

The boy-god Horus is naked and only wears a cap with a uraeus on the forehead. He sits sideways on the legs of his mother who supports his shoulders as he sucks from her left breast. The color contrast between the bronze and gilded bronze sections creates a greater solemnity and an effective play of light. (A.A.)

STATUE OF MIN
Bronze; Height 14.2 cm
Purchased in 1885, Provenance unknown
Twenty-sixth Dynasty (664-525 bc)

ROOM 19

The hieroglyphic inscription along the base identifies the god as Min but various elements show that he has been assimilated to other, more easily identified deities. The god advances with his left leg advanced and wearing a short skirt with two straps that cross over his chest and back. Both the skirt and cone-shaped headdress relate him to the figure of Rashef, the Asiatic

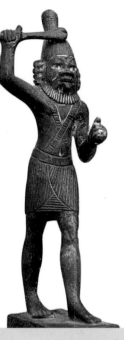

warrior god who appeared in Egypt during the Twelfth Dynasty; Rashef was associated with the Asiatic gods Anat, Astarte, and Qadesh as well as Min. Even the position of the arms is typical of the iconography of Rashef: to underline his bellicose appearance, his right arm is raised as it brandishes a club while his left arm (that probably once held a spear and shield) is bent forwards. The face is that of Bes, the monstrous but benevolent god, who is shown with his tongue protruding.

Representations of this sort were common during the Late Period when the evolution of Egyptian religious beliefs had arrived at a single god, able to multiply himself "millions" of times, as recited in Egyptian hymns. The assimilation of Bes with the sun god resulted in pantheistic forms such as this that were to culminate in the concrete realization of "mixed" divine beings, apparently monstrous, yet in reality the explicit expression of a unique divine figure. (A.A.)

STATUE OF A FALCON
Bronze with gold inlays
Height 22.5 cm
Sais, Found in 1893
Twenty-sixth Dynasty (664-525 bc)

ROOM 19

This bronze statue found at Sais in 1893 is a splendid example of the high technical quality achieved. It was made using the lost wax technique in which a wax model was enclosed in clay; the clay was allowed to dry, then the wax melted and the metal poured into the resulting clay mold. This particular example was given gold encrustation to highlight the plumage and features of the head, and to decorate the chest. Adornment is provided by an amulet in the shape of a heart with a sun disk hanging from a wide necklace, and the red crown and uraeus

serpent of which only the lower sections remain. The base on which the falcon stands bears an inscription that says a certain Imhotep, the son of Padineith and Iah, ordered the statue.

Generally these precious objects were donated to a temple as homage to the deity. The magical properties of the inscription allowed the owner named to participate magically in daily temple rites that the common people were not allowed to attend. Following the same principle, high functionaries left

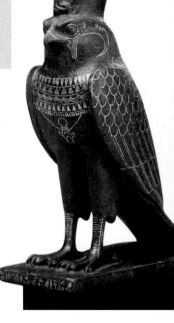

statues of themselves in the courtyards of temples so that they could magically participate in processions and festivals. (A.A.)

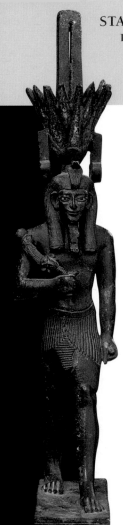

STATUE OF NEFERTEM
BRONZE; HEIGHT 41.5 CM
SAQQARA, SERAPEUM
SAIT PERIOD (664-525 BC)

ROOM 19

Nefertem, the third god in the trinity worshipped at Memphis, is the son of Ptah and Sekhmet. The statue depicts the god advancing with his left leg forward, wearing the *shendyt* short skirt, and holding a scimitar in his left hand. The element that characterizes the god is the large and elaborate headdress that represents an open lotus flower with two plumes. Carefully engraved, the petals of the flower were made to stand out with small flakes of blue enamel but little trace of it is left today. Finely worked amulets linked to fertility, *menat* symbols, hang from the sides of the flower. The upper parts are decorated with a goddess with the head of a lion; she stands with a papyrus scepter in hand, a sun disk on her head (right-hand *menat*), and a uraeus serpent on her forehead (left-hand *menat*). The lower half is decorated with the *udjat* eye.

The lotus flower, in particular the young god who emerges, is connected with one of the Egyptian cosmogonies: when a lotus plant emerged from primordial Chaos, it opened and thereby gave life to the sun god. Nefertem represents the young sun, the god of the primordial lotus. A similar sculpture was found in Tutankhamun's tomb that represented the young king emerging from a flower, just like Nefertem, as an illustration of the ancient Egyptian myth of creation.
(A.A.)

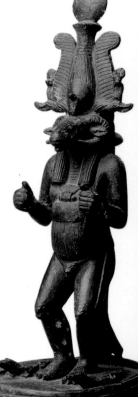

STATUE OF AMUN-RA PANTHEO
BRONZE; HEIGHT 23,2 CM
PROVENANCE UNKNOWN
UNCERTAIN DATE

ROOM 19

The statue is an example of the development of Egyptian religious beliefs during their latest phase. This sort of deity – known as "pantheos" or "metaphysics" – is an attempt to represent the multiple aspects of the complexity of the divine being in a single figure. It combines pairs of opposites that complement one another to form a whole in accordance with Egyptian understanding. This logic sees the elements brought together as variants of a single theme. This statue is identified as the god Amun-Ra by an inscription on the base. The statue combines various divine and demoniac figures. The "head" is a combination of a ram's head and a jackal's head that wears the *atef* crown on its wig. The god is naked with the phallus represented by a leonine protome, his legs slightly flexed, and also the knees decorated with a lion's head. On the stomach is a gigantic scarab with bird's wings that cover the kidneys; the back is a falcon with a long tail that reaches the base and wings closed over the legs. The feet rest between two crocodiles on the oval base surrounded by a serpent, Uroboro, that bites its own tail. The serpent represents the boundary between the ordered world and Chaos, the place where the cyclical regeneration of the universe magically occurs. (A.A.)

STATUE OF AMUN PANTHEO
BRONZE; HEIGHT 45 CM
SAQQARA; EXCAVATION BY J.E. QUIBELL (1912)
UNCERTAIN DATE

ROOM 19

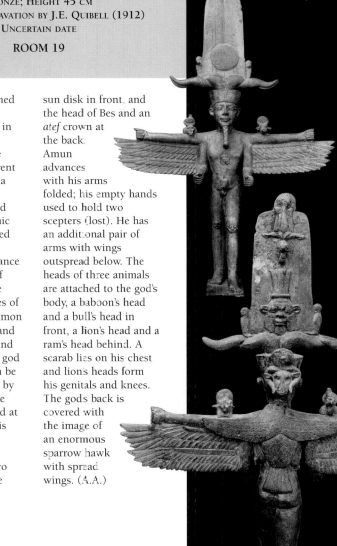

The statue formed part of the magical Egyptian pantheon in which hybrid gods were created by the syncretism of different divine aspects into a single figure. Such statues were imbued with great apotropaic power and were used to hold malign influences at a distance using the powers of their various divine components. Images of this kind were common in the Late Period and are seen on stelae and small amulets. The god in this example can be identified as Amun by the headdress in the form of a ram's head at the back. Above this are two large ram's horns flanked by uraeus serpents, two plumes with a large sun disk in front, and the head of Bes and an *atef* crown at the back. Amun advances with his arms folded; his empty hands used to hold two scepters (lost). He has an additional pair of arms with wings outspread below. The heads of three animals are attached to the god's body, a baboon's head and a bull's head in front, a lion's head and a ram's head behind. A scarab lies on his chest and lion's heads form his genitals and knees. The gods back is covered with the image of an enormous sparrow hawk with spread wings. (A.A.)

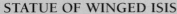

STATUE OF WINGED ISIS
Bronze; Height 41.5 cm
Saqqara, Serapeum
Uncertain date

ROOM 19

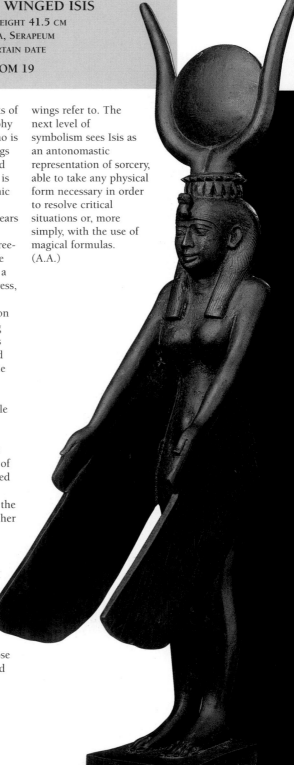

The statue consists of a particular iconography of the goddess Isis who is shown with open wings and her arms stretched forward. The goddess is wrapped in a long tunic that leaves her ankles uncovered, and she wears a broad necklace. Her face is framed by a three-part wig topped by the body of a vulture and a typical Hathor headdress, i.e. with a sun disk between cow's horns on a flared head-covering decorated with uraeus serpents. The polished surface gives the statue a special light.

The wings are associated with the role played by Isis in the Egyptian pantheon, mainly as the goddess linked to the mystery of life reborn – personified in the god Osiris. Her particular function in the myth of Osiris allows her to be presented as a guardian deity par excellence, able to aid those who request her help, to heal sickness, and to assist the suffering. It is these powers to assist and comfort those in need that her spread wings refer to. The next level of symbolism sees Isis as an antonomastic representation of sorcery, able to take any physical form necessary in order to resolve critical situations or, more simply, with the use of magical formulas. (A.A.)

No date has been officially recognized for the appearance of this particular type of stela (also known as a "Horus stone"). The engravings on the stelae were incantations against the bites of snakes and scorpions for which medicine had no remedy and seem to be linked to private magic rather than the official version expressed by healing statues. Placed in public places, healing statues acted as intermediaries between the human and divine spheres but their intrinsic function was the same as that of the stones. It is believed that Horus stones were sometimes placed at the feet of healing statues. The magical texts with which they were engraved were always more or less the same and associated the boy Horus with the *typus* of the sufferer and the goddess Isis with the *typus* of the sorcerer that aided and healed the son who had invoked her help. As occurred with magical statues, the stela was bathed with water and, having thus been charged with positive magical power, it was collected and drunk by the sufferer in the hope of a miraculous cure.

The dominant figure in these stones is the child Horus with the standard side braid falling to his shoulder to denote his young age. The head of the god Bes can be seen over Horus. The god is naked, seen from the front with his feet on two crocodiles and his large hands each holding a couple of snakes, as well as a scorpion and an oryx in his right hand and a lion in the left. These animals might be construed as being forces of the god Seth (Seth represents evil in the Egyptian *pantheon*) or, as another hypothesis suggests, as "weapons" of the god. In this way, the crocodiles would not just be personifications of evil defeated by the god, but also an emanation of the god himself, able to drive evil away.

(A.A.)

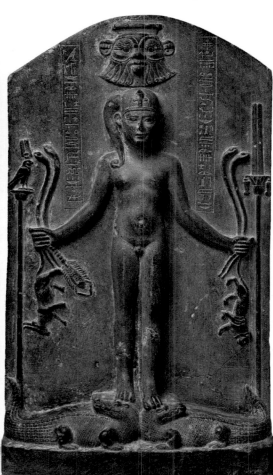

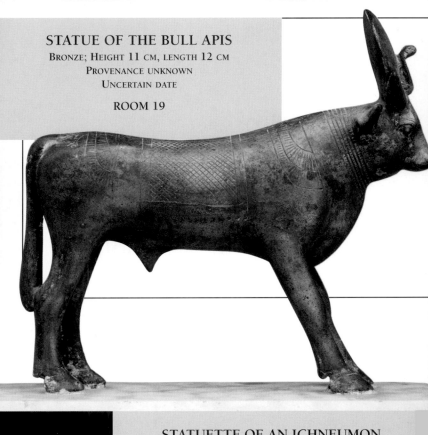

STATUE OF THE BULL APIS
BRONZE; HEIGHT 11 CM, LENGTH 12 CM
PROVENANCE UNKNOWN
UNCERTAIN DATE

ROOM 19

STATUETTE OF AN ICHNEUMON
BRONZE; HEIGHT 26 CM
SAQQARA, SERAPEUM; FOUND IN 1860
UNCERTAIN DATE

ROOM 19

The ichneumon is a type of mongoose also referred to as the "Pharaoh's mouse"; it belongs to the carnivorous family of *Viverridae* that hunt mice, birds, and snakes. It was their ability to catch snakes that led them to be identified with the sun god Atum who defeated the terrifying serpent Apopis.

The animal was a manifestation of several deities and became part of their mythological histories. The ichneumon appears in tomb paintings from the Old Kingdom and by the Middle Kingdom had developed into a sacred creature. Many bronze statues of this animal have been found dating from the Late Period and Ptolemaic Period.
(A.A.)

The bull, a sacred animal in ancient Egypt, is shown with a sun disk and uraeus serpent between his horns. The animal's physical force was associated with his sexual potency making him a symbol of fertility and rebirth. For this reason, many civilizations connected bulls with agricultural activities and the festival of the New Year that celebrated the cyclical rebirth of the cosmos.

This statue is of the bull Apis which was worshipped at Memphis, though Heliopolis and Armant worshipped the bulls Mnevis and Buchis respectively. During the Late Period, Apis became a manifestation of Ptah and was considered an intermediary between the divine and human worlds. He lived in a sacred enclosure at the temple of Ptah in Memphis, where he was raised and nursed, together with his

mother, also held in great honor Physical signs such as a white star on his forehead represented his sacredness.

At Saqqara in 1851, Auguste Mariette discovered the necropolis reserved for sacred bulls at Memphis known as the Serapeum; it contained the embalmed bodies of bulls buried in gigantic sarcophaguses using the same rites as those used for the most important people. (A.A.)

STATUE OF ANUBIS
BRONZE
HEIGHT 14.8 CM
SAQQARA, SERAPEUM
UNCERTAIN DATE

ROOM 19

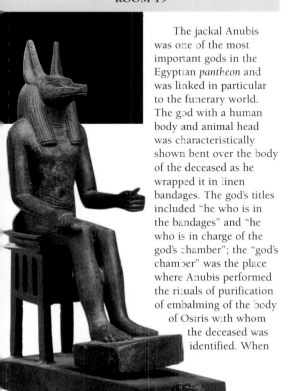

The jackal Anubis was one of the most important gods in the Egyptian *pantheon* and was linked in particular to the funerary world. The god with a human body and animal head was characteristically shown bent over the body of the deceased as he wrapped it in linen bandages. The god's titles included "he who is in the bandages" and "he who is in charge of the god's chamber"; the "god's chamber" was the place where Anubis performed the rituals of purification of embalming of the body of Osiris with whom the deceased was identified. When

the embalming was completed, an hourly recital guided the passage of the deceased from the state of the "dead" to the state of the "living." This "rite of passage" was linked to a particular liturgy (in Egyptian, "Sakhu") that has survived on rolls of papyrus, sarcophaguses, and the walls of tombs and temples. The deceased and the participants in the ritual were transposed into the world of the gods and, by wearing his mask, the funeral priest became Anubis.

The photograph shows the god with the head of a jackal, a three-part wig, and a large necklace. He sits on a throne with his feet on a stool and would have held the *ankh* symbol in his right hand and a scepter in his left, but both are now missing. Traces of gilding remain on the wig, skirt, and necklace. (A.A.)

STATUE OF IMHOTEP

BRONZE; HEIGHT 21.5 CM
PROVENANCE UNKNOWN
GRECO-ROMAN PERIOD (3RD-2ND CENTURY BC)

ROOM 19

Imhotep is officially recognized as the architect and superintendent of works for the great funerary complex of Djoser that centered on the stepped pyramid at Saqqara. The monument signalled the beginning of monumental stone architecture, a symbolic innovation.

Imhotep achieved uncontested fame in the centuries that followed and was eventually divinized in the Late Period and assimilated with the god Asclepius. From the time of the New Kingdom, he was considered the patron of writing and science and was recognized in literature as one of the great "wise men" of the past. During the Ptolemaic Period, Imhotep – with Amenhotep, the son of Hapu – was worshipped on the upper terrace of the temple at Deir al-Bahari where the faithful and sick gathered to request grace from the two gods of medicine.

This statue represents Imhotep seated with his hands holding a papyrus. He wears a skirt, sandals, and a necklace with encrustations of gold. On the base, a hieroglyphic inscription describes him as the "son of Ptah" in recognition of his work around Memphis where the cult of Imhotep was most widespread.

Even the papyrus bears a hieroglyphic inscription that defines him as "he who listens to prayers" in the same way that the intermediaries between the human and divine spheres were defined. These figures were considered able to transpose the everyday problems and needs of ordinary people to the gods. The question of whether Egyptian temples were open areas where the public could pray to the particular god remains unanswered. (A.A.)

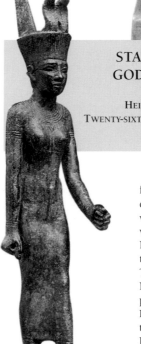

STATUE OF THE GODDESS NEITH

BRONZE
HEIGHT 14 CM; SAIS
TWENTY-SIXTH DYNASTY (664-525 BC)

ROOM 19

This statue comes from ancient Sais (present day Sa al-Hagar) which was the main place of worship of the goddess Neith and the capital of the country during the Twenty-seventh Dynasty. Neith had been very popular during the Early Dynastic Period and at the start of the Old Kingdom, but she was eclipsed during the Middle and New

Kingdoms. The hieroglyph of her name, two bows united, defines her character: predominantly "the lady of hunting" and a warrior able to ward off danger, she was also considered a protectress and sorcerer.

The statue shows her advancing with her left arm forward and the right down her side. Her hands probably held the *uas* scepter and *ankh* symbol but have been lost. She wears a long tunic and the red crown with two uraeus serpents on the front. (A.A.)

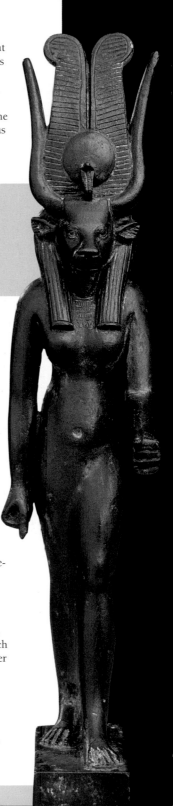

STATUE OF THE GODDESS HATHOR
BRONZE; HEIGHT 27.2 CM
SAQQARA, SERAPEUM
LATE PERIOD (664-332 BC)

ROOM 19

The statue shows Hathor in her appearance as a goddess-cow. In accordance with the Egyptian manner of representing the gods – half human and half animal – Hathor is shown in all her mystery as a celestial cow, the mother goddess of heaven who feeds and weans her children. Her name, literally the "estate of Horus," underlines her celestial role. As a divine mother, she was also assimilated with Isis who sometimes appeared as a cow. Hathor was also a goddess of love and, therefore, of song, dance, and rapture. Her benevolent aspect to humanity meant she was also transposed to the funerary sphere where she was considered to be benevolent to the dead. Her name was often linked to the necropolis at the mountain in Thebes and to the area of Deir al-Bahari where her sanctuary once stood before Hatshepsut built her own funerary temple. Hathor had many places of worship, even far away as Sinai and Nubia.

Here Hathor is advancing with her left leg advanced, her left arm stretched forwards, and the right hanging by her side. Once, she probably held the *uas* scepter and the *ankh* symbol in her left and right hands respectively. The cow's head with wide ears is covered by a striped three-part wig and also wears the false beard. A "broad necklace" emerges from below her beard and adorns her long garment. Two finely engraved ostrich feathers stand between her horns with the sun disk and a uraeus serpent; these elements are considered as Hathor's headdress and can be seen on other goddesses assimilated to Hathor. (A.A.)

The cat was one of the ancient Egyptians' favorite animals, in particular during the late period. Fondness for cats is clear from the wall decorations in private tombs during the New Kingdom when they were often shown seated with their owner. There are many images of cats and kittens like this one in which the group is portrayed on a rounded base that follows the lines of the

STATUE OF A CAT AND KITTENS
BRONZE
LENGTH 9.5 CM
PROVENANCE UNKNOWN
UNCERTAIN DATE

ROOM 19

mother lying on her side. Two of the four kittens are held in the mother's paws, one sits looking at the observer and the other is on its rear legs stretching out a paw to its mother's

face in play. A scene of this type was linked to the concept of maternal protection which was synonymous with birth.
(A.A.)

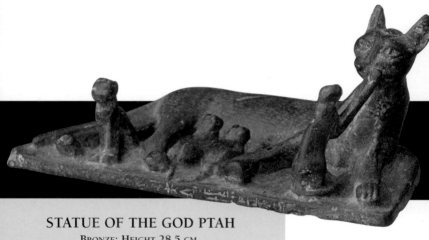

STATUE OF THE GOD PTAH
BRONZE; HEIGHT 28.5 CM
SAQQARA, SERAPEUM
SAIT PERIOD (664-525)

ROOM 19

The god Ptah was an artisan, blacksmith, founder, and, as such, was considered the guardian deity of these arts. He is identified by his headdress – a tight smooth cap – also used by the foreman of the skilled craftsmen shown in representations inside mastabas. Ptah's body is wrapped in a mummy-shaped cloth

that only leaves his hands uncovered. The right hand holds the *ankh* symbol and the left the *uas* scepter that touches the false beard. The peculiarity of Ptah's beard is its shape; it is not curved, as are those of other divinities, but straight like that worn by the pharaoh. It might be thought that the sovereign took this attribute from

the god as Ptah was the main god in Memphis, the kingdom's most ancient capital. A broad necklace adorns the cloak and widens to its full extent across Ptah's shoulders.

Ptah always remained the demiurge god of Memphis to whom one of the Egyptian cosmogonies, in which he was known as the "shaper of the earth," was linked. In the beginning there was Nun, the primordial waters, then Ptah created the gods, men, and all living

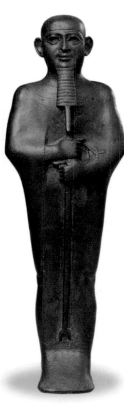

creatures, plus the land, rivers, and oceans through the power of the spoken word. In Memphis in particular, Ptah was associated in a triad (a typical construct of the Egyptian pantheon) with the goddess-lion Sekhmet and the god Ptah, Nefertem being considered their son. He was also given a funerary connotation and assimilated to the divine forms of Sokar and Osiris as a tutelary deity of the Memphite necropolis. During the Late Period his name was entwined with that of the sacred bull Apis and the divinized Imhotep whose father he was considered to be. The sacred bull was supposed to live in the middle of Ptah's temple complex in Memphis, and each successive bull was buried with all honors in a specific necropolis known as the Serapeum at Saqqara. (A.A.)

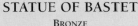

STATUE OF BASTET
BRONZE
HEIGHT 42 CM
KOM KIBRIT, FOUND IN 1914
UNCERTAIN DATE

ROOM 19

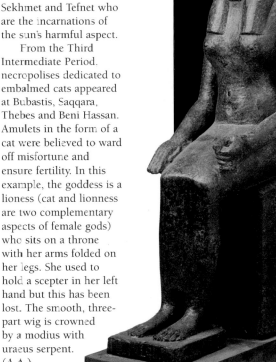

Bastet was the goddess of Bubastis (Tell Basta, the capital of the 18th *nome* of Lower Egypt and a strategically important area for control of the routes to the eastern coasts of the Mediterranean. Bastet was represented from earliest times as a woman with the head of a cat and holding in her hands several instruments connected with her cult. She was identified with other goddesses such as the lioness Sekhmet, Tefnet, Mehet, and Hathor of Dendera. In the New Kingdom Bastet became associated with Mut of Thebes and in general with the concept of goddess-mother. Bastet represents the eye of the sun in its beneficent aspect as opposed to Sekhmet and Tefnet who are the incarnations of the sun's harmful aspect.

From the Third Intermediate Period. necropolises dedicated to embalmed cats appeared at Bubastis, Saqqara, Thebes and Beni Hassan. Amulets in the form of a cat were believed to ward off misfortune and ensure fertility. In this example, the goddess is a lioness (cat and lionness are two complementary aspects of female gods) who sits on a throne with her arms folded on her legs. She used to hold a scepter in her left hand but this has been lost. The smooth, three-part wig is crowned by a modius with uraeus serpent. (A.A.)

This fine bronze object worked with damascening and thin sheets of gold is in the style of a wide necklace adorned with drops and lotus flowers and a row of uraeus serpents. Maat is shown in the center, the goddess of justice and cosmic order kneeling with her wings spread in a sign of protection. The plume on her head is

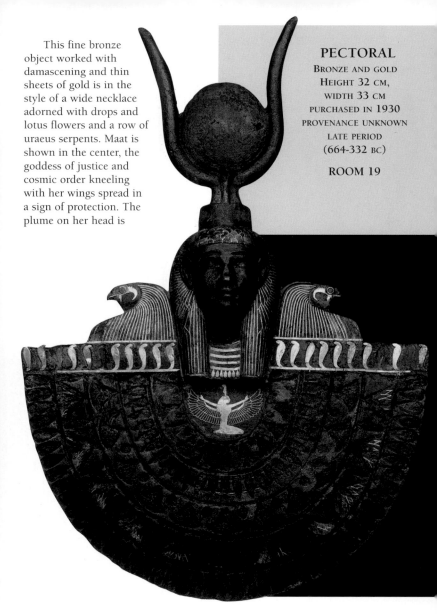

PECTORAL
BRONZE AND GOLD
HEIGHT 32 CM,
WIDTH 33 CM
PURCHASED IN 1930
PROVENANCE UNKNOWN
LATE PERIOD
(664-332 BC)

ROOM 19

characteristic of this goddess and simultaneously an ideogram of her name.

Two symmetrical falcon heads lie at either end of the pectoral, ringing the neck of the goddess

Hathor to form the focus of the composition. The cow's head headdress with sun disk in the center is modeled in high relief like the head of the goddess; its clean simplicity lightens the filled fields of the

necklace originally decorated with gold damascening.

The use of the object remains obscure though it was most certainly considered to have the power to ward off evil. (M.S.C.)

STATUE OF THE GODDESS MAAT

Lapis lazuli, Gold: Height 7.2 cm
Huber Collection, Khartoum
Ptolemaic Period (305-30 bc)

ROOM 19

This perfectly preserved statue cleverly uses color to highlight the two attributes that identify the figure as the goddess Maat: the cobra on her forehead and the tall curved plume on her head. Maat is crouching but only her head seems to be modeled. A smooth, three-part wig frames her face but leaves her ears visible. As shown by the gold ring at the back, this was a pendant that was probably worn at the neck as an amulet. Its value is to be linked to the meaning of Maat in Egyptian religious belief. Maat represented the First Order, the perfect organization of the cosmos and its creatures at the moment of the creation of the universe. This was an order that was not to be to altered or its cycles to be interrupted in any way. Maat stood for everything that made the cosmos function in a state of perfection and immutability: Justice, Truth, and Harmony though there has never been an official translation of the name Maat.

Even during the Old Kingdom, it seems Maat was divinized and closely linked to the sun god. During the reign of Thutmosis III, temple reliefs show the scene of the king "offering Maat" to the deity in which the pharaoh held a statue similar to the example in the photograph. In offering Maat, the pharaoh received Maat in exchange which was a form of legitimization of his power and a guarantee that the power of the monarch would be enough to maintain Order and chase away Disorder. The pharaoh was the guarantor of Maat on earth, the only individual with enough power to maintain perfect order for eternity.

Maat was also present in the scene of the "weighing of the heart" when divine judgement was made on the deceased; if the heart was as light as Maat (placed on the other end of the scale), the deceased was allowed to enter the world of the dead. (A.A.)

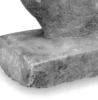

The sistrum was a typical musical instrument of ancient Egypt and used exclusively by women or the king during ceremonies. Temple and tomb illustrations reveal that sistrums were played by singers or princesses to accompany sacred ritual song and dance. When the instrument was shaken by the handle, the small bars (the three for this exampleare now lost) fixed to the frame made a rhythmic sound.

The sistrum was particularly sacred to the goddess Hathor and was used to soothe her during festivals. The goddess was generally depicted as a decorative motif at the end of the handle as in this case; we see the cow's head and ears wearing a wig with curly ends.

The goddess wears the modius on her head which has from a rectangular *naos* topped by a V-shaped molding and enclosed in two spirals from which a cobra looks out.

The *naos* model of sistrum is the oldest and existed uninteruptedly from the end of the Old Kingdom until the Roman Period. A second model appeared during the New Kingdom and became highly popular during the Greco-Roman period. (A.A.)

STATUE OF A CROCODILE WITH A FALCON'S HEAD

LIMESTONE; HEIGHT 9 CM, LENGTH 36 CM
AL-MANSURA; UNCERTAIN DATE

ROOM 19

The statue represents an unknown god with the body of a crocodile and the head of a falcon. It might be Soknopaios (a form of the crocodile god Sobek with a falcon's head) which literally meant "Sobek, lord of the island"; Soknopaios was worshipped from the second century BC to the third century AD throughout Fayum. Excavation work has unearthed a temple dedicated to this god at the site Soknopaiou Nesos, present day Dimai. Numerous papyruses and *ostrakas* have been found referring to the god who was associated with an oracle invoked by the sick. (A.A.)

STATUE OF ISIS-SELKET

GREY ALABASTER
HEIGHT 18.8 CM
SAQQARA, SERAPEUM
UNCERTAIN DATE

ROOM 19

The statue represents a goddess formed by the combination of Isis with the goddess-scorpion Selket; identification is provided by the goddess' headdress and the scorpion decoration on the front of the throne. In one of her traditional poses, Isis crouches on her heels beside Osiris' death bed with her sister Nephthys, mourning the death of her brother and husband. The image of Osiris on a tablet rests on her knees.

The funerary aspects of Isis and Selket combine well as both were guardians of the royal sarcophagus and canopic vases with the goddesses Nephthys and Neith. Selket is the guardian deity of the falcon-headed vase with Qebehsenuef, one of the four sons of Horus. The goddess-scorpion Selket more generally appears as a woman with a scorpion's head but was also represented as a lionness or serpent. Her cult existed from the first dynasties and she can be found in the *Pyramid Texts*. (A.A.)

STATUE OF A COBRA WITH TWO LIZARDS

BRONZE; HEIGHT OF THE COBRA 11.5 CM
BASE: HEIGHT 4 CM, LENGTH 15 CM,
WIDTH 8.5 CM; SAIS; UNCERTAIN DATE

ROOM 19

The bronze group comes from ancient Sais (modern Sa el-Hagar) which was the capital of Egypt during the XXVI dynasty. A coiled cobra rests on a particularly high base with a lizard on either side. The cobra was an emblematic creature symbolizing divine and royal protection and was primarily identified with Uto, the goddess of the crown of Lower Egypt. Uto's connection with the sun god Ra assimilated her to many goddesses and the symbol of the cobra became a hieroglyph for female divinity. The lizard is commonly found sunning itself in Egyptian fields and bones and mummies of the creature found in Fayum are evidence of a cult dedicated to the animal. Like all creatures that shed skin, it was a symbol of regeneration as is made clear in Chapter 182 of the *Book of the Dead*. (A.A.)

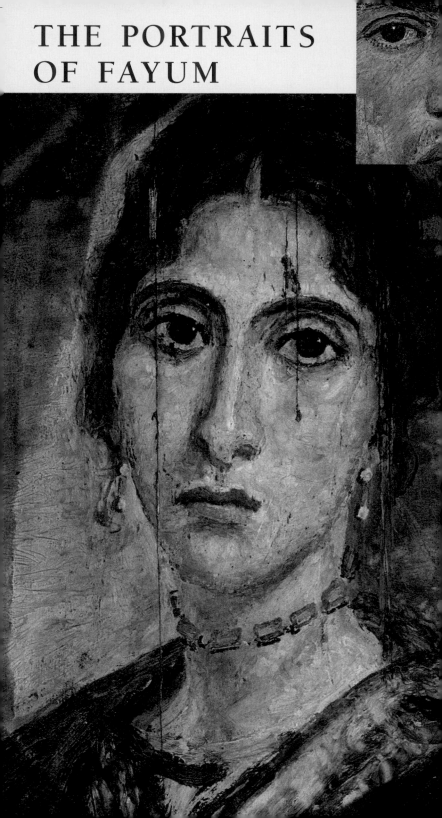

THE PORTRAITS
OF FAYUM

The series of paintings known to us as the "Fayum portraits" – the area where this kind of painting was most widespread – is a rich corpus of portraits on wood made during the Roman imperial era. The paintings were inserted between the bandages of the mummy or on the linen shrouds that covered it at a point corresponding to the face of the deceased. The religious and funerary validity of this practice is rooted in the long tradition of the sarcophagus representing the deceased but it also reflects the uniquely Roman taste for portraits and iconographic realism.

From the time of Tiberius (14-37 AD) until the end of the 4th century AD, portrait painting increasingly became the most successful expression of the reciprocal penetration of Egyptian and Roman cultures that were far more integrated in death than in life.

For the most part, one of two painting techniques was used: tempera, which employed pigments mixed with a binder that was soluble in water, or encaustic painting, which used colors emulsified with hot, molten wax.

In addition to paintings on wood, the Ptolemaic tradition of painting funerary masks on cartonnage continued. In general, the typologies of the masks were conventional and free from characterizing features but, at the start of the Roman Period, new technical and stylistic solutions

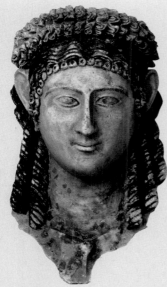

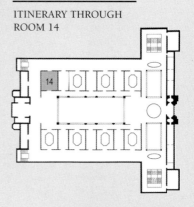

CHAPTER 16
FIRST FLOOR

ITINERARY THROUGH
ROOM 14

558 PORTRAIT
OF A YOUNG WOMAN
Encaustic painting on wood; Height 42 CM, width 23 CM; Hawara; Excavation by W.M.F. Petrie (1888); Roman Period (1st century AD).

559 FUNERARY
MASK OF A WOMAN
Plaster
Height 29.5 CM
Width 18 CM
Tuna (1895)
Roman Period
(30 BC-313 AD).

were introduced with the use of new materials like plaster. From the time of the Romans, the two sexes were differentiated by their hairstyles, jewelry, and facial features; additionally, the head was occasionally raised from the bust as if the deceased was watching the world of the living.

The faces were generally those of the new settlers or of centurions and their families who were in Egypt following in the train of the emperors. On the social scale, the Romans formed the privileged, wealthy élite compared to the overwhelming majority of Egyptians and Hellenes. Hellenes was the name applied by the Romans not just to the Greeks but to all races resident in Egypt that were not Egyptian. Mixed marriages, though not encouraged by the central authority, were not rare and some of the portraits show people with African features.

Observing a practice in use in all Roman provinces, the individuals were portrayed in accordance with styles that were current in Rome itself, whether of jewelry, hairstyles, the cut of a beard, or the design of clothes with the result that every detail contributes to the dating of a portrait.

It is not clear if the portraits were painted during the lifetime of the individuals or after death. It is difficult to credit the first hypothesis in the case of children and young, but X-ray examinations have shown that there were remarkable similarities between the age of the deceased and their portraits. Censuses taken in Egypt by the Romans reveal that the average life span was rather short.

Indications of frames found on the panels – in some cases framed portraits have been found placed beside the mummy, not among the bandages – suggest that the paintings were carried in procession at the time of death and then left hanging in the houses, like domestic *lares*, perhaps for years, before being placed in the tomb with the embalmed bodies. It is thought that the mummies may have received the same treatment, being placed in special "ancestor chambers" before burial, and sarcophaguses have been found with front panels that opened to allow the mummy inside to be viewed.

Regional variants of the portraits exist both in the style and the shape of the panels at the top: for example, the local traditions at Hawara, al-Rubayat and Antinoopolis were curved, cut at the corners, or profiled in the shape of the shoulders.

Following the discovery of the first large collection of portraits at al-Rubayat in Fayum in 1887 by a group of farmers (the T. Graf collection), other finds were made including those of Petrie at Hawara (1888-89 and 1910-11), Grenfell and Hunt at Tebtunis (1899-1900), and Gayet at Antinoopolis, Middle Egypt (1897).

Currently the number of "Fayum portraits" has exceeded one thousand panels or fragments and the latest discoveries at al-Hibe near Thebes, and at al-Alamein on the Mediterranean coast confirm the diffusion of an artistic type that specialized in depicting the physical reality of individuals that was practised by *ante litteram* "photographers" of late antiquity. (M.S.C.)

561 PORTRAIT OF YOUNG BOY; Painted wood; Height 37 cm; Fayum; purchased in 1895; Roman Period (30 BC - 313 AD).

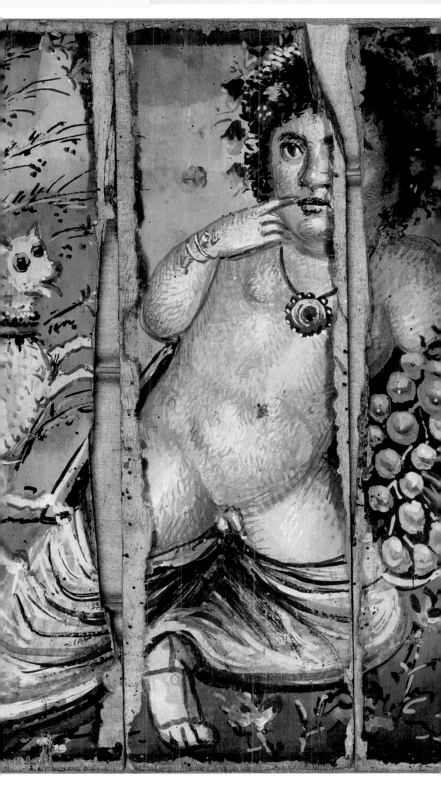

MASK OF A MAN
PAINTED PLASTER
HEIGHT 32 CM, WIDTH 27.5 CM
PROVENANCE UNKNOWN
ROMAN PERIOD (MID-2ND CENTURY AD)

ROOM 14

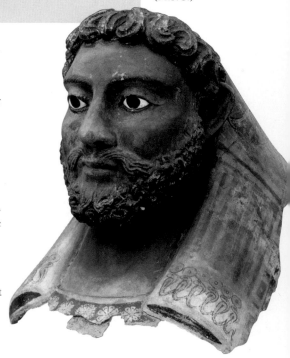

Plaster masks placed on the mummy over the area of the face were the natural development of the *cartonnage* masks (or gold for sovereigns) during the pharaonic period.

The man's face is framed by thick curly hair and a full beard and his eyes are made from an opaque material. A noteworthy feature is the transformation of the traditional Egyptian wig into a sort of scarf wrapped around the head of the deceased that bears the image of the sun disk on the nape of the neck. The stripes at the side simulate the fall of the hair down the neck turning it into a decorative feature completely removed from its original function. (M.S.C.)

FUNERARY MASK
CARTONNAGE GILDED AND PAINTED
HEIGHT 42 CM, WIDTH 26 CM, LENGTH 40 CM
PROVENANCE UNKNOWN
ROMAN PERIOD (1ST CENTURY AD)

ROOM 14

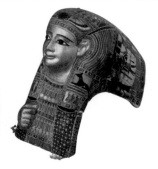

The rich decoration of this mask follows the traditional themes of Egyptian funerary iconography. The lips have a slight "archaic" smile, the face and hand are painted gold (like the flesh of the gods), and the winged sun disk flanked by two cobras in the center of the head has been added to protect the deceased. The bands of the wig are edged with uraeus serpents and decorated with mirror images of Anubis, the god who presided over embalming, who holds a lotus flower between his paws to guarantee rebirth in the Afterlife.

The style and workmanship are very similar to those of the masks from Meir in Middle Egypt. (M.S.C.)

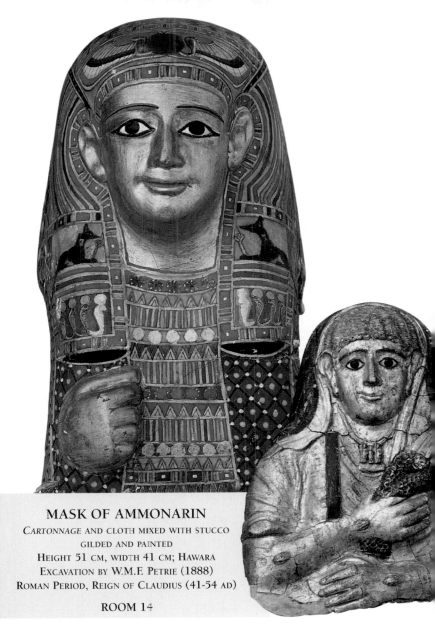

MASK OF AMMONARIN
CARTONNAGE AND CLOTH MIXED WITH STUCCO
GILDED AND PAINTED
HEIGHT 51 CM, WIDTH 41 CM; HAWARA
EXCAVATION BY W.M.F. PETRIE (1888)
ROMAN PERIOD, REIGN OF CLAUDIUS (41-54 AD)

ROOM 14

This mask covered the head and bust of the mummy of a woman whose name, Ammonarin, is written in gold letters on the black band of the gauze that covers her head. As in many similar examples, most of the decoration is molded directly in the plaster that overlays the *cartonnage*.

Both wrists are adorned with spiral bracelets in a form popular during the Roman Period, that of a snake. Her right hand grasps a bunch of red flowers tied with a ribbon and her neck is adorned by a gold choker from which three figures hang: the small figure in the center, possibly Harpocrates, is flanked on either side by Demeter wearing a modius and carrying a torch. (M.S.C.)

PORTRAIT OF A MAN

ENCAUSTIC PAINTING AND TEMPERA ON WOOD
HEIGHT 39.5 CM, WIDTH 23 CM
PROVENANCE UNKNOWN
ROMAN PERIOD (EARLY 3RD CENTURY AD)

ROOM 14

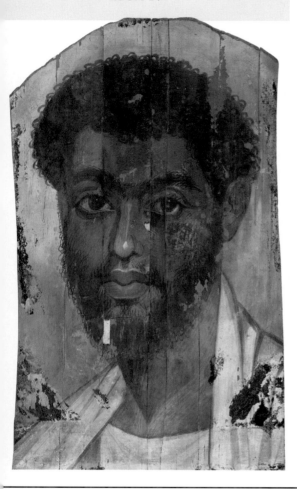

The decidedly African features of this young man have been rendered using soft, delicate tones that are not unfaithful to the strongly realistic style that characterized portraiture during the Roman Period.

The technique of mixing tempera and encaustic painting was rare but successfully renders the light that modulates the colors of the surface of the face and gives depth to the figure. The dark flesh tones and black hair and beard stand out from the pale gray background in a chromatic contrast accentuated by the white *chiton* and cloak shadowed with green. The portrait was painted at the start of the 3rd century AD. (M.S.C.)

PORTRAIT OF A YOUNG WOMAN

ENCAUSTIC PAINTING ON WOOD
HEIGHT 42 CM, WIDTH 21 CM
FAYUM
ROMAN PERIOD (MID-2ND CENTURY AD)

ROOM 14

The sad expression of this young woman is accentuated by her large black eyes and thick curved eyebrows. Heavy brushstrokes skilfully heighten the pale flesh tones of her face and clothes and give luster to the silvery light of the

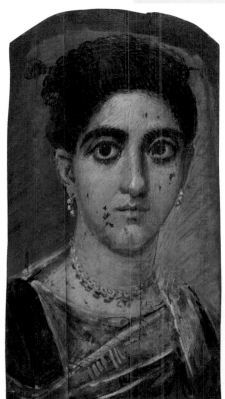

pearls in her earrings.

Her hair is simply tied in a chignon and held by a pin in a style that was popular at the time of Trajan (98-117 AD) but the style of the painting, the workmanship of the earrings, and wide use of reflected light suggest a date closer to the early reign of Antoninus Pius. (M.S.C.)

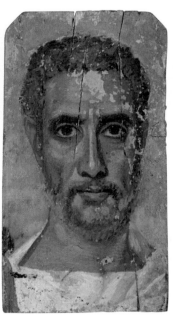

PORTRAIT OF A MAN
ENCAUSTIC PAINTING ON WOOD
HEIGHT 34 CM, WIDTH 18.5 CM
PROVENANCE UNKNOWN
ROMAN PERIOD
(FIRST HALF OF 2ND CENTURY AD)

ROOM 14

The painting gives a faithful portrayal of the face of a middle-aged man. He has been depicted with masterly contrasts of light accentuated by the transparency of the encaustic. Despite his increasing age, the brightness of his gaze is clearly depicted in the large, deep-set eyes and made more intense by his thick dark eyebrows separated by vertical lines. His hollow cheeks are edged by a soft, greying beard that matches the color of the short curls of his hair. He wears a white tunic covered by a greenish cloak over his left shoulder and a purple *clavus* over the other.

The faint melancholy of the portraits found in Fayum here has a calmer, more intimist mood that reflects the spiritual awareness of a man facing death in his maturity. (M.S.C.)

PORTRAIT OF A WOMAN

TEMPERA ON WOOD
HEIGHT 35 CM, WIDTH 19.5 CM
AL RUBAYAT; ROMAN PERIOD (SECOND HALF
OF THE 2ND AND EARLY OF 4TH CENTURY AD)

ROOM 14

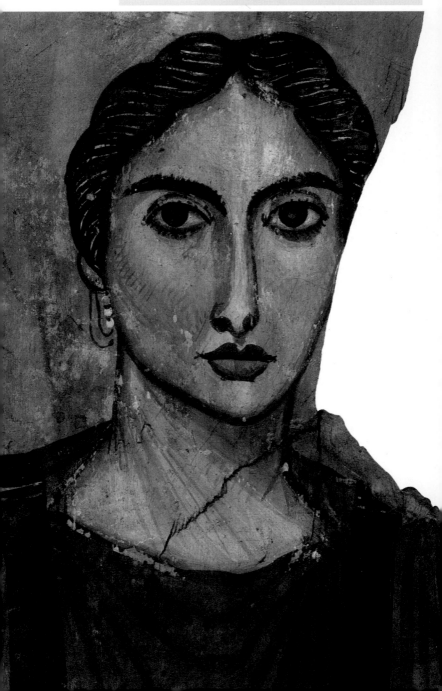

This female portrait is stylistically very close to the Late-ancient and Byzantine iconographic tradition although the rather perfunctory execution and lack of characterizing details means it might be dated anywhere between the second half of the 2nd century and the start of the 4th century AD.

It is defined by strong chromatic contrasts and delicate brushstrokes of strong color as the tempera technique used is unable to give the three dimensional effects achieved with encaustic painting; the result is that the figure seems flat, her eyes are dull and inexpressive, and her personality is hardly revealed by her long lower lashes and thick dark eyebrows. The proportions of her features are poorly handled as her nose is too long for the oval of her face; in addition, the slight twist of the neck is exaggerated by the thick wrinkles of her skin. (M.S.C.)

PORTRAIT OF A YOUNG WOMAN
ENCAUSTIC PAINTING ON WOOD
HEIGHT 31 CM, WIDTH 22 CM
FAYUM
ROMAN PERIOD (END 1ST CENTURY AD)

ROOM 14

The panel shows a patrician woman with well-defined, elegant features whose hairstyle and small densely clustered ringlets tell us she lived during the second half of the 1st century AD.

Her face is young and fresh, illumined by the transparency of her enormous bright eyes that are gracefully framed by her slender eyebrows. The woman wished to show off her jewels in the portrait that was to perpetuate her earthly image. A pair of typical double pendant earrings, *crotalia*, dangle from her ears and a restrained gold necklace with a half-moon pendant encircles her long smooth neck. Her dress is only suggested but it is undoubtedly the *chiton* normally worn by women of her rank, colored dark purple with wide bands at the sides. (M.S.C.)

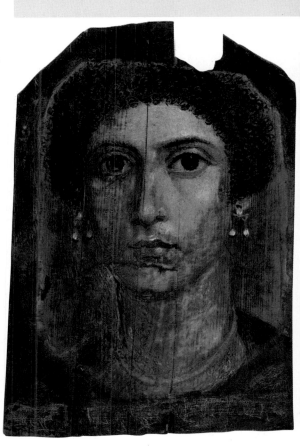

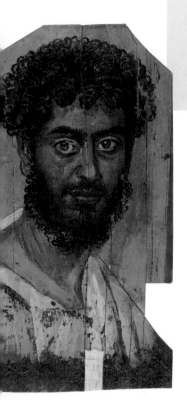

PORTRAIT OF A MAN

ENCAUSTIC PAINTING ON WOOD
HEIGHT 41 CM, WIDTH 21.5 CM
FAYUM
ROMAN PERIOD (1ST CENTURY AD)

ROOM 14

The emphasis placed on the size of the eyes in the faces found in Fayum portraits reflects a less abstract spirituality than that of the pharaonic artistic traditions. We see the typical Roman *pietas* in the gaze that the new masters of Egypt were unable to disown, despite embracing the religion of Osiris.

The rather dark-toned painting portrays a young man of moderate African features with fleshy lips in a half-smile, and heavy bags below his slightly bulging eyes that sparkle with life. The mode used to depict his hair and beard – in ringed, fluffy curls – is typical of the reign of Hadrian, the Roman emperor who most admired Greek culture, though some scholars consider the work to have been painted during the age of Antoninus (Edgar, 1905). (M.S.C)

PORTRAIT OF TWO BROTHERS

ENCAUSTIC PAINTING ON WOOD; DIAMETER 61 CM
ANTINOOPOLIS
EXCAVATION BY M. GAYET (1899)
ROMAN PERIOD (2ND CENTURY AD)

ROOM 14

These two figures have traditionally been considered brothers portrayed together in the communion of death. Evident physical differences are due to the differing ethnic origin of their parents, Egyptian and Roman or Greek. Mixed marriages between the new masters of Egypt and local people were in fact quite common at this time, although it meant the loss of social and fiscal privileges enjoyed by "pure" Roman families. The artist has produced an effective portrayal of the personalities of the two men by transforming their facial peculiarities – such as the size of the eyes and the shape of the mouth – into elements of intense emotional force.

The strong and slightly Negroid facial features of the elder man are reflected in the lifelike depiction of the thick, black, curly hair, the high cheekbones emphasized by the slight shadow of the shaved beard, and the fleshy mouth clearly delineated beneath the thin moustache. He has a serious, almost severe, gaze that penetrates the observer with the austerity of a man who is the victim of an irrevocable destiny. He wears a white *chiton* and a cloak with a crimson colored flap.

In contrast, this intensity is softened by the innocent expression of a boy unprepared for death; his lips part in a sad smile and his large, dark, deeply marked eyes convey painful

colors of his cloak held by an expensive green *cabochon* clasp mounted on gold filigree. The fine quality of the clothes and the execution of the portrait suggest the pair belonged to a well-to-do family, probably nobles, who lived in

of bronze statues of gods. Mercury is clearly identifiable on the right with his winged sandals, short mantle, and wand, while the statue on the left depicts a god with his head crowned by rays and a three-part headdress. It might be

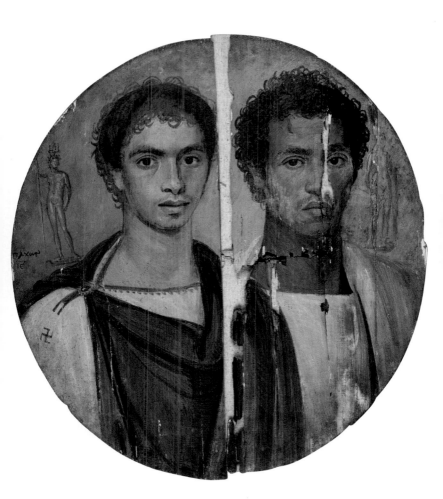

amazement at his knowledge of an early death. His clothes are more elaborate: his *chiton* is trimmed and embroidered with purple and matches the bright

Antinoopolis where several of the most valuable portraits on wood were found.

The two male figures drawn above the portraits seem to be reproductions

Antinoo-Osiris's transfiguration (Parlasca, 1969). The date of creation is debated; it is probably from Adrian empire (first half of the 2nd century AD). (M.S.C.)

PORTRAIT OF A WOMAN

ENCAUSTIC PAINTING ON WOOD
HEIGHT 38 CM, WIDTH 21 CM; HAWARA
EXCAVATION BY W.M.F. PETRIE (1888)
ROMAN PERIOD (LATE 1ST CENTURY)

ROOM 14

Hawara is the site of the cemetery of the city of Arsinoe (the ancient Crocodilopolis) in Fayum. The proximity of the Greco-Roman necropolis to the ancient pyramidal complex of Amenemhat III (Twelfth Dynasty) shows that the places "sanctified" by the pharaohs in the past were especially attractive to the new masters of Egypt.

The portraits from this area were mostly painted on cedar which, being imported, was considered a symbol of status. The portraits were slimmer and curved at the upper end to facilitate their insertion among the mummy's bandages.

This intense young woman with the severe expression was called Demos and died at the age of twenty four. This information is given in an inscription on a strip of cloth that was applied to her bust when she was buried. Epigraphs are very rare among the Fayum portraits which usually supply only the name and age or profession of the deceased.

Demos wears two strings of emeralds with a string of gold balls and a pair of earrings made from gold and pearls. Her hair is carefully curled and held in place in a chignon by a long gilded pin; the overall style would suggest that she died during the reign of Domitian (81-96 AD) (M.S.C.)

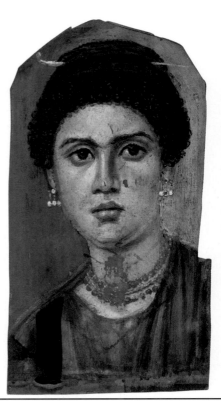

PORTRAIT OF A BOY

ENCAUSTIC PAINTING ON WOOD
HEIGHT 35.5 CM, WIDTH 16.5 CM
FAYUM
ROMAN PERIOD (LATE 1ST - EARLY 2ND CENTURY AD)

ROOM 14

The laurel crown is a recurring element in Fayum portraiture which was used to define the athleticism, youth, and nobility of the figure represented. In this case, the individual is a child

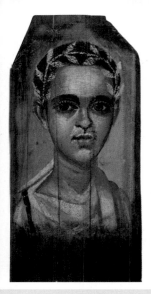

with large eyes framed by long hair and a vague smile on his lips. A radiant light caresses the surfaces of the boy's face, playing down his childish features, but a dark shadow falls over his innocent gaze like a presage of an early death. The purple *clavus* and a white cloak, both symbolic of his high social class, lie over his slender shoulders. (M.S.C.)

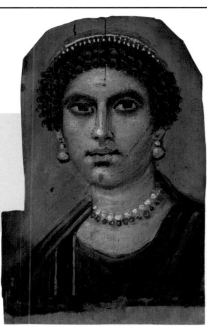

PORTRAIT OF A WOMAN
Encaustic painting on wood
Height 35 cm, width 21.5 cm; Hawara
Excavation by W.M.F. Petrie (1888-1889)
Roman Period (mid-1st century ad)

ROOM 14

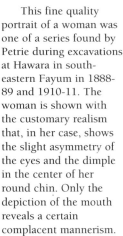

This fine quality portrait of a woman was one of a series found by Petrie during excavations at Hawara in south-eastern Fayum in 1888-89 and 1910-11. The woman is shown with the customary realism that, in her case, shows the slight asymmetry of the eyes and the dimple in the center of her round chin. Only the depiction of the mouth reveals a certain complacent mannerism.

She wears two necklaces of pearls and emeralds and circular twin gold earrings that comparison with the many Roman jewels found throughout the empire indicates could be either spherical or semi-spherical. Her hair has been carefully styled in three rows of curls and is adorned by a diadem created with tiny silver beads.

As occurred during the pharaonic era when artists based their work on the iconography of the court, the fashions adopted by the imperial family were copied by the upper echelons of the social hierarchy both in Italy and the other provinces. Naturally the styles of jewelry and hairstyles cannot be considered as completely trustworthy criteria for dating the portraits, especially given the addition of local variants, but they certainly aid in approximating the right period.

The general style of the painting and the ornaments in this case suggest a date of around 65-70 ad at the time Nero's reign was ending and the era of the Flavians was beginning. (M.S.C.)

MUMMIES

The end of the Twentieth Dynasty signalled the abandonment of the royal necropolises in the Valley of the Kings and the inevitable raids on its tombs. Only the devotion of the Theban priests allowed the bodies of their deceased kings to be preserved when they removed the mummies from their tombs and hid them collectively elsewhere. The mummies were discovered in two hiding places – the cachette at Deir al-Bahari (DB 320) and the tomb of Amenhotep II in the Valley of the Kings (KV 35) – which were respectively discovered by the Egyptian Antiquities Service (1881) and by Victor Loret (1898). (A.A.)

572 THE GOD ANUBIS LEANING OVER THE MUMMY (DETAIL FROM SENNEDJEM'S TOMB)
West Thebes, Deir al-Medina, Tomb of Sennedjem
Discovered by the Egyptian Antiquities Service (1886)
Nineteenth Dynasty, Reign of Rameses II (1279-1212 BC)

573 MUMMY OF RAMESES II
Found in the Cachette at Deir al-Bahari; Officially discovered by the Egyptian Antiquities Service (1881)
Nineteenth Dynasty, Reign of Rameses II (died in 1212 BC)

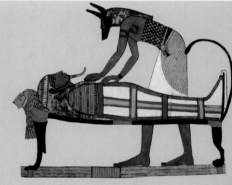

CHAPTER 17
FIRST FLOOR

17

ITINERARY THROUGH
ROOMS 52 AND 56

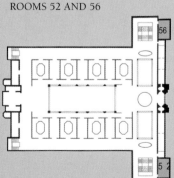

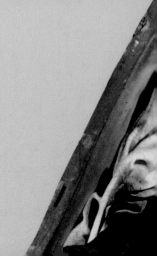

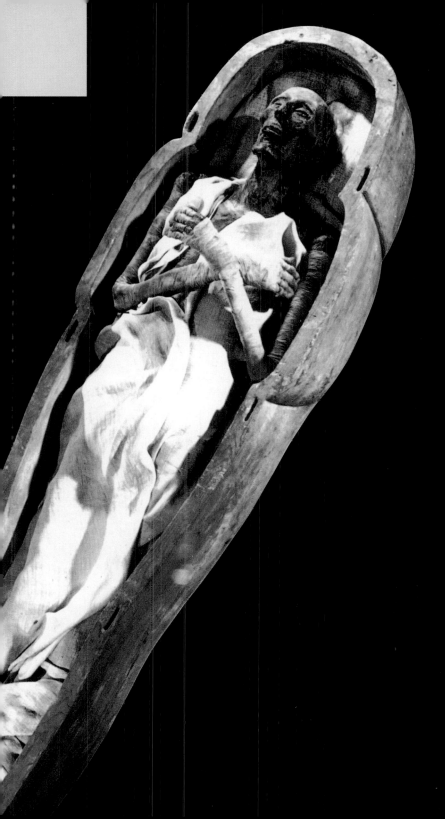

MUMMY OF AMENHOTEP I
FOUND IN THE CACHETTE IN DEIR AL-BAHARI
OFFICIALLY DISCOVERED
BY THE EGYPTIAN ANTIQUITIES SERVICE IN 1881
EIGHTEENTH DYNASTY, AMENHOTEP I
(DIED IN 1504 BC)

ROOM 56

As was the case with Ahmose, Thutmosis II, and Rameses VIII, the burial place of Amenhotep I is not known. During the 1990's, a German team excavated the Theban necropolis of Dra Abu al-Naga where a very large tomb was found that might have belonged to Amenhotep I.

His mummy, found in the cachette at Deir al-Bahari (DB 320), bears a series of labels that commemorate the various episodes the mummy experienced: it was restored in year 6 of the Reign of Smendes, again in year 10 of the reign of Siamun, and finally placed in DB 320 during the Reign of Sheshonq I (Twenty-second Dynasty). (A.A.)

MUMMY OF THUTMOSIS II
FOUND IN THE CACHETTE IN DEIR AL-BAHARI
OFFICIALLY DISCOVERED
BY THE EGYPTIAN ANTIQUITIES SERVICE IN 1881
EIGHTEENTH DYNASTY, THUTMOSIS II (DIED IN 1479 BC)

ROOM 56

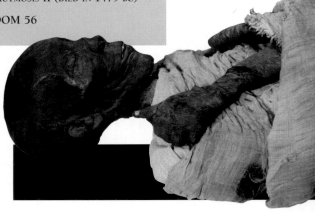

The original burial place of Thutmosis II also remains unknown. He reigned for just three years and no grave goods were found with his body. Various theories have been put forward: that he was buried with his father, Thutmosis I (though where is also unknown), that he was buried in tomb 42 in the Valley of the Kings, or tomb DB 358 in Deir al-Bahari. The body was finally hidden in the cachette at Deir al-Bahari where it was found in a sarcophagus with a label that recorded its removal in year 6 of the reign of Smendes (Twenty-first Dynasty). (A.A.)

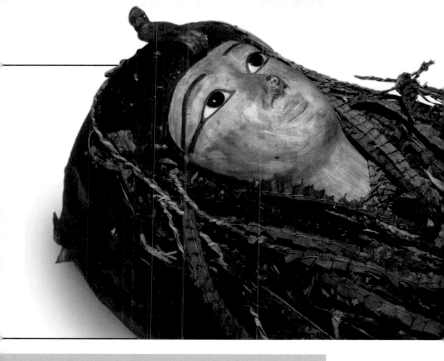

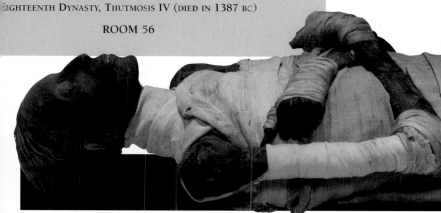

MUMMY OF THUTMOSIS IV
Found in the Tomb of Amenhotep II
in the Valley of the Kings
Discovered by V. Loret (1898)
Eighteenth Dynasty, Thutmosis IV (died in 1387 bc)

ROOM 56

Victor Loret found two distinct groups of mummies in two annexes of the burial chamber of Amenhotep II (KV 35) in 1898. The mummy of Thutmosis IV lay with eight other famous figures including Amenhotep III, Merenptah, Sety II, Siptah, Rameses IV, Rameses V, and Rameses VI, and with the body of a woman referred to as "Unknown woman D."

It appears as though all the mummies were placed there at the same time, probably in year 12 or 13 of Smendes' reign (circa Twenty-first Dynasty, 1057 bc). (A.A.)

The mummy of the father of Rameses II was found in a sarcophagus in the cachette at Deir al-Bahari; the lid was engraved with two large cartouches bearing the name of the sovereign and, lower down, three labels written during the Pontificates of Herihor and Pinudjem II (Twenty-first Dynasty) listing the names and titles of those involved in the transferral of the bodies.

Sety I's original tomb is considered to be the most splendid in the Valley of the Kings (KV 17). It is also known as "Belzoni's Tomb" after the name of its discoverer in 1817. (A.A.)

MUMMY OF SETY I
FOUND IN THE CACHETTE IN DEIR AL-BAHARI (DB 320)
OFFICIALLY DISCOVERED
BY THE EGYPTIAN ANTIQUITIES SERVICE IN 1881
NINETEENTH DYNASTY, SETY I (DIED IN 1279 BC)

ROOM 56

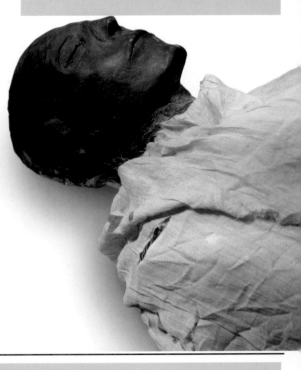

MUMMY OF RAMESES II
FOUND IN THE CACHETTE IN DEIR AL-BAHARI
OFFICIALLY DISCOVERED
BY THE EGYPTIAN ANTIQUITIES SERVICE IN 1881
NINETEENTH DYNASTY, RAMESES II (DIED IN 1212 BC)

ROOM 56

The mummy of the most glorious pharaoh in Egyptian history was found in the cachette at Deir al-Bahari (DB 320). For the superb exhibition on Rameses the Great held in the Louvre Museum in 1976, the mummy left Egyptian soil by plane and was welcomed in France with all the honour that is given to an important head of state. The mummy was the subject of detailed restoration and study before being returned to Egypt eight months later. One of the characteristics of the mummy is the thick fair hair that has survived. (A.A.)

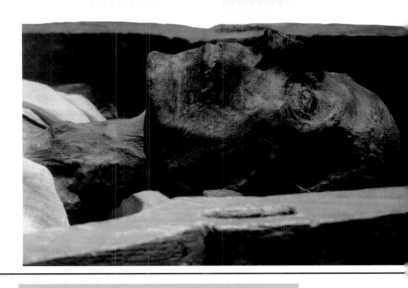

MUMMY OF MERENPTAH
Found in the Tomb of Amenhotep II
in the Valley of the Kings
Discovered by V. Loret (1898)
Nineteenth Dynasty, Merenptah (died in 1202bc)

ROOM 56

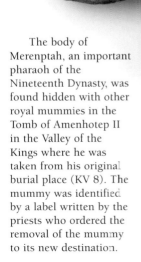

The body of Merenptah, an important pharaoh of the Nineteenth Dynasty, was found hidden with other royal mummies in the Tomb of Amenhotep II in the Valley of the Kings where he was taken from his original burial place (KV 8). The mummy was identified by a label written by the priests who ordered the removal of the mummy to its new destination.

Generally, the labels placed on the bandages of the mummies have been found to tell the truth whereas those on the sarcophaguses that contained them are often inexact. (A.A.)

THE MUSEUM FOR THE VISITOR IN A HURRY

For those who have little time available to dedicate to the Museum, here is a route for a rapid but complete tour of the most important objects from Egyptian culture from its origin until the end of the Roman domination. The reader is advised, in any case, to peruse the Introductions to the various chapters in the guide which are indispensable to an understanding of this millenary civilization and to an appreciation of its less evident aspects, too.

GROUND FLOOR

The Predynastic and Early Dynastic Periods
Room 43: this room contains the objects from the earliest period of Egyptian history, from its origins to the start of the Third Dynasty: *Narmer's Tablet* (pp. 28-29) and the *wooden panels from the Tomb of Hesira* (p. 48).

The Old Kingdom
Room 47: *the three Triads of Menkaura* (pp. 52-53) stand out from the other sculptural masterpieces.
Room 42: *the statue of Khafra* (pp. 68-69) and *the statue of a scribe* (p. 70) are the most important examples of sculpture during the Old Kingdom.
Room 32: representation of the deceased inside the tomb in various iconographic forms – *Rahotep and Nofret* (pp. 78-79) and *the dwarf Seneb* (p. 81). See *the false door of Iteti* (p. 80) as an example of funerary architecture.

The Middle Kingdom
Room 26: *the pharaoh Mentuhotep II* brought an end to the troubles of the First Intermediate Period and reunified Egypt (pp. 102-103).
Room 22: an example of private funerary worship in *the small sanctuary of Nakht* (p. 113).
Room 16: *the double statue of Amenemhat III* (p. 123) is representative of the power of royal statuary during the Middle Kingdom.

The New Kingdom
Room 12: *the big statue of Amenhotep II protected by the goddess-cow Hathor* dominates the room (p. 150); it was placed at the entrance to the *painted shrine of Thutmosis III*, Amenhotep's father (p. 151), in Deir al-Bahari. *The two statues of Amenhotep, son of Hapu* (p. 154), represent the apex of private sculpture under Amenhotep III in one of ancient Egypt's most flourishing periods. Not to be missed *the relief depicting the Queen of Punt* (pp. 156-157) taken from the Temple of Hatshepsut at Deir al-Bahari.
Room 3: dedicated to the Amarnian Period. *Pharaoh Amenhotep IV*, who established the new capital at Tell al-Amarna organized his life around the worship of Aten, the shining sun disk (p. 183). He inaugurated a new religious era that was reflected in every form of art; *the two colossal statues* (p. 172) were an original interpretation of

the figure of the pharaoh in the second part of his reign when iconographic realism assumed exaggerated forms. These can be compared to the harmonious representations of *the king as officiator* (p. 176) and of his wife *Nefertiti* (pp. 178-179).
Room 10: note *the colossal statue of Rameses II with the god Horun* (p. 197).

The Third Intermediate Period and the Late Period
Room 20: the tendency to base the art of these unstable periods on the models of the past, in an attempt at association with the continuity of the ancient traditions, can be seen in *the small statue of Osorkon III* (p. 216) kneeling as he pushes a sacred bark. It follows the statuary of the Eighteenth Dynasty.
Room 24: the harmonious proportions and search for aesthetic perfection seen in "classical" statuary characterized the works of the Late Period, for example, *the three schist sculptures of Psamtek* (pp. 222-223), the *bust of Montuemhat* (p. 224) and *the statue of the goddess Taweret* (p. 229), a masterpiece of Saite art.

The Greco-Roman Era
Room 34: the idealized features of *Alexander the Great* can be seen in an alabaster head (p. 247) which is identified as the Macedonian leader on the basis of traditional iconography.

Room 49: *the inlaid sarcophagus of the High Priest Petosiri* should not be missed (p. 253).

Room 50: a late Roman sculpture of *the bust of a prince*, made of valuable red porphyry (p. 251).

FIRST FLOOR

The grave goods of Tutankhamun

Much of the floor is filled with the treasures found by Howard Carter in the Tomb of Tutankhamun.

Room 45: *the statues of the ka of the young pharaoh* (pp. 262-263).

Room 35: *the inlaid gold throne* (pp. 278-279) and *the games board* (p. 282).

Room 20: *the alabaster lamp* (p. 286) and *the head of the king that emerges from a lotus flower* (p. 291).

Rooms 10 and 9: *the funerary beds decorated with animal protomas* (pp. 294-297) and the elegant set of *canopic vases* (pp. 302-303).

Room 3: contains the treasure of the king, in particular, *the solid gold mask* (pp. 310-311), *the gold statuette of the king crouching* (p. 313), his *corslet* (p. 320-321), *the necklace with the lunar boat* (p. 324), and *the two pectorals with a scarab* (pp. 327-329).

Jewelry

Room 4: the room contains masterpieces of Egyptian jewelry from the First Dynasty until the Roman Period. Exceptionally well-manufactured, they testify to the Nile craftmen's creativity and stylistic and subject continuity. Note *the falcon's head with a headdress* (p. 340), *the necklace in the name of Amenemhat III* (p. 348), *the diadem belonging to Princess Khnumit* (p. 355), *the necklace belonging to Neferuptah* (p. 360), *the earrings belonging to Sety II* (p. 375), and *the diadem decorated with Serapis* (p. 384).

The treasures of Tanis

Room 2: contains the treasures of the royal tombs of the sovereigns from the Twenty-first and Twenty-second Dynasties which had their residence at Tanis in the north-eastern Delta. In particular, note *the necklace belonging to Psusennes I* (p. 401), *the cup* (p. 405) and *gold funeral mask* (p. 407) belonging to General Undjebauendjed, the silver *sarcophagus with the head of a falcon belonging to Sheshonq II* (p. 414) and *the gold mask belonging to Psusennes I* (p. 423).

Grave goods and sarcophaguses

Room 17: *the sarcophagus of the noblewoman Aset* (p. 438) stands out for the originality of the iconography of the deceased who is shown as a living being.

Room 27: *model of a livestock census* (p. 446).

Room 37: models with troops of Nubian archers and Egyptian lancers (pp. 458-459).

Room 21: *wooden sarcophagus of Neferi* (p. 465).

Room 31: *sarcophagus of Djedhorefankh* (pp. 466-467).

Lunette 48:

The display cases contain small objects of great beauty, in particular, *the head of Queen Tiy*, wife of Amenhotep III and mother of Akhenaten (p. 480), and *the shawabty of Lieutenant Hat* (p. 488).

The grave goods of Yuya and Tuya

Room 43: especially important is *the series of wooden* (p. 496) *and limestone vases* (p. 497) painted to imitate more valuable materials.

Daily life

Room 34: *hair pin* (p. 524) and *cosmetics spoon* (p. 525).

Ostrakas and papyruses

Room 24: do not miss *the ostrakon of a lute player* seen from above (p. 530) or *the papyrus of the Book of the Dead from the Tomb of Pinudjem* (pp. 532-533).

The gods

Room 19: this room gives an overview of the complex pantheon of Egyptian gods and of the multiple manifestations of the divine entity. Note *the sarcophagus of a falcon* (p. 538), *the magic stela of Horus on crocodiles* (p. 547), *the statuette of famous architect Imhotep* who was divinized during the Late Period (p. 550), and *the statue of the goddess Maat* (p. 555).

The portraits of Fayum

Room 14: there are many examples of this form of worship after death during the Roman Period but *the portrait of the two brothers* on a wooden board (pp. 568-569) deserves special attention. (M.S.C.)

LIST OF OBJECTS
GROUND FLOOR

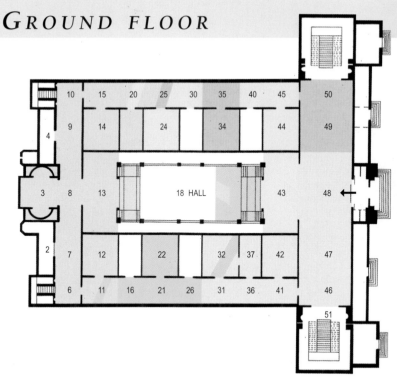

FIRST FLOOR

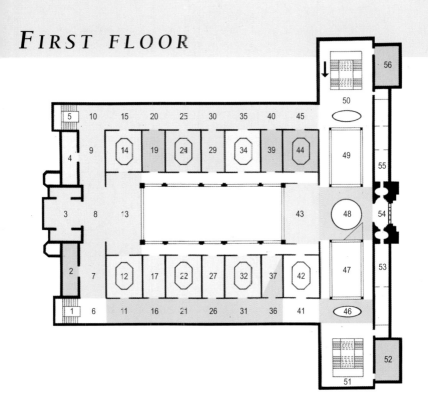

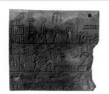

LABEL OF DJER
HEIGHT 8.5 CM, 9.5 CM
JE 70144
ROOM 43 - PAGE 24-25

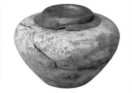

SEALED VASE
HEIGHT 7.2 CM, DIAMETER 10.5 CM
JE 34942
ROOM 43 - PAGE 27

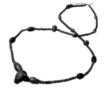

NECKLACE
LENGTH 61.5 CM
JE 87515
ROOM 43 - PAGE 32

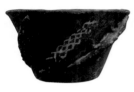

BOWL WITH APPLICATION
HEIGHT 11 CM, DIAMETER 19.5 CM
JE 38284 - CG 18804
ROOM 43 - PAGE 25

NARMER'S TABLET
HEIGHT 64 CM, WIDTH 42 CM
JE 32169 - CG 14716
ROOM 43 - PAGE 28-29

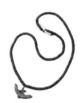

NECKLACE
LENGTH 77 CM
JE 87494
ROOM 43 - PAGE 33

DISC OF HEMAKA
DIAMETER 8.7 CM
JE 70164
ROOM 43 - PAGE 26

STATUE OF HETEPDIEF
HEIGHT 39 CM
JE 34557 - CG 1
ROOM 43 - PAGE 30

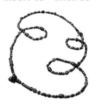

NECKLACE
LENGTH 82 CM
JE 43127
ROOM 43 - PAGE 33

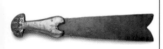

KNIFE
LENGTH 30.6 CM
JE 34210 - CG 64868
ROOM 43 - PAGE 27

JUBILEE VASE
HEIGHT 37 CM, DIAMETER 28 CM
JE 64872
ROOM 43 - PAGE 31

LOTUS-FLOWER VASE
HEIGHT 7 CM
JE 71299
ROOM 43 - PAGE 34

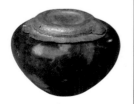

SEALED VASE
HEIGHT 4.2 CM, DIAMETER 6.5 CM
JE 34941
ROOM 43 - PAGE 27

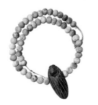

NECKLACE
LENGTH CM 29
JE 87499
ROOM 43 - PAGE 32

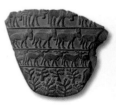

FRAGMENT OF A TABLET
HEIGHT 19 CM, WIDTH 22 CM
JE 27434 - CG 14238
ROOM 43 - PAGE 35

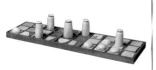

SENET
HEIGHT 5 CM, WIDTH 4 CM
JE 45038 AND 98212
ROOM 43 - PAGE 36

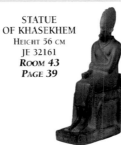

STATUE
OF KHASEKHEM
HEIGHT 56 CM
JE 32161
ROOM 43
PAGE 39

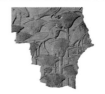

FRAGMENT OF A RELIEF
HEIGHT 102 CM
JE 56007
ROOM 47 - PAGE 46

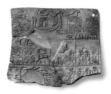

LABEL OF AHA
HEIGHT 4.8 CM, WIDTH 5.6 CM
JE 31773 - CG 14142
ROOM 43 - PAGE 36

FRAGMENT OF PLASTER
HEIGHT CM 27, WIDTH 20 CM
CG 1744
ROOM 32 - PAGE 42

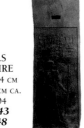

PANELS
OF HESIRE
HEIGHT 114 CM
WIDTH 40 CM CA.
JE 28504
ROOM 43
PAGE 48

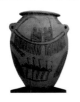

VASE WITH DECORATION
HEIGHT 22 CM, DIAMETER 15 CM
JE 64910
ROOM 43 - PAGE 37

STATUE OF MERSUANKH
AND TWO DAUGHTERS
HEIGHT 43.5 CM, WIDTH 21 CM
JE 66617
ROOM 46 - PAGE 44

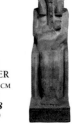

STATUE
OF DJIOSER
HEIGHT 142 CM
JE 49158
ROOM 48
PAGE 49

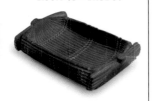

BASKET-SHAPED TRAY
HEIGHT 4.8 CM, LENGTH 22.7 CM
JE 71298
ROOM 43 - PAGE 38

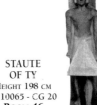

STAUTE
OF TY
HEIGHT 198 CM
JE 10065 - CG 20
ROOM 46
PAGE 44

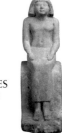

STATUE
OF MERETITES
HEIGHT 39 CM
JE 87807
ROOM 47
PAGE 50

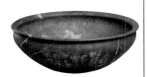

VASE WITH NAMES
OF PHARAOHS
HEIGHT 12 CM, DIAMETER 23 CM
JE 88345
ROOM 43 - PAGE 38

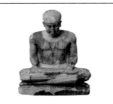

STATUE OF PTAHSHEPSES
HEIGHT 42 CM
CG 83
ROOM 32 - PAGE 45

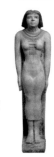

STATUE
OF SATMERIT
HEIGHT 53 CM
JE 87806
ROOM 47
PAGE 50

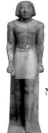

STATUE OF NEFERHERENPTAH
HEIGHT 65 CM
JE 87804
ROOM 47
PAGE 50

MENKAURA TRIAD
HEIGHT 92.5 CM
JE 40679
ROOM 47 - PAGE 52-53

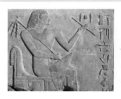

RELIEF FROM THE MASTABA OF I
HEIGHT 112 CM, WIDTH 502 CM
CG 1536- 1537
ROOM 46 - PAGE 58-59

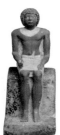

STATUE OF ITISEN
HEIGHT 37 CM
JE 87805
ROOM 47
PAGE 50

STATUETTE OF NEFEREFRA
HEIGHT 34 CM
JE 98171
ROOM 47 - PAGE 54

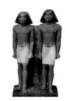

STATUE OF NIMAATSED
HEIGHT 57 CM
CG 133
ROOM 46 - PAGE 60

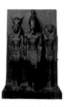

STATUETTE OF A WOMAN PREPARING BEER
HEIGHT 28 CM
JE 66624
ROOM 47
PAGE 51

HEAD OF USERKAF
HEIGHT 45 CM
JE 90220
ROOM 47 - PAGE 55

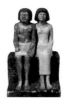

STATUE OF AK AND HETEP-HER-NOFRET
HEIGHT 49 CM; JE 35204
ROOM 46 - PAGE 61

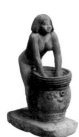

MENKAURA TRIAD
HEIGHT 93 CM
JE 40678
ROOM 47 - PAGE 52-53

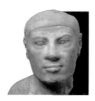

HEAD OF URKHUI
HEIGHT 35 CM
JE 72221
ROOM 47 - PAGE 56

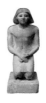

STATUE OF KAEMKED
HEIGHT 43 CM
CG 119
ROOM 46 - PAGE 62

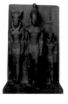

MENKAURA TRIAD
HEIGHT 95.5 CM
JE 46499
ROOM 47 - PAGE 52-53

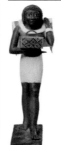

STATUE OF A BEARER
HEIGHT 36.5 CM
JE 30810 -
CG 241
ROOM 46
PAGE 57

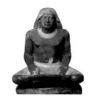

STATUE OF A SCRIBE
HEIGHT 51 CM, WIDTH 41 CM
JE 30272 - CG 36
ROOM 46 - PAGE 63

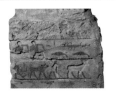

WALL FRAGMENTS
HEIGHT 61.5 CM, WIDTH 138 AND 124 CM
JE 43809
ROOM 41 - PAGE 64

STATUE OF A SCRIBE
HEIGHT 51 CM
JE 30272 - CG 35
ROOM 42 - PAGE 70

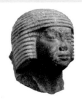

HEAD OF A STATUE
HEIGHT 30.5 CM
JE 87816
ROOM 36 - PAGE 74

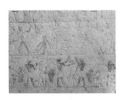

**RELIEF OF THE MASTABA
OF KAEMREHU**
H. 97 CM, L. 236 CM; CG 1534
ROOM 41 - PAGE 65

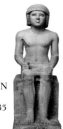
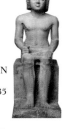
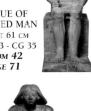

**STATUE OF
A SEATED MAN**
HEIGHT 61 CM
JE 30273 - CG 35
*ROOM 42
PAGE 71*

RESERVE HEAD
HEIGHT 25.5 CM
JE 46216 - CG 6005
ROOM 31 - PAGE 74

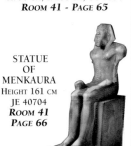

**STATUE
OF
MENKAURA**
HEIGHT 161 CM
JE 40704
*ROOM 41
PAGE 66*

STATUE OF A SCRIBE
HEIGHT CM 48
CG 59
ROOM 42 - PAGE 71

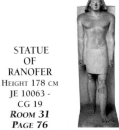
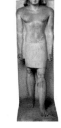

**STATUE
OF
RANOFER**
HEIGHT 178 CM
JE 10063 -
CG 19
*ROOM 31
PAGE 76*

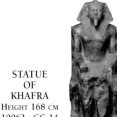

RELIEF FROM A MASTABA
HEIGHT 122 CM, WIDTH 110 CM
JE 40027
ROOM 41 - PAGE 67

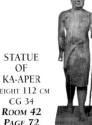
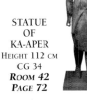

**STATUE
OF
KA-APER**
HEIGHT 112 CM
CG 34
*ROOM 42
PAGE 72*

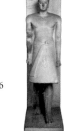

**STATUE
OF
RANOFER**
HEIGHT 186 CM
JE 10064 -
CG 18
*ROOM 31
PAGE 77*

**STATUE
OF
KHAFRA**
HEIGHT 168 CM
10062 - CG 14
*ROOM 42
PAGE 68-69*

FALSE-DOOR STELA OF IKA
HEIGHT 200 CM, WIDTH 150 CM
JE 72201
ROOM 42 - PAGE 73

**STATUES OF
RAHOTEP AND NOFRET**
HEIGHT 121 CM AND 122 CM
CG 3 AND 4
ROOM 32 - PAGE 78-79

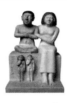

FALSE-DOOR STELA OF ITETI
HEIGHT 360 CM, WIDTH 210 CM
JE 15157 AND 39134
ROOM 32 - PAGE 80

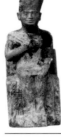

**SMALL
STATUE
OF KHUFU**
HEIGHT 7.5 CM
JE 36143
ROOM 37
PAGE 87

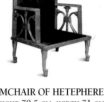

ARMCHAIR OF HETEPHERES
HEIGHT 79.5 CM, WIDTH 71 CM
JE 53263
ROOM 37 - PAGE 90

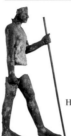

**THE DWARF SENEB
AND HIS FAMILY**
HEIGHT 43 CM, WIDTH 22.5 CM
JE 51280
ROOM 32 - PAGE 81

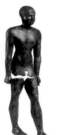

**STATUE
OF PEPY I**
HEIGHT 177 CM
JE 33034
ROOM 32
PAGE 84

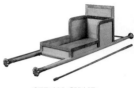

**SEDAN CHAIR
OF HETEPHERES**
HEIGHT 52 CM, LENGTH 99 CM
JR 52372
ROOM 37 - PAGE 91

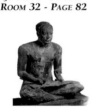

THE "GEESE OF MAYDUM"
HEIGHT 27 CM, LENGTH 172 CM
JE 34571 - CG 1742
ROOM 32 - PAGE 82

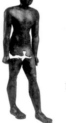

**STATUE
OF
MERENRA**
HEIGHT 65 CM
JE 33035
ROOM 32
PAGE 85

CASKET OF HETEPHERES
HEIGHT 21.8 CM, WIDTH 33.7 CM
JE 53265-53266-52281
ROOM 37 - PAGE 91

MITRI AS A SCRIBE
HEIGHT 76 CM, WIDTH 50 CM
JE 93165
ROOM 32 - PAGE 83

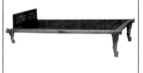

BED OF HETEPHERES
HEIGHT 21.5-35.5 CM, WIDTH 97 CM
LENGTH 178 CM; JE 53261
ROOM 37 - PAGE 88

BUST OF A QUEEN
HEIGHT 12 CM
JE 39741
ROOM 22 - PAGE 93

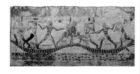

**RELIEF OF A CONTEST
BETWEEN FISHERMEN**
LENGTH 145 CM
JE 30191 - CG 1535
ROOM 32 - PAGE 86

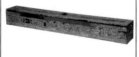

**CANOPY HOLDER
OF HETEPHERES**
LENGTH 157.5 CM; JE 72030
ROOM 37 - PAGE 89

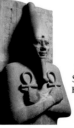

**OSIRIAN
PILLAR OF
SENUSRET I**
HEIGHT 470 CM
JE 48851
ROOM 22
PAGE 94

STELA OF IBI
HEIGHT 49 CM
CG 20525
ROOM 21 - PAGE 97

**STATUE
OF
MENTUHOTEP II**
HEIGHT 138 CM
JE 36195
*ROOM 26
PAGE 102-103*

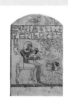

STELA OF DEDUSOBEK
HEIGHT 28.5 CM, WIDTH 18.5 CM
CG 20596
ROOM 21 - PAGE 108

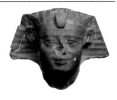

HEAD OF SENUSRET I
HEIGHT 38 CM
JE 45489 - CG 42007
ROOM 22 - PAGE 98

PILLAR OF SENUSRET I
HEIGHT 434 CM, WIDTH 95 CM
JE 36809
ROOM 32 - PAGE 104-105

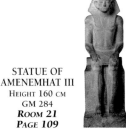

**STATUE OF
AMENEMHAT III**
HEIGHT 160 CM
GM 284
*ROOM 21
PAGE 109*

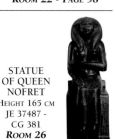

**STATUE
OF QUEEN
NOFRET**
HEIGHT 165 CM
JE 37487 -
CG 381
*ROOM 26
PAGE 99*

**STATUE
OF VIZIER
ANKHU'S
FATHER**
HEIGHT 115 CM
CG 42034
*ROOM 21
PAGE 106*

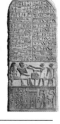

**STELA
OF
NEMTYEMHAT**
HEIGHT 57 CM
WIDTH 23 CM
CG 20088
*ROOM 21
PAGE 110*

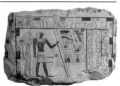

STELA OF A GENERAL
HEIGHT 80 CM, WIDTH 55 CM
JE 45969
ROOM 32 - PAGE 100

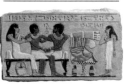

STELA OF AMENEMHAT
HEIGHT 30 CM, WIDTH 50 CM
JE 45626
ROOM 21 - PAGE 106

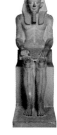

**STATUE
OF
SENUSRET I**
HEIGHT 200 CM
JE 31139 -
CG 414
*ROOM 22
PAGE 111*

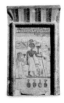

**STELA WITH V-SHAPED
CORNICE**
HEIGHT 56 CM; CG 1753
ROOM 32 - PAGE 101

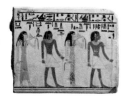

STELA OF NIT-PTAH
HEIGHT 23 CM, WIDTH 30 CM
JE 45625
ROOM 21 - PAGE 107

**STATUETTE OF
SENUSRET I**
HEIGHT 56 CM
JE 44951
*ROOM 22
PAGE 112*

NAOS OF NAKHT
HEIGHT 38 CM
CG 70037
ROOM 22 - PAGE 113

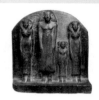

UKH-HOTEP'S FAMILY
HEIGHT 37 CM, WIDTH 30 CM
CG 459
ROOM 22 - PAGE 118

STATUE OF AMENEMHAT III
HEIGHT 100 CM
GM 506
ROOM 16 - PAGE 124

PILLAR OF SENUSRET I
HEIGHT 180 CM - GM 306
ROOM 22 - PAGE 114

STATUE OF A GODDESS
HEIGHT 162 CM
JE 36359
ROOM 22 - PAGE 119

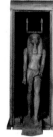

**STATUE
OF THE *KA*
OF
AUIBRA-HOR**
HEIGHT OF THE
STATUE 170 CM,
NAOS CM 207
JE 30948 -
CG 259
ROOM 11
PAGE 125

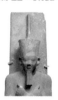

PILLAR OF SENUSRET I
HEIGHT 180 CM - CG 398
ROOM 22 - PAGE 115

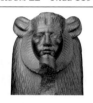

SPHINX OF AMENEMHAT III
HEIGHT 150 CM, LENGTH 236 CM
JE 15210 - CG 394
ROOM 16 - PAGE 120-121

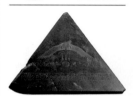

PYRAMIDION
OF AMENEMHAT III
HEIGHT 140 CM; JE 35122
HALL - PAGE 126

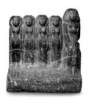

**STATUARY GROUP WITH
SOBEKHOTEP**
HEIGHT 35 CM, WIDTH 32 CM
JE 43094
ROOM 22 - PAGE 116

**DOUBLE STATUE
OF AMENEMHAT III**
HEIGHT 160 CM; JE 18221
ROOM 16 - PAGE 122

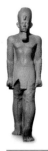

**STATUE OF
SENUSRET III**
HEIGHT 315 CM
CG 42011
HALL
PAGE 127

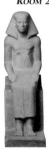

**STATUE
OF THE
MAJORDOMO
SAKAHERKA**
HEIGHT 62 CM
JE 43928
ROOM 22
PAGE 117

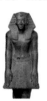

STATUE OF AMENEMHAT III
HEIGHT 90 CM
JE 45626
ROOM 16 - PAGE 123

**SARCOPHAGUS OF PRINCE
THUTMOSIS' CAT**
HEIGHT 64 CM; CG 5003
ROOM 11 - PAGE 132

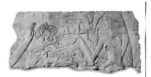

FRAGMENT OF RELIEF
HEIGHT 36 CM, WIDTH 75 CM
TR 17/6/24/10
ROOM 7 - PAGE 133

STELA OF SHERI
HEIGHT 50 CM, WIDTH 31.5 CM
CG 34173
ROOM 12 - PAGE 141

STATUE OF SENENMUT WITH NEFERURA
HEIGHT 60 CM
JE 36923 - CG 42116
ROOM 12 - PAGE 146

STELA WITH THE ROYAL FAMILY OF AMARNA
HEIGHT 44 CM; JE 44865
ROOM 3 - PAGE 134

STELA OF NEBAMUN
HEIGHT 34.5 CM, WIDTH 23.5 CM
CG 34107
ROOM 12 - PAGE 141

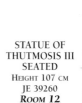

STATUE OF THUTMOSIS III SEATED
HEIGHT 107 CM
JE 39260
ROOM 12 PAGE 147

HEAD OF A QUEEN
HEIGHT 18 CM
JE 45547
ROOM 3 - PAGE 135

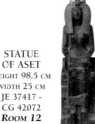

STATUE OF ASET
HEIGHT 98.5 CM
WIDTH 25 CM
JE 37417 -
CG 42072
*ROOM 12
PAGE 142*

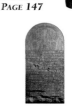

STELA FOR TETISHERI
HEIGHT 225 CM, WIDTH 106.5 CM
JE 31409 - CG 34026
ROOM 12 - PAGE 148

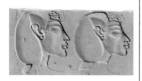

MODEL FOR SCULPTURE
HEIGHT 23 CM, WIDTH 31 CM
JE 59294
ROOM 3 - PAGES 136-137

STATUE OF THUTMOSIS IV WITH HIS MOTHER TIA
HEIGHT 115 CM, WIDTH 69 CM
CG 42080
ROOM 12 - PAGE 143

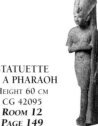

STATUETTE OF A PHARAOH
HEIGHT 60 CM
CG 42095
*ROOM 12
PAGE 149*

STELA OF NEFERMENU
HEIGHT 37 CM, WIDTH 23.5 CM
JE 34058
ROOM 12 - PAGE 140

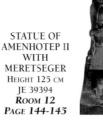

STATUE OF AMENHOTEP II WITH MERETSEGER
HEIGHT 125 CM
JE 39394
*ROOM 12
PAGE 144-145*

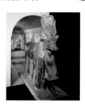

STATUE OF HATHOR WITH AMENHOTEP II
HEIGHT 225 CM, LENGTH 227 CM;
JE 38575; *ROOM 12 - PAGE 150*

SHRINE OF THUTMOSIS III
HEIGHT 225 CM, WIDTH 157 CM
LENGTH CM 404; JE 38575
ROOM 12 - PAGE 151

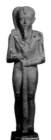

STATUE OF THE GOD KHONSU
HEIGHT 152 CM
CG 38488
ROOM 12
PAGE 155

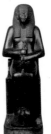

STATUE OF ISIS SEATED
HEIGHT 176 CM
JE 89616
ROOM 11
PAGE 160

HEAD OF AMENHOTEP III
HEIGHT 38 CM
JE 38597
ROOM 12 - PAGE 152

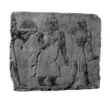

WALL RELIEF
HEIGHT 49.3 CM MAX, WIDTH
45 CM MAX; JE 14276 - CG 89661
ROOM 12 - PAGE 156-157

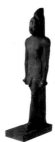

STANDING STATUE OF THUTMOSIS III
HEIGHT 200 CM
JE 38234 BIS -
CG 42053
ROOM 11
PAGE 161

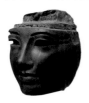

HEAD OF A WOMAN
HEIGHT 20 CM, WIDTH 15 CM
JE 38248 - CG 42101
ROOM 12 - PAGE 153

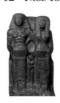

SENNEFER AND SENAY
HEIGHT 120 CM
JE 36574 - CG 42126
ROOM 12 - PAGE 158

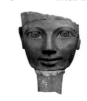

HEAD OF HATSHEPSUT
HEIGHT 61 CM, WIDTH 55 CM
JE 56259 A - 56262
ROOM 11 - PAGE 162

STATUE OF AMENHOTEP
HEIGHT 117 CM
JE 36368 - CG 42127
ROOM 12 - PAGE 154

STATUE OF LADY IBENTINA
HEIGHT OF THE STATUE 31.8 CM
NAOS 62 CM; JE 63666
ROOM 12 - PAGE 159

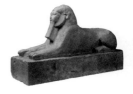

SPHINX OF HATSHEPSUT
HEIGHT 62 CM
JE 53113
ROOM 11 - PAGE 163

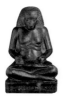

STATUE OF AMENHOTEP
HEIGHT 128 CM
JE 44861
ROOM 12 - PAGE 154

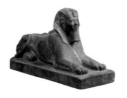

SPHINX OF THUTMOSIS III
HEIGHT 21 CM, WIDTH 21 CM
LENGTH 61 CM; CG 42069
ROOM 12 - PAGE 159

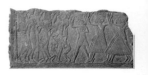

FRAGMENT OF A RELIEF
HEIGHT 51 CM, LENGTH 105 CM
JE 4872
ROOM 7 - PAGE 164-165

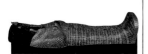

SARCOPHAGUS FROM TOMB 55 (KV)
LENGTH 185 CM
JE 39627
ROOM 8 - PAGE 166

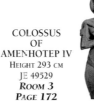

COLOSSUS OF AMENHOTEP IV
HEIGHT 293 CM
JE 49529
*ROOM 3
PAGE 172*

SMALL SLAB OF AKHENATEN
HEIGHT 10 CM, WIDTH 11 CM
JE 28186
ROOM 3 - PAGE 177

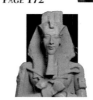

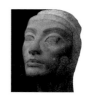

AMARNA-PERIOD MASK
HEIGHT 17 CM; JE 59289
ROOM 3 - PAGE 167

COLOSSUS OF AMENHOTEP IV
HEIGHT 185 CM
JE 49528
ROOM 3 - PAGE 172

HEAD OF NEFERTITI
HEIGHT 35.5 CM
JE 59286
ROOM 3 - PAGE 178-179

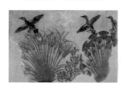

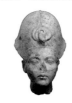

PORTRAIT OF NEFERTITI
HEIGHT 27 CM, WIDTH 16.5 CM
JE 59396
ROOM 3 - PAGES 168-169

FRAGMENT OF PAVING
HEIGHT 101 CM, WIDTH 160 CM
JE 33030 AND 33031
ROOM 3 - PAGE 174

HEAD OF AKHENATEN
HEIGHT 24.5 CM
JE 67921 A
ROOM 3 - PAGE 180

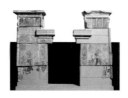

ARTIST'S STUDY
HEIGHT 23.5 CM, WIDTH 22.3 CM
JE 48035
ROOM 3 - PAGE 170

ALTAR
HEIGHT 98 CM, WIDTH 118 CM
JE 65041
ROOM 3 - PAGE 175

AKHENATEN WITH HIS DAUGHTER
HEIGHT 39.5 CM, WIDTH 16 CM
JE 44866
ROOM 3 - PAGE 181

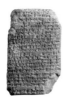

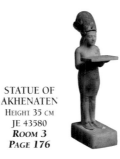

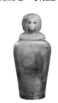

ACCADIAN TABLET
HEIGHT 13 CM, WIDTH 8 CM
JE 28179 - CG 4743
ROOM 3 - PAGE 171

STATUE OF AKHENATEN
HEIGHT 35 CM
JE 43580
*ROOM 3
PAGE 176*

CANOPIC VASE
HEIGHT 38.8 CM
JE 39637
ROOM 3 - PAGE 182

SCENE OF WORSHIP
HEIGHT 53 CM, WIDTH 48 CM
TR 10/11/26/4
ROOM 3 - PAGE 183

STATUE OF AMENHOTEP III
HEIGHT 700 CM
GM 610
HALL - PAGE 187

KING WITH OSIRIAN TRIAD
HEIGHT 139 CM, WIDTH 116 CM
JE 49537
ROOM 9 - PAGE 192

HEAD OF PRINCESS
HEIGHT 25 CM
JE 44870
ROOM 3 - PAGES 184-185

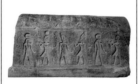

NAOS OF RAMESES II
HEIGHT 156 CM, LENGTH 271 CM
JE 37475 - CG 70003
HALL - PAGE 188

BUST OF RAMESES II
HEIGHT 80 CM, WIDTH 70 CM
CG 616
ROOM 9 - PAGE 193

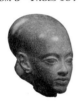

HEAD OF PRINCESS
HEIGHT 14 CM
JE 65040
ROOM 3 - PAGES 184-185

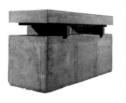

HATSHEPSUT'S SARCOPHAGUS
HEIGHT 90 CM, WIDTH 73 CM
LENGTH 199 CM; JE 47032
HALL - PAGES 188-189

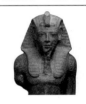

BUST OF MERENPTAH
HEIGHT 91 CM, WIDTH 58 CM
JE 31414 - CG 607
ROOM 10 - PAGE 194

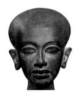

HEAD OF PRINCESS
HEIGHT 21 CM
JE 44869
ROOM 3 - PAGES 184-185

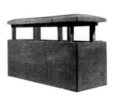

HATSHEPSUT'S SARCOPHAGUS
HEIGHT 100 CM, WIDTH 87.5
LENGTH 245 CM; JE 52344
HALL - PAGE 189

RAMESES II WITH ENEMIES
HEIGHT 99 CM, WIDTH 50 CM
JE 46189
ROOM 10 - PAGE 195

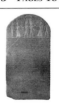

STELA OF MERENPTAH
HEIGHT 318 CM, WIDTH 163 CM
JE 31408 - CG 34025
ROOM 13 - PAGE 186

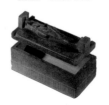

MERENPTAH'S SARCOPHAGUS
HEIGHT 89 CM, WIDTH 120 CM
LENGTH 240 CM; JE 87297
HALL - PAGES 190-191

STATUE OF TUTANKHAMUN
HEIGHT 285 CM, WIDTH 73 CM
JE 59869
ROOM 10 - PAGE 196

**RAMESES II
AND THE GOD HORUN**
Height cm 231; JE 64735
Room 10 - Page 197

WIFE OF NAKHTMIN
Height 85 cm
JE 31629 - CG 779 b
Room 15 - Page 201

**STATUE OF TJAY
AND HIS WIFE NAIA**
Height cm 90; CG 628
Room 14 - Page 206

BUST OF MERIT-AMUN
Height 75 cm, width 44 cm
JE 31413 - CG 600
Room 15 - Page 198

STELA OF RAHOTEP
Height 157 cm
JE 48845
Room 15 - Page 202

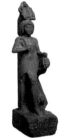

**STATUE OF
RAMESES VI
WITH A
PRISONER**
Height cm 74
JE 37175 -
CG 42152
*Room 14
Page 207*

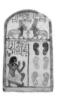

STELA OF BAY
Height 24.5 cm, width 14 cm
JE 43566
Room 15 - Page 199

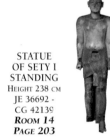

**STATUE
OF SETY I
STANDING**
Height 238 cm
JE 36692 -
CG 42139
*Room 14
Page 203*

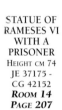

FRAGMENT OF A RELIEF
Height 70 cm, width 75 cm
JE 69306
Room 14 - Page 208

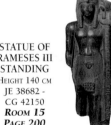

**STATUE OF
RAMESES III
STANDING**
Height 140 cm
JE 38682 -
CG 42150
*Room 15
Page 200*

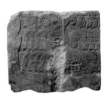

COLUMN OF THUTMOSIS IV
Height 162 cm, diameter 96 cm
JE 41560
Room 14 - Page 204

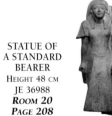

**STATUE OF
A STANDARD
BEARER**
Height 48 cm
JE 36988
*Room 20
Page 208*

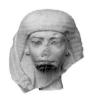

STATUE OF NAKHTMIN
Height 34 cm
JE 31630 - CG 779 a
Room 15 - Page 201

STATUE OF RAMESSENAKHT
Height 75 cm, width 43 cm
CG 42162
Room 14 - Page 205

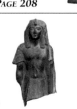

**STATUE OF SETY I
AS A STANDARD BEARER**
Height 22 cm; CG 751
Room 25 - Page 209

CUBE STATUE OF HOR
Height 51 cm
JE 37150
Room 25 - Page 210

BLOCK STATUE OF AHMES
Height 70 cm, width 30 cm
JE 36579
Room 25 - Page 217

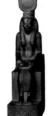

STATUE OF ISIS
Height 90 cm
Width 20 cm
38884
Room 24
Pages 222-223

**STATUE OF
PETIAMONNEBNESUTTAUY**
Height 72 cm; JE 36908
Room 24 - Page 211

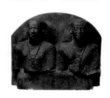

**STATUE OF MONTUEMHAT
AND HIS SON NESPTAH**
Height 34 cm; CG 42241
Room 25 - Page 218

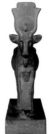

**STATUE OF
HATHOR WITH
PSAMTEK**
Height 96 cm
Width 29 cm
CG 784
Room 24
Page 222-223

BUST OF PSAMTEK
Height 14 cm
JE 36554
Room 40 - Page 214

HEAD OF SHABAKA
Height 97 cm
CG 42010
Room 25 - Page 219

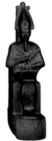

**STATUE OF
OSIRIS**
Height 89.5 cm
Width 28 cm
CG 38358
Room 24
Page 222-223

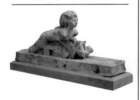

STATUE OF OSKORKON III
Height 18 cm
JE 37426 - CG 42197
Room 20 - Page 216

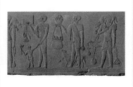

BAS-RELIEF OF HORHOTEP
Height 126 cm
JE 46591
Room 24 - Page 220

STATUE OF THE VIZIER HOR
Height 96 cm
JE 37512
Room 24 - Page 224

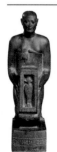

**STATUE OF
PSAMTEK-
SANEITH**
Height 44.5 cm
CG 726
Room 25
Page 216

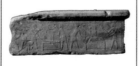

**BAS-RELIEF OF
NEFERSESHEM-PSAMTEK**
Height 30 cm; JE 10978
Room 24 - Page 221

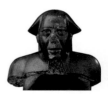

BUST OF MONTUEMHAT
Height 50 cm
JE 31884
Room 24 - Page 224

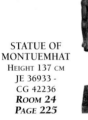

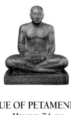

**STATUE OF
MONTUEMHAT**
HEIGHT 137 CM
JE 36933 -
CG 42236
ROOM 24
PAGE 225

STATUE OF PETAMENHOTEP
HEIGHT 74 CM
JE 37341
ROOM 24 - PAGE 230

HEAD OF A WOMAN
HEIGHT 65 CM
JE 39468
ROOM 50 - PAGE 235

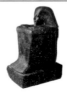

**STATUE OF THE VIZIER
NESPAQASHUTY**
HEIGHT 78 CM; JE 36665
ROOM 24 - PAGE 226

BLOCK STATUE OF HOR
HEIGHT 109 CM
JE 36575 - CG 42226
ROOM 30 - PAGE 231

**BUST-PORTRAIT
OF A WOMAN**
HEIGHT 61 CM; JE 47108
ROOM 34 - PAGE 236

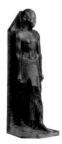

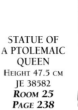

**STATUE
OF AHMES**
HEIGHT 95 CM
JE 37075
ROOM 24
PAGE 227

**STATUE OF
AMENIRDIS**
HEIGHT 170 CM
JE 3420 -
CG 565
ROOM 30
PAGE 232

BUST OF A ZEUS
HEIGHT 17.5 CM
CG 27439
ROOM 34 - PAGE 237

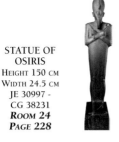

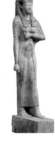

**STATUE OF
OSIRIS**
HEIGHT 150 CM
WIDTH 24.5 CM
JE 30997 -
CG 38231
ROOM 24
PAGE 228

STELA OF PIANKHY
HEIGHT 180 CM, WIDTH 184 CM
JE 48862
ROOM 30 - PAGE 233

**STATUE OF
A PTOLEMAIC
QUEEN**
HEIGHT 47.5 CM
JE 38582
ROOM 25
PAGE 238

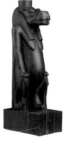

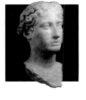

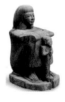

**STATUE
OF THE
GODDESS
TAWERET**
HEIGHT 96 CM,
WIDTH 38 CM
CG 39194
ROOM 24
PAGE 229

HEAD OF A WOMAN
HEIGHT 35 CM
JE 43268
ROOM 34 - PAGE 234

CUBE STATUE
HEIGHT 18.7 CM
JE 91118
ROOM 25 - PAGE 239

PORTRAIT OF PANEMERIT
Height 30 cm
JE 151154 - CG 27493
Room 34 - Page 240

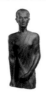

STATUE OF HOR
Height cm 83
JE 38310
Room 34 - Page 243

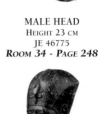

MALE HEAD
Height 23 cm
JE 46775
Room 34 - Page 248

STELA
Height 35 cm, width 25 cm
CG 27537
Room 34 - Page 240

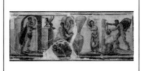

PAINTING WITH MYTHOLOGICAL SCENE
Height 98 cm, width 239 cm
JE 63609
Room 34 - Page 244

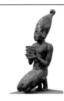

HEAD OF A KING
Height 46 cm
JE 28512 - CG 838
Room 34 - Page 248

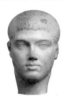

PORTRAIT OF SEVERUS ALEXANDER
Height 23 cm; CG 27480
Room 34 - Page 241

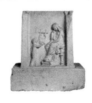

FUNERARY STELA OF NIKO
Height 69 cm, width 53 cm
CG 9259
Room 34 - Page 245

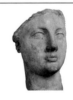

STATUETTE OF A KNEELING SOVERIGN
Height 26 cm; JE 91436
Room 35 - Page 249

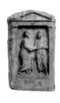

FUNERARY STELA
Height 43 cm, width 24 cm
CG 217
Room 34 - Page 242

STELA OF PTOLEMY V
Height 72 cm, width 50 cm
JE 54313
Room 34 - Page 246

FEMALE HEAD
Height 73 cm
CG 27468
Room 50 - Page 250

HEAD OF A PTOLEMAIC QUEEN
Height 10 cm; JE 39517
Room 34 - Page 242

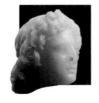

HEAD OF ALEXANDER THE GREAT
Height 10 cm; CG 27476
Room 34 - Page 247

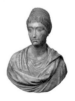

BUST-PORTRAIT OF A WOMAN
Height 61 cm; JE 44672
Room 50 - Page 250

PORTRAIT OF A PRINCE
HEIGHT 57.6 CM
CG 7257
ROOM 50 - PAGE 251

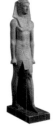

STATUE OF
PTOLEMAIC
KING
HEIGHT 280 CM
CG 701
ROOM 50
PAGE 252

SARCOPHAGUS
OF PETOSIRIS
HEIGHT 195 CM; JE 46592
ROOM 49 - PAGE 253

First 1 *floor*

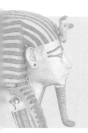

OSTRICH-FEATHER FAN
HEIGHT 105.5 CM, WIDTH 18.5 CM
JE 62001
ROOM 13 - PAGES 258-259

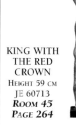

KING WITH
THE RED
CROWN
HEIGHT 59 CM
JE 60713
ROOM 45
PAGE 264

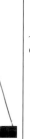

TUTANKHAMUN
ON A LEOPARD
HEIGHT 85.6 CM
JE 60715
ROOM 40
PAGE 266-267

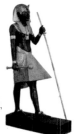

STATUE
OF THE *KA*
HEIGHT 192 CM,
JE 60707
ROOM 45
PAGE 262

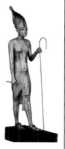

KING WITH
THE WHITE
CROWN
HEIGHT 75.3 CM
JE 62360
ROOM 40
PAGE 264

TUTANKHAMUN
ON A BOAT
HEIGHT 69.5 CM
JE 60709
ROOM 40
PAGE 266-267

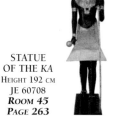

STATUE
OF THE *KA*
HEIGHT 192 CM
JE 60708
ROOM 45
PAGE 263

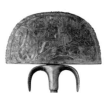

VOTIVE SHIELD
HEIGHT 88 CM, WIDTH 55 CM
JE 61576
ROOM 45 - PAGE 265

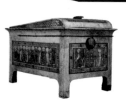

SMALL CHEST
HEIGHT 39 CM, LENGTH 49.5 CM
JE 61476
ROOM 40 - PAGE 268

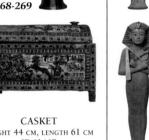
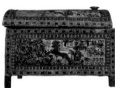

SMALL SARCOPHAGUS
HEIGHT 78 CM
JE 60698
ROOM 40
PAGE 268-269

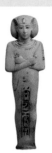

SHAWABTY WITH NUBIAN WIG
HEIGHT 54 CM
JE 60835
ROOM 40
PAGE 273

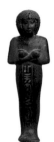

FAÏENCE *SHAWABTY*
HEIGHT 30 CM
JE 87852
ROOM 35
PAGE 277

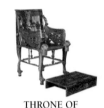

CASKET
HEIGHT 44 CM, LENGTH 61 CM
JE 61467
ROOM 40 - PAGE 270-271

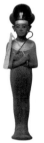

SHAWABTY WITH NEMES
HEIGHT CM 48
JE 60828
ROOM 40
PAGE 274

FAÏENCE *SHAWABTY*
HEIGHT 30 CM
JE 61054
ROOM 35
PAGE 277

SHAWABTY WITH THE RED CROWN
HEIGHT 63 CM
JE 60823
ROOM 40
PAGE 272

SHAWABTY WITH THE BLUE CROWN
HEIGHT CM 48
JE 60830
ROOM 40
PAGE 274

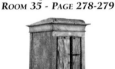

THRONE OF TUTANKHAMUN
HEIGHT 102 CM, WIDTH 60 CM
JE 62028
ROOM 35 - PAGE 278-279

SHAWABTY WITH THE WHITE CROWN
HEIGHT 61.5 CM
JE 60824 A
ROOM 40
PAGE 272

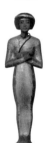

SHAWABTY WITH NUBIAN WIG
HEIGHT 54 CM
JE 60833
ROOM 40
PAGE 275

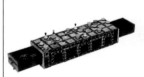

SHRINE FOR STATUE
HEIGHT 50.5 CM, LENGTH 48 CM
JE 61481
ROOM 35 - PAGE 280-281

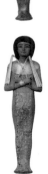

SHAWABTY WITH TWO FLAILS
HEIGHT CM 52
JE 60838
ROOM 40
PAGE 273

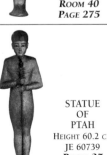

STATUE OF PTAH
HEIGHT 60.2 CM
JE 60739
ROOM 35
PAGE 276

GAMES BOARD
HEIGHT 5.9 CM, WIDTH 9 CM
JE 62059
ROOM 35 - PAGE 282

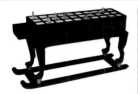

GAMES BOARD
HEIGHT 8.1 CM, LENGTH 46 CM
JE 62058
ROOM 35 - PAGE 282

PERFUME CONTAINER
HEIGHT 70 CM
JE 62114
ROOM 20 - PAGE 287

HEAD OF TUTANKHAMUN
HEIGHT CM 30
JE 60723
ROOM 20 - PAGE 291

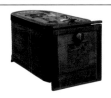

CASKET
HEIGHT 31.7 CM, LENGTH 64.5 CM
JE 61490
ROOM 30 - PAGE 283

ALABASTER BASIN
HEIGHT 37 CM, LENGTH 58.3 CM
JE 62120
ROOM 20 - PAGE 288

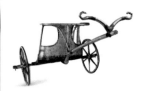

CEREMONIAL CHARIOT
HEIGHT 118 CM, LENGTH 250 CM
JE 61989
ROOM 13 - PAGES 292-293

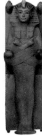

**THE KING
ON THE
CATAFALQUE**
LENGTH 42.2 CM
WIDTH 12 CM
JE 60720
*ROOM 30
PAGE 284*

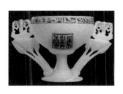

**CUP IN THE FORM
OF A LOTUS FLOWER**
HEIGHT 18.3 CM; JE 67465
ROOM 20 - PAGE 289

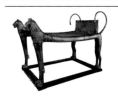

FUNERARY BED
HEIGHT 156 CM, LENGTH 181 CM
JE 62911
ROOM 10 - PAGES 294-297

CEREMONIAL SEAT
HEIGHT 102 CM, LENGTH 44 CM
JE 62030
ROOM 25 - PAGE 285

**VASE IN THE FORM
OF AN IBEX**
HEIGHT 27.5 CM; JE 62122
ROOM 20 - PAGE 289

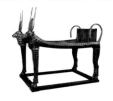

FUNERARY BED
HEIGHT 188 CM, LENGTH 208 CM
JE 62013
ROOM 10 - PAGES 294-297

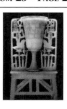

ALABASTER LAMP
HEIGHT 51.4 CM
JE 62111
ROOM 20 - PAGE 286

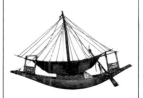

MODEL OF A BOAT
LENGTH 118 CM
JE 61239
ROOM 20 - PAGE 290

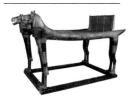

FUNERARY BED
HEIGHT 134 CM, LENGTH 236 CM
JE 62012
ROOM 9 - PAGES 294-297

MANNEQUIN OF TUTANKHAMUN
Height 76.5 cm; JE 60722
Room 9 - Pages 298-299

FIRST SHRINE
Height 275 cm, Length 508 cm
JE 60664
Room 8 - Pages 306-307

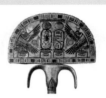

FAN
Length 125 cm
JE 62000
Room 8 - Page 309

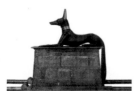

SIMULACRUM OF ANUBIS
Height 118 cm, length 270 cm
JE 61444
Room 9 - Pages 300-301

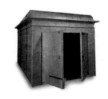

SECOND SHRINE
Height 225 cm, Length 374 cm
JE 60660
Room 8 - Pages 306-307

MASK OF TUTANKHAMUN
Height 54 cm, width 39.3 cm
JE 60672
Room 3 - Page 310-311

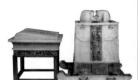

CONTAINER FOR CANOPIC VASES
Height 85.5 cm, length 54 cm
JE 60687
Room 9 - Pages 302-303

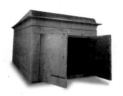

THIRD SHRINE
Height 215 cm, Length 340 cm
JE 60667
Room 8 - Pages 306-307

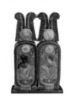

DOUBLE BALSAM HOLDER
Height 16 cm, width 8.8 cm
JE 61496
Room 3 - Page 312

SHRINE FOR CANOPIC VASES
Height 198 cm, length 153 cm
JE 60686
Room 9 - Page 304

FOURTH SHRINE
Height 190 cm, length 290 cm
JE 60668
Room 8 - Pages 306-307

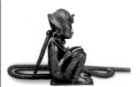

GOLD STATUETTE OF THE CROUCHING PHARAOH
Height 5.4 cm; JE 60702
Room 3 - Page 313

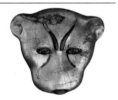

LEOPARD HEAD
Height 16.5 cm
JE 62631
Room 8 - Page 305

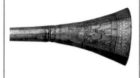

TUTANKHAMUN'S HORN
Length 58.2 cm
JE 62007
Room 8 - Page 308

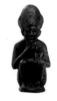

STATUETTE OF THE PHARAOH
Height 5.8 cm; JE 60718
Room 3 - Page 313

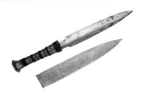

IRON DAGGER
Length 34.2 cm
JE 61585
Room 3 - Page 314-315

*DJED
AMULET*
Height 9 cm
JE 61778
*Room 3
Page 318*

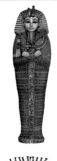

**WRAPPING
FOR
INTERNAL
ORGANS**
Height 39
Width cm 11
JE 60690
*Room 3
Page 323*

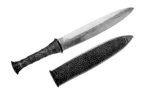

GOLD DAGGER
Length 31.9 cm
JE 61584
Room 3 - Page 314-315

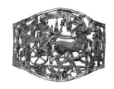

GOLD PLAQUE
Height 6.2 cm, width 8.5 cm
JE 87847
Room 3 - Page 319

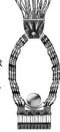

**NECKLACE
WITH LUNAR
BOAT**
Height 23.5 cm,
width 10.8 cm
JE 61897
*Room 3
Page 324*

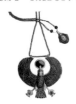

NECKLACE WITH A FALCON
Length of the chain 65 cm, width
of the pendant 9 cm; JE 61891
Room 3 - Page 316

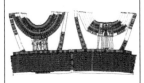

TUTANKHAMUN'S CORSLET
Height 40 cm, width 85 cm
JE 62627
Room 3 - Pages 320-321

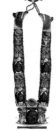

**NECKLACE
WITH
A SCARAB**
Necklace:
Length 50 cm,
Pectoral:
Width 11.8 cm
JE 61896
*Room 3
Page 325*

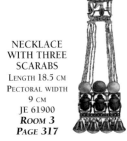

**NECKLACE
WITH THREE
SCARABS**
Length 18.5 cm
Pectoral width
9 cm
JE 61900
*Room 3
Page 317*

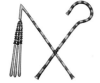

FLAIL AND SCEPTER
Length 33.5 cm
JE 61760 and JE 61762
Room 3 - Page 322

BRACELET
Diameter 5.4 cm
JE 62360
Room 3 - Page 326

COLLAR OF HORUS
Width 35 cm
JE 61899
Room 3 - Page 318

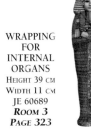

**WRAPPING
FOR
INTERNAL
ORGANS**
Height 39 cm
Width 11 cm
JE 60689
*Room 3
Page 323*

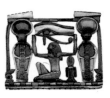

COUNTERPOISE
Height 6.9 cm, width 8.2 cm
JE 61898
Room 3 - Page 326

PECTORAL WITH A SCARAB
HEIGHT 14.9 CM, WIDTH 14.5 CM
JE 61884
ROOM 3 - PAGE 327

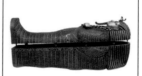

SECOND SARCOPHAGUS
HEIGHT 78.5 CM, WIDTH 68 CM
LENGTH 204 CM; JE 60670
ROOM 3 - PAGE 332-333

MIRROR BELONGING TO SATHATHORIUNET
HEIGHT 28 CM; JE 44920 - CG 52663
ROOM 4 - PAGE 341

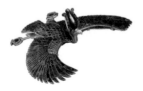

PECTORAL WITH VULTURE
HEIGHT 14.1 CM, WIDTH 16.4 CM
JE 61894
ROOM 3 - PAGE 328

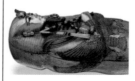

INNER SARCOPHAGUS
HEIGHT 51 CM, WIDTH 51.3 CM
LENGTH CM 187; JE 60670
ROOM 3 - PAGE 334

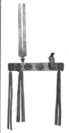

DIADEM BELONGING TO SATHATHOR-IUNET
HEIGHT 44 CM
WIDTH 19.2 CM
JE 44919 -
CG 52641
ROOM 4
PAGE 342

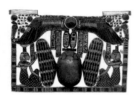

PECTORAL WITH A SCARAB
HEIGHT 16.5 CM, WIDTH 24.4 CM
JE 61948
ROOM 3 - PAGE 329

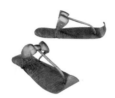

GOLD SANDALS
LENGTH 29.5 CM
JE 60680
ROOM 3 - PAGE 335

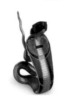

URAEUS OF SENUSRET II
HEIGHT 6.7 CM, WIDTH 3 CM
JE 46694 - CG 52702
ROOM 4 - PAGE 342

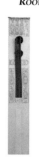

SCRIBE'S TABLET
HEIGHT 30.3 CM
WIDTH 4.7 CM
JE 62081
ROOM 3
PAGE 330

PENDANT WITH THE HEAD OF HATHOR
HEIGHT 5.5 CM; JE 86780
ROOM 4 - PAGE 336

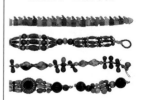

BRACELETS OF DJER
LENGTH VARIES BETWEEN
10.2 AND 15.6 CM; JE 35054
ROOM 4 - PAGE 343

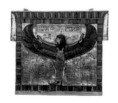

PECTORAL DEPICTING NUT
HEIGHT 12.6 CM, WIDTH 14.3 CM
JE 61944
ROOM 3 - PAGE 331

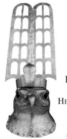

FALCON'S HEAD
HEIGHT 37.5 CM
JE 32158
ROOM 4
PAGE 340

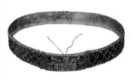

BELT OF PTAHSHEPSES
HEIGHT 4.5 CM, LENGTH 90 CM
JE 87078
ROOM 4 - PAGE 344

SHELL SHAPED CONTAINER
LENGTH 5.3 CM; JE 92656
ROOM 4 - PAGE 344

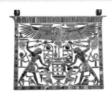

NECKLACE IN THE NAME OF AMENEMHAT III
PECTORAL HEIGHT 7.9 CM; JE 30876
ROOM 4 - PAGE 348

NECKLACE OF URET
LENGTH 62.9 CM
JE 98783 - 98790C - 98971C - 98792C - 98793C
ROOM 4 - PAGE 352

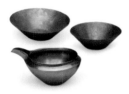

VESSELS OF HETEPHERES
HEIGHT VARIES BETWEEN 2.4 AND 5.2 CM; JE 52404, JE 52405, JE 52406
ROOM 4 - PAGE 345

NECKLACE BEARING THE NAME OF SENUSRET III
PECTORAL HEIGHT 6.1 CM; JE 30875
ROOM 4 - PAGE 349

BELT OF URET
LENGTH 84 CM
JE 98787 - 98790A - 98791A - 98792A - 98793A
ROOM 4 - PAGE 352

BELT OF SATHATHOR
LENGTH 70 CM
JE 30858 - CG 53123 AND CG 53136
ROOM 4 - PAGE 346

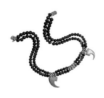

ANKLET OF MERERET
LENGTH 34 CM
JE 30884A, JE 30923
ROOM 4 - PAGE 350

BRACELETS AND ANKLETS OF URET; BRACELETS: JE 98785A, B - 98788A, B - 98790D - 98792D - 98793D; ANKLETS: JE 98784 A, B - 98789 - 98780A, B - 98790D - 98792D - 98793D; *ROOM 4 - PAGE 353*

GIRDLE OF MERERET
LENGTH 60 CM
JE 30879 AND JE 30923 - CG 53075
ROOM 4 - PAGE 346

PENDANT OF MERERET
HEIGHT 4.6 CM
JE 53070
ROOM 4 - PAGE 350

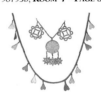

JEWELS OF KHNUMIT
JE 31126, JE 31124, JE 31127
JE 31125, JE 31121
ROOM 4 - PAGE 354

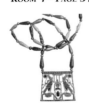

NECKLACE BEARING THE NAME OF SENUSRET II
PECTORAL HEIGHT 4.9 CM; JE 30857
ROOM 4 - PAGE 347

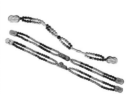

BRACELETS OF URET
LENGTH 15 CM; JE 98786 A, B - 98781 A, B - 98790 B - 98791 B - 98792 B - 98793 B
ROOM 4 - PAGE 351

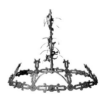

DIADEM OF KHNUMIT
DIAMETER 64 CM
CG 52860
ROOM 4 - PAGE 355

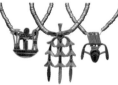

BRACELETS OF KHNUMIT
FASTENERS: HEIGHT VARIES
BETWEEN 1.9 AND 3.3 CM
CG 52958, CG 52956, CG 52955
ROOM 4 - PAGE 356

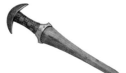

DAGGER OF ITA
LENGTH 26.8 CM
JE 31069
ROOM 4 - PAGE 361

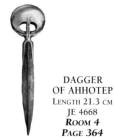

DAGGER
OF AHHOTEP
LENGTH 21.3 CM
JE 4668
ROOM 4
PAGE 364

FASTENER OF SATHATHOR
HEIGHT 2.7 CM
JE 30862
ROOM 4 - PAGE 357

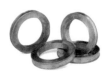

BRACELETS OF AHHOTEP
DIAMETER 10.4 CM
JE 4697
ROOM 4 - PAGE 362

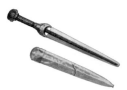

DAGGER OF AHMES
LENGTH 28.5 CM
JE 4665
ROOM 4 - PAGE 365

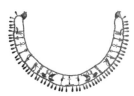

NECKLACE OF KHNUMIT
LENGTH 35 CM
JE 31116 - CG 53018
ROOM 4 - PAGE 358

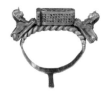

BRACELET OF AHHOTEP
HEIGHT 8.2 CM, WIDTH 11 CM
JE 4680
ROOM 4 - PAGE 362

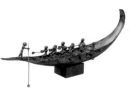

MODEL BOAT
LENGTH 48 CM
JE 4680 - CG 52642
ROOM 4 - PAGE 366

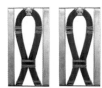

CLASPS OF BRACELETS
OF KHNUMIT
HEIGHT CM 3,9
JE 31091 - CG 52044, CG 52045
ROOM 4 - PAGE 359

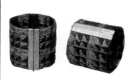

BRACELETS OF AHHOTEP
HEIGHT 3.6 CM, DIAMETER 5.4 CM
JE 4686, JE 4687
ROOM 4 - PAGE 363

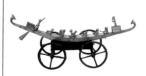

MODEL BOAT
LENGTH 43.3 CM
JE 4681, JE 4669
ROOM 4 - PAGE 366

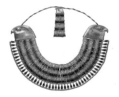

NECKLACE OF NEFERUPTAH
HEIGHT 10 CM, LENGTH 36.5 CM
JE 90199
ROOM 4 - PAGE 360

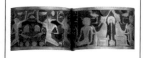

BRACELET OF AHHOTEP
HEIGHT 3.4 CM, DIAMETER 5.5 CM
JE 4684 - CG 52069
ROOM 4 - PAGE 364

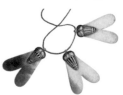

NECKLACE WITH
FLY PENDANTS
LENGTH OF THE CHAIN 59 CM
JE 4694 - CG 52671
ROOM 4 - PAGE 367

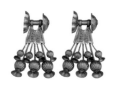

NECKLACE WITH SCARAB
Length 202 cm
JE 4695
Room 4 - Page 368

SMALL CUP
Height 9.4 cm
JE 3º872
Room 4 - Page 371

EARRINGS OF SETY II
Height 13.5 cm
JE 39675
Room 4 - Page 375

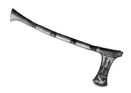

CEREMONIAL AXE OF AHMES
Length 47.5 cm
JE 4673
Room 4 - Page 368

VASE WITH COW HANDLE
Height 11.2 cm
JE 39870
Room 4 - Page 372

BRACELETS OF SETY II
Width max 6.5 cm
JE 39688
Room 4 - Page 376

EARRING
Diameter 3.9 cm
JE 97864
Room 4 - Page 369

VASE
Height 7.6 cm
JE 39887
Room 4 - Page 373

NECKLACE WITH PECTORAL
Pectoral: height 11 cm
JE 31379
Room 4 - Page 376

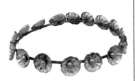
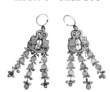

VASE WITH GOAT HANDLE
Height 16.5 cm
JE 39867 - CG 53262
Room 4 - Page 370

SMALL DIADEM
Diameter 17 cm
JE 39674
Room 4 - Page 373

EARRINGS
Length 11.5 cm
JE 28328
Room 4 - Page 377

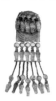
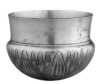

BRACELETS OF RAMESES II
Diameter 7.2 cm
JE 39873
Room 4 - Page 371

**EARRINGS IN THE NAME
OF RAMESES XI**
Height 16 cm; JE 6086
Room 4 - Page 374

CUP
Height 9.2 cm
JE 3584 - CG 53274
Room 4 - Page 378

PATERA
HEIGHT 3.2 CM
JE 3583 - CG 53275
ROOM 4 - PAGE 378

RING
DIAMETER 2.3 CM
JE 67885
ROOM 4 - PAGE 382

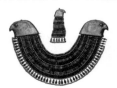

COLLAR OF NUBHOTEP
EXTERNAL DIAMETER 32 CM
JE 30939, JE 30940 , JE 30945
ROOM 4 - PAGES 386-387

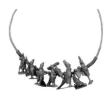

NECKLACE WITH PENDANTS
DIAMETER 12.5 CM
JE 45206
ROOM 4 - PAGE 379

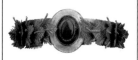

BRACELET WITH AGATE
DIAMETER 9 CM
JE 98537
ROOM 4 - PAGE 383

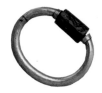

**BRACELET
OF SHESHONQ**
DIAMETER 7.7 CM; JE 72186
ROOM 4 - PAGE 388

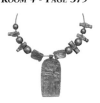

NECKLACE
DIAMETER 14 CM
JE 45206
ROOM 4 - PAGE 380

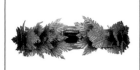

BRACELET WITH AGATE
DIAMETER 9 CM
JE 98538
ROOM 4 - PAGE 383

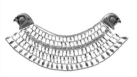

NECKLACE OF KHNUMIT
OVERALL DIMENSIONS: HEIGHT
CM 3.8, WIDTH CM 4.3; JE 30942
ROOM 4 - PAGE 389

GOLD BRACELET
DIAMETER 8 CM
JE 38082
ROOM 4 - PAGE 381

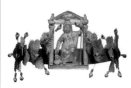

DIADEM WITH SERAPIS
DIAMETER 22 CM
JE 98535
ROOM 4 - PAGE 384

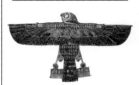

PENDANT OF AMENEMOPE
WIDTH 37.5 CM
JE 86036
ROOM 2 - PAGE 393

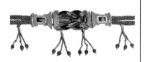

NECKLACE
LENGTH 42 CM
JE 67881
ROOM 4 - PAGE 382

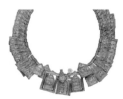

**PECTORAL WITH
PENDANTS**
WIDTH 38 CM; JE 98536
ROOM 4 - PAGE 385

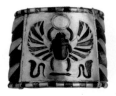

ANKLET OF PSUSENNES I
HEIGHT 5.5 CM, DIAMETER 6.6 CM
JE 85781
ROOM 2 - PAGE 395

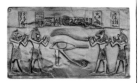

PLAQUE OF PSUSENNES I
HEIGHT 9.9 CM, WIDTH 16.6 CM
JE 85821
ROOM 2 - PAGE 394

PECTORAL OF PSUSENNES I
HEIGHT 10.5 CM
JE 85788, JE 85799
ROOM 2 - PAGE 399

CUP OF UNDJEBAUENDJED
DIAMETER 16 CM
JE 85906
ROOM 2 - PAGE 403

SWORD HILT
HEIGHT 16 CM
JE 85854
ROOM 2 - PAGE 396

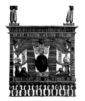

PECTORAL OF PSUSENNES I
HEIGHT 13.8 CM
JE 85796, JE 85791, JE 85795
ROOM 2 - PAGE 400

CUP OF UNDJEBAUENDJED
DIAMETER 16.5 CM
JE 87743
ROOM 2 - PAGE 403

NECKLACE OF PSUSENNES I
LENGTH 56 CM
JE 85755, JE 85756
ROOM 2 - PAGE 396

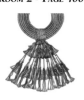

NECKLACE OF PSUSENNES I
CLASP: HEIGHT 6.2 CM
JE 85751
ROOM 2 - PAGE 401

CUP OF UNDJEBAUENDJED
DIAMETER 18.4 CM
JE 87742
ROOM 2 - PAGE 404

**WATER JUG
OF PSUSENNES I**
HEIGHT 38 CM; JE 85892
ROOM 2 - PAGE 397

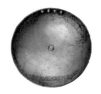

PATERA OF PSUSENNES I
DIAMETER 15.2 CM
JE 85905
ROOM 2 - PAGE 402

CUP OF UNDJEBAUENDJED
DIAMETER 15.5 CM
JE 87741
ROOM 2 - PAGE 405

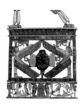

PECTORAL OF PSUSENNES I
HEIGHT 12 CM
JE 85786
ROOM 2 - PAGE 398

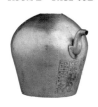

**JUG WITH SPOUT
OF AMENEMOPE**
HEIGHT 12 CM; JE 86099
ROOM 2 - PAGE 402

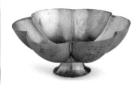

CUP OF UNDJEBAUENDJED
DIAMETER 13.3 CM
JE 87740
ROOM 2 - PAGE 405

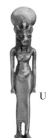

**PENDANT OF
UNDJEBAUENDJED**
HEIGHT 7.2 CM
JE 87718
ROOM 2
PAGE 406

**FUNERARY MASK
OF AMENEMOPE**
HEIGHT 30 CM; JE 86059
ROOM 2 - PAGE 409

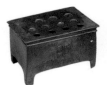

**BRAZIER
OF RAMESES II**
HEIGHT 24 CM, WIDTH 26.5 CM
JE 85910
ROOM 2 - PAGE 415

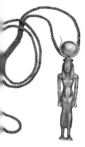

**PENDANT
DEPICTING
ISIS**
HEIGHT 11 CM
JE 87716
ROOM 2
PAGE 406

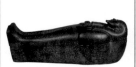

**SARCOPHAGUS
OF PSUSENNES I**
LENGTH 220 CM
JE 85911
ROOM 2 - PAGE 410-411

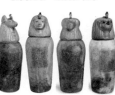

**CANOPIC VASES
OF PSUSENNES I**
HEIGHT VARIES BETWEEN 41 TO 38 CM
JE 85915, JE 85914, JE 85917, JE
85916; *ROOM 2 - PAGE 416-417*

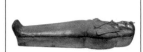

**FUNERAL MASK OF
UNDJEBAUENDJED**
HEIGHT 22 CM; JE 87753
ROOM 2 - PAGE 407

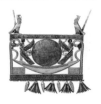

**SARCOPHAGUS
OF PSUSENNES I**
LENGTH 185 CM
JE 85917
ROOM 2 - PAGE 412-413

PECTORAL OF SHESHONQ I
HEIGHT 7.8 CM
JE 72171
ROOM 2 - PAGE 418

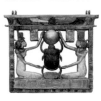

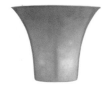

**PECTORAL OF
AMENEMOPE**
HEIGHT 9.8 CM; JE 86037
ROOM 2 - PAGE 408

BASIN OF PSUSENNES I
HEIGHT 17 CM
JE 85893
ROOM 2 - PAGE 414

PECTORAL OF SHESHONQ II
HEIGHT 7 CM
JE 72172
ROOM 2 - PAGE 419

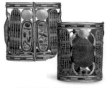

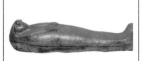

**BRACELETS OF
PSUSENNES I**
HEIGHT 7 CM, DIAMETER 8 CM
JE 86027, JE 86028
ROOM 2 - PAGE 408

**SARCOPHAGUS
OF SHESHONQ II**
LENGTH 190 CM
JE 72154
ROOM 2 - PAGE 414

SANDALS OF PSUSENNES I
LENGTH 23.3
JE 85842
ROOM 2 - PAGE 420

MASK OF SHESHONQ II
HEIGHT 26 CM, WIDTH 23 CM
JE 72163
ROOM 2 - PAGE 421

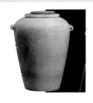

POT OF HATSHEPSUT
HEIGHT 33.5 CM
JE 57203
ROOM 12 - PAGE 428

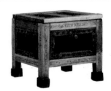

CASKET OF RAMESES IX
HEIGHT 21.5 CM
JE 26271
ROOM 12 - PAGE 431

BRACELETS OF SHESHONQ II
HEIGHT 4.6 CM, DIAMETER 7 CM
JE 72184B
ROOM 2 - PAGE 421

COW'S HEAD
HEIGHT 46 CM
JE 32367
ROOM 12 - PAGES 428-429

**FUNERARY MASK FOR THE
MUMMY OF A FOETUS**
HEIGHT 16 CM
JE 39711
ROOM 12 - PAGE 432

**PECTORAL
OF
SHESHONQ II**
HEIGHT 15 CM,
LENGTH OF
CHAIN 75 CM
JE 85786
*ROOM 2
PAGE 422*

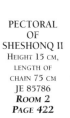

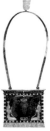

WINGED COBRA
HEIGHT 44 CM, LENGTH 65 CM
CG 24629
ROOM 12 - PAGE 429

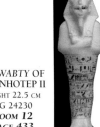

*SHAWABTY OF
AMENHOTEP II*
HEIGHT 22.5 CM
CG 24230
*ROOM 12
PAGE 433*

MASK OF PSUSENNES I
HEIGHT 48 CM, WIDTH 38 CM
JE 85913
ROOM 2 - PAGE 423

ANKH SIGN
HEIGHT 42 CM, WIDTH 21 CM CA
JE 32491
ROOM 12 - PAGE 430

URAEUS SERPENT
HEIGHT 23 CM
JE 39628
ROOM 12 - PAGE 433

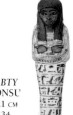

*SHAWABTY
OF KHONSU*
HEIGHT 21 CM
JE 27234
*ROOM 17
PAGE 425*

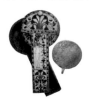

MIRROR WITH CASE
CASE: LENGTH 28 CM, MIRROR:
LENGTH 12.5 CM; JE 26278
ROOM 12 - PAGE 430

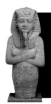

SHAWABTY OF RAMESES VI
HEIGHT 26 CM
JE 96857 - CG 48415
ROOM 12 - PAGE 434

SHAWABTY CONTAINER OF HENUTTAUY
HEIGHT 58 CM; JE 26272B
ROOM 12 - PAGE 435

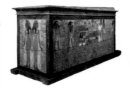

SARCOPHAGUS OF KHONSU
HEIGHT 125 CM, LENGTH 262 CM
JE 27302
ROOM 17 - PAGES 440-441

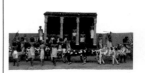

MODEL OF LIVESTOCK CENSUS
LENGTH 173 CM; JE 46724
ROOM 27 - PAGE 446

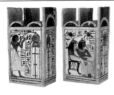

SHAWABTY CONTAINER OF KHONSU
HEIGHT 35.6 CM; JE 27299
ROOM 17 - PAGE 436

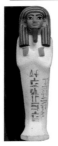

SHAWABTY OF AMENHOTEP
HEIGHT 29 CM
JE 66247
ROOM 22 PAGE 442

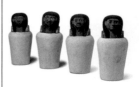

CANOPIC VASES OF INEPUHOTEP
HEIGHT 34 CM; JE 46774
ROOM 27 - PAGE 447

DOOR OF THE TOMB OF SENNEDJEM
HEIGHT 135 CM; JE 27303
ROOM 17 - PAGE 437

NAOS WITH FALCON
HEIGHT 69.5 CM
TR 18/11/24/46
ROOM 22 - PAGE 442

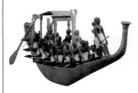

MODEL WITH A BOAT
HEIGHT 61 CM; JE 46716
ROOM 27 - PAGE 448

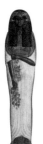

SARCOPHAGUS OF THE LADY ASET
HEIGHT 193.5 CM
JE 27309
ROOM 17 PAGE 438

SCARAB
LENGTH 11 CM
TR 15/1/25/44
ROOM 22 - PAGE 444

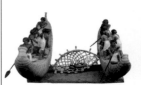

MODEL WITH A FISHING SCENE
HEIGHT 31.5 CM; JE 46715
ROOM 27 - PAGE 449

SARCOPHAGUS OF SENNEDJEM
HEIGHT 184.5 CM
JE 27299
ROOM 17 - PAGE 439

STELA OF DJEDDJEHUTYIUANKH
HEIGHT CM 27.6; TR 25/12/24/20
ROOM 22 - PAGE 445

MODEL OF WEAVERS AT WORK
HEIGHT 25 CM ; JE 46723
ROOM 27 - PAGE 450

MODEL OF A HOUSE AND GARDEN
Height 43 cm; JE 46721
Room 27 - Page 450

THREE BEARERS OF OFFERINGS
Height cm. 59; CG 250
Room 32 - Page 454

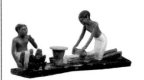

MODEL OF A WOMAN STEEPING AND ANOTHER POKING A FIRE
Length 60 cm; CG 243
Room 32 - Page 456

CARPENTRY WORKSHOP
Height 26 cm
JE 46722
Room 27 - Page 451

STATUE OF A MAN HOEING
Height 29 cm; CG 245
Room 32 - Page 455

MODEL OF A MAN ROASTING A DUCK
Height cm 24; CG 245
Room 32 - Page 457

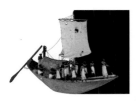

MODEL OF A SAILING BOAT
Length 124 cm; JE 46720
Room 27 - Page 452

CIRCULAR OFFERINGS TABLE OF HORUS
Diameter 83 cm; JE 53151
Room 32 - Page 455

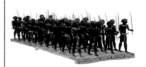

TROOP OF NUBIAN ARCHERS
Length 190.2 cm; CG 257
Room 37 - Pages 458-459

FUNERARY MASK
Height 50 cm
TR 7/9/33/1
Room 27 - Page 453

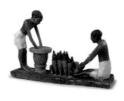

MODEL SHOWING THE PREPARATION OF BREAD AND BEER
Height 35 cm
CG 244; *Room 32 - Page 456*

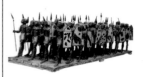

TROOP OF EGYPTIAN LANCERS
Length 169.8 cm; CG 258
Room 37 - Pages 458-459

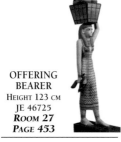

OFFERING BEARER
Height 123 cm
JE 46725
*Room 27
Page 453*

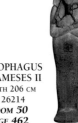

MODEL OF A WOMAN POKING THE FIRE
Length 30.5 cm; JE 30820
Room 32 - Page 457

SARCOPHAGUS OF RAMESES II
Length 206 cm
JE 26214
*Room 50
Page 462*

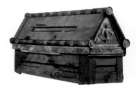

WOODEN SARCOPHAGUS
LENGTH 199 CM
JE 33101
ROOM 21 - PAGE 464

SARCOPHAGUS
OF MAATKARA
LENGTH 223 CM
JE 26200
ROOM 46
PAGE 470

SARCOPHAGUS OF ASHAYT
LENGTH 250 CM
JE 47267
ROOM 48 - PAGE 476

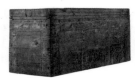

SARCOPHAGUS OF NEFERI
LENGTH 265 CM
JE 28088
ROOM 21 - PAGE 465

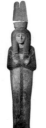

SARCOPHAGUS
OF AHMES
NEFERTARI
LENGTH 378 CM
CG 61003
ROOM 46
PAGE 471

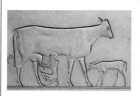

SARCOPHAGUS OF KAUIT
LENGTH 262 CM
JE 47397
ROOM 48 - PAGE 477

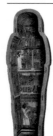

SARCOPHAGUS
OF
DJEDHOREFANKH
LENGTH 203 CM
TR 23/11/16/2
ROOM 31
PAGE 466-467

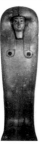

SARCOPHAGUS
OF AHHOTEP
LENGTH 212 CM
CG 28501
ROOM 44
PAGE 472

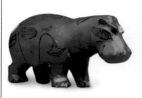

STATUETTE OF
HIPPOPOTAMUS
HEIGHT 11.5 CM; JE 21365
ROOM 48 - PAGE 478

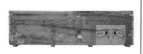

SARCOPHAGUS OF KHUY
LENGTH 189 CM
JE 36445
ROOM 37 - PAGE 468

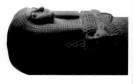

SARCOPHAGUS OF AHMES
MERITAMUN
LENGTH 313.5 CM; JE 53140
ROOM 46 - PAGE 473

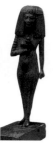

STATUETTE
OF HENUT-
NAKHTU
HEIGHT 22.2 CM
CG 804
ROOM 48
PAGE 479

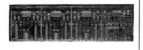

SARCOPHAGUS OF SENBI
LENGTH 212 CM
JE 42948
ROOM 37 - PAGE 469

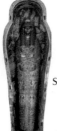

SARCOPHAGUS
OF PAKHAR
HEIGHT 189 CM
CG 6122-6121
ROOM 48
PAGE 474-475

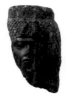

HEAD OF TIY
HEIGHT 7.2 CM
JE 38257
ROOM 48 - PAGE 480

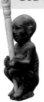

KOHL STICK HOLDER
HEIGHT 9.5 CM
JE 44902
ROOM 48 - PAGE 481

*VASE IN SHAPE
OF A PAPYRUS*
HEIGHT 18 CM, WIDTH 8 CM
JE 97892
ROOM 48 - PAGE 485

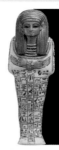

*SHAWABTY
OF PTAHMES*
HEIGHT 20 CM
CG 48406
ROOM 48
PAGE 489

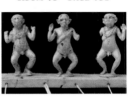

FIGURINES OF THREE
DANCING DWARVES
HEIGHT 7.8 CM; JE 63858
ROOM 48 - PAGE 482

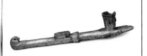

CENSER IN SHAPE
OF AN ARM
LENGTH 55 CM
JE 30700
ROOM 48 - PAGE 486

FUNERARY MASK OF YUYA
HEIGHT 33 CM; JE 95316
ROOM 43 - PAGE 490

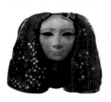

HEAD OF A STATUE OF A
WOMAN
HEIGHT 10.5 CM; JE 39390
ROOM 48 - PAGE 483

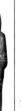

STATUETTE OF
THUTMOSIS III
HEIGHT 18 CM
JE 88888
ROOM 48
PAGE 486

FUNERARY MASK OF TUYA
HEIGHT 40 CM
JE 95254
ROOM 43 - PAGE 494

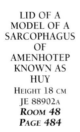

LID OF A
MODEL OF A
SARCOPHAGUS
OF
AMENHOTEP
KNOWN AS
HUY
HEIGHT 18 CM
JE 88902A
ROOM 48
PAGE 484

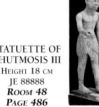

STATUETTE OF HEDGEHOG
HEIGHT 5.3 CM
JE 30742
ROOM 48 - PAGE 487

STATUETTE OF THE *BA*
OF YUYA
HEIGHT 13.5 CM; JE 95312
ROOM 43 - PAGE 495

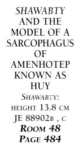

SHAWABTY
AND THE
MODEL OF A
SARCOPHAGUS
OF
AMENHOTEP
KNOWN AS
HUY
SHAWABTY:
HEIGHT 13.8 CM
JE 88902B , C
ROOM 48
PAGE 484

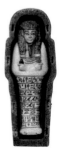

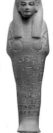

SHAWABTY
BELONGING TO
LIEUTENANT
HAT
HEIGHT 20 2 CM
JE 39590
ROOM 48
PAGE 488

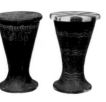

POTS
HEIGHT 20.5 CM
JE 95257, JE 95255
ROOM 43 - PAGE 496

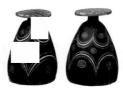

POTS
HEIGHT 14 CM
JE 95283, JE 95274
ROOM 43 - PAGE 496

JEWEL BOX BELONGING TO TUYA
HEIGHT 41 CM; JE 95248
ROOM 43 - PAGE 502

TILES WITH PICTURES OF PRISONERS
MAX HEIGHT 26 CM; CG 27525
ROOM 44 - PAGE 506

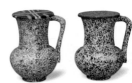

POTS
HEIGHT 19 CM
JE 95281, JE 95278
ROOM 43 - PAGE 496

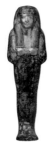

SHAWABTY **BELONGING TO TUYA**
HEIGHT 27.7 CM
CG 51037
ROOM 43
PAGE 503

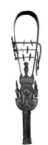

SISTRUM
HEIGHT 42.7 CM
TR 14/5/75/1
ROOM 44
PAGE 507

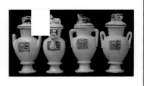

FOUR VASES IN THE NAME OF YUYA
HEIGHT 25 CM; CG 51102
ROOM 43 - PAGE 497

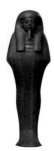

MAGICAL STATUE
HEIGHT CM 25.5
JE 95347
ROOM 43
PAGE 504

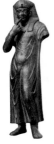

STATUETTE OF HARPOCRATES
HEIGHT 26.7 CM
CG 26964
ROOM 39
PAGE 508

CHAIR BELONGING TO PRINCESS SATAMUN
HEIGHT 77 CM
JE 95342
ROOM 43 - PAGES 498-499

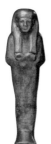

SHAWABTY **OF TUYA**
HEIGHT 27 CM
JE 95362
ROOM 43
PAGE 505

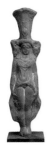

STATUETTE OF ISIS-APHRODITE
HEIGHT 31.5 CM
CG 67928
ROOM 39
PAGE 509

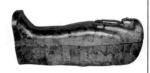

SARCOPHAGUS OF YUYA
LENGTH CM 204
JE 95232
ROOM 43 - PAGE 500-501

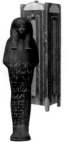

SHAWABTY **OF YUYA WITH ITS BOX**
HEIGHT 29.8 CM
JE 95372
ROOM 43
PAGE 505

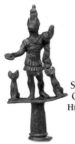

STATUETTE OF ANUBIS
HEIGHT 14.8 CM
CG 27694
ROOM 39
PAGE 509

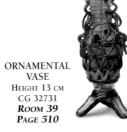

ORNAMENTAL
VASE
Height 13 cm
CG 32731
Room 39
Page 510

DECORATED FLASK
Height 30.5 cm
JE 54502
Room 39 - Page 513

SPOON IN THE
SHAPE OF A
MARJORAM LEAF
Length 26.5 cm
CG 45133
Room 34
Page 518

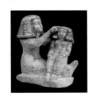

PHIAL
Height 10.3 cm
CG 32731
Room 39 - Page 511

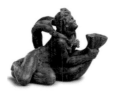

MALE FIGURE WITH
GOATSKIN
Height 8.5 cm; CG 26752
Room 39 - Page 514

STATUETTE OF A WOMAN
WITH A GIRL
Height 6.3 cm; JE 33732
Room 34 - Page 518

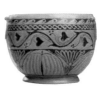

FAÏENCE VASE
Height 7.2 cm
JE 49802
Room 39 - Page 511

STATUETTE
OF THE
GOD
BES
Height 34 cm
CG 27123
Room 39
Page 515

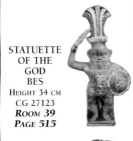

WOODEN FIGURINE
OF A FEMALE
Height 23 cm
JE 36274
Room 34 - Page 520

VASE
Diameter 17 cm
JE 37662
Room 39 - Page 512

TERRACOTTA
ISIS-
APHRODITE
Height 29.5 cm
CG 26961
Room 39
Page 515

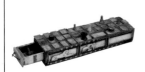

SENET BOARD
Length cm 26.5
CG 68005
Room 34 - Page 520

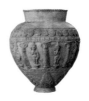

VASE WITH DECORATION
Height cm 14
JE 44160
Room 39 - Page 512

KOHL
HOLDER
Height 9.4 cm
CG 44575
Room 34
Page 517

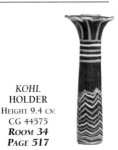

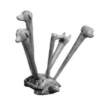

GAME OF THE DOG
AND JACKAL
Length of the support 5.5 cm
CG 44474
Room 34 - Page 521

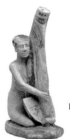

**STATUETTE
OF HARPIST**
HEIGHT 18.5 CM
JE 44419
ROOM 34
PAGE 522

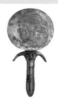

MIRROR
HEIGHT 24.9 CM
CG 44034
ROOM 34 - PAGE 525

DECORATED *OSTRACON*
HEIGHT 28.5 CM
CG 25139
ROOM 24 - PAGE 529

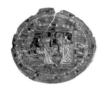

DIAPHRAGM OF A DRUM
DIAMETER 25 CM
JE 25993
ROOM 34 - PAGE 522

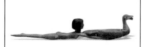

MAKE-UP SPOON
LENGTH 30.5 CM
CG 45117
ROOM 34 - PAGE 525

DECORATED *OSTRACON*
HEIGHT 10.5 CM
JE 63805
ROOM 24 - PAGE 530

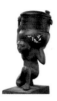

UNGUENTARY OF SIAMUN
HEIGHT 14 CM
JE 44745
ROOM 34 - PAGE 523

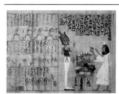

**FUNERARY PAPYRUS
OF NESPERENNEBU**
HEIGHT 35 CM, LENGTH 300 CM
SR 11487
ROOM 24 - PAGE 526

OSTRACON **WITH IMAGES
OF THE PHARAOH**
HEIGHT 18 CM; JE 25147
ROOM 24 - PAGE 531

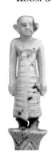

HAIR PIN
TOTAL LENGTH
14.5 CM,
HEIGHT OF THE
FIGURINE
3.9 CM
JE 25741
ROOM 34
PAGE 524

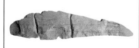

OSTRACON **WITH THE
PLAN OF A ROYAL TOMB**
LENGTH 83.5 CM
CG 25184
ROOM 24 - PAGE 528-529

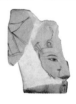

OSTRACON **WITH IMAGES
OF THE PHARAOH**
HEIGHT 42 CM; JE 25144
ROOM 24 - PAGE 531

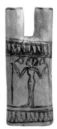

KOHL
CONTAINER
HEIGHT 13 CM
CG 3978
ROOM 34
PAGE 524

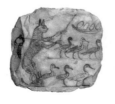

DECORATED *OSTRACON*
HEIGHT 11 CM
JE 63801
ROOM 24 - PAGE 528

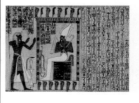

BOOK OF THE DEAD
OF PINUDJEM I
LENGTH 450 CM; SR VIII.11488
ROOM 24 - PAGE 532-533

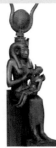

**STATUE
OF ISIS AND
HORUS**
HEIGHT CM 46.5
JE 39483
ROOM 19
PAGE 534

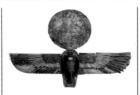

WINGED SCARAB
HEIGHT 77 CM
JE 46356
ROOM 19 - PAGE 539

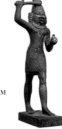

**STATUE
OF MIN**
HEIGHT 14.2 CM
JE 27043
ROOM 19
PAGE 542

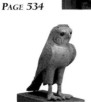

STATUE OF FALCON
HEIGHT 19 CM
JE 46388
ROOM 19 - PAGE 535

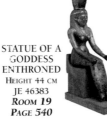

**STATUE OF A
GODDESS
ENTHRONED**
HEIGHT 44 CM
JE 46383
ROOM 19
PAGE 540

STATUE OF A FALCON
HEIGHT 22.5 CM
JE 30335
ROOM 19 - PAGE 543

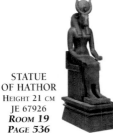

**STATUE
OF HATHOR**
HEIGHT 21 CM
JE 67926
ROOM 19
PAGE 536

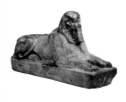

SMALL SPHINX
LENGTH 43 CM
JE 46393
ROOM 19 - PAGE 540

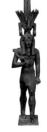

**STATUE
OF
NEFERTEM**
HEIGHT
41.5 CM
CG 38076
ROOM 19
PAGE 544

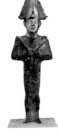

**STATUE
OF OSIRIS**
HEIGHT 16.2 CM
CG 38312
ROOM 19
PAGE 537

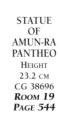

**STATUE
OF OSIRIS**
HEIGHT 29.2 CM
JE 38258
ROOM 19
PAGE 541

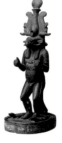

**STATUE
OF
AMUN-RA
PANTHEO**
HEIGHT
23.2 CM
CG 38696
ROOM 19
PAGE 544

**SARCOPHAGUS
OF A FALCON**
HEIGHT 88 CM; JE 46351
ROOM 19 - PAGE 538

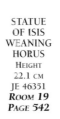

**STATUE
OF ISIS
WEANING
HORUS**
HEIGHT
22.1 CM
JE 46351
ROOM 19
PAGE 542

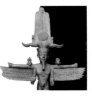

**STATUE OF AMUN
PANTHEO**
HEIGHT 45 CM; JE 43462
ROOM 19 - PAGE 545

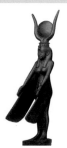

STATUE
OF WINGED
ISIS
Height
41.5 CM
CG 38891
ROOM 19
PAGE 546

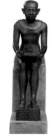

STATUE
OF
IMHOTEP
Height
21.5 CM
CG 38045
ROOM 19
PAGE 550

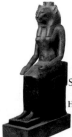

STATUE OF
BASTET
Height 42 CM
JE 45391
ROOM 19
PAGE 553

STELA OF "HORUS
ON CROCODILES"
Height 44 CM; CG 9401
ROOM 19 - PAGE 547

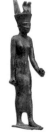

STATUE
OF THE
GODDESS
NEITH
Height 14 CM
JE 30324
ROOM 19
PAGE 550

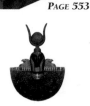

PECTORAL
Width 33 CM
JE 53671
ROOM 19 - PAGE 554

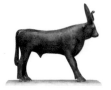

STATUE OF THE BULL APIS
Height 11 CM
TR 3/2/19/23
ROOM 19 - PAGE 548

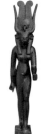

STATUE
OF THE
GODDESS
HATHOR
Height
27.2 CM
CG 39134
ROOM 19
PAGE 551

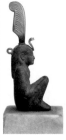

STATUE
OF THE
GODDESS
MAAT
Height 7.2 CM
CG 38907
ROOM 19
PAGE 555

STATUETTE OF AN
ICHNEUMON
Height 26 CM; JE 8662
ROOM 19 - PAGE 548

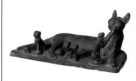

STATUE OF BASTET
Length 9.5 CM
TR 22/2/22/3
ROOM 19 - PAGE 552

SISTRUM
Height 19 CM
JE 38808
ROOM 19 - PAGE 556

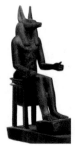

STATUE
OF ANUBIS
Height
14.8 CM
CG 38527
ROOM 19
PAGE 549

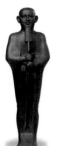

STATUE OF
THE GOD
PTAH
Height
28.5 CM
CG 38445
ROOM 19
PAGE 552

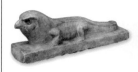

STATUE OF A CROCODILE
WITH A FALCON'S HEAD
Length 36 CM; JE 21868
ROOM 19 - PAGE 556

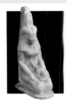

STATUE
OF ISIS-SELKET
HEIGHT 18.8 CM; JE 38987
ROOM 19 - PAGE 557

MASK OF A MAN
HEIGHT 32 CM
CG 33158
ROOM 14 - PAGE 562

PORTRAIT OF A MAN
HEIGHT 34 CM
CG 33234
ROOM 14 - PAGE 565

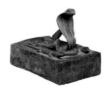

UREAUS WITH LIZARDS
HEIGHT 11.5 CM
JE 30837
ROOM 19 - PAGE 557

FUNERARY MASK
HEIGHT 42 CM
TR 18/8/19/1
ROOM 14 - PAGE 562

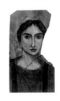

PORTRAIT OF A WOMAN
HEIGHT 35 CM
CG 33248
ROOM 14 - PAGE 566

PORTRAIT OF A YOUNG
WOMAN
HEIGHT 42 CM; CG 33243
ROOM 14 - PAGE 558

MASK OF AMMONARIN
HEIGHT 51 CM
CG 33128
ROOM 14 - PAGE 563

PORTRAIT OF A WOMAN
HEIGHT 31 CM; CG 33244
ROOM 14 - PAGE 567

FUNERARY MASK
OF A WOMAN
HEIGHT 29.5 CM; CG 33187
ROOM 14 - PAGE 559

PORTRAIT OF A MAN
HEIGHT 39.5 CM
CG 33242
ROOM 14 - PAGE 564

PORTRAIT OF A MAN
HEIGHT 41 CM
CG 33252
ROOM 14 - PAGE 568

PORTRAIT OF A CHILD
HEIGHT 37 CM
JE 32568
ROOM 14 - PAGE 560

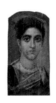

PORTRAIT OF A YOUNG
WOMAN
HEIGHT 42 CM; CG 33253
ROOM 14 - PAGE 564

PORTRAIT OF TWO
BROTHERS
DIAMETER CM 61; CG 33267
ROOM 14 - PAGES 568-569

PORTRAIT OF A WOMAN
HEIGHT 38 CM
CG 33237
ROOM 14 - PAGE 570

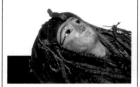

MUMMY OF AMENHOTEP I
JE 61058
ROOM 56 - PAGE 574

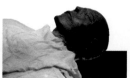

MUMMY OF SETY I
JE 61077
ROOM 56 - PAGE 576

PORTRAIT OF A BOY
HEIGHT 35.5 CM
CG 33260
ROOM 14 - PAGE 570

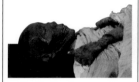

MUMMY OF THUTMOSIS I
JE 61066
ROOM 56 - PAGE 574

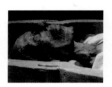

MUMMY OF RAMESES II
JE 61078
ROOM 56 - PAGE 576

PORTRAIT OF A WOMAN
HEIGHT 35 CM
CG 33241
ROOM 14 - PAGE 571

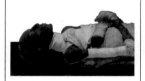

MUMMY OF THUTMOSIS IV
JE 61073
ROOM 56 - PAGE 575

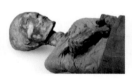

MUMMY OF MERENPTAH
JE 61079
ROOM 56 - PAGE 577

GLOSSARY

Agemina: a metal working technique consisting of the inlay of threads or sheets of silver or gold in bronze.
Amun: the "King of the Gods" who formed the Theban triad with Mut and Khonsu.
Amulets: talismans whose purpose was to ward off negative influences; in a funerary context, they guaranteed vital functions to the deceased.
Ankh: a hieroglyph and an amulet, the symbol of life.
Anubis: the god who presided over embalming and who accompanied the deceased in the Afterlife.
Apis: the sacred bull, a symbol of virility and fertility.
Apopis: an evil serpent that rose up each morning to battle

the rising Sun but which was always defeated.
Apotropaic: that which protects and wards off evil influences.
Atef: a crown typically worn by Osiris, composed of a tiara topped by a sun disk and flanked by two plumes.
Aten: sun disk which became the only god during the reign of Amenhotep IV.
Atum: god that represented the sun as Ra-Atum (referred to the evening sun).
Ba: bird with a human head that depicts one of the components of the human spirit.
Bastet: goddess of joy and music depicted with the head of a cat.
Bes: beneficent spirit in the form of a dwarf who frightened away evil spirits.

Book of the Amduat (Book of that which is in the Underworld): describes the night time journey of the sun through the land of the dead, divided into twelve parts like the hours required for Ra to make the journey. At the end of the nightime journey, the sun god – identified with Osiris – is reborn to make his daytime journey across the sky.
Book of the Dead: collection of magic-religious formulas used to ensure survival of the deceased in the Afterlife. Appeared during the Eighteenth Dynasty.
Book of the Doors: guide for the deceased to pass through the doors and by the guardians in the Underworld.

Canopic vases: the four vases that contained the internal organs of the deceased.

Cartouche: elongated form of the hieroglyph, *shenu*, from the verb *shen* ("to surround") which contained the birth and coronation names of the pharaoh.

Clavus: purple band that adorned Roman tunics; in Roman Egypt they signified affiliation to Rome.

Cartonnage: light material made from layers of linen soaked in stucco; it was used in the manufacture of mummy-shaped sarcophaguses and funerary masks.

Champlevé and cloisonné: techniques used in jewelry in which glass paste or colored stone was used to fill cavities made with metal.

Desheret: red crown that symbolized dominion over Lower Egypt.

Divine beard: false beard tied to the chin of the gods and the kings.

Djed: pillar that had an ancient and undefined origin; during the historical epoch it represented the spine of Osiris but was also a protective amulet.

Ennead: Atum, Shu, Tefnet, Geb, Nut, Osiris, Isis, Set, and Nephthys – the nine gods that made up the cosmogony of Heliopolis.

Geb: personification of the earth and the husband of Nut.

Hathor: the guardian goddess of women, music, and the dead; depicted with the head and ears of a cow.

Hathoric: of the goddess Hathor, for example, referring to the headdress with a sun disk between cow's or a female face with a cow's horns and ears.

Heget: the white crown that symbolized Upper Egypt.

Heqa: scepter in the form of a crozier.

Hemhem: headdress formed by three *atef* crowns on ram's horns and flanked by uraeus serpents.

Horus: son of Osiris and Isis and the guardian god of the pharaoh; depicted as a falcon or with the head of a falcon.

Ibis: the Nile bird sacred to the god Thoth.

Imentit: goddess of the West who pampered the dead.

Isis: goddess, the sister and wife of Osiris and the mother of Horus.

Ka: one of the animating spirits of man that represented the vital force.

Kalathos: wicker basket; by extension the headdress of the god Serapis.

Khepri: god that represented the morning sun; depicted as a scarab.

Khepresh: blue crown with metal studs.

Khnum-Ra: god creator of life and living species, depicted with the head of a ram.

Khonsu: god of the moon, son of Amun and Mut.

Kohl: black cosmetic used around the eyes.

Lotus: primordial plant from which the sun was born at the start of the world.

Maat: goddess that personified cosmic order; she was connected with the concepts of truth and justice and depicted with an ostrich plume on her head

Menat: necklace with a counterpoise.

Mertseger: goddess worshipped at Deir al-Medina, depicted as a cobra.

Min: mummy-shaped god who was the guardian deity of fertility.

Montu: warrior god with a human body and the head of a falcon.

Mummy: taken from the Persian word "mumia" indicating an dried body wrapped in bandages.

Mut: goddess, wife of Amun and depicted as a vulture.

Naos: small shrine that generally contained the statue of a god.

Nefertem: god who personified the primordial lotus from which the sun was born.

Neith: domestic and warrior goddess who had multiple roles; she was depicted wearing the red crown of Lower Egypt but sometimes wore a shield with two arrows on her head. She was a primordial goddess, the creator of the gods and all creatures. Her cult reached its apex during the Saite epoch.

Neheh: scepter in the form of a scourge or flail.

Nekhbet: guardian goddess of Upper Egypt, depicted as a vulture.

Nemes: headdress of lined or striped material worn by the pharaoh.

Nephthys: goddess, the sister of Isis and the wife of Seth.

Nome: administrative district of ancient Egypt.

Nun: goddess that represented the primordial ocean.

Nut: goddess that personified the heavenly vault, depicted as a woman arched over the earth.

Ostrakon: fragment of limestone or ceramic on which text or sketches were scratched.

Protoma: decorative element of the head and upper torso of a person or animal.

Pshent: double crown symbol of the pharaoh's dominion over Upper and Lower Egypt.

Ptah: god creator depicted as a mummy with the *was* scepter.

Pylon: monumental portal of a temple.

Pyramid Texts: written on the walls of the burial chambers in the pyramids from the time of the last pharaoh of the Fifth Dynasty, Unas; they were a set of magic and religious formulas that allowed the pharaoh to overcome obstacles in his path during his journey to the Afterlife.

Pyramidion: small pyramid placed on top of obelisks or large pyramids.

Ra: ancient god who symbolized the sun, depicted as a man with the sun disk on his head, sometimes with the head of a falcon or a ram during his night journey through the Underworld.

Ra-Horakhty: god that combined the characteristics of Ra and Horus.

Sarcophagus Texts: magic-religious formulas and rituals written on wooden sarcophaguses between the First Intermediate Period and the Middle Kingdom; their purpose was to ensure survival of the deceased in the Afterlife.

Sed festival: royal jubilee of the pharaoh celebrated after a certain number of years, generally thirty.

Sekhem: a scepter that symbolized authority.

Serapis: god from the Ptolemaic era that combined the Egyptian characteristics of the gods Osiris and Apis with the Greek characteristics of Zeus and Pluto.

Serdab: area in a funerary structure reserved for the statue of the deceased; a small slit in the structure level with the eyes of the statue allowed the deceased to participate in celebrations held in his honor.

Serekh: stylized representation of the facade of an Archaic royal palace.

Seth: god of chaos and the murderer of Osiris; he was depicted with a human body and the head of an unidentifiable animal.

Shawabty: small statues that took the place of the deceased in physical work to be undertaken in the Afterlife.

Shendyt: short skirt with pleated bands that crossed in front and partially covered a piece of fabric with horizontal folds.

Sobek: god crocodile generally depicted with a human body and the head of a crocodile.

Sons of Horus: the four mummy-shaped spirits that protected the internal organs of the deceased: they were Imset with the human head, Hapi with the head of a baboon, Duamutef with the head of a jackal, and Qebehsenuef with the head of a falcon.

Tit: protective amulet known as "Isis' knot."

Thoth: the god who invented writing and the sciences; depicted with a human body and the head of an ibis or baboon.

Torus: cylindrical architectural feature; it bounded the V-shaped molding around doors in Egyptian monuments.

Uadjet: guardian goddess of Lower Egypt, depicted as a cobra.

Udjat: the eye of Horus used as an amulet.

Uraeus serpent: cobra that adorned the forehead of the sun gods and the pharaoh.

Was: scepter generally used by male gods and a symbol of power.

BIBLIOGRAPHY

ABBO B. ET AL., Tanis. L'or des pharaons. Galeries Nationales du Grand Palais, Paris 1987. EXHIBITION CATALOGUE

Aldred C., Old Kingdom Art in Ancient Egypt, London 1949
- ID., Middle Kingdom Art in Ancient Egypt, London 1950
- ID., Jewels of the Pharaohs. Egyptian Jewellery of the Dynastic Period, London 1971
- ID., Akhenaten king of Egypt, London 1988. French edition (1997), translated and presented by A.P. Zivie, and brought up to date with fundamental new discoveries relating to Akhenaten.

ARNOLD D., Der Tempel des Königs Mentuhotep von Deir el-Bahari, Archäologische Veröffentlichungen 8, 3 vols, Mainz 1974-1981

ASTON D.A., The Shabti Box: A Typological Study, Oudheidkundige Medelingen uit het Rijsksmuseum van Oudheden te Leiden 74, Leiden 1994

BALOUT L. / ROUBET C. / DESROCHES-NOBLECOURT CH. ET AL., La Momie de Ramses II - Contribution scientifique à l'Égyptologie, Paris 1985

BARGUET P., Le temple d'Amun-Rê à Karnak. Essai d'exégèse, Cairo 1962

BIERBRIER M.L., The Tomb-builders of the Pharaohs, Cairo 1989

BLACKMAN A.M., "The Significance of Incense and Libation in Funerary and Temple Rituals," in Zeitschrift für

Ägyptische Sprache und Altertumskunde 50, 1912, pages 69-75

BONGIOANNI A., "Considérations sur les noms d'Aten et la nature du rapport souverain-divinité à l'époque amarnienne", in Göttinger Miszellen 6, (1993), pages 43-51

BONGIOANNI A. / TOSI M., La spiritualità dell'antico Egitto (I Concetti di akh, ba e ka), Rimini 1977

BONNET H., Reallexikon der ägyptischen Religionsgeschichte, Berlin 1952

BOTHMER B.V., Egyptian Sculpture of the Late Period 700 B.C. to A.D. 100, New York 1960

BOWMAN A.K., Egypt after the Pharaohs, London 1986 Bresciani E., Letteratura e poesia dell'Antico Egitto, Turin 1902

BUDGE E.A.W., The Mummy - A Handbook of Egyptian Funerary Archaeology, Cambridge University Press 1925

CARTER H., "A tomb prepared for queen Hatshepsut and other recent discoveries at Thebes," in Journal of Egyptian Archaeology 4, 1917, pages 107-118

CERNY J., L'identité des Serviteurs dans la Place de la Vérité et les ouvriers de la nécropole royale de Thèbes, in Revue de l'Egypte Ancienne, II, Paris 1929

CLÈRE J.J., Les chauves d'Hathor, Orientalia Lovaniensia Analecta 63, Leuven 1995

CORTEGGIANI J.P., L'Egypte des pharaons au Musée du Caire, Paris 1986

DARESSY G., "Les sépultures des prêtres d'Amun à Deir el-Baharî," in Annales du Service des Antiquités de l'Égypte 1, 1900, pages 141-148
- ID., "Les cercueils des prêtres d'Ammon (Deuxième trouvaille de Deir el-Bahari)," in Annales du Service des Antiquités de l'Égypte 8, 1907, pages 3-38

DE BUCK A., The Egyptian Coffin Texts, 7 vols, Chicago 1935-1961

DE PUTTER T. / KARLSHAUSEN C., Les pierres utilisées dans la sculpture et l'architecture de l'Egypte pharaonique, Connaissance de l'Egypte ancienne 4, Bruxelles 1992

DESROCHES NOBLECOURT C., Concubines du mort, Bulletin de l'Institut Français d'Archéologie Orientale LIII, Cairo 1953
- ID. (ED.), Ramsès le Grand, Paris 1976.

EDGAR C.C., "Catalogue général des antiquités Égyptiennes du Musée du Caire: Graeco-Egyptian Coffins, Masks and Portraits", Cairo 1905 EXHIBITION CATALOGUE

FAULKNER R.O., The Ancient Egyptian Pyramid Texts, Oxford 1969

FRANKFORT H., Ancient Egyptian Religion, New York 1948

GRIMM G. / DIETER J., Kunst der Ptolomär-und Römerzeit im Ägyptischen Museum Kairo, Mainz 1975

HAYES W.C., *Royal Sarcophagi of the XVIII dynasty*, Princeton 1935

HELCK W., *Zur Verwaltung des Mittleren und Neuen Reiches, Probleme der Ägyptologie 3*, Leiden 1958

HOFFMAN M.A., *Egypt Before the Pharahos*, New York 1979

HORNUNG E., *Der Eine und die Vielen - Ägyptische Gottesvorstellungen*, Darmstadt 1973

HORNUNG E./ STAEHELIN E., *Studien zum Sedfest*, Geneva 1974

HORNUNG H., *Tal der Könige*, Zürich 1982

HOULIHAN P.F., *The Animal World of the Pharaohs*, Cairo 1996

KACZAMARCZYK A./ HEDGES R.E.M., *Ancient Egyptian Faïence*, Warminster 1983

KEES H., *"Der Vezir Hori, Sohn des Jutjek,"* in *Zeitschrift für Ägyptische Sprache und Altertumskunde 83*, 1958, pages 129-138

KELLEY A., *The Pottery of Ancient Egypt (Dynasty I to Roman Times)*, I-III, Toronto 1976

KITCHEN K.A., *The Third Intermediate Period in Egypt (1100-650 A.C.)*, Warminster 1973

KOZLOFF A. / BRYAN B. ET AL., *Aménophis III, le Pharaon-Soleil, Galeries Nationales du Grand Palais*, Paris 1993 Exhibition catalog

LABOURY D., *La statuaire de Thoutmosis III. Essai d'interprétation d'un portrait royal dans son contexte historique, Aegyptiaca Leodiensia 5*, Liège 1998

LANGE K. / HIRMER M., *Ägypten, Architektur, Plastik, Malerei in drei Jahrtausenden*, München 1967

LAUER J.-P., *La Pyramide à Degrés*, I-II, Cairo 1936; II , Cairo 1939

- ID., *Saqqarah, la nécropole royale de Memphis*, Paris 1977

LECLANT J., *Montouemhat quatrième prophète d'Amun prince de la ville, Bibliothèque d'Étude 35*, Cairo 1962

- ID. (ED.). *Le Temps des Pyramides, Univers des formes I*, Paris 1978

- ID. (ED.), *L'Empire des Conquérants, Univers des formes II*, Paris 1979

- ID. (ED.), *L'Egypte du Crépuscule, Univers des formes III*, Paris 1980

MARIETTE A., *Les Mastabas del l'Ancien Empire*, Paris 1882-1889

Martin G.T., *The Royal Tomb at El Amarna*, I-II, London 1974 & 1989

MORENZ S., *Ägyptische Religion*, Stuttgart 1977

NICHOLSON P.T.- SHAW I. (EDS.), *British Museum Dictionary of Ancient Egypt*, London 1995

NICHOLSON P.T. - SHAW I.(EDS.), *Ancient Egyptian Materials and Technology*, Cambridge 2000

NIWINSKI A., *"The Bab el-Gusus Tomb and the Royal Cache in Deir el-Bahari,"* in *Journal of Egyptian Archaeology 70*, 1984, pages 73-81

- ID., *21st Dynasty Coffins from Thebes - Chronological and Typological Studies, Theben 5*, Mainz am Rhein 1988

- ID. *Studies on the Illustrated Theban Funerary Papyri of the 11th and 10th Centuries B.C.*, Freiburg 1989

PARLASCA K., *Ritratti di mummie*, in A. Adriani (ed.), *Repertorio d'arte dell'Egitto greco-romano*, II serie: 1, Palermo 1969; II e III, Rome 1977 & 1980

PIANKOFF A., *The Shrines of Tutankhamun*, New York 1955

POSENER G., *De la divinité du pharaon, Cahier de la Société asiatique 15*, Paris 1960

POSENER-KIÉGER P., *Les archives du temple funéraire de Néferirkaré-Kakaï (les papirus d'Abousir)*, 2 vols, Bibliothèque d'Étude 65.1/2, Cairo 1976

PUSCH E.B., *Das Senet Brettspiel im Alten Ägypten*, Berlin 1979

QUIBELL J.E., *Catalogue Genéral des Antiquités Égyptiennes du Musée du Caire: The Tomb of Yuaa and Thuiu*, Cairo 1908

REDFORD D.B., *Akhenaten: the Heretic King*, Princeton 1984

REDFORD D.B. / SMITH R.W., *The Akhenaten Temple Project*, Warminster 1976

REEVES N. / WILKINSON R.H., *The Complete Valley of the Kings*, Cairo 1996

RÜBSAM W.J.R., *Götter und Kulte in Faijum während der griechisch-römisch-byzantinischen Zeit*, Bonn 1974

SALEH M., *Das Totenbuch in den thebanischen Beamtengrabern des Neuen Reiches*, Mainz 1984

SALEH M./SOUROUZIAN H., *The Egyptian Museum Cairo. Official Catalogue*, Cairo 1987

SCHÄFER H., *Principles of Egyptian Art, (English Edition)*, Oxford 1986

STADELMANN R., *"Totentempeln III,"* in *Lexikon der Ägyptologie VI*, pages 706-711

- ID., *Die ägyptischen Pyramiden*, Mainz 1985

STRUDWICK N., *The Administration of Egypt in the Old Kingdom*, London 1985

TAYLOR J.H., *"Aspects of the History of the Valley of the Kings in the Third Intermediate Period,"* in Reeves C.N. (ed.), *After Tut'ankhamun: Research and Excavations in the Royal Necropolis at Thebes*, London 1992

Toutankhamun et son temps. Petit Palais, Paris 1967.

EXHIBITION CATALOGUE

TIRADRITTI F. (ED.), *Treasures of the Egyptian Museum*, Cairo 1998

TRIGGER B.G./ KEMP B.J./ O'CONNOR D. / LLOYD A.B., *Ancient Egypt, A Social History*, Cambridge 1983

VALBELLE D., *Les ouvriers de la tombe. Deir el-Médineh à l'époque Ramesside, Bibliothèque d'Étude 96*, Cairo 1985

VANDIER J., *Manuel d'Archéologie Egyptienne*, I-VI, Paris 1952-1978

VANDIER D'ABBADIE J., *Catalogue des ostraca figurés de Deir el-Médineh*, Cairo 1936-1959

VON BECKERATH J., *Handbuch der ägyptischen Königsnamen, Münchner Ägyptologische Studien 20*, Munich-Berlin 1984

WILDUNG D., *Imhotep und Amenemhotep, Münchner Ägyptologischen Studien 36*, München - Berlin 1977

ID., *Sesostris und Amenemhet - Ägypten im Mittleren Reich*, München 1984

WILKINSON R.H., *The Complete Temples of Ancient Egypt*, London 2000

WINLOCK H.E., *Models of Daily Life in Ancient Egypt, Publications of the Metropolitan Museum of Art, Egyptian Expedition XVIII*, 1955

INDEX

BIOGRAPHIES OF THE AUTHORS

Zahi Hawass is the Director of the archaeological site of Giza and Saqqara, Professor of Archaeology at the University of Cairo.

Araldo De Luca, one of the best photographers in the world of statuary and jewelry; for White Star Publications he contributed the photographs for the volumes *The treasures of the Egyptian Museum* (1999) and *Tutankhamun* (2000).

Alessandro Bongioanni teaches at Turin University and has published numerous articles in Italian and international magazines; he has been involved with the cataloging of objects in the Egyptian Museum in Turin.

Maria Sole Croce graduated in Egyptology at Turin University and studied at the Faculty of Oriental Studies at Zurich University; she has worked for the Egyptian Museum in Turin for a number of years and been a member of the excavation team of the Mission Archéologique Française at Boubasteion.

Alessia Amenta graduated in Literature and obtained a PhD in Egyptology at "La Sapienza" University in Rome; she has participated in several excavations in Italy and Egypt.

Daniela Comand graduated in Egyptology at Turin University with a thesis on foreign cultural influences felt at Deir al-Medina during the Ramessid; she has worked with the Egyptian Museum in Turin since 1990.

Silvia Einaudi graduated in Egyptology at Turin University and works with the Egyptian Museum in Turin.

Marcella Trapani has published various articles in specialist journals in Italy and abroad. She is currently the Egyptologist at the Superintendency in the Egyptian Museum in Turin where she works on exhibitions and publications for the scientific community and the general public.

ACKNOWLEDGMENTS

The Editor would like to thank: S.E. Farouk Hosny – the Egyptian Minister of Culture; Gaballah Ali Gaballah – Secretary-General of the Supreme Council for Antiquities; S.E. Francesco Aloisi di Larderel – the Italian Ambassador to Egypt; Ali Hassan – the former Secretary-General of the Supreme Council for Antiquities; Mohamed Saleh – Director of the Egyptian Museum in Cairo from 1981 to 1999; Carla Maria Burri – Director of the Italian Cultural Institute in Cairo; Samir Gharib – Artistic consultant to the Egyptian Minister of Culture; Nabil Osman – President of the Egyptian Information Center; Ahmed Hosen - Director of the Cairo Press Center; Gamal Shafik of the Cairo Press Center for his organization of the photographic service; The staff and curators of the Egyptian Museum in Cairo; Alessandro Cocconi – Photographic assistant

PHOTOGRAPHIC CREDITS